THE MUSIC OF
BLACK AMERICANS

A HISTORY

THIRD EDITION

ALSO BY EILEEN SOUTHERN

The Buxheim Organ Book

Readings in Black American Music

Anonymous Pieces in the Ms. El Escorial IV.A.24

Biographical Dictionary of Afro-American and African Musicians

*African-American Traditions in Song, Sermon, Tale, and Dance,
1600s–1920: An Annotated Bibliography*
(with Josephine Wright)

African-American Theater (Nineteenth-Century
American Musical Theater, vol. 9)

Samuel Arnold: "Obi; or, Three-Finger'd Jack"
(with Robert Hoskins)

Also of Interest:

New Perspectives on Music: Essays in Honor of Eileen Southern

THE MUSIC OF
BLACK AMERICANS

A HISTORY

THIRD EDITION

Eileen Southern

Professor Emerita of Music and Afro-American Studies, Harvard University

W · W · NORTON & COMPANY · NEW YORK · LONDON

Copyright © 1997, 1983, 1971 by W. W. Norton & Company, Inc.

All rights reserved
Printed in the United States of America

The text of this book is composed in Sabon
with the display set in Gill Sans
Composition and manufacturing by Maple-Vail Book Manufacturing Group
Book design by Jack Meserole
Cover illustration: Royce M. Becker Design

Library of Congress Cataloging-in-Publication Data

Southern, Eileen.
    The music of black Americans : a history / Eileen Southern. —3rd ed.
        p.   cm.
    Discography:
    Includes bibliographical references (p.) and index.
    ISBN 0-393-03843-2—ISBN 0-393-97141-4 (pbk.)
    1. Afro-Americans—Music—History and criticism.   I. Title.
ML3556.S74   1997
780'.89'96073—dc20   96-28811

W. W. Norton & Company, Inc. 500 Fifth Avenue, New York, NY 10110
http://www.wwnorton.com

W. W. Norton & Company Ltd., 10 Coptic Street, London WC1A 1PU

1 2 3 4 5 6 7 8 9 0

To Joseph

Contents

PART ONE

SONG IN A STRANGE LAND
1619–1775

PART TWO

LET MY PEOPLE GO
1776–1865

Illustrations

The Music of Black Americans: A History

Preface

The purpose of this book is to help the reader understand and appreciate the several genres and many styles of music which, taken together, define African-American music in the United States. I have chosen a chronological ordering of the materials, tracing the history of black music from its origin in Africa through its manifestations in colonial America and then in the United States, up to the present time.

In the twenty-five years since the first edition of this book was published, important developments have occurred in the field of African-American music that call for recognition and for an assessment of their impact on American music at large. Most striking has been the ever-increasing interest of students, scholars, and black-music enthusiasts generally in researching and writing the history of the music. They have also compiled bibliographies, discographies, and indexes; written dissertations; published biographical writings and musical criticism; and collected recorded music and musical scores. As a result, there is now a substantial, recent literature on African-American music that can be examined and evaluated.

In revising the work, it has been my aim to bring the text up to date, based on my own research and that of others in the field during the past two decades. I have inserted new material throughout the book, rewritten passages as necessary, restructured parts of the text, divided an extensive chapter in two, and added an entirely new chapter, "Currents in Contemporary Arenas."

Among other notable features of this revision is the treatment of black women musicians, not only as professional associates of their male counterparts, but also as composers and performers in their own rights. In discussing the music itself, I have paid close attention to the details that attended the evolution of black music in the last quarter of the twentieth century, particularly gospel and popular musics such as rap. Finally, I have updated and greatly expanded the Appendices. The sheer quantity of publications that has appeared in the last two decades (many of uneven quality) prevents any attempt at exhaustive coverage of the literature. Rather, the bibliographies, though selective, are comprehensive.

Readers seeking additional sources of information will find that a number of the one-volume works include comprehensive bibliographies and discographies; examples are William Austin's *Music in the Twentieth Century,* Frank Tirro's *Jazz: A History,* and *We'll Understand It Better By and By* (gospel), edited by Bernice Johnson Reagon. Finally, of course, there are the authoritative *New Grove* dictionaries, which began publication in 1980 and which provide a wealth of information about music. The four-volume *New Grove Dictionary of American Music* (1986) and the two-volume *New Grove Dictionary of Jazz* (1988) are particularly useful for their expansive coverage of African-American music and musicians, offering a sharp contrast to the way the subject is neglected in earlier reference books.

Serious study of African-American music requires getting to know the music, which means listening to it and, if possible, performing it. One should sing the slave songs, the hymns, the "tunes" of jazz pieces, the themes of the classical compositions. The centrality of the melodic theme in the performance of African-American music is all-embracing; knowing the tune is essential for appreciating the variations that frequently follow its statement (or accompany it), whether in a spiritual, a bebop piece, a gospel song, or an extended jazz work. For the convenience of the reader, my text includes a number of simple songs suitable for informal singing.

In recent years several new anthologies of recorded music have made examples of the various styles of black music much more accessible. The largest collection, *New World Recorded Anthology of American Music,* includes a fine variety of jazz, theater, and folk music, but very little of the classical music of black composers. Indeed, as regards the availability of black-composer recordings, the scene generally is bleak. I have listed under the heading *Sound Recordings* titles of some works, many of which are out of print but may be found in libraries or private collections. Most useful is the nine-volume Columbia Records *Black Composers Series,* but it is woefully inadequate in representing the music of black composers for the past 250 years.

To be sure, a mere handful of works may be found in conventional sources such as the *Schwann Record and Tape Guide,* but most often the recordings (and scores) have been published by small, independent companies ("indies") that come and go, or by the composers themselves. It is not an over-statement to suggest that most black classical music still exists only in manuscript format.

African-American academic journals, *The Black Perspective in Music* and the *Black Music Research Journal,* contain annual lists of new music. Readers seeking more information about these works may apply directly to the Center for Black Music Research (Columbia College, Chicago), or write directly to the composers. They are relatively easy to find, as most are members of college music faculties and can be reached through their institutions. They are almost always pleased to learn that someone wishes to perform their music.

Music scores are in the same dismal situation as recordings. Many scores that were actually published are now out of print. More often, however, the original scores never left the composers' music shelves except to be used for a local rehearsal or performance and then returned to the shelves until needed again.

To compensate for the paucity of scores and recordings, the reader should seize every opportunity to hear live African-American music—or, at least, tune in to radio and television broadcasts of the music. Urban residents have an advantage in finding listening opportunities, but the expansion of cable television and computer networking both hold promise of spreading even the less popular forms of black music. The nation's major concert halls and religious temples regularly program the sounds of African-American music from one season to the next, as do also the intimate supper clubs, Broadway stages, festival venues, and the like.

The performers need not be professional: that little storefront church on the corner might be the spiritual home of another Mahalia Jackson; the Sunday afternoon tea at the local YMCA might be featuring another Leontyne Price; the bunch of teenage boys harmonizing on a corner under the street light might be a future rapper Ice-T and his posse; it may be a future André Watts who is playing a new concerto by George Walker at the monthly concert of the community African-American Symphony Orchestra. Outside a rather seedy bar on a Saturday night, we might hear the plaintive wail of a future B. B. King, fresh from a tour on the "chitlin' circuit." The music is everywhere! Often, one needs only to stop and listen.

A number of people have provided assistance to me over the years that this work has been in preparation, either through their publications or by personal communication. I acknowledge my debt to the scholar historians whose research and publications in the field of African-American history have inspired me and provided a model of sorts for my work in the history of African-American music. Similarly, I am indebted to the music historians whose publications in the history of American music have alerted me to issues involving relationships between genres that call for investigation.

In the prefaces to the first two editions of this book, I expressed my appreciation to colleagues, students, relatives, friends, and professional-musician associates for their useful suggestions and assistance in many ways. For this edition I have again benefited from their good will, and I remain grateful.

It would be impossible to name them all, but special mention must be made of Alfred Bradford who has supplied me with newspaper and magazine clippings through the years, thus making it easier for me to keep abreast of important events. My sister Stella Hall, my daughter April Reilly, and my son-in-law John Reilly gave close, careful readings to the text and were helpful in calling my attention to errors and omissions. Several colleagues who read portions of the text shared with me their critical observations, as did the professional musicians with whom I talked. I am grateful to all of them.

My heartfelt thanks also go to the scholars who reviewed this work in its entirety: among them, Ronald Riddle, Doris McGinty, Josephine Wright, and Richard Crawford. Their advice has been carefully considered, and much of it is reflected in the pages of the book. Professor Crawford, through his critical reading of both previous editions, has provided insightful observations and his valuable suggestions. Finally, I remain appreciative to Michael Ochs, music editor at W. W. Norton, for his enthusiasm and devoted care in guiding this book through production. Also I thank copy editor Kathryn Talalay, editorial assistant Martha Graedel, and Neil Ryder Hoos, photo coordinator at Norton, for their help and advice.

This book is dedicated with deep gratitude to my husband, as were the two previous editions. As researcher, typist, data-entry clerk, proofreader, critical reviewer, and generally right-hand man in every way, he has made this book possible. I can never adequately express my appreciation for his patience and encouragement.

THE MUSIC OF
BLACK AMERICANS

A HISTORY

THIRD EDITION

PART ONE

SONG
IN A
STRANGE
LAND

1619–1775

*For they that carried us away
captive required of us a song; and they
that wasted us required of us mirth,
saying, Sing us one of the songs of Zion.
How shall we sing the Lord's song in a
strange land?*

—Psalm 137: 3, 4

IMPORTANT EVENTS

1619 First arrival of Africans in the English colonies: Jamestown, VA.

1620 Landing of the Pilgrims: Plymouth, MA.

1626 Founding of New Amsterdam. Eleven Africans brought in as indentured servants.

1630 Founding of Boston, MA. Cultural center and largest city in the colonies as late as 1743.

1638 Beginning of the New England slave trade with the arrival of the first black men on the ship *Desire:* Boston, MA.

1640 Publication of the first book in the English colonies, the *Bay Psalm Book:* Boston, MA.

1641 Earliest record of a slave baptized and taken into the church: Dorchester, MA. Enactment of the famous "Body of Liberties" laws in Mass., giving tacit approval to the institution of slavery.

1644 Earliest record of the manumission of slaves: New Amsterdam, NY.

1646 Earliest mention of manumission in New England: New Haven, CT.

1661 First of the so-called Black Codes giving statutory recognition to the institution of slavery: VA.

1664 New Amsterdam taken over by the British; renamed New York.

1667 Law passed by the Virginia Assembly stating that the baptism of slaves did not exempt them from bondage.

1670 Founding of Charles Town, SC, only "city" in the South during the colonial period.

1681 Founding of Philadelphia, cultural center and largest city in the colonies on the eve of the American Revolution.

1688 Germantown protest: pioneer attack on the institution of slavery by the Quakers: Germantown, PA.

1693 Founding of the Society of Negroes, at Boston, MA.

1701 Establishment of the Society for the Propagation of the Gospel in Foreign Parts (called the SPG), missionary organization of the Established Church of England that operated missions to the slaves in the colonies during the years 1702–85.

1704 Establishment of one of the earliest schools for slaves by the SPG; taught by Elias Neau at Trinity Episcopal Church, New York, NY.

1707 Publication of *Hymns and Spiritual Songs* by Isaac Watts, which influenced the development of black American hymnody: London (American edition, Boston, 1739).

1712 New York City slave insurrection.

1717 Publishing of *The Psalms of David, Imitated . . .* by Isaac Watts: London (first American edition, Philadelphia, 1729).

1723 Earliest record of a black army musician—Nero Benson, trumpeter: Framingham, MA.
Founding of the Associates of Doctor Bray, allied society of the SPG, which operated schools for slaves during the years 1758–75.

1729 First public concert in the colonies: Boston, MA.

1735 Five slaves baptized by the Reverend Jonathan Edwards at the Northampton, MA., revival of the "Great Awakening" movement.

1739 Slave uprising, the "Stono Conspiracy," near Charles Town, SC.

1741 Founding of the first permanent Moravian settlement, with black men among the first settlers: Bethlehem, PA.
New York City slave conspiracy.

1742 Negro School House opened by Alexander Garden, with two educated slaves as teachers (until 1764): Charles Town, SC.

1756 First of the French and Indian Wars (1756–63).

1764 Founding of the first Methodist Society in the colonies at Baltimore, MD.

CHAPTER 1

The
African
Legacy

"ABOUT the last of August came a Dutch man-of-warre that sold us twenty Negars." This statement, dated 1619, in the *Generall Historie of Virginia* by Captain John Smith, refers to the first arrival of black men in the English colonies on the mainland (i.e., the eastern seaboard of the present United States).[1] They were to continue to come for more than two hundred years, brought at first in small groups (called "parcels"), then later by the shiploads, clamped in irons and wedged into foul vessels so closely together that there was hardly enough room for movement. The Africans came for the most part from the west coast of Africa—from the area now occupied by the lands of Senegal, Guinea, Gambia, Sierra Leone, Liberia, Ivory Coast, Ghana, Togo, Benin, Nigeria, Cameroon, Gabon, and parts of the Congo and Zaire. Before the arrival of whites on Africa's west coast, the area was dominated by such empires as Ghana, Mali, Songhay, Kanem-Bornu, and the Mossi, Hausa, and other states. With the collapse of some of the older empires, new ones came into existence. During the period of the transatlantic slave trade, the powerful kingdoms, states, and city-states included Ashanti, Benin, Dahomey, the Delta states, Gambia, Oyo, and Senegal.

Olaudah Equiano, one of the first Africans to write a book in the English language, described the area from which slaves were taken in his autobiog-

---

[1]A. G. Bradley, ed., *Travels and Works of Captain John Smith* (1624: Edinburgh, 1910), p. 541.

raphy, *The Interesting Narrative of the Life of Olaudah Equiano, or Gustavus Vassa the African. Written by Himself* (1789):

> That part of Africa, known by the name of Guinea, to which the trade for slaves is carried on, extends along the coast about 3400 miles, from Senegal to Angola, and includes a variety of kingdoms.[2]

White traders gave to the region such names as the Gold Coast, the Ivory Coast, and the Slave Coast. The first white travelers in the region found a wide variety of political organizations: some were highly organized, with kings, governors, and noblemen (for example, the palace chiefs and town chiefs of Benin); others were loosely formed into clans, tribes, or similar kinship groups. Regardless of the political makeup of West Africa, however, the most important divisions were the ancient ones that separated peoples into groups according to their clans, or their villages of origin, or their descent from common ancestors. Thus the various peoples included such nations as the Akan, Fon, Yoruba, Ibo, Fanti, Fulani, Ashanti, Jolof, Mandingo, Bakongo, and Baoulé.

MUSIC IN WEST AFRICA

We know a considerable amount about the music of West Africa during the slave-trade period (1619–ca. 1860 in the United States), despite the paucity of written indigenous records. In the first place, the oral traditions of modern Africa offer reliable clues to the past, for many musical practices of today are remarkably similar to those of two centuries ago. Perhaps even more important is the information to be found in writings of the early European travelers and traders in Africa. Some of these chronicles provide surprisingly rich details about one or more aspects of African music and occasionally include musical examples and illustrations of musical instruments.[3]

The Role of Music in Society

One of the most striking features of African life was the importance given to music and the dance, and travelers seldom failed to comment upon this. The earliest report in the English language comes from Richard Jobson, an English sea captain sent to Africa by the Company of Adventurers of London in 1620 to explore the Gambia River area with a view to assessing its potential for trade. After returning to England he published *The Golden*

---

[2]Equiano, *The Interesting Narrative of the Life of Olaudah Equiano* (London, 1789), p. 3.
[3]Generally, discussion of musical matters is scattered throughout the books published by the European traders rather than concentrated in one place. In the following notes, all pages including significant discussion of music will be cited with the first mention of the titles.

Trade or a Discovery of the River Gambra and the Golden Trade of the Aethiopians, in which he observed:

> There is without doubt, no people on the earth more naturally affected to the sound of musicke than these people; which the principall persons do hold as an ornament of their state, so as when wee come to see them their musicke will seldome be wanting. . . . Also, if at any time the Kings or principall persons come unto us trading in the River, they will have their musicke playing before them, and will follow in order after their manner, presenting a shew of state.[4]

A century later trader James Houstoun wrote, "I visited King Conny in his Castle, who received me with the usual ceremonies of their Country, Musicke, Drums, and Horns."[5] Equiano the African states, "We are almost a nation of dancers, musicians, and poets."[6] Other accounts of the period offer similar testimony to the primacy of music in the lives of the African peoples.

Occasions for Music Making

For almost every activity in the life of the individual or the community there was an appropriate music; it was an integral part of life from the hour of birth to beyond the grave. Equiano points out:

> Thus every great event, such as a triumphant return from battle or other cause of public rejoicing, is celebrated in public dances, which are accompanied with songs and music suited to the occasion. The assembly is separated into four divisions, which dance either apart or in succession, and each with a character peculiar to itself. The first division contains the married men, who in their dances frequently exhibit feats of arms and the representation of a battle. To these succeed the married women, who dance in the second division. The young men occupy the third, and the maidens the fourth. Each represents some interesting scene of real life, such as a great achievement, domestic employment, a pathetic story, or some rural sport; and as the subject is generally founded on some recent event, it is therefore ever new. This gives our dances a spirit and variety which I have scarcely seen elsewhere.

There was ceremonial music for the festivals commemorating agricultural rites, celebrating the installation of kings or bringing together important chiefs of the nation, and reenacting historical events of significance. Thomas Edward Bowdich gives a full description of one such festival, called the Yam Customs, in his book, *Mission from Cape Coast to Ashantee.* A scientific writer, Bowdich was sent to Africa in 1817 by the African Committee of London to establish commercial relations with the Ashanti. He was also an amateur musician and painter; he recorded African melodies in

---

[4]Richard Jobson, *The Golden Trade* (London, 1623), pp. 105–7.
[5]James Houstoun quoted in Elizabeth Doonan, *Documents Illustrative of the History of the Slave Trade* (Washington, D.C., 1930–35), v. 2, p. 288.
[6]Equiano, *Narrative,* pp. 7–8.

notation, described instruments and performance practice with precision, and included several watercolor scenes of African life in his book. All these things make his report extremely valuable for the music historian. When Bowdich's mission arrived at Kumasi, the capital of Ashanti (now in Ghana), he tells us that:

> Upwards of 5000 people, the greater part warriors, met us with awful bursts of martial music, discordant only in its mixture; for horns, drums, rattles, and gong-gongs were all exerted with a zeal bordering on phrenzy. . . . We were halted whilst the captains performed their Pyrrhic dance in the centre of a circle formed by their warriors.[7]

The dance lasted for about a half hour, after which the Englishmen were escorted by the warriors through the streets of the town to an open square near the palace. They were totally unprepared for the "magnificence and novelty" of the scene that lay before them.

> The king, his tributaries, and captains, were resplendent in the distance, surrounded by attendants of every description. . . . The sun was reflected, with a glare scarcely more supportable than the heat, from the massy gold ornaments, which glistened in every direction. More than a hundred bands burst at once on our arrival, [all playing] the peculiar airs of their several chiefs; the horns flourished their defiances [i.e., fanfare melodies], with the beating of innumerable drums and metal instruments, and then yielded for a while to the soft breathings of their long flutes, which were truly harmonious; and a pleasing instrument, like a bagpipe without the drone, was happily blended. At least a hundred large umbrellas, or canopies, which could shelter thirty persons, were sprung up and down by the bearers with brilliant effect, being made of scarlet, yellow, and the most shewy [i.e., showy] cloths and silks. . .

Special kinds of music were called for during preparations for war or for embarking upon a major hunting expedition; similarly, there were musical rituals associated with victory celebrations, whether in observation of the defeat of an enemy or of a successful hunt. Among all the nations, one of the most important festivals occurred when local rulers and chiefs paid homage to the king in the nation's capital. The crowds who filled the town at such times included not only chiefs and their followers but also envoys and merchants from other states, traders from within and without the country, and villagers from miles around. Typically, these festivals lasted for many days—the Annual Customs of Dahomey, for example, took several weeks.[8]

Then there was the music involved in religious rites—veneration of the deities, of the lesser divinities and spirits, and of the ancestors. Bowdich observes that the Ashanti thought it "absurd" to worship God in any way

[7]Edward Bowdich, *Mission from Cape Coast Castle to Ashantee* (London, 1819), pp. 31–40, 358–69, 449–52.

[8]Robert Noris, *Memoirs of the Reign of Bossa Ahadee, King of Dahomey* (London, 1789), pp. 86, 104–5, 109.

other than through singing and chanting. Closely related to religious rites were those associated with funerals, particularly of important persons of the community and royalty. Among some peoples of Angola (now the Congo and Zaire) there was a tradition for litigation music. In presenting cases to the judge-chief, the litigants chanted their arguments to the accompaniment of drums and song. All this music was ceremonial and ritualized, and frequently performed in conjunction with dance and / or drama by professional musicians.

But a large part of the music making in Africa took place on a less formal, highly socialized level that brought together members of the community in either selective groups or as a whole to share in common experiences. There was music appropriate for celebrating the birth of a child, the appearance of the first tooth, the onset of puberty, initiation rites, betrothal ceremonies, and similar events of an individual's life. Usually, singing groups were sex-differentiated; slave trader Theophilus Conneau describes a women's-children's group he saw in 1826:

> The usual dance was proposed. A huge bonfire was made in the yard, and a circle formed by women and children. A female drummer soon made her appearance, and a tam-tam struck their national dance, accompanied with song.[9]

Occasions associated with children, adolescent girls, and funerals, in particular, generally called for musical performance by women.

On the other hand, warrior songs, hunting songs, fishermen and boating songs, and other kinds of cooperative-work songs were the province of the men. Bowdich's reference to the songs of the Canoe men identifies an important work activity in a land where waterways provided the chief means of transportation. As agricultural peoples, West Africans had a wide variety of songs associated with planting, harvesting, cattle raising, preparation of food, selling in the market and on the street, and similar activities. There were many times, of course, when men and women sang together; traveler Hugh Clapperton witnessed such an occasion in 1829:

> The walls of Boussa . . . appeared very extensive, and are at present under repair. Bands of male and female slaves, accompanied by drums and flutes, and singing in chorus, were passing to and from the river with water, to mix the clay they were building with.[10]

Finally, there was recreational music, both formal and informal. Conneau reports on the kind of entertainment offered a chief at the end of the day: "After dinner several female singers were introduced and amused us with a concert. I cannot say much in favor of their voices or melodies, but still, some of their instruments were certainly ingenious enough. . . ." Group

[9]Conneau in Mable Smythe, ed., *A Slaver's Logbook* (Englewood Cliffs, NJ, 1976), pp. 54, 63, 96, 130–32, 136, 171.
[10]See also Hugh Clapperton, *Journal of a Second Expedition into the Interior of Africa* (London, 1829), pp. 14, 24, 71, 86–87, 98.

music making in the community for recreational purposes was invariably accompanied by dancing, a point to which we shall return.

Professional Musicians

Every village had its master musicians, singers, and instrumentalists, who provided music for formal activities of the community. Often they were attached to the courts of kings or chiefs as royal horn blowers, royal drummers, and praise singers; frequently their positions were inherited from their fathers to be passed on in turn to their sons. Whether royal or independent musicians, they were expected to be virtuoso performers and to know the traditional history and literature of the people. Jobson compares the African minstrels, called griots, to Irish bards:

> They have a perfect resemblance to the Irish Rimer, sitting in the same manner as they doe upon the ground, somewhat remote from the company; and as they use [the] singing of Songs unto their musicke, the ground and effect whereof is the rehearsall of the ancient stock of the King, exhalting his antientry, and recounting over all the worthy and famous acts by him or them [that] hath been achieved: singing likewise *extempore* upon any occasion is offered, whereby the principall may be pleased; wherein diverse times they will not forget in our presence to sing in the praise of us white men, for which he will expect from us some manner of gratification.

Trader Mungo Park cites some of the duties of those he called Jillikea or singing men: to sing "extempore songs" (that is, improvise both tunes and texts) in honor of their patrons, to recite the historical events of their kings and nations, and to accompany the warriors in the fields, stimulating them to fight by recounting the heroic deeds of their ancestors. The singing men used their talents to "divert the fatigue" of the group with which he was traveling and to obtain for them "a welcome from strangers." Griots did not limit their praise songs to their patrons; they were willing to sing for anyone who gave them money—"solid pudding for empty praise." Park notes also a second class of singers:

> ... devotees of the Mahomedan faith, who travel about the country, singing devout hymns, and performing religious ceremonies, to conciliate the favour of the Almighty, either in averting calamity, or in insuring success to any enterprize.[11]

Master musicians were highly esteemed by the people. Bowdich observes that the gold horn blower and the master of the bands sat with the official members of the king's household, "surrounded by a retinue and splendor which bespoke the dignity and importance of their offices."[12] Others noted

---

[11]Mungo Park, *Travels in the Interior Districts of Africa* (New York, 1800), pp. 200–2, 275–76, 319–21.
[12]See also William Smith, *A Voyage to Guinea* (London, 1744), pp. 20–22, 219.

that musicians generally sat near the king or chief, an indication of their high rank. Mungo Park was particularly impressed by the exalted status of poet-musicians in Africa, who "are much employed and respected by the people, and very liberal contributions are made for them," while in Europe "neglect and indigence . . . commonly attend the votaries of the Muses." It should be remarked that singing women as well as singing men shared in this adulation.

Musical Instruments and Performance Practice

Early travelers in Africa most often encountered percussive instruments—that is, instruments belonging to the classes of membranophones and idiophones. The membranophones, or drums, came in all sizes and shapes, ranging in length from ten or twelve inches to ten or twelve feet, and in diameter from two or three inches to several feet. Bowdich says that most often drums were made of

> hollow'd trunks of trees, frequently carved with much nicety, mostly open at one end, and of many sizes: those with heads of common skin (that is of any other than Leopard skin) are beaten with sticks in the form of a crotchet rest [i.e., ♩]; the largest are borne on the head of a man, and struck by one or more followers; the smaller are slung round the neck, or stand on the ground; in the latter case they are mostly played with the inside of the fingers, at which the natives are very expert: amongst these drums are some with heads of leopard skin, (looking like vellum,) only sounded by two fingers, which are scraped along, as the middle finger is on the tamborine, but producing a much louder noise.

His testimony is corroborated by many others. A traveler among the Ibo peoples found two drum-types, the one made from a hollow log, and the other made by cutting a gourd or calabash in half and drawing a skin tightly over the opening.[13] Major Dixon Denham describes a drum "made of a hollow block of wood about three feet high, with a skin drawn tensely over the top by means of braces."[14] Conneau refers to a drum made from the "trunk of a tree four feet in diameter and hollowed or bored out to the consistency of two inches thick; its length was ten feet and only one end was covered with a bullock hide." Mungo Park names the "tangtang, a drum open at the lower end" and the tabulu, a talking drum. In 1705 a traveler saw a drum in the shape of an hourglass.[15]

The drum, of all instruments, was most frequently chosen as a royal or sacred instrument, as is true in modern-day Africa. Performance groups for

---

[13]James Hawkins, *A History of a Voyage to the Coast of Africa* (Troy, NY, 1797), pp. 100–1.
[14]Dixon Denham *et al., Narrative of Travels and Discoveries in Northern and Central Africa* (London, 1828), v. 1, pp. 241–42, 274–76, 282; v. 2, pp. 58, 233, 236, 256, 365, 402–4.
[15]William Bosman, *A New and Accurate Description of the Coast of Guinea* (London, 1721), pp. 115–18, 220, 422–23.

"Jelleman of Soolima [and] Jelleman of Kooranko." From *Travels of Soolima in the Timannee* (1825) by Alexander G. Laing.

drums varied as much as drum sizes; there might be a single player or duo, or there might be small and large ensembles. Europeans noted with surprise that Africans played drums with the fingers or the palms of the hands or "crooked sticks."

Idiophones (instruments made of any materials capable of producing sound) were represented by an endless variety of bells, castenet-types, gong-gongs made of iron, sticks, and rattles, as well as the tuned xylophones and hand pianos (or thumb pianos). Like the drum, the xylophone came in many sizes and materials. Generally referred to as *balafou* or *balafoo*, it might be large with twenty or more keys or small enough to hang by a strap around the neck. Conneau describes one of the latter:

This was something like an harmonica: a board the size of a tea waiter with a light open frame at the extreme ends. On this frame were tied two strings made of cane, and on it reposed several pieces of bamboo well cleaned from the pith. These pieces were gradually made, one larger than the other, declining in size and placed in rotation; under them were placed seven gourds also gradually declining in size. This instrument was carried with a strap around the neck and played with two wooden hammers covered with gutta-percha.

Its harmony was peculiar. The female musician who played it had fastened to her elbows, wrists, ankles, and knees a lot of small bells which she managed to sound as she struck the harmonica and danced in the meantime.

Jobson tells us that the xylophone was the "principall instrument" in Gambia; called Ballards, it stood a foot above the ground and had "seventeen wooden keyes." The player, sitting on the ground, struck the keys with sticks "about a foote long," of which the ends were covered with "some soft stuffe." Gourds hanging underneath each key, "like bottles," received the sound and returned it again with "extraordinary loudness." Like the drum, the xylophone was a popular instrument for accompanying the dance. Traveler Alexander Gordon Laing describes a dance accompanied by six single and one double *ballafou*.[16]

The thumb piano, also called *mbira* or *sansa,* came in several sizes and was as popular in the slave-trade period as in modern times. Equiano the African associates the *mbira* with female performance:

> We have many musical instruments, particularly drums of different kinds, a piece of music which resembles a guitar, and another much like a stickado. These last are chiefly used by betrothed virgins, who play on them on all grand festivals.

Bowdich calls the instrument an *oompoochwa* and compares it to "a Staccado nearly deprived of its tone":

> The Oompoochwa is a box, one end of which is left open; two flat bridges are fastened across the top, and five pieces of thin curved stick, scraped very smooth, are attached to them, and (their ends being raised) are struck with some force by the thumb.

Aerophones (wind instruments) were not as prevalent as the other instrument classes—at least, not in so wide a variety. The sources refer to several kinds of flutes: small flutes with three sound holes; instruments resembling panpipes made of small, one-tone flutes joined together in graduated lengths; long flutes; and instruments similar to bagpipes. Horns and trumpets were made from elephant tusks and horns of other animals. Bowdich points out that "the horns form their loudest sounds . . . are generally very large, and, being graduated like the flutes, their flourishes have a martial and grand effect." Like drums, horns could be used as talking instruments. Major Denham reports on trumpets and clarinet types:

> The Sultan returned to the town, preceded by several men blowing long pipes, not unlike clarionets, ornamented with shells, and two immense trumpets from twelve to fourteen feet long, borne by men on horseback, made of pieces of

[16]Alexander Gordon Laing, *Travels in . . . Western Africa* (London, 1825), pp. 104–5, 132–33, 141–42, 148, 154–59, 186–87, 191–92, 228–46, 249–51, 428–32.

hollow wood, with a brass mouth-piece, the sounds of which were not unpleasing.

Chordophones (string instruments) included lute or fiddle types, harp and lyre types, zither types, and a simple musical bow that apparently was unique to Africa. Bowdich describes the musical bow, or *bentwa,* as

> . . . a stick bent in the form of a bow, and across it, is fastened a very thin piece of split cane, which is held between the lips at one end, and struck with a small stick; whilst at the other it is occasionally stopped, or rather buffed, by a thick one; on this they play only lively airs, and it owes its various sounds to the lips.[17]

Lute types were typically made of gourds or calabashes, the tops covered with deer skins or skins of other animals, with two large holes cut for the "sound to escape." Fiddle types might be "made of a narrow box, its open top covered with alligator or antelope skin, with a long stick used as a neck and a bridge to support the strings." The strings, made from horse or cow hair, varied in number from one to as many as seven or eight, and the instrument was bowed or plucked, depending upon the customs of the people. Clapperton gives a detailed description of a violin made of a gourd that he saw in Dahomey. It had

> . . . three strings of horsehair, not in single hairs but a number for each string untwisted, the bow the same; the body of the violin was formed of half a long gourd; the bridge, two cross sticks; the top, the skin of a guana stretched tightly over the edges; the neck was about two feet long, ornamented with plates of brass, having a hollow brass knob at the end.

In regard to harps, the sources distinguish between large harps, as for example the *korro* with eighteen strings, and small harps, as the *simbing* with seven strings. Conneau compares the sound of the harp he heard to that of an American banjo. Bowdich comments upon its suitability as accompaniment for long, narrative songs, its strings being made of the fibrous roots of the palm wine tree, thus producing a "full, harmonious, and deep" tone.

While large bands of instruments might include a variety of types—such as the band heard by Bowdich at the Yam Customs in Kumasi—small ensembles usually consisted of drums, small flutes, and one or two chordophones. Jobson reports on a string instrument played "in consortship with a little drumme" for accompanying the dance. Performers generally attached small jingling idiophones to their wrists, elbows, knees, and ankles—small rings of iron and rattles—which added percussive elements to the musical sound as performers struck their drums and xylophones or plucked strings of the chordophones or the thin strips of thumb pianos.

[17]See also James E. Alexander, *Transatlantic Sketches* (Philadelphia, 1833), p. 212.

These subsidiary sounds were an essential element of performance style. The Ballards player heard by Jobson, for example, had large iron rings on his arms, to which were attached horizontally extending iron bars that had "upon them smaller rings and juggling toyes."

For performers who could not produce the subsidiary buzzing sounds themselves, there were always others to assist. Clapperton encountered a traveling violinist attended by two boys, who added percussive effects to his singing and playing by beating hollow gourds filled with pebbles and beans against their palms.

> His voice [was] clear and melodious. . . . He accompanied his instrument with his voice, the boys joining in [the] chorus. His songs were extempore. I should have taken one down, but found they were all about myself.

When there was nothing else at hand, a performer might simply beat a stick against an instrument or on the ground, or could resort to hand clapping and foot stomping.

The singing style was distinctive for its high intensity and use of such special effects as falsetto, shouts, groans, and guttural tones. A strong, clear voice was favored, but Europeans generally described the sounds of the African voice as "a rude noyse," "a strong nasal sound," or "very loud and shrill." During the musical-dance performance spectators participated by joining in the song refrains, clapping hands, tapping feet, or even entering the dance ring on occasion. According to tradition, they shouted words of encouragement (or disapproval) to the performers, just as during the palaver, they were accustomed "to give a groan or sigh at any remarkable or affecting description."

Although the only pointed discussion of rhythm comes from Bowdich, it is obvious that this element of African music was as important in the past as it is today.[18] Whether playing fast or slowly, performers maintained strict time, that is, handled their complex rhythms so as to intensify the basic pulse, which may have been produced by drums, idiophones, or even hand clapping. Scholars of African music refer to this metronomic element in the music as the *time line*. Bowdich points out that "it is always perfect, and the children will move their heads and limbs, whilst on their mother's backs, in exact unison with the tune which is playing."

In regard to melody, Bowdich again is the only informant who writes with authority; the others generally avoid technical language. To be sure, Park notes that a song improvised in his honor had a "sweet and plaintive air," but he does not, or cannot, explain why this was so. Bowdich includes the music for twenty-three songs in his book and attempts to identify the scales as major or minor. Careful examination of the music suggests, however, that the scales were predominantly pentatonic and modal, as in the following example:

[18]Bowdich's discussion of musical elements appears on pp. 449–52.

Empoöngwa song (Gabon)

Andantino

We are indebted to Bowdich for recording the melodies in notation. It was a difficult task because of the African propensity for embellishing melodies, but he was aware of the problem and made a special effort to solve it.

> I was fortunate enough to find a rare instance of a native able to play the radical notes of each tune [that is, the melodic skeleton without ornamentation]; he is the best player in the country [on the *sanko,* a string instrument]. . . . To have attempted anything like arrangement, beyond what the annexed airs naturally possess, would have altered them, and destroyed the intention of making them known in their original character. I have not even dared to insert a flat or sharp.

Melodic improvisation was as characteristic a feature of the music as was singing "extempore," that is, text improvisation. The first affected the second to some extent: a singer would invent a song on the spot, then naturally change the repetitions in the melody to fit the ever-changing text. But instrumental music also was affected by improvisation. Bowdich observes that the embellishing figures of melodies fell into two classes: those improvised on the spot and those belonging to a traditional repertory:

> Their graces [i.e., embellishing figures] are so numerous, some extempore, some transmitted from father to son, that the constant repetition only can distinguish the commencement of the air [i.e., melody]: sometimes between each beginning they introduce a few chords, sometimes they leave out a bar, sometimes they only return to the middle, so entirely is it left to the fancy of the performer.

In essence, the musical performance consisted of repeating a relatively short musical unit again and again, with variation in its repetition. The short tune of the Gabon song, above, fills only three measures in transcription. By comparing one repetition (mm. 4–6) with the basic tune (mm. 1–3), we can perceive how performers might have varied their tunes.

Some instruments were given diatonic tunings but others were tuned to produce chromatics within the octave. To the European ear, these tunings seemed quite random, according to no definite plan. Bowdich observes, for example, that the eight-string *sanko* was tuned from middle C to the octave above according to the sound of the C-major scale, but he could not discern a pattern in the tunings of other instruments he heard.

A Kerrapee song

When performance involved more than one person, harmonic elements might be introduced into the music: singers might sing parts of the song at the interval of a third, a fourth, or a fifth below the basic melody; or they might perform the song in parallel intervals throughout.

A very old Ashantee air

A Fantee dirge

A favorite performance practice involved a lead singer supported by one or two others, or by a group, functioning as a chorus to sing refrains. This resulted in musical structures in antiphonal style—that is, alternating solo vs. solo, or solo and small ensemble, or solo and group—for which modern scholars generally use the term *call-and-response*.

An Accra fetish hymn

Music and Poetry

Equiano the African reminds us that music, poetry, and the dance were inextricably interlinked and, as we have seen, poet and musician typically were one and the same person. Poetic language was distinctive for its use of imagery and figures of speech, which—to quote Bowdich—were "hyperbolical and picturesque." The Accras, for example, instead of saying "Good night," said, "Sleep till the lighting of the world." A New Year's song observed that "the year's ends have met." Song texts generally reflected personal or community concerns. The texts might speak of everyday affairs or of historical events; texts might inform listeners of current happenings or praise or ridicule persons, including even those listening to the song. More than one informant reports how the people would sit "all around in a Circle laughing, and with uncouth Notes, blame or praise somebody in the Company." But the most important texts belonged to the historical songs that recounted heroic deeds of the past and reminded the people of their traditions.

Without exception the European travelers were amazed at the "extempore" singing, and quite a few found themselves serving as the subject of a song—sometimes to their extreme discomfiture. Mungo Park was delighted with the song improvised about him and wrote down the words in his book, thus giving us the earliest example of an African song translated into a European language. The song was composed under unusual circumstances. Park had been compelled to seek shelter in a small village, but was unsuccessful in finding someone who would take him in, and so had to spend the entire day sitting under a tree without food.

Toward evening, as thunderclouds threatened and Park began to give up hope of finding a place for the night, a woman passing by took pity on him and invited him into her home. She gave him supper and directed him to a mat where he could sleep. The woman and her companions spent the greater part of the night spinning cotton; as they worked, they lightened their labors with songs, one of which was extemporized on the subject of Park himself. Park listened carefully, observing that the song "was sung by one of the young women, the rest joining in a sort of chorus." The following is Park's literal translation of the spinners' song:

> The winds roared, and the rains fell;
> The poor white man, faint and weary,
> Came and sat under our tree.
> He has no mother to bring him milk,
> No wife to grind his corn.

CHORUS   Let us pity the white man
> No mother has he to bring him milk,
> No wife to grind his corn.

The song of the spinners represents a typical African poetic form—the alternation of stanza and chorus, with the quite common feature of the reappearance of the stanza refrain as part of the chorus.

The African predilection for call-and-response performance was reflected in poetic form as well as in musical form, as is illustrated in the following example recorded by Major Denham:

> Give flesh to the hyenas at daybreak,
>> Oh, the broad spears!
> The spear of the Sultan is the broadest,
>> Oh, the broad spears!
> I behold thee now—I desire to see none other,
>> Oh, the broad spears!
> My horse is as tall as a high wall,
>> Oh, the broad spears!
> He will fight against ten—he fears nothing,
>> Oh, the broad spears!
> He has slain ten; the guns are yet behind,
>> Oh, the broad spears!
> The elephant of the forest brings me what I want,
>> Oh, the broad spears!
> Like unto thee, so is the Sultan,
>> Oh, the broad spears! . . .

In performance, speech and music frequently were integrated, with varying degrees of gradation among the four kinds of expression—speech, recitative, chant, and song. To some travelers the singing seemed to be "almost all recitative." A song might move into speech and back to singing during its performance; a story might employ songs during the course of the narrative. Call-and-response structure made ample allowance for the interjection of speech into song; for example, the group might speak or chant refrains instead of singing them.

Music and the Dance

If anything appeared more exotic to the early European travelers than musical performance, it was the dance. They observed that dancing was the "diversion of the evenings" for the people, that "all the night the people continue dancing, until he that playes be quite tyred out." And when the musicians were forced to rest, others took their place, and the dancing continued until dawn. Again and again the travelers describe the various kinds of dances they witnessed—some flavoring their accounts with disapproval, others, with admiration. Like music, dance was a form of communication as well as creative expression and recreation; there were dances for celebrating the important events of the individual or community life—fertility, initiation into adulthood, war, worship, death, and similar kinds of human concerns.

Different nations cultivated different dance forms, of course, but certain formations and body attitudes seem to have been prevalent among all the peoples. In 1620 Jobson noticed the "bended bodies" and "crooked knees" of the women dancers and how the men dance "with their swords naked in their hands," while all the time "the standers-by seeme to grace the dancers, by clapping their hands together after the manner of keeping time." Over a century later, a traveler in Sierra Leone noticed that

> Men and Women make a Ring in an open part of the Town, and one at a time shews his Skill in Antick Motions and Gesticulations, yet with a great deal of

"Funeral Ceremony at Annabon." Engraving by J. W. Cook from William Allen's *Narrative of the Expedition Sent . . . to the River Niger,* 1848.

Agility, the company making the Musick by clapping their hands together during the time, helped by the louder noise of two or three Drums. . . .[19]

Other observers have commented on the circle formation of the dancers and the predilection for "principally confining [movement] to the head and upper parts of the body" and for "scarcely moving their feet" or using a shufflelike step. Also distinctive were the exhibitions of individual skill and the placement of the musicians in the center of the ring. The sword or stick dances of the males are mentioned frequently, and every description refers to the bystanders clapping their hands, "evincing by acclamation and gesture their unqualified approbation."

A dance observed by Major Denham in 1826 might be regarded as typical:

The dance was performed by men armed with sticks, who springing alternately from one foot to another, while dancing round in a ring, frequently flourished their sticks in the air, or clashed them together with a loud noise. Sometimes a dancer jumped out of the circle, and springing around on his heel for several minutes, made his stick whirl above his head at the same time with equal rapidity; he would then rejoin the dance. In the center of the ring there were two drummers, the drums standing on the ground.[20]

In modern Africa, music and dance may be integrated with drama, particularly on occasions associated with worship or festivals. Undoubtedly such music-dance-drama combinations occurred in the past, and the spectacle witnessed in 1825 by Major Alexander Gordon Laing at Talaba, Soolima (now Senegal) clearly fits the description (although the term *drama* is not used). Thirty warriors on horseback and 2,000 on foot staged mock battles on the parade grounds in front of the king and his guests for more than half an hour, accompanied by a band of over one hundred musicians. This was followed by a performance involving a Jelle, or singing man, in elaborate costume, ten women "fancifully dressed out in fine cloths," the War-Master (principal military chief), and a number of warriors engaging in dialogue, song, pantomime, and dance.[21]

Summary

Although the musical cultures of West Africa during the slave-trade period varied from nation to nation, the cultures shared enough features to constitute an identifiable heritage for Africans in the New World. From the accounts of explorers and traders, to which can be added evidence deduced from modern oral traditions, we learn of the primacy of music as an integral

[19]John Atkins, *A Voyage to Guinea, Brasil, and the West Indies* (London, 1737), pp. 53, 64. See also Francis Moore, *Travels Into the Inland Parts of Africa* (London, 1737), pp. 64, 109–10; Laing, *Travels,* pp. 311–13.

[20]Denham, *Narrative,* p. 402.

[21]Laing, *Travels,* pp. 228–38.

part of everyday life, of distinctive performance practices, and of the prevalent musical instruments.[22] Moreover, it is possible to imagine how the music might have sounded since many instruments of the past are still used today, a number of songs were preserved in notation, and much music has been transmitted orally through the generations. Music making was generally a communal activity involving the interaction of soloists or leaders with the group as the chorus. Music served not only in the conventional roles of enhancing worship rituals and providing recreational outlets, but also offered a means of communication and a way of sharing in collective experiences, whether of the past or present. Finally, the integration of music with dance and / or dramatic elements was a characteristic feature of the cultures.

THE AFRICAN DIASPORA

The precise number of Africans transported to the New World via slave ships on the so-called Middle Passage is unknown; it has been estimated by some to be ten million, by others, fifteen million or more. Although black men entered the New World as early as 1501 with the first explorers, and slavery became established in the West Indies during the second decade of the century, it was not until the seventeenth century that Africans were imported into the mainland colonies.

From Indentured Servitude to Slavery

According to reliable estimates there were 1,980 colonists on the mainland of America in 1625—180 in the Plymouth Colony and 1,800 in Virginia. The records do not indicate the number of black people included in the population figures for Virginia at that time; it is not likely that Plymouth had any at all. By 1649, Virginia's population had increased to 15,000 whites and 300 blacks. In 1626 the Dutch West India Company brought eleven black men from Angola into New Amsterdam, a settlement at the mouth of the Hudson River, to work as the "Company's Negroes" about the village as builders, domestics, and farm hands. Two years later three black women were brought in from Angola. Sometime before 1638 New England saw its first black men, and by the middle of the century black folk on the streets of colonial America were common.

The earliest African arrivals in the colonies had the status of indentured servants, as did many whites and Native Americans of the period. Already by 1644 Governor Kieft of New Amsterdam had manumitted (released from bondage) the original eleven men of Angola and their wives for "long and faithful service"; and the records show that black indentured servants

---

[22]For discussions of traditional music in Africa see Francis Bebey, *African Music* (New York, 1975) and Joseph H. Kwabena Nketia, *The Music of Africa* (New York, 1974).

in Virginia began to secure their freedom in the 1650s, having served out their time. During the second half of the seventeenth century, the importation of Africans into the colonies increased. More and more black captives were given contracts that made them "servants for life" instead of "servants for a time." Eventually they received no indentures at all.[23]

It was during this period that black slavery became established, at first by custom, then by law. From North to South the colonists began to enact laws ensuring that the incoming Africans would be held in lifetime servitude. Although a Massachusetts law of 1641 prohibited enslavement, it was easy to evade the law; slave traders had only to see to it that the Africans they imported were captured in wars or sold to them by others.

> There shall never be any bond slavery, villenage, or captivity among us unless it be lawful captives taken in just wars, and such strangers as willingly sell themselves or are sold to us. And these shall have all the liberties and Christian usages which the law of God, established in Israel concerning such persons, does morally require. This exempts none from servitude who shall be judged thereto by authority.[24]

During the 1660s the codes of the colonies giving statutory recognition to black slavery came swiftly: Virginia in 1661, Maryland in 1663, New York and New Jersey in 1664. Later the colonies of Pennsylvania, Delaware, New England, and the Carolinas followed suit. By 1700 the "peculiar institution" of slavery was a reality throughout the thirteen colonies.

African Retentions in the New World

Africans were taken to the New World in chains, stripped to the bare skin, and those that came to the mainland colonies generally were separated from their families and communities. But though they could bring no material objects with them, they retained memories of the rich cultural traditions they had left behind in the motherland and passed these traditions down to their children. The importance given to music and dance in Africa was reflected among the slaves in the colonies, as will be seen—in the songs they sang, in their dancing and folk festivals. In addition, there were specific customs that persisted throughout their long years of acculturation into the lifestyle of the dominant society in the United States. (To be sure, the African experience was reflected as well in other areas, particularly in folk literature and religion.) The function of music as a communal activity, for example, led to the development of slave-song repertories that provided some measure of release from the physical and spiritual brutality of slavery. Despite

---

[23]See further in Robert Beverley, *The History of Virginia in Four Parts* (London, 1722), p. 235.

[24]The Massachusetts Body of Liberties, 1641, is reprinted in many places; for example, *The Annals of America*, ed. Mortimer G. Adler (Chicago Encyclopaedia Britannica, 1976), v. 1: *Discovering a New World, 1492–1754*, p. 167.

the interaction of African and European cultural patterns in black communities, with the resultant emergence of new, *African-American* patterns, there persisted among black folk musicians a predilection for certain performance practice, certain habits, certain musical instruments, and certain ways of shaping music to meet their needs in the new environment that had roots in the African experience.

CHAPTER 2

The
Colonial
Era

W HETHER they were gentlemen adventurers in Virginia, religious dissenters in New England, wealthy merchants in the Hudson Valley,
or black and white indentured servants, the first settlers landing on
the shores of the Atlantic seaboard were confronted with the tremendous
task of clearing the "hideous and desolate wilderness" and building a place
in which to live. During the first decades of the colonial experience, the
cultural and social life of the people was necessarily that of a frontier community, and there was little time for the cultivation of the arts. To be sure,
back in the countries from which they emigrated the settlers had participated in the musical life characteristic of the seventeenth century. The white
settlers brought their psalm books to the New World and later imported
musical instruments. The black folk brought their memories of the rich traditions of Africa. Together the settlers, black and white, were to lay the
foundation for a phenomenal subsequent development of music in America.

MUSIC IN THE COLONIES

Colonial society in the seventeenth century was basically a rural society, and
its music was primarily a vocal music, organized in relation to the needs of
the meetinghouse (or church), the home, and the community. For the majority of the settlers the meetinghouse provided not only religious guidance but
also social diversion. In the town it was the tavern or "ordinary" that served
as the chief social institution for all classes of society—the "better sort,"

"the middling sort," and the "inferior classes." At the beginning of the eighteenth century, however, town dwellers constituted only about 8 percent of the population. In 1720, they were concentrated in Boston (with a population of 12,000), Newport (3,800), New York (7,000), Philadelphia (10,000), and Charles Town (3,500).[1]

Undoubtedly it was the lack of organized recreational activities that stimulated so great an interest in dancing among the colonists, for dancing was the favorite form of social entertainment everywhere—from Boston in New England to Charles Town in the South—and with everyone, white settlers and black. The favorite instrument for dance music was the violin, played by white and black fiddlers. Except for the fife, trumpet, and drum music of the militia, dance music was the chief type of instrumental music performed in the colonies during the early years.

Vocal music remained dominant throughout most of the eighteenth century. The rapidly developing cities, however, soon began to stimulate the production of a wider variety of music, a music for the "concert room" and the "ballroom" as well as for the meetinghouse and the tavern. It became evident, as Benjamin Franklin wrote in 1743, that the "first drudgery of settling new colonies, which confines the attention of people to mere necessaries," was just about over and that there were many people "in every province in circumstances that set them at ease."[2] The colonists could afford to cultivate the fine arts. They purchased instruments for use in their homes: "vialls" (viols) of all sizes, the more popular violins, virginals (small harpsichords), "hautboys" (oboes), "guittars," flutes, "fortepianos," and "harmonicas" (mechanically controlled musical glasses invented by Benjamin Franklin). In 1714 the first permanent church organ, the "Brattle organ," was installed in King's Chapel in Boston. In 1729 the first public concert held in the colonies took place in Boston, a "Concert of Musick on Sundry Instruments."

Charles Town (later, Charleston), the cultural metropolis of the South, was regarded by some as the musical center of the entire eastern seaboard during the early eighteenth century. Certainly it was the port of entry for most professionals coming from England to perform or teach music in the colonies. It was there that the first performance of an opera in the colonies took place, in 1735, the one-act ballad *Flora: Or Hob in the Well*. As early as 1735 musicians of Charles Town were giving public concerts in honor of St. Cecilia, the patron saint of music, and in 1762 they orga-

[1]See further in Carl Bridenbaugh, *Cities in the Wilderness* (New York, 1939), p. 143. Estimates are that Boston had about 2,000 blacks, and New York, over 1,600 (p. 220). By the 1750s blacks comprised approximately 8 percent of the population in Boston, 14 percent in New York, 20 percent in Newport, and more than half of Charleston's population. See also Bridenbaugh, *Cities in Revolt* (New York, 1955), pp. 88, 285, 333; Lorenzo Greene, *The Negro in Colonial New England* (New York, 1942), pp. 84, 87, 338.

[2]Quoted in James Truslow Adams, *A History of American Life* (New York, 1927), v. 3: *Provincial Society, 1690–1763,* frontispiece.

nized the first colonial group devoted exclusively to music, the St. Cecilia Society.

Music schools and dancing schools sprang up in the towns, and in the rural areas itinerant music and dancing masters provided instruction, particularly south of the Delaware River, where the plantation was the chief unit of settlement. The musicians of colonial America came from all classes: there were professional emigrants from Europe, native professionals, "gentlemen amateurs" and amateurs among the lower classes, and musician-domestics—both indentured servants and slaves, both black and white.

PRIMARY SOURCES OF INFORMATION

Understandably, the black inhabitants of colonial America left few written records of their cultural activities. After recovering from the initial shock of being uprooted from their ancestral homes and forcibly integrated into an alien society, they had to learn to adjust—first, to the traumatic experience of slavery itself, then to the master group's language, culture, and way of life. Invariably black men and women had to do these things without help. Indeed, most frequently there was strong opposition to their acquiring any knowledge or skill that did not relate directly to their value as servants. In order to piece together the history of the black musician we must turn to documents of the dominant society—to their colonial newspapers, town and court records, legislative journals, and to the various diaries, letters, personal narratives, missionary reports, travel journals, and fiction of white colonists and travelers to the New World.

The Colonial Newspaper

The colonial newspaper provides a rich source of information about slave musicians.[3] From the beginning, the advertising columns in newspapers (the *Boston News-Letter*, established in 1704, was the first permanent one) regularly carried listings of slaves "for sale" or "for hire." Numerous listings included references to the possession of musical skills by slaves, for their market value was thereby greatly increased. In March, 1766, for example, the *Virginia Gazette* advertised:

> TO BE SOLD. A young healthy Negro fellow who has been used to wait on a Gentlemen and plays extremely well on the French horn.

On August 6, 1767, a prospective slave buyer reading the *Virginia Gazette* was offered yet a bigger bargain:

[3]See further in Lathan N. Windley, *Runaway Slave Advertisements. A Documentary History from the 1730s to 1790.* 4 vols. (Westport, CT: Greenwood Press, 1983). This collection contains 6,000 advertisements collected from twenty-one colonial newspapers.

TO BE SOLD a valuable young handsome Negro Fellow about 18 or 20 years of age; has every qualification of a genteel and sensible servant and has been in many different parts of the world. . . . He . . . plays on the French horn. . . . He lately came from London, and has with him two suits of new clothes, and his French horn, which the purchaser may have with him.

Judging from the evidence, slave musicians most frequently were fiddlers. Numerous examples, such as the following one from the *New York Gazette-Post-Boy*, can be cited to illustrate this:

TO BE SOLD. A Negro Indian Man slave, about forty years of age, well known in town, being a fiddler. [June 21, 1748]

Similar advertisements appeared in other newspapers of the time:

. . . he plays remarkably well on the violin.
. . . a Virginia-born Negro . . . can play upon the violin.
. . . a Negro Man slave, about 38 years old . . . can read and play on the Fiddle.

"Runaway" listings invariably gave more information about slaves than did "for sale" advertisements. The slaveholders omitted no details of personal appearance or habits that would help to identify the fugitives; for example, the clothing worn (generally made of "Negro cloth"), the color of the skin (ranging from black to "whitish"), the tools or other articles taken away (sometimes a gun), and the presence of identifying marks on the body (frequently the owner's initials branded on the cheeks). The possession of musical skills was considered to be noteworthy, as the following examples indicate:

RUN AWAY . . . a Negro Man about 46 years of age . . . plays on the Violin and is a Sawyer. [*Virginia Gazette*, April 24, 1746]

RUN AWAY . . . a likely Negro Man named Damon . . . was born in the West Indies, beats the drum tolerably well, which he is very fond of. [*Virginia Gazette*, April 17, 1766]

CAESAR: Absented himself from my Plantation . . . plays well on the French horn. [*South Carolina Gazette*, April 19, 1770]

A slave fugitive of Poughkeepsie, New York, could play two instruments:

RUN AWAY: Negro man named Zack . . . speaks good English, plays on the fife and German flute, had a fife with him. [*Poughkeepsie Journal*, 1791]

A South Carolinian could whistle and also fiddle:

RUN AWAY: Dick, a mulatto fellow . . . a remarkable whistler and plays on the Violin. [*South Carolina Gazette*, June 4, 1772]

Were the matter not so grim, one might be inclined to smile at the phrasing of some of the listings:

RUN AWAY . . . a Negro Man named Derby, about 25 years of age, a slim black Fellow, and plays on the Fiddle with his Left Hand, which he took with him. [*Virginia Gazette*, May 14, 1772]

RUN AWAY: a Negro fellow named Peter, about 44 years of age . . . he carried away a fiddle, which he is much delighted in when he gets any strong drink.

[*Virginia Gazette,* May 4, 1769]

RUN AWAY: a Mulatto fellow named John Jones, about 26 years old . . . is a mighty singer. [*Maryland Gazette,* April 14, 1745]

RUN AWAY: Negro man named Robert . . . speaks good English, is a fiddler and took his fiddle with him.

[*New York Packet & American Advertiser,* September 2, 1779]

Of a girl it was related that she was "fond of Liquor and apt to sing indecent and Sailors' songs" when intoxicated. Other examples, too numerous to cite here, could be drawn from colonial newspapers attesting to the prevalence of musical abilities among the slaves. In the *Virginia Gazette* alone, the advertisement sections contained more than sixty references to black musicians during the years 1736–80, forty-five of which were to black violinists or fiddlers. It is noteworthy that some references were made to fiddle *makers,* as distinguished from performers:

RUN AWAY . . . a black Virginia born Negro fellow named Sambo, about 6 ft. high, about 32 years old. He makes fiddles, and can play upon the fiddle, and work at the carpenter's trade. [August 18, 1768]

Other Primary Sources

Other sources of information are the town and court records and the assembly journals of the time, which frequently reveal items of musical interest among the dry lists of facts. Thus we learn, for example, that the slave Nero Benson served as a trumpeter in the company of Captain Isaac Clark in 1723 in Framingham, Massachusetts.[4] The trial records of the New York City slave revolt in 1741 show that one of the slaves involved was a fiddler: a man named Jamaica, a slave of Ellis, who was "frequently at Hughson's [tavern] with his fiddle."[5] On October 5, 1765, the two young drummers who marched through the streets of Philadelphia beating "crepe-festooned" drums to call the citizenry to a town meeting on the State House grounds were black boys.[6]

Most informative of all, of course, are the various kinds of personal writing, nonfiction and fiction, that have come down from the colonial period. Travelers who remarked on a slave's singing or instrumental playing, local historians who cited the names of black musicians in villages and

[4]In regard to Benson, see William Barry, *History of Framingham, Massachusetts, from 1640 to the Present Time* (Boston, 1847), p. 157.

[5]Herbert Aptheker, *A Documentary History of the Negro People in the United States* (New York, 1951), p. 4.

[6]See Harold D. Eberlin and Cortlandt van Dyke Hubbard, *Diary of Independence Hall* (New York, 1948), p. 109;

towns or described slave festivals, diarists who jotted down notes about their musically inclined servants, novelists who recreated scenes of slave merrymaking—all represent valuable sources of information about the musical activities of black colonists.

Of the writings of New Englanders, the most useful is the diary kept over a span of fifty-five years (1674–1729) by the Puritan judge Samuel Sewall of Boston.[7] Sewall was very fond of music and, moreover, was the precentor (or deacon) in his church, one of his duties being to lead congregational singing. Because of his talent he was frequently called upon to lead group singing on the many and varied occasions in the Puritan way of life that called for psalm singing: religious services on weekdays, weddings, funerals, meetings of the town council, holiday celebrations, and social gatherings in the home. Sewall's diary is of value, then, for two reasons: it throws light on musical practices of his time; and it reveals the extent to which black people participated in community life. Consequently, we learn indirectly from Sewall about the musical activities of the blacks.

In regard to musical practices in the South, the letters and reports of clergymen who worked among the slaves as missionaries are particularly revealing. In addition to filing official documents with their supervisors, the missionaries wrote to their benefactors in England for various kinds of supplies. Some of the letters were published in contemporary books, such as the *Letters from the Rev. Samuel Davies and Others; Shewing the State of Religion in Virginia, S.C., &c Particularly Among the Negroes* (London, 1761) and Benjamin Fawcett, *A Compassionate Address* (London, 1755).

The South also had its celebrated diarists, among them, William Byrd II of Westover, Virginia, and Philip Vickers Fithian. Although these diaries were not as extensive as Sewall's, they offer lively descriptions of the southern way of life for the aristocracy and their indentured servants, black and white.

CONGREGATIONAL SINGING; PSALMODY AND HYMNODY

Singing in the Meetinghouse

In New England, where Sabbath services were held mornings and evenings, African Americans joined in the singing from the special pews where they sat separately from the whites (sometimes the pews were marked "BW" for black women and "BM" for black men). Along with other members of the congregation they waited for the precentor to "line out" the

---

[7]Sewall's diary has been published in several editions; among them, *Collections of the Massachusetts Historical Society,* Fifth Series, vols. 5–7 (Boston, 1878–82). Dates are given for quotations rather than page numbers so that any edition of the diary can be consulted for further information.

psalm and "set the tune" according to traditional procedures. The Reverend John Cotton provided explicit instructions in a treatise of 1647:

> it will be a necessary helpe, that the lines of the Psalme, be openly read before-hand, line after line, or two lines together, that so they who want either books or skill to reade, may know what is to be sung, and joyne with the rest in the dutie of singing.[8]

In the colony of New York it was the Dutch Reformed Church that ordered, in a church law of 1645, the precentor or *voorzanger* to "tune the psalm" for congregational singing. The procedure consisted in the precentor's chanting one line (or two lines) at a time, ending on a definite pitch, and the congregation following with the singing of the same line, generally with some elaboration of the tune. (This practice, called "lining out," later became a characteristic feature of hymn singing in black churches and still lingers on in many places.) It was the precentor's responsibility not only to start the psalm tune on the right pitch, but also to sing loudly and clearly enough to lead the congregation in the singing.

People learned to sing psalm tunes by rote, in the same way they learned folksongs, and inevitably they altered the tunes a little each time they sang. The most popular of the early psalters, called the *Bay Psalm Book*, contained no music in its first edition (1640) but suggested the names of appropriate tunes to which the psalm texts could be fitted. This psalter was the first book printed in the English colonies. A 1698 edition of the psalter included thirteen tunes: *Oxford, Litchfield, Low Dutch, York, Windsor, Cambridge Short, St. David's, Martyrs, Hackney, 119th Psalm, 100th Psalm, 115th Psalm*, and *148th Psalm*. Any psalm could be sung to a variety of tunes, the choice being restricted by the need to match the metrical system of psalm and tune.

A comparison of the King James version of Psalm 19:1–6 (a) with the metrical version of the same psalm as it appeared in the *Bay Psalm Book* (b) illustrates the difference between the two:

(a)   The heavens declare the glory of God;
                       and the firmament sheweth his handywork.
                   Day unto day uttereth speech,
                       and night unto night sheweth knowledge.
                   There is no speech nor language,
                       where their voice is not heard.
                   Their line is gone out through all the earth,
                       and their words to the end of the world.
                       In them hath he set a tabernacle for the sun,
                   Which is as a bridegroom coming out of his chamber,
                       and rejoiceth as a strong man to run a race.
                   His going forth is from the end of the heaven,

---

[8]Quoted in Gilbert Chase, *America's Music,* 2nd ed. rev. (New York, 1966), p. 31.

and his circuit unto the ends of it:
and there is nothing hid from the heat thereof.

(b)   The heavens doe declare
the majesty of God:
also the firmament shews forth
his handy-work abroad.
Day speaks to day, knowledge
night hath to night declar'd.
There neither speach nor language is,
where their voyce is not heard.
Through all the earth their line
is gone forth, & unto
the utmost end of all the world,
their speaches reach also:
A Tabernacle hee
in them pitcht for the Sun.
Who Bridegroom like from's chamber goes
glad Giants-race to run.
From heavens utmost end,
his course and compassing;
to ends of it, & from the heat
thereof is hid nothing.

A favorite tune used for the singing of Psalm 19 was the *Cambridge Short Tune*. Since it has the same metrical scheme as the psalm text—that is, short meter—each syllable of the psalm text can be matched by a note in the melody.

Cambridge Short Tune

The small repertory of melodies in general use increased the probability of most members of the community being willing and able to learn to sing psalms, whether or not they could read or had access to psalters. In contemporary psalters and hymnals the meters most often applied to singing the psalms are long meter (8.8.8.8), common meter (8.6.8.6), and short meter (6.6.8.6). Among the other psalm collections (some of them containing tunes) available to the early settlers were Thomas Ravenscroft's *Whole Booke of Psalmes,* the popular Ainsworth Psalter (mentioned by Longfellow in *The Courtship of Miles Standish*), the Sternhold and Hopkins, the Tate and Brady, and the Allison Psalters.

Psalm Singing in the Community

We know from contemporaneous sources that the singing of psalms was not confined to the meetinghouse. In many places in the North, when a colonial family gathered for prayer services in the home, the "light of the blazing fire glowed on the dark shining faces intermixed familiarly with the master's children." Black servants sang with their masters on special occasions, as on October 3, 1688, at Sewall's house: "Have a Day of Prayer at our House: . . . Sung *Cambridge Short Tune,* which I set"; and at weekly prayer meetings, such as the one held at Sewall's house on January 1, 1718: "Privat Meeting at our House . . . Sung clauses out of the 143rd Psalm."

Psalm singing was essential at a wedding ceremony or at funeral service. Sewall took personal charge of the wedding of "Mr. John Wait's Bastian and Mrs. Thair's Negro Jane" in January 1701. Although Sewall did not describe this wedding, his descriptions of others in his diary offer insight into common practices among the household servants. After the brief ceremony held in the "Hall" of his house, Sewall would have set the psalm tune—perhaps *York* or *Low Dutch*—"in a very good key, which made the singing with a good number of voices very agreeable." For wedding refreshments "cake and sack-posset" would have been served.

When the community gathered for public ceremonies such as the King's Birthday or Election Day, psalm singing was again in order. Sewall described a typical ceremony that took place on May 20, 1691: "Election Day [was] very fair and comfortable weather. Led the South Company into the Common, there prayed with them. . . . The 122nd Psalm was sung. Mr. Allen got me to set the Tune, which was *Windsor.*"

The singing of psalms by the colonists, black and white, was not confined to formal occasions. Like their contemporaries in Europe, they believed that:

> The first and chief Use of Musick is for the Service and Praise of God, whose gift it is. The second Use is for the Solace of Men, which as it is agreeable unto Nature, so it is allow'd by God, as a temporal Blessing to recreate and cheer men after long study and weary labor in their Vocations.[9]

When black colonists began to organize their own meetings, it was natural that they should include the singing of psalms. The earliest of these orga-

[9]John Playford, *Brief Introduction to the Skill of Musick* (London, 1687), p. 3.

nizations, the Society of Negroes, was formed in October 1693, when a group of servants went to Puritan minister Cotton Mather for help in forming a "Meeting for ye Welfare of [those] . . . that were Servants." The Society drew up nine rules for its governance, of which the first stated:

> It shall be our Endeavour to Meet in the Evening after the Sabbath [service]; and Pray together by Turns, one to begin and another to conclude the Meeting; And between the two *Prayers,* a Psalm shall be Sung and a *Sermon* repeated.[10]

The Reform Movement

The traditional way of singing psalms, without recourse to musical notation and without the aid of instrumental accompaniment, inevitably led to the development of undesirable practices with regard to congregational singing. People forgot the psalm tunes or changed the tunes slightly as they sang. Had there been instrumental accompaniment for the singing, it would have sufficed to keep the congregation on pitch, but the use of instruments in the meetinghouse was frowned upon in most places (but not among the Anglicans) and absolutely forbidden in Reformed Puritan churches. The precentor could not always be depended upon to provide good leadership; sometimes he himself forgot the tune, or set the pitch too high, or embellished the melody so freely that the singers following his leadership became confused.

Deacon Sewall, for example, experienced several embarrassing moments during his years as leader of congregational singing. The black worshipers in attendance at church on those occasions contributed as much to the confusion, no doubt, as did the white worshipers. On October 25, 1691, Sewall wrote:

> Capt. Frary's voice failing him in his own Essay, he calls to me to set the Tune, which accordingly I doe. . . . The Tune I guess'd at was in so high a Key that I could not reach it.

On December 28, 1705, Sewall again realized that he himself was to blame:

> [He] Spake to me to set the Tune. I intended *Windsor* and fell into *High Dutch,* and then essaying to set another Tune went into a Key much too high. So I pray'd Mr. White to set it; which he did well, *Litchfield Tune.* The Lord humble me and Instruct me, that I should be the occasion of any Interruption in the Worship of God.

Years later, Sewall was still having difficulties, as on February 2, 1718:

> In the morning I set *York Tune* and in the 2[d] going over, the gallery carried it irresibly to St. David's which discouraged me very much.

---

[10]Mather entered eight of the rules in his diary for 1693; the ninth was printed later when the full document was printed as a broadside sheet. Reprint in *Massachusetts Broadsides, Ballads, Etc. Printed in Massachusetts 1639–1800* (Boston, 1922), p. 29, no. 201.

On February 23, 1718, the very same thing happened again.

The occurrences in Sewall's church were not unusual; similar ones were taking place in churches all over the land. Some learned clergymen began to agitate for the improvement of psalm singing in the church, making such allegations as:

> Tunes are now miserably tortured, and twisted, and quavered in some Churches, into an horrid Medley of confused and discordant Noises . . . and besides no two men in the Congregation quavering alike, or together, which sounds in the Ears of a Good Judge like five hundred different tunes roared out at the Same Time.

or:

> the same person who sets the Tune and guides the Congregation in Singing, commonly reads the Psalm, which is a task so few are capable of performing well, that in Singing two or three staves the Congregation falls from a cheerful Pitch to downright Grumbling. . . .[11]

By the 1720s a movement was definitely under way to improve the quality of congregational singing.

The conventional approach to the singing of the psalms, called the "common way," was "grave and serious." Tunes were sung in a very slow tempo with much ornamentation of the melodic lines. The reformers wanted to replace the old style with a new one, called "regular singing," which emphasized singing by rules, in a strict tempo, and with exact pitches. The ordinary people clung to their old ways for as long as they could, for they liked the slow melodies with flourishes and shakes on the notes, but the reformers eventually won out. Singing schools, and later singing societies, were organized where people could receive instruction in "correct singing"—that is, could learn to sing the psalm tunes as written. Organs were brought into the church to accompany the congregational singing and to keep the singing on pitch. Trained singers were organized into church choirs that took over the responsibility for performing difficult religious music— for example, the anthems—and leading the congregation in its singing. Psalters and hymnals containing tunes were gradually used more and more, so that people could follow the music as they sang.

The Growth of Hymnody

During the 1730s a religious movement called the "Great Awakening" swept the colonies, bringing with it a demand for the use of livelier music in the worship service. The "new" songs of the movement were *hymns;* for texts they employed religious poems instead of the scriptural psalms. In

---

[11]The two statements are quoted in Chase, *America's Music,* pp. 26, 33. The first is from Thomas Walter, *The Grounds and Rules of Musick Explained . . .* (Boston, 1721); the second is from an article that appeared in the *New England Courant* in 1724.

1707 the English minister Dr. Isaac Watts published a book, *Hymns and Spiritual Songs,* that became immensely popular in the colonies, especially among the black folk, because of the freshness and vitality of the words. In 1717 he published another collection of his attractive hymns, entitled *The Psalms of David, Imitated in the Language of the New Testament and Apply'd to the Christian State and Worship.*

Before long, people began to neglect the psalms, preferring to sing hymns instead, especially since the latter were fitted to lively tunes. One after the other, the various Protestant denominations in the colonies adopted the hymns of Watts, and the "Era of Watts" in the history of American religious music was under way.[12] The following example shows a Watts hymn based on Psalm 19.

A Morning Hymn, Isaac Watts, based on Psalm 19; *Old Hundredth Tune*

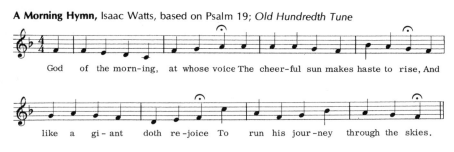

God of the morn-ing, at whose voice The cheer-ful sun makes haste to rise, And

like a gi-ant doth re-joice To run his jour-ney through the skies.

2. From the fair chambers of the east
   The circuit of his race begins,
   And without weariness or rest
   Round the whole earth he flys and shines.
3. O like the Sun may I fulfil
   Th' appointed Duties of the Day,
   With ready Mind and active Will
   March on and keep my heavenly Way.
4. But I shall rove and lose the Race,
   If God my Sun should disappear,
   And leave me in this World's wild Maze
   To follow every wand'ring Star.

In 1737 a hymnal published by John Wesley, George Whitefield, and other students at Oxford University launched Wesley's career as a hymnal compiler and became the first of a long series of official Methodist hymnals. The book, *A Collection of Psalms and Hymns,* included thirty-five hymns written by Watts, the remainder being contributed by a number of other men, among them Wesley's father and brother Charles, who with Wesley had founded the Methodist Church in 1729. Wesley had been influenced in his decision to compile a hymnal by the music of the Moravians, members of a

---

[12]See further in Louis F. Benson, *The English Hymn* (New York, 1915), pp. 359 ff.

religious sect of German origin, who came to the colonies in 1735 on the same ship as the Wesley brothers. The deeply moving hymns sung by the Moravians while on shipboard impressed the Wesleys and, consequently, affected considerably the development of Methodist hymnody—and thus, as we shall see, indirectly affected Negro hymnody as well.

RELIGIOUS INSTRUCTION AND PSALMODY

Patterns of Slavery in North and South

In New England the white population was of predominantly English stock and belonged, for the most part, to the Congregational Church. The middle colonies, on the other hand, were settled by a variety of ethnic and religious groups: Dutch settlements were clustered around the Hudson and Delaware Rivers, Germans were in Pennsylvania, Swedes and Finns on the lower Delaware, and the English everywhere. Among the religious groups most interested in the plight of black men and women were the Quakers first and foremost; the Moravians; the Congregationalists to some extent; the Catholics; and the Methodists (beginning in the late eighteenth century).

Throughout the region slavery assumed a milder form than in the southern colonies, although in some places the harsh and severe treatment of black slaves provoked more than one rebellious uprising. Generally, slavery tended to be paternalistic, slaves being regarded as part of the family. They were listed as members of the family (usually taking the family's surname) on the "household baptism plan"; they lived in the home and worked alongside their masters in the field, shop, or kitchen. The attitude of the Puritan Cotton Mather toward his black servants was shared by many of his contemporaries, not only in Massachusetts but in the other colonies:

> I would always remember that my servants are in some sence [sic] my children, and by taking care that they want nothing which may be good for them, I would make them as my children. . . . Nor will I leave them ignorant of anything, wherein I may instruct them to be useful. . . .[13]

With its large plantations the South resembled rural England, and the wealthy planters, many of them originally members of English nobility or landed gentry, led lives similar in some ways to those of English country gentlemen. The isolation of the plantation necessarily encouraged the development of considerable self-sufficiency on the part of the master family and the slaves. One of the richest and most powerful of the southern aristocrats, William Byrd II of Westover, Virginia, wrote in 1726:

---

[13]This excerpt from Mather's "Sermon to Masters and Servants" is reprinted several places; for example, Carter G. Woodson, *The Education of the Negro Prior to 1881* (New York, 1915), p. 337.

> I have my flocks and my birds, my bond-men and bond-women, and every soart
> of trade among my own servants, so that I live in a kind of independence on
> everyone but providence.[14]

The isolation of the plantation also gave the master unusual power over
his family and slaves. He interpreted the slave codes and unwritten traditions as he willed; he made of the institution of slavery either the brutal
experience that it was for most black men and women or something better,
which at times and in certain places approximated the relatively humane
condition of slavery in New England.

Conversion and Religious Instruction in the North

One of the major concerns of colonial clergymen was the matter of con-
verting the so-called heathen of the New World, the African Americans and
the Native Americans, to Christianity. And the act of conversion automatically included religious instruction. In New Amsterdam, as early as 1638,
the citizens petitioned "Dominie" Bogardus, governor of the colony and
pastor of the Dutch Reformed Church, for a "schoolmaster to teach and
train the youth of both Dutch and blacks in the knowledge of Jesus Christ."
When in 1641 a "Negro woman belonging to Rev. Stoughton of Dorchester
[Massachusetts] . . . was received into the Church and baptized"—possibly
the earliest slave baptism in the colonies—it was pointed out that she was
"well approved . . . for sound knowledge and true godliness."[15]

White or black, servant or master, religious instruction was not only an
essential prerequisite for membership in the church, but was also a basic
part of daily life. A Massachusetts law of 1648, for example, instructed "all
masters of families doe once a week (at the least) catechize their children
and servants in the grounds and principles of Religion."[16] A teacher's contract of 1682 in New York included among its articles of agreement:
"School shall begin with the Lord's prayer and close by singing a Psalm."[17]

During the years 1702–85 the Society for the Propagation of the Gospel
in Foreign Parts (hereafter referred to as SPG) sent clergymen to the colonies
to minister to the slaves and to convert them to Christianity. This missionary
organization of the Established Church of England was established in 1701.
In association with their work the missionaries founded schools for the religious instruction of black folk. As early as 1704 the SPG appointed Elias
Neau to open a catechizing school, which he conducted in his home in New

---

[14]Quoted in Hugh Jones, *The Present State of Virginia,* ed. Richard Morton (1724; Chapel
Hill, 1956), p. 8.

[15]The statement about the baptism in 1641 appears in John Winthrop's *Journal* and is
reprinted in Greene, *Negro in Colonial New England,* p. 257.

[16]Quoted in Marcus W. Jernegan, *Laboring and Dependent Classes in Colonial America,
1607–1783* (Chicago, 1931), p. 91.

[17]Quoted in Alice Morse Earle, *Colonial Days in Old New York* (New York, 1896), p. 31.

York. Within a year the group had increased to thirty persons, and Neau moved the school to Trinity Church. Psalm singing was included, of course, in the daily program.

In 1726 the rector and vestry of Trinity observed that "upwards of a hundred English and Negro servants" attended the catechism on Sundays and sang psalms at the close of instruction. In the same church the Reverend Richard Charlton reported to his superior in 1741 that forty-three Negroes were studying psalmody with the church organist, Johann Clemm (= Klemm). In 1745 Charlton wrote, "I have got our Clark to raise a Psalm when their instruction is over, and I can scarce express the satisfaction I have in seeing 200 Negroes and White Persons with heart and voice glorifying their Maker." In 1751 Joseph Hildreth reported that about twenty Negroes came to him regularly in the evenings for instruction in singing psalms.

Another religious group that concerned itself with teaching slaves was the Associates of Doctor Bray, an allied society of the SPG that was founded in 1723.[18] The records show that slaves received regular training in the charity schools operated by the society in Philadelphia during the years 1758–75, in New York (1760–75), in Newport (1760–75), and in Williamsburg (1760–75). As in other places, psalmody instruction included not only teaching the tunes but also how to sing the psalms correctly. The instructors here and elsewhere would have had access to the first music-instruction books published in the colonies: *An Introduction to the Singing of Psalm-Tunes, In a plain & Easy Method* (Boston, 1721) by the Reverend John Tufts, and *The Grounds and Rules of Musick Explained, or An Introduction to the Art of Singing by Note* (Boston, 1721) by the Reverend Thomas Walter.

When schoolmasters began in the eighteenth century to operate schools independently of the church, they retained psalm singing in the curriculum as a matter of course. We may be sure, for example, that psalmody was studied by the Negroes attending the school operated by Nathaniel Pigott in Boston, which announced in a newspaper advertisement (1728) that it was opened for the "Instruction of Negroes in Reading, Catechizing & Writing."[19] The same would have been true in Samuel Keimer's school in Philadelphia, although his objective, as stated in a newspaper advertisement (1723), was simply to teach the slaves to "read the Holy Writ in a very uncommon, expeditious and delightful manner."[20]

There was yet one other religious sect that gave musical instruction to

[18]The fullest account of the work of the SPG and Thomas Bray's Associates with the slaves is in Edgar Pennington, "Thomas Bray's Associates and Their Work Among the Negroes," *American Antiquarian Society Proceedings*, new series, 48 (1938): 311–403. The quotations about religious instruction of the slaves at Trinity Church are in Pennington, pp. 385–91.
[19]Quoted in Greene, *Negro in Colonial New England*, p. 238.
[20]Quoted in Edward Turner, *The Negro in Pennsylvania* (Washington, D.C., 1911), p. 128.

converted black colonists—the Moravians, who settled first in Georgia, then permanently at Bethlehem, Pennsylvania, in 1741. One of the members of the first Moravian settlement at Bethlehem, the "Sea Congregation," was Andrew the Negro (Andreas der Mohr).[21] Andrew participated in the special activities assigned to the "single men," one of which was the Saturday-evening twilight serenade, a gathering together of all the single men to sing hymns outside the buildings on the settlement grounds. Single and married people took part in the evening prayer services, generally in the form of song services. The entire congregation also celebrated "love feasts"—that is, services with emphasis on the taking of communion and the singing of psalms, hymns, and other spiritual songs.

The records do not indicate whether Andrew played an instrument in one of the Moravian ensembles, such as the *Collegium musicum* or the trombone choir. Members of the settlement took part in musical activities to the extent of their capabilities. Whether singer or instrumentalist, Andrew would have received excellent instruction in music from the musical leader of the settlement, Prylaeus, who was a demanding taskmaster. By 1747, at least four others had joined the congregation: another Andrew, Maria Magdalena, Johannes, and Jupiter. The extraordinary musical activity of the Moravians far surpassed that of other contemporary settlements; Bethlehem in particular became a musical center where visitors came from near and far to hear impressive performances of choral and instrumental music.

Missionary Activities in the South

In the South as in the North, there was concern for the souls of the slaves, and efforts were made to convert them. In some instances slaves attended church with their masters, sitting in the galleries or on the floors of churches; or they listened to the sermon through open windows from outside the church. Some slaveholders arranged for clergymen to preach to slave congregations in separate services at the church, or they brought ministers to the plantations to preach.

Not all clergymen were conscientious about their responsibilities for the souls of the slaves. In 1758 the Reverend Samuel Davies wrote that "thousands of Negroes are neglected or instructed just according to the character of the established clergy in their several parishes."[22] Ultimately, the amount of religious training given to the slaves depended upon their masters, however diligent the clergymen. Even slaveholders who were inclined toward humane treatment of their slaves hesitated to grant them religious instruc-

---

[21]See further in Joseph Levering, *A History of Bethlehem, Pennsylvania, 1741–1892* (Philadelphia, 1903), pp. 122 ff.

[22]*Letters from the Rev. Samuel Davies and Others . . .* (London, 1761), p. 9.

tion and baptism, at first because of the widely circulated idea that slaves who were received into the church would automatically achieve freedom. To refute this, the Virginia Assembly passed a law in 1667 specifically stating that the baptism of slaves did not exempt them from bondage and urging masters to encourage their slaves to accept Christianity. Maryland passed a similar law in 1671.

The slave owners were reluctant to allow their slaves to be converted, however, for additional reasons. The Reverend Hugh Jones pointed out in his book *The Present State of Virginia from Whence Is Inferred a Short View of Maryland and North Carolina* (1724): "As for baptising Indians and Negroes, several of the people disapprove of it; because they say it often makes them proud, and not as good servants."[23] There was yet an even more compelling reason. Unlike in the North, where the black population reached early a relatively stable level, throughout the colonial period large numbers of Africans were still being imported into the southern colonies.

This continuous influx, resulting in ever-increasing numbers of black men and women in the South, contributed to the slaveholders' well-founded fears of slave conspiracies and uprisings. As a consequence, the South paid a great deal of attention to all possible means of keeping the slaves under firm control. To allow the slaves to congregate together, for whatever reason, was simply not considered wise under the circumstances. Governor Spotswood of Virginia stated plainly in 1710 his objections to any kind of slave assemblage:

> We are not to depend on either their stupidity, or that babel of languages among them; freedom wears a cap, which can without a tongue call together all those who long to shake off the fetters of slavery.[24]

The Established Church of England exerted a strong and widespread influence on southerners, white as well as black, especially through its missionary society, the SPG. Each parish was provided with a minister-schoolmaster, who had to make periodic reports to the bishop of London or his representative in the colonies on the religious and educational conditions in his parish.

There are extant a number of documents attesting to the activities of colonial clergymen among the slaves, stating how many adults were taken into the church, how many infants baptized, how many slaves given religious instruction, and how many taught the basic rudiments of reading and writing. Religious instruction, moreover, always included the teaching of psalms and hymns. The slaves preferred the musical activities of the religious experience above all else.

In 1742 the Reverend Alexander Garden, Commissary of the Bishop of

---

[23]Jones, *Present State,* p. 99.
[24]Quoted in Jones, p. 8.

London for South Carolina, opened a "School House" in Charles Town and staffed it with two black men, Harry and Andrew, whom he himself had educated. The school thrived for twenty-two years, reaching an enrollment of more than seventy children and a large number of adults before it was forced to close in 1764.[25] Most religious instruction, however, took place under less formal circumstances—on the plantation or in the church edifice.

In 1755 Samuel Davies (later to become president of Nassau Hall, i.e., Princeton University) wrote from Virginia to his superiors in London.[26]

> The Negroes above all the Human Species that I ever knew have an Ear for Musick, and a kind of extatic Delight in *Psalmody;* and there are no Books they learn so soon or take so much pleasure in, as those used in that heavenly Part of divine Worship.

On January 6, 1761, another missionary, the Reverend Mr. Wright, wrote to London in a similar vein:

> My landlord tells me, when he waited on the colonel at his countyseat two or three days, they heard the Slaves at worship in their lodge, singing Psalms and Hymns in the evening, and again in the morning, long before break of day. They are excellent singers, and long to get some of Dr. Watts' Psalms and Hymns, which I encouraged them to hope for.

The psalms and hymns of Dr. Watts, so beloved by the slaves, were published in colonial editions as early as 1729 (*Psalms of David, Imitated,* in Philadelphia) and 1739 (*Hymns and Spiritual Songs,* in Boston). The missionaries acknowledged the preference of black folk for the hymns of Dr. Watts and requested Watts' hymnals along with Bibles in their orders sent to London. The Reverend Mr. Hutson wrote on July 11, 1758:

> This is accompanied with the warmest gratitude for the late parcel of Books received from the Society, to distribute among the poor with us. . . . I was extremely glad of the Books for their sakes, especially the Bibles, Dr. Watts' Psalms and Hymns, and the Compassionate Address.

In 1760 the Reverend Mr. Todd lamented that he had been "obliged to turn sundry empty away who have come to me for Watts Psalms and Hymns."

In no way did religious instruction for black folk in the South attain the level that it did in the North; at no time did it reach an equivalent proportion of the black population. Indeed, during the colonial period most black folk were hardly touched by efforts of the missionaries. They lived in their separate quarters on the plantations and farms away from the whites, and

---

[25]See further in Frederick Dalchro, *An Historical Account of the Protestant Episcopal Church in South Carolina* (Charleston, 1820), pp. 148, 156–58, 174, 192–93. See also Pennington, "Thomas Bray's Associates," p. 337.

[26]A reprint of excerpts from *Letters from the Rev. Samuel Davies, and Others* is in RBAM. The "others" referred to in the title include Reverends Wright, Hutson, and Todd.

used their holiday Sundays "to dig up their small lots of ground allowed by their Master for potatoes, peas, etc."[27] and to divert themselves in dancing or watching cock fights. In many places slaves were made to work on Sundays, despite the colonial laws requiring slaveholders to set aside Sundays as free days.

RECREATIONAL MUSIC

Holiday Celebrations

For the most part the colonists in the North and in the South observed the same holidays: New Year's Day, Easter, Pentecost or Whitsunday, Election Day, Militia or Muster Day, and Christmas. The Puritans, to be sure, had fewer holidays than others; in 1699 a contemporary complained, "Election, Commencement and Training Days are their only Holy Days." The observance of Christmas was especially avoided among the Puritans. The special gala days of the "middling and inferior sort" were the annual fairs held in many towns and villages. For the gentry, celebrations of the birthdays of "prince and proprietary" or military events provided not only the public ceremonies which they shared with their fellow citizens, but also offered opportunities for holding exclusive formal dances, assemblies, and other kinds of special "Entertainments."

Sewall wrote about a typical celebration of the King's Birthday on October 14, 1685:

> Many Guns fired, and at night a Bonfire on Noodles Island in remembrance of the King's Birthday. Some marched through the streets with Viols and Drums, playing and beating by turns.

Sewall did not identify the musicians as black or white, but contemporaneous sources attest to the fact that black folk generally joined the boisterous crowds that roamed the streets on holidays, some playing their fiddles, drums, and trumpets.

Militia Day, also called Training or Muster Day, never failed to attract a large gathering of bystanders, including slaves. More than likely, many a black fifer "picked up" the skill of playing his instrument on these occasions. In the early years all servants, including "Negars" and Indians, were compelled to undergo military training. Every company had at least one fifer (or trumpeter) and one drummer. During the 1650s colonial fears of Negro and Indian uprisings led to precautionary laws exempting the nonwhites from military service. In later years they were allowed to enroll for

---

[27]Philip Vickers Fithian, *Journal and Letters . . .*, ed. Hunter D. Farish (1900; Williamsburg, 1957), p. 70.

service only as drummers, fifers, trumpeters, or pioneers. In times of emergency, to be sure, the colonists conveniently forgot their laws and pressed black men into service as fighters, particularly during the French and Indian War.

New Year's Day was an occasion for merrymaking everywhere. In some places men went from house to house firing gun salutes, finally gathering on the village green for a day of riotous fun. In Boston, trumpets instead of guns were used for New Year's Day saluting. In 1705 the trumpeter who gave a New Year's salute to Judge Sewall was a black musician:

> Colonel Hobbey's Negro came about 8 or 9 mane and sends in by David to have leave to give me a Levit [trumpet blast] and wish me a merry new year. I admitted it: gave him 3 Reals. Sounded very well.

Twice a year in the South, at Christmas and at Easter, the slaves were given a respite of several days from work to celebrate their jubilees. Christmas was the most joyous festival of the year. Fithian wrote about one Christmas Eve: "Guns are fired this Evening in the Neighborhood and the Negroes seem to be inspired with new life." The days following Christmas were spent in merrymaking and dancing to the music of the fiddle or banjo—most often the fiddle. On Easter Sunday, people dressed in their finest and went to church—"all the Parish seemed to meet together, High, low, black, white, all came out." Afterward, the slaves were "disbanded till the [following] Wednesday morning." Their chief mode of diverting themselves during the Easter vacation was dancing to fiddle music. But then the favorite form of entertainment for their masters, too, was dancing![28]

Social Diversions of the Colonists

A variety of informal social activities were available to colonial villagers, participated in by white and black alike: church and house raisings, maple sugarings, cornhuskings, etc., most of these generally followed by dancing to the music of the fiddle. When there was no special activity taking place, people gathered together in taverns, where they danced and sang "wanton ditties." By the beginning of the third decade of the eighteenth century, people living in towns could listen to concerts performed in concert rooms, in taverns, or in homes. Dancing, however, was more popular. During the 1730s and 1740s, dancing assemblies were organized in Newport, New York, Philadelphia, and some smaller towns, with membership limited, for the most part, to the aristocracy. The Philadelphia Assembly foundered at times because of the combined influence of the staid Quakers and the "Great Awakening" movement, but eventually gained a reputation for being one of the most brilliant and exclusive assemblies in the colonies.

[28]Fithian, *Journal*, p. 89.

Slave Dance Musicians

In the North black musicians provided much of the dance music for the colonists of all classes; they played for country dances, balls in the towns, and frequently for dancing schools, too. One of the best-known fiddlers in New England was Sampson, slave of Colonel Archelaus Moore. For many years Sampson "afforded fine fun for frolicsome fellows in Concord [Massachusetts] with his fiddle on Election Days."[29] The fiddler Polydor Gardiner of Narragansett was in great demand for parties and dances, as were also Caesar, slave fiddler of East Guilford, and Barzillai (Zelah) Lew, fiddler of Groton. In Wallingford, Connecticut, Colonel Barker's slave Cato "ranked high as a fiddler in the community" and provided music "for balls on the nights preceding the annual Thanksgiving and other occasions when dancing was expected." Of another slave in the area, Robert Prim, it was said that he and his violin were "indispensable requisites at every party or merrymaking." Although few other names of black dance musicians have been preserved for posterity, most of the colonial villages and towns had access to some fiddler on whom they could rely to furnish music for their dances, and very often that fiddler was a black man, slave or free.[30]

Slave musicians also played in some of the dancing schools that were established in the towns to prepare the socially minded citizens for the great amount of dancing that took place. After all, slaves were reliable, skilled enough, affable, and cheap. An anecdote of old New York reports on the slave Caesar, who drove the coach that took the young ladies to the dancing school, played for the dancing, and then served as a waiter during refreshment time. The dancing began at one o'clock in the afternoon. "Caesar, on their arrival, tuned his three-string fiddle, the gentlemen appeared . . . and at it they went, dancing and skipping for dear life until 8 o'clock."[31]

All over the South slaves played for the dancing of their masters at balls, assemblies, and special "Entertainments" in the plantation ballrooms and "palaces" of the colonial governors. As an urban center, Charles Town offered opportunity for the "better sort" to live as did their counterparts in cities of the North and in European capitals—to attend concerts, plays, balls, assemblies, and other sophisticated entertainments. There were singing schools and dancing schools, which attracted men as well as women. Any young gentleman was "presumed to be acquainted with Dancing, Boxing, playing the Fiddle, & Small-Sword, & Cards."[32] In Charles Town,

---

[29]Nathaniel Bouton, *The History of Concord* (Concord, Mass., 1856), p. 252.

[30]Reference to Cato and Prim in Charles Henry Davis, *History of Wallingford, Connecticut* (Meriden, CT., 1870), pp. 341, 344. See also Greene, *Negro in Colonial New England*, pp. 249 ff.

[31]John F. Watson, *Annals and Occurrences of New York City and State . . .* (Philadelphia, 1846), p. 212.

[32]Quotation from Fithian, *Journal*, p. 161.

because of the tremendous demand for skilled and unskilled labor, the slaves were able to develop their talents and skills to a greater extent than in any other colonial town. Black men worked at all trades, crafts, and arts. They seriously competed with white laborers and actually took over some trades—to such an extent that in 1744 some white artisans petitioned the commons house for relief from the ruinous competition.

In addition to Charles Town, the villages of Annapolis in Maryland, and Richmond and Williamsburg (called Middle Plantation from 1633 to 1699) in Virginia provided social and cultural activities for the southern colonists, some of whom maintained townhouses in the villages in addition to their plantation residences. Wherever there were dancing and music, there was apt to be a slave musician playing the fiddle or flute or French horn for the dancers, whether in the town or on the plantation.

It may be assumed that black musicians occasionally participated in more formal musical activity as well. In 1752, for example, the president of the Tuesday Club in Annapolis—a club whose motto was "fiddlers, fools and farces" but whose chief activity seems to have been composing music—complained that the members' musical compositions were of low quality, that "only the ditties of a visiting Negro boy showed talent."[33]

The royal governor in Williamsburg gave splendid affairs, at which the colonists performed country dances, minuets, and reels, including their favorite *Sir Roger de Coverley* or the *Virginia Reel*. Interestingly enough, colonists were also fond of a special type of lively jig called by some the "Negro Jig." In 1774 Nicholas Cresswell, an Englishman traveling in Maryland, saw one of these:

> 37 Ladies dressed and powdered to life. All of them fond of dancing. . . . Betwixt the country dances they have what I call everlasting Jigs. A couple gets up and begins to cut a jig (to some Negro tune). Others come and cut them out, and these dances always last as long as the Fiddler can play.[34]

This reference to a "Negro tune" may well represent the earliest record of the influence of slave music on the white colonists. Fithian, too, writes about whites dancing "giggs," but does not identify the music to which such dancing was done. There is a *Negro Jig* in a dance collection of 1782, *A Selection of Scotch, English, Irish and Foreign Airs,* published by James Aird in Scotland. There is no way of knowing whether this piece was of slave origin, or whether it was composed in imitation of a slave dance tune. The implication is clear, however, that the colonists were developing an awareness of the distinctive qualities of so-called "Negro music" and using this music for dancing.

Few names of black dance musicians in the South have come down to

---

[33]Lubov Keefer, *Baltimore's Music* (Baltimore, 1962), p. 18.
[34]*The Journal of Nicholas Cresswell, 1774–1777,* ed. Lincoln MacVeagh (New York, 1924), pp. 52–53. See further about the Negro Jig in Dena Epstein, *Sinful Tunes and Spirituals* (Urbana, 1977), p. 122.

A slave fiddler plays for colonial dancers. From an engraving by Howard Helmick in "Old Maryland Homes and Ways" by J. W. Palmer, *Century Magazine,* 1894.

us from the colonial period. Generally, the records simply indicate that some slaves were especially valued for their musical skills; for example, the "accomplished black fiddler" on the plantation of Richard Bailey in Acomorack County, Virginia. We do know, however, that the young slave fiddler belonging to Charles Carrol of Annapolis was named John Stokes and that Simeon (Sy) Gilliat (d. 1820), the slave violinist owned by Baron Botetourt of Williamsburg (royal governor of Virginia), was reputed to be very skilled.[35]

[35]Reference to Virginia fiddler in Philip A. Bruce, *Social Life of Virginia in the Seventeenth Century* (Richmond, 1907), p. 181; discussion of Sy Gilliat in Samuel Mordecai, *Richmond in By-Gone Days* (Richmond, 1856), pp. 180, 310–11; excerpted in RBAM, pp. 135–37.

What kind of music did the colonists have for their dancing? Contemporaneous accounts mention most often the music of violins. It is probable that for gala occasions oboes and transverse flutes were added to the string ensembles. The fact that the dance tunes in a popular collection, *Thompson's Compleat Collection of 200 Favourite Country Dances Performed at Court . . .* , were arranged or "Set for the Violin, German flute & Hautboy" suggests such a probability. Moreover, the references to slave musicians point out that most often they were violinists and flutists, a phenomenon perhaps to be attributed more to the demands of the white colonists for dance musicians than to mere coincidence or to any preference for these instruments among the black people.

Several excellent sources of dance music were available to colonial dance musicians, of which . . . the two best-known collections were published in England. In addition to the Thompson collection, there was one even better known and more popular, *The English Dancing Master or Plaine and Easie Rules for the Dancing of Country Dances with the Tune to Each Dance,* by John Playford, author of several other music manuals. These two books contained a varied repertory of traditional ballad tunes, country dance tunes, and the more formal court-dance melodies. Consequently, dance musicians could provide music for all of the colonists' favorite dances; for example, *Pea Straw, Faithful Shepherd, Arcadian Nuptials, Lady Hancock,* and *Boston's Delight.* Some of the tunes in the Playford collection, such as *Greensleeves* or *Sellinger's Round* or *Paul's Steeple,* were extremely popular in the colonies.

Social Singing

None of the white colonists in the North, not even the Puritans, limited themselves exclusively to the singing of psalms. They sang the old ballads brought with them from Europe, and they called upon various kinds of worksongs—sea chanties, weavers' songs, sugar-making songs, etc.—to ease their labors. As early as the seventeenth century, some clergymen began to speak out against the people's excessive attention to secular music.

Some of the "idle, foolish ballads" sung by the settlers were Yankee versions of English ballads; for example, *Barb'ry Ellen (Barbara Allen)* or *Dirante, My Son (Lord Randall, My Son).* When ballad makers needed tunes for topical songs they drew upon the melodies of old favorites, such as the tune *Derry Down, Down, Down (The Three Ravens)* for a text about the notorious Kitty Crow in 1765, or the *Boston Come All Ye* tune for a satirical text entitled *The Paxton Expedition* (ca. 1764). One of the most popular songs of all was the *Yankee Song:*

> Corn stalks twist your hair off,
> Cart-wheel frolic round you.
> Old fiery dragon carry you off,
> And mortar pessel pound you.

The tune with different words later became better known as *Yankee Doodle.*

In singing schools the colonists could learn to sing not only psalms, but also secular songs, "catches, glees, [and] canons . . . with sobriety and ease." Consequently, what was not picked up in the tavern or on the street could be learned from a singing master. Black folk sang all kinds of songs at all times. They sang psalms along with the white settlers and turned to hymns in the eighteenth century along with everyone else. They sang the old African songs as long as they could remember them—especially on the occasions of special slave festivals, as we shall see. In the taverns and on the streets they sang the ballads and ribald songs of the white colonists. And when they tired of singing those or had exhausted the repertory, they made up their own songs, stumbling a bit over the unfamiliar English or Dutch or Swedish or German or French words (depending upon where they lived), but managing, nevertheless, to express their ideas in these alien tongues.

Slave Recreational Activities

In addition to participating in the recreational activities of white colonists, slaves also developed their own traditions of merrymaking. As early as 1702 the city fathers of Philadelphia complained that "Negroes commonly meete together in a riott and tumultuous manner on the first day of the week." Many a white clergyman protested against the way the Sabbath was observed by the slaves "in frolicking, dancing, and other profane courses." In 1709, for example, Dr. LeJau, one of the first SPG missionaries, regretted that "It has been customary among them to have their feasts, dances, and merry meetings upon the Lord's Day."[36] The planters, however, generally accepted the fact that the slaves, having no other free time during the week and not being admitted into the church for one reason or another, should use Sundays as a day of rest and diversion. English traveler Nicholas Cresswell wrote in his journal in 1774:

> Mr. Bayley and I went to see a Negro Ball. Sundays being the only days these poor creatures have to themselves, they generally meet together and amuse themselves with Dancing to the Banjo. . . . They all appear to be exceedingly happy at these merrymakings and seem if they had forgot or were not sensible of their miserable condition.[37]

As a matter of fact, the attitude of the slaves toward the Sabbath was not very different from that of their white counterparts. Fithian's diary reveals:

> A Sunday in Virginia dont seem to wear the same Dress as our Sundays to the Northward. Generally here by five o'clock on Saturday every face (especially the

---

[36]Francis LeJau, *The Carolina Chronicle of Dr. Francis LeJau, 1706–1717,* ed. Frank Klingberg (Berkeley, 1956), p. 61.
[37]Cresswell, *Journal,* p. 18.

Negroes) looks festive and cheerful. All the lower class of people, & the Servants, & the slaves, consider it a Day of Pleasure and Amusement & spend it in such Diversions as they severally choose.[38]

Colonial records contain few references to exclusively black musical activities. Chroniclers of life in the eighteenth century generally seem to have been unconcerned about what happened in the slave quarters, and visitors to the plantations were not curious enough—in those times—to spy. The colonists, of course, were aware that a great deal of dancing went on to the music of fiddles, most of them homemade. In Maryland Cresswell noticed that the slaves were playing a different kind of string instrument and described it:

> This instrument (if it may be so called) is made of a Gourd something in the imitation of a Guitar, with only four strings and played with the fingers in the same manner.[39]

Cresswell noted further that the music of the banjo was accompanied by the singing of "very droll music indeed," the slaves singing about their masters and mistresses "in a very satirical manner."

Cresswell's description of a banjo (1774) is apparently the earliest such reference in colonial writings, although these instruments may have been found among the slaves even in the seventeenth century. Obviously, however, they were not common during colonial times. The singing at Cresswell's "Negro Ball" reflects the African propensity for musical improvisation. The singers vied with one another in poking fun at their masters—a practice reported again and again by chroniclers—making up their verses as they sang and each trying to outdo the previous singer. The white observer noted that the "poetry [was] like the music—rude and uncultivated." The music was evidently African, for no other kind would have been appropriate for the slaves' dancing, which to Cresswell was "so irregular and grotesque" that he was "not able to describe it."

DEVELOPMENT OF MUSICAL SKILLS

One persistent question, for which there seems to be no satisfactory answer, is how the slaves, lacking personal possessions and control of their time, developed instrumental skills. Although the African heritage gave them a natural talent for and inclination toward making music, they came to the New World emptyhanded, and upon arrival had to acquaint themselves with strange instruments and different ways of handling them. To be sure, some of the instruments were similar to those the Africans had known in their own country, but the instruments were not identical. In music—as in

[38]Fithian, *Journal*, p. 137.
[39]Cresswell, p. 18.

language, religion, and customs—the Africans had to adjust to the ways of their white masters.

Only tentative answers, based on the meager evidence available, can be offered to the question. With regard to the acquiring of instruments, it is obvious that many slave musicians must have fashioned their own instruments from whatever materials were at hand. In some instances slave owners purchased instruments for their slaves. The following excerpt from a letter written in 1719 by a Philadelphian Quaker supports both these suppositions:

> Thou knowest Negro Peter's Ingenuity In making for himself and playing on a fiddle without any assistance. As the thing in them [i.e., the musical impulse] is Innocent and diverting and may keep them from worse Employment, I have to Encourage [him] in my Service promist him one from England. Therefore buy and bring a good strong well-made Violin with 2 or 3 Sets of spare Gut for the Suitable Strings. Get somebody of skill to Chuse and by [buy] it. . . .[40]

How widely the practice of buying musical instruments for slaves was followed during the colonial period is a question that cannot be satisfactorily answered until more evidence comes to light.

With regard to the development of skill in playing an instrument, we may assume that most slaves taught themselves to play. There is documentary evidence for such an assumption in the case of nineteenth-century slave musicians. It is thus logical to accept the notion that colonial slaves also might have taught themselves, especially since they were closer to the African tradition, and would have remembered the musical activities they pursued before coming to the New World. The curious phrasing in a newspaper "runaway" advertisement throws considerable light on the question of how other slaves might have learned to play musical instruments:

> Whereas Cambridge, a Negro Man belonging to James Oliver of Boston doth absent himself sometimes from his Master: said Negro plays well upon a flute, and not so well on a Violin. This is to desire all Masters and Heads of Families not to suffer said Negro to come into their Houses to teach their Prentices or Servants to play, nor on any other Accounts. All Masters of Vessels are also forbid to have anything to do with him on any Account, as they may answer it in the Law. N. B. Said Negro is to be sold: Enquire of said Oliver.
>
> [*Boston Evening Post*, October 24, 1743]

This advertisement suggests that in Boston, at least, slaveholders followed the practice of engaging slave musicians to teach their slaves and, as well, their apprenticed white servants. (Slaves are commonly referred to as servants in colonial sources.) Who taught the slave music-teachers? Did they "pick up" their skills, or were they apprenticed out to white professional musicians? Undoubtedly both questions may be answered in the affirmative. At any rate, there is nothing in the available evidence to suggest that slaves

---

[40]Turner, *Negro in Pennsylvania*, p. 42.

as a group were given instrumental lessons—that is, in the same way as they were taught to sing correctly in psalmody classes.

Under the circumstances, then, the musical instruments favored by the slaves would have had to fulfill three conditions: first, the instruments had to offer a minimum of technical difficulties in the learning process, so that they could be learned with little or no professional help; second, the instruments had to be easily available and so easily handled that the slaves could carry them around and practice them at odd times of the day or night, whenever there were a few extra minutes to spare; third, the instruments had to be useful, so that once the slaves had learned to play them they would have opportunities to perform for others.

In the South, too, the slaves managed to find ways to develop their musical skills despite the restrictions of the social structure. Those fortunate enough to live on the great plantations or in homes of wealthy townsmen were generally exposed to a high level of cultural activity. Fithian's journal and letters are valuable for the information they contain about life in the South. The young Princeton graduate, who spent two years (1773–74) as a "Plantation Tutor of the Old Dominion" to the children of the aristocrat Robert Carter, gives a vivid description of the mode of life for the wealthy and, as well, for indentured servants, white and black. Fithian's employer had a large collection of musical instruments on his plantation, Nomini Hall: "a Harpsichord, Forte Piano, Harmonica, Guittar, Violin, & German Flutes . . . & at Williamsburg [the site of his townhouse] a good Organ." Almost every evening in the Carter home the members of the family played chamber music. The slaves, who moved freely about the house and among the members of the family, listened to the music along with their masters and doubtless "picked out" pieces on the musical instruments whenever they found opportunities to do so.

To teach the sons and daughters of the wealthy colonists, itinerant music masters traveled from plantation to plantation, staying several days at each place, depending upon the number of persons to be given musical instruction. Mr. Stadley, the German music master who taught the Carter children, generally remained three or four days each time he came to Nomini Hall, chiefly to instruct the young women in the art of playing the violin and "Forte Piano." With Mr. Stadley in the house, the evenings provided occasions for playing more demanding chamber music and singing, to which a professional added a great deal of zest.

It was inevitable that musically inclined slaves should benefit from the periodic visits of music masters to the plantations. Those who worked about the house would have been able to listen to the instruction of the music masters and to observe how passages could be executed on various instruments. Frequently, young people of slaveholding families taught the slaves to play flutes and violins themselves. Fithian, for example, commented more than once upon the close relationship existing between "several Negroes, & Ben & Harry [the Carter boys]." More than once, the young Carters were chased from the schoolroom where they had been dancing with some slaves to the music of fiddles. Finally, in some instances, slaveholders arranged for black folk to be given lessons; such a practice equipped the slave with sufficient musical skill to play for plantation dances or to entertain visiting guests.

Students took their slaves with them to the College of William and Mary in Williamsburg (established in 1693). Some contemporaries thought it unfortunate that there were not special quarters for the slaves, similar to the "apartment" for the Native Americans. "There is very great occasion for a quarter for the Negroes and inferior servants belonging to the college," wrote Hugh Jones in 1724.[41] For the slaves, however, the circumstance was fortunate; they lived in the rooms of their young masters and undoubtedly attended classes with them on various occasions. More than likely, many a slave at the college learned to "play very well on the Violin" or to "play extremely well on the French horn" from attending music classes which were taught by "masters from the town" rather than by members of the regular faculty.[42]

The evidence suggests that some slaves in Charles Town and other urban centers of the South must have been taught to play by professional musicians, just as slaves were trained in bricklaying, carpentry, soldering, etc. Despite the laws against the teaching of black slaves, intrepid southerners taught them any number of skills and trades. As we have seen, Commissary Alexander Garden operated a Negro School House (1742–64), using as teachers two young slaves whom he himself had educated. The course of study included psalmody, along with reading, writing, and catechism.

Another school for slaves in Charles Town was maintained by a Mr. Boulson, who in 1740 turned his dancing school and concert room into a school for slaves after he was converted by the evangelist George Whitefield. The records fail to indicate the subjects taught by Mr. Boulson to his fifty-three black students, but it is improbable that the former music master would neglect singing.[43]

Slaves frequently played the fiddle for dancing in the home and for dancing classes. Many were the nights at Nomini Hall, for example, when "John the Waiting Man played" and the young ladies spent the evening "merrily in dancing." Just as there were itinerant music masters for young southerners, so were there itinerant dancing masters. The dancing teachers held classes in rotation at the plantation homes of their scholars, giving instruction at each place for several days in succession. Their pupils traveled with them from one plantation to the other, remaining as guests in the house where the dancing classes were being held.

[41]In regard to the teaching of music and dancing to college students, see Jones, *Present State,* pp. 11, 19, 250.
[42]Quotations about slave instrumentalists from contemporary slave advertisements.
[43]Bridenbaugh, *Cities in the Wilderness,* p. 451.

Generally, itinerant dancing masters traveled with their own musician. Resident dancing masters in the larger towns, however, selected their fiddlers from among those available, white or black:

> If any gentlemen living in the Country are disposed to send their children to Charlestown, they may be boarded with George Logan, who also intends to open his School to teach to dance, next Monday being the 19th Instant. He will likewise go into the Country if he meets with Encouragement. Any white Person that can play on the Violin, or a Negro may be employ'd by the said Logan living in Union Street.   [*South Carolina Gazette,* September 17, 1737]

SLAVE FESTIVALS IN THE AFRICAN TRADITION

Black folk in the English colonies found ways to carry on some of their traditional African practices despite the bonds of slavery. Perhaps the most spectacular of these practices occurred in the slave gatherings and festivals that took place throughout the colonial period in northern cities where there were large concentrations of black folk. Although the slaves that were brought into the colonies originally came from a wide area of West Africa (and parts of East Africa) and represented many different nations, they shared enough traditions of music and dancing to enable them to participate in collective dances with ease. Moreover, slaves who spoke different African languages were generally able to communicate with each other, as Equiano pointed out in his book: "I understood them, though they were from a distant part of Africa."[44]

'Lection Day Festivities

A colonial holiday observed solely by black folk in New England was " 'Lection Day." On this occasion the blacks elected their own "governors" (or "kings" in New Hampshire), in elaborate ceremonies that paralleled those of Election Day for the white population. The custom seems to have originated in Connecticut about 1750 and lasted, in some New England towns, as late as the 1850s. Depending upon the place, the holiday was observed in May or June. Generally, slaves were given the vacation period from Wednesday to the following Sunday in which to elect their rulers and to celebrate.

First in the order of events would be the election parade. A parade in Hartford, Connecticut, often involved as many as one hundred slaves, either mounted on horseback or marching, two by two, on foot. The procession of slaves, dressed in their finest apparel, would advance with colors flying to the music of fifes, fiddles, "clarionets," and drums. But the Hartford parades were unusually elaborate affairs. In most places the processions

---

[44]*The Life of Olaudah Equiano . . .* (New York, 1791), p. 60.

marched or rode to the music of fifers and drummers. To be sure, only the best musicians were given the honor of playing for an election parade. It was said, for example, that King Caesar of Wallingford, Connecticut, was always escorted by an "indefatigable drummer and a fifer of eminence."[45]

After the election ceremony came the merrymaking, consisting of games, wrestling, jumping, singing, and dancing to the music of fiddles. In 1756, an observer of the celebration in Newport, Rhode Island, found the singing exotic:

> Every voice in its highest key, in all the various languages of Africa, mixed with broken and ludicrous English, filled the air, accompanied with the music of the fiddle, tambourine, banjo and drum. . . .

One writer reported on the kind of dancing that took place, noting that the slaves "shuffled and tripped" to the sounds of the fiddles.[46]

Although black folk in the North were fairly well integrated into community activities—at least, to the extent possible for a servant class—they nevertheless engaged in their own African style of merrymaking as well. And the festivities undoubtedly brought back race memories, if not individual memories, of the elaborate ceremonies attendant upon the election and inauguration of chiefs and kings in Africa.

Pinkster Celebrations

"Pinkster Day," the name given to Pentecost Sunday (or Whitsunday, in the Anglican Church), originally was a principal holiday of the Dutch in the Netherlands settlements. Later it was adopted by the English in New York, in parts of Pennsylvania, and in Maryland. It seems that the earliest reference to the popular name of the holiday occurred in a Sermon Book of 1667 by Adrian Fischer, "Story of the Descent of the Holy Ghost on the Apostles on 'Pinckster Dagh.' " After the first day or so of Pinkster—the celebration was often prolonged for as much as the full week after Pentecost—black men and women took over completely with their Congo dances, dancing as they had in Africa. The festivals attracted large crowds of white spectators from both city and rural sections. Local historians wrote about "Pinkster, the Carnival of the Africans," and novelists incorporated scenes from the "great Saturnalia of the New York Blacks" in their fictional works, in the same way as writers described the exotic dancing of the black celebrants in the Place Congo of New Orleans at the beginning of the nineteenth century.[47]

Except for scattered references here and there, the earliest, full, extant

[45]Orville Platt, "Negro Governors," *New Haven Historical Society Quarterly* 6 (1900): 321, 326.
[46]Platt, pp. 324, 331.
[47]See, for example, James Fenimore Cooper, *Satanstoe* (New York, 1845), pp. 65–70.

description of the Pinkster festival is a lengthy ode of some forty-five or more stanzas that was published in 1803 in reference to the dancing at Albany, New York. The title page reads as follows:

A
PINKSTER ODE
For the Year 1803.
Most Respectfully Dedicated To
CAROLUS AFRICANUS, REX;
Thus Rendered in English:
KING CHARLES,
Captain-General and Commander in Chief
of the
PINKSTER BOYS.
By His Majesty's Obedient Servant,
ABSALOM AIMWELL, Esq. [pseud.]
Albany:
Printed Solely for the Purchasers and Others,
1803.

King Charles (ca. 1699–1824), the leading spirit of the dancing at Albany, played the master drums and also "called" the dances; his instrumental forces included the banjo, fiddles, fifes, drums, and the "hollow drum." The author of the ode leaves no doubt that the festival was African in tone, although his only specific reference to Africa is in a verse about Charles "leading on the Guinea dance."

Another vivid portrayal of the Albany festivals occurs in an account published in 1857 by an octogenarian, Dr. James Eights.[48] Since Eights states that he was an eyewitness of the dancing on more than one occasion during his boyhood, it may be assumed that he saw it during the 1770s. He tells us that the Pinkster grounds were laid out in the form of an "oblong square," on a hill that is now the site of the state capitol. Along the perimeter of the square were erected stalls, booths, and tents that featured exhibitions of wild animals, rope dancing, bareback riding, and other attractions common to a fair. The center was left clear for dancing. Few blacks were to be seen on the Monday after Pentecost, for it was considered "ungenteel for the colored nobility to make their appearance on the commencing day." But on the second day, about ten o'clock in the morning, a "deputation [from the assembled multitude] . . . anxiously desirous to pay all proper homage to his majesty their king," would gather to wait upon the leading spirit of the festival, Old King Charley, the venerable sovereign of the blacks.

[48]Reprinted from the *Cultivator:* James Eights, "Pinkster Festivities in Albany," *Collections on the History of Albany,* v. 2 (Albany, 1867), pp. 323–27. The entire article is reproduced in RBAM, pp. 41–48. Eights is identified as an octogenarian in an anonymous article, "Albany, Fifty Years Ago," *Harper's New Monthly Magazine* (March 1857): 453.

At this time Charley, who had been brought from Angola and was said to have been a prince back in Africa, was over seventy years old, tall, thin, and extremely agile. He customarily wore the costume of a "British brigadier of the olden times," and made a very colorful appearance as he slowly advanced toward the center of the square, dressed in a scarlet coat ornamented with tracings of golden lace, his "small clothes" of new yellow buckskin, his black shoes with silver buckles, and a tricornered cocked hat upon his head.

New couples joined the performance from time to time as fatigued dancers dropped out, forced to stop from exhaustion. The principal instrument for the dance music was a drum made from a wooden eel-pot with a cleanly dressed sheepskin drawn tightly over its wide end:

> Astride this rude utensil sat Jackey Quackenboss, then in his prime of life and well known energy, beating lustily with his naked hands upon its loudly sounding head, successively repeating the ever wild, though euphonic cry of *Hi-a-bomba, bomba, bomba,* a full harmony with the thumping sounds. These vocal sounds were readily taken up and as oft repeated by the female portion of the spectators not otherwise engaged in the exercises [that is, dances] of the scene, accompanied by the beating of time with their ungloved hands, in strict accordance with the eel-pot melody.

The dancing grew more rapid and furious as the day wore on.

On the next day the occurrence was repeated, and the next day, and the next. By the end of the week all the celebrants, black and white, must have welcomed the Sabbath, which became quite literally a day of rest, and the "ancient city was at length again left to its usual quietude."

In a later account of the Albany festival, Old King Charley was described as being well over one hundred years old, but still the ruler of the festival. No longer did he dance; instead he took over the drum beating, using a drum made from a box with a sheepskin head, and was accompanied by the singing of "some queer African airs." After Charley withdrew from the dancing, the celebration was observed with less enthusiasm, but continued, nevertheless, until 1811 when the town council of Albany prohibited further erection of stalls on "Pinkster Hill."

In Manhattan the favorite gathering place for Pinkster celebrations was the site now known as City Hall Park. Black folk "collected in thousands in those fields," coming into the city from as far away as thirty or forty miles. Although the festival lasted only three days in Manhattan and "was not celebrated with as much vivacity as at Albany," it nevertheless was a time of great excitement for both white spectators and black participants. Hundreds upon hundreds of people watched the black celebrants sing African songs, strum banjos, and dance to the music of drums constructed by drawing skins over the ends of hollow logs.

Other Slave Gatherings

The Revolutionary War brought an end to the Manhattan slave festivals, but after the war the tradition of public slave dances was revived in a different form. On holidays, and particularly for Pinkster celebrations, the slaves would come in from Long Island and New Jersey to the city markets—and as well from the city itself—to engage in friendly dancing contests. Butchers of the markets and other bystanders would toss in a little money so that prizes could be offered to the best dancers. Music for the dancing, which consisted of jigs and breakdowns, was provided in a novel manner: the slaves produced a kind of percussion music by beating their hands on their thighs and stomping their heels. Over the years these practices resulted in the development of some "excellent dancers." Catherine Market, near the Bowery, was the favorite gathering place for the slave-dance competitions, but there was also dancing at Bear Market in Maiden Lane.[49]

Contemporaneous accounts refer to yet another colonial town where whites gathered to watch the slaves perform traditional African dances and songs. In Philadelphia, where semiannual fairs were held until the time of the Revolution, the last days of the fairs were given over to the slaves for their own "jubilees." The dancing on these occasions was similar to that of the New York slaves. They danced in Potter's Field (now Washington Square), divided into small groups according to their "nations" or tribes. The dancing of the slaves lasted for many hours at a time:

> . . . the Blacks joyful above, while the sleeping dead reposed below. In that field could be seen at once more than one thousand of both sexes, divided into numerous little squads, dancing and singing, each in their own tongue, after the customs of their several nations in Africa.[50]

In Boston the slaves and free blacks congregated about the wharves in an area called "New Guinea," but there is no evidence that group dancing ever took place there.

During colonial times, slave festivals were held only in the North. Such gatherings were possible in places where slavery was relatively benign, where indulgent owners allowed their slaves time off for frolics, where town authorities were not afraid to let huge masses of slaves assemble, where some black leaders were respected by the local white townspeople as well as their own people—and none of these conditions existed in the southern colonies. The next site of African festivals in the United States was to be in nineteenth-century New Orleans, where the mingling of diverse cultures—Spanish, French, British, German, and African—encouraged the development and the flowering of music and dance to an extent previously unknown in the New World.

---

[49]See further in Thomas F. Devoe, *The Market Book* (New York, 1862), pp. 322, 344–45.
[50]John Fanning Watson, *Annals of Philadelphia* (Philadelphia, 1850), 2nd ed. rev., v. 2, p. 265.

It is quite evident that the festivals described above represent African survivals among black people in the English colonies, despite the pressures exerted upon them by the slavery experience to accommodate the folk ways and customs of the dominant culture. The once prevalent "myth of the Negro past"—that enslavement caused them to lose their every vestige of the African heritage—is nowhere more firmly refuted than in the areas of music and dance and, more specifically, than by the occurrence of the slave festivals.[51]

An equally significant, though less dramatic, survival of "Africanisms" is represented by the storytelling and singing of black women in New England who, in their own way, kept alive the African traditions. For example, Lucy Terry of Deerfield and Senegambia of Narragansett, Rhode Island, won wide recognition for their gifts in this regard. Lucy, who called herself Luce Bijah, married a free black man, Abijah Prince. After gaining her own freedom, she made her home a gathering place for slaves and free men and women of the community, a place where they could listen to tales and songs of old Africa. Indeed, American literature contains numerous references to female slaves of colonial times who kept young audiences spellbound, and adults, too, with their ancient tales.

Slaves in the colonial South danced and sang in the traditional African ways when gathered together for diversion, as did their northern counterparts. But with the exception of Cresswell, few onlookers recorded any such activities, and the slaves obviously could not keep records because they had not been allowed to learn how to write. There is, however, one eyewitness account of an occasion in the South where African music might have been performed. In 1739 there was a slave uprising on a plantation in Stono, near Charles Town. The "Angola Negroes" who began the revolt were joined by other slaves, and all proceeded down the road toward St. Augustine, burning and killing as they went. Along the way they stopped in a field "and set to dancing, singing and beating Drums by way of triumph."[52]

By the time of the American Revolution, black people were an integral part of colonial society. Comprising over 20 percent of the population, black men and women performed much of the labor in the colonies, both in towns and on the plantations. They participated in the musical activities to whatever extent was allowed; in the meetinghouse they sang psalms and hymns along with the white worshipers. And, as we have seen, they began organizing their own groups as early as 1693—a fact that did not go unnoticed by white colonists. Gentleman-farmer Hector St. John de Crèvecoeur, a French immigrant who settled about 1760 in Orange County, New York, wrote:

---

[51]See further in Melville J. Herskovits, *The Myth of the Negro Past* (New York, 1941).

[52]See further in Edwin C. Holland, *A Refutation of the Calumnies Circulated Against the Southern and Western States* . . . (Charleston, 1822), pp. 68–69, 81.

Our blacks divide with us the toils of our farms; they partake also of the mirth and good cheer of the season. They have their own meetings and are often indulged with their masters' sleighs and horses. You may see them at particular places as happy and merry as if they were freemen and freeholders. . . .[53]

Neither did the musicality of the black slaves go unnoticed by the colonists, who were impressed by their singing. Samuel Davies, for example, wrote:

I can hardly express the pleasure it affords me to turn to that part of the Gallery where they [the slaves] sit, and see so many of them with their Psalm or Hymn Books, turning to the part then sung, and assisting their fellows who are beginners, to find the place; and then all breaking out in a torrent of sacred harmony, enough to bear away the whole congregation to heaven.[54]

Others grew to depend upon the services of the slave fiddler: "If we have not the gorgeous balls, the harmonious concerts, the shrill horn of Europe, yet we dilate our hearts as well with the simple Negro fiddle."[55]

[53]Hector St. John de Crèvecoeur, *Sketches of Eighteenth-Century America, Or More Letters from An American Farmer,* ed. Henri Bourdin *et al.* (New Haven, 1925), p. 148.
[54]Davies, *Letters,* p. 14.
[55]Crèvecoeur, *Sketches,* p. 96.

PART TWO

LET
MY
PEOPLE
GO

1776–1865

When Israel was in Egypt's land,
Let my people go.
Oppress'd so hard they could not stand,
Let my people go.

Go down, Moses,
Way down in Egypt land.
Tell ole Pharaoh
To let my people go.

—Negro Spiritual

IMPORTANT EVENTS

1775 The American Revolution (1775–83).

1775 The Dunmore Proclamation, promising freedom to all slaves who joined the British army; caused liberalizing of colonial laws that prohibited the enlistment of Negroes as servicemen. Organization of first anti-slavery society by the Quakers: Philadelphia, PA.

1776 The Declaration of Independence; Philadelphia, PA.

1778 First enactment of laws offering freedom to slaves who served in the American army for a number of years.

1780 Pennsylvania passed a law providing for the gradual abolition of slavery.

1781 Philadelphia selected as the capital of the United States (until 1800).

1782 Publication of *Selection of Scotch, English, Irish and Foreign Airs* by James Aird, which included first known printing of *Yankee Doodle* and a *Negro Jig:* Glasgow, Scotland.

1783 Slavery abolished by law in Massachusetts, followed by similar laws in other New England states.
Northwest Territory ceded to the United States.

1784 First black men, Richard Allen and Absalom Jones, granted licenses to preach (by the Methodists): Old St. George's Methodist Episcopal Church, Philadelphia, PA.
Formal organizing of the Methodist Church in the United States at the "Christmas Conference": Baltimore, MD.

1787 Founding of the Free African Society in Philadelphia.
Beginning of Negro freemasonry with Prince Hall's organization of African Lodge No. 1 (under warrant from the Grand Lodge of England) at Boston, MA.
Slavery prohibited in the Northwest Territory, but provision made for the return of fugitive slaves.

1788 Founding of first black church in the United States at Savannah, GA: First African Baptist Church.

1789 Publication of *The Interesting Narrative of the Life of Olaudah Equiano, or Gustavus Vassa the African. Written by Himself:* London, England.

1790 First census taken in the United States; black population more than three-quarters of a million, including 59,000 free blacks.

1792 First law passed by Congress authorizing the formation of military bands (other than fife-and-drum corps); law amended in 1803.

1794 Dedication of the first independent black churches in the North at Philadelphia: St. Thomas African Episcopal Church and Bethel African Methodist Episcopal Church.

1796 Founding of the second independent black church in the North at New York: the African Methodist Episcopal Zion Church.

1800 Gabriel Prosser slave revolt: Richmond, VA.
Beginning of the "Second Awakening" or the "Great Revival." First historic camp meeting held in Logan County, KY.

1801 Publication of first hymnal designed for the express use of black folk, *A Collection of Hymns and Spiritual Songs from Various Authors, by Richard Allen, Minister of the African Methodist Episcopal Church* (two editions): Philadelphia, PA.

1803 Louisiana Purchase.

1808 Congressional Act abolishing the slave trade (1807); went into effect on January 1.

1812 War of 1812 (1812–15).

1816 Organization of the American Colonization Society, whose aim was to repatriate black men and women to Africa.

1819 Spanish Cession (Florida Territory).

1821 Establishment of the American colony of Liberia on the west coast

IMPORTANT EVENTS

of Africa with 130 American blacks.

Founding of the African Grove Theatre at New York.

1822 Denmark Vesey insurrection in Charleston, SC.

1827 Publication of the first Negro newspaper, *Freedom's Journal*: New York, NY.

1829 Publication of *Appeal . . .* by David Walker, militant black abolitionist

1830 First National Convention of the Free People of Color in September at Philadelphia, PA.; Richard Allen elected president.

1831 Nat Turner slave revolt: Southampton County, VA.

1833 Organization of the American Anti-Slavery Society: Philadelphia, PA.

1842 Founding of the New York Philharmonic Society.

1843 First organized white minstrel show, the Virginia Minstrels: the Bowery Amphitheatre, New York, NY.

1845 Annexation of Texas Territory.

1846 Annexation of Oregon Territory.

1848 Mexican Cession (New Mexico and California Territories).

The "Gold Rush" to California.

1850 Compromise of 1850. Abolition of the slave trade in Washington, D.C.

1852 Publication of *Uncle Tom's Cabin* by Harriet Beecher Stowe.

1853 Aborted slave revolt in New Orleans; involved 2,500 slaves.

1856 Establishment of the first Negro college, Wilberforce University, at Wilberforce, OH.

1857 Dred Scott decision of the Supreme Court, affirming that a slave could not be recognized as a citizen of the United States.

1860 Census indicated 4,441,830 African Americans in the United States, including 488,070 free persons.

1861 Abraham Lincoln inaugurated as sixteenth president of the United States.

1861 Civil War (1861–65).

1863 The Emancipation Proclamation issued by Lincoln became effective on January 1, stating that "all persons held as slaves within any State or designated part of the State, the people whereof shall be in rebellion against the United States, shall be then, thenceforward, and forever free." (Slaves freed only in confederate states).

1865 Enactment of the Thirteenth Amendment, which abolished slavery throughout the United States. Establishment of the Bureau of Refugees, Freedmen, and Abandoned Lands (called the Freedmen's Bureau), which aided the newly freed slaves and established schools for them.

CHAPTER 3

Two Wars
and the
New Nation

D URING the first half of the eighteenth century, England was too preoccupied in its struggle with France to pay much attention to the American colonies. But with the attainment of victory in the Seven Year's
War in Europe and the French and Indian War in the New World (both
wars, 1756–63), England began to enforce a policy regarded by the colonists as threatening to their political and economic freedom. Their vigorous
protests against the new imperial policy included denunciation not only of
the series of intolerable Acts passed by England, but also of the slave trade.
Some of the colonists, in affirming their right to freedom from England,
began to realize that the same right of freedom might apply as well to black
men and women. And the slaves themselves began to agitate for their freedom in the courts and legislative assemblies as early as 1766. In 1773, for
example, a "Grate number of Blacks" sent a petition to the governor and
General Court of Massachusetts asking for freedom from the "state of
slavery."

BLACK MUSICIANS IN THE ARMED SERVICES

Extant military records often fail to list the race of servicemen in the American wars of the eighteenth and early nineteenth centuries, and town and
other civic records—which are the chief sources of information about black
servicemen—are often incomplete. To be sure, meager bits of information
about black servicemen may sometimes be obtained from local histories.

When army rolls do refer to race, the lists often include such enigmatic entries as "A Negro Man" or "A Negro, name not known." Only occasionally will an entry give a full citation of name, race, and classification—such as "Negro Bob, drummer." For all these reasons, few names of black army musicians have come down to us. We know, however, that a typical assignment for a black man was that of drummer. Indeed, a Virginia Act of 1776 specifically stated that black men "shall be employed as drummers, fifers, or pioneers."

The Revolutionary War

The first blood shed in the colonists' struggle for freedom was that of a runaway slave, Crispus Attucks, in the Boston Massacre of 1770. More than one American historian has commented upon the significance of this occurrence, that a fugitive slave should have been willing to risk his life in a fight for the freedom of his country when he himself was not free. But Attucks was not the only black man to join the War for Independence, he was merely the first. More than five thousand African-Americans fought in the Revolutionary War against England. Since some had fought in the French and Indian War despite laws excluding them from military service, there were precedents for their entrance into the Revolutionary War. Among the black soldiers who fought in the Battle of Bunker Hill in the spring of 1775 was Barzillai Lew, a drummer and fifer of Chelmsford, Massachusetts. Lew had also fought in the French and Indian War.

In November 1775, General George Washington issued orders prohibiting the further recruitment of Negroes. About the same time, and unknown to Washington, a royal governor of Virginia, Lord Dunmore, issued a proclamation that promised freedom to all slaves and indentured servants who should join His Majesty's troops. Hundreds of slaves responded to the call, some to join the British lines, others simply to seek freedom as best they could. The colonies were forced to liberalize their policy in view of the Dunmore Proclamation, and eventually black men were actively recruited (except in Georgia and South Carolina), generally with the understanding that their services would automatically grant them freedom. Most black men fought in integrated units in both the North and the South. In New England, however, there were all-black companies attached to regiments of Connecticut, Rhode Island, and Massachusetts. The black battalion of Massachusetts, called the "Bucks of America," was under the command of a black colonel, George Middleton.

The names of black army musicians appearing in the records include: William Nickens, drummer in a Virginia company; Negro Tom, drummer in Captain Benjamin Egbert's regiment of Orangetown, New York; drummer Negro Bob of the First Company of Rangers, South Carolina; fifer Richard Cozzens and drummer Scipio Brown of Rhode Island regiments; and Jabez

Jolly and Simeon Crossman, both drummers in Massachusetts regiments. Barzillai Lew, mentioned above, fought throughout the war in Massachusetts. In addition to these, there are numerous references to anonymous black army musicians. Each of the black detachments of New England, for example, had a drummer and a fifer.

The typical composition of a Negro company is indicated in a proposal made to the General Assembly of Massachusetts by one Thomas Kench, an officer in an artillery regiment stationed at Castle Island in Boston Harbor. According to Kench, the command should be white and consist of the regular officers and an orderly sergeant. The black soldiers should include three sergeants, four corporals, two drummers and fifers, and eighty-four rank and file. The Bucks, of course, represented a typical black company; incidentally, its leader, Colonel George Middleton, was a fiddler. Only one name of a navy musician seems to have been preserved from anonymity, that of Nimrod Perkins of Virginia, drummer on the galley the *Diligence*.

The martial music of the Revolutionary War period emanated primarily from fifes and drums; occasionally, trumpets were used. According to the Orderly Book of a Virginia general, each regiment was allowed a "Fifer-Major" and a "Drummer-Major," whose duties were "to practice the young fifers and drummers between the hours of eleven and one o'clock every day, and to take care that they perform their several duties with as much exactness as possible." It was not until 1792 that the first laws were passed by Congress for the formation and regulation of true military bands (as distinguished from fife-and-drum corps). The duties of service musicians in the War for Independence included performing at ceremonies of an official nature as well as sounding calls, and more than likely, they were required to provide entertainment at times. We may be sure that fiddles were used at such times, particularly where black soldiers were present.

The armed-services musicians played spirited marches in the field for their comrades-at-arms and on parade before their countrymen and women. A large body of war songs developed during the war, many of them using familiar tunes for verses of topical interest—about the defeat of a British general, about the Boston Tea Party, about "Liberty's call" or "the American hero." One popular hymn, *Chester*, represented the contribution to the war effort of the renowned composer William Billings of Massachusetts. According to some, this hymn tune, fitted with a special patriotic text, was so well liked that it became the theme song of the revolution. But it could not compete with an older song (composer unknown) that served as a rallying point for the whole country—the infectious *Yankee Doodle*. Hundreds of verses were sung to the lively melody, and it was quoted in one of the new nation's first overtures, Benjamin Carr's *Federal Overture* (1794).

Black servicemen apparently sang the same songs as did their fellows; they seem not to have developed special musical traditions as they were to do in later wars. Undoubtedly there was much improvisatory singing among the black soldiers as they sat around the campfires at night or worked at their tasks during the day. Just as they had satirized their masters, mistresses, and fellow slaves in their songs back home, so must they have extemporized songs about the white officers and soldiers, their new mode of life, their army adventures, and the civilians they encountered. But no one bothered to write down the music of the black soldier, and so it is lost, as are most of the names of those who sang and played it.

The War of 1812

The number of black men who served in the War of 1812 was small by comparison with the roll of Revolutionary War black servicemen, although here again, the records rarely refer to race. Most Negroes seemed to have entered the navy, undoubtedly because at the beginning of the war they were excluded from joining the army. History preserves the names of three navy musicians: George Brown, a bugler on the *Chesapeake;* Cyrus Tiffany, a fifer on the *Alliance,* who fought in the Battle of Lake Erie; and Jessie Wall, a fifer on the frigate *Niagara.*

In 1814 General Jackson issued a proclamation allowing black men to enlist in the army, and later they fought in some strategic battles, especially in Louisiana. Throughout the period of the war, as during the revolution, slaves went over in considerable numbers to the British lines in response to promises of freedom.

There is very little on record concerning black army musicians in the War of 1812. A New Orleans newspaper carried an item referring to Jordan B. Noble (ca. 1796–1890) of the Seventh Regiment of Infantry as a "matchless drummer"; he "beat his drum during all and every fight, in the hottest hell of the fire, and was complimented by [General Andrew] Jackson himself after the battle."[1] Noble became a professional soldier and fought in three later wars, including the Civil War. It was said that the "colored Creoles" of Louisiana who fought in the Battle of New Orleans had their own special war song, *En Avan' Grenadié* ("Go forward, grenadiers; he who is dead requires no ration"), which they sang along with *La Marseillaise* and other songs. And that is the sum of the knowledge we have.

We know, however, that more black musicians must have been active during the war because of the number of all-black brass bands that began to appear soon after the war—especially in New Orleans, Philadelphia, New York, and sections of New England. For example, the Third Company of Washington Guards (Philadelphia) employed a Negro band under the leadership of Frank Johnson that was destined to become internationally famous. The black musicians who composed the military bands of the early

---

[1]See further in Grace King, *New Orleans: The Place and the People* (New York, 1895), p. 256; also the *New Orleans Daily Picayune,* June 21, 1890.

nineteenth century undoubtedly acquired their training—as well as access to instruments—during the War of 1812.

THE POST-REVOLUTIONARY PERIOD

During the 1780s the southern states suffered a severe depression, chiefly due to the decline in prices of their main crops—tobacco, rice, and indigo. For a while it seemed that "the peculiar institution" of slavery itself might go into a decline. But the invention in 1793 of the cotton gin by a Yankee schoolteacher, Eli Whitney, effected a complete reversal of the situation and ushered in a period of economic prosperity for the southern planters. The Industrial Revolution had created a great market for cotton goods and, consequently, for cotton fiber wherever it could be produced. With the invention of Whitney's machine, which separated the cotton seed from the fiber, southern planters were able to employ their slave labor solely in the cultivation of the crop. The growing of cotton became extremely profitable, and by 1815 most of the planters had switched over from the cultivation of tobacco and rice to that of cotton. Now there was an increased demand for slaves! Consequently, the beginning of the nineteenth century saw a renewed flourishing of the slave trade, with New England's ships taking the lead in supplying southern planters with the human cargo.

Meanwhile, anti-slavery groups, which had begun to appear even before the War for Independence, pressed for legislation against the slave trade. Finally, on March 2, 1807, Congress passed a law prohibiting the importation of African slaves into the States after January 1, 1808. The law was openly flouted for many years, however, and slavery became more firmly established in the South than ever before. In the North slavery slowly died away. Beginning as early as 1780 in Pennsylvania, laws were passed that provided for its gradual abolition. In 1787 Congress prohibited slavery in the newly acquired Northwest Territory (ceded by Great Britain to the United States in 1783), although at the same time it provided for the obligatory return of fugitive slaves to their owners. By 1783 complete emancipation had come for the black colonist of Massachusetts, the first to be freed; by 1830 slavery had all but disappeared in the northern states.

Musical Activities in the New Nation

After the war the musical life of the States resumed at the point where it had slackened earlier: concerts, plays, and operas began to flourish again, singing and dancing schools reopened, and the people returned with gusto to their singing of hymns and ballads. Professional musicians continued to come to the States in increasing numbers, particularly from England. The activity of these foreign musicians combined with that of the Americans to stimulate a flourishing of the arts that evoked admiration from travelers unprepared for such vigorous cultural activity in so young a republic.

The foreign musicians settled chiefly in the larger cities—Boston, New York, Philadelphia, Charleston, and New Orleans in the French-owned Louisiana Territory—where they gave lessons "on the pianoforte, harpsichord and violin"; joined orchestras or organized them where none existed; inaugurated concert series, established music publishing houses, and opened music stores; founded music societies, and collaborated with theatrical companies in presenting plays and operas to the public. Philadelphia early established itself as the chief center of music publishing, with a prolific output of psalm and hymn collections, instruction books, and collections of the "newest country dances" and "latest songs." New Orleans took the lead in producing operas and was the first city to have a permanent opera company.

Both American and foreign musicians responded to the great demand emanating from the vigorous musical activity of the land; they wrote hymn tunes and arrangements, anthems, marches, ballads, dances, and incidental music for plays. Moreover, they wrote "instructors" for their students or incorporated such material in their song collections. In a typical collection, five to ten pages were given over to a discussion of music theory, entitled perhaps "A Plain and Concise Introduction to Music" or "Easy Introduction to the Grounds of Music" and covering such subjects as "the gamut," staves and clefs, note values, musical signs, sol-fa syllables and "transposition of the mi," time and key signatures, intervals, and syncopation. If music students of the period did not learn theory, it was through no fault of the professional musicians.

There is evidence that in several places black students were included among those taught by established musicians. The Englishman William Tuckey, for example, who had come to the colonies before the war, became the organist and choirmaster at Trinity Church in New York and taught music to the pupils of the church's charity school, some of them African Americans. It was Tuckey's church choir that in 1770 presented the first performance of music from Handel's *Messiah* heard in the United States. In New Orleans, some of the French, German, and Italian musicians who were associated with opera companies and orchestras taught Negro students— who themselves became music teachers, composers, and conductors. The Congregational minister and musician Andrew Law (1749–1821), was associated with two of the earliest black music teachers in the North.

Black Singing-School Masters

One of the first black music teachers in the new nation was Newport Gardner (né Occramer Marycoo; 1746–1826). Nothing is known of his childhood except that he was fourteen years old when he was brought to the colonies from Africa and sold to Caleb Gardner, a prominent merchant of Newport, Rhode Island. The African lad showed a great interest in music, and Mrs. Gardner arranged for him to study with "a singing master named Law [who] occasionally came to Newport to give lessons." Since Andrew Law (mentioned above) conducted a singing school in Newport during the year 1783, it seems likely that he was the teacher in question, and we have some indication of what Gardner learned, for Law published several books, including *Select Harmony* (1779), *The Art of Singing* (1794), and *The Rudiments of Music* (1783). In his books Law discusses "toning and tuning the voice," articulation and pronunciation, music theory (that is, "voice parts, cliffs [i.e., clefs], sharps and flats"), accent, "The swell of soft and Loud," time, and mode.[2]

It was said of Gardner that he "read and wrote music with ease" and "possessed a voice remarkably strong and clear." A contemporary writer, John Ferguson, wrote in 1830:

> Newport Gardner ... early discovered to his owner very superior powers of mind. He taught himself to read, after receiving a few lessons on the elements of written language. He taught himself to sing, after receiving a very trivial initiation into the rudiments of music. He became so well acquainted with the science and art of music, that he composed a large number of tunes, some of which have been highly approved by musical amateurs, and was for a long time the teacher of a very numerously-attended singing school in Newport.[3]

In 1791 Gardner won money in a lottery that enabled him to purchase freedom for himself and his family. He rented the "upper chamber" of a house on High Street in Newport for his singing school and developed a large clientele, including among his students his former mistress. Gardner also was active in the community; he served as a deacon in the First Congregational Church, where the Reverend Samuel Hopkins was pastor; and, beginning in 1808, he was headmaster of a school for black children founded by the African Benevolent Society. Hopkins encouraged Gardner's ambition to return to Africa as a missionary and gave him special training to that purpose. In 1824 Gardner was one of the founders of the first black church in Newport, the Colored Union Church. A year later he was ordained a deacon by the Congregational Church in Boston, and early in 1826 he sailed to Liberia as a missionary.

Gardner began to write music when he was only eighteen (1764). It is possible that a song, *Crooked Shanks,* attributed to a composer named Gardner (no first name given) in the collection *A Number of Original Airs, Duettos and Trios* (1803), may be one of his "large number of tunes" that "was popular with amateurs" of his time.

[2]See further about Law in Richard Crawford, *Andrew Law, American Psalmodist* (Evanston, IL, 1968). The fact of Gardner's study with Law is discussed in George Champlain Mason, *Reminiscences of Newport* (Newport, 1884); reprint of chapter about Newport Gardner in RBAM, pp. 36–40.

[3]John Ferguson, *Memoir of the Life and Character of Rev. Samuel Hopkins* (Boston, 1830); reprint of passages about Gardner in BPIM 4 (July 1976): 202–5.

The *Boston Recorder and Telegraph* published an advertisement for his choral piece *Promise Anthem* on January 13, 1826:

> *Promise Anthem* for Sale at 90 Washington Street. The music composed by Dea. Newport Gardner, a native of Africa.

Promise Anthem was sung both in Newport and in Boston; although the music is not extant, the text[4] has been preserved (based on Jeremiah 30:1–3, 10; St. Mark 7:27–28).

> The word that came to Jeremiah from the Lord, saying:
> Write thou all the words which I have spoken unto thee in a book.
> For lo! the days come, saith the Lord, that I will bring again the captivity of my people Israel and Judah, saith the Lord;
> and I will cause them to return to the land that I gave to their fathers, and they shall possess it.
> Therefore, fear thou not, O my servant Jacob, saith the Lord; neither be dismayed, O Israel;
> For lo! I will save thee from afar, and thy seed from their captivity,
> And Jacob shall return and be in rest and quiet, and none shall make him afraid. Amen.
>
> Hear the words of the Lord, O ye African race, hear the words of promise.
> But it is not meet to take the children's bread and cast it to the dogs.
> Truth, Lord, yet the dogs eat of the crumbs that fall from their master's table.
> O African, trust in the Lord. Amen.
> Hallelujah. Praise the Lord. Praise ye the Lord. Hallelujah. Amen.

There is some evidence that black singing-school masters set up schools in other places, but few names have come down to us. A teacher in New York is identified only as "Frank the Negro" by his former teacher, Andrew Law. In 1786 Frank had "about forty scholars." In Philadelphia, a John Cromwell conducted a singing school during the 1820s; some of his students later received recognition for their skills in singing and in playing brass instruments.[5]

Black Benevolent and Fraternal Societies

The postwar period brought freedom to large numbers of slaves in the North, who began to unite with other free blacks to organize various kinds of self-help and fraternal societies. In Newport, Rhode Island, for example, black freedmen in 1780 had organized an African Union Society. In 1787 a group in Philadelphia organized the Free African Society under the leadership of Richard Allen (1760–1831) and Absalom Jones (1746–1818). In Charleston, South Carolina, a society organized about 1793 called itself

[4]Text of *Promise Anthem* in Ferguson, *Memoir.*
[5]Robert Stevenson, *Protestant Church Music in America* (New York, 1966), p. 93. John Cromwell is discussed in the *Philadelphia Tribune,* December 21, 1912.

The Brown Fellowship. And Bostonians called their organization, formed in 1796, the African Society of Boston. Although begun as mutual-aid and moral-reform societies, these groups soon included religious services among their activities and eventually became involved with establishing schools for their children. Both kinds of activities included musical performance.

It was in Boston that the first fraternal group was organized, a Masonic lodge, called African Lodge No. 1, under the leadership of Methodist minister Prince Hall (1735–1805). When the Grand Lodge of Massachusetts refused to give the group a charter, they obtained one from a branch of the British Masons in 1787. All these groups gave freedmen the opportunity to share ideas and to gain experience in managing their own affairs, which had been denied them under slavery. Religion was deeply integrated into the lives of Africans in the motherland, and it continued to exert influence over them in the New World, even as they adopted the Protestant religions of their owners. In time they realized that religious societies could meet their needs and accomplish the aims of the benevolent and fraternal groups, as well.

THE BLACK CHURCH

Toward the end of the eighteenth century a movement for the establishment of separate black congregations gradually gained momentum, primarily because of the growing impatience of black worshipers with the discrimination they encountered in white churches. In some places white congregations encouraged the organization of all-black congregations; in other places they bitterly opposed such groups.

For the most part, however, the white churches were too preoccupied with their own problems—those involved with establishing their independence from the European mother churches—to be overly concerned with the problems of their black members. Although the first Methodist Society in the colonies, for example, dates from 1764 with the congregation of Robert Strawbridge in Baltimore, Maryland, it was not until 1784 that the American church was formally organized and its bishops selected at the "Christmas Conference" in Baltimore.

The Earliest Black Congregations

The first self-governing congregations were Baptist groups organized in Georgia, and one of the first black men to receive permission to preach (as an exhorter) to slaves was George Leile (ca. 1751–?), himself the slave of a Baptist deacon. As early as 1774 Leile traveled up and down the Savannah River, preaching to slaves on the plantations that bordered the river. Eventually he founded a small congregation at Silver Bluff, South Carolina, near the Georgia boundary line. The church was broken up during the Revolutionary War, however, and in 1782 Leile went to Kingston, Jamaica, where he continued to work with Baptist groups.

The earliest permanent congregation in the nation was the First African Baptist Church at Savannah, Georgia, formed in 1788 by Andrew Bryan (1737–1812), who was ordained a Baptist minister that year. Like Leile a slave, Bryan purchased his freedom two years later and moved his congregation into a new building in 1794. In Boston, black men and women, under the leadership of Thomas Paul (1773–1831), organized the African Baptist Church in 1805 and the next year built a meeting house which still stands today as the oldest black church building in the United States. In about 1808 Paul went to New York City to help establish the Abyssinian Baptist Church there. Philadelphia also saw its First African Baptist Church the same year.

Among other important black congregations of the early nineteenth century were the First African Presbyterian Church in Philadelphia, founded in 1807, and the St. Philips Episcopal Church in New York, founded in 1818. The amount of independence gained by these congregations varied from place to place; some had white ministers, particularly in the South, and / or were governed by white councils; but all enjoyed more freedom to worship as they pleased than was possible for them in the white mother churches. To be sure, in the South most of the independent congregations were dissolved early in the century, primarily in response to the Denmark Vesey uprising in 1822 and the Nat Turner insurrection in 1831. Since the leaders of these revolts were preachers, the southern states blamed religious groups for fomenting terrorism and enacted repressive laws that were particularly destructive to religious groups. It was not until after the Civil War that independent congregations reappeared in the South.

Methodist Dissenters

We have not yet discussed black Methodist dissenters, and with good reason: their withdrawals from the white mother churches proved to have serious, unforeseen consequences. Black people had been welcomed into Methodism from the earliest period of its establishment in the colonies; indeed, one of the first converts in the 1760s was Aunt Annie, a slave of the Sweitzer family in Baltimore. Ex-slaves were present at the church's "Christmas Conference" in 1784—among them, "Black Harry" Hoosier, an itinerant preacher of some notoriety, and Richard Allen, who would later become a celebrity—and by the end of the century black worshipers constituted about one-fifth of the total membership of the Methodist Church. In sum, Methodism had a special appeal for the lowly of both races, and black folk found its preachments and practices especially suited to their spiritual needs.

Nevertheless, black Methodists became increasingly impatient and frustrated during the 1780s over the discrimination they met in white churches. As early as 1787 in Baltimore, black Methodists organized themselves into

A Sunday morning at the African Episcopal Church of St. Thomas. *(Courtesy the Historical Society of Pennsylvania)*

an autonomous group; later they purchased a building and by 1812 had attracted a dynamic leader, Daniel Coker (ca. 1785–ca. 1825), who helped them incorporate the church in 1816 as the African Methodist Episcopal Bethel Society. In 1796 black Methodists in New York left the John Street Methodist Episcopal Church to form their own congregation, naming their worship place "Zion Chapel."

But it was in Philadelphia that the withdrawal movement reached its culmination. Some of the members of the Free African Society, particularly Richard Allen, had always been interested in organizing an independent religious society. By August 1791 plans were well underway for building an African Church, supported by such eminent white citizens as Benjamin Rush. In the meanwhile, members of the Society were still attending Old St. George's Methodist Church. In 1784 the church licensed Allen and Jones to preach—they were the first black men to receive preaching licenses from the Methodist Church—and in 1786 Allen became an assisting pastor with an assignment to preach at the 5:00 A.M. services.

Under Allen's leadership the black membership of Old St. George's increased so dramatically that some of the whites became alarmed. In 1792, after the church completed a construction project which included adding a gallery, they demanded that the black members be "removed from their original seats" to places in the new gallery. Allen relates the incident in his autobiography:

> We expected to take the seats over the ones we formerly occupied below, not knowing any better, we took those seats. . . . Just as we got to the seats, the elder said, "Let us pray." We had not been long upon our knees before I heard considerable scuffling and low talking. I raised my head and saw one of the trustees, H. . . M . . ., having hold of the Rev. Absalom Jones, pulling him up off his knees, and saying, "You must get up, you must not kneel here." Mr. Jones replied, "Wait until prayer is over." Mr. H. M. said, "No, you must get up now, or I will call for aid and force you away." Mr. Jones said, "Wait until prayer is over and I will get up and trouble you no more." With that he [the trustee] beckoned to one of the other trustees, William White, to pull him up. By this time prayer was over, and we all went out of the church in a body, and they were no more plagued with us in the Church.

Allen and his followers were particularly annoyed because they

> . . . had subscribed largely towards finishing St. George's Church, in building the gallery and laying floors, and just as the house was made comfortable . . . were turned out from enjoying the comforts of worshipping therein.[6]

The plans for building an African church, however, were moving along smoothly. By the summer of 1794 the new building was ready for occupancy, and on July 17, 1794, the congregation of the African Episcopal Church of St. Thomas held its dedication services. Yes, the new church became Episcopalian! Despite the objections of Allen and Jones, the majority of the black group voted in favor of an alignment with the Church of England, and they were encouraged by the white St. Paul's Episcopal Church. Absalom Jones accepted the ministry of the church, was ordained a deacon the next year, and in 1804 became the first black Episcopal priest in the nation.

Allen determined to remain within the folds of Methodism, although the local white clergy strongly opposed the organization of an independent black group. By the summer of 1794 he was successful in finding a home for his small band of followers—an old frame blacksmith shop on a lot he himself had purchased—and the church was dedicated on July 29, 1794. In 1799 Allen was ordained a Methodist deacon. Later he explained that he felt the "emotional natures" of his people should not be swallowed up in a cold, intellectual ritual:

> I was confident that no religious sect or denomination would suit the capacity of the colored people so well as the Methodists, for the plain simple gospel suits

[6]*The Life Experience and Gospel Labours of the Right Reverend Richard Allen* (Philadelphia, 1887), pp. 25–26. Recent research reveals that the incident described by Allen probably took place in 1792, not in 1787 as implied by Allen. See further in Milton C. Sernett, *Black Religion and American Evangelicalism* (Metuchen, NJ, 1975), pp. 218–20.

The Reverend Richard Allen (1760–1831) engraved by John Sartain. *(Courtesy New York Public Library, Special Collections)*

best for any people, for the unlearned can understand, and the learned are sure to understand.[7]

Richard Allen's Hymnals

Although Allen was not a formally trained minister, he was extremely intelligent and highly articulate. At the time he organized the first congregation of the African Methodist Episcopal Church (hereafter referred to as AME Church), he had had extensive experience as both an itinerant and a resident minister. Because he knew and appreciated the importance of music to his people, one of his first official acts as AME minister was to publish a hymnal for the specific use of his congregation. The importance of this first hymnal designed expressly for an all-black congregation cannot be overemphasized; whereas Allen might have used the official Methodist hymnal—and, as a good Methodist, should have done so—instead he consciously set about to collect hymns that would have a special appeal to the members of his congregation, hymns that undoubtedly were long-time favorites of black Americans. Thus the hymnal provides an index to the hymns popular among black congregations (the AME in particular) of the new nation.

[7]Allen, p. 29.

These hymns represent the black worshipers' own choices, not the choices of white missionaries and ministers.[8]

Undoubtedly Allen began developing a repertory of his favorite hymns early in his career; when he became minister of his own church, he would have taught those hymns to his people and included their favorites in the worship service as well. In 1801 his collection of hymns, titled *A Collection of Spiritual Songs and Hymns Selected from Various Authors by Richard Allen, African Minister,* was printed by John Ormrod, who had the previous year printed *The Articles of Association of the AME Church of the City of Philadelphia* for him. The collection consists of fifty-four hymn texts, without tunes, drawn chiefly from the collections of Dr. Watts, the Wesleys, and other hymn writers favored by the Methodists of that period, but also including hymns popular with the Baptists. Within the same year an enlarged second edition of the hymnbook was printed by T. L. Plowman, with the title page this time reading *A Collection of Hymns and Spiritual Songs from Various Authors, by Richard Allen, Minister of the African Methodist Episcopal Church.*[9] Ten additional hymns were added to the collection, making a total of sixty-four, and a few changes were made in some texts of the original corpus. As was not unusual at the time, Allen neither provided authors' names nor indicated appropriate melodies for his hymns.

The wording of the title chosen by Allen was not novel for the time; indeed, it was rather common, its earliest use dating back to a revised edition of the *Bay Psalm Book* printed in 1651 with the title *The Psalms, Hymns and Spiritual Songs of the Old and New Testaments.* The original inspiration for the title was the Scriptural passage:

> Let the word of Christ dwell in you richly in all wisdom, teaching and admonishing one another in Psalms and Hymns and Spiritual Songs, singing with grace in your hearts unto the Lord. [Col. 3:16]

How and where did the self-educated ex-slave minister find the hymns for his collection? Hymnbook compilers typically gathered their material from the large number of hymnals already in print. Augustus Toplady, for example, wrote in the preface to his collection of 1776 that a few of the hymns were of his own authorship and the remainder he had selected after examining "between forty and fifty volumes." It is not probable, however, that Richard Allen would have had access to any large number of hymnals, nor would he have had the time for examining them had they been available. In addition to his responsibilities as minister to the fledgling church, Allen had to earn a living; at various times in his life he was a teamster, brickyard worker, woodcutter, shoemaker, and day laborer. It may be assumed, therefore, that some of the pieces Allen used must have been

---

[8]Braithwaite, J. Roland, ed. *Richard Allen: A Collection of Hymns and Spiritual Songs* (Nashville, TN, 1987), p. x.
[9]See RBAM pp. 52–61, for a list of the hymns and reprints of eight hymns.

selected from the hymnals to which he had access as an itinerant preacher traveling the Pennsylvania–Delaware circuit and as an assistant minister at Old St. George's Methodist Episcopal Church. Others may have been in oral circulation among Methodists and Baptists of the area—in the same way that folksongs circulated. Finally, it seems clear that Allen himself must have written some of the hymns.

There are several bases for assuming that Allen wrote hymn texts. From time to time he published sermons, doggerel verses, tracts, and other kinds of religious writings; and his autobiography, *The Life Experience and Gospel Labours of the Right Reverend Richard Allen, Written by Himself and Published by His Request* (publ. 1887), includes two hymns, *The God of Bethel heard her cries* and *Ye ministers that are called to preaching.* It is possible, therefore, that he might have been the author of some of the hymns in his collection. Others might have been written by elders of the church, or by members; some of the homely verses certainly suggest the hand of amateurs.

We can attribute some of the texts to well-known writers of the period by searching through contemporaneous hymnals for concordances. Thus we find that Isaac Watts is represented by no fewer than thirteen hymns; his verses had been favorites among black folk ever since colonial times, when missionaries to the slaves reported that the slaves took "extatic delight" in singing the psalms and hymns of Dr. Watts. Allen realized the power of a Watts hymn, such as *There is a Land of Pure Delight,* to inspire his people to believe that their wretched existence on earth would be followed by a blissful one in heaven:

There is a land of pure delight,
Where saints immortal reign.
Infinite day excludes the night,
And pleasures banish pain.

There everlasting Spring abides.
And never-with'ring flowe'rs:
Death, like a narrow sea divides
This heav'nly land from ours.

Sweet fields beyond the swelling flood,
Stand dress'd in living green;
So, to the Jews, old Canaan stood,
While Jordan roll'd between.

Allen's hymnal, like many others of the period, includes no melodies; consequently, we have no way of knowing which tunes actually were used for singing the hymns. But some logical assumptions can be made. In the first place, the melody repertory was limited: a single tune would have been drawn upon for the singing of any number of hymns as long as the metrical patterns of tune and hymn text matched. The evidence suggests that a deacon "lined out" the hymn for congregational singing, selecting an appropriate tune according to whether it was short meter, common meter, or long meter, thus following in the tradition of Protestant practices for centuries past.

It may be assumed that tunes consistently linked with specific hymns in other hymnals were used for the singing of those hymns by Allen's congregation. The tune *Newark,* for example, is associated with the text *Now begins the heav'nly theme* (No. 31 in Allen's hymnal) in several collections published during the years 1776–1805, and it was undoubtedly used by the Bethelites. On the other hand, there is strong evidence to support an assumption that Bethel drew upon popular songs of the period as a source of tunes, or composed its own tunes.

This had been a common practice among Protestants ever since the origin of their religion—some of Martin Luther's best chorale melodies were borrowed from German folksong or popular song. Nevertheless, it upset the church fathers that black Methodists were debasing, so to speak, the music of the church. Visitors to the black church in 1804 made satirical remarks about the singing they heard, not so much about the sound of the singing as about the kinds of songs that were sung.[10] John Fanning Watson, one of the leading Methodist church fathers of the city, complained in 1819:

> We have too, a growing evil, in the practice of singing in our places of public and society worship, *merry* airs, adapted from old *songs,* to hymns of our composing: often miserable as poetry, and senseless as matter.... Most frequently [these hymns are] composed and first sung by the illiterate *blacks* of the society.[11]

And a visitor to the church, William Faux, wrote in 1820:

> After sermon they began singing merrily, and continued, without stopping, one hour, till they became exhausted and breathless. "Oh! come to Zion, come!" "Hallelujah, &c." And then, "O won't you have my lovely bleeding *Jasus,*" a thousand times repeated in full thundering chorus to the tune of "Fol de rol." While all the time they were clapping hands, shouting and jumping, and exclaiming, "Ah Lord! Good Lord! Give me *Jasus!* Amen."...[12]

This quotation not only gives some text refrains of songs improvised by black worshipers, but also is the earliest reference to a specific popular tune used for that purpose. All available evidence suggests that the following is the tune that Faux heard. It is the only song of the period with the "Fol de rol" text:[13]

---

[10]William Colbert's comments about the singing at Bethel Church in 1804 are cited in Don Yoder, John Fanning *Pennsylvania Spirituals* (Lancaster, Pennsylvania, 1961), p. 27.

[11]Watson, *Methodist Error* (Trenton, New Jersey, 1819); passages about the singing of black Methodists reprinted in RBAM, pp. 62–64.

[12]William Faux, *Memorable Days in America* (London, 1823), p. 420.

[13]See Patricia Havlice, *Popular Song Index* (Metuchen, NJ, 1975), p. 216. The song was popular on the English stage from the late eighteenth century through the first half of the nineteenth and, consequently, would have been known to the Englishman Faux as well as Americans in this period. See further in *Journal of the Folk Song Society* 5 (1914–16): 163–64. A modern source for the song is Helen Creighton, *Songs and Ballads from Nova Scotia* (New York, 1966), pp. 164–65.

Bil - lie Tay-lor was a smart young fel - ler, Full of mirth and full of glee, And he did his mind dis - ki ver To a la - dy fair to see. Fol de rol de rol de ri - do, fol de ray, Fol de rol, de rol, de ri - do.

Allen's hymnal was significant in more ways than one: in addition to its position in music history as the first anthology of hymns collected for a black congregation, it was also the first to employ the so-called wandering refrains—that is, refrain verses or short choruses attached at random to orthodox hymn stanzas. The idea of adding a refrain to a hymn was highly novel at the beginning of the nineteenth century; the only other extant examples are in a hymnbook published by the Native American minister Samson Occom in 1774. But Allen's practice of adding *any* refrain to *any* hymn—hence, the "wandering refrain"—apparently was unique! This was a kind of improvisation, and it must have introduced a great deal of informality into the worship service.

There is yet one other aspect of performance practice that should be noted. A Russian traveler, Paul Svin'in, visited Bethel Church in 1811. Accustomed to the restrained style of the Greek Orthodox worship service, he found Bethel's service much too unusual for his taste. However, his account of the singing is of special value because of the information it provides about musical practices. When Svin'in and his friend arrived at the church, the minister was reading from the psalms.

> . . . At the end of every psalm the entire congregation, men and women alike, sang verses in a loud, shrill monotone. This lasted about half an hour. When the preacher ceased reading, all turned toward the door, fell on their knees, bowed their heads to the ground and set up an agonizing, heart-rending moaning. Afterwards, the minister resumed the reading of the psalter and when he had finished sat down on a chair; then all rose and began chanting psalms in chorus, the men and women alternating, a procedure which lasted some twenty minutes. . . .[14]

[14]Pavel Petrovich Svin'in, secretary to the Russian Consul General, lived in Philadelphia during the years 1811–13 and later published a book about his experiences. See further in *Picturesque United States of America, 1811, 1812, 1813, Being a Memoir on Paul Svinin . . .* by Avraham Yarmolinsky (New York, 1930), p. 20.

Two features of this part of the service are worthy of note: the choral response given by the congregation to the reading of each psalm, and the singing of the psalms in alternation by the men and the women. Both procedures point back to the traditional African predilection for antiphonal singing. The loudness of the singing and the "heart-rending moaning" are also typically in the African tradition—the singers singing with all their might and becoming totally involved in the experience.

INDEPENDENT BLACK DENOMINATIONS

The black churchmen who led the movement to establish independent congregations within Methodism soon discovered that their freedom had severe limitations, despite their physical separation from the mother churches. Under the rules of the Methodist Church, white elders still controlled the activities of the black churches and still owned the buildings, regardless of the amount of money invested by black members in their churches. Richard Allen and his congregation chafed under the stifling conditions and struggled for many years with the mother church. Finally the matter reached the Pennsylvania Supreme Court, where Bethel won its case; on January 1, 1816, the church became totally autonomous. The way was paved for the organization of the world's first black denomination.

In April 1816 several black Methodist congregations met together in Philadelphia to plan for setting up a General Conference, and drew up an Ecclesiastical Compact for the fledgling denomination, to be called the African Methodist Episcopal Church. Daniel Coker and Allen were elected to a dual bishopric, but Coker later resigned; consequently, Allen became the Church's first bishop. Thereafter followed a period of organizing the church program, setting up congregations, and establishing rules and procedures. In 1817 the Church published its first official document, *The Doctrines and Discipline of the African Methodist Episcopal Church*. By the next General Conference in May 1818, there were sixteen congregations in the Church, representing almost seven thousand members. During the following decades, membership increased enormously; congregations were established throughout the North and, for a brief period, in the South at Charleston. That church was short-lived, as we will see, and its leadership went north, including two preachers who would later become bishops, Morris Brown and Daniel Payne.

Black Methodists founded two other denominations during these years. In New York they obtained a charter in 1821 for the African Methodist Episcopal Zion Church (hereafter referred to as the AMEZ Church) and elected James Varick (1750?–1828) their first bishop. Like the AME Church, this denomination became quite large over the years and had many congregations. In Wilmington, Delaware, Peter Spencer and William Anderson founded the Union African Methodist Episcopal Church in 1805 and incorporated it in 1813. Although that Church did not expand to the same extent as the others, by 1906 it included no fewer than two hundred congregations.

Denominational Hymnals

Richard Allen was in charge of publications for the new AME denomination and, predictably, one of the first was a hymnal, in 1818. The introduction to the collection of 314 hymns stated:

> To the members of the African Methodist Episcopal Church: Beloved brethren. In April last, we presented you with the Discipline of our Church. It was requisite that we should exhibit to the Christian world the rules of government and articles of faith by which we intended to be influenced and governed. In doing this, we were under the necessity of laying before the public a plain statement of facts; which, we are happy to find, have given general satisfaction.
>
> Having become a distinct and separate body of people, there is no collection of hymns, we could with propriety adopt. However, we have for some time been collecting materials for the present work; and we trust the result of our labour will receive the sanction of the congregations under our charge.
>
> In our researches, we have not passed over a selection of Hymns because [they were] esteemed and used by a particular denomination; but have endeavoured to collect such as were applicable to the various states of Christian experience.
>
> A number of new hymns have been introduced into this work, in consequence of the estimation in which they were held. And we flatter ourselves, the present edition will not suffer by a comparison with any collection of equal magnitude.
>
> It may be proper to inform the congregations that our Hymn Book is designed to supersede those heretofore used among us.
>
> We exhort you to retain the spirit of singing; always recollecting that it is a part of Divine worship. When the spirit and the understanding are united, it is believed to be a service acceptable in the sight of God, and beneficial to the souls of the people. [Signed by] Richard Allen, Daniel Coker, James Champion.

In 1808 Allen had published a new edition of the 1801 hymnal, but like the earlier version, it was of small pocket size and unpretentious. The hymnal of 1818 was impressive by comparison; it shared some 244 concordances with the official Methodist hymnal, including many of the Watt's hymns so beloved by black Christians. Significantly, only fifteen hymns of the 1801 collection were carried over into the new edition. Were the earlier hymns too homely for a proud, new denomination? By the second decade of the century, many of these hymns were to be associated with a new genre, called "camp-meeting hymn" (to be discussed later), which was not quite respectable in the eyes of Methodist clergymen. But the discarded hymns were not forgotten by black worshipers, as we shall see; verses taken from the hymns lived on in the folk music of the people, the "spirituals."

The AME Church consistently published its own hymnals rather than use those of the white mother churches, as did most other black congregations. In the 1837 edition, each hymn carries identification of its scriptural text, its meter (that is, long, short, common, mixed, etc.), and an appropriate tune for singing the hymn; in 1898 music was included for the first time. Throughout its history the AME hymnal has contained hymns written by black authors and composers. Two other denominational hymnals merit comment at this point: in 1822 Peter Spencer published the *Union African Hymn Book* for his Ezion Union African Church in Wilmington, and in 1838 Christopher Rush and other members of his church published *Hymns for the Use of the African Methodist Episcopal Zion Church in America.*

Importance of the Black Church

The black church stands tall in the center of the black experience in the United States. It was the first institution to be controlled solely by blacks, and it has remained their most powerful institution up to the present time. From the beginning the church was more than a religious community: the church set up Infant Schools and Sunday Schools to care for its children and educate the ex-slaves; it sponsored benevolent and moral-reform societies; it organized literary and debating societies and library rooms; and it promoted recreational programs for its members. In short, the church undertook the responsibility for providing black communities with all the opportunities and activities denied them by a racist populace in the North and a slaveholding populace in the South.

In the area of music the church played the particularly important role of patron. It sponsored singing schools for children and adults and offered showcases for the display of talent within the black community through its promotion of concerts and artist recitals. It fostered the development of talent among the young, even to the extent of raising money for necessary musical study. Perhaps most important of all, it provided a place where black folk could experiment with composing all kinds of religious music, from the spiritual to formal anthems and similar set pieces.

THE CAMP MEETING

The camp meeting, an American institution that evolved during the "Second Awakening," was a revival movement that dominated the religious life of America's frontier communities during the period 1780 to 1830. Its participants were the common people, black and white, of all the Protestant denominations; its format, that of a continuous religious service spread out over several days, often an entire week. Religious services took place in a forest or woods, the members of the huge temporary congregations worshiping in large tents and living in small tents. The historic first camp meeting was held in Logan County, Kentucky, in July 1800, and drew thousands of participants. A Presbyterian minister, the Reverend James McGready, was the leading spirit in organizing the meeting, but various denominations were represented among the several preachers involved in the conduct of the services and the handling of the large crowds. Eventually the camp-meeting movement came to be dominated by Methodist ministers, who taught their own Methodist hymns to the campers in the early years. From Kentucky the idea of camp meetings traveled in all directions—northeast into West Virginia, Maryland, Delaware, Pennsylvania, and up to the northern states; east into Virginia and on into the Carolinas; south into Tennessee and down into the Deep South.

The camp meeting was primarily an interracial institution; indeed, sometimes there were more black worshipers present than white. Foreign visitors to the States were greatly impressed by what they saw and heard at camp meetings, there being no European prototypes for the vast assemblages in forest groves. The visitors filled their diaries and travel journals with detailed descriptions of the people attending these meetings, of the sermons, of the procedures, and, above all, of the singing—especially the songs of black folk. Ex-slaves, too, provided descriptions of camp meetings in their writings.

At night the scene of a meeting was an awesome sight. Huge campfires burned everywhere, so that it seemed as if the "whole woods stood in flames." From three to five thousand people or more were assembled in the huge main tent, called a *tabernacle,* to listen to the preacher-for-the-evening address them from an elevated stand. On benches below the elevation sat the other preachers. Then there were rows of seats for the people— according to some reports, one side for the Negroes and the other side for the white congregation. Other accounts state, however, that the black folk had to *stand,* not sit, in a narrow space reserved for them behind the preachers' elevation; undoubtedly, practices varied from place to place. Robert Todd, a Methodist historian who was active in the Pennsylvania–Maryland–Delaware–Virginia area, says that "a portion of the circle to the rear of the preacher's stand [was] invariably set apart for the occupancy and use of the colored people."[15]

Occasionally black ministers preached to camp-meeting assemblies. Precedents for black ministers addressing white or interracial congregations had been set by the Methodists in their early "itinerating" practices, which sent ministers to preach in rural areas, hunting up all those who "dwelt in the wilderness." The first of the English Methodist missionaries to come to America (who later became the first bishop of the American Methodist Church), the Reverend Francis Asbury, often was accompanied by Black Harry Hoosier in his travels, estimated to have totaled over 270,000 miles.

[15]Robert W. Todd, *Methodism of the Peninsula* (Philadelphia, 1886), p. 181. In regard to blacks in camp meetings, see also Frederick Douglass, *My Bondage and My Freedom* (Boston, 1853); reprint of passages about music in RBAM pp. 82–87.

On some occasions Black Harry substituted for Asbury and was well received. And Daniel Coker addressed a gathering of five thousand at a camp meeting in Maryland.[16]

Some time during the second decade of the century, as early as 1818 if not before, black churches began sponsoring their own camp meetings, led by the AME churches. By the 1820s camp meetings under black leadership were common in the Philadelphia—Baltimore—New York circuit. These meetings drew worshipers by the thousands and included whites as well as blacks.[17]

Singing in the Camp Meeting

To both participants and observers, the singing was one of the most impressive aspects of camp meetings. When the people sang their hymns and spirituals, they instantaneously formed a "superb choir." After attending a camp meeting in Georgia, the Swedish novelist Fredrika Bremer wrote:[18]

> A magnificent choir! Most likely the sound proceeded from the black portion of the assembly, as their number was three times that of the whites, and their voices are naturally beautiful and pure.

According to a report on a camp meeting held in Pennsylvania in 1838, where there were seven thousand in attendance, the Negroes sang louder than any others, although they were greatly outnumbered:

> Their shouts and singing were so very boisterous that the singing of the white congregation was often completely drowned in the echoes and reverberations of the colored people's tumultuous strains.

The blacks customarily continued singing in their segregated quarters long after the whites had retired to their tents for the night, and sometimes sang all night long. More than a dozen contemporary writers commented upon this unusual practice. Fredrika Bremer observed that although the meeting she attended had lasted long past midnight, the black worshipers did not go to sleep afterward:

> On the black side [of the camp] . . . the tents were still full of religious exaltation, each separate tent presenting some new phasis. . . . In one [tent] . . . a song of the spiritual Canaan was being sung excellently. . . . At half-past five . . . the hymns of the Negroes, which had continued through the night, were still to be heard on all sides.

Black campers made their influence felt in the camp-meeting movement in yet another way—much to the discomfiture of the church fathers. John F.

---

[16] *Journal of Daniel Coker* (Baltimore, 1820), p. 18.
[17] See further about early camp meetings sponsored by black churches in Benjamin J. Leedom, *Westtown Under the Old and New Regime . . .* (Würzburg, Germany, 1882), pp. 166–72.
[18] Fredrika Bremer, *The Homes of the New World* (New York, 1853), v. 1, pp. 306–17.

Watson observed this in his discussion of the "errors" made by Methodists of the time:

> Here ought to be considered too, a most exceptional error, which has the toler-ance at least of the rulers of our camp meetings. In the *blacks'* quarter, the coloured people get together, and sing for hours together, short scraps of dis-jointed affirmations, pledges, or prayers, lengthened out with long repetition *choruses.* These are all sung in the merry chorus-manner of the southern harvest field, or husking-frolic method, of the slave blacks. . . .

Such practices he condemned, pointing out that

> . . . the example has already visibly affected the religious manners of some whites. From this cause, I have known in some camp meetings, from 50 to 60 people crowd into one tent, after the public devotions had closed, and there continue the whole night, singing tune after tune, (though with occasional epi-sodes of prayer) scarce one of which were in our hymn books.[19]

Some of the practices of the black campers affected camp-meeting sing-ing to such an extent that church leaders were moved to protest. First, the black campers were holding songfests away from proper supervision, and this was undesirable in the eyes of the church fathers. They were singing songs of their own composing, which was even worse in the eyes of the officials. The texts of the composed songs were not lyric poems in the hal-lowed tradition of Watts, but a stringing together of isolated lines from prayers, the Scriptures, and orthodox hymns, the whole made longer by the addition of choruses or the injecting of refrains between verses. Finally, for their composed religious songs they used tunes that were dangerously near to being dance tunes in the style of slave jubilee melodies. None of this was acceptable to the orthodox. Nevertheless, from such practices emerged a new kind of religious song that became the distinctive badge of the camp-meeting movement.

The Camp-Meeting Hymn

Just as the "Great Awakening" movement in the eighteenth century had stimulated a revolt among the common people against the staid psalmody of the religious establishment and had ushered in the livelier hymnody, so the "Second Awakening" of the early nineteenth century brought a reaction against the now antiquated hymns. In the noisy, folksy atmosphere of the camp meeting, songs of a different kind were demanded. There were no hymnbooks in the early years of the movement; the campers had either to sing from memory or to learn songs in the meetings.

Most of the congregation was illiterate and, at any rate, it would have been difficult to read by the light of flickering campfires or torches. As a result the same kind of procedures were developed at camp meetings as had

[19]Watson, *Methodist Error,* pp. 63–64.

been practiced among Negroes. Song leaders added choruses and refrains to the official hymns so that the people could join in with the singing. They introduced new songs with repetitive phrases and catchy tunes. Spontaneous songs were composed on the spot, often started by some excited preacher and developed by the crowds who shouted "Hallelujah" and similar praise words or phrases between the preacher's lines. The new songs were called "spiritual songs," as distinguished from the hymns and psalms. True, the term "spiritual song" had been in use for over a century, but now it acquired a different meaning, being used to designate the camp-meeting hymn.

The distinctive features of the camp-meeting hymn and the spiritual song were the chorus and / or refrain, the popular tune or folksong-style melody, and the rough and irregular couplets that made up the texts, which often referred to everyday experiences as well as scriptural concepts. The choruses were freely added to any of the standard hymns, and eventually there developed a body of these "wandering verses," which became immensely popular with camp-meeting congregations. As we have seen, Richard Allen's hymnal of 1801 apparently was the first to include such "wandering verses":

> Hallelujah to the Lamb,
> Who has purchased our pardon;
> We will praise him again
> When we pass over Jordan.
> [Chorus sung with Hymns Nos. 1 and 50]

> There's glory, glory in my soul;
> Come, mourners, see salvation roll.
> [Couplet in Hymn No. 14]

> Firm united let us be,
> In the bonds of charity;
> As a band of brothers join'd,
> Loving God and all mankind.
> [Chorus of Hymns Nos. 45 and 56]

In addition to adding choruses to hymns they knew, the camp meeters also composed songs on the spot, drawing upon popular melodies of the time for tunes or inventing their own tunes to fit the improvised texts. Again, Watson is a witness, for he was one of the first clergymen to pay heed to the evolvement of the spiritual in stating that the "senseless songs" were "most frequently composed and first sung by the illiterate blacks of the Society" and that the songs consisted of "short scraps of disjointed affirmations, pledges, or prayers, lengthened out with long repetition *choruses.*" Moreover, Watson set down two of the refrains he heard: *Touch but one string, 'twill make heaven ring* and *Go shouting all your days* in connection with *glory, glory, glory.*

From the perspective of the present, it is possible to perceive a connective link between "wandering verses" attached to hymns and improvised spirituals, particularly those in the black tradition. One of the verses heard by Watson, for example, which is also attached to Hymn No. 14 in Allen's hymnal, reappears in a Negro spiritual text as follows:[20]

> Oh shout, oh shout, oh shout away,
> And don't you mind,
> And glory, glory, glory in my soul.
>
> And when 'twas night I thought 'twas day,
> I thought I'd pray my soul away,
> And glory, glory, glory in my soul!
>
> O Satan told me not to pray
> He want my soul at de judgement day
> And glory, glory, glory in my soul!
>
> And every where I went to pray,
> There some thing was in my way,
> And glory, glory, glory in my soul!

Another of the verses Watson heard the black worshipers singing appears in this spiritual:

> CHORUS O my King Emanuel, my Emanuel above,
> Sing glory to my King Emanuel.
>
> If you walk de golden street,
> And you join de golden band,
> Sing glory be to my King Emanuel.
>
> *Chorus.*
>
> *If you touch one string,*
> *Den de whole heaven ring.*[21]
> Sing glory be to my King Emanuel.
>
> *Chorus, etc.*

There were at least two other favorite camp-meeting verses that belonged to the Negro tradition, according to contemporaneous sources:

> Roll, Jordan, roll

and

> Shout, shout, we are gaining ground;
> Glory, Hallelujah.

[20]The two spirituals were published in *Slave Songs of the United States* (New York, 1867), by William Allen *et al.*: *O shout away* (No. 92) and *King Emanuel* (No. 35). The similarities in text between the two spirituals and the refrains heard sung by the blacks in Philadelphia suggests the early origins of some of the slave songs in the 1867 collection.

[21]Author's italics. Hymn No. 14 in Allen's hymnal.

In his book *Methodist Error,* Watson discussed the latter along with several other verses "composed and first sung by Blacks."

Shouts in the Camp Meeting

Watson reported on a curious activity of the Negroes that took place while they were singing in their quarters after the all-camp services were ended. To him it seemed that the singers were almost dancing, and indeed they were:

> With every word so sung, they have a sinking of one or [the] other leg of the body alternately; producing an audible sound of the feet at every step, and as manifest as the steps of actual Negro dancing in Virginia, etc. If some, in the meantime, sit, they strike the sounds alternately on each thigh.[22]

This is the earliest account of a religious dance ceremony of African origin, the "ring shout," that was to be described many, many times in nineteenth- and twentieth-century American literature. Watson apparently did not take note of the circle formation of the dancers, but he did observe the thigh slapping. As we have seen, the slaves who danced in the markets of New York City accompanied themselves with percussive sounds produced in this manner. And during the period when Watson was writing, the slaves in New Orleans were drawing crowds of whites to the Place Congo on Sunday afternoons to watch a similar form of dancing. (This point will be discussed in a later chapter.)

There was another camp-meeting practice that allowed the African American to indulge in their traditional "shuffle step" dancing—the "farewell march around the encampment." Robert Todd reported on a typical occurrence in a northern slave state:

> Usually the tide of enthusiasm on the colored side of the encampment arose and intensified as the days and nights rolled by; and reached the climatic point on the last night of the meeting. By general consent, it was understood that, as to the colored people, the rules requiring quiet after a certain hour, were, on this last night, to be suspended; and great billows of sound from the tornado of praise and singing rolled over the encampment, and was echoed back from hill and wood for miles away, until the morrow's dawning.

With the sunrise, the black campers would begin knocking down the plank partitions that separated the white quarters from their quarters. Then they would begin the "grand march round de campment,"

> accompanied with leaping, shuffling, and dancing, after the order of David before the ark when his wife thought he was crazy; accompanied by a song appropriate to the exciting occasion. . . . The sound of the hammer aforesaid became the signal for a general arising all around the camp; and, in a few moments, curtains were parted; tents thrown open; and multitudes of faces

---

[22]Watson, *Methodist Error,* p. 63.

peered out into the early dawning to witness the weird spectacle. Sometimes the voices of the masters and veterans among the white people would echo back, in happy response, the jubilant shout of the rejoicing slaves.[23]

ETHIOPIAN MINSTRELSY

Blackface minstrelsy was a form of theatrical performance that emerged during the 1820s and reached its zenith during the years 1850–70. Essentially it consisted of an exploitation of the slave's style of music and dancing by white men, who blackened their faces with burnt cork and went on the stage to sing "Negro songs" (also called "Ethiopian songs"), to perform dances derived from those of the slaves, and to tell jokes based on slave life. Two basic types of slave impersonations were developed: one in caricature of the plantation slave with his ragged clothes and thick dialect; the other portraying the city slave, the dandy dressed in the latest fashion, who boasted of his exploits among the ladies. The former was referred to as Jim Crow and the latter, as Zip Coon.

Antecedents of Minstrel Songs

So-called Negro songs had been in circulation in England as early as the mid-eighteenth century; they were performed on the concert stage and published in song collections. In the United States contemporaneous sources report the singing of "Negro songs" as early as 1769, the year when Lewis Hallam the Younger sang *Dear Heart! What a Terrible Life I Am Led* in his role as Mungo in Bickerstaffe's comic opera, *The Padlock,* at the John Street Theatre in New York. In the following years Charles Dibdin and Joseph Tyler attracted attention as singers of Negro songs, sung either during the course of plays or between the acts.

Another singer of Negro songs was Mrs. Graupner, who sang *The Negro Boy* "in character" (that is, in blackface with appropriate costume) at the end of the second act of Southerne's play *Oroonoko* on December 30, 1799, at the Federal Theatre in Boston. The earliest reference to a Negro dance appeared in a New York newspaper, the *New York Journal,* in regard to a performance by a Mr. Tea, a "Negro Dance, in Character," in a stage entertainment on April 14, 1767.[24]

The best known of the songs—all of them published in American collections and all generally portraying the black man sympathetically as either a tragic or pitiful figure—were *Negro Philosophy, Poor Black Boy, An African*

---

[23]Todd, *Methodism,* p. 183.
[24]This account, which corrects errors previously published in several sources about the first performances of so-called Negro songs in the United States, is based on S. Foster Damon, "The Negro in Early American Songsters," *Papers of the Bibliographical Society of America* 28 (1934): 133–41.

Love Song, The Negro Boy (also entitled *I Sold a Guiltless Negro Boy*), *The Desponding Negro,* and *The Negro's Humanity* (also entitled *A Negro Song*).

The last of these was a versified arrangement of the genuine African song recorded by Mungo Park in the eighteenth century. Park had sent the original words to his friend Georgiana Cavendish, the Duchess of Devonshire, who "versified" the text—that is, changed the verses so that they would rhyme and altered some of the phrasing that to her was crude. She, in turn, arranged for the new text to be set to music by an "eminent composer," Giacomo Gotifredo Ferrari. The song was later set to music by other composers, both in its original form and in the Devonshire version, and became extremely popular on both sides of the Atlantic.

> The loud wind roar'd, the rain fell fast,
> The white man yielded to the blast;
> He sat down, beneath our tree,
> For weary, sad, and faint was he,
> And ah, no wife, or mother's care.

CHORUS
> For him, the milk or corn prepare,
> The white man shall our pity share;
> Alas, no wife, or mother's care,
> For him, the milk or corn prepare.

> The storm is o'er, the tempest past,
> And mercy's voice has hush'd the
> blast;
> The wind is heard in whispers low,
> The White Man, far away must go,
> But ever in his heart will bear
> Remembrance of the Negro's care.

> *Repeat Chorus*

Growth of the "Ethiopian" Music

In the early years of the nineteenth century, entertainers and songwriters began to treat the black man less sensitively than earlier, presenting him instead as a comic figure to be ridiculed—as in the songs *The Negro and the Buckra Man* (1816) and *The Guinea Boy* (1816), and in the play *Obi; or Three-Fingered Jack* (1812). Those who helped to develop the new sentiment included blackface entertainers George Nichols and George Washington Dixon, among many others; but the high point was reached in 1829 by Thomas Dartmouth Rice, later called "Daddy Rice, Father of American Minstrelsy."

As the story goes, Rice was in Louisville, Kentucky, when he heard the singing of an old, deformed stable-groom and conceived the idea of imitating the black stable-hand in a stage act. Rice observed that the man sang a funny little song as he went about his work, that he moved with a curious shuffle, made almost ludicrous by the deformity, and that every so often, at a certain point in the song, he gave a little jump into the air. According to minstrel-historian T. Allston Brown, the song belonged to the folk tradition of slaves in Kentucky:[25]

> I went down to creek, I went down a fishing
> I axed the old miller to gimmy chaw tobacker
> To treat old Aunt Hanner.
>
> CHORUS   First on the heel tap, den on de toe
> Ebery time I wheel about I jump Jim Crow.
>
> I goes down to de branch to pester old miller,
> I wants a little light wood;
> I belongs to Capt. Hawkins, and don't care a d——n.
>
> *Repeat Chorus*

When Rice impersonated the stable-hand on the stage—song, dance, old clothes, blackface, and all—the act was hugely successful with audiences, and Rice's future was made. He went from one theater to another, singing his *Jim Crow Song* to great applause, and became known as "Jim Crow Rice." To be sure, Rice "doctored" the song lyrics to insure that his singing was as ridiculous as his dancing was grotesque:[26]

> Come listen all you galls and boys, I's jist from Tuckyhoe;
> I'm goin' to sing a leetle song, My name's Jim Crow
> Weel about and turn about, And do jis so
> Ev'ry time I weel about and jump Jim Crow.
>
> Oh, I'm a roarer on de Fiddle
> And down in old Virginny
> They say I play de skyentific
> Like Massa Pagannini.

The published song has many, many verses, and there are many versions of the song in print. On stage the minstrel sang improvised verses, as well, that alluded to current topics of interest and to local events. But all the verses share in common the one theme—to disparage the black man and his life style. And indeed, that was the theme of all the minstrel or Negro songs during the period.

Credit for organizing the first, full-length minstrel entertainment goes to

---

[25]Brown, "The Origin of Negro Minstrelsy," in Charles H. Day, *Fun in Black* . . . (New York, 1874); reprint of excerpts in BPIM 3 (Spring 1975): 77–80. Text of song on p. 79.

[26]Text from a *Jim Crow Song* published by E. Riley (New York, 1832). Originally consisting of forty-seven stanzas, it is only one of dozens of texts written for the song in the nineteenth century.

a quartet of white minstrels—William "Billy" M. Whitlock, Daniel "Dan" Emmett, Frank Bower, and Dick Pelham—who called themselves the Virginia Minstrels. They performed between the acts of stage entertainments, beginning in January 1843, at first at the Chatham Theatre in New York, then moving to the Bowery Amphitheatre, and later to the Park Theatre. In March they took their show to Boston's Masonic Temple, where they gave the first full-length Ethiopian Concert. Thereafter they toured at home and abroad to wildly enthusiastic audiences until the group was disbanded in July 1843.

Another highly successful group of the time was the Christy Minstrels, organized in 1844 and consisting of E. P. Christy, George Christy, Lansing Durand, and Tom Vaughan. Before long there literally were hundreds of blackface minstrels playing on the stages of the United States and crossing the Atlantic to tour in Europe.

For more than four decades, Ethiopian minstrelsy was the most popular form of theatrical entertainment in the United States and, to the rest of the world, America's unique contribution to the stage. To obtain materials for their shows, the minstrels visited plantations, then attempted to recreate plantation scenes on the stage. They listened to the songs of the black folk as they sang at work in the cotton and sugar cane fields, on the steamboats and river docks, and in the tobacco factories. The melodies they heard served as bases for minstrel songs, and they adapted the dances they saw to their needs.

The musical instruments originally associated with plantation "frolics" became "Ethiopian instruments"—banjos, tambourines, fiddles, and bone castanets. In its established form, the minstrel show consisted of three parts: the first contained songs and jokes; the second, called the *olio*, comprised a variety of specialty acts and ensemble numbers. Typically, the performance concluded with a "walk around finale," an act in which some of the performers sang and danced up front (on the stage) and the remainder of the company gave support from the back. Essentially, as the minstrel E. P. Christy pointed out, white minstrels tried "to reproduce the life of the plantation darky" and to imitate the "Negro peculiarities of song."

The subject of minstrelsy received a great deal of attention in the nineteenth century; in periodicals and books, writers discussed its history and its merits. One historian, writing in the 1870s, identified the slave origins of some of the songs made famous on the minstrel stage. Black stevedores sang *Clare de Kitchen,* for example, on Mississippi riverboats before Nichols arranged it for use on the minstrel stage. Another example is the slave song beginning

> As I was gwine down Shinbone Alley
>> Long time ago;

which became

O'er the lake where dropped the willow,
Long time ago![27]

To be sure, by the time minstrels had altered the verses and the tunes, few of the original folk elements remained in the minstrel songs, but no one forgot that the black man was behind it all.

An essay published in *Knickerbocker Magazine* in 1845 contains insightful comments on the relationship between minstrel materials and the songs and dances of the slaves, including the following query and answer:

> Who are our true rulers? The Negro poets, to be sure. Do they not set the fashion, and give laws to the public taste? Let one of them, in the swamps of Carolina, compose a new song, and it no sooner reaches the ear of a white amateur, than it is written down, amended (that is, almost spoilt), printed, and then put upon a course of rapid dissemination, to cease only with the utmost bounds of Anglo-Saxondom, perhaps with the world. Meanwhile, the poor author digs away with his hoe, utterly ignorant of his greatness.

The author, J. Kinnard, remarks further:

> But our national melodists have many imitators. Half the songs published as theirs are, as far as the words are concerned, the productions of "mean whites"; but base counterfeits as they are, they pass current with most people as genuine negro songs. Thus is it ever with true excellence! . . .
> But the music and dancing are all Sambo's own. No one attempts to introduce any thing new *there*. In truth they, with the chorus, constitute all that is essentially permanent in the negro song. The blacks themselves leave out old stanzas, and introduce new ones at pleasure.[28]

Kinnard probably erred in assuming that minstrel songwriters did not change the original slave melodies, but he was correct in perceiving that the stage songs generally omitted the characteristic choruses of genuine slave songs and that such stage dances as breakdowns, double-shuffles, toe-and-heels, and jubas were genuine.

Some of the nation's most talented songwriters contributed songs to the Ethiopian vogue that swept over the United States. "Respectable voices" were raised in criticism of Ethiopian music, proclaiming it to be representative of the "lowest dregs of music," and composers were admonished to write more refined music, such as the sentimental ballads and elegant salon pieces preferred in polite circles. But the public clamored for Ethiopian melodies, and songwriters gave it such songs as *Old Dan Tucker, Dandy Jim from Caroline, Zip Coon, Jim Along Josey, Coal-Black Rose, Rosa Lee,* and *Dearest May,* in addition to others that will be discussed below. Everyone sang these songs; the music became a part of American tradition.

Among the songwriters, the most gifted was Stephen Foster (1826–

[27][J. Kinnard], "Who Are Our National Poets," *Knickerbocker Magazine* 26 (1845); reprint in BPIM 3 (Spring 1975): 83–94. Quotation on p. 85.
[28]Kinnard, pp. 88–89, 94.

1864), called "America's Troubadour" and recognized as the greatest American songwriter of the nineteenth century, who furnished more than his share to minstrelsy's immortal repertory. He began writing Ethiopian songs about 1845 and from the beginning was successful, producing such songs as *Old Uncle Ned* and *Oh! Susanna* (both 1848). His best-known songs, which were widely sung by Christy's Minstrels, were written during the 1850s and included *Camptown Races, My Old Kentucky Home, Old Folks at Home, Old Black Joe, Old Dog Tray,* and *Massa's in de Cold, Cold Ground.*

Black Entertainers in Ethiopian Minstrelsy

Unlikely as it may seem today, in view of minstrelsy's derogatory depiction of black folk on the stage, a few genuine black entertainers were involved in Ethiopian minstrelsy almost from the beginning. In New Orleans, there were two minstrel-song singers, although neither blackened his face. Signor Cornmeali (d. 1842) or Mr. Cornmeal (his real name is unknown) first attracted attention as a street vendor who sang Ethiopian melodies, particularly *My Long Tail Blue* and *Old Rosin the Beau* as well as his own vending song about Indian meal, *Fresh Corn Meal,* in a highly novel manner. His talent and his popularity with the citizens of New Orleans landed him on the stage of the St. Charles Theatre in 1837 and again in 1840 at the Camp Street Theatre. Minstrel-historian Brown states that Cornmeali "furnished [George] Nichols with many airs, which he turned to account."[29]

Nichols was not the only blackface minstrel to be influenced by Cornmeali; in 1838 Thomas "Daddy" Rice added a skit to his act called "Corn Meal" after hearing the black singer perform in New Orleans. Another black entertainer who provided Nichols with material was John "Picayune" Butler (d. 1864), who played the banjo on street corners in New Orleans as early as the 1820s. His best known song was *Picayune Butler is Going Away,* and he became famous along the Mississippi River, "from Cincinnati to New Orleans," for his banjo skills. In 1857 Butler competed in a banjo competition in New York and would have won, according to eyewitnesses, had he not been indisposed. Even though he broke two of his four banjo strings, he plucked through the required waltz, reel, schottische, polka, and jig with artistry. A collection of 1858 includes an anonymous song written in his honor, *Picayune Butler's Come to Town.*

Then there was William Henry Lane (ca. 1825–1852), better known as Master Juba, who was the only black entertainer to tour with the early major minstrel groups. Little is known of Lane's early career, except that he was reputed to have studied dancing with one Uncle Jim Lowe, a black reel-and-jig dancer of the period. Juba began his dancing career in the notorious "Five Points" district of the city of New York. By 1842 he was so famous

[29]Brown, p. 78.

C. W. Pell's Serenaders. *(Courtesy Harvard Theatre Collection)*

that English novelist Charles Dickens identified him as "the greatest dancer known." Dickens visited a dance hall of "Five Points" in that year and later wrote about the experience in his book *American Notes for General Circulation* (1842). Juba advanced his career by engaging in dance contests during the early 1840s and winning a number of them. About 1846 he joined Charley White's Serenaders as a tambourine player and banjoist, then in 1849 went to England, where he toured with Richard Pell's Ethiopian Serenaders and became an idol of the entertainment world.

As the principal black professional minstrel of the antebellum period, Juba was a link between the white world and authentic black source materials; his dancing contributed to the preservation of artistic integrity in the performance of black dances on the minstrel stage. A critic observed in the *Illustrated London News:*

> Juba is a musician as well as a dancer. To him the intricate management of the nigger tambourine is confined, and from it he produces marvellous harmonies. We almost question where, upon a great emergency, he could not play a fugue upon it. . . . The great Boy [a reference to Dickens] immortalized him; and he deserved the glory thus conferred. [August 5, 1848]

Another black minstrel, Japanese Tommy (né Thomas Dilworth [or Dilward?]) should be noted here, although he belongs to a later generation. He began his career in 1853 with Christy's Minstrels and later played with other well-known groups, including Bryant's Minstrels, Sam Hague's Georgia Slave Troupe, and Charles Hicks's Georgia Minstrels. Violinist, singer, and dancer, he was a dwarf; his diminutive size undoubtedly attracted as much attention as his performances.

Black folk sang the minstrel songs just as did the whites. Here was a curious kind of interaction. The minstrel songs, originally inspired by genuine slave songs, were altered and adapted by white minstrels to the taste of white America in the nineteenth century, and then were taken back again by black folk for further adaptation to *their* musical taste. Thus the songs passed back into the folk tradition from which they had come. By all accounts the slaves sang these songs with the same "touching pathos" that they sang their own songs. There was, however, an obvious difference between the two kinds of songs that observers could not help but note. H. G. Spaulding wrote in the *Continental Monthly* (1863):

> ... a tinge of sadness pervades all their melodies, which bear as little resemblance to the popular Ethiopian melodies of the day as twilight to noonday.[30]

And W. H. Russell commented in *My Diary, North and South:*

> The oarsmen, as they bent to their task, beguiled the way singing in unison a real Negro melody, which was unlike the works of the Ethiopian Serenaders as anything in song could be unlike another.[31]

The practices of "Ethiopian" minstrels in the nineteenth century established unfortunate stereotypes of black men—as shiftless, irresponsible, thieving, happy-go-lucky "plantation darkies"—that persisted into the twentieth century on the vaudeville stage, in musical comedy, on the movie screen, radio, and television. And yet, blackface minstrelsy was a tribute to the black man's music and dance, in that the leading figures of the entertainment world spent the better part of the nineteenth century imitating his style.[32]

---

[30]Henry G. Spaulding, "Under the Palmetto," *Continental Monthly* (August 1863); reprint in KATZ pp. 3–8. For quotation, see p. 8.

[31]William H. Russell, *My Diary* . . . (London, 1863), p. 211.

[32]See further in Robert C. Toll, *Blacking Up: The Minstrel Show in Nineteenth-Century America* (New York, 1974).

CHAPTER 4

Antebellum
Urban
Life

I N 1800 the federal census classified as Negro slightly more than a million
persons in the United States; by 1840 the number had increased to
almost three million; and by 1860, the date of the last census enumeration before the Civil War, there were 4,441,830, of whom 3,953,760 were
slaves and 488,070 were free. In 1800 almost 19 percent of the black population was free; by 1860, less than 13 percent was free. Although the black
population doubled in size during the first half of the nineteenth century,
the proportion of those that were free remained the same, and during the
years 1840–60 it fell considerably.

At the beginning of the nineteenth century, about 10 percent of the black
population of the United States lived in urban communities. In the North
most black people, whether living in urban or rural areas, would be free by
1827, the year the last of the manumission laws became effective. In the
South there were free blacks communities in Baltimore, Maryland; Washington, D.C.; Richmond, Virginia; Charleston, South Carolina; Mobile,
Alabama; and New Orleans, Louisiana. Their presence there exerted a considerable influence upon urban life, and the character of urban life, in turn,
brought about a greater relaxation of the strict disciplines of slavery than
was possible on isolated plantations and farms. Although the majority of
free black men in cities were employed in personal services or common
labor occupations, there were many with skills of various kinds who followed the trades. Moreover, there were black men who operated small busi-
nesses and practiced in such professions as law, medicine, dentistry,
teaching, ministry, and music.

A considerable number of urban slaves worked as artisans and craftsmen under the "hiring-out" system, wherein they reported to employers other than their masters, but the masters received the wages. In many instances, formal contracts were signed, as they were for apprentices, and the slaves worked for periods as long as a year or longer. This system brought common laborers as well as skilled ones to the towns, where they were employed in factories, textile mills, construction, and as household servants. Particularly on the waterfront, "hired-out" slaves were used as firemen, roustabouts, and stevedores. For most black folk in the South outside New Orleans, the pleasures of city life were limited, centering around their homes, the churches, the shops and taverns, and the occasional public dances given by various societies or institutions in the larger cities. In some places, slaves were allowed to find their own housing as well as their employment, a circumstance that frequently resulted in the formation of ghetto areas inhabited chiefly by black folk. As a consequence, however, slaves gained the opportunity to mingle with other slaves, with free Negroes, and with working-class whites.

In their efforts to achieve economic security, free black men and women often managed to overcome almost insurmountable obstacles, including discriminatory legislation and the hostility of white laborers. City slaves saw about them the possibility for a better life, and many of them took advantage of it. They learned to read and write, despite the laws everywhere that prohibited the instruction of slaves; they developed skills that enabled them to compete for jobs; and they saved money to purchase their freedom. They discovered, as did ex-slave Frederick Douglass, that "a city slave is almost a free man, compared with a slave on the plantation."[1]

BLACK MUSICIANS AND THE GENERAL STATE OF MUSIC

What kinds of music did black folk produce in the nineteenth century before the Civil War? As during the colonial period, slave musicians continued to serve their masters by providing music for entertainment and dancing. Among themselves the slaves sang their own folksongs—about their work, their places of abode, their loves, their frolics and jubilees, their religion, political events—about whatever was closest to their hearts or minds. Early in the nineteenth century, some free black folk began to establish themselves as professional musicians. It was no easy thing to do. As we have noted, European musicians were in firm control of music making in America: they filled the important posts in theaters and churches; they gave the concerts and directed the musical institutions, which they, for the most part, had

[1]For all quotations from Frederick Douglass, see reprint of passages from his autobiography in RBAM pp. 82–87.

organized. Native-born white musicians, who had achieved recognition in the eighteenth century for their psalms, hymns, and anthems, added popular music to the list in the nineteenth century.

It was a time of impressive beginnings in the new nation. In Boston a Philharmonic Society was organized in 1810 that gave public concerts for fourteen years, the Handel and Haydn Society was formed in 1815, and the Boston Academy of Music was established in 1832. In New York the Philharmonic Society was founded in 1842 (making it the oldest symphony orchestra in the country). In Philadelphia a Musical Fund Society was started.

At first glance, it would seem that America had no place for black musicians in the scheme of things. But several ameliorating factors entered into the picture. First, slave musicians had established the tradition of providing dance music for white America, and it was to be some time before black America was seriously challenged in that field. Second, there was a tremendous demand for other kinds of music from the steadily expanding and increasingly prosperous population, which could afford to pay for the things it demanded. America wanted to hear band music, for example, and was sometimes willing to listen to the music of black bandsmen as long as the music was well played. America wanted music teachers, and in some places the color of a person's skin was less important than the ability to impart instruction. America needed music to which it could dance—quadrilles, cotillions, jigs, and quicksteps—sentimental ballads to sing, lively tunes to whistle, and salon pieces to play on the "fortepianos." Finally, America was curious about the black concert artist, so recently removed from the bonds of slavery. The public often attended the concerts of black performers out of mere curiosity, but remained to acclaim the sound of a beautiful voice or the exhibition of extraordinary technique.

There is ample data for the study of the musical activities of black folk during the antebellum period. A considerable number of published autobiographies and narratives of former slaves provide first hand information about the quality of life for black men and women during these years. White Americans wrote letters, local histories, fiction, travel narratives, diaries, and miscellaneous nonfiction works in which they referred to the music of black folk. At the same time the country was flooded with visitors from abroad who also kept diaries, wrote letters back to Europe, and published accounts of their travels in the States. To these visitors the activities of Native Americans and African Americans—and especially the music of the latter—were among the more exotic attractions of the New World. Other sources of information are newspapers, of which there were many more in the nineteenth century than in the preceding one, and periodicals, which sprang up for the first time during these years. Certain kinds of knowledge can be obtained, of course, from various types of official records—military, legislative, court, and civic.

With regard to the documentation of the actual music, the picture is not so bright. Black composers wrote a considerable quantity of art music, some of which was published by such established houses as J. L. Peters in New York, John Church in Cincinnati, and Oliver Ditson in Boston. Much more of this music, however, remains unpublished—some of it in manuscript form in various libraries, a great deal of it apparently lost. As for the music of the common people and the slaves, even less is extant. A few songs were written down in personal narratives and periodicals, but it was not until the 1840s that the first collections of slave songs began to be published.

The turn of the century was for black people in the North a period of transition from slavery to freedom and, therefore, a time of difficult adjustments. They struggled not only to improve their economic condition, but also to gain a measure of respect from a hostile white society convinced of their inferiority. Black writers and their white sympathizers repeatedly pointed out the accomplishments of distinguished Negroes as proof that "the powers of the mind are disconnected with the color of the skin" and that "black men are not naturally inferior to the whites, and unsusceptible of attainments in arts and sciences."

They pointed to Benjamin Banneker (1731–1806), the gifted mathematician and astronomer; to James Derham (1762–?), the first black physician in the nation; to the Reverend Prince Hall (1735–1807), founder of Negro freemasonry; to the poets Phillis Wheatley (1753–1794) and Jupiter Hammon (1717–1787); and to the writer Olaudah Equiano (Gustavus Vassa, 1745–1801). Predictably, some of the intense pursuit of respectability by the emerging black middle class reflected itself in their cultural activities. For those Negroes who managed to attain various levels of affluence, the most acceptable modes of social diversion were literary-society meetings, concerts, and musical evenings in the home.

URBAN MUSIC IN THE NORTH

A monograph published anonymously in 1841, *Sketches of the Higher Classes of Colored Society in Philadelphia. By a Southerner* [Joseph Willson], provides interesting glimpses into the social life of economically secure Negroes at that time. Judging from contemporary evidence, free middle-class Negroes lived in much the same way in other large cities of the nation. The anonymous author defines his use of the term "upper class" to mean "those whose incomes enable them to maintain the position of house holder and their families in comparative ease and comfort." He points out that "among no people is the pursuit of knowledge more honored," and cites as evidence the establishment in 1833 of the Philadelphia Library Company of Colored Persons (the first institution of its kind), which not only served as a book repository, but also sponsored concerts, lectures, debating societies, and trained young men in public speaking.

More relevant to the present discussion is the author's statement that

"Music is made a prominent part of the amusements on all occasions of social meeting together of friends." Almost every parlor contained a pianoforte; young ladies were expected to exhibit skill in piano playing, singing, and painting, as well as in the traditional literary and culinary arts. Like their white fellow-citizens, middle-class African Americans filled their houses with stuffed furniture and bric-a-brac and their cultural life with musical soirées and parlor parties. Our anonymous author wrote:

> It is rarely that the Visitor in the different families where there are 2 or 3 ladies will not find one or more of them competent to perform on the pianoforte, guitar or some other appropriate musical instrument; and these, with singing and conversation on whatever suitable topics that may offer, constitute the amusements of their evenings at home. The love of music is universal; it is cultivated to some extent—vocal or instrumental—by all.[2]

The kind of music cultivated in black middle-class homes was the trite and rather superficial music favored by white society during this period of America's growth. Music historian Gilbert Chase has used the phrase "music in the genteel tradition" to apply to this type of music, which was

> . . . characterized by the cult of the fashionable, the worship of the conventional, the emulation of the elegant, the cultivation of the trite and artificial, the indulgence of sentimentality, and the predominance of superficiality.[3]

The musical taste of the new nation was in a formative stage and, influenced by the foreign musicians who poured into the country from the politically restless countries of Europe, the public strained after what it considered to be aristocratic. Much of the music heard at the fashionable recitals held in the cities was frivolous; the singing was intended to draw tears or induce chills, the instrumental performances were meant only to dazzle with their brilliance. The nineteenth century was the time of the sentimental ballad and the salon piece full of endless runs, arpeggios, and trills.

Much of the social and cultural activity in the urban black community of the period centered around the black church. Whereas there were fewer than a dozen black churches at the beginning of the nineteenth century, by the fourth decade of the century that number had more than tripled. In New York, for example, there were ten churches, and in Philadelphia there were as many as sixteen. These churches organized Sabbath Schools for adults, day schools for children, and singing schools for musical amateurs; the churches sponsored Sacred Music Concerts and Juvenile Sacred Music Concerts and, as well, lectures on sacred music from time to time.

From 1827 on, black newspapers served to facilitate communication among black communities, particularly those on the eastern seaboard. The most enduring newspapers were *Freedom's Journal* (the first black newspa-

---

[2][Joseph Willson] *Sketches of the Higher Classes of Colored Society . . .* (Philadelphia, 1841), p. 58.
[3]Chase, *America's Music,* p. 165.

per in the United States, 1827–29); *The Rights of All* (1829); the *Weekly Advocate* (1837); the *Colored American* (1837–42); papers published by Frederick Douglass during the years 1847–63, the *North Star, Frederick Douglass's Paper,* and *Douglass' Monthly;* and the *Anglo-African* (1859). These newspapers, along with some of their white counterparts, published announcements of musical events, advertisements for concerts and singing schools, and, periodically, editorials about music. Occasionally, full programs for forthcoming concerts were published, which listed not only pieces to be performed and names of performers but also the instruments used for solo performances.

Musicians performed on programs of the various literary and debating societies organized by African Americans, among them, the Philomathean and Phoenixonian in New York and the Demosthenian Institute and Minerva Literary Association (a women's group) in Philadelphia. Indeed, almost any occasion in the black community called for music: the dedication of a church, celebration of political anniversaries, anti-slavery lectures, masonic events, funerals, and similar activities. Finally, there was recreational music, which included dance music for the fancy dress balls that black folk gave occasionally in urban areas, as well as music in the dance halls, taverns, and grog shops where they gathered in their leisure time.

In summary, music played an important role in black urban communities. In the city of Philadelphia, for example, a survey made in 1849 by the Society of Friends[4] indicated that in a black population of 9,076, thirty-two were professional musicians—men whose livelihood depended entirely upon their musical activities. This is a high proportion for an oppressed people denied opportunities for self-advancement both by law and tradition. And it is a relatively large proportion of the total number who were engaged in professional activities at that time. Obviously the social and economic climate of white Philadelphia encouraged black folk to enter musical careers, for it is hardly probable that they could have succeeded working entirely within the black community. It must also be assumed that they had access to high-level instruction so that they could develop their skills to the extent necessary for professional activities.

To be sure, there were other classes of black musicians in urban areas of the nation—part-time musicians, who combined music making with working at other trades. There were barber-musicians, boot- and shoe-maker-musicians, brick-maker-musicians, and tanner-musicians. These men, most of them self-taught, followed in a hallowed American tradition; the renowned William Billings and many other native white composers were self-taught artisan-musicians. One energetic black musician of Philadelphia was obviously very talented and very busy, if we may credit his description of himself as "Portrait Sign and Ornamental Painter, Daguerreotypist, Teacher of Photography, the Guitar and Singing."

[4]See further in *A Statistical Inquiry into the Condition of the People of Color of the City and Districts of Philadelphia* (Philadelphia, 1849).

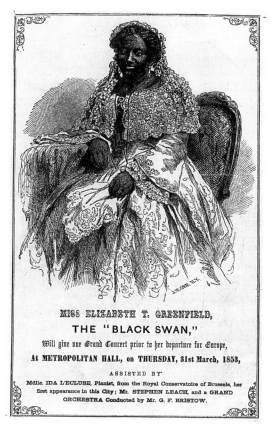

MISS ELIZABETH T. GREENFIELD,
THE "BLACK SWAN,"
Will give one Grand Concert prior to her departure for Europe,
At METROPOLITAN HALL, on THURSDAY, 31st March, 1853,

ASSISTED BY

Mdlle. IDA L'ECLUSE, Pianist, from the Royal Conservatoire of Brussels, her
first appearance in this City; Mr. STEPHEN LEACH, and a GRAND
ORCHESTRA Conducted by Mr. G. F. BRISTOW.

Handbill for a concert by Elizabeth Taylor Greenfield. *(Courtesy Harvard Theatre Collection)*

The Concert Stage

At the beginning of the nineteenth century, Philadelphia was the cultural and intellectual center of black America, and it is not surprising that the first "school of black musicians" should have emerged there. The nation's first black concert singer, Elizabeth Taylor Greenfield (ca. 1824–1876), was called "the Black Swan," because of her "remarkably sweet tones and wide vocal compass."[5] Born a slave in Natchez, Mississippi, she was taken to Philadelphia as an infant, where she was adopted by a Quaker, Mrs. Greenfield. Elizabeth's guardian arranged for her to study music as a child, despite the Society of Friends' ban on musical pursuits, and allowed her to sing at private parties. Elizabeth made her debut in 1851, singing before the Buffalo Musical Association and thereby establishing her reputation as an artist.

She toured extensively during the years 1851–53 under the management

[5]Quoted in James M. Trotter, *Music and Some Highly Musical People* (Boston, 1878), pp. 77–78.

of Colonel J. H. Wood, then went to London, England, in April of 1853 to study voice. Under the patronage of the Duchess of Sutherland and Harriet Beecher Stowe, she studied with George Smart, organist for Queen Victoria's Chapel Royal, and sang at a number of concerts, including a command performance for the Queen. After returning to the United States, she continued to tour periodically and conducted a music studio in Philadelphia. During the 1860s she organized and directed an opera troupe, which contributed greatly to the musical life of the black community.

Greenfield was the best-known black concert artist of her time, and her musical activities were widely covered in the press; an excerpt follows:

> Any one who went to the concert of Miss Greenfield on Thursday last, expecting to find that he had been deceived by the puffs of the American newspapers, must have found himself most agreeably disappointed. . . .
>
> After he [the pianist] had retired, there was a general hush of expectation to see the entrance of the vocalist of the evening; and presently there appeared a lady of a decidedly dark color, rather inclined to an embonpoint, and with African formation of face. . . . The amazing power of the voice, the flexibility, and the ease of execution took the hearers by surprise. . . . The higher passages of the air were given with clearness and fullness, indicating a soprano voice of great power. . . . She can, in fact, go as low as Lablache, and as high as Jenny Lind— a power of voice perfectly astonishing. It is said she can strike thirty-one full, clear notes; and we could readily believe it. [*Globe,* Toronto, May 12–15, 1852]

Thomas Bowers (ca. 1826–1885) acquired his title, "the Colored Mario," because of the similarity of his voice to that of the Italian opera tenor Giovanni Mario. Bowers studied voice with Greenfield and toured with her in 1854 under Wood's management. Throughout his career he combined music teaching with singing as a soloist and in concerts with others. His sister, Sarah Sedgewick Bowers, called "the Colored Nightingale," was also a professional singer.

Sacred Music Concerts

The evidence suggests that black churches began sponsoring Sacred Music Concerts during the 1820s. A typical American concert of this period consisted of a series of solo songs, sung by both men and women, interspersed with an occasional duo or small ensemble number. When black artists began to give concerts, they followed in the tradition established by their white counterparts. The chief distinction of the Sacred Music Concert was that it also included choral numbers, primarily excerpts from oratorios and other sacred works. We know from newspaper advertisements what kind of music was performed at the concerts given by black artists: most often it was the music of Chappell and Handel in the early part of the nineteenth century; toward the middle of the century, composers such as Bellini, Gluck, Haydn, and Mozart were more popular. Frequently, these programs included compositions of black composers William Appo, Francis Johnson, and Robert C. Jones.[6]

In order to obtain the necessary training for concert singing, black choristers attended singing schools operated by their churches or privately. Soloists and instrumentalists, however, were professionals who studied with private teachers. Understandably, their numbers were small; it was not uncommon for musicians of Philadelphia to travel to New York, Baltimore, Boston, or even Washington, D.C., for concert appearances. Best known of these traveling artists were the choral directors Morris Brown, Jr., Robert Jones, and Jacob Stans, and the orchestra directors William Appo, James Hemmenway, Francis Johnson, and Aaron J. R. Connor.

The format of the concerts remained constant over the years. Typically, a concert opened with an overture for orchestra, then followed with choral numbers from oratorios or anthems, and duos or trios. Part Two of the concert opened with a voluntary on the organ or another orchestral composition, then continued with choral works, arias or duos, and more anthems. Frequently, the congregation joined in singing a hymn at the beginning and / or end of the program. On at least one occasion, a full oratorio was performed: Haydn's *Creation* at the First African Presbyterian Church in Philadelphia on March 14, 1841. The musical forces included a fifty-piece orchestra conducted by Johnson and a chorus of 150 voices conducted by Brown.

During the early years of the Sacred Music concerts, the performing groups drew support from both the churches and the community. As stated above, singing schools were set up where "young ladies and gentlemen of color" could learn the "science and practice of vocal music." As early as 1827 (and perhaps earlier), St. Philips Episcopal Church in New York was operating a singing school that met on Tuesday and Friday evenings. John Cromwell was the leading black singing-school master in Philadelphia during the early 1820s; two of his students, Morris Brown, Jr., and Robert Johnson, later opened their own schools. In New York there were William Appo and a white teacher, William C. Webster, who used the Pestalozzian system; in Boston there was Pulaski Flanders, also white.

The older black churches pioneered in the sponsoring of the concerts, among them, St. Philips and the First Presbyterian Church in New York, St. Thomas and the First and Second Presbyterian Churches in Philadelphia, and the Belknap Baptist Church in Boston. We may assume that the first such concerts were given in the mid-1820s; in April 1827, for example, the African Harmonic Society of Philadelphia advertised that it was holding its second Sacred Concert on April 13 at the First African Presbyterian Church, and in September of that year St. Philips in New York sponsored a Concert of Sacred Music.

---

[6]See further in Eileen Southern, "Musical Practices in Black Churches of Philadelphia and New York, ca. 1800–1844," *Journal of the American Musicological Society* 30 (1977): 298–312.

By the 1830s, the responsibility for promoting concerts was being taken over by musical and literary groups, such as the Union Harmonic Society, the Amateur Society (of Boston), the Garrison Juvenile Society, the Phoenixonian Society, and similar organizations. Admission was usually twenty-five cents. The concerts given at Boston's Belknap Church under direction of Susan Paul, daughter of the minister, received much attention in the press, as did also concerts of the Garrison Juvenile Choir and of singing-school youth groups. Judging from the programs published in newspapers, care was taken to select appropriate music for the children to sing.

Grand Concerts and Concert Troupes

By mid-century, Grand Concerts of secular music and Musical Soirées were gradually replacing the Sacred Music Concerts in black communities. As was common during that time, these concerts consisted of performances by several soloists and, sometimes, of small ensembles. When the Philomathean and Phoenixonian Societies of New York held an "Exhibition," for example, "for the benefit of the unfortunate captives of the Amistad Schooner," the ensemble that performed under the direction of William Appo included three violins, violoncello, double bass, flute, two "clarionets", horn, trumpet, and trombone. Small companies traveled from one place to another giving concerts, but except for one or two, they won little recognition outside their own communities. We have already observed that Greenfield's opera troupe in Philadelphia was well received by the public. The other exception was the Luca Family Singers of Connecticut.

"Singing family" troupes were in vogue in the United States during the mid-century years, and it is probable that the black Luca Family may have been inspired by the white Hutchinson Family, who toured extensively at home and abroad. The Luca troupe comprised the father, John W. Luca; the mother, Lisette; her sister, Diana Lewis; and the four boys, John, Jr., (ca. 1832–1910), Simeon (ca. 1834–1854), Alexander (ca. 1836–189?), and Cleveland (1838–1872). All the boys played instruments as well as sang; Cleveland was the piano accompanist. The Lucas first attracted wide attention in May 1850, when they sang at a convention of the Anti-Slavery Society at the Tabernacle in New York.

They toured widely until 1860, using a wagon to carry their instruments and piano. After Simeon's death in 1854, contralto Jennie Allen occasionally sang with the troupe, and they also performed as a trio. After Cleveland went to Africa to teach music at the invitation of President Roberts of Liberia, the troupe was disbanded. In 1859 the Lucas and Hutchinsons joined forces to present concerts in Ohio, generally to favorable press notices:

> The Hutchinsons and Lucas sang to quite a full audience at West's Hall last evening. The performance could not, coming from troupes possessing talent varied and of the higher order, be otherwise than good. These bands, when they

united, made a palpable hit. Their combined concerts are almost invariably successes. [Sandusky (Ohio) paper, March 1, 1859]

To be sure, not all communities welcomed interracial concerts, as the following excerpt from a newspaper of Fremont, Ohio, indicates:

> The Hutchinsons—Asa B., Lizzie C., and little Freddy—accompanied by the
> Luca family, gave a concert at Birchard Hall on last Wednesday evening. The
> house was not more than a paying one. When we went to the concert, we antici-
> pated a rare treat; but alas! how woefully were we disappointed! . . . We have,
> perhaps, a stronger feeling of prejudice than we should have felt under other
> circumstances, had their abolition proclivities been less startling; but to see
> respectable white persons (we presume they are such) travelling hand in hand
> with a party of negroes, and eating at the same table with them, is rather too
> strong a pill to be gulped down by a democratic community.
> [February 25, 1859][7]

Bands and Orchestras

After the death of Francis "Frank" Johnson (1792–1844), an editorial
in the Philadelphia *Public Ledger* of April 6, 1844 stated:

> Frank was one of the most celebrated personages of Philadelphia. His talents as
> a musician rendered him famous all over the Union, and in that portion of
> Europe which he had visited, while his kindness of heart and gentleness of
> demeanor endeared him to his own people, and caused him to be universally
> respected in this community. It will be a long time before his place can be simi-
> larly filled.

Johnson was indeed a celebrity for all times! During his short career he
accumulated an amazing number of "firsts" as a black musician: first to win
wide acclaim in the nation and in England; first to publish sheet music (as
early as 1818); first to develop a "school" of black musicians; first to give
formal band concerts; first to tour widely in the nation; and first to appear
in integrated concerts with white musicians. His list of achievements also
included "firsts" as an American, black or white: he was the first to take a
musical ensemble abroad to perform in Europe and the first to introduce
the promenade concert to the United States.

Little is known of his early life; reputedly he was born in Martinique
in the West Indies and migrated to the United States in 1809, settling in
Philadelphia. He began to attract wide attention in 1818 when Willig published his *Six Setts of Cotillions* and the press noted the popularity of his
dance orchestra. In a book published in 1819, Johnson is identified as
"leader of the band at all balls, public and private; sole director of all serenades, acceptable and not acceptable; inventor-general of cotillions; to
which add, a remarkable taste in distorting a sentimental, simple, and beau-

---

[7]Trotter, *Music,* pp. 102–3.

Frank Johnson (1792–1844) with his silver trumpet. *(Courtesy Charles L. Blockson Collection)*

tiful song, into a reel, jig, or country-dance. . . ."[8] It may be that he began his career in the band led by Matt Black, which was active after the War of 1812.

Johnson's military bands were equally popular with the public. According to one source, the Third Company of Washington Guards in Philadelphia organized the first Johnson band after the war in 1815. After that company was disbanded other Philadelphia regiments employed the band. Then in 1821 Johnson began an association with the Philadelphia State Fencibles and remained with that elite regiment for many years. His early band consisted primarily of woodwinds, supplemented by a French horn or two, a serpent, cymbals, bells, triangles, and drums. During parades a drummer and fifer played at intervals to give the bandsmen periods of rest. To play for dances, his bandsmen substituted string instruments for their winds, and thereby changed from a military band to "Johnson's Celebrated Cotillion Band" or "Johnson's Fine Quadrille Band."

As keyed brass instruments were introduced into the United States during the 1820s and '30s, Johnson gradually introduced them into his bands; by the mid-1830s, the Johnson band had become a brass band. He also used such exotic instruments as the bell harmonicon, harp, and ophicleide in his concerts. His various bands were widely praised for excellence. A British

[8]Robert Waln, *The Hermit in America* (Philadelphia, 1819); reprint of excerpts from chapter titled "The Cotillion Party" in RBAM, pp. 122–24. For quotation, see pp. 123–24.

traveler on tour in the States heard one of them at a Fourth of July celebration in Albany, New York, and observed:

> The only military bands I ever remember to have heard superior to it was the royal band that attends at the Palace of St. James in London and the band of the National Guards in Paris.[9]

In the fall of 1837 Johnson sailed to London, England, with four of his best bandsmen—William Appo, Aaron Connor, Edward Roland, and Francis Seymour—and in December began a series of concerts at the Argyll Rooms.[10] Since the programs for his concerts were published in the London newspapers, we know that his group played arias from operas by Bellini, Rossini, and Hartman; instrumental pieces by Mozart and DeBeriot; comic songs; and arrangements of English and American patriotic songs. Johnson played two solos (on violin and keyed bugle); Connor sang; three of the men sang in a trio; and all five played a movement for brass band. Johnson himself wrote all the arrangements.

During his six-month stay, he is reputed to have given a command performance for Queen Victoria, who presented him with a silver bugle, but efforts to document this have been unsuccessful. More important for his career development, however, was the fact that he heard the latest, most fashionable music as well as the traditional classics, and heard some of the leading musicians of the time in performance, among them, Johann Strauss. But it was the "promenade concert" that impressed him most. An invention of Philippe Musard, who in 1833 introduced to Paris the concept of combining a program of light classical music with a promenade, the concert was first presented in London in January 1838, under the direction of Pilati, who had directed Musard concerts in Paris. Johnson took in all the details of these concerts: the programs consisting of operatic airs and quadrilles; the use of the "new" cornet-à-pistons and ophicleide; the arrangements to which the audience could promenade between Parts One and Two of the program; and the small admission fees.

Johnson returned to the United States greatly inspired by his European experience; he chose the Christmas season of 1838–39 to introduce "Concerts à la Musard" to Philadelphia—indeed, to the nation, for this seems to have been the first such concert in the United States. They were wildly successful; the press reported that thousands attended each night, and hundreds had to be turned away. Each winter thereafter Johnson staged a series of concerts in Philadelphia; beginning in 1840 he advertised them as "Grand Promenade Concerts à la Musard." During the 1843–44 season, he combined musical forces with leading vocal artists of Philadelphia to produce

---

[9]Quotation from J. Silk Buckingham reprinted in Joel Munsell, *Annals of Albany* (Albany, 1871) v. 9, p. 309.

[10]See further in Eileen Southern, "Frank Johnson of Philadelphia and His Promenade Concerts," BPIM 5 (Spring 1977): 3–29.

the first integrated concerts in the history of the nation. His death in April 1844 cut off a fascinating experiment in breaking through the rigid walls of segregation.

Johnson spent the fashionable winter seasons in Philadelphia, where he also conducted a well-attended music studio; in the summers he played at Saratoga Springs, New York, at Cape May, New Jersey, or at White Sulphur Springs in Virginia; the remainder of the year he toured throughout the North, into Canada, and on one occasion into the slave state of Missouri. Although no official list of his bandsmen exists, we can learn from the press the names at least of those who played solos on his concerts: in addition to Appo, Connor, Roland, and Seymour, there were Dennis Carter, Edward Augustus, Joseph Gordon, Edward Johnson, Robert C. Kennedy, William Jackson, James Richards, and E. Toulou. After Johnson's death, Joseph Anderson (ca. 1816–1873) took over leadership of the Frank Johnson Brass and String Bands and maintained their excellence up to the time of the Civil War.

Johnson's stature was so great that, in retrospect, he seems to dwarf other black bandmasters of his time. But during the period several bands won wide recognition for excellence. Indeed, black bands had a monopoly on providing dance music for the aristocracy in urban areas during most of the nineteenth century, particularly in the South. In Philadelphia along with Johnson there were two highly competitive bands directed by James Hemmenway and Isaac Hazzard. Aaron Connor left the Johnson band in 1846 and successfully organized his own group. All these organizations played for balls and assemblies, dancing schools, and concerts, and were in residence at the fashionable resorts during the summers.

There were bands in New York, as well as Philadelphia, during the antebellum period, but few names have been preserved in contemporary literature. A writer pointed out in 1883, "Forty years ago nearly every regimental band in New York was composed of black musicians."[11] And the press, black and white, frequently reported upon these bands when they played for parades or traveled to other towns to give concerts. We do have the names of some of the musicians who played on Sacred Music Concerts and similar kinds of programs—and who probably also played in the brass bands.

The press mentioned most often the Plet brothers, Anastase and Cherry (violin and clarinet), William Brady (double bass), John D. Connor (trombone), Amity Dennis (clarinet), Abel Howard (violoncello), G. Howard (violin), Peter Howard (clarinet), William Jackson (violin), A. LaCost (flute), W. P. Mariner (violoncello), William Noland (trumpet), and Elijah Smith (horn). The men most often cited as leaders of the orchestra were William Appo (horn), Aaron J. Connor (violin), and Anastase Plet.

In nearby Newark, New Jersey, Peter O'Fake (1820–1884) won recogni-

---

[11]Quoted from the *American Art Journal* 39 (May 19, 1883) in Epstein, *Sinful Tunes* p. 160.

tion for his musical skills as a choral director and leader of a society dance orchestra that played for balls of the aristocracy in the city and at resorts in the summers. In 1847 O'Fake performed at a concert with the (white) Jullien Society in New York, an unusual occurrence for that period because of the rigid segregation practices in force. In 1848, he reputedly conducted the Newark Theater orchestra for an evening's performance—also an unprecedented activity for a black man. O'Fake was a composer of sorts; his quadrille *The Sleigh Ride* was said to have such realistic effects that dancers imagined themselves actually "in the enjoyment of a veritable sleigh ride."

Newburgh, New York, contributed its share of black musicians to the period. In 1827 a band "consisting of men of average talent" was organized by Samuel Dixon; called Dixon's Brass Band, the men wore uniforms of yellow pants and red coats.[12] And during the late 1840s, Dubois Alsdorf (1827–1907) organized a brass band and a society dance orchestra that remained in high demand for several decades. He also conducted a dancing school for the aristocracy, which sponsored annual balls; his sons, also musicians, maintained the school until 1930. Alsdorf was one of the first black musicians to become a member of the Musicians Protective Association (AFM Local 291).

Like New York, Boston was the home of a number of brass bands and orchestras during the antebellum years, beginning as early as the 1790s, but none achieved lasting fame. We cannot hope to know the full story about black bands and orchestras in the antebellum period, but judging from the numerous references in contemporaneous literature to such activities, the few names that have come down to us represent only the tip of the iceberg. For the record, it should be noted that in the Midwest the well-known bands included the Union Valley Brass Band, the Scioto Valley, and Roberts bands (all flourished in Ohio during the 1850s) and the bands of Joseph Gillam and Obediah Wood in Detroit, Michigan, which dated from the 1840s.

Composers

Francis Johnson stood tall in the center of a small "school" of black composers during the antebellum period. A prolific composer and arranger, he wrote more than two hundred compositions including cotillions, quadrilles, quick-steps and other marches, stylized dances, sentimental ballads, patriotic songs, arrangements of operatic airs, and even Ethiopian minstrel songs. Much of his music survives in printed form or manuscript. Johnson's activity as director of military bands and society dance orchestras, as music teacher, violinist, and performer on the Kent (keyed) bugle obviously dictated the kinds of music he wrote and arranged.

In his early career, when his primary activity was playing for balls, parades, and dancing schools, he spent much of his time making arrange-

[12]William Carter White, *A History of Military Music in America* (New York, 1944), p. 53.

ments for his patrons of the "latest, most fashionable music," of which a large part was "imported at great expense" from abroad.[13] After his return from England in 1838, he began to give concerts and, consequently, paid more attention to writing original music. He became celebrated for his *Voice Quadrilles,* "performed by him and his Band at his Soiree Musicales in London, and the principal cities in the United States, with most distinguished success," which introduced the novelty of bandsmen singing as they played (much to the annoyance of some dancers).[14] Other popular compositions included a "Bird Waltz," in which could be heard the "chirping of the canary bird [via Johnson's flute obbligato] so distinctly and so natural that the keenest perception cannot discover the difference"; the *Philadelphia Fireman's Quadrille,* in which Johnson "with his bugle" could be heard to "distinctly cry, 'Fire!' 'Fire!' "; and his *New Cotillions and March, With the National Airs arranged for and performed at the Grand Ball Given at the New Theatre In Honour of Our Illustrious Guest General LaFayette.*

The public wanted dramatic effects from Johnson, and that is what they got. To be sure, programmatic pieces were generally popular with the American public during this period, particularly "battle pieces," such as *The Battle of Prague* by Franz Kotzwara, which Johnson arranged for performance by his band. The more realistic the effects used to imitate sounds of the battle—and other sounds of real life—the more impressed were the audiences. Johnson's *New Railroad Gallop,* for example, promised that "In the introduction will be heard the getting up of steam, [then] trying the fassett, passengers about entering the cars, moving ahead rather slow, then in full speed, bell rings, letting off steam, &c."

Johnson's musical scores only suggest how his bands must have sounded. In the first place, we have only piano arrangements of band music or melodic skeletons. This was the common practice of the period; composers left few band or orchestra scores but rather made arrangements that could be sold to the ever-increasing numbers of amateur singers and pianists in the nation. Second, even after Johnson's scores have been reconstructed for performance by instrumental groups, the music hardly seems extraordinary—despite the elaborate flute, violin, and trumpet obbligatos and vocal embellishments—with its predominantly diatonic harmonies, straightforward rhythms, and scalar-triadic melodies. Johnson's style was attuned to the musical climate in which he lived, and his scores do not differ substantially from those of his white American contemporaries—for example, John Hill Hewitt (1801–1890).

Since Johnson competed successfully with white musical organizations

---

[13]The quotations that follow are from advertisements published in contemporaneous newspapers, particularly Philadelphia's *Public Ledger.*

[14]See Charles Jones and Lorenzo Greenwich, *A Choice Collection of the Works of Francis Johnson,* 2 vols. (New York, 1980). Also Francis Johnson in RBAM, pp. 125–34.

for public patronage against the overwhelming odds of race discrimination, his music must have gained something in performance that is not evident in the scores. Based on the admittedly scanty evidence available, that "something" must have been his ability to "distort" commonplace music into stimulating and distinctive music. To translate the word *distort* into modern parlance, we might surmise that it meant infusing the music with rhythmic complexities such as are found in black folk music or twentieth-century jazz. Thus Johnson stands at the head of a long line of black musicians whose performance practice made the essential difference in the transference of musical scores into actual sound.

The popularity of Johnson's music would explain why, when Philadelphia was preparing for the visit of General LaFayette in 1824, a city father stated: "Nothing could be more natural than that the black master of melody should be engaged to play at the Lafayette Ball."[15] It would also explain why his music found its way into collections along with pieces of Beethoven, Braham, Burgmüller, Czerny, and arrangements of Bellini, Donizetti, and Weber—as in, for example, *The Lady's Musical Library, Embracing the Most Popular and Fashionable Music* (Philadelphia, 1842, 1843) or *Taw's Musical Miscellany, No. 8.*

A description of Johnson's music room by one of his wealthy white students offers some insight into Johnson the composer and teacher:

> The wall was covered with pictures and instruments of all kinds, and one side of the room was fixed with shelves whereon were thousands of musical compositions, constituting a valuable library. Bass drum, bass viols, bugles and trombones lay in admirable confusion on the floor; and in one corner was an armed composing chair, with pen and inkhorn ready, and some gallopades and waltzes half finished.[16]

The Philadelphia School

Johnson is credited with having further developed the talents of other black musicians in Philadelphia, although in one or two instances he may have served more as a role model than teacher. Like Johnson, these composers wrote music that reflected their activities as leaders of bands and dance orchestras and as studio teachers. Aaron J. R. Connor (d. 1850), an important member of the Johnson bands, seems to have worked in the master's shadow for many years, but after Johnson's death in 1844 Connor formed a band and began to publish songs and piano arrangements of band music. His best-known pieces were *My Cherished Hope, My Fondest*

---

[15]Ellis Paxson Oberholtzer, *Philadelphia: A History of the City* (Philadelphia, 1912), v. 2, p. 140.

[16]Philip English Mackey, ed., *A Gentleman of Much Promise. The Diary of Isaac Mickle, 1837–1845* (Philadelphia, 1977), p. 196.

Dream, a song published in the *Anglo-African Magazine* (1859), and the dance compositions *Chestnut Street Promenade Quadrilles, American Polka Quadrilles,* and *The Evergreen Polka.*

James Hemmenway (1800–1849) had a brief tenure in Johnson's band, but for the most part, led his own group, which found a permanent home as the resident orchestra for Philadelphia's Washington Hall for many years. He is remembered for his *Philadelphia Hop Waltz, General Lafayette's Trumpet March and Quickstep,* and *The New Year and Courtesy Cotillion.* An early song, *That Rest So Sweet Like Bliss Above,* was published in Philadelphia's elite journal *Atkinson's Casket* in 1829.

Isaac Hazzard (ca. 1804–1865) seems to have had no contact with Johnson as mentor or patron; on the contrary, he was a strong competitor for the patronage of the aristocracy. Hazzard played for dancing schools, led dance orchestras, played for parades, and conducted a music studio. He did not, however, give concerts. Among his most popular pieces were *The Miercken Polka Waltz* and *The Alarm Gun Quadrille.*

William Appo (ca. 1808–188?) began his career in Johnson's band, as we have seen, and accompanied the group to England in 1837. Later he settled in New York, where he ran a music studio and won wide recognition in black communities as an orchestral director. Black contemporary Daniel Payne called him "the most learned musician of the race." His compositions included sacred music as well as secular: the anthem *Sing unto God* and a men's chorus commissioned by the Utica Clay Glee Club of Utica, New York, entitled *John Tyler's Lamentation.* Another New York composer was William Brady (d. 1854), whose surviving compositions include *Anthem for Christmas* and *Carnival* [sic] *Waltz.*

Composers in Other Cities

Although a native of Boston, Henry F. Williams (1813–1903) came into contact with the Philadelphia musicians when he performed with the Frank Johnson bands for a short while during the 1840s (after Johnson's death). He also led his own groups before returning to Boston, where he was active as a composer, performer, arranger, and music teacher. After Johnson, he was the best-known black composer of the period. His songs *Lauriett* and *The Coquette (I Would I'd Never Met Thee)* were extremely popular, and his anthem for Thanksgiving, *O, Give Thanks,* found favor with church choirs. Of his numerous marches and stylized dances, best known were the *Rose Schottische, Sunny Side Polka,* and the *Parisien Waltzes* (which went into several editions).

Joseph William Postlewaite (1827–1889) of St. Louis, Missouri, belongs to a somewhat later generation but is included here because he was active during the antebellum period. He began publishing his compositions as early as 1849 and in the late 1850s organized a band, which played for society dances and other social entertainments and for parades. Like his contemporaries, Postlewaite wrote primarily dances and marches, which he published in piano arrangements for his own use. By the 1860s he was identified in the press as director of no fewer than four bands and orchestras. His best-known compositions included the *St. Louis Greys Quick Step* (which went into ten editions), the *St. Louis National Guards Quick Step, Dew Drop Scottisch, Iola Waltz,* and *Galena Waltz.*

Justin Miner Holland (1819–1897) began his musical studies in Boston at the age of fourteen. He studied further with eminent local teachers, with members of Ned Kendall's Brass Band, with professional teachers at the Oberlin Conservatory, and with private teachers in Mexico. In 1845 he settled in Cleveland, writing music and conducting a music studio. Holland was one of the few American composers whose works were known both in the United States and abroad. He published three collections—*Holland's Comprehensive Method for the Guitar* (1874), *Holland's Modern Method for the Guitar,* and *Gems for the Guitar*—and a number of individual pieces.

These composers were talented craftsmen, and they are historically important as the first black composers to publish music—this during a period when the majority of black men and women in the nation were still enslaved. Black composers typically wrote music upon demand: if their groups had to play for parades, they wrote quick-steps; when they were called upon to play for a ball, they wrote quadrilles and cotillions or arranged operatic airs into dance music.

The title pages of their compositions carry dedications to the organizations or persons who commissioned the music and made it possible for them to write the next piece. They also offered their services to amateur poets who might wish musical settings of verses written to lady loves. In summary, black composers were thoroughly pragmatic in their attitudes toward producing music for public consumption; in the nineteenth century that public wanted sheet music to sing and to play on pianofortes in genteel parlors and music for balls and parades.

There was no hint of racial themes in the music of the antebellum years, except perhaps in the case of Johnson, who published a piece in honor of Haiti when France finally recognized that black republic's independence on April 17, 1825. (Haiti had declared her independence in 1804.) His title page reads as follows: "*Recognition March of the Independence of Hayti,* for Pianoforte and Flute, composed expressly for the Occasion and Dedicated to President J. P. [Jean Pierre] Boyer by his humble servant with every sentiment of Respect."

The absence of racial themes should hardly justify comment—white composers were not concerned with race matters either—except that, outside the world of music, black Americans were fighting desperately for their civil rights and for the emancipation of their brothers and sisters in slavery. And Philadelphia was a hotbed of political activity, the site of national conventions of black folk, beginning as early as 1830, seeking to improve their condition, and an important station on the Underground Railroad. Indeed, Johnson may have written his piece in direct response to the activities of colonialization groups that thought emigration to Haiti was the solution to the problems of black oppression in the United States.

Black composers wrote music in the styles of the time and employed conventional forms. In their songs graceful melodies ornamented with vocal flourishes are supported by arpeggiated or Alberti-bass accompaniments that emphasize tonic, subdominant, and dominant harmonies. The stylized dances are charming, lilting, or spirited, according to the character of the dance, and the marches are appropriately lively with effective bravura passages. Johnson, in particular, was given to adding flute and trumpet obbligato solos to his piano arrangements. This music was not only popular during its time but also was long-lived; when the Board of Music Trade of the United States published its *Complete Catalogue of Sheet Music and Musical Works, 1870,* it listed many compositions by black composers, although some of these pieces were more than thirty years old by that date.

Not all the Philadelphia composers were well-trained professionals. One of the most popular songs of the period, *Listen to the Mocking Bird,* was written by a street whistler-guitarist, Richard Milburn (ca. 1817–18??). According to the evidence, Milburn only received twenty copies of the music as payment for his song, which was arranged and published by Septimus Winner using the pen name Alice Hawthorne. Such practices were common, however, during the nineteenth century (and into the twentieth); many a writer received a few dollars for a song which later sold thousands of copies to make a small fortune for the buyer or publisher. Indeed, Winner himself sold Milburn's song to Lee and Walker for five dollars; during the years 1855–1905, the song sold twenty million copies. But Milburn was even cheated out of the credit as the original writer, for later editions of the best-selling song dropped his name from the cover, and America forgot that *Listen to the Mocking Bird* was written by a black man.

Music in the Theater

Whereas Philadelphia was the first city of the black concert stage, New York early took the lead in regard to black theater. In the summer of 1821 a group of amateurs under the leadership of Henry Brown organized a dramatic troupe, which staged its first production in September of that year at the African Grove Theatre on the corner of Bleecker and Mercer Streets, "in the rear of the one-mile stone on Broadway."[17] Typically, for that period, the production consisted of several kinds of dramatic entertainments: a trag-

[17]An account of the origin of the African Grove Theatre Company and information about its first productions appear in New York's *National Advocate,* August 3, 1821; September 21, 1821; September 25, 1821; October 1, 1821; and October 27, 1821. Some of the later published accounts include factual errors.

Sheet music cover for *Listen to the Mocking Bird*, 1855. *(Courtesy New York Public Library, Schomburg Center for Research in Black Culture)*

edy, ballet, and a ballad opera, with songs and dances interspersed among these events (see facing page). Over the years the African Grove staged Shakespeare's *Othello, Hamlet,* and *Richard the Third,* such lighter works as *The Poor Soldier, Obi; or, Three-Fingered Jack,* and the musical extravaganza *Tom and Jerry; or, Life in London.*

Thanks to information found in newspapers of the period (particularly New York's *National Advocate*), extant playbills, and descriptions by visitors to the theater, we know quite a bit about the performances at the African Grove. Sometimes music came at the end of the evening's program, as on August 3, 1822, when "some fashionable songs were sung at the conclusion"; among them, *Eveleen's Bower* by the leading lady. On another night, the featured play was followed by songs and dances, and then by another play. A three-piece ensemble, consisting of violin, clarinet, and bass fiddle, played "a lively tune" as an overture before the curtain rose. A male trio sang some comic songs, followed by a soloist singing *Is There a Heart*. Two solo dances were performed, including a hornpipe danced by one of the actresses. After the final curtain of the evening the ensemble struck up another lively number, this time a march.[18]

The ballad *Is There a Heart That Never Lov'd* evidently was a great favorite at the African Grove, for it was performed on several occasions. Undoubtedly, the singing of this sentimental song, written by English composer John Braham, and similar ones, brought tears to the eyes of listeners of that time:

> Is there a heart that never lov'd
> Or felt soft woman sigh?
> Is there a man can mark unmoved
> Dear woman's tearful eye?
> Oh, bear that man to some distant shore
> Or solitary cell,
> Where none but savages roam,
> Where love doth never dwell.

The police closed down the African Grove several times. All audiences were boisterous in those times, but the Grove was especially plagued by white hoodlums, who were determined to break up the company. Nevertheless, the black thespians persevered in their efforts to produce theater for many years, despite overwhelming hostility on the part of whites. In its heyday, the Grove was a tourist attraction for visitors to the city, in the same way that Harlem would become some hundred years later. A traveler from Scotland wrote in his journal: "One of the theatres is for the black people of the city; it is really worth one's while to go there for a few nights for the novelty of the thing."[19]

The African Grove made important contributions to black American history in several respects, other than the fact that it was the nation's first black theater. It was there, in June 1823, that a play by a black writer was produced for the first time in American history. Written by Henry Brown, the company's director, *The Drama of King Shotaway* was "founded on

[18]Simon Snipe, *Sports of New York: Containing an Evening at the African Theatre* . . . (New York, 1823).
[19]Peter Neilson, *Recollections of a Six Years' Residence* . . . (Glasgow, 1830), p. 20.

Playbill for an evening of entertainment "by persons of Colour" at the African Grove Theatre, New York City, October 1, 1821. *(Courtesy New-York Historical Society)* facts taken from the insurrection of the Caravs in the island of St. Vincent in the West Indies." Presumably, the play referred to personal experiences of its playwright, for Brown had migrated to the United States from the West Indies. Then, also, the Grove made a special effort to adapt plays written by whites to the circumstances of its black audiences. Thus the English musical *Tom and Jerry* was provided with an extra scene in the African Grove production that referred to selling slaves on the auction block in Charleston, South Carolina. In a later production of *Tom and Jerry* on June 7, 1823, the African Grove changed its locale, producing *Tom and Jerry; or, Life in New York,* in which scenes of slaves dancing in the city's Fulton Market were added.[20]

Finally, the African Grove served as a training ground for future professionals, of whom at least two became celebrated. James Hewlett (d. 184?), the principal actor of the company, toured music halls as a single attraction, singing ballads and imitating famous actors. After leaving the Grove, he toured in England twice and advertised himself as "The New York and London Coloured Comedian." But it was Ira Aldridge (1807–1867) who went to the British Isles in 1824 and later won renown as both a tragedian and a comic actor. Most celebrated for his portrayal of Othello to Edmund Kean's Iago, he was also acclaimed for other tragic roles. But he was equally famous for his singing roles, such as Mungo in the ballad opera *The Padlock* (libretto by Bickerstaffe; music by Charles Dibdin), and for his solo performance on the Spanish guitar.

Indirectly, Aldridge was responsible for preserving an early example of a slave song (possibly the earliest), *Opossum up a Gum Tree.* English actor Charles Mathews visited the African Grove Theatre one evening during the 1822–23 season and, hearing Aldridge sing the song, he wrote down the words:

> Opossum up a gum tree,
> On de branch him lie;
> Opossum up a gum tree,
> Him think no one is by.
>
> Opossum up a gum tree,
> Nigger him much bewail;
> Opossum up a gum tree,
> He pulls him down by the tail.

Later, Mathews used the song in his performances, but he changed the words to such an extent that it was no longer a slave song but rather an Ethiopian song.

---

[20]This discussion is based primarily on playbills for the African Grove. But see also George Odell, *Annals of the New York Stage* (New York, 1927–49), v. 3, pp. 34 ff., 70–71, 224, 228, 293; Laurence Hutton, *Curiosities of the American Stage* (New York, 1891), p. 133; Gerald Bordman, *American Musical Theatre* (New York, 1978), pp. 7, 11.

Opossum him creep softly,
Raccoon him lay mum;
Pull him by the long tail,
Down opossum come.

Jin kum, jan kum, beangash,
Twist 'em, twist 'em, run;
Oh, the poor opossum,
Oh, the sly raccoon.[21]

There are fleeting references in contemporary sources to other black thespian groups. In 1837 a company directed by Messrs. Rhodes and Little staged plays and ballad operas in a Philadelphia theater on Pine Street above Sixth Street. On March 25, 1837, it was scheduled to produce *The Indian Hunter, A Sailor's Dream,* and "other interesting pieces."[22] In New Orleans, the Marigny Theatre offered vaudeville and musical comedies for a few months in 1838, and a theater called Theatre de la Renaissance produced comedies, dramas, comic operas, and vaudeville during the winter season of 1840. A company named The Negro (or Creole) Dramatic Company gave annual performances during the years 1859–70.[23]

All these theater productions involved the performance of music—in the ballad operas and musical comedies, in the solo songs, and in the orchestra pits. We have noted that the African Grove used a three-piece ensemble to play overtures and accompaniments. On the other hand, it seems that the New Orleans theater employed a full orchestra, which was directed by Constantin Deburque. To a limited extent, black musicians participated in white theater activities. Several travelers in the South point out that in some places theater orchestras as well as dance orchestras were composed entirely of black musicians (generally slaves). And in Philadelphia, a traveler reported seeing four black musicians in the orchestra at the Walnut Street Theatre in 1826—William and Joseph Appo and the two Newton brothers.

Balls and Holiday Celebrations

The favorite recreation of black Americans was dancing, just as it was for white Americans in the antebellum period. Ever so often organizations or private individuals sponsored elaborate fancy-dress balls, for which they engaged the services of the city's leading dance orchestras and caterers—the same ones who performed for the elite white assemblies. In 1828, for example, Frank Johnson's orchestra played for such an affair in Philadelphia, and it was reported widely in both white and black newspapers.

But race leaders were somewhat sensitive about the press reports of the

[21]Charles Mathews, *Sketches of Mr. Mathews' Celebrated Trip to America* (London, 1824), p. 9.

[22]See further in regard to the Philadelphia theater in the *Public Ledger,* March 27, 1837.

[23]Regarding black theater in New Orleans, see the *Freeman* of Indianapolis, January 15, 1910.

dances, primarily because the white reporters adopted a supercilious tone in their accounts and gave more attention to ridiculing the dancers than to reporting the balls as social events. Moreover, the general feeling was that with so many black people living in slavery, their free brothers and sisters should not indulge in such frivolities as fancy-dress balls, that energies were better spent on anti-slavery activities and cultural activities that uplifted the race. Nevertheless, the dancing continued, as can be gathered from sporadic remarks in the press and other contemporary sources. Ironically, contemporaneous literature includes many anecdotes about indulgent slaveholders in the South giving balls and other kinds of social entertainments for their favorite slaves and sometimes even renting hotels or dance halls and engaging the finest caterers and musicians available to serve at the affairs.

There were no guilt associations, however, with the celebration of holidays, particularly January 1, which memorialized the law prohibiting the importation of slaves into the United States beginning in 1808; July 5, which commemorated the abolition of slavery in the state of New York in 1827; and August 1, which commemorated the final emancipation of slaves in all the colonies of Great Britain in 1838. Throughout the North, and in some southern urban areas, black folk participated in parades and memorial services on those days, followed by merrymaking (including dancing, no doubt) in the evenings. Brass bands, of course, had important roles to play on holidays, and performers were given opportunities to exercise their talents.

Descriptions of the celebrations in New York in 1827 have come down to us. One celebrant wrote about the festivities in the city of New York:

> [There was] a real, full-souled, full-voiced shouting for joy, and marching through the crowded streets, with feet jubilant to songs of freedom. . . .[24]

At Albany, New York, a formal parade began at 11:00 A.M. The African Band, accompanied by three marshals, led the procession, which wound its way "through numerous streets," according to the *Albany Argus and Daily City Gazette*. Banners were on display at the Second Baptist Church, where the special services were to be held. After the performance of "appropriate music," an oration was delivered by the church's minister.

Dance Halls and Dives

It was inevitable that many of the newly freed slaves in the city of New York should find themselves unprepared to cope with the bitter competition of the free market, especially those who were without skills and had no experience in taking care of their own affairs. The government gave them

---

[24]James McCune Smith, Introduction to Henry Highland Garner, *A Memorial Discourse* (Philadelphia, 1865), p. 24.

no such aid as it had given, for example, to the refugees of the Haitian Revolution who poured into New York in the early 1800s, and some ex-slaves gravitated toward a life of crime and idleness. One of the neighborhoods in Manhattan inhabited by such ex-slaves and working-class whites, the so-called "Five Points" area, earned for itself the unsavory reputation of being one of the worst slums in the United States. But it also won a measure of fame when Charles Dickens visited there in 1842 and wrote about his experience in his book *American Notes*.[25]

Each dance hall in the area had its own fiddler who played for the dancing. Almack's, called Dickens's Place after the English author had visited there, was "the assembly room of the Five Point fashionables." Pete Williams, its black owner, was an amateur actor and a drama enthusiast, who occasionally presented shows for his patrons. For the most part the performances were staged by the waitresses, who doubled as singers and dancers. A visitor, George Foster, found the music to be "of no ordinary kind":

> It is Saturday night, and the company begins assembling early, for Saturday night is a grand time for thieves, loafers, prostitutes and rowdies, as well as for honest, hard-working people. Already the room—a large, desolate-looking place, with white-washed walls garnished with wooden benches—is half full of men and women, . . .
>
> In the middle of one side of the room a shammy platform is erected, with a trembling railing, and this is the "orchestra" of the establishment. Sometimes a single black fiddler answers the purpose; but on Saturday nights the music turns out strong, and the house entertains, in addition, a trumpet and a bass drum. With these instruments you may imagine that the music at Dickens's Place is of no ordinary kind. You cannot, however, begin to imagine *what* it is. You cannot *see* the red-hot knitting-needles spirted out by that red-faced trumpeter, who looks precisely as if he were blowing glass, which needles aforesaid penetrating the tympanum, pierce through and through your brain without remorse. Nor can you perceive the frightful mechanical contortions of the bass-drummer as he sweats and deals his blows on every side, in all violation of the laws of rhythm, like a man beating a baulky mule and showering his blows upon the unfortunate animal, now on this side, now on that. If you could, it would be unnecessary for us to write.[26]

This was assuredly "red-hot" music, played long before such words as "jazz" or "ragtime" had entered the vocabulary of popular music cognoscenti. According to Foster, one of the favorite pieces of the dancers was *Cooney in de Holler,* a variant of the popular *Opossum Up a Gum Stump.* From all evidence, the following melody was associated with the song during this period:

[25]Charles Dickens, *American Notes for General Circulation* (London, 1842), p. 37; reprint in BPIM 3 (Spring 1975): 81–82.

[26]George G. Foster, *New York by Gas Light* (New York, 1850), pp. 72–76; reprint of excerpts in RBAM, pp. 138–41. For source of quotations above, see p. 139.

Cooney in de Holler

On the night that Dickens visited Almack's a "corpulent black fiddler" was joined by "his friend who plays the tambourine." The English author was particularly impressed by the dancing of a "lively young Negro, wit of the assembly and the greatest dancer known." This was undoubtedly the world-renowned black dancer known as "Juba" (that is, William Henry Lane). The dancer performed the "single shuffle, double shuffle, cut and cross cut . . . spinning about on his toes and heels like nothing but the man's fingers on the tambourine."[27] Though neither Dickens nor Juba himself may have been aware of it, the shuffle steps of the dancing and the drumming accompaniment on the tambourine were in the African tradition.

The dance halls of "Five Points" are regarded by some as the antecedents of Harlem's famous "black-and-tan cabarets" of the 1920s. The dance musicians who played in "Five Points" were musical illiterates, but they "beat out hot music" that stimulated the dancers to wild and frenzied dancing. And as the Harlem cabarets were to do in the next century, some of the dance halls—particularly Dickens's Place—lured European tourists and other curious persons to watch the dancing and marvel at the music. Journalist George Foster found the same kind of activities in the dance halls of Philadelphia, particularly Dandy Hall, when he visited there during the years 1848–49.

Street Vendors and Itinerant Musicians

On the streets of large cities, the street vendors and hucksters, calling out their wares or offering their services, were a familiar sight. Their cries, although typically more song fragments than true songs, are nevertheless a part of the musical tradition of black folk in the United States. As a class the street vendors generally remained anonymous, but a few became legendary figures in their communities because of their unusual voices or because they plied their trade for such a long time. One such vendor was Henry Anderson (b. 1800), "The Hominy Man" of Philadelphia, who first attracted attention

[27]Dickens, *American Notes for General Circulation* (New York, 1842), p. 36.

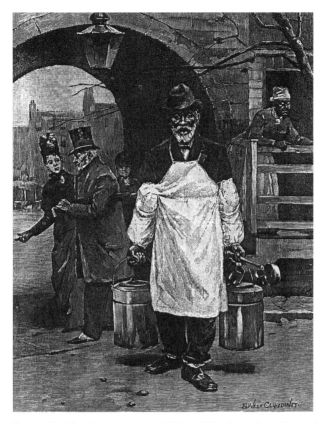

"A Southern Oyster Peddler." Engraving by B. West Clinedinst, from *Harper's Weekly*, 1889.

in about 1828 because of his strong, resonant "tenor robusto" and the fact that his were "the most musical of all cries." The message was a simple one:

> Hominy man come out today
> For to sell his homi*nay.*

or

> De hominy man is on his way
> From de navy yard
> Wid his harmony.[28]

As we have seen, a New Orleans street vendor Signor Cornmeali used his street cries as a stepping stone to appearances on the professional stage.

The call of the street vendor was intended to carry a distinct message and rarely, therefore, left the listener in doubt of its meaning. Sometimes the

---

[28]First version is from John Thomas Scharf, *History of Philadelphia* (Philadelphia, 1884), v. 2, p. 930; second version is from Oberholtzer, *Philadelphia,* v. 2, p. 95.

calls were just a phrase or two sung in a "novel manner." Sometimes they were parodies of folksongs. Ex-slave William Wells Brown heard the following version of the spiritual *I Am Going to Glory* and commented: "A woman with some really fine strawberries put forth her claims in a very interesting song; the interest centered more upon the manner than the matter":[29]

I live four miles out of town,
I am going to glory;
My strawberries are sweet and sound,
I am going to glory.
I fotch them four miles on my head,
I am going to glory;
My child is sick, my husband dead,
I am going to glory.
Now's the time to get them cheap,
I am going to glory;
Eat them with your bread and meat,
I am going to glory.
Come sinner get down on your knees,
I am going to glory;
Eat these strawberries when you please,
I am going to glory. . . .

For each black musician who achieved a national reputation during the antebellum period, there were hundreds of humble part-time musicians who followed their trades and picked up extra money by playing for dances at night, on weekends, and during holidays. An English traveler, John Maude, encountered one of these Jacks-of-all-trades on the sloop *Nancy*. The black man, Nicholas, who had purchased his own freedom and that of his wife, performed "well on the violin" and was "very smart." When the boat reached its destination Maude and his party arranged for Nicholas to play for some dancing, about which he wrote in his diary:

Went on shore; took with us Nicholas and his violin, the fiddle soon got the girls together; we kicked up a dance and kept it up till midnight.

Black fiddlers also invaded college campuses. At Princeton College in 1789, for example, an observer was shocked when he came across some undergraduates

. . . dancing up and down the entry as a Negro played upon a violin with twenty students hallooing and tearing about.[30]

One of the best-known itinerant musicians of the nineteenth century was Solomon Northup of Saratoga Springs, New York, who became even

[29]William Wells Brown, *My Southern Home* (Boston, 1880), p. 211.
[30]John Maude, *Visit to the Falls of Niagara in 1800* (London, 1826), pp. 3, 16; in regard to black fiddlers at Princeton, see Joseph Marks, *America Learns to Dance* (New York, 1957), p. 57.

better known for the "slave narrative" he wrote than for his fiddling. His book, *Twelve Years a Slave . . . ,* presents a vivid account of how he, a free man, was kidnapped by slave raiders, sold into slavery in Louisiana, then rescued twelve years later.[31] One of many ex-slave narratives that appeared in the mid-nineteenth century, Northup's book is highly regarded by scholars for its reliability and historical value.

Northup's experiences before his abduction may be taken as typical for black violinists in the North trying to earn a livelihood with music. He tells us that he had "numerous calls to play upon the violin," and that "throughout the surrounding villages [his] fiddling was notorious [*sic*]." In the summer he worked at the United States Hotel in Saratoga Springs; in the winter he relied upon his violin playing. As a matter of fact, Northup's fiddle was his undoing. When two men offered him a job playing with a show, he followed them to Washington, D.C., where he was drugged and kidnapped. He had been promised one dollar for each day's work, three dollars for each night's playing (the standard payment at the time), and the cost of his travel expenses back to Saratoga Springs.

MUSIC OF THE BLACK CHURCH, I

Although a number of black-church histories were published in the nineteenth century, few include information about musical practices. For that reason alone, the writings of Daniel Alexander Payne (1811–1893) are invaluable, particularly his *Recollections of Seventy Years* (1888) and *History of the African Methodist Episcopal Church* (1891). But Payne is also important because of his insightful commentary; over his long years of association with the AME Church as minister, church historian, college president, and bishop, his sharp eyes missed little of importance in the history of the church. It is fair to assume that some of Payne's observations about music in the AME churches apply as well to other independent, urban black congregations of the antebellum period; the scanty evidence available in contemporary literature supports such an assumption.[32]

Music in the Worship Service

During formal worship services, the music consisted of psalms, hymns, and anthems. Black congregations generally used the hymnals of the white denominations to which they belonged, except for the AME and AMEZ churches, which published their own. The black Episcopalians were the first to introduce the trained choir into the worship service; and the St. Thomas

---

[31]Solomon Northup, *Twelve Years a Slave* (Cincinnati, 1853); reprint of passages about music in RBAM, pp. 93–102.
[32]See further in Southern, "Musical Practices."

Episcopal Church in Philadelphia was the first to purchase a pipe organ. When the organ was installed in early 1828, it provoked much comment in the press, as did also the employment of a young black woman, Ann Appo (ca. 1809–1828), as church organist. Churches that could not afford to buy pipe organs used harps and harmoniums (reed organs) to accompany congregational singing.

By 1830 it appears that the progressive urban churches of all denominations had introduced choral singing into their services; but some congregations found it difficult to accept the idea of allowing a trained choir to assume major responsibility for music in the worship service. At the beginning of the nineteenth century, common practice called for the deacon to "line out" the psalms and hymns—that is, to chant one or two lines at a time, followed by congregational singing of the lines—and some Methodist and Baptist churches clung to the old traditions as long as they could. Payne gives a colorful account of how Bethel Church in Philadelphia made the painful changeover from the old to the new, from singing in the "common way" to singing by note, led by a choir (see below).[33] The transition began in December 1841, when the congregation moved into a new building; some of the forward-looking members set aside a gallery for a choir to use at the dedicatory services. Later, these members attempted to introduce choral singing into the regular services, but this caused an uproar among the elder members, who resisted the ideas of both singing by note and employing a trained choir.

One of the church elders, Joseph Cox, wrote about the struggle in his diary on December 23, 1841:

> The singing today was not good, there being an opposition because the old people are opposed to note singing. Elymus Johnson, the person appointed by them, is weakly, and the other would not help him. So we had dull music today.

That the "old people" lost out is evident from an entry Cox made in his diary on June 9, 1842:

> The musical department of the Bible Class Association of Bethel . . . will give their first vocal soiree of choruses from eminent authors on next Thursday eve, the 23rd inst. . . .

The progressive members of Bethel had won their case, but it caused great dissension among the members. As Payne wrote,[34]

> The first introduction of choral singing into the A.M.E. Church took place in Bethel, Philadelphia, Pa., between 1841 and 1842. It gave great offense to the

---

[33]Daniel Payne, *History of the African Methodist Episcopal Church* (Nashville, 1891), pp. 452 ff.

[34]The quotations that follow are from Daniel Payne, *Recollections of Seventy Years* (Nashville, 1888); reprint of passages about music in RBAM, pp. 65–70.

older members, especially those who had professed personal sanctification. Said they: "You have brought the devil into the Church, and therefore we will go out." So, suiting the action to the word, many went out of Bethel, and never returned.

The split in Bethel's congregation failed, however, to solve the dispute. Although Payne had only recently become associated with the AME Church, he was drawn into the fray:

> So great was the excitement and irritation produced by the introduction of the choir into Bethel Church that I, then a local preacher and school-master, was requested by the leader of the choir and other prominent members in it to preach a special sermon on sacred music. This I did as best I could. In my researches I used a small monograph on music written by Mr. Wesley [founder of the white English Methodist Church], but drew my information chiefly from the word of God. The immediate effect of that discourse was to check the excitement, soothe the irritation, and set the most intelligent to reading as they had never done before.

Payne observed that similar "excitements" and "irritations" occurred when choirs were introduced into other churches of the sect, "not only in the cities but also in the large towns and villages." Conservative members withdrew from churches in many places, with the result that large congregations were supplanted by smaller ones. In Chicago the minister, the Reverend Elisha Weaver, actually was impeached by his congregation in 1857 for introducing vocal and instrumental music into the church. From the vantage point of the present time, the parallels are obvious between the development of white Protestant musical traditions in the colonial period and the growth of similar traditions in the independent black churches of the nineteenth century.

The first use of musical instruments in the church also caused conflict among black Methodists, although not to the same extent as the introduction of choral singing. The earliest performance of instrumental music in an AME church took place in Baltimore in 1848, the occasion being a concert of sacred music presented under the direction of James Fleet of Washington, D.C. In a second concert of sacred music given in the same year, William Appo directed a seven-piece string ensemble. It was not long before AME congregations everywhere began to develop great pride in their choirs, their organs, and the concerts presented in their churches. When he was writing his memoirs in 1888, Payne was very proud of the state of music in AME churches. He observed:

> In a musical direction what progress has been made within the last forty years! There is not a Church of ours in any of the great cities of the republic that can afford to buy an instrument which is without one; and there are but few towns or villages where our Connection exists that are without an instrument to accompany the choir.

And as we have seen, black urban churches took the lead in sponsoring concerts and similar activities until other community organizations had developed to the point of being able to assume such responsibilities.

Camp Meetings and Bush Meetings

Black churches also sponsored camp meetings throughout the nineteenth century, led primarily by Methodists and Baptists. Black folk in the North broke away from white camp meetings as early as the second decade of the century, and the evidence suggests that AME congregations were the first to thus establish their independence, holding their own meetings as early as August 1818, in Bucks County, Pennsylvania. Newspaper advertisements informed communities of the dates and places of camp meetings and of arrangements made for transportation from the cities to the wooded sites where they were held. Attendance might rise as high as four or five thousand people at these gatherings, which lasted from three or four days to a week. Although sponsored by black churches, the meetings attracted whites both as participants and as guest preachers.

At bush meetings—that is, smaller meetings held in wooded areas without use of tents—the same practices were observed. Payne was greatly upset when he encountered the following "heathenish" practices at one of them:

> After the sermon, they formed a ring, and with coats off sung, clapped their hands and stamped their feet in a most ridiculous and heathenish way. I requested the pastor to go and stop their dancing. At his request they stopped their dancing and clapping of hands, but remained singing and rocking their bodies to and fro. . . . After the sermon in the afternoon, having another opportunity of speaking alone to this young leader of the singing and clapping ring, he said: "Sinners won't get converted unless there is a ring. . . . The Spirit of God works upon people in different ways. At campmeeting there must be a ring here, a ring there, a ring over yonder, or sinners will not get converted. . . ."[35]

These performances obviously reflected deep-rooted African traditions.

Informal Religious Practices

A rather delightful tradition in some urban churches was the "sacred serenade." An editorial in the *Colored American* on October 24, 1840, commented:

> Some of our unequalled vocalists and excellent musicians are sometimes in the practice, late at night, of visiting their friends, and exercising their extraordinary skill in entertaining them with songs of the night. We were on Tuesday night last so entertained and were awakened from our slumbers by the harmony of voices and the sweet accords of music, the charm and solemnity of which is always enhanced by the stillness of night. We hope the next time they visit us (for they

[35]Payne, *Recollections*, p. 69.

are welcome) that they will not, just as they have aroused us from our slumber, retire as in this case, but repeat their anthems, that we may not be awakened in vain.

Payne stated that "no one but those who have had their slumbers broken by those sacred serenades can realize their sweetness and power."

It is evident from contemporary sources that church fathers found it difficult to keep Africanisms from creeping into religious services, whether in urban or rural areas. Again and again, writers remark about the unusual practices they observed when visiting black churches, particularly in regard to singing, from Boston in the North to Cincinnati in the Midwest to Savannah in the South. Payne represents the prevailing attitude among the clergy in his efforts "to modify the extravagances indulged in by the people."

He reports that he met Praying and Singing Bands in many places. These groups would meet *after* the formal worship services, generally at night, to spend two or more hours in praying, dancing holy dances, and singing songs he labeled "corn-field ditties" (actually, the precursors of Negro spirituals):

> The man who had the most powerful pair of lungs was the one who made the best prayer, and he could be heard a square off. He who could sing loudest and longest led the "Band," having his loins girded and a handkerchief in hand with which he kept time, while his feet resounded on the floor like the drum-sticks of a bass drum. In some places it was the custom to begin these dances after every night service and keep it up till midnight. . . . Someone has even called it the "Voudoo Dance."[36]

The AME Church felt so strongly about the encroaching Africanisms that it passed a special resolution at its annual conference in 1841: "Resolved, that our preachers shall strenuously oppose the singing of fuge [*sic*] tunes and hymns of our own composing in our public places and congregations."

None of the suppressive measures worked! Throughout the nineteenth century large numbers of black Christians improvised their spiritual songs in urban churches and on rural plantations, thus contributing to the development of a repertory of Negro spirituals that would have enormous impact upon American music of the twentieth century—indeed, upon world music. And the black Christians continued to engage in holy dances, called "shouts," that would affect the development of both their sacred and secular dances in the future.

URBAN MUSIC IN THE SOUTH

New Orleans—A Musical Center

In the early nineteenth century, New Orleans was undoubtedly the most musical city in the land. Sometimes as many as three opera companies were

---

[36]Payne, *Recollections,* p. 70.

playing at the same time; there were plays and concerts and balls and street parades and, most stirring of all, the yearly celebrations of Carnival or Mardi Gras. Thomas Ashe, a traveler to the city in 1806, stated that among the French residents "the concert, dance promenade and *petit souper* [were] conducted with as much attention as at Paris or Rome."[37]

New Orleans was certainly the most exotic city in the land. In 1803, the year of the Louisiana Purchase, its Spanish, French, African, English, Irish, and German traditions were fusing into something that was new and different, into a truly American culture. Its Negro population, the largest of any American city, constituted more than one-third of the city's total, numbering over twelve thousand people. Peculiar to the city's social structure was a rigid caste system, which distinguished between whites, blacks (who were mostly slaves), and so-called "creoles of color" (who were generally free mulattos, quadroons, or octoroons). To a greater extent than in any other city, the caste class distinctions were reflected in social and cultural activities, particularly those of nonwhites.

Vocal Music

Although the black folk of New Orleans concentrated their attention on instrumental music, vocal music was hardly neglected. At the opera houses, segregated sections were reserved for free Negroes and for slaves. Visitors to the city were surprised to note that even the slaves hummed operatic arias as they walked through the streets. In the cathedrals, visitors noted that the black folk added both warmth and volume to the singing during Mass, where women made up the larger part of the congregations.

In 1842 four nuns "of color" established the first convent for black women in the United States—the Convent of the Holy Family. Some of the most moving ceremonies of the year occurred there during Passion Week—on Good Friday, Holy Saturday, and Easter Sunday. A white visitor to the services, Julia Bishop, wrote in a magazine article about the singing on Easter:

> *Kyrie eleison,* they sing *Kyrie, Kyrie, Kyrie eleison.* All the singers are women and they have brought to the song service the rich quality of the Negro voice, musical in its wildest state, and now trained to the most perfect melody. But the voices have also brought with them that pathetic touch which lingers around the gayest notes and which training has never been able to remove and even the Gloria in Excelsis which presently arises thrills to the heart with its grand and lofty melancholy.[38]

---

[37]Thomas Ashe, *Travels in America, 1806* (London, 1809), p. 312.
[38]Julia T. Bishop, "Easter Morn in a Colored Convent," *Ladies Home Journal* (April 1899): 10.

Brass Bands and Orchestras

New Orleans had a great fondness for brass bands, shared by the black and white populations alike.[39] Any event was used as a pretext for a parade, and the same musicians who played in the dance orchestras at night could be found parading the streets during the day. A newspaper item in the *New Orleans Picayune* (1838) called it "a real mania for horn and trumpet playing." Negroes had their own brass bands, the members recruited from among free blacks or colored creoles, who took their musical activities very seriously. They studied music with the players associated with the French Opera House and the city orchestras; some of them went to Paris to complete their studies. As a result, the Negro bands and orchestras of New Orleans maintained high levels of musicianship.

It was not always necessary for a talented Negro to obtain his own musical instruction; the demand for bandsmen was so great that often a patron could be found who was willing to advance a Negro's music education. In 1820, for example, the New Orleans Independent Rifle Company advertised for "two young men of color," offering not only to teach them to play but also to provide them with keyed bugles, uniforms, and a monthly salary.

One of the best-known bandsman in the city was Jordan Noble (ca. 1796–1890), a veteran of four wars. "The matchless drummer," as he was called, marched in many parades during the antebellum years and occasionally gave "field-music concerts," using the drums he had played in the wars.

Black bands also flourished in other urban areas of the South where there were free black communities. In Richmond, Virginia, for example, the thirteen-member band attached to the Richmond Light Infantry Blues in 1841 was "regularly instructed in martial music by a competent teacher . . . and properly uniformed at the expense of the company."[40] Sometimes the bands included slaves as well as free men, as did Allen's Brass Band of Wilmington, North Carolina, which was active during the 1850s–60s.[41]

A Symphony Orchestra

During the 1830s musicians of New Orleans organized a Negro Philharmonic Society that was composed of more than one hundred members. In addition to presenting concerts, the society arranged for performances by visiting artists. Some of the players also provided music at the Theatre de la Renaissance for the "free colored," where the orchestra was under the direc-

---

[39]See further about the music of black musicians in New Orleans in Henry Kmen, *Music in New Orleans* (Baton Rouge, 1966).

[40]"The Richmond Light Infantry Blues of Richmond, Virginia," *Tyler's Quarterly Historical Magazine* 1 (July 1919): 16.

[41]Nancy R. Ping, "Black Musical Activities in Antebellum Wilmington, North Carolina," BPIM 8 (Fall 1980): 151–52.

tion of Jacques Constantin Deburque (1800–1861), violinist and music teacher. Deburque and Richard Lambert were the permanent directors of the symphony orchestra; Lambert was also a noted music teacher and the patriarch of a family that produced several professional musicians in later generations. When the symphony orchestra performed works calling for special instrumentation, professional white musicians would join the group.

Dance Orchestras and Recreational Music

In such cities as Baltimore, Charleston, Louisville, and New Orleans there were occasional balls for black folk, slave and free, and sometimes these were quite elaborate affairs. In 1856, for example, when the Falls City Hotel in Louisville gave a New Year's Eve Ball for the slaves it owned or hired, the event was described with extravagant phrases in the local newspaper. Readers were assured that the hotel owners "exerted themselves to render their colored guests comfortable and their entertainment agreeable." Black musicians, of course, provided the music for dancing. More typically, however, they played in taverns and on the streets for their fellow black folk. A visitor to Richmond in 1799, Thomas Fairfax, remarked about one of these street troubadours:

> After going to bed I was entertained with an agreeable serenade by a black man, who had taken his stand near the Tavern, and for the amusement of those of his colour, sung and played on the Bangoe. He appeared to be quite adept on this African instrument, which though it may not bear a comparison with the Guitar is certainly capable of Conveying much pleasure to the musical ear. Its wild notes of melody seem to Correspond to the state of Civilization of the Country where this Species of music originated.[42]

Music for dancing in taverns was also provided by fiddles, flutes, clarinets, tambourines, and drums.

Black Fiddlers and White Dancers

As before the American Revolution, music for the dances of white society in the nineteenth century was generally provided by slaves. More frequently than in earlier times, the dance orchestras consisted of two or three musicians and were occasionally interracial. The traveler Thomas Ashe noticed in 1806, for instance, that the orchestra for a ball held in Wheeling, West Virginia, was composed of two black banjo players and a white lutenist.

In Richmond, the black fiddler-slave Sy Gilliat of colonial fame was still active in the 1800s. The leading figure at the city's balls, he appeared at

---

[42]Thomas Fairfax, *Journey from Virginia to Salem, Massachusetts* (London, 1836); quoted in Julian Mates, *The American Musical Stage Before 1800* (New Brunswick, N.J., 1962), p. 80.

dances wearing the same kind of court dress as he had worn for years, complete with brown wig, and his manners remained as courtly as ever. Local historian Samuel Mordecai affirms that the most exciting event in Richmond of those days was the annual Race Ball, which took place at the end of a week of horse racing. It customarily opened with a dignified *minuet de la cour,* but after this bow to convention the dancers "commenced the reel, like a storm after a calm." The music of "Sy Gilliat's fiddle and the flute or clarionet of his blacker comrade, London Briggs" was quite "fast and furious," and the dancers cut "all sorts of capers" to it, dancing not only reels, but contradances, congos, hornpipes, and jigs.[43]

After Gilliat's death, his place as a leading dance musician was taken by the violinist George Walker. A newspaper advertisement acclaimed Walker as "the best leader of a band in all eastern and middle Virginia":

> FOR HIRE: either for the remainder of the year or by the month, week or job, the celebrated musician and fiddler, George Walker. All persons desiring the services of George Walker are notified that they must contract for them with us, and in no case pay to him or any other person the amount of his hire without a written order from us. George Walker is admitted by common consent, to be the best leader of a band in all eastern and middle Virginia.
>
> [*Richmond Daily Enquirer,* June 27, 1853]

Black orchestras played for much of the dancing that took place in New Orleans, whether the dances were for whites, slaves, or colored creoles. To have a white dance-orchestra play for an affair was a novelty. In 1834, for example, the promoter of a great ball made a special appeal to the snobbish by promising the performance of a "new band, fresh from Europe"—obviously a white group.

At a large affair the dance orchestra might be composed of from five to eight players; typically, "a clarionet, three fiddles, two tambourines, and a bass drum." It was the job of one of the players to call out the dance figures. Benjamin Latrobe's comment about the caller he heard at a *Grand Bal* dur-

Fiddler playing for a cotillion, from *Harper's Weekly,* 1875.

[43]Mordecai, *Richmond;* reprint of passages about black musicians in RBAM, pp. 135–36.

ing Carnival time (that is, Mardi Gras) in 1819 is colored by his bias, but is nevertheless worth quoting because of the first hand details it provides:

> ... a tall, ill-dressed black, in the music gallery who played the tambourine standing up, and in a forced and vile voice called the [dance] figures as they changed.[44]

The slave orchestras that played for parties held in town mansions or on the plantations near New Orleans were generally small ensembles, sometimes simply fiddle, flute, and fife, or perhaps two fiddles, flute, triangle, and tambourine. It was not uncommon to find dance music being provided by a single fiddler. Dance fiddlers were in great demand, and a good one, such as Massa Quamba, could charge as much as three dollars per night for his services.

At white balls, sections were often set aside for black men and women, where they could listen to the music but could not dance. The so-called "Quadroon Balls" were, like the Place Congo dances, an exotic New Orleans tradition. The special attractions of these balls were the beautiful, colored creole girls—the quadroons and octoroons—and only white males were admitted as guests. Ironically, the music for these balls was provided by orchestras composed of male "creoles of color."

AFRICAN TRADITIONS IN THE SOUTH

Dancing in the Place Congo

One of the most exotic sights of old New Orleans was the slave dancing that took place in the Place Congo (now Beauregard Square). The slaves' custom of assembling on Sundays and church holy days to dance in public squares must have begun before 1786, for in that year a local ordinance was passed forbidding such dancing until after the close of religious services. In 1799 a traveler saw "vast numbers of slaves" assembled together on the levee and "dancing in large rings."[45]

The most detailed contemporary description of dancing in the Place Congo is found in the journal of Benjamin Henry B. Latrobe, the famous architect, who spent some time in New Orleans during the years 1818–20. "Accidentally stumbling upon an assembly of Negroes" who met on Sunday afternoons to dance in the Place, Latrobe counted five or six hundred dancers gathered there, all of them "formed into circular groups."[46] From the narrative of William Wells Brown, *My Southern Home*, we learn that "not

[44]Benjamin H. B. Latrobe, *Impressions Respecting New Orleans* (New York, 1905), p. 172.
[45]Cited in Epstein, *Sinful Tunes*, p. 84.
[46]Latrobe, *Impressions*, pp. 179–81.

"The Bamboula." From an engraving by Edward W. Kemble, in "The Dance in Place Congo" by George W. Cable, *Century Magazine,* 1886.

less than two or three thousand people would congregate to see the dusky dancers," who represented six different African tribes: "Kraels, Minahs, Congos and Mandringas, Gangas, Hiboas, and Fulas."[47]

At about three o'clock in the afternoon the dancers would begin to gather, each tribe assembling in a different part of the square. There were no trees or grass, for over the years the ground had been worn hard by the feet of the dancers. Each group had its own orchestra, consisting generally of drums in several sizes (made of "gum stumps" that had been "dug out" and covered with sheepskin heads), banjos (made of Louisiana gourds), and rattles (made from the jawbones of horses). The dancing would build up in excitement, becoming wilder and more frenzied as the afternoon wore on, until men and women would fall fainting to the ground. Their places were quickly taken, however, by other couples. By nine o'clock the dancing would have come to an end, the spectators gone home, and the square deserted.[48]

Latrobe "crowded near enough" to observe the performance of several groups at close range and later wrote in his diary about the instruments and the dance steps:

> The music consisted of two drums and a stringed instrument . . . , [one of which was] a cylindrical drum, about a foot in diameter. . . . The drum was an open-staved thing held between the knees. . . . They made an incredible noise. The most curious instrument, however, was a stringed instrument, which no doubt was imported from Africa. On the top of the finger board was the rude figure of a man in a sitting posture, and two pegs behind him to which the strings were

[47]Brown, *Southern Home,* pp. 121–22.
[48]Brown, pp. 121–22.

fastened. The body was a calabash. It was played upon by a very little old man, apparently eighty or ninety years old.[49]

The largest of the rings formed by the dancers was not over ten feet in diameter. In some instances the ring of dancers "walked, by way of dancing, round the music in the center." Here the walking movements must have involved the kind of shuffle step characteristic of West African dancing. In one instance two dancers, both women, were in the center of the ring. "They held each a coarse handkerchief extended by the corners in their hands and set to each other in a miserably dull & slow figure, hardly moving their feet or bodies." Again, here is a reference to the shuffle step. As noted above, the dances began slowly, but gradually quickened, building up into wild, frenzied movements.

The vocal music accompanying the dances obviously comprised chants rather than genuine songs, and these were repeated over and over again for as long as five or six hours. As much as fatigue, it was the combination of the incessant chanting and the exciting music that sent the dancers into a state of ecstacy and eventually caused them "to fall fainting to the ground."

Obviously, the entire performance of the Place Congo dance was in the same African tradition as the Pinkster dances in New York and the jubilees in Philadelphia. The instruments and the performance practice were like those described by witnesses of the eighteenth-century slave festivals in the North and, moreover, like those reported by travelers to Africa during the eighteenth and nineteenth centuries.

John Conny Festivals

Another slave festival of the antebellum period that revealed links to West Africa was the John Conny (or John Kuner, John Canoe, John Connu, Junkanoo) festival associated with the Christmas season in towns on the eastern shores of North Carolina (particularly Wilmington) and Virginia (particularly Norfolk). Contemporaneous sources report that the participants in the general merrymaking wore costumes, masks, and head-dresses distinctive for the cow horns they sported as they made their rounds from house to house, asking for Christmas gifts, or paraded through the streets. The festival had its own songs, especially composed for the occasion, and musical accompaniment was provided by a drum type called a "gumbo box," jawbones, cow horns, triangles, and other percussive instruments.[50]

There was an actual King John Conny in African history (flourished in the 1720s on the Coast of Guinea), and the New World festival obviously

---

[49]Latrobe, pp. 170–81.

[50]Description of festival in Linda Brent, *Incidents in the Life of a Slave Girl* (Boston, 1861). See also Ping etc., "Black Musical Activities," BPIM 8 (Fall 1980): 139–160. Rosita Sands, "Junkanoo," BPIM 17 (Fall 1989): 93–108.

represents an African survival. Since the festival was celebrated with much vigor in the West Indies, particularly the Bahamas, it may well have entered the United States by that route rather than directly from Africa.

Voodoo

The most immediate impetus to the rise of voodoo practices in Louisiana was the emigration of slaves and free black people from the island of Santo Domingo at the time of the Haitian Revolution in 1804. This institutionalized cult of ritual worship undoubtedly existed long before Haitian refugees arrived in New Orleans, for Louisiana began to import slaves from the West Indies as early as 1716. Voodoo seems to have flourished in pockets of the South through the nineteenth century and into the twentieth; contemporaneous sources specifically mention voodoo ceremonies taking place in Missouri, Georgia, and Florida. The few descriptions that are extant, however, refer only to rites observed in New Orleans.

There is no question that Haiti was the central place where African religious traditions—primarily of Dahomey (now Benin) but also of other West African nations—were syncretized with Catholic beliefs and practices to produce vaudou (called voodoo in the United States). Essentially the ceremonies centered upon worship of the snake deity Damballa (or Da) through singing, dancing, and spirit possession. In New Orleans names given to other deities included Legba or Papa Limba (identified with St. Peter), Blanc Dani (identified with St. Michael), and Agasu (identified with St. Anthony).

The secret rituals might take place at any time, but on St. John's Eve (June 23) there was always an annual celebration, which outsiders were sometimes allowed to attend. One observer persuaded an old woman to sing a voodoo song for him:

> Heron mande, heron mande,
> Tigi li papa,
> Heron mande, heron mande, heron mande,
> Dosi dans godo!
> Ah tingwaiye, ah tingwaiye! ah tingwaiye
> Ah waiyah, ah waiyah, ah tingwaiye,
> Tigi li papa!
> Heron mande,
> Ahwaya! Ah tingwaiye,
> Ahwaya! Ah tingwaiye.

She could not tell him the meaning of the words; she knew only that the song was "very, very old and had come from Santo Domingo."[51]

The instrumental music at the ceremony was produced by an old man

[51]James W. Buel, *Metropolitan Life Unveiled* (St. Louis, 1882), pp. 520–29. See also Brown, *Southern Home*, pp. 68–69.

"The Voodoo Dance." From a drawing by Edward W. Kemble in "Creole Slave Songs," *Century Magazine*, 1886.

sitting "astride of a cylinder made of thin cypress staves hooped with brass and headed by a sheepskin," which he beat with two sticks; a man with "two sheep shank-bones" and a woman with the "leg-bones of a buzzard or turkey," both of them beating on the sides of the cylinder; a young man "vigorously twirling a long calabash . . . made of a Louisiana gourd a foot and a half long, and filled with peebles"; and players on a banjo and a tam-tam.

THE ANTI-SLAVERY MOVEMENT

Abolitionists in the North were not satisfied with emancipating the black folk in their own region; they would settle for nothing less than complete freedom for all slaves in the United States. The anti-slavery movement, which had its beginnings in the colonial period, increased in numbers and became very militant. As early as 1817 publications began to appear vigorously denouncing slavery. In 1831 the New England Anti-Slavery Society was formed, followed in 1833 by the organization of the American Anti-Slavery Society; periodicals were published, pamphlets distributed, and lecturers sent out into the field. Black men and women fought alongside whites against "the peculiar institution" of slavery, many serving as full-time agents and orators; among them, Frederick Douglass (ca. 1817–1895), William Wells Brown (1816–1884), and a woman given at birth the name of Isabella, which she later changed to Sojourner Truth (1797–1885).

Anti-Slavery Songs

At a typical anti-slavery meeting the lecture platform was shared by speakers (one or two of them black) and singers—or, at least, a song leader. Songs were an indispensable part of the program, being used to "put fire" into the meetings. Frequently the platform singers had composed their own song texts; Sojourner Truth was acclaimed, for example, both for her oratory and her original songs, which often were deeply religious in nature. In 1849 William Wells Brown published some of the most popular anti-slavery songs in a collection, *The Anti-Slavery Harp*. In accordance with the common practice of the time, only song texts were included, but there are references to suitable tunes.

That list of suitable tunes provides an index of songs in vogue among

Anti-slavery song, **The Sweets of Liberty** (to the tune *Is There a Heart That Never Loved*), Braham

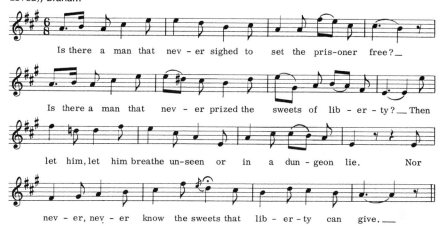

2. Is there a heart so cold in Man
   Can galling fetters crave?
   Is there a wretch so truly low,
   Can stoop to be a slave?
   O, let him, then, in chains be bound,
   In chains and bondage live;
   Nor never, never know the sweets
   That liberty can give.
3. Is there a breast so chilled in life,
   Can nurse the coward's sigh?
   Is there a creature so debased,
   Would not for freedom die?
   O, let him, then, be doomed to crawl
   Where only reptiles live;
   Nor never, never know the sweets
   That liberty can give.

the common people, black and white, at the mid-century. Since the words of the anti-slavery songs were all-important, it was essential that only well-known tunes be used, so that audiences would give all their attention to the texts. Predictably, songs from the British Isles dominate the list: *Auld Lang Syne, Flow Gently Sweet Afton, Kathleen O'More, Long, Long Ago,* and *Gaily the Troubadour* (the last two by the English song writer Thomas Haines Bayly). There are three minstrel songs, *O Susannah, Old Rosin the Beau,* and *Dandy Jim;* the sentimental ballad *Is There a Heart;* and three hymn tunes, *Lenox, My Faith Looks Up to Thee,* and *When I Can Read My Title Clear.* It is noteworthy that among these other tunes suggested for use, several were special favorites of black folk; for example, *Old Rosin the Beau, Is There a Heart,* and *When I Can Read My Title Clear.*

The white singing troupe, the Hutchinson family, became so closely associated with the movement, touring with the abolitionists and contributing a number of original songs, that its members were sometimes referred to as "the minnesingers of American freedom." The Hutchinsons also toured independently, beginning in 1842, and carried anti-slavery songs (as well as popular ballads, temperance songs, and women's suffrage songs) to audiences all over America and the British Isles.

The Underground Railroad

One of the earliest activities of the abolitionists was the Underground Railroad, which was not a railroad at all but a loosely knit organization existing for the sole purpose of helping fugitive slaves to escape. As early as the eighteenth century there had been people who came to the assistance of fugitive slaves, especially among the Quakers. At the beginning of the nineteenth century various persons began to develop ways of giving systematic aid to fugitives, and so secret pathways of "underground roads" were planned, with "stations," "conductors," and sometimes even travel vehicles. Most of the traveling was done at night, the fugitives moving on foot, guided by the North Star or following along well-known water routes. During the day, they hid out at the "stations," where they received food, rest, and directions for continuing the journey.

All "lines" led North, from southern plantations to "stations" in Ohio, Pennsylvania, New Jersey, New York, and eventually to Canada—especially after the passage of the Fugitive Slave Law in 1850. The slaves often had to disguise themselves, mulattos posing as white persons, women posing as men and vice versa. Elaborate codes were worked out, so that messages could be sent from station to station, via the "grapevine telegraph," when fugitives were on the way. The story of the Underground Railroad is fascinating, full of hair-raising, breathtaking adventures that cannot be recounted here. Some of the scenes in Harriet Beecher Stowe's novel *Uncle Tom's Cabin* (1852) vividly recreate aspects of the journey along the Railroad.

"The Underground Railroad," painting from about 1890 by Charles T. Webber. *(Courtesy Cincinnati Art Museum)*

An essential part of the operation was the preliminary planning; prospective travelers had to be informed first of the possibility of escaping, then given specific instructions for departure. Songs played a significant role in the activities of the Underground Railroad. Frederick Douglass, whose first plans for escape in 1835 failed, later wrote about the songs he and his fellow slaves sang during the period they were plotting the escape:[52]

> We were, at times, remarkably bouyant, singing hymns and making joyous exclamations, almost as triumphant in their tone as if we had reached a land of freedom and safety. A keen observer might have detected in our repeated singing of
>
> > "O Canaan, sweet Canaan,
> > I am bound for the land of Canaan,"
>
> something more than a hope of reaching heaven. We meant to reach the *north*— and the north was our Canaan.

Douglass wrote also about another song that inspired him to escape from slavery:

> "I thought I heard them say,
> There were lions in the way,
> I don't expect to stay
> > Much longer here.

[52]Douglass, *My Bondage,* p. 87.

> Run to Jesus—shun the danger—
> I don't expect to stay
> Much longer here."

was a favorite air, and had a double meaning. In the lips of some, it meant the expectation of a speedy summons to a world of spirits; but in the lips of *our* company, it simply meant, a speedy pilgrimage toward a free state, and deliverance from all the evils and dangers of slavery.

The purpose of some songs was to alert the slaves that a "conductor" was on the way. Many conductors made trip after trip into the South to personally lead caravans of slaves off the plantations, the white operators posing as slaveholders, slave traders, peddlers, or anyone else they thought could gain the confidence of slaveowners. One of the leading conductors of the organization was the ex-slave Harriet Tubman (1820?–1913), called the "black Moses of her race." After escaping from slavery herself, she made innumerable trips back into the South to help others to escape. It is said that she always used a special song to disclose her presence to the slaves:

> Dark and thorny is de pathway
> Where de pilgrim makes his ways;
> But beyond dis vale of sorrow
> Lie de fields of endless days.

When the slaves heard this song, whether or not they could see the singer, they knew that their "Moses" had come after them, and they would begin to make preparations for leaving.[53]

Those who were left behind would have been consoled by such songs as *Bound to Go* or *Members, Don't Get Weary*. Many of the old songs that the slaves had been singing for years must have been sung with special meaning when an escape plot was in the air. Such songs as *Steal Away to Jesus; Swing Low, Sweet Chariot; Brother Moses Gone to de Promised Land; I Hear from Heaven To-Day; Good News, de Chariot's Coming; Oh, Sinner, You'd Better Get Ready;* and numbers of others with similar texts undoubtedly served as "alerting" songs. Then there were songs that served as "maps," the best known of which was *Follow the Drinkin' Gourd,* which directed the fugitives to always travel in the direction of the Big Dipper.[54]

It is possible that when an escape plot was in the air, traditional songs were provided with parody verses specifically stating meeting places and departure times. No such versions survive, however. Most of the records of the Underground Railroad activities were systematically and carefully destroyed, and understandably so, for the penalties of discovery were too great to risk taking chances.

---

[53]Sarah Bradford, *Harriet, the Moses of Her People* (New York, 1886), p. 37.
[54]For other versions of this song, which is in public domain, and discussion of its possible origin, see H. B. Parks, "Follow the Drinking Gourd," *Publications of the Texas Folk Lore Society* 7, ed. by J. Frank Dobie (Austin, 1928), pp. 81–84.

Follow the Drinkin' Gourd, traditional

Fol-low ____ the drink-in' gourd! Fol-low ____ the
drink-in' gourd. _ For the old man is a-wait-in' for to
car-ry you to free-dom If you fol-low the drink - in' gourd. When the
sun comes back and the first quail calls, _ Fol-low ____ the
drink-in' gourd, _ For the old man is a-wait-in' for to
car-ry you to free-dom if you fol-low the drink - in' gourd.

MUSIC OF THE BLACK CHURCH, II

For the first decades of the nineteenth century, the black churches provided not only religious guidance but also the greatest opportunities for fellowship and education among black folk. After 1820, however, the enactment in most southern states of stringent laws (designed to control the movement of black people more closely) sharply curtailed religious and other group activities. Southerners had been greatly upset by the Gabriel Prosser conspiracy in 1800 at Richmond, Virginia, and the Denmark Vesey revolt in 1822 at Charleston, South Carolina. When the next decade brought about an even larger and more destructive insurrection, the Nat Turner revolt of 1831 in Virginia, the South strengthened the Black Codes everywhere, and an unprecedented period of harassment began for black men and women.

Since some whites believed black Methodists to have had a hand in the Vesey plot, the brunt of the attack on black institutions fell upon the AME Church, which found continuation of its work impossible; many of its preachers moved North. Bishop Daniel Payne, for example, had been teaching at a school for free black folk in Charleston, but was forced to leave that city in 1834. Particularly affected by the move was Charleston, a stronghold of independent black Methodism. Black preachers of other denominations were either discouraged from preaching or forbidden outright. The formal religious life of the black southerner in cities came under the control of whites, who generally handled it indifferently. Sometimes Negroes were allowed to sit in segregated pews or on the floors of white churches; sometimes special services were held for them, before or after the regular services for whites. Most often, Negroes did not go to church at all.

These practices continued until after the Civil War. In many southern urban areas black men and women took refuge in secret meetings. While there is no direct evidence as to the effect of all of this on religious music in the South, there can be little doubt that in their secret religious meetings they turned away from Protestant psalms and hymns, in favor of music more responsive to their special needs—that is, to songs of their own creation. More than one preacher, black and white, felt it necessary to reprove them for "outlandish" religious practices.

Music Instruction in Sabbath Schools

Sabbath schools provided one of the few opportunities for black folk of all ages to meet together in educational pursuits. In some urban churches Negroes were taught hymns and psalms; in exceptional instances they actually studied psalmody. There was, to be sure, great danger in all of this; a Charleston law of 1800, for example, gave the police authority to "break down gates or windows" in dispersing groups gathered together "for the purpose of mental instruction of the blacks." Nevertheless, such instruction continued, even after Negro church activities were curtailed by the authorities. Frederick Douglass, like other black leaders, held Sabbath school classes in the home of a free black man in Baltimore, Maryland, with the express purpose of teaching his forty scholars of all ages to read.

The white minister Charles Colcock Jones of Savannah, Georgia, had very strong convictions about the importance of music in religious instruction for the black worshiper and devoted several passages to the subject in his book *The Religious Instruction of the Negroes in the United States* (1842). He stated that not only should scholars be taught psalms and hymns, but they should be taught "how to sing them." Jones recommended highly some of the hymns of Dr. Watts; for example, *There Is a God Who Reigns Above, I'm Not Ashamed to Own My Lord,* and *When I Can Read My Title Clear.* Included among the hymns written by other writers he recommended was the popular *Blow Ye the Trumpet, Blow.*

Significantly, Jones wanted black folk to learn psalms and hymns so that they would desist from singing songs of their own creation:

> One great advantage in teaching them good psalms and hymns, is that they are thereby induced to lay aside the extravagant and nonsensical chants, and catches and hallelujah songs of their own composing; and when they sing, which is very

often while about their business or of an evening in their houses, they will have something profitable to sing.[55]

Jones's attitude corresponded with that of most white preachers and missionaries during the nineteenth century—and of some black preachers too. Negroes were reproved for their love of music and dancing, to the degree that when they joined the church they gave up dancing and "fiddle-sings," singing only psalms and hymns. When the Swedish traveler Fredrika Bremer asked some slaves in South Carolina to sing their own folksongs for her, she was informed that they " 'dwelt with the Lord,' and sang only hymns."

Many a traveler and local historian commented upon the psalm and hymn singing of city slaves in the South. In Richmond, for example, the singing of the slaves who worked in the tobacco factories was a special attraction of the city. Historian Mordecai observed:

> Many of the negroes, male and female, employed in the factories, have acquired such skill in psalmody and have generally such fine voices, that it is a pleasure to listen to the sacred music with which they beguile the hours of labour. Besides the naturally fine voice and ear for music which seems to have been given to the black race . . . many of the slaves in Richmond have acquired some knowledge of music by note, and may be seen, even in the factories, with their books of psalmody open on the work-bench.[56]

SONGS ON THE WATERFRONT

As a group, the most musical black folk of the antebellum period may well have been the men working on the waters and waterfronts of the United States—on the eastern seaboard, the Gulf Coast, the Mississippi River and its two big tributaries, the Missouri and the Ohio. Negroes were employed as stevedores on the wharfs and on the levees; they loaded cargos, fired engines, and worked in food services on the boats that plied back and forth between waterfront cities. In many instances they also served as entertainers, providing shows of the vaudeville type for the boat passengers at the end of the day's labor and music for dancing afterward. Stevedores always sang as they worked. The black writer Martin Delany commented upon their songs in *Blake: or the Huts of America* (1859):

> In the distance, on the levee and in the harbor among the steamers, the songs of the boatmen were incessant. Every few hours landing, loading and unloading, the glee of these men of sorrow was touchingly appropriate and impressive. . . . If there is any class of men anywhere to be found whose sentiments of song and words of lament are made to reach the sympathies of others, the black slave-

---

[55]Charles C. Jones, *Religious Instruction of the Negroes* (Savannah, GA, 1842), p. 265.
[56]Mordecai, *Richmond*, p. 27.

"Scene on a Mississippi Steamer." From an engraving, "The Parting Song," by A. R. Waud, *Harper's Weekly,* 1867.

boatmen are that class . . . they are seemingly contented by soothing their sorrows with songs apparently cheerful, but in reality wailing lamentations.[57]

Nineteenth-century literature is replete with references to the singing of the black watermen and anecdotes about their behavior. The stevedore and roustabout songs reflected the lifestyle of the singers, and their texts often were unprintable. One of the oldest roustabout song texts on record is the following, heard in the Philadelphia area about 1800:

> Nancy Bohannan, she married a barber,
> Shave her away, shave her away;
> He shaved all he could, he couldn't shave harder,
> Shave her away, shave her away.[58]

Beginning in the 1830s song collectors began to write down the songs, but accounts written before the Civil War typically include only descriptions of performance practice and song texts. In 1853 Fredrika Bremer was particularly impressed, for example, by the singing of black firemen on board the Mississippi River steamer *Belle Key.* As the firemen flung wood into the engine fires:

> . . . the Negro up aloft on the pile of fire-wood began immediately an improvised song in stanzas, and at the close of each [stanza] the Negroes down below joined

[57]Martin Delany, *Blake,* ed. by Floyd J. Miller (Boston, 1970), p. 100.
[58]Scharf, *History of Philadelphia,* v. 2, p. 931.

in vigorous chorus. . . . They, amid their . . . fantastic song, keeping time most exquisitely, hurled one piece of fire-wood after another into the yawning fiery gulf.[59]

Some song collectors of the period were uncomfortably aware that they might be missing some exotic song materials in devoting so much time to the collecting of spirituals and plantation songs. An anonymous "gentleman of Delaware" emphasized this point in 1867:

> We must look among their non-religious songs for the purest specimens of negro minstrelsy. . . . Some of the best *pure negro* songs I have ever heard were those that used to be sung by the black stevedores, or perhaps the crews themselves, of the West India vessels, loading and unloading at the wharves in Philadelphia and Baltimore. I have stood for more than an hour, often, listening to them, as they hoisted and lowered the hogsheads and boxes of their cargoes; one man taking the burden of the song (and the slack of the rope) and the others striking in with the chorus. They would sing in this way more than a dozen different songs in an hour . . . generally rather innocent and proper in their language, and strangely attractive in their music; and with a volume of voice that reached a square or two away. . . .[60]

When Lafcadio Hearn, a white journalist, went to Cincinnati in 1869 he found that more than two-thirds of the stevedores and longshoremen there were black. He was fascinated by their roustabout songs, which obviously had a long history, and wrote down the texts of several. One of the "most melancoly of these plaintive airs" was *O Let Her Go By.*

> I'm going away to New Orleans,
> Good-bye, my love, good-bye;
> I'm going away to New Orleans,
> Good-bye, my love, good-bye;
> O let her go by.
>
> She's on her way to New Orleans,
> Good-bye, my love, good-bye;
> She's bound to pass the Robert E. Lee,
> Good-bye, my love, good-bye;
> O let her go by.
>
> I'll make this trip and I'll make no more,
> Good-bye, my love, good-bye;
> I'll roll these barrels and I'll roll no more,
> Good-bye, my love, good-bye;
> O let her go by.
>
> An' if you are not true to me,
> Farewell, my lover, forever;
> An' if you are not true to me,

[59]Bremer, *Homes,* v. 2, p. 174.
[60]Allen, *Slave Songs,* p. vii.

> Farewell, my lover, forever;
> O let her go by.[61]

On shore the stevedores and boatmen found amusement and comradeship in waterfront shacks, dives, and "dance halls" where the music was similar to that heard in the "Five Points" cafés in the city of New York. Although few chroniclers seem to have ventured into these waterfront hangouts until after the Civil War, the curious who began to explore such spots in the 1870s and 1880s found well-established traditions of distinctive African-American song and dance.

Black watermen carried their special worksongs, along with other kinds of Negro folksongs, up and down the rivers—from Wheeling, West Virginia, and Cincinnati on the Ohio River; from Omaha, Nebraska, Kansas City and St. Louis on the Missouri River; to the towns on the Mississippi itself, Cairo, Illinois, Memphis, Tennessee; and finally, to New Orleans. The same songs or similar ones could be heard on the Gulf Coast in Mobile, Alabama; and on the Atlantic coast in Savannah, Georgia; Charleston, South Carolina; Norfolk, Virginia; and in northern ports. The watermen were truly itinerant musicians, and may have been responsible, more than any other single force, for the spread of Negro folksongs from one community to another, white as well as black.

[61]Lafcadio Hearn, "Levee Life," the *Cincinnati Commercial* (March 17, 1876): 2; reprint in *The Selected Writings of Lafcadio Hearn*, ed. Henry Goodman (New York, 1949).

CHAPTER 5

Antebellum
Rural
Life

A T the beginning of the nineteenth century the vast majority of slaves in
the United States lived on plantations in the South. The slave population had increased rapidly since the time of the first United States
census enumeration in 1790 from somewhat fewer than 700,000 to
3,953,760 in 1860. Although slaves were generally concentrated in the
lower southern states on plantations where such crops as cotton and rice
were produced on a large scale, only about one quarter of the whites in
the South were slaveholders. Of this group fewer than 15 per cent owned
plantations with more than twenty slaves. In essence, the majority of slaves
belonged to small planters and lived on plantations where their numbers
ranged from two or three to about fifteen.

PRIMARY SOURCES OF INFORMATION

There is a variety of sources from which can be drawn information that
gives us insight into slave life on the plantation. Black Americans themselves
left slave narratives, fiction that includes realistic scenes of slave life, journals, histories, personal writings, and articles in newspapers and periodicals.
Travelers from Europe wrote at great length about the new nation in their
journals and diaries, frequently offering the kind of detail that was overlooked by both black and white Americans. Then there were northerners
who traveled in the South for the first time and found much there of the
strange and exotic to comment upon, as well as northerners who took up

residence in the South for short or long periods of time. There were southern slaveholders and other apologists for slavery who left written records; there were those who were against slavery and wrote about it; and there were the missionaries to the slaves, who represented a special viewpoint, whether anti- or pro-slavery.

THE MUSICAL SOURCES

By the time of the Civil War the music of black folk in the United States had developed its own characteristic style. As we have pointed out, white observers had begun to notice differences between African-style music and European music as early as 1637. They revealed this awareness by the kinds of observations they made—by the things that caught their attention and by the things they left unsaid. The early writers spoke largely about performance practice—about concepts of sound, instruments, and the black folks' attitude toward music making. While the writers were vaguely aware that the music itself was different, they were unable to explain its divergencies and, unfortunately, did not preserve any of the music.

Later observers paid closer attention to what they saw and heard. They jotted down the words of songs, remarked on how they were sung, described in detail the body movements of dancers and workers, commented upon the instruments used, how the instruments were constructed and how played. Finally came the song collectors, who patiently listened to the "weird and barbaric madrigals" or "sweet, impressive melodies" and attempted to record them in European musical notation.

Few of these people were professional musicians, however, and errors were inevitably made in the process of transcribing.

It must be remembered, too, that their work was accomplished without the aid of the phonograph, an indispensable item of equipment for the modern-day folksong collector. Moreover, they rarely had the opportunity to hear a song performed several times in succession; they were required to "catch the tune" the first time, for the same song, if sung a day later or by a different person, would have been altered—sometimes beyond recognition.

Isolated examples of slave-song texts began to appear in periodicals and books early in the nineteenth century. As early as 1800 some listeners were able to catch and write down refrains they heard in the slave songs, and during the 1830s came the earliest attempt to notate the music of the improvised songs. But it was not until 1867 that the first collection of plantation songs appeared in print, *Slave Songs of the United States,* edited by William Allen, Charles Ware, and Lucy McKim Garrison. In addition to the songs they themselves found, the editors drew upon the private collections of their friends, particularly those who worked among the ex-slaves in the Sea Islands of South Carolina and Georgia during the 1860s. This important, historic anthology will serve as the primary source of information in our discussion of the slave songs.

Because of the relatively large number of these songs published during the nineteenth century, it is possible to discuss their texts and musical features with some degree of authority. Besides the 1867 collection, the repertory of the Fisk Jubilee Singers and the Hampton Students was published in the last quarter of the century; from time to time there appeared other collections. All in all, the slave-song repertory recorded in musical notation during the nineteenth century comprises no fewer than six hundred songs.[1] Whether or not they were aware of it, the first American collectors of black folksongs were a part of the same nationalistic movement that swept over Europe in the nineteenth century. Political nationalism had its musical counterpart, and one of its concerns was the collection and codification of the national folklore heritage of a country.

During the same period that some Americans were collecting slave melodies, other collectors were tracking down the folk music of British origin in the United States—notably, Francis Child, a professor at Harvard University, and the Englishman Cecil Sharp. In Europe folklorists began exploring their folk roots as early as 1742, when the first volume of a genuine collection of folk songs, *Ancient British Music,* was published by John Parry and Ivan Williams. By the mid-nineteenth century the folklore-collection movement was well on its way. For their part, nationalist composers consciously employed folksongs or folksong idioms in their music or wrote music in the spirit of folk music.

DAILY LIFE ON THE PLANTATION

Life on the plantation was highly organized socially with several ranks within the system, except on the smallest plantations. At the top, of course, was the slaveholder and his family; just below, the overseer. Typically, the overseer had the responsibility for managing the plantation, although in some instances he shared this responsibility with the slaveholder. The overseer's assistant, called a "driver," was a slave (there might be several drivers), who looked after the details of management, helped to train new slaves, and performed a myriad of other supervisory tasks about the plantation. Because the nature of his duties often forced him into brutality along with the whites, in some places he was as much dreaded by slaves as the overseer, despite his status. The slaves most respected on the plantation were the artisans, craftsmen, carpenters, bricklayers, and other skilled laborers, along with the religious leaders—the preacher and / or exhorter.

---

[1]This estimated figure includes songs published in periodicals, fiction, and nonfiction, in addition to the several collections of slave songs published during the last quarter of the century.

Below this group in social position were the house servants and the coachman. On a small plantation, however, house servants might be part-time workers who spent the remainder of their time in the fields. Finally, at the bottom of the social hierarchy, were the field hands, who comprised the majority of the slaves.

Just as the facts of social rank were firmly established in the minds of the slaves, so were the routines of daily life.[2] Slaves went to work at dawn, awakened in some places by the blowing of the conch horn, and toiled until sundown, whether they lived on cotton, rice, sugar cane, tobacco, or any other kind of plantation. A traveler in Virginia in the eighteenth century observed:

> The Negro is called up about daybreak, and is seldom allowed time enough to swallow three mouthfuls of homminy, or hoe-cake, but is driven out immediately to the field of hard labor . . . the noon meal . . . [consists of] homminy and salt and, if his master be a man of humanity, he has a little fat, skimmed milk, rusty bacon or salt herring to relish his homminy or hoecake. . . . They then return to severe labour . . . until dusk in the evening, when they repair to the tobacco-houses, where each has his task in stripping alloted him, which employs him some hours. . . . It is late at night before he returns to his second scanty meal.[3]

The routines varied little from place to place. Food rations, too, were surprisingly similar throughout the South: a peck of corn and a pint of salt with two or three pounds of salt pork on some plantations. Here and there were slaveholders who prided themselves on giving their slaves fresh meat occasionally, and in some places slaves were able to supplement their meager diets by hunting and fishing, growing vegetables in the tiny plots around their cabins, and "filching" food from the "big house." Generally, however, "ole missus" kept the food stores locked and carried the keys on her person.

Depending upon the kind of work to be done, slaves toiled either in "gangs," supervised by overseers or drivers or even the planters themselves, or under the "task system," wherein individuals had to complete a certain amount of work each day. Under both systems the lash was heavily used to get as much work as possible from the slaves, even under the most lenient of masters. The lash failed to distinguish between men and women, old and young, sick and well, healthy adolescents and pregnant mothers; it provided the answers to most of the slaveholder's problems. And if, during the course of the whippings, a slave was beaten to death—as happened again and

---

[2]Documentation for the facts of slave life is available in the hundreds of slave narratives published in book format during the nineteenth century, as well as the immense collection deposited in the Library of Congress Slave Narrative Collection. In recent years a multivolume collection of these narratives has been published by George P. Rawick, gen. ed., *The American Slave: A Composite Autobiography* (Westport, CT, 1977–79), 48 vols. including Supplement, Series 1; Supplement, Series 2.

[3]John F. D. Smyth, *A Tour in the United States of America* (London, 1784), v. 1, p. 46.

again—the system itself protected slaveholders from prosecution, even where murders were witnessed by people other than slaves.

Sundays brought a break in the monotonous routines of daily life where planters exempted their slaves from work; in some places, slaves were also given Saturday afternoon off. In addition, Christmas and Easter typically brought longer periods of respite from work, from one or two days to as much as a week. Finally, the nature of the work itself often dictated interruptions in daily routines—or, at least a change of activities—as, for example, in the fall when crops had to be harvested. To be sure, there were some slaves who arranged for their own furloughs, making excursions at night to neighboring plantations to visit family members or loved ones, attend religious meetings, or simply to dance and make merry.

It was important, however, that slaves leaving the plantation without passes should evade the patrols, or the "pattyrollers," as the slaves called them. Especially organized to enforce the Black Codes, the patrol systems in the South were strengthened after each slave insurrection and particularly after the Nat Turner rebellion in 1831. Composed of local whites, the patrols had the authority to challenge slaves (and free blacks as well) caught without passes and to break up their assemblages. Needless to say, the patrols could not prevent the slaves from moving about without permission but only caused them to move with greater caution. They became familiar with all the bypaths and crosscuts in the areas surrounding their plantations and learned how to use the stars as a guide at night, the time of their greatest wanderings.

Tragic events occurred all too frequently to break the monotony of everyday routines. Most dreaded of all by the slaves was the separation of families when the slaveholder decided to sell some of his slaves. This might happen for any number of reasons: a slave became too obstreperous to handle, the master needed money, or a master's death left slaves to be divided among his heirs. Since it was the general practice not to inform slaves of impending sales, they were often caught unawares, which only served to deepen their grief. Although sales might take place privately as well as publicly, the traditional day for slave auctions was January 1; the slaves called it "Heartbreak Day."

Death of course also brought separations to the slave community. The "burying" generally was a hasty event that took place at night within twenty-four hours of the death. Family and friends might sit up all night mourning the deceased in prayer and song, but they were expected to be about their work at daybreak as usual. Some time later—from a few days to as much as six months—at a time convenient for the master, a proper funeral would be held to memorialize the deceased. It was not uncommon for several persons to be so eulogized at the memorial service. This practice was not wholly a reflection of what was expedient for the master but undoubtedly also pointed back to African traditions.

Burial rites occupy an integral position in West African societies because

"A Negro Funeral in Virginia." From a drawing by A. B. Frost, *Harper's Weekly, 1880.*

of the importance of ancestor veneration in their religions. Not only must proper attention be given to the interment of the deceased but also to the canonization funerary ceremonies, called "second burial" in some societies, that follow at a later time. The fact that vestiges of this tradition lingered on among the slaves is indicated by some of their practices; for example, in many places they distinguished between the two kinds of rites, calling the first a "burying" and the second, "the funeral." As in Africa, there was a time lapse between the two ceremonies.[4]

SONGS OF NARRATION AND SOCIAL COMMENT

Music was a primary form of communication for the slaves, just as it had been for their African forebears. Through the medium of song the slaves could comment on their problems and savor the few pleasures allowed them; they could voice their despair and hopes, and assert their humanity in an environment that constantly denied their humanness. As in the African tradition, the songs of the slaves could tell their history and reveal their everyday concerns. Slaves sang of the passes needed in order to move about and of the dangers of getting caught.

> Hurrah for good old massa,
> He give me the pass to go to the city;
> Hurray for good old missus,

[4]African-style funeral rites are discussed in many places; see, for example, Albert J. Raboteau, *Slave Religion* (New York, 1978).

> She boil the pot and give me the licker [that is, the juices];
> Hurrah, I'm going to the city.[5]

If passes were not forthcoming, then one had to watch sharply for the patrols. One of the most widely dispersed pattyroller songs was:

> Run, nigger, run, the patty-roller catch you,
> Run, nigger, run, for it's almost day;
> Massa was kind and Missus was true,
> But if you don't mind, the patty-roller catch you.

Sometimes the songs were merely cries in the field—"cornfield hollers," "cottonfield hollers," "whoops," or "water calls." A slave's call or cry could mean any one of a number of things: a call for water, food, or help, a call to let others know where he or she was working, or simply a cry of loneliness, sorrow, or happiness. One cry might be answered by another from a place far distant. In 1853 a traveler in South Carolina described such a cry:

> Suddenly one [a slave] raised such a sound as I had never heard before, a long, loud musical shout, rising and falling, and breaking into falsetto, his voice ringing through the woods in the clear frosty night air, like a bugle call. As he finished, the melody was caught up by another, and then, another, and then, by several in chorus.[6]

Death was a constant companion, and the slaves sang about it, too.

I Know Moonlight, from *Slave Songs of the United States*

> I know moon-light, I know star-light; I lay dis bod-y down.

> 2. I walk in de moonlight, I walk in de starlight;
>   I lay dis body down.
> 3. I know de graveyard, I know de graveyard,
>   When I lay dis body down.

The tragic tale of the father or mother sold away from loved ones was recounted again and again in the song literature:[7]

Sold Off to Georgy, from Hungerford

> 1. Fare - well, fel - low sar - vants! O - ho! O - ho! I'm

---

[5]Brown, *Southern Home,* p. 96.
[6]Frederick Law Olmsted, *Journey in the Seaboard Slave States* . . . (New York, 1856), v. 2, p. 19.
[7]James Hungerford, *The Old Plantation* . . . (New York, 1859); reprint of passages about music in *RBAM,* pp. 71–81. See p. 73 for boat song.

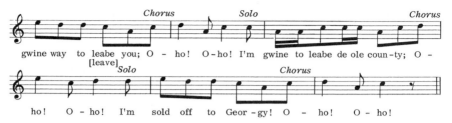

gwine way to leabe you; O - ho! O-ho! I'm gwine to leabe de ole coun-ty; O -
[leave]
ho! O - ho! I'm sold off to Geor-gy! O - ho! O - ho!

2. Farewell, ole plantation, (Oho! Oho!)
   Farewell, de ole quarter, (Oho! Oho!)
   Un daddy, un mammy, (Oho! Oho!)
   Un master, un missus! (Oho! Oho!)
3. My dear wife un one chile, (Oho! Oho!)
   My poor heart is breaking; (Oho! Oho!)
   No more shall I see you, (Oho! Oho!)
   Oh, no more foreber! (Oho! Oho!)

I'm Gwine to Alamby, from *Slave Songs of the United States*

1. I'm gwine to A - la - ba-my, Oh _____
For to see my mam-my, Ah _____

2. She went from Ole Virginny,—Oh,
   And I'm her pickaninny,—Ah.
3. She lives on the Tombigbee,—Oh,
   I wish I had her wid me,—Ah.
4. Now I'm a good big nigger,—Oh,
   I reckon I won't git bigger,—Ah.
5. But I'd like to see my mammy,—Oh,
   Who lives in Alabamy,—Ah.

Many a traveler commented upon the "wild hymns of sweet and mournful melody" sung by men and women of the slave coffles on the long journey from "Virginny" into the lower South. Gathered together into groups that sometimes numbered in the hundreds, slaves were handcuffed, two by two, and attached to a long chain that ran down the center of the double file. Men on horseback accompanied the coffles, wielding long whips to "goad the reluctant and weary," and fiddlers among the slaves were forced to play on their instruments. Thus the grim procession took on the bizarre aspect of a nightmarish parade. And the slaves sang about this too.

See these poor souls from Africa
Transported to America:

The Coffle Gang. "There is not a village or road that does not behold the sad procession of manacled outcasts, whose chains and mournful countenances tell that they are exiled by force from all that their hearts hold dear." From George Carleton, *The Suppressed Book about Slavery,* 1864.

> We are stolen and sold to Georgia, will you go along with me?
> We are stolen and sold to Georgia, go sound the jubilee.
>
> See wives and husbands sold apart,
> The children's screams!—it breaks my heart;
> There's a better day a-coming, will you go along with me?
> There's a better day a-coming, go sound the jubilee.
>
> O gracious Lord! When shall it be
> That we poor souls shall all be free?
> Lord, break them Slavery powers—will you go along with me?
> Lord, break them Slavery powers, go sound the jubilee.
>
> Dear Lord! Dear Lord! When Slavery'll cease,
> Then we poor souls can have our peace;
> There's a better day a-coming, will you go along with me?
> There's a better day a-coming, go sound the jubilee.[8]

It was common practice to force slaves to sing and dance under the most tragic of circumstances. Just as on the slave ships the captured Africans were made to dance and sing during their "airings" on deck, so in the slave pens of the States, they often had to sing and dance before being put up for sale on the auction block.

There was usually a slave fiddler available to play for such dancing— often one of the slaves who, himself, was up for sale. Solomon Northup described his experience as follows:

[8]The text of the song appears in several sources; see, for example, William Wells Brown, *The Anti-Slavery Harp* . . . (Boston, 1849), p. 29.

[The] keeper of the slave pen in New-Orleans, was out among his animals early in the morning. With an occasional kick of the older men and women, and many a sharp crack of the whip about the ears of the younger slaves, it was not long before they were all astir, and wide awake. . . . In the first place we were required to wash thoroughly, and those with beards, to shave. We were then furnished with a new suit each, cheap, but clean. . . . During the day he exercised us in the art of "looking smart," and of moving to our places with exact precision.

After being fed, in the afternoon, we were again paraded and made to dance. Bob, a colored boy, who had some time belonged to Freeman, played on the violin. Standing near him, I made bold to inquire if he could play the "Virginia Reel." He answered he could not, and asked me if I could play. Replying in the affirmative he handed me the violin. I struck up a tune, and finished it. Freeman ordered me to continue playing, and seemed well pleased, telling Bob that I far excelled him—a remark that seemed to grieve my musical companion very much.[9]

Frequently a song summed up all the things the slaves most hated, from a relatively minor irritation, such as having the mistress demand a personal service at the end of an exhausting day, to the dreaded "laying on" of a hundred lashes when a slave failed to meet his work quota.

Dere's No Rain, from *Slave Songs of the United States*

Dere's no rain to wet you. O yes, I want to go home, Want to go home.

2. Dere's no sun to burn you.—O yes, etc.
3. Dere's no hard trials.
4. Dere's no whips a-crackin'.
5. Dere's no stormy weather.
6. Dere's no tribulation.
7. No more slavery in de kingdom.
8. No evil-doers in de kingdom.
9. All is gladness in de kingdom.

No More Auction Block for Me, from *Slave Songs of the United States*[10]

1. No more auc-tion block for me, No more; no more;

No more auc-tion block for me, ma-ny thou-sand gone.

[9]Northup, *Twelve Years a Slave*; reprint of passages about music in RBAM, pp. 93–102. See p. 96 for quotation.
[10]See also Gustavus D. Pike, *The Jubilee Singers* . . . (Boston, 1873), p. 186.

2. No more peck o' corn for me, &c.
3. No more driver's lash for me, &c.
4. No more pint o' salt for me, &c.
5. No more hundred lash for me, &c.
6. No more mistress' call for me, &c.

WORKSONGS

Singing accompanied all kinds of work, whether it consisted of picking cotton, threshing rice, stripping tobacco, harvesting sugar cane, or simply doing the endless small jobs on the plantation, such as clearing away the underbrush or repairing fences. Music served the double function of alleviating the monotony of the work and, at the same time, spurring workers on to fresh efforts. And many planters recognized the importance of using a song leader to obtain the maximum amount of work from a gang. Sometimes these leaders were even excused from labor so that they could devote all their energies to the singing, or they were given extra rewards as incentives.

Masters and overseers everywhere generally encouraged slaves to sing as they worked; ex-slave Frederick Douglass reported:

> Slaves are generally expected to sing as well as to work. A silent slave is not liked by masters or overseers. *"Make a noise"* and *"bear a hand,"* are the words usually addressed to the slaves when there is silence amongst them. This may account for the almost constant singing heard in the southern states. There was, generally, more or less singing among the teamsters, as it was one means of letting the overseer know where they were, and that they were moving on with the work.[11]

But the singing of mournful songs was discouraged; as one planter explained:

> When at work I have no objection to their whistling or singing some lively tune, but no *drawling* tunes are allowed in the field, for their motions are almost certain to keep time with the music.[12]

A different type of song was that of the lone workers as they went about the assignment of mending a fence or building a barn or cooking a meal. With no necessity for coordinating their work movements with others, their songs could take on the nature of deeply personal utterances. Tempo, text, melody—all these things reflected their moods of the moment. If they felt gay, their fingers flew and a worksong cheered all who might be listening; if they felt melancholy, the same song might be sung so mournfully as to slow up activity and to depress all within hearing.

[11]Douglass, *My Bondage;* reprint of passages about music in RBAM, pp. 82–87. See p. 83 for quotation.
[12]"Management of Negroes," *DeBow's Review* 10 (March 1851): 328.

A plantation's repertory of worksongs developed according to the kinds of work performed by the slaves. Work in the fields called for coordinated movements, as a song collector pointed out in 1868:[13]

> Long ago, when the mowing-machine and reaper were as yet unthought of, it was not uncommon to see, in a Kentucky harvestfield, fifteen or twenty "cradlers" swinging their brawny arms in unison as they cut the ripened grain, and moving with the regulated cadence of the leader's song. The scene repeated the poet's picture of ancient oarsmen and the chanter seated high above the rowers, keeping time with staff and voice, blending into one impulse the banks of the trireme.
>
> For such a song strong emphasis of rhythm was, of course, more important than words. Each mower kept his stroke and measured his stride by musical intervals. A very favorite song for these harvesting occasions commenced thus:

Rise Up In Due Time, from John Mason Brown

During a woodcutting song hundreds of slaves, paired off in twos in front of the trees, marked "the blows by the song":

> A cold frosty morning,
> The niggers feeling good,
> Take your ax upon your shoulder,
> Nigger, talk to the wood.

Corn songs were sure to be included in any plantation repertory; since the peck of corn was a staple item of the slave's diet, they were all concerned with that crop regardless of what was raised on the plantation where they lived. Songs intended to aid in the coordination of movements fall into a different category from songs describing the work, which were intended for singing in social context. The following is an example of the former:[14]

Roun' de Corn, Sally, from Hungerford

[13] John Mason Brown, "Songs of the Slave," *Lippincott's Magazine* 2 (December 1868); reprint in KATZ, pp. 23–30. See p. 27 for quotation and worksong, *Rise Up in Due Time.*
[14] Hungerford, *The Old Plantation,* p. 75.

Chorus — Roun' de corn, Sal - ly! Solo — Hoo-ray, hoo-ray, ho! Chorus — Roun' de corn, Sal - ly!

Solo — Hoo - ray for all de lub - ly la - dies! Chorus — Roun' de corn, Sal - ly! Fine

Solo — Dis lub's er thing dat's sure to hab you, Chorus — Roun' de corn, Sal - ly!

Solo — He hole you tight, when once he grab you, Chorus — Roun' de corn, Sal - ly!

Solo — Un ole un ug - ly, young un prit - ty, Chorus — Roun' de corn, Sal - ly!

Solo — You need - en try when once he git you, Chorus — Roun' de corn, Sal - ly! D.C.

> 2. Dere's Mr. Travers lub Miss Jinny;
> He thinks she is us good us any.
> He comes from church wid her er Sunday,
> Un don't go back ter town till Monday.
> Hooray, hooray, ho! etc.

All over the rural South the population—whites as well as blacks, and particularly the white small planters and common laborers—looked forward to such work festivals as log rolling, hog killing, corn shucking (corn-husking), and rice threshing to give some respite from the heavy labor of everyday life and to bring some brightness into the monotony of existence. On such occasions it was the custom of the people in a community to gather at one plantation, the planters coming in from miles around and bringing with them their slaves. The work to be done was then tackled by the entire group and followed by feasting and dancing.

Paine provides vivid descriptions of the corn-shucking jubilees that involved small planters and their slaves in Georgia:

> A farmer will haul up from his field a pile of corn from ten to twenty rods long, from ten to twenty feet wide, and ten feet high. . . . It is so arranged that this can be on a moonlight evening. The farmer then gives a general "invite" to all the young ladies and gentlemen in the neighborhood, to come and bring their slaves; for it takes no small number to shuck such a pile of corn. . . .
>
> The guests begin to arrive about dark, and in a short time, they can be heard in all directions, singing the plantation songs, as they come to the scene of action.

When they have all arrived, the Host makes the following propositions to his company, "You can shuck the pile, or work till eleven o'clock, or divide the pile and the hands, and try a race."

The last offer is generally accepted. Each party selects two of the shrewdest and best singers among the slaves, to mount the pile and sing, while all join in the chorus. The singers also act the part of sentinels, to watch the opposite party—for it is part of the game for each party to try to throw corn on the other's pile.[15]

Singing was essential to the success of the evening. No huge work project was successfully tackled at a jubilee without singing, whether shucking corn, rolling logs, or threshing rice. Mallard, in recalling the rice frolics on his plantation, thought first of the singing of the workers:

The dirt floor is beaten hard and swept clean and the sheaves of golden rice arranged upon it side by side. And now the stalwart laborers, with their hickory flails, beat off the heads of grain from the yellow straw. . . . The rhythmical beat of the numerous flails is accompanied by a recitative and improvised song of endless proportions, led by one musical voice, all [the others] joining in the chorus, and can be heard a mile.[16]

There are numerous references in the sources to the singing of the slaves as they marched along the roads leading to the site of the work jubilee. The slaves assembled from plantations as far as six to eight miles away and merged into large gangs as they met on the road. Their "rich deep voices," which could be heard for miles around, would swell out in a huge roar as the singers came in on the refrains of the song.

Ex-slave William Wells Brown cites the following as an example of a "marching" corn song sung in 1820 as the slaves marched down the road to the site of the corn-shucking festival:

> All them pretty gals will be there,
> Shuck that corn before you eat;
> They will fix it for us rare,
> Shuck that corn before you eat.
> I know that supper will be big,
> Shuck that corn before you eat;
> I think I smell a fine roast pig,
> Shuck that corn before you eat. . . .[17]

Perhaps even more common than the corn songs were the songs of the boatmen. The boat or canoe was the prevalent mode of transportation in the South, and few travelers failed to comment on the plaintive, melancholy singing of the boatmen as they "kept time and tune to their oars with extem-

---

[15]Lewis W. Paine, *Six Years in a Georgia Prison* (New York, 1851); reprint in RBAM, pp. 88–92. See p. 90 for quotation.
[16]Robert Q. Mallard, *Plantation Life before Emancipation* (Richmond, 1892), pp. 21–22.
[17]Brown, *Southern Home*, pp. 91–92.

poraneous chants." In Georgia, the English actress Frances Anne Kemble wrote in her diary in 1838:

> My daily voyages up and down the river have introduced me to a great variety of new musical performances of our boatmen. . . . When the rowing is not too hard, they accompany the stroke of their oars with the sound of their voices. . . . The chorus strikes in with the burden [i.e., the refrain], between each phrase of the melody, [which is] chanted by a single voice.[18]

When a Maryland planter complained about the "low-spirited" songs of his boatmen, one of them answered, "De boat-songs is always dat way, marster . . . dat is mo' er less." To his master's request for a "lively little song" that he was singing when "hanging tobacco at the barn," the slave answered, "But dat's a corn song; un we'll hab ter sing it slow ter row to."[19]

The slaves distinguished among song types according to the function of the songs, as in the African tradition, and were concerned that their activities be accompanied by appropriate songs. But there were few hard and fast rules; often it was merely a matter of adjusting the tempo, as one of the editors of the *Slave Songs of the United States* pointed out:

> As the same songs . . . are sung at every sort of work, of course the *tempo* is not always alike. On the water, the oars dip "Poor Rosy" to an even *andante;* a stout boy and girl at the hominy mill will make the same "Poor Rosy" fly, to keep up with the whirling stone; and in the evening, after the day's work is done, "Heab'n shall-a be my home" [the refrain of *Poor Rosy*] peals up slowly and mournfully from the distant quarters.[20]

Poor Rosy, from *Slave Songs of the United States*

[18]Frances Anne Kemble, *Journal of A Residence on a Georgian Plantation* (New York, 1863), p. 218.
[19]Hungerford, *The Old Plantation*, pp. 73–74.
[20]Allen, *Slave Songs*, pp. xxii–xxiii.

2. Got hard trial in my way,
   Heav'n shall-a be my home.
O when I talk, I talk wid God,
   Heav'n shall-a be my home.
3. I dunno what de people want of me,
   Heav'n shall-a be my home.

One old slave, who had seen more than her share of tragedy, said, "I likes 'Poor Rosy' better than all the songs, but it can't be sung without a *full heart and a troubled spirit.*"

Slaves recorded the circumstances of their daily lives in song just as assuredly as if they had kept diaries or written biographies. Obviously, the larger part of the antebellum repertory has been lost, but the reports that have come down to us testify to the powerful role that music played in their lives.

The slaves often sang together as they returned from the fields to their quarters at the end of the day, particularly on plantations where the gang system was in use and all of them would have stopped work at the same time. The songs were carried through the gathering dusk to the ears of the white residents in the big house, conveying a message of hopelessness and despair, even though the words of the songs were unintelligible at so great a distance. Again at night, such songs could be heard coming up from the slave quarters, sung by the tired workers as they sat on their cabin doorsteps or by their cabin fires before going to bed.

"Evening at the Quarters." From an anonymous drawing in *Harper's New Monthly Magazine,* 1887.

"Negro Village on a Southern Plantation." From *Aunt Phillis's Cabin* by Mary H. Eastman, 1852.

RECREATIONAL MUSIC

Slaves spent their Sundays in various ways—tending vegetable plots, caring for their clothes, going to religious services, hunting and fishing, playing games—in short, doing all the things for which they had no time during the week. But their favorite recreational activity was dancing, and few plantations were without a fiddler, at least, to provide the music. Many slaveholders acknowledged the importance of giving their workers regular breaks from the monotonous grind of daily labor and saw to it that appropriate conditions prevailed on weekends. Two articles published in a southern trade journal in 1851 illustrate the slaveholder's viewpoint.[21] A planter of considerable means states:

> I have a good fiddler, and keep him well supplied with catgut, and I make it his duty to play for the Negroes every Saturday night until twelve o'clock. . . . Charley's fiddle is always accompanied with Ihurod on the triangle and Sam to "pat." . . .

A "small planter" admits to having "a fiddle in my quarters, and though some of my good old brethren in church would think hard of me, yet I allow dancing; ay, I buy the fiddle and encourage it. . . ." He would do more if he could afford it:

> [I] would build a house large enough, and use it for a dance house for the young, and those who wished to dance, as well as for prayer meetings, and for church

[21]"Management of Negroes," *DeBow's Review* 10 (June 1851): 625; 11 (October 1851): 372.

on Sunday—making it a rule to be present myself occasionally at both, and my overseer always. I know the rebuke in store about dancing, but I cannot help it. I believe Negroes will be better disposed this way than any other.

The slaves were proud of their dancing prowess and considered the "measured, listless and snail-like steps" of white society cotillions inferior to their own lively reels and jigs. All contemporary accounts of slave dancing emphasize its vigor and vitality. A visitor to Virginia in 1784 observed with amazement that after a day of hard labor the slave, instead of retiring to well-earned rest, walked six or seven miles in the night to the site of a dance, where

> he performs with astonishing ability, and the most vigorous exertions, keeping time and cadence, most exactly, with the music . . . until he exhausts himself, and scarcely has time, or strength, to return home before the hour he is called forth to toil the next morning.[22]

Lewis Paine reports an amusing episode in Georgia when, after a log rolling, masters and slaves had begun dancing at the same time. As the slave musicians became more and more intoxicated with the spirit of the dancing, they played faster and "wilder," until finally the whites could keep up no longer and withdrew from the dancing. This was exactly what the slave dancers desired! They sang out, "Now show de white man what we can do!" and threw themselves with wild abandon into their "frolic."[23]

Dance Music

Slave fiddlers had their own methods for producing "hot" music as the dancing became wilder and more abandoned.

> A boy would stand behind the fiddler with a pair of knitting needles in his hands. From this position the youngster would reach around the fiddler's left shoulder and beat on the strings in the manner of a snare drummer.[24]

The fiddler sang and stomped his feet as he played, the boy handling the needles all the while. An expert fiddler "could stomp the left heel and the right forefoot and alternate this with the right heel and the left forefoot, making four beats to the bar."

Holiday dances were generally all-night affairs. When the fiddler grew tired, the slaves provided a different kind of dance music by "pattin' juba." Basically, this procedure involved foot tapping, hand clapping, and thigh slapping, all in precise rhythm. There seem to have existed, however, a number of ways to accomplish this feat. According to Paine, in Georgia the

---

[22]Smyth, *A Tour,* p. 46.
[23]Paine, *Six Years,* p. 89.
[24]W. C. Handy, *Father of the Blues* (New York, 1941), p. 5.

patter tapped his foot in regular time while he alternately clapped his hands lightly and slapped his thighs. On the plantation in Louisiana where Northup was enslaved, the patting was performed by

striking the hands on the knees, then striking the hands together, then striking the right shoulder with one hand, the left with the other—all the while keeping time with the feet, and singing, perhaps, this song:

"Harper's creek and roarin' ribber,
Thar, my dear, we'll live forebber;
Den we'll go to the Ingin Nation,
All I want in dis creation,
Is pretty little wife and big plantation."[25]

Solomon Northup tells us that the juba song typically was "one of those unmeaning songs, composed rather for its adaptation to a certain tune or measure, than for the purpose of expressing any distinct idea." And patting juba made "a most curious noise, yet in such perfect order that the slaves had no difficulty in dancing to it."

There were as many ways to pat juba (or juber) as there were patters. On a Maryland plantation, a boy sang the "words of a jig in a monotonous tone of voice, beating time meanwhile with his hands alternately against each other and against his body."[26] The principal "juber rhymer" on that plantation was a girl named Clotilda, who improvised the verses for the dancing and *recited* them in a "shrill sing-song voice, keeping time to the measure . . . by beating her hands sometimes against her sides, and patting the ground with her feet." After each stanza, she paused a bit—perhaps to collect her thoughts for the next improvised stanza—but continued to beat her hands and pat her foot without ceasing.

Numerous variants of the juba song were current in the nineteenth century. Generally they had in common only the juba refrain and the idea of indicating in the verse the steps to be followed in the dancing. The following is an example of Clotilda's juba song as preserved by Hungerford:

JUBER DANCE

Laudy! how it make me laugh
Ter see de niggers all so saf';
See um dance de foolish jig,
Un neber min' de juber rig.
Juber!

(Negroes dancing every one after his or her own fashion, but keeping time to the beat.)

Juber lef' un Juber right;
Juber dance wid all yo' might;

[25]Northup, *Twelve Years a Slave*, p. 100.
[26]Hungerford, *The Old Plantation*, pp. 78–79.

> Juber here un Juber dere,
> Juber, Juber, ebery where.
> > Juber!

(The dancers get into confusion in their frantic efforts to follow the directions. *Clotilda* rebukingly,

> > "Git out, you silly breed!
> > Can't you dance de Juber reed?")
> > Once ole Uncle Will
> > Gwine ullong de side de hill,
> > Stump his toe uggin er weed,
> > Un spill all his punkin seed.
> > > Juber!

(Ludicrous imitations of Uncle Will stumbling and trying to recover himself, and to prevent his pumpkin seed from falling at the same time. *Uncle Will,* with great disgust, "Imperdin piece!")

> > Dere's ole Uncle Jack
> > Hab er pain in his back;
> > Ebery time he try ter skip
> > Den he hab ter get er limp.
> > > Juber!

(Active skips suddenly changed to a variety of awkward limps expressive of great pain in the back. *Uncle Jack,* angrily, "De outrageous hussy!")

> > Guess I knows er nigger gal—
> > Dere she is, her name is Sal—
> > Un she hab to min' de baby,
> > Show us how she rock de cradle.
> > > Juber!

(A variety of swaying motions, intended to represent cradle-rocking in a ridiculous view. *Sall,* a daughter of Aunt Kate, and nurse of a baby sister, indignantly, "I alwus said Clotildy was crazy!")

> > Ebery body know Aunt Jinny,
> > Nothing ken be said uggin her;
> > When she fever nigger take,
> > My! how dat ole lady shake.
> > > Juber! *etc.*

In addition to instrumental dance music and pattin' juba, the dance-music repertory of the slaves included "fiddle-sings," "jig-tunes," and "devil songs." Regretfully, few of these were preserved. Most of the song collecting took place on plantations where slaves, having been converted to Christianity, came to regard dancing as sinful and no longer indulged in it. As suggested above, there were collectors who realized that they might be neglecting an important repertory in failing to record the nonreligious music, but apparently they were in the minority. There might have been other reasons—one of them that the texts of dance songs tended to be non-sensical. Who would bother to record such an absurdity as the following except, perhaps, a slave:[27]

> Who's been here since I've been gone?
> Pretty little gal wid a josey on.
>> Hog eye!
>> Old Hog eye!
>> And Hosey too!
> Never see de like since I was born.

A number of dance songs have come down to us, however, from Catholic Louisiana, where dancing was not discouraged. Six such songs are included in the *Slave Songs of the United States,* all "obtained from a lady who heard them sung before the war on the Good Hope Plantation, St. Charles Parish, Louisiana," according to the editors of that 1867 collection.[28] A song titled *Calinda* accompanied a kind of contradance in which the two lines of dancers faced each other, advancing and retreating in time to the music. The *bamboula* was a lively couple-dance accompanied by the song *Musieu Bainjo;* its name probably points to the African bamboo-drum music originally associated with the dance. Four songs in the 1867 collection served as accompaniment songs for the group dance *coonjai* (counjaille): *Belle Layotte* (Pretty Layotte), *Remon, Aurore Bradaire,* and *Caroline.* The 1867 collection includes a description of the music for the dancing:

> When the *Coonjai* is danced, the music is furnished by an orchestra of singers, the leader of whom—a man selected both for the quality of his voice and for his kill in improvising—sustains the solo part, while the others afford him an opportunity, as they shout in chorus, for inventing some neat verse to compliment some lovely *danseuse,* or celebrate the deeds of some plantation hero. The dancers themselves never sing, as in the case of the religious "shout" of the Port Royal negroes; and the usual musical accompaniment, besides that of the singers, is that furnished by a skilful performer on the barrel-head-drum, the jawbone and key, or some other rude instrument.[29]

Musical Instruments

The most common plantation instruments were the fiddle and the banjo. Some slaves purchased their instruments with money earned from working in their free time, and others received instruments as gifts from their masters or other whites, but most had to content themselves with homemade instruments.

[27]Song text from Northup, *Twelve Years a Slave,* p. 100.
[28]Quotation from Allen, *Slave Songs,* p. vii.
[29]Allen, p. 114.

Depending upon the place and custom, various kinds of materials were used for the fiddles and banjos. Given a good knife, some pine boards, and gut from a slaughtered cow that had been carefully cut into strips, dried, and treated, a skilled craftsman could produce a fairly good fiddle. In some places, fiddles were made of gourds and the strings and bows were made of horsehair. A banjo might be made from half of a fruit with a very hard rind, such as a calabash or gourd, by stretching a thin skin or piece of bladder over the opening, adding two or three strings made from gut, and raising the strings on a bridge. Banjos were also constructed by stretching the tanned hide of a groundhog or woodchuck over a piece of timber fashioned like a cheesebox. Sometimes the bowl of the gourd was not cut away, and the instrument had the appearance of a mandolin. While there seem to be no references to slaves playing "store-bought" mandolins, we know that after emancipation the instrument became popular among black folk musicians.

For other than string instruments, the slaves used any and every kind of material that could be forced to produce a musical sound—old pieces of iron, ribs of a sheep, jawbones of a cow or horse, pieces of wood and sticks, even a jawbone and key in Louisiana, the key being rubbed against the bone. Slaves made flutes of all kinds from natural materials, and made pan-pipes of "canes, having different lengths for different notes, and blowed like mouth organs."

In the deep South there were laws that expressly prohibited the slaves "using and keeping drums, horns or other loud instruments which may call together or give sign or notice to one another."[30] Slaveholders were well aware of the African tradition for "talking instruments," and made every effort to eliminate that source of secret communication among the slaves. On the other hand, in the upper South horns were often used for practical purposes: the conch horn, for example, to call slaves to work at daybreak, or a long-trumpet type at tobacco auctions in Virginia.

The most frequent combination of instruments for dancing coupled the fiddle and the banjo, to which might be added various kinds of small percussions, such as triangles, tambourines, castenets, and sticks. As mentioned above, homemade percussions of unlikely origin were used also. One account mentions music played on a "banjor (a large, hollow instrument with three strings)" and a "quaqua (somewhat resembling a drum)."[31] In the mid-nineteenth century, a Virginian recalled that dancing on Sundays "resounded with the sounds of jollity—the merry strains of the fiddle [and] the measured beats of the quaw sticks. . . ."[32]

[30]Quoted in Paine, *Six Years,* p. 127.
[31]Smyth, *A Tour,* p. 46.
[32]Mallard, *Plantation Life,* p. 162.

Other Recreational Activities

On their holidays, in addition to dancing, slaves engaged in "swapping tales" and singing songs, particularly about Brer Rabbit and his animal friends or John the slave. Since these tales frequently included songs during the course of the narrative, the results were a type of cantefable. The true ballad or narrative song—called "ballet" by the slaves—seems not to have had as important a place in the repertory as in the African and European traditions; at least, we do not find such songs in the antebellum repertory. The slaves sang about the adventures of animals and about the experiences of their Biblical heroes (a point to which we shall return), but not about themselves.

It may well be that the simple, unvarying routines of slave life precluded the development of a song type dependent upon the adventures of a hero or heroine. Without control of their own bodies, slaves had few adventures. They knew in advance the consequences any of their actions might have and knew that there was nothing they could do to avert the consequences. Only three or four songs in the repertory can be remotely classified as story songs and one of these is an animal song. There must have been hundreds of these animal songs in circulation, just as there were hundreds of folktales about Brer Rabbit and his friends, but only one, *Charleston Gals,* has come down to us from this period in a musical source.

The satirical song also is poorly represented in the surviving repertory, but the evidence informs us that it was prevalent all over the South. Indeed, one of the earliest reporters of slave singing, Nicholas Cresswell, states: "In their songs they generally relate the usage they have received from their Masters or Mistresses in a very satirical manner." And most observers noticed how easily the slaves slipped a derisive verse or two about white listeners into songs they were improvising, thus following in a hallowed African tradition for satire.

A song called *Away Down in Sunbury* is provided with just one stanza in the 1867 collection, but one can easily imagine that succeeding stanzas, continuing in the same satirical vein, related other instances where the slave deceived the unsuspecting master:

> O massa take that bran' new coat and hang it on the wall,
> That darky take the same ole coat and wear it to the ball.
>
> CHORUS O don't you hear my true love sing,
> O don't you hear him sigh,
> Away down in Sunbury
> I'm bound to live or die.

The slaves were not averse to shooting a few barbs at each other in both secular and religious songs. A creole song pokes fun at the city dandy:

Musieu Bainjo, from *Slave Songs of the United States*

[Look at that puffed-up Mr. Banjo over there,
See how he puts on airs.
   Hat perched on the side of his head, Mr. Banjo,
   Fancy cane in his hand, Mr. Banjo,
   New boots that go squeak, squeak, Mr. Banjo. . . .]

The first verses of a song entitled *O Daniel* aim at deflating the ego of a self-righteous member of the church:

> You call yourself church-member,
> You hold your head so high,
> You praise God with your glittering tongue,
> But you leave all your heart behind.

In another example, *On to Glory,* the final stanza includes a little chastisement for a wayward sister:

> There's Chloe Williams, she makes me mad,
> For you see, I know she's going on bad;
> She told me a lie this afternoon,
> And the devil will get her very soon.

Then there is a song that begins:

> Hypocrite and the concubine,
> Living among the swine;
> They run to God with the lips and tongue,
> Living among the swine;
> They run to God with the lips and tongue,
> And leave all the heart behind.

There are numerous references in the literature to the play activities of children and to their "play-party" songs. Predictably, their favorite game was a juvenile version of the shout; whites always allowed the children to shuffle around in their rings, even where adults were forbidden to do so. Although few children's plantation songs from the antebellum period are extant, the evidence suggests that a repertory of such songs did exist. Children also sang religious songs when at play, as an observer noticed in 1855, and he cited the titles of songs the children sang as they circled around a tree with hands joined: *I'm Going Way up Yonder, See God Feeding the Lambs,* and *When I Get over Jordan.*[33]

ENTERTAINMENT FOR THE MASTERS

Slaves frequently were called upon to entertain their masters at the "big house," particularly when there were guests. The kinds of entertainment demanded varied, depending upon the occasion and the taste of the planters. Sometimes, no more was requested than a song to dispel the tedium of the moment; then again, a slave might be expected to perform serious music, as in the case of Solomon Northup, who said, "Frequently I was called into the house to play before the family, mistress being passionately fond of music." The following excerpts from slave narratives suggest general practices:

Ex-slave Isaac Williams wrote:

When our masters had company staying with them, they would often collect all the slaves for a general jubilee frolic.[34]

Another report suggests the value placed upon the slave's ability to improvise:

Charlie could make up songs about de funniest things. . . . Marsa say, "Come here, Charlie, and sing some rhymes for Mr. H." "Don't know no new ones, Marsa," Charlie answered. "Come on, you black rascal, give me a rhyme for my company, one he ain't heard."[35]

Fiddlers were always in great demand. Rare was the plantation that did not have someone around like Old John Drayton, who played for all the dances on his plantation. His fellow slaves were very proud of Drayton's fiddling. An old ex-slave from another plantation boasted:

I was a good fiddler; used to be a fiddler for the white girls to dance. Just picked it up, it was a natural gift. I could still play if I had a fiddle. . . . Played all those old-time songs . . . *Soldier's Joy, Jimmy Long Josey, Arkansas Traveler,* and *Black-eyed Susie.*

He fair make the fiddle talk. When Master give a dance he always calls upon John. Yes sir, that man sure could play. When he saw down on the fiddle and pull out that tune, "Oh, the Monkey Marry to the Baboon Sister," he make a parson dance.[36]

[33]Charles G. Parsons, *Inside View of Slavery* (Boston, 1855), p. 276.
[34]Isaac Williams, *Sunshine and Shadow of Slave Life*(East Saginaw, MI, 1885), p. 61.
[35]Milton Meltzer, ed., *In Their Own Words* (New York, 1964), p. 47.
[36]B. A. Botkin, *Lay My Burden Down* (Chicago, 1945), p. 11.

The Music For The Dance, by A. B. Frost

"The Music for the Dance." From a drawing by A. B. Frost, *Harper's Weekly,* 1891.

A good violinist found that his fiddle gained him entry into places otherwise closed to slaves and exempted him of many a day of hard work in the fields. Nothing could better illustrate this than the experience of Solomon Northup in Louisiana. His master's wife induced her husband Edwin, a crude, vicious man, to buy a violin for Northup because she was "passionately fond of music." As a consequence, Northup was frequently called upon to play for the Epps family in the evenings. When Northup finally obtained his freedom "Mistress Epps was actually affected to tears," primarily because she no longer would have someone to play for her on the violin.

As the owner of Northup, Epps received numerous requests for his slave's services from townsmen and planters on neighboring plantations. The white people in the nearby villages got to know him well:

> [They] always knew there was to be a jollification somewhere, whenever Platt Epps [Northup's slave name] was seen passing through the town with his fiddle in his hand. "Where are you going now Platt?" and "What is coming off tonight, Platt?" would be interrogatories issuing from every door and window, and many a time when there was no special hurry, yielding to pressing importunities, Platt would draw his bow, and sitting astride his mule, perhaps, discourse musically to a crowd of delighted children, gathered around him in the street.[37]

[37]Northup, *Twelve Years a Slave,* p. 99.

To the slaveowner went all payments, of course, for his slave's fiddling, but Northup sometimes received a little money for his musical exertions. On one occasion he collected seventeen dollars in tips—a large sum for a slave to receive at one time. To play for dances of the planters the slave musician could not get by with only reels and jigs; he was expected to be able to play minuets and cotillions as well. The demands upon his violin technique, consequently, were almost as great as if he had been a city-slave musician.

The slave orchestras that played for the slaveholders' quadrilles and cotillions might consist of as few as two instruments or as many as half a dozen, depending upon the importance of the ball and the wealth and social position of its hosts. The basic core of the orchestra was composed of violins, violoncellos, and perhaps double basses, to which might be added flutes, oboes, clarinets, and French horns.

IMPORTANCE OF MUSIC TO THE SLAVES

White observers in the nineteenth century often misunderstood the singing and dancing of slaves, interpreting such activities as indicative that the slaves were unfeeling and uncaring, that they somehow were lacking in the normal human responses to oppression, loss of loved ones, and deprivation of freedom. Often the whites saw the blacks on their plantations as "a large flock of cheerful and contented slaves . . . ever merry and ever working with a song." On one occasion a slave, when questioned by Fredrika Bremer about his apparent good humor, responded:

> We endeavor to keep ourselves up as well as we can. What can we do unless we keep a good heart? If we were to let it weaken, we should die.[38]

More observant listeners heard the plaintive melancholy overtones in the singing and were occasionally startled by "wild and unaccountable" melodies.

Frederick Douglass and Solomon Northup were the most articulate of the ex-slaves who tried to explain the meaning of slave songs. Douglass observed in the 1845 edition of his autobiography that slaves sang most when they were unhappy. He remembered in particular the singing of two slaves on his Maryland plantation when they made their monthly trips to the Great House Farm for supplies.

> While on their way, they would make the dense old woods, for miles around, reverberate with their wild songs, revealing at once the highest joy and the deepest sadness. They would compose and sing as they went along, consulting neither time nor tune. . . . "I did not, when a slave, understand the deep meanings of those rude, and apparently incoherent songs. I was myself within the circle, so that I neither saw nor heard as those without [the circle] might see and hear. They told a tale which was then altogether beyond my feeble comprehension;

[38]Bremer, *Homes*, v. 2, p. 106.

there were tones loud, long and deep, breathing the prayer and complaint of souls boiling over with the bitterest anguish. Every tone was testimony against slavery, and a prayer to God for deliverance from chains."[39]

And Northup represented the hundreds of thousands who could not conceive of having to endure the "weariness, and fear, and suffering, and unremitting labor" of slavery without a violin or banjo to console them. He wrote:

> It was my companion—the friend of my bosom—triumphing loudly when I was joyful, and uttering its soft, melodious consolations when I was sad. Often, at midnight, when sleep had fled affrighted from the cabin, and my soul was disturbed and troubled with the contemplation of my fate, it would sing me a song of peace. On holy Sabbath days, when an hour or two of leisure was allowed, it would accompany me to some quiet place on the bayou bank, and, lifting up its voice, discourse kindly and pleasantly indeed.[40]

THE WORSHIP SERVICE

Up until the Civil War, the great majority of slaves remained outside the Christian Church; it has been estimated that only a small proportion of them actually were admitted to membership in the church. Three kinds of religious experiences were available to the relatively few who were converted to Christianity: in some places slaves attended the churches of their masters, where they sat in galleries and back pews or worshiped in separate services. In other places, slaves worshiped in their own churches or plantation Praise Houses under the leadership of white ministers. One planter pointed with pride to his record in this regard:

> I also employ a good preacher, who regularly preaches to them on the Sabbath Day, and it is made the duty of every one to come up clean and decent to the place of worship. As Father Garritt regularly calls on Brother Abraham (the foreman of the prayer meetings) to close the exercises, he gives out and sings his hymn with much unction.[41]

Finally, there were black congregations led by black preachers but supervised by whites. Almost without exception these were Baptist congregations. As the Baptist church is autonomous—that is, free from the regulation of a national body, as was not the case with the AME or AMEZ Churches—it was possible for local whites to control these congregations without interference from outsiders. There seems to have been only one AME congregation in the South, for example—a church in Charleston, South Carolina—but that church was broken up after the Denmark Vesey insurrection in 1822.

---

[39]Douglass, *My Bondage*, pp. 83–84.
[40]Northup, *Twelve Years a Slave*, pp. 99–100.
[41]"Management of Negroes," *DeBow's Review* 10 (June 1851): 625; 11 (October 1851): 372.

To be sure, many slaveholders disallowed any kind of religious services for their slaves. Despite the stringent laws of the South prohibiting the assembling of black folk, the slaves managed to hold religious meetings in secret. Modern scholars refer to the religious community of slaves that existed outside the formal church as "the invisible institution" or "the invisible church."

The secret meetings were often held at midnight after the masters had gone to bed. They also took place at sunrise on Sundays, since slaveholding families customarily slept late on Sunday mornings, and the patrols, after their all-night duty, retired at dawn.

Contemporary slave literature is replete with anecdotes about all the things slaves did to escape detection. A common practice was to meet in the deep woods, in remote ravines or gullies, or in secluded thickets (called "brush arbors"). The preachers and exhorters would speak over a kettle of water in order to drown the sound, or the group would turn a kettle upside down in the center of the gathering so that the kettle would absorb the sound of the singing. Predictably, the practices of the "invisible church" were reflected in the slave songs:

> I sought my Lord in de wilderness,
> In de wilderness, in de wilderness;
> I sought my Lord in de wilderness,
> For I'm a-going home.

or:

> As I went down in de valley to pray,
> Studying about dat good old way,
> When you shall wear de starry crown,
> Good Lord, show me de way.
> O mourner, let's go down,
> Let's go down, let's go down
> O mourner, let's go down,
> Down in de valley to pray.[42]

On plantations where masters were interested in the religious development of their slaves or were inclined to be lenient, mid-week prayer meetings and Sunday evening meetings were not uncommon. Whether whites were present or not, the slaves generally adhered to conventional forms of worship in their formal services. Such services might be held in the cabin of the preacher or the "exhorter," in a "cotton house," or even in a special "praise house" set aside for the slaves.

If the leader of the service was able to read, he read a chapter from the Bible. Another slave read a psalm and lined it out for congregational singing, and the leader followed this with a prayer. If the leader could not read, he delivered a brief "exhortation" based on a passage of the Bible that he

---

[42]From the Slave Narrative Collection.

had memorized. The congregation then sang a psalm or hymn from memory, and the service closed with prayer. Amazingly, there usually was someone on the plantation who could read the Bible and who taught others to do so—this, despite laws in all of the southern states prohibiting the teaching of slaves to read and write.

Almost as important as the exhorter was the song leader. An ex-slave explained it in this way:

> I was the singing man. I led the hymns. I learned them all by heart, and lined them off for the people to follow.[43]

A white listener commented thus:

> One hears the elder "deaconing" a hymn-book hymn, which is sung two lines at a time, and whose wailing cadences, borne on the night air, are indescribably melancholy.[44]

The slaves, led by the singing man, sang the old long-meter hymns as slowly as the American colonists had sung psalms a century earlier. Sometimes the song leader was an older woman. She might have been the same person who attended the small children during the day while their parents worked, who taught them to "say their prayers, repeat a little catechism and sing a few hymns."

Spirituals

The first references in print to the religious folksongs of black Americans as a distinctive genre began to appear early in the nineteenth century, as we have seen, although writers invariably used the term *hymn* to apply to these songs. First, there were the black Methodists of Philadelphia adding choruses and refrains of "their own composing" to the standard Protestant hymns in Richard Allen's hymnal of 1801. Then a few years later, in 1804, a visitor to Allen's church ridiculed the "kind of songs" being sung at the church, implying that they were not orthodox hymns.[45] Finally, in 1819 John Fanning Watson publicly aired the matter, protesting that the black members of the Society were singing their improvised hymns in public places and at camp meetings. By 1841 this practice had become so widespread that the AME Church felt it necessary to pass a resolution at its Annual Conference directing preachers to "strenuously oppose" the singing of the specially composed hymns in "public meetings."

It is not known precisely when the term *spiritual* was first used in print to apply to the religious folksongs of the black American. Obviously, the term points back to the three species of sacred song early set up in the his-

---

[43]Orland Armstrong, *Old Massa's People* (Indianapolis, 1931), p. 242.
[44]Allen, *Slave Songs,* p. xiii.
[45]Jones, *Religious Instruction,* p. 265.

tory of Protestantism—psalms, hymns, and spirituals—which, in turn, points to the Scriptures, Col. 3:16. In the introduction to *Slave Songs of the United States,* the editors use the term *spiritual* (or *sperichil*) without bothering to define it, an indication that the term must have been in common usage by the 1860s. By that time the spiritual repertory must have been quite extensive and undoubtedly included many songs of ancient vintage. As we have observed, verses of some of the songs in the *Slave Song* collection can be traced back to Richard Allen's historic hymnal of 1801 and Watson's publication of 1819.

Over the years black men and women would have had ample freedom to develop a repertory of religious songs, away from the surveillance of whites, in the independent black churches, segregated camp and bush meetings, and "invisible churches" on the plantations. Predictably, they classified the spirituals in the same way as they did secular songs. There were spirituals for singing in the worship service, for singing while "jes' sittin' around," and for singing to accompany the shout—such as the "ring spirituals," "running spirituals," and "shout spirituals." Ex-slaves also referred to "funeral hymns" as a special type, and undoubtedly there were other classes of spirituals for appropriate occasions.

The question of whether spirituals should be sung at the formal worship service was controversial. Many white clergymen—for example, plantation missionary Charles Colcock Jones, as we have seen—wanted the slaves to desist entirely from singing their own spirituals. Other southern preachers, however, were more lenient; for example, the Reverend Robert Q. Mallard, Jones's son-in-law, generally allowed his slaves to sing their own "improvised spirituals" at religious services on the plantation and admired their enthusiasm, particularly when they sang:

> My brother, you promised Jesus,
> My brother, you promised Jesus,
> My brother, you promised Jesus,
> To either fight or die.
>
> Oh, I wish I was there
> To hear my Jesus's orders,
> Oh, I wish I was there
> To wear my starry crown.[46]

Many black preachers not only were permissive about the singing of spirituals, but were even encouraging.

The Shout

After the regular service a special one, purely African in form and tradition, frequently was held in the same room. The most detailed account of

---

[46]Mallard, *Plantation Life,* p. 162.

this rite in any nineteenth-century source is given in the 1867 collection of *Slave Songs,* but numerous other sources also describe it.

> The true "shout" takes place on Sundays or on "praise" nights through the week, and either in the praise-house or in some cabin in which a regular religious meeting has been held. Very likely more than half the population of the plantation is gathered together. . . . The benches are pushed back to the wall when the formal meeting is over, and old and young, men and women . . . all stand up in the middle of the floor, and when the "sperichil" [spiritual] is struck up, begin first walking and by-and-by shuffling round, one after the other, in a ring. The foot is hardly taken from the floor, and the progression is mainly due to a jerking, hitching motion, which agitates the entire shouter, and soon brings out streams of perspiration.

Generally, the gathering divided itself into two groups, shouters (that is, dancers) and singers. The latter, "composed of some of the best singers and of tired shouters stand at the side of the room to 'base' the others, singing the body of the song and clapping their hands together or on the knees." The dancers participated in the singing according to how they felt. Sometimes they danced silently; sometimes they sang only refrains of the song; sometimes they sang the entire song along with the singers. The descriptive passage concludes:

> Song and dance are alike extremely energetic, and often, when the shout lasts into the middle of the night, the monotonous thud, thud of feet prevents sleep within half a mile of the praise-house.[47]

For the participants the shout was not under any circumstances to be construed as a dance, and strictly observed rules insured that the line between "shouting" and dancing was firmly drawn. Only songs of a religious nature were sung, and the feet must never be crossed (as would happen in the dance). Among strict devotees, the feet must not even be lifted from the ground. Presumably, any song could function as a shout song or "running spiritual." In practice, however, the slaves preferred some songs to the exclusion of others, and a special body of these songs was developed among them.

In performance, a ring spiritual was repeated over and over as the shouters moved around in a circle, often for as long as four and five successive hours. The song thus took on the character of a chant, a "wild monotonous chant," and its text became the "repetition of an incoherent cry." Although the ring of shouters moved slowly at the beginning, the tempo of the music and the pace of the circling gradually quickened so that the performance eventually displayed "signs of frenzy." The religious fervor of the participants and the loud monotony of the music combined to produce a state of ecstasy in all present, and shouters often fell to the ground in a state of

---

[47]Allen, *Slave Songs,* pp. xiii–xv.

complete exhaustion. Their places were quickly taken by others, however, and the ring dance continued.

It can readily be seen that this religious performance belongs to the same tradition as the eighteenth-century "jubilees" and Pinkster dances, the Place Congo dancing in New Orleans, the circle dances at camp meetings, and the "Methodist praying bands" in urban areas. Here were the same ring formations, the loud chanting, the shuffling movements, the intense concentration of the participants, and the gradual build-up of the performance to a wild and frenzied state. The only missing element was the instrumental music of drums and string instruments, and to a certain extent this was compensated for by the hand clapping of the singers.

Some nineteenth-century writers thought that only the Baptists had shouts. The editors of *Slave Songs* thought that the shout was "confined to South Carolina and the States south of it." From the vantage point of the present we can see, however, that the shout belonged to no one denomination nor to any one region. It simply represented the survival of an African tradition in the New World.

Among the spirituals most closely associated with the shout throughout the South were *Oh, We'll Walk Around the Fountain; I Know, Member, Know Lord; The Bells Done Ring; Pray All the Members; Go Ring That Bell*; and *I Can't Stay Behind.*

While white observers admitted the strange attraction of the shout, they generally disapproved of it, regarding the holy dance as barbaric and even lascivious. Knowing nothing of African traditions, the observers failed to appreciate the two most important elements of the shout: (1) shouters used dance as a means of communication with God in the same way as song and prayer are used; and (2) shouters reached the highest level of worship when the Holy Spirit entered their bodies and took possession of their souls. Nowhere in the history of the black experience in the United States was the clash of cultures—the African versus the European—more obvious than in the differing attitudes taken toward ritual dancing and spirit possession.

I Can't Stay Behind, from *Slave Songs of the United States*

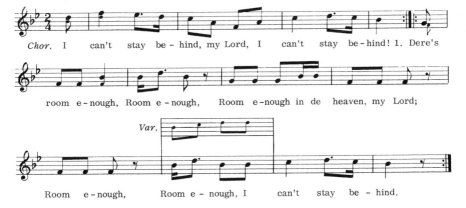

2. I been all around, I been all around,
   Been all around de Heaven, my Lord.
3. I've searched every room—in de Heaven, my Lord.
4. De angels singin'—all round de trone.
5. My Fader call—and I must go.
6. Sto-back, member; sto-back, member.

OTHER RELIGIOUS SERVICES

In addition to conducting worship services, the plantation preacher was called upon to preside at baptisms, weddings, revival and camp meetings, and funerals. Depending upon the occasion, musical performances might be lively and cheerful or solemn and mournful. Weddings, for example, called for a sermon, prayers, and religious songs, but after the ceremony the solemn mood gave way to dancing to the music of fiddles, banjos, and other instruments.

Funeral processions to the gravesite were marked by the intoning of doleful spirituals and somber hymns, and at the grave the slaves frequently practiced rites that clearly were rooted in the African tradition. The numerous descriptions of slave funerals that have come down to us refer to pine-knot torches flickering in the night, the singing of "wild chants" in wailing tones, the antiphonal responses of the mourners to the prayers and moans of the preacher or exhorter, and the ritual dancing to the accompaniment of drums and other percussion. More than one observer noted that on the return from the grave, the tone of the occasion changed and the music was apt to be lighter, even festive—reflecting the belief of some that death freed the slave to return home to Africa, and of others, that death freed the slave from a life of unremitting sorrow. As a slave pointed out,

> On de way home from de funeral, de mules would perk up a little in dey walk and a faster hymn was sung on the way home. When we got home, we was in a good mood from singing de faster hymns. . . .

Slaves, like the white observers, commonly used the word "hymn" to apply to either hymns or spirituals; we know from examples cited in the literature that spirituals were widely sung at slave funerals.

AN ORIGIN FOR THE SPIRITUAL

Rarely is it possible to identify the author of a folksong or to pinpoint its original form. Typically, folksongs are created by nonprofessional musicians, altered by other singers and passed along from one generation to the next by oral transmission. In the process, the music is adapted to the taste of both those who sing and those who listen. The changes that take place become a part of the original song and inevitably the music takes on a different form than it originally had. Over the span of years the authors' names are forgotten.

There are three choices available to the folk composer who wishes to create a new song. Consciously or unconsciously, he or she may (1) improvise upon a song already in existence; (2) combine material from several old songs to make the new one; or (3) compose the song entirely of new materials. The African tradition favors the first process. Indeed, variation is so strong a factor in this tradition that changes are introduced into songs with each new performance. Above all, music in the African tradition is functional. Consequently, the melody of a song often serves chiefly as a vehicle for the text, and is constantly adjusted to fit, even as the singer extemporizes from one verse to the next.

As we have seen, slave music was squarely in the African tradition with respect to improvisation. Much of the evidence indicates that a large number of the slave songs represent "variations upon a theme"—that is, the songs seem to be altered versions of other songs. No doubt many of these songs—the social songs, in particular—were brought over from Africa and passed down from parents to children. Almost every contemporaneous source contains references to slaves born in Africa who helped to keep African traditions alive in their communities during the eighteenth and nineteenth centuries. And the continuous influx of new slaves into the 1860s helped to revive traditions that were in danger of dying out, whether the newcomers came from Africa, the West Indies, or another state on the mainland.

To return to the choices available to the folk composer, it seems that the black composer might often have resorted to the second in producing the spirituals: selecting snippets of materials from preexistent songs to compose new ones. We have already observed the importance of the Bible in providing a storehouse of materials for the slave composer and, in a previous chapter, discussed the relationship of Protestant hymn to the spiritual. With a little imagination, we can recreate the process by which the slave composer might have combined verses from hymns with "short scraps of disjointed affirmations [and] pledges or prayers," and "lengthened out" the resultant text with "long repetition choruses" (words quoted from Methodist church father John Watson.

The following hymn was popular among black folk as far back as 1801, when it was published in Richard Allen's hymnal, and through the antebellum years it was cited several times as a favorite among black singers.

> Behold the awful trumpet sounds,
>   The sleeping dead to raise,
> And calls the nations underground:
>   O how the saints will praise!
>
> Behold the Saviour how he comes
>   Descending from his throne

> To burst asunder all our tombs
>   And lead his children home.
>
> But who can bear that dreadful day,
>   To see the world in flames:
> The burning mountains melt away,
>   While rocks run down in streams.
>
> The falling stars their orbits leave,
>   The sun in darkness hide:
> The elements asunder cleave,
>   The moon turn'd into blood!
>
> Behold the universal world
>   In consternation stand,
> The wicked unto Hell are turn'd
>   The Saints at God's right hand.
>
> O then the music will begin
>   Their Saviour God to praise,
> They all are freed from every sin
>   And thus they'll spend their days!

After singing this hymn, the slave composer with vivid imagination seizes upon the significance of the awesome events that will take place on Judgment Day according to the text, and has a personal response, "My Lord, what a morning!" Proceeding to enumerate the events, the slave composer then uses motives from the hymn but rephrased in the slave's own words. The result is an entirely new song with its own form and music, for obviously the old hymn tune no longer fits.

> My Lord, what a morning,
> My Lord, what a morning,
> My Lord, what a morning,
> When the stars begin to fall.
>
> You'll hear the trumpet sound,
> To wake the nations underground,
> Looking to my God's right hand,
> When the stars begin to fall.
>
> You'll hear the sinner mourn
> To wake the nations underground, etc.
>
> You'll hear the Christians shout,
> To wake the nations underground, etc.

The slave repertory of the nineteenth century includes many variations on the theme of the original hymn. One spiritual, *In That Great Getting-Up Morning,* is a song of almost epic proportions. The chorus establishes the basic mood of the spiritual:

In That Great Getting-Up Morning, traditional

In that great   get-ting-up morn-ing,   Fare you   well!   Fare you well!

In that great   get-ting-up morn-ing,   Fare you   well!   Fare you well!

After a lengthy introduction, beginning "I'm a-going to tell you about the coming of the Saviour," the slave composer takes the first stanza of the hymn, expands it into a little story, and gives the trumpet to Gabriel, who holds a lengthy conversation with the Lord about how he is to blow:

The Lord spoke to Gabriel

[Throughout the song the refrain follows each line of the text, as in the first stanza.]

> Go look behind the altar
> Take down the silver trumpet
> Blow your trumpet, Gabriel
>
> Lord, how loud shall I blow it
> Blow it right calm and easy
> Do not alarm my people
> Tell 'em to come to judgement
>
> Gabriel blow your trumpet
> Lord, how loud shall I blow it
> Loud as seven peals of thunder
> Wake the living nations

Further instructions are given to Gabriel and he is forewarned of what will happen upon the sounding of the trumpet—all this in accordance with the text of the original hymn, but in the idiomatic language of the slaves.

> Place one foot upon the dry land
> Place the other on the sea
> Then you'll see the coffins bursting
> See the dry bones come a-creeping
>
> Hell shall be uncapped and burning
> Then the dragons shall be loosened
> Where you running poor sinner?
> Where you running poor sinner?
>
> Then you'll see poor sinners rising
> Then you'll see the world on fire
> See the moon a-bleeding
> See the stars a-falling
>
> See the elements a-melting
> See the forked lightning

> Then you'll cry out for cold water
> When the Christians shout in glory
>
> Hear the rumbling of the thunder
> Earth shall reel and totter
> Then you'll see the Christians rising
> Then you'll see the righteous marching

The song concludes with the arrival of the Christians in heaven:

> See them marching home to heaven
> Take the righteous home to glory
> There they'll live with God forever
> On the right-hand side of my Saviour

Other spirituals that belong to this "family" include *And de Moon Will Turn to Blood; In Dat Great Day; O, Rocks, Don't Fall on Me;* and *Steal Away, Steal Away.*

Sometimes a spiritual will draw upon more than one hymn. In the following example, the hymn cited above serves as a source for all the lines except line 7 (here italicized).

> When every star refuses to shine,
> Rocks and mountains don't fall on me;
> I know that King Jesus will-a be mine,
> Rocks and mountains don't fall on me.
> The trumpet shall sound and the dead shall rise,
> Rocks and mountains don't fall on me;
> *And go to the mansions in-a the skies,*
> Rocks and mountains don't fall on me.

The seventh line points to a hymn written by Isaac Watts, which appears in Richard Allen's 1801 collection and is still a favorite of black congregations today. The first stanza is as follows:

> When I can read my title clear
> To mansions in the skies,
> I'll bid farewell to ev'ry fear
> And wipe my weeping eyes.

An interrelation between other spirituals and Protestant hymns can be demonstrated in the same way. It must be remembered that in every instance, the spiritual is a refashioning of verses and motives from the parent hymn or hymns and *not* simply a different version of the hymn. The spiritual is another song type with its own text, music, and distinctive stylistic features. Typically, the melodies of the slave songs represent original composition rather than a borrowing of old tunes. Not that the slaves were averse to appropriating tunes for their improvised songs from other repertories of the period—popular songs, Anglo-American folksongs, minstrel songs, and even hymns. But, as song collector Thomas W. Higginson pointed out, "As they learned all their songs by ear, they often strayed into wholly new versions, which sometimes became popular, and entirely banished the others." In essence, the plantation songs were reshaped by the process of "communal recreation" into characteristic African American folksongs, no matter what the original sources of text and melodic materials.

There is a final class of spiritual that should be mentioned; the homiletic spirituals, which originated with the folk preacher and were taught to the congregation by him or the deacon. Black ministers took seriously the admonition of Dr. Isaac Watts:

> Ministers are to cultivate gifts of preaching and prayer through study and diligence; they ought also to cultivate the capacity of composing spiritual songs and exercise it along with the other parts of worship, preaching and prayer.

The congregations contributed their share to the composition of these songs, their interjected expressions developing into song refrains.

Sometimes an excited preacher would be carried away by his emotion and compose a song on the spot—that is, during the sermon itself. More than one contemporary writer witnessed such occurrences. William Wells Brown writes, for example, of visiting a church in Nashville, Tennessee, where the sermon was preached by "an educated minister from Cincinnati" whose aim was "to set the congregation to shouting."[48] Although Brown disapproved of the procedures, he remained for the service and later described what had happened. At a certain point in the sermon, the minister took from his pocket a letter and said, "When you reach the other world you'll be hunting for your mother, and the angel will read from this paper." This statement was repeated again and again as the minister walked back and forth on the pulpit platform. His voice grew higher and higher in pitch as he repeated the words, until he was almost singing.

The congregation became excited; soon various members began to cry out: "Let that angel come right down now and read that letter," "Yes, yes, I want to hear the letter," "Come, Jesus, come or send an angel to read the letter," "Lord, send us the power," in addition to the more usual cries, "Amen," "Glory, Hallelujah," "Yes, Lord." It does not take too much imagination to recreate the scene, for parallel occurrences can be found today among black churches in rural areas and in ghetto areas of the cities. The spirituals that originated in the emotionally charged atmosphere of the religious service have been called "preaching spirituals" by some modern writers.

[48]Brown, *Southern Home*, pp. 192–93.

CHARACTER OF THE FOLK MUSIC

Typically the slave songs consist of four-line stanzas alternating with four-line choruses and, within that structure, an alternation of solo verses with refrains, thus reflecting traditional African call-and-response performance practices. There are a few extant examples, however, of three-line stanzas. In regard to the individual verses or lines of the song, some stanzas have all tetrameter verses (that is, lines with four stresses or accents) and other kinds of stanzas alternate tetrameter lines with trimeter lines (three accents to the line), as in so-called ballad meter.

EXAMPLE 1. I meét little Rósa eárly in the mórning (4)
Ó Jerúsalem! eárly in the mórning. (4)
And I aśked her, Hów [do] you dó, my daúghter, (4)
Ó Jerúsalem! eárly in the mórning. (4)
I meét my móther eárly in the mórning, (4)
Ó Jerúsalem! eárly in the mórning. (4)

EXAMPLE 2. I wánt to gó where Móses tród, (4)
Ó the dýing Laḿb. (3)
For Móses góne to the prómised lańd, (4)
Ó the dýing Laḿb. (3)
To dŕink from spŕings that néver run dŕy, (4)
Ó the dýing Laḿb. (3)

Repetition is an important element of the music; the most prevalent stanzaic forms—in addition to the one in which alternating lines are refrains—are the *aaab* form (with three repeated lines and a refrain) and the *aaba* form (with two repeated lines, one new line, then a repeat of the first line). Occurring less frequently is the *abcd* form (with no repetition of text). Stanza and chorus are linked through the recurrence of refrain lines common to both, regardless of the form of either.

We'll run and never tire, (a)
We'll run and never tire, (a)
We'll run and never tire, (a)
Jesus sets poor sinners free. (R)

Way down in the valley, (a)
Who will rise and go with me? (b)
You've heard talk of Jesus, (c)
Who set poor sinners free. (R)

The lightning and the flashing, (a)
The lightning and the flashing, (a)
The lightning and the flashing, (a)
Jesus sets poor sinners free. (R)

Of course, not all of the slave songs employ the typical forms as outlined above. Sometimes a text, while utilizing the predictable repetition, reflects an unusual arrangement of words into patterns:

Bow low, Mary, bow low, Martha,
For Jesus come and lock the door,
And carry the keys away.

Sail, sail, over yonder
And view the promised land.
For Jesus come and lock the door,
And carry the keys away.

Weep, O Mary, bow low, Martha,
For Jesus come and lock the door,
And carry the keys away.

Sail, sail, my true believer,
Sail, sail, over yonder;

Mary, bow low, Martha, bow low,
For Jesus come and lock the door,
And carry the keys away.

Generally, the musical form of the song is the same as the poetic form, but not always. Prevalent musical patterns are *abab, abac,* and *aaab* (with each letter representing a musical phrase). The repetition of musical lines may be relatively literal, with unimportant changes in pitch, or sequential in that phrases are repeated on a higher or lower pitch level. In the case of the latter, it is conventional to indicate the form as *aa'bc* (see chorus of example on p. 165). The following song has an *aaab* form:

Sabbath Has No End, from *Slave Songs of the United States*

2. Gwine to follow King Jesus, I really do believe.
3. I love God certain.
4. My sister's got religion.
5. Set down in the kingdom.
6. Religion is a fortune.

Melody and Scales

As written down in the documents, most melodies use the tones of the major or pentatonic scales, which tend to produce bright, cheerful melodies. But according to contemporaneous reports the slaves' singing rarely was bright and cheerful; it was generally described as plaintive, mournful, or wild. Bremer wrote about a song, for example: "I wish I could give you an idea of [it], so fresh was the melody, and so peculiar the key."[49] Even in their gayest songs there were "overtones of melancholy." It seems unlikely that the majority of the slave songs were actually in the major or pentatonic modes. Probably, these songs, like many Negro folksongs of the twentieth century, did indeed use the major and pentatonic scales but with some tones of these scales flatted or "bent" to a lower pitch.

There are just enough hints in the *Slave Songs* to suggest how this alteration may have operated. In many songs, the editors have used accidentals to indicate such alterations. Most frequently in a major melody, it is the seventh tone of the scale that is flatted, indicating that the tone was sung lower than normally (as C D E F G A B♭ C). Frequently, such a song includes both flatted and normal seventh tones, as in the following song, which uses the altered D-major scale: D E F♯ G A B C C♯ D:

Roll, Jordan, Roll, from *Cabin and Plantation Songs*

The song collectors who transcribed the songs were aware of the complications involved. Lucy McKim Garrison, one of the editors of *Slave Songs of the United States,* wrote in 1862:

> It is difficult to express the entire character of these negro ballads by mere musical notes and signs. The odd turns made in the throat, and the curious rhythmic

[49]Bremer, *Homes,* v. 1, p. 371.

effect produced by single voices chiming in at different irregular intervals, seem almost as impossible to place on the score as the singing of birds or the tones of an Aeolian Harp.[50]

A year later another transcriber admitted to the same difficulty in his recording of melodies:

> The tunes to which these songs are sung, are some of them weird and wild—barbaric madrigals—while others are sweet and impressive melodies. The most striking of their barbaric airs it would be impossible to write out.[51]

And the compiler of the Hampton spirituals reported in 1872:

> Tones are frequently employed which we have no musical characters to represent. Such, for example, is that which I have indicated as nearly as possible by the flat seventh. . . . The tones are variable in pitch, ranging through an entire octave on different occasions, according to the inspiration of the singer.[52]

Obviously then, the songs as written down in extant collections must represent only an approximation of slave music as it actually sounded. Some of them include more than one altered or "bent" tone. In the example on p. 191, both the sixth and seventh tones of the scale are ambiguous.

To be sure, the observations of reporters were not altogether incorrect; a small number of the songs actually are based on the minor scale. And there are a few songs that use tones of the medieval church modes (Dorian, Phrygian, Lydian, Mixolydian, Aeolian); for example, the following song suggests the minor but actually uses tones of the Dorian mode (as D E F G A B C D).

Dis Is de Trouble of de World, from *Slave Songs of the United States*

*(What you doubt for?) etc.

[50]Allen, *Slave Songs,* p. vi.

[51]Spaulding, "Under the Palmetto," *Continental Monthly* (August 1863), reprint in KATZ, p. 5.

[52]M. F. Armstrong and Helen W. Ludlow, *Cabin and Plantation Songs,* Henry P. Fenner, arr. (New York, 1874), p. 172.

Finally, there are some songs with pitch implications so vague that it is difficult to decide which scale serves as a basis for the melodies.

According to the testimony of nineteenth-century writers, the slaves also sang melodies using only one, two, or three tones. None of these are preserved, however. Significantly, these melodies were labeled as African and were associated with rituals of various types. Latrobe, watching the dancers in the Place Congo of New Orleans, observed:

> The women squalled out a burden [that is, refrain] . . . consisting of two notes.[53]

And the Swedish traveler Fredrika Bremer relates that she persuaded an elderly slave in Charleston, South Carolina, to sing for her "an Ethiopian death-song, which seemed to consist of a monotone vibration upon three semi-tones."[54] Although no written examples of two- or three-tone melodies are preserved in American sources, we can obtain some understanding of the nature of these songs by referring to African music—for in some parts of Africa such songs are common.

The songs vary in regard to compass—that is, the difference in pitch between the lowest and the highest notes of a melody. Few songs have compasses smaller than an octave, and many extend over a range of a tenth or a twelfth. Within the confines of the melodic range there is an emphasis on pentatonic patterns, even when the melodies derive from six- or seven-tone scales. One example will illustrate this point. The following melody uses the tones of the E♭-major scale, but because of the persistent emphasis on the tones E♭-F-G-B♭-C it suggests the pentatonic instead of the major:

Jesus on de Water-Side, from *Slave Songs of the United States*

[53]Latrobe, *Impressions*, p. 51.
[54]Bremer, *Homes*, v. 2, p. 394.

Rhythmic Features

Rhythm is the most striking feature of slave music, as is true in all African-derived music, and it was impossible for the song collectors to indicate in conventional notation the rhythmic complexities of what they heard. Editor Allen admitted the problem:

> What makes it all the harder to unravel a thread of melody out of this strange network is that, like birds, they [that is, the black singers] seem not infrequently to strike sounds that cannot be precisely represented by the gamut, and abound in "slides from one note to another and turns and cadences not in articulated notes." . . . There are also apparent irregularities in the time [that is, rhythm], which it is no less difficult to express accurately.[55]

Nevertheless, certain general observations can be made. Except for the field hollers, which have their own free rhythmic patterns, the slave songs show a decided preference for simple duple meters. In performance, the steady beats of a song's meter were sustained by hand clapping and foot tapping.

Modern scholars use various terms to refer to the African tradition for

> conceiving music as structured along a theoretical framework of beats regularly spaced in time . . . whether or not the beats are expressed in actual melodic or percussion tones. . . . Since this metronome sense is of such basic importance . . . it is assumed without question or consideration to be part of the perceptual equipment of both musicians and listeners and is, in the most complete way, taken for granted.[56]

The basic pulse of the music is supplied by drums and other percussions in Africa, but by clapping and / or stomping in the United States because the use of drums was prohibited. Against the fixed rhythms of the pulse, the melodies moved freely, producing cross-rhythms that constantly clashed with the pulse patterns. It has become conventional to notate the cross-rhythms of the slave melodies as syncopation, but in reality, the phenomenon is more complex than that. While it is true that in some songs there is syncopation because of the shifting of melodic accents from strong to weaker beats, in other songs the melodies are moving in different rhythms than those of the basic pulse. What results is no longer simple syncopation but rather polyrhythms or multimeters.

The song collectors failed to indicate this in musical notation, or could not do so because of their musical limitations, but one has only to listen to twentieth-century black singers performing folk music to appreciate the complexities of the songs. If modern folk performances so vividly illustrate the phenomenon of cross-rhythms against the basic pulse, how much more

---

[55]Quotation from Allen in *Slave Songs*, pp. v–vi.
[56]Discussion of the "metronome sense" in Richard Waterman, "African Influence on the Music of the Americas," *Acculturation in the Americas*, ed. Sol Tax (Chicago, 1952), p. 211. See also Joseph H. Kwabena Nketia, *The Music of Africa* (New York, 1974).

obvious it must have been in antebellum times when the folk singers were closer to their African roots—which is where it all began. The following example suggests how a syncopated melody might have been accompanied by a pulse consisting of clapping and tapping. On the other hand, the example on p. 194 seems to represent a multimetric song in that the melody actually moves in groupings of three eighth notes against duple pulses.

Nobody Knows de Trouble I've Had, from *Slave Songs of the United States*

2. I pick de berry and I suck de juice, O yes, Lord!
   Just as sweet as the honey in de comb, O yes, Lord!
3. Sometimes I'm up, sometimes I'm down,
   Sometimes I'm almost on de groun'.
4. What make ole Satan hate me so?
   Because he got me once and he let me go.

Musical Texture

Normally we classify music as (1) *monophonic,* when there is just the melody, one note at a time; (2) *polyphonic,* when there are two or more melodies going on simultaneously; or (3) *homophonic,* when the melody has subsidiary accompanying parts.

Although the slave songs have come down to us as monophonic music and the sources report on unison singing, with everyone singing the same melody (although some at the octave), the evidence contradicts this testimony. Again and again the choral singing of blackfolk is described in terms of homophony (that is, melody with accompanying tones); writers refer to "a torrent of sacred harmony" or to the "barbaric madrigals." Both descriptions imply more than one sound at a time. The editor of *Slave Songs of the United States* frankly admitted the difficulties he encountered in trying to transfer the songs he heard to musical notation on a staff:

> The voices of the colored people have a peculiar quality that nothing can imitate; and the intonations and delicate variations of even one singer cannot be reproduced on paper. And I despair of conveying any notion of the effect of a number singing together, especially in a complicated shout. . . . There is no singing in *parts,* as we understand it, and yet no two [singers] appear to be singing the same thing.

He continues to describe in detail what happens during the course of the singing. The lead singer always began the song. The others joined the singing on the refrains, or even in the verses if they knew the words. Most often, however, the lead singer improvised new words for the verses as he or she sang. Those who constituted the chorus called themselves "basers"; when they came in on the refrains, they were "basing" the leader.

> . . . the "basers" themselves seem to follow their own whims, beginning when they please and leaving off when they please, striking an octave above or below (in case they have pitched the tune too low or too high), or hitting some other note that chords, so as to produce the effect of a marvellous complication and variety, and yet with the most perfect time, and rarely with any discord.[57]

It is important to emphasize that individuals might begin to sing the refrain before the leader concluded his or her solo, and that the leader might begin the next solo before the chorus had finished. Scholars refer to this phenomenon as *overlapping call-and-response* patterns. Obviously, these procedures produced unorthodox harmonic sounds, as Allen observed, but the diverse elements were tied together because of the governance of the strong rhythms.

Collector William Barton made an effort in a few songs to catch some of the "extra tones" that he heard accompanying melodies. He introduces *In Dat Great Day* with these sentences:

[57]Allen, *Slave Songs,* pp. iv–vi.

In theory the song is sung in unison, and there is no harmony proper. But in practice the more independent singers introduce grace notes and slurs, and the higher and lower voices range above and below in fifths and thirds in the more descriptive portions [of the text], especially in the latter verses. In this song the melody of "O Israel, O Israel" is given in the first line [that is, the soprano part] where those words are used, and in the notes which run nearest the tonic; but as the song proceeds this simple theme is worked out quite elaborately and with much greater variety than the notes here indicate.[58]

In Dat Great Day, from Barton

2. Don' you see de dead arisin'? etc.
3. Don' you heah de trumpet soundin'?
4. Don' you see dem tombs a-bustin'?
5. Yes, we'll see our chillen risin'.
6. Don' you see de chariot comin'?
7. Don' you see de sinnah tremblin'?
8. Don' you heah de saints a-shoutin'?

To summarize, the slave songs were not typically sung in unison, despite evidence to the contrary in the music sources, where most of the songs are written down as melodies. And yet the term *polyphonic,* in its true meaning, hardly applies to the singing, for the slaves did not believe themselves to be singing different melodies at the same time. Perhaps the best descriptive word is *heterophony,* in that the singers followed the lead melody for the most part but allowed themselves to wander away from it when its tones were too high, or when the text called for special emphasis, or simply when their whims indicated the need for more variety.

[58]William E. Barton, *Old Plantation Hymns* (Boston, 1899); reprint in KATZ, p. 116.

Poetic Language and Themes

The song texts are marked by vivid imagery, with emphasis on meta-phoric figures of speech. A slave sings "my brother's sitting on the tree of life"; he exults "I cast my sins in the middle of the sea." Sometimes he thinks of his sins as a heavy load on his back: "my sins so heavy I can't get along." To be sure, there is always the possibility of forgiveness: "Jesus give me a little broom for to sweep my heart clean." Often his wretched existence makes him long for the security of his infancy: "Rock o' my soul in the bosom of Abraham."

Occasionally, the technique of personification is used. The slave reminds himself: "Death's gonna lay his cold icy hand on me." He sings, "Death go from door to door" in his search for quarry; "he knock down some, and he cripple up some." In some songs the "mournful" thunder or the "lumbering" thunder "rolls from door to door," "calling home God's children," or the "forked" lightning calls God's children home.

Above all, the language is forceful and direct. The slave longs to "go home" where there is "no rain to wet," "no sun to burn," and "no whips a-cracking." He holds onto his brother or sister "with a trembling hand." If he remains in the wilderness too long, his "head will get wet with the midnight dew." He says to his wayward brother "O Sinner, ain't you tired of sinning?" Trouble becomes a "gloomy cloud," but it can be dispelled because "the sun give a light in the heaven all around."

The use of rhyme was apparently not essential to slave singers, probably because the songs originated as improvisations. Since the lead singers extemporized the words of a song as they went along, they had no time to think about rhyme, so great was their concern for the ideas they wanted to express. Perhaps during the choral response they could think ahead a bit, but not always to the extent of perfecting the rhyme. The next time the song was sung, the leader might improvise different words in response to a different set of circumstances, or a different person might lead the singing.

There are some words, some phrases, some lines that reappear so consistently from song to song that they can be regarded as "wandering" phrases and verses. Obviously at one time these wandering bits of text were associated with specific songs, but it is now impossible to trace them back to the original settings. There are, for example, the places to which the slaves refer to their songs—the wilderness, the valley, Jerusalem, Jericho, and the promised land. Any of these may be accompanied by adjectives—for example, "the lonesome valley" or "new Jerusalem." To get to one's destination, one travels up or down the road, which is "rocky" or "stormy" or "rough" or "heavenly," depending upon the circumstances. Occasionally there are references to chariots, but the slave knew from experience that the chief mode of travel was necessarily by foot. Then there are the ubiquitous allusions to water—particularly to the Jordan river or stream or banks—and to the boats that sail on the water, or to ships—particularly the Ship of Zion.

Predictably, musical themes and motives appear again and again: all must sing, trumpets must be blown, bells must ring, harps must be played, and all must "jine de band." Finally, there are the refrains that do not refer to specific themes or ideas, which might be attached to any spiritual, whether or not appropriate or related to the text; the most common examples are "Roll, Jordan, roll," "Glory, Hallelujah," "I look to the East and I look to the West" (or "Bury me in the East and bury me in the West" or "There's a fire in the East and fire in the West"), and "Ashes to ashes and dust to dust."

The slaves had their Scriptural heroes, their favorite—judging by the number of times they sang about him—being Jacob. Needless to say, their antihero was Satan. Among the other revered heroes, about whom they sang constantly, were Daniel, Moses, and Gabriel, the trumpet blower. But few of the important figures of the Old Testament were neglected, and many of the New Testament were lauded. Essentially, the spirituals retell the stories of the Bible in song; to cite only a few examples, the stories about Adam and Eve, David and Goliath, Ezekiel and the wheel, Jonah and the whale, John the Baptist, Paul and Silas, Mary and Martha, and, above all, Jesus himself. Into these stories the slaves put all the drama and excitement lacking in their own lives, but at the same time reshaped the original material to their own concerns.

Invariably, religious concepts are interpreted in the light of the slave's everyday experiences. Numerous examples could be cited but one will suffice to illustrate this point. In the *Slave Songs* there is a spiritual, *Pray All de Members,* with a text about prayer and symbolic journeys to Jericho and Jerusalem. Suddenly, the sixth and seventh stanzas jerk the listener back to the concrete everyday world: "Patrol around me, Thank God he no catch me."

Now there are no patrols in the spiritual world waiting to catch unwary pilgrims, and one cannot help thinking that the singer is concerned not so much with a journey to Jerusalem as with a trip to the next plantation for a secret religious meeting, perhaps, or to freedom in the North. Jerusalem and Jericho are being used as code names for actual places, and the maker of the song simply has neglected to invest the patrols with similar symbolic garb. We know, of course, from the testimony of ex-slaves that the religious songs, more than any others, often had double meanings and were used as code songs.

Again and again the same themes are represented in the folksongs, both religious and nonreligious. Some of these themes can be anticipated, for they are the themes of any oppressed people who are determined "to overcome." First, there is *faith*—faith that someday slavery will be no more. Slaves know that Jesus will come to rescue them, whether they are wrestling with Jacob, fighting Satan, or searching for a way out of the wilderness. Closely associated with faith is *optimism*. A song proclaims that the winter will soon be over; other songs remind the slaves that the sun is shining and the bells are ringing. *Patience* is necessary. If the slaves cannot depend upon inner resources, then they must pray to the Lord for help, ask Jesus to give more patience. At the same time, the song makers cry out, "how much longer?" They are discouraged, weary, and ill, their bodies wracked with pain and fever. They even welcome death as a reliever of their misery. The *weariness* theme sounds in almost all the songs, sometimes in the opening verses but more frequently in the later ones. Surprisingly, for a so-called meek people, there is a great deal of emphasis on the theme of *fighting*. True, the fight is frequently symbolic—a fight with Satan or Jacob or sin. But in numerous instances all pretense is dropped; the slave plans to fight until he dies.

Despite their isolation on the plantations, the slaves were aware of the bitter conflict shaping in the United States during the middle decades of the nineteenth century that was to result in the Civil War. There was constant movement from plantation to plantation and from state to state—particularly from Virginia to the states in the deep South—as slaves were sold, exchanged, or sent out "for hire." The news was spread of aborted slave revolts, of the militance of the abolitionists and their Underground Railroad to freedom. Eventually, a body of plantation war songs developed in the South, in response to the unsettled condition of the nation.

Performance Practice

Generally, but not always, the opening verses of Negro folksongs tend to be syllabic—that is, there is one note for each syllable. Succeeding verses are another matter! Once a pattern has been set, any number of syllables may be sung on a single pitch. One of the editors of the *Slave Songs* explained it thus:

> Neither should any one be repelled by any difficulty in adapting the words to the tunes. The negroes keep exquisite time in singing, and do not suffer themselves to be daunted by any obstacle in the words. The most obstinate Scripture phrases or snatches from hymns they will force to do duty with any tune they please, and will dash heroically through a trochaic tune at the head of a column of iambs with wonderful skill.[59]

The single most important element of the slave music was its performance as, indeed, is true of black folk music in the twentieth century. It was the performance that shaped the song into an entity, that finally determined its melody, texture, tempo, rhythmical patterns, text, and effect upon listeners. The song as recorded in musical notation represents only a skeleton that indicates stable notes of the melody, the basic pulse, and persistent refrain texts. All else might vary from performance to performance. If there is any

---

[59]Allen, *Slave Songs*, p. iv.

one aspect of performance that almost all the contemporary sources agree upon, it is the fact that the slaves improvised their songs.

> All these songs are peculiarly improvisations. . . . This improvisation goes forward every day. . . . The rhyme comes as it may, sometimes clumsily, sometimes no rhyme at all, sometimes most wonderfully fresh and perfect.[60]

By gathering together diverse threads of discussion in the sources, we can arrive at some generalizations about the performance practice in the nineteenth century that ultimately determined the character of the folk music. In the first place, there was high musical density, defined by one modern scholar as a profusion of musical activities going on simultaneously within a relatively short musical space.[61] Editor William Allen described it as follows in 1867:

> We have aimed to give all the characteristic variations [for the songs] which have come into our hands, whether as single notes or whole lines, or even longer passages; and of words as well as tunes. . . . It may sometimes be a little difficult . . . to determine precisely [the relationship between all these things]. . . . However much latitude the reader may take in all such matters, he will hardly take more than the negroes themselves do. . . . The rests [in the notated songs], by the way, do not indicate a cessation in the music, but only in part of the singers. They overlap in singing, as already described, in such a degree that at no time is there any complete pause.[62]

Natural pauses in the melody were filled in with clapping, stomping, pattin', vocal outbursts, and, in the case of dance music, strumming or slapping string instruments, shaking rattles, and beating sticks, bones, and other percussive instruments.

The voice quality cultivated by black singers was strong, intense, and clear; contemporaneous accounts refer to the "far-sounding harmony," "vigorous chorus," or the "great billows of sound" produced by the slaves' singing. When the slaves gathered for corn-shucking jubilees, in some places as many as three hundred or more would participate in the singing as they marched along the roads, their "rich, deep voices swelling out" on the refrains. Even the singing of two slaves as they walked through a forest "would make the dense old woods, for miles around, reverberate with their wild songs." When the slaves sang psalms and hymns during their religious services, they sang "loud and slow." One observer thought the male voices seemed "oftener tenor than any other quality," and a number of writers remarked the free use of falsetto, particularly in the field hollers but also in other song types.

There is evidence that singers showed a predilection for variety in timbre

---

[60]Bremer *Homes*, v. 2, p. 108.
[61]Olly Wilson, "The Significance of the Relationship Between Afro-American Music and West African Music," BPIM 2 (Spring 1974): 16.
[62]Allen, *Slave Songs*, p. xxl.

at all points along the continuum. A song might move from speechlike sounds (described as "recitative" or "shrill monotone," for example) through ranges of the musical compass to screaming and yelling, all within the confines of a single performance. Or a singer might jump from speech to melody or yell and vice versa. The performer displayed an equal concern for variety in accompanying sounds: at any one point in the performance a listener could distinguish between the high, medium, and low, the sharp and muffled, the clear and buzzing.

Few observers commented upon instrumental performance practice, aside from pointing out the slave's obvious love for the instrument he or she played. One writer's acute observation in 1857 is invaluable:

> The banjo is of all instruments the best adapted to the lowest class of slaves. . . . They *talk* to it, and a skillful performer can excite the most diverse passions among the dancers [italics mine].[63]

When we add testimony from articulate slaves such as Solomon Northup, who called his violin "my companion—the friend of my bosom," a logical assumption is that the slaves regarded their instruments as equal partners in the making of music—not simply as accompanists. This concept undoubtedly contributed a great deal to the unique sound of slave music and, as we shall see, has profound implications for the development of black music in the twentieth century.

Then, there was the obvious influence of the dance upon performance; by all accounts, musical performance was inseparable from some kind of body movement—if not in the course of dancing or working, then movement involved in providing accompaniment for singing and dancing. An old man drummed on a board as he sang; the fiddler tapped his foot as he played; a boy patted juba as he recited the words of a dance song. One writer attempted to define this phenomenon:

> Without any teaching, the Negroes have contrived a rude kind of opera, combining the poetry of motion, of music, and of language . . . all the Negro songs were intended to be performed as well as sung and played.[64]

Finally, there is the importance given to communal participation; among the black folk there was no audience, only performers and nonperformers. The affair moved along in call-and-response style, the group following the soloist with refrains or, in another setting, the onlookers responding to the preacher or the tale teller or the "shouter" with cries of approval (or disapproval)—"Yes, Lord," "I say now," "Wake em, brudder," "Stan' up to 'em, brudder."

---

[63]John Dixon Long, *Pictures of Slavery* . . . (Philadelphia, 1857), p. 17.
[64][J. Kinnard], "Who Are Our National Poets," reprint in BPIM (Spring 1975): 83–94. Quotation on p. 87.

Summary

Based on the evidence, it can be assumed that during the nineteenth century the foundations were laid for a distinctive African-American folk music, that African and European traditions were blended in such a way as to produce a new music genre. The sources tell us that in the eighteenth century black Americans continued to sing African songs and to perform African dances, while at the same time they learned the psalms, hymns, and popular songs of the whites, as well as their jigs and reels. To be sure, these practices continued into the nineteenth century, lingering longer in some places than in others. But certainly by the time of the Emancipation Proclamation in 1863, it appears that the new black folk music with its own special traditions had established itself throughout the nation.

It was a music predominantly African in tone, developed by black folk living in urban communities and by the slaves on the plantations. The character of the music changed very little as black Americans moved from slavery to freedom and from the nineteenth century into the twentieth. All the stylistic features that have been discussed in this chapter as representative of black folk music appear in the folk music of the twentieth century as well, and music continued to play a primary role in the lives the people.

CHAPTER 6

The War Years
and
Emancipation

THE 1860s were ushered in by a bitter intersectional war between white pro-slavery and anti-slavery forces, bringing drastic changes in the existing relationship between black men and white men in the United States. In the years just before the war, several events forewarned of the trouble to come. One of the first was the Compromise of 1850, which was intended to settle both the problem of the fugitive slave and the question of whether slavery should be permitted in the territories being annexed to the United States—California, Utah, and New Mexico (including what is now Arizona). The compromise was unsuccessful; abolitionists only increased their efforts in helping slaves to escape, and slaveholders stepped up their activities in recovering the fugitives, often kidnapping free black men and women as well as runaways. The publication of Harriet Beecher Stowe's anti-slavery novel, *Uncle Tom's Cabin*, in 1852 served to widen further the growing gulf between North and South. When the Supreme Court decided in 1857 that a Negro could not be regarded as a citizen of the United States and, consequently, had no civil rights (in the so-called Dred Scott case), many of the abolitionists were convinced that war was inevitable if the slaves were ever to be freed.

Then came John Brown's raid on the federal arsenal at Harpers Ferry, Virginia, in 1859. He had planned—with the help of ardent abolitionists like himself, including several black men—to obtain enough ammunition in his raid to open fire on the slaveholders of Virginia. These plans were thwarted and Brown was hanged, but in the process he became a martyr to the cause of freedom. In 1860 an aroused people voted into the presidency of the United States a man who was determined to prevent the country from falling apart and who had pronounced anti-slavery sentiments, although he was not an abolitionist.

When President Abraham Lincoln was called upon to defend Fort Sumter on April 12, 1861, against an attack by secessionists, he called out federal troops, and the War Between the States began. As in previous wars, black men offered their services to the Union—and, as in previous wars, their offers were at first rejected. It was not until the fall of 1862 that they were permitted to enlist for service. Among the first troops to be organized were the First South Carolina Volunteer Regiment, the Fifty-fourth Massachusetts Regiment, a New Orleans regiment called the *Corps d'Afrique,* and the First Regiment of Kansas Colored Volunteers.

By the end of the Civil War in 1865, more than 186,000 black men had been inducted into the army as the "United States Colored Troops."[1] They had been organized into the various existing kinds of regiments—166 in all, including 137 regular infantry, 13 heavy artillery, 10 light artillery, and 6 cavalry. Most troops were led by white commanding officers, but some regiments were staffed by black officers. Relatively large numbers of black musicians performed in army bands and afterward put to good use the skills they had developed during the war. In the Confederate army, slaves were employed in essential noncombatant services and in important war industries. Many southerners took their slaves with them to the front, mostly to serve as body servants, but also to perform other duties. The slave Josephus Blake and two fellows, for example, played fifes and drums for the regiment of their master, General John B. Gordon.

In addition to the black serviceman and the southern slave laborer, there was yet a third role played by the black man during the war years—that of "contraband of war." The term was applied to the fugitive slaves who fled by the thousands to the Union army lines, were settled in contraband camps, and placed under the supervision of federal forces. So much confusion resulted from the government's handling of the contrabands that various private elements among the whites organized themselves to assist the refugees. Chief among the newly established groups were educational missions and freedmen's relief associations.

The whites, who as commanding officers, supervisors in contraband camps, and agents of educational missions, came into contact with blacks were usually northerners, and most frequently these contacts represented their first close association with African Americans. They brought to the experience a sincere desire to help and, at the same time, considerable curiosity about the recipients of their aid. They recorded their impressions and the events of everyday life among the black folk in a steady stream of pub-

[1]Of this number, approximately 52,000 were from the North; the remainder (more than two-thirds) were from slave states. See further in John Hope Franklin, *From Slavery to Freedom* (New York, 1967), 3rd. rev. ed., pp. 290 ff.

Band of the 107th United States Colored Infantry. *(Courtesy Library of Congress)*

lished letters, journals, diaries, and narratives that ebbed only in the closing years of the nineteenth century. For the most part, the persons responsible for disseminating information about the musical practices of the African American and for collecting examples of their songs during the 1860s were members of this group of concerned northerners.

Best known was Colonel Higginson of the South Carolina Volunteer Regiment—Harvard graduate, minister, and abolitionist. Higginson first published an article in the *Atlantic Monthly* (June 1867) about the black man's songs and later wrote a book, *Army Life in a Black Regiment,* that contained additional information. The compilers of the historic 1867 collection, *Slave Songs of the United States,* were all members of an educational mission that had been sent in 1861 to Port Royal on the coast of South Carolina, and most of them were members of later missions sent to one or another of the islands off the coast of South Carolina and Georgia.

Among those who contributed songs to the 1867 collection were Charlotte Forten (1838–1914), a young black teacher from Philadelphia, and Laura M. Towne, a white teacher from New England. Forten worked with the ex-slaves on Helena Island, South Carolina, during the years 1862–64, and described the impressive singing she heard all about her in a journal, which later was published. She also submitted articles to the *Atlantic Monthly,* entitled "Life on the Sea Islands" (May, June 1864), that included song texts and description of performance practice. Towne began teaching on the island in 1862 and remained there until her death in 1901. Her journal, which like Forten's was published later, offers astute observations about musical practices and includes song texts. Finally, there was Elizabeth Botume, another Sea Islands teacher, who although not a contributor to

Slave Songs, left a book, *First Days Amongst the Contrabands* (1893), containing very useful information about the music of the ex-slaves.

MUSIC IN THE UNION ARMY

One of the first acts of the white commanding officers of Negro regiments was to procure instruments and music instructors for the formation of bands. In Massachusetts, for example, a special fund of $500 was contributed early during the recruiting stage to Colonel Robert Gould Shaw's Fifty-fourth Regiment for the purchase of musical instruments and uniforms, and a musician of the Fifty-eighth Regiment of New York was obtained to instruct the band. During the first months of organization a great deal of attention was given to drilling and evening parades. Recruits for the First Regiment of Kansas Colored Volunteers spent as many as five hours daily in drills and ended each day with a dress parade. The Fifty-fifth of Massachusetts had its first evening parade even before uniforms and arms had arrived from the government. White army bands and special drum corps composed of young black boys were used to provide music for drills during the period when black soldiers were being taught how to play band instruments.

Black soldiers brought to army life their love of music. More than one officer was entranced by the continuous singing that went on day and night in army camps and later wrote about it in a regimental history, a camp diary, or a personal memoir. Black ex-soldiers, too, have left written records of army life that included references to group singing. Since the report of Colonel Higginson agrees with the published records of other army men, we quote from it as representative of life in a black army camp. The white officer strolling among his men as they sat around evening campfires rarely failed to be amazed by the wide variety of activities in which they were engaged. While some men were cleaning their guns or rehearsing their drills, others were swapping stories and jokes, especially at the expense of their white officers. To be sure, these were typical scenes in the white camps as well, but the religious activities of the black soldier probably were unmatched by parallel scenes among the whites. Higginson wrote:[2]

> The everlasting "shout" is always within hearing, with its mixture of piety and polka, and its castenet-like clapping of the hands. Then there are quieter prayermeetings, with pious invocations and slow psalms, "deaconed out" from memory by the leader, two lines at a time, in a sort of wailing chant. . . . Elsewhere, it is some solitary old cook, some aged Uncle Tiff, with enormous spectacles, who is perusing a hymn-book by the light of a pine splinter, in his deserted cooking booth of palmetto leaves.

[2]Thomas W. Higginson, *Army Life in a Black Regiment* (Boston, 1870); reprint of excerpts in RBAM pp. 175–202. See pp. 178–79, 175 for quotations.

Of course, not all activity was of a serious nature:

> By another fire there is an actual dance, red-legged soldiers doing right-and-left, and "now-lead-de-lady-ober," to the music of a violin which is rather artistically played, and which may have guided the steps, in other days, of Barnwells and Hugers.

On rainy evenings, "mingled sounds of stir and glee" would come from the tents to the ears of the commanding officers:

> . . . a feeble flute stirs somewhere in some tent, not an officer's,—a drum throbs far away in another . . . and from a neighboring cook-fire comes the monotonous sound of that strange festival, half pow-wow, half prayer-meeting, which they know only as a "shout."

For the shout the men would have crowded into one tent or hut, singing at the "top of their voices . . . quaint, monotonous, endless, negro-Methodist chants." Invariably the excitement would spread to other parts of the camp, and soldiers from all over would join in the performance—inside and outside the enclosure—all "steadily circling like dervishes." Higginson and others marveled that the shout should take place "not rarely and occasionally, but night after night."

In some places black soldiers formed glee clubs that occasionally gave concerts for the community, gaining thereby not only good will but also money for the company fund. Service units came into contact with members of the community on many occasions, the most common of which were the periodic drills and parades and the celebration of holidays to which spectators were invited. The historian of the Fifty-fifth Massachusetts describes one such occasion:

> On the 4th of July, 1863, a festival was prepared for the regiment by the ladies in the vicinity. Music and dancing, with games and prizes were the order of the day, and in the evening a display of fireworks from the high embankment of the railroad overlooking the camp. The leader of the regimental band was presented with a silver cornet. . . .[3]

But it was the black soldiers' singing of folksongs that most frequently drew the attention of commanding officers and friends of the regiments. Higginson was moved thereby to record the texts of the songs sung by his men. He explained his action:

> The war brought to some of us, besides its direct experiences, many a strange fulfillment of dreams of other days. For instance, the present writer had been a faithful student of the Scottish ballads, and had always envied Sir Walter [Scott] the delight of tracing them out amid their own heather, and of writing them down piecemeal from the lips of aged crones. It was a strange enjoyment, therefore, to be suddenly brought into the midst of a kindred world of unwritten

---

[3]Charles B. Fox, *Record of the Service of the 55th Regiment of Massachusetts Volunteer Infantry* (Boston, 1868), p. 2.

songs, as simple and indigenous as the Border Minstrelsy, more uniformly plaintive, almost always more quaint, and often as essentially poetic.

This interest was rather increased by the fact that I had for many years heard of this class of songs under the name of "Negro Spirituals," and had even heard some of them sung by friends from South Carolina. I could now gather on their own soil these strange plants, which I had before seen as in museums alone.[4]

Singing was for black servicemen not only a recreational activity, but a release from the predictable tensions involved in fighting a war, particularly one in which the problem of the freedom of the race was to be settled. Black soldiers sang, along with their own folksongs, the war songs of white composers that were popular with all servicemen, such as George Root's *Tramp, Tramp, Tramp, Battle Cry of Freedom,* and *Just Before the Battle, Mother;* Henry Clay Work's *Marching Through Georgia;* Patrick S. Gilmore's *When Johnny Comes Marching Home;* and Walter Kittredge's *Tenting on the Old Camp Ground.* But their all-time favorite was *John Brown's Body.* The four-phrase melody for this song belonged originally to a campmeeting song composed in 1852 by a white song-leader, William Steffe. To the original chorus, "Glory, Glory, Hallelujah," an anonymous soldier added some stanzas about John Brown.

John Brown's Body, William Steffe

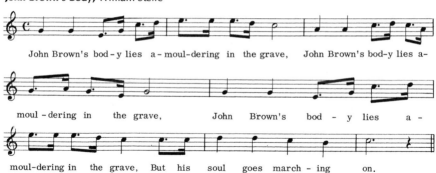

In 1862 Julia Ward Howe wrote a stirring poem, *The Battle Hymn of the Republic,* to be sung to the popular tune, which was used for both stanzas and chorus. Black soldiers seemed to prefer their own texts, however, and used the tune for marching songs, camp songs, social songs, and even religious songs. Among the different versions that were in circulation during the war years was this one:

> We are done with hoeing cotton, we are done with hoeing corn,
> We are colored Yankee soldiers, as sure as you are born;
> When Massa hears us shouting, he will think 'tis Gabriel's horn,
> As we go marching on.

[4]Higginson, *Army Life,* pp. 172–73.

John Brown's Body came to be the unofficial theme song of black soldiers. Early in the war it was invested with a special sentiment for them. Historians report, for example, that when the band of the Fifty-fourth of Massachusetts, one of the first black regiments to go South, played the melody as the soldiers marched down State Street in Boston en route to Battery Wharf, tears came to the eyes of the proud black women watching the parade and the mother of the white commanding officer, Mrs. Shaw. Another popular song was the so-called *Negro Battle Hymn,* also known as *They Look Like Men of War.*

Under informal circumstances, soldiers on the march used the "route step"—that is, they were allowed to talk and sing and were not required to keep in step but could simply remain four abreast as long as they did not lag behind. Higginson provides a description of route stepping, on an occasion when his men were "at the top of exhilaration."[5] To everybody, known or unknown, who gathered along the roads to watch them pass, they would sing out greetings: "Howd' you, brother?" His "laughing and utterly unmanageable drummers" heartily greeted the grave little boys on the roadside with, "Dem's de drummers for de nex' war!" They flirted with the girls and saluted the venerable kerchiefed matrons, singing briskly all the while. When Higginson reined up to watch them pass, the strains of one company's songs blended with those of the preceding and following companies.

> Such an odd mixture of things, military and missionary, as the successive waves of song drifted by! First, "John Brown", of course; then, "What make old Satan for [to] follow me so?" then, "Marching Along"; then, "Hold your light on Canaan's shore"; then, "When this cruel war is over" (a new favorite, sung by a few); yielding presently to a grand burst of the favorite marching song among them all, and one at which every step instinctively quickened, so light and jubilant its rhythm,—
>
> > "All true children gwine [going] in de wilderness,
> > Gwine in de wilderness, gwine in de wilderness,
> > True believers gwine in de wilderness,
> > To take away de sins ob de world,"—
>
> ending in a "Hoigh!" after each verse,—a sort of Irish yell. For all the songs, but especially for their own wild hymns, they constantly improvised simple verses, with the same odd mingling,—the little facts of to-day's march being interwoven with the depths of theological gloom, and the same jubilant chorus annexed to all. . . .

William Barton recorded several "war songs" in his collection, *Hymns of the Slave and Freeman.* His comments about the improvisatory nature of the verses in these songs support Higginson's statement. Sometimes only a single line represents the stable element, the rest of the song being "built up

---

[5]Higginson p. 171.

as occasion demands." In the following song, however, the entire chorus was typically sung without alternation.[6]

Stay in the Field, from Barton

O stay in the field, chil-der-en-ah, Stay in the field, chil-der-en-ah.

Stay in the field, Un - til the war is end - ed.

1. { I've got my breast-plate, sword and shield, / And I'll go march-ing thro' the field, } Till the war is end-ed.

2. Satan thought he had me fast,
Till the war is ended;
But thank the Lord I'm free at last,
Till the war is ended.

MUSIC IN THE CONFEDERATE ARMY

Little is known about the activities of Negro musicians in the Confederate army except that slaves were pressed into service as fifers and drummers. But there is evidence in the official records of the army that suggests that some may have been given the rank of musician or bugler. An act entitled "An Act for the payment of musicians in the army not regularly enlisted" reads as follows:

> The Congress of the Confederate States of America do enact, That whenever colored persons are employed as musicians in any regiment or company, they shall be entitled to the same pay now allowed by law to musicians regularly enlisted: Provided, That no such persons shall be employed except by consent of the commanding officer of the brigade to which said regiments or companies may belong. Approved April 15, 1862.

MUSIC IN THE CONTRABAND CAMP

Life in the contraband camp was in many ways similar to life on the plantation. Black people lived in special quarters under supervision of the whites and worked at jobs that would aid in the war effort. The ex-slaves adjusted

[6]Barton, *Old Plantation Hymns;* reprint in KATZ, p. 100.

Sheet music cover for *Hymn of the Freedman*. *(Courtesy of the author)*

to the incredible inconveniences of camp life, to the lack of sufficient clothing and, occasionally, of adequate food. It was enough for them that freedom was in the air! Elizabeth Botume, like other writers of her time, noticed that songs, too, were in the air, night and day. Her campers had been forced to resort to very primitive means in order to obtain the basic food staple of the camp:[7]

> This hominy was ground between two flat stones, one of which was stationary and the other was moved by hand by means of an upright stick inserted in a groove in the stone. It was a slow and tedious process, but always enlivened by songs . . . and jokes of the colored people when grinding. At night the older people came and ground by the light of a pine torch fastened to a post. All night long I could hear the whizzing of the wheel and the shouts of the people. I have dropped to sleep hearing,—
>
> > "O believer, go ring that bell, ring that bell,
> >   ring that bell,
> > O believer, go ring that bell, ring that charming bell."
>
> the words and the tunes mingling with my dreams. When I awoke in the morning they were still singing, but it was now—
>
> > "Roll Jordan, roll Jordan, roll Jordan, roll."

When the camp held its periodic festivals, there was always the ubiquitous shout. The favorite shout spirituals among all the contrabands were *I Can't Stay Behind* and *Nobody Knows the Trouble I've Had.*

The whites who lived in contraband camps were sometimes asked to fulfill unusual requests. Botume, for example, was once asked to "funeralize"—that is, to read the burial service for a funeral and lead the singing. She wrote later in her diary, "I lined the hymns as distinctly as possible, which the entire crowd sang loud and slow in a minor tune." Funerals were invariably held at night. The ex-slaves believed that the spirit remained with the body until daylight, then went home to God as the morning stars disappeared. All night long the friends of the deceased would sit together in a watch meeting, called a "setting up," chanting and clapping their hands. At dawn would begin the long procession from the burial site, the marchers beating muffled drums and singing spirituals. On one occasion Botume was reminded of the *Pilgrim's March* in Wagner's opera, *Tannhäuser,* as the tones of the spirituals "reverberated through the arches of 'God's first temple.' "

EMANCIPATION

Over the years the slaves had developed a sizable repertory of songs about the day when freedom should come. While few song texts of this kind are

[7]Elizabeth Botume, *First Days Amongst the Contrabands* (Boston, 1893), pp. 135, 103, 222.

preserved, and understandably so, there are numerous references to them. As the war tensions mounted throughout the nation, black folk were restricted more and more. In Georgetown, South Carolina, for example, slaves were whipped for singing the following spiritual on the occasion of Lincoln's election:

> We'll fight for liberty,
> We'll fight for liberty,
> We'll fight for liberty,
> Till the Lord shall call us home;
> We'll soon be free,
> Till the Lord shall call us home.[8]

In the fall of 1862, President Lincoln issued a preliminary proclamation stating that on January 1, 1863, "all persons held as slaves within any State, or designated part of the State, the people whereof shall be in rebellion against the United States shall be then, thenceforward and forever free." Black men assembled in "rejoicing meetings" all over the land on the last night of December in 1862, waiting for the stroke of midnight to bring freedom to those slaves in the secessionist states. At the contraband camp in Washington, D.C., the black assemblage sang over and over again:

> Go down, Moses,
> Way down in Egypt land;
> Tell old Pharaoh,
> Let my people go.

Then, according to William Wells Brown, "a sister broke out in the following strain, which was heartily joined in by the vast assembly"[9]

> Go down, Abraham,
> Away down in Dixie's land;
> Tell Jeff Davis
> To let my people go.

In a lowly cabin in South Carolina a slave said to those gathered there, "by the time I counts ten, it will be midnight and the land will be free. . . ." A man began to sing:

> Oh, brethren, my way, my way's cloudy
> Go send dem angels down

[Throughout the song the refrain follows each line of text, as in the first stanza.]

> There's fire in the east an' fire in the west
> An' fire among the Methodists
> Ole Satan's mad and I'm glad

---

[8]Benjamin Quarles, *The Negro in the Civil War* (Boston 1953), p. 51.
[9]Following quotations from William Wells Brown, *The Negro in the American Rebellion* (Boston, (1867), pp. 118–19, and Brown, *Southern Home*, pp. 155–56.

He missed the soul he thought he had
I'll tell you now as I told before
To the promised land I'm bound to go
This is the year of Jubilee
The Lord has come to set us free

In some places the first songs that came to the lips of the huge assemblies of Negroes gathered in great halls or in open fields were not spirituals but beloved hymns that had been consolation for decades. At Tremont Hall in Boston, for example, it was *Blow Ye the Trumpet, Blow.* At a celebration at Camp Saxton in South Carolina, where white and black had assembled, it was a patriotic hymn that the freed slaves began to sing after the speeches and the band music—*My Country 'Tis of Thee.* A handful of black people began the singing, and others joined in. When some whites also attempted to join the singing, Colonel Higginson waved them to silence; the "new citizens" of the Union alone sang all the verses of their new national hymn.

New Year's Day took on a special significance for black people of the nation. Formerly known as "Heartbreak Day" because of the custom of holding big slave auctions on that day, the first day of the year now became associated with freedom and hope for the future. For many years after 1863, celebrations were held in Negro communities in honor of the Emancipation Proclamation. In 1866 celebrations were especially important, for in 1865 Congress added the Thirteenth Amendment to the Constitution, abolishing slavery in *all* the states; the 1863 Act had eliminated slavery only from those states that had seceded from the Union.

The slaves had wisely refrained from singing their freedom songs in the presence of whites before Emancipation; now they came out into the open. From this period dates such songs as *No More Auction Block for Me, I Want Some Valiant Soldier, Babylon Is Fallen, Bobolishion's* [Abolition's] *Coming, Before I'd Be a Slave, The Massa Run,* and *Done wid Driber's Dribin'* (i.e., the slave driver's or overseer's driving).

Done wid Driber's Dribin', traditional

1. Done wid dri-ber's dri-bin', Done wid dri-ber's dri-bin',
Done wid dri-ber's dri - bin', Roll, Jor - dan, roll.

2. Done wid massa's hollerin',
3. Done wid missus' scoldin'.

Of these songs, *Before I'd Be a Slave* was destined to be long-lived. Barton heard the song many times during the 1880s.[10] He associated it especially

[10]Barton, *Old Plantation Hymns,* p. 98.

with an old ex-slave, Uncle Joe Williams, to whom slavery had not been unkind, but who nevertheless had looked forward to freedom as eagerly as the most persecuted of slaves. This was the song Williams "loved to sing, sitting before his door in the twilight":[11]

Before I'd Be a Slave (Oh, Freedom), from Barton

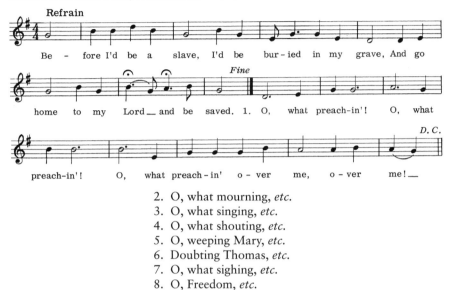

2. O, what mourning, *etc.*
3. O, what singing, *etc.*
4. O, what shouting, *etc.*
5. O, weeping Mary, *etc.*
6. Doubting Thomas, *etc.*
7. O, what sighing, *etc.*
8. O, Freedom, *etc.*

Half a century later, during the early 1960s, the song was adopted by workers in the Civil Rights movement in the United States and in a few short years had spread throughout the world, a musical standard-bearer for those—regardless of race, color, or religion—in search of equal opportunity to achieve the good things in life.

[11]Barton, p. 98.

PART THREE

BLOW YE THE TRUMPET

1865–1919

Blow ye the trumpet, blow
The gladly-solemn sound
Let all the nations know
To earth's remotest bound
The year of Jubilee is come
Return ye ransom'd sinners, home.

—PROTESTANT HYMN

IMPORTANT EVENTS

1865 First large migration of ex-slaves to urban areas.
First permanent black minstrel troupes; black showman Charles "Barney" Hicks organizes the Georgia Minstrels.
Founding of the Oberlin Conservatory of Music at Oberlin, OH.

1866 Passage of the Civil Rights Act, which gave citizenship to black men and guaranteed them equal treatment under the law.

1867 First publication of a collection of spirituals and plantation songs: *Slave Songs of the United States,* edited by William Allen, Charles Ware, and Lucy McKim Garrison.
Founding of two conservatories of music in Boston, the Boston Conservatory and the New England Conservatory; also of the Cincinnati Conservatory and Chicago Musical College.
Establishment of the first of the philanthropists' foundations that worked to advance Negro education, the Peabody Education Fund. Later came the John F. Slater Fund (1892); the General Education Board, supported by John D. Rockefeller (1902); the Julius Rosenwald Fund (1912).

1869 Completion of the first transcontinental railroad, the Union Pacific.

1870 Founding of the Colored Methodist Episcopal Church (called C.M.E.; name changed to Christian M. E. in 1954).

1871 First tour of the Fisk University Jubilee Singers; followed by tours of the Hampton Students and professional jubilee troupes.

1872 World Peace Jubilee produced by Patrick S. Gilmore at Boston; performers include the Fisk Jubilee Singers and the Hyers Sisters.

1876 Celebration of the Centennial of American Independence at Philadelphia.
Organization of the first permanent black musical-comedy troupe, the Hyers Sisters Comic Opera Co.

1880 Organization of black Baptist congregations into the National Baptist Convention, U.S.A.

1883 Founding of the Metropolitan Opera Company at New York.

1885 Founding of the National Conservatory of Music at New York.

1887 Invention of the disc recording method by Emile Berliner; his enterprise was the beginning of the Victor Recording Company.

1890 First enactment of Jim Crow legislation in the South that enforced segregation of black people in the areas of education, housing, transportation, and recreation.

1895 Founding of the Church of God in Christ.
Gussie Davis, Tin Pan Alley composer, wins prize as second most popular songwriter in the nation in competition sponsored by the *New York World.*
Founding of the American Federation of Musicians.

1896 Founding of the Church of Christ, Holiness.
Organizing of Black Patti's Troubadours.

1898 First musicals written and produced by black people play on Broadway: *A Trip to Coontown* by Cole and Johnson; *Clorindy; or, The Origin of the Cakewalk* by Cook Dunbar. Followed in first decade of the twentieth century by Walker and Williams musicals and by Cole and Johnson musicals.

1899 Publication of the *Maple Leaf Rag* by Scott Joplin.

1900 First grand opera productions by Theodore Drury at NY (1900–8).

1901 Bert Williams and George Walker recorded singing songs from black musicals.
First known recording of black musicians.

1902 First incorporation of a black musician's union, Chicago's Local 208, into the American Federation of Musicians.

IMPORTANT EVENTS

First known recording of a black music group: the Dinwiddie Colored Quartet by the Victor Talking Machine Company.

1904   First performance of a black musical show abroad: *Walker and Williams in Dahomey* at the Shaftesbury Theatre in London.

1905   Founding of the Niagara Movement under leadership of W. E. B. Du Bois in protest of race discrimination and lynching at Niagara Falls, Canada.

Founding of first permanent black theater by Bob Motts at Chicago.

Founding and incorporation of first black symphony in the North: Philadelphia Concert Orchestra; E. Gilbert Anderson, conductor.

Incorporation of second black musician's union in the nation: the New Amsterdam Musical Association of New York (founded in 1900).

1906   The Azusa Street Revival at Los Angeles (1906–9) under leadership of William Seymour.

1908   Appointment of first black bandmasters to the U.S. Army: Ninth and Tenth Cavalry regiments, Twenty-Fourth and Twenty-Fifth Infantry regiments.

1909   Founding of the NAACP (National Association for the Advancement of Colored People, incorporating the Niagara Movement) at New York.

1910   Incorporation of the Clef Club at New York (music-contracting company).

1911   First performance (private) of a Negro folk opera written by a black composer: *Treemonisha* by Scott Joplin.

Founding of the National League on Urban Conditions among Negroes (called the National Urban League).

1912   First in a series of four annual concerts (1912–15) given by black sym-phony orchestras at Carnegie Hall in New York.

Publication of the *Memphis Blues* by W. C. Handy.

1913   Organization of the first black-theater circuit by black showman Sherman H. Dudley; led to the formation of T.O.B.A. (the Theatre Owners Booking Association) in 1920.

1914   World War I (1914–18)

First in a series of three annual "All-Colored Composers Concerts" (1914–16) given at Orchestra Hall in Chicago.

Institution of the Spingarn Medal awards by the NAACP for achievement by a black individual.

Founding of ASCAP (American Society of Composers, Authors, and Publishers).

Publication of the *St. Louis Blues* by W. C. Handy.

1915   First publication of a jazz arrangement, *Jelly Roll Blues* by Ferdinand Morton.

1916   Beginning of huge migration of black men and women out of the South into the North and West.

First publication of a collection of solo arrangements of spirituals, *Jubilee Songs of the United States of America* by Harry T. Burleigh.

First publication of a collection of gospel hymns written by a black songwriter, *New Songs of Paradise* by Charles A. Tindley.

1917   First recording of a jazz band, the Original Dixieland Jazz Band (a white group) at New York.

1918   Jazz concert of James Reese Europe's 369th Infantry Band at the Théâtre des Champs-Elysées "conquers Paris."

1919   Founding of the National Association of Negro Musicians.

CHAPTER 7

After
the War

THE year 1865 brought to an end the enslavement of more than four million black men and women. By the thousands the ex-slaves fled the hated plantations to urban areas of the South, to the North, and out into the great plains of the West. Inevitably there was a tremendous amount of suffering, for the ex-slaves were suddenly thrust without preparation into a new way of life. The federal government set up the Bureau of Refugees, Freedmen, and Abandoned Lands (called Freedmen's Bureau) to provide basic food and health services, to arrange for employment, and to establish schools. The American Missionary Association and various other religious groups also assisted in the establishment of schools, and hundreds of teachers came down from the North to work in them. Among the Negro institutes and colleges founded just after the war were Atlanta, Biddle Memorial (now Johnson C. Smith), Fisk, Hampton, Howard, and St. Augustine.

It had been rumored that each ex-slave family was to receive "forty acres and a mule" from the government as a start toward building a new life, but this proved to be unfounded. Some amount of land was distributed to ex-slaves, however, particularly under the Southern Homestead Act. The newly freed also received help from another quarter—the black church. With the demise of slavery, blacks were no longer forced to attend the churches of the whites, and they began to organize their own. Those independent Negro churches already in existence, the AME and AME Zion denominations, greatly expanded their membership, and a new denomination, the Colored Methodist Episcopal Church (now Christian Methodist Episcopal Church) appeared on the scene.

Despite the initial migration of thousands out of the South, within a few years most of the newly freed slaves were resettled there and engaged in agricultural occupations as before. They worked under a system called "sharecropping," wherein the landowners provided land and tools for the workers, whose responsibility it was to raise crops. At harvest time the workers were given a share of the crops as pay for their labor. The built-in evils of the system militated against the ex-slaves' prospects of improving their lot. In some ways they were worse off than they had been under slavery. The southern states began to pass the so-called Jim Crow laws that infringed upon the rights of black men and women in every area of daily life. Their precarious situation was not helped by the emergence of white secret societies such as the Ku Klux Klan, whose avowed purpose was to reestablish control over the black population and maintain "white supremacy." Under cover of darkness, hooded white riders tore black men from their homes—beat them, tarred and feathered them, and lynched them.

SONGS OF THE PEOPLE

In keeping with their traditions, the ex-slaves sang about their experiences—their new freedom, their new occupations, the strange ways of the city, current events, and their feelings of rootlessness and loneliness. Above all the newly freed sought self-identity. Slavery had deprived them of their names, homelands, and families. The original African names of their forbears had long ago been forgotten, the land of Africa no longer beckoned after almost two hundred and fifty years of exile, and their relatives had been dispersed, for the slave auction block had separated husband from wife, mother from child, brother from sister, and lover from lover. Now that freedom had come, some freedmen and freedwomen set out in search of long-lost loved ones. The black singer recounted their adventures, too. In an uneasy society that used the slightest pretext for putting black men in prison, large numbers of them found themselves behind bars. Consequently, a new type of song was born, the prison song.

Many erstwhile black farmers sought work in lumber camps, on steamboats, in coal and iron mines, on the cattle range, in factories, and on railroads. Even before the completion in 1869 of the first transcontinental railroad, the Union Pacific, hundreds of ex-slaves were following the railroad tracks in search of jobs. As they worked they sang such songs as:

> Captain, go side-track yo' train,
> Captain, go side-track yo' train,
> Number three in line, a-coming in on time,
> Captain, go side-track yo' train.

The most popular railroad song of all was a ballad about John Henry, the black, 220-pound, "steel driving" railhand who became a folk hero to his people.[1] No one could work as long as John Henry could; the women would all come out just to watch him work and to hear him make the cold steel ring. Many versions of his story came into being, the tale of a proud, hard-working "hammer man" who refused to let a "new-fangled steel drill beat him down," but who "hammered himself to death" in the struggle of man against the machine.

John Henry, traditional

John Hen-ry tol' his Cap-'n That a man was a natch'-al __
Cap-'n says to John Hen-ry, "Goin' to bring me a steam-drill

man: An' be-fore he'd let that steam-drill beat him down, He'd fall
roun'; Take that steam-drill out up-on __ the __ job, Goin' to

dead wid his ham-mer in his han'__ He'd fall dead wid his ham-mer in his han'.
whip that__ steam-drill down__ Goin'to whip that__ old__ steam-drill down."

John Henry says to his Cap'n,
"Send me a twelve-poun' hammer aroun',
A twelve-poun' wid a four-foot handle,
An' I beat yo' steam-drill down,
An' I beat yo' steam-drill down."
John Henry went down on de railroad.
Wid a twelve-poun' hammer by his side,
He walked down de track, but he never come back,
'Cause he laid down his hammer an' he died,
Yes, he laid down his hammer an' he died.

Railroad songs of the nineteenth century were not usually ballads, how-ever, but long, drawn-out, monotonous chants. William Barton describes the singing of some of these songs in his book. Only the leader sang the words of the verses; the workers sang out the refrains, which came at irregu-lar intervals, "just often enough to quicken the lagging interest of any who may have dropped out." The melody was apt to be quite dull, using chiefly the sixth and eighth tones of the scale, but its rhythm was sharp, setting the pace for the work activity—the spades sinking into the clay and the picks stabbing the ground in time to the music. Barton writes:

To hear these [railroad] songs . . . at their best, one needs to hear them in a rock tunnel. The men are hurried in after an explosion to drill with speed for another double row of blasts. They work two and two, one holding and turning the drill,

---

[1] For a discussion of the John Henry myth, worksongs, and ballads, see Guy B. Johnson, *Tracking Down a Negro Legend* (Chapel Hill, 1929).

the other striking it with a sledge. The sledges descend in unison as the long low chant gives the time [i.e., the rhythm]. . . . Imagine the effect of it all, the powder smoke filling the place, the darkness made barely visible by the little lights on the hats of the men, the echoing sounds of men and mules toward the outlet loading and carting away the rock thrown out by the last blast, and the men at the heading droning their low chant to the *chink! chink!* of the steel. A single musical phrase or a succession of a half dozen notes caught on a visit to such a place sticks in one's mind forever.[2]

The men who worked on steamboats and on the levees of the river towns continued to contribute material to the store of "water" songs built up during antebellum days. Ex-slaves who came into possession of land for the first time found themselves concerned about things that formerly had interested only their masters—such as, for example, the price of cotton, the weather, or the boll weevil. Often their songs about the vagaries of land ownership were parodies of spirituals, such as the following one heard by William Wells Brown:[3]

> Sing yo' praise, bless de Lamb,
> Getting plenty money;
> Cotton's gwine up, 'deed it am,
> People, ain't it funny?

CHORUS: Rise, shine, give God the glory, glory, [*Repeat three times.*]

> Don't you think it's gwine to rain?
> Maybe was, a little;
> Maybe one ole hurricane
> 'S bilin' in the kittle!

Repeat Chorus

Out on the western plains black cowboys joined the crews that drove millions of longhorns over the Chisholm and the Western Trails, from the Rio Grande to such cattle towns as Dodge City, Kansas. Between the years 1868 and 1895 more than five thousand black cowboys went up the trails, delivering the Texas cattle to railroad centers for shipment to northern and eastern markets. On the lonesome journeys they sang the sad, lonely songs that cowboys sang as well as their own plaintive songs. At night around the campfires the black cowboys entertained their trail mates with songs and sometimes fiddle music. A typical trail crew of eight cowboys invariably included two or three black men.

Best known of the black cowboys was Nat Love, or Deadwood Dick as he called himself. Unfortunately, Love left no records of his musical activities—he cared little about music and did not discuss it in his autobiography. Some names of black cowboy minstrels have been preserved, however, in

---

[2]Barton, *Old Plantation Hymns;* reprint in KATZ, p. 107.
[3]Brown, *Southern Home,* p. 175.

other sources of the period. Big Jim Simpson, for example, was a cowboy-fiddler who came up the Chisholm Trail from Texas and finally settled down on the Flying-E Ranch in Wyoming. Among the cowboys who rode with Billy the Kid in the Lincoln County bloody feud were George Washington and Sabrien Bates, both black fiddlers. Blind Sam and his brothers settled down as entertainers in Deadwood City during the 1870s after spending many years fighting Native Americans. And old Jim Perry, respected in the West as an all-around cowboy, also built up a reputation as a fiddler.

DISSEMINATION OF THE SPIRITUALS

The Fisk Jubilee Singers and Other Student Groups

The postwar spirituals, like the social songs, employed the old forms and musical idioms of the slave songs, but the content of these songs reflected the new status of the singers and the different circumstances under which they lived. The growing importance of the railroad in the lives of black men, for example, revealed itself in the number of songs that included phrases about "getting on board the Gospel train" and about the railroad-car wheels "rumbling through the land." Although the folksongs of the Negro began to appear in print early in the 1860s, the songs were unknown to most whites of the country. It remained for a group of young black students to bring the songs to the attention of the American public and eventually to the people of Europe. This was as it should have been, for as we have seen, the beauty and "quaint charm" of the spirituals derived as much from the way in which they were sung as from the music itself.

The singers were students at the newly established Fisk University in Nashville, Tennessee, which opened its doors in 1866. Fisk's administrator John Odgen asked George L. White, one of the school's young white teachers, to devote his leisure hours to music instruction. In addition, White gave a thorough training in musicianship to selected students who showed great promise. Wisely, he let them sing "their own music" as well as standard classical music. In 1867 the students under White's direction presented a concert to the Nashville public and were well received. Encouraged, White began to take his singers on short trips to nearby towns. In 1871 he conceived the idea of taking the singers on a tour in order to raise money to help with the building program at Fisk, which remained continuously in financial straits during those early years.[4]

This was not a decision lightly made. The students were not minstrel singers; their program included no jokes, no dances, no catchy tunes. The American public had not yet heard the religious music of the slaves and had

[4]J. B. T. Marsh, *The Story of the Jubilee Singers; With Their Songs,* rev. ed. (Boston, 1880), p. 175.

The Fisk Jubilee Singers. *(Courtesy New York Public Library, Schomburg Center for Research in Black Culture)*

given no indication that it was ready to hear it. With great misgivings but determined, White set out on October 6, 1871, with eleven singers, a "skillful young Negro pianist" (Ella Shepherd), and a teacher-chaperon (Miss Wells)—on borrowed funds! The experiment was not an immediate success. In Cincinnati a newspaper critic wrote:

> This is probably the first concert given by a colored troupe in this temple, which has resounded with the notes of the best vocalists in the land.[5]

When Henry Ward Beecher, the noted preacher, sponsored their presentation, the newspapers referred to the singers as Beecher's Negro Minstrels.

Despite several depressing incidents, White determined to continue with the tour. It was in Columbus, Ohio, after a sleepless night, that he conceived the idea of giving his singers a name. For many years the slaves had talked about their "year of jubilee" when slavery should be ended; why not call the singers the "Fisk Jubilee Singers"? The name had a euphonious sound and it caught on with the public. In Boston a newspaper reporter wrote that when the Jubilee Singers sang *Home, Sweet Home* to an audience that had heard the renowned Jenny Lind sing it, the song as presented by the black students was "rendered with a power and pathos never surpassed." The format of the Fisk Jubilee Singers' concerts was similar to that of concerts presented by white artists of the time, except that a large number of spirituals were included. Among audience favorites were the slave songs *Keep Me from Sinking Down; O Brothers, Don't Stay Away; Go Down, Moses;* and

[5]Quoted in Pike, *The Jubilee Singers,* p. 82.

such popular songs as *Old Folks at Home, A Temperance Medley,* and *Home, Sweet Home.*

The event that catapulted the singers to fame took place in Boston on the occasion of the mammoth World Peace Jubilee, produced by Patrick Sarsfield Gilmore in Boston in 1872. Just three years earlier in Boston he had put on a colossal show, the National Peace Jubilee, that amazed the nation with its chorus of ten thousand and its orchestra of one thousand. For the World Peace Jubilee, Gilmore's chorus was doubled to twenty thousand singers and the orchestra to two thousand instrumentalists. World-famous soloists were imported from Europe to participate, and Johann Strauss the Younger was invited to direct the huge orchestra in the playing of *The Blue Danube Waltz.*

The musical results of the daring venture were disastrous; the forces were simply too big to be handled. What is significant, however, is that for the first time black singers were included in a big musical production in the United States. On June 22, 1872, the sixth day of the festival, special stands were erected on the huge stage to accommodate the local black chorus of 150 voices, the Fisk Jubilee Singers, and the Hyers Sisters, who appeared along with the festival chorus. According to an eyewitness report, it was during the singing of the popular *The Battle Hymn of the Republic* that the Fisk Singers attracted attention. The local black chorus was to sing the verses of the song and the rest of the choral forces were to come in on the refrains. The orchestra began on too high a pitch, however, and the opening verses were a "painful failure." The Fisk Singers sprang to the rescue; singing out strongly with their well-trained voices, they easily reached the high notes. J. B. T. Marsh gives an account in his book, *The Story of the Jubilee Singers,* of the historic occasion:

> Every word . . . rang through the great Coliseum as if sounded out of a trumpet. The great audience was carried away with a whirlwind of delight. . . . Men threw their hats in the air and the Coliseum rang with cheers and shouts of, "The Jubilees! The Jubilees forever!" Mr. [Patrick Sarsfield] Gilmore brought the Singers from their place below and massed them upon his own platform, where they sang the remaining verses.

The reputation of the Fisk Jubilee Singers was made! They went on to sing at places in the United States that had never before heard folk music of black America, before crowned heads of Europe, and before the common people in Germany, Switzerland, and Great Britain. Everywhere the Singers "carried their audiences by storm" and won acclaim from the critics. Within seven years they raised $150,000, a tremendous sum for those days, and turned it over to the university to help with the erection of a new building on the campus named Jubilee Hall.

In the winter of 1872–73, students at two other schools—Hampton Institute in Virginia and the Fairfield Normal Institute in South Carolina—were organized into singing groups and taken on tours to raise money for their schools. Like the Fisk Jubilee Singers, these groups sang spirituals and

Handbill for a concert by the Fisk Jubilee Singers, 1873. *(Courtesy Fisk University Library)*

other "plantation songs"; and like the Jubilees met with success. Other struggling Negro colleges were inspired to send out spiritual-singing fund-raisers, and a tradition was established that lasted through the twentieth century. Perhaps equally important, a large part of the Western world was introduced to the folksongs of black America.[6]

Professional Jubilee Singers

Inevitably, the success of the Fisk and Hampton student singers inspired emulation. So many spurious groups appeared in imitation of the Fisk Singers that Fisk University gave up its promotion of concert tours in 1878. Thereafter, Frederick J. Loudin, a member of the university singers since 1875, took over direction of the now-private group and brought in new singers. In 1884, Loudin's Jubilee Singers embarked upon a six-year tour around the world that brought fame not only to the singers but also to Fisk, for most audiences were unaware that the university no longer sponsored the group.

Orpheus McAdoo, like Loudin a former member of the Fisk Singers, formed spin-off groups from the Fisk Singers and took his Jubilee Singers to South Africa and Australia. Again, audiences confused his groups with the original Fisk Jubilee Singers. In any event, the Negro folksongs were disseminated into far-flung lands; by the end of the nineteenth century there were few places in the world that had not heard black America's spirituals and plantation songs.

Among the groups that began to tour in the 1880s were the Canadian Jubilee Singers of Ontario, Canada, who performed primarily in Great Britain. There were dozens of other groups, of whom the best known were the Wilmington (North Carolina) Jubilee Singers, Slayton's Jubilee Singers, the Sheppard Jubilee Singers, and the MacMillen and Sourbeck Jubilee Singers (which later changed its name to Stinson's Jubilee Singers). One of the Stinson's singers, Billy Mills, was the grandfather of four brothers who would later win fame as the Mills Brothers quartet.

BLACK ETHIOPIAN MINSTRELSY

Minstrel Troupes

The coming of freedom brought ex-slaves the opportunity to explore an entertainment field, Ethiopian minstrelsy, in which they long had been active

---

[6]A relatively large number of slave-song collections was published during the last quarter of the nineteenth century in both England and the United States. Some of the collections appeared in several editions; for example, the Fisk Jubilee Song collections ran through no fewer than eighteen editions during the years 1872–1902. See further in Eileen Southern and Josephine Wright, *African-American Traditions . . .* (Westport, CT, 1990).

as amateurs. Nineteenth-century literature is replete with anecdotes about masters calling their talented slaves to the "big house" to perform for guests, and from its beginning Ethiopian minstrelsy was a conscious imitation of the black man's songs, dances, and humor by white performers in blackface. Now the public could see genuine black faces on the stage.

Although troupes composed of black entertainers date back to the 1840s, it was not until 1865 that the first permanent black minstrel troupes were formed.[7] In April of that year, white entrepreneur W. H. Lee organized a troupe of fifteen ex-slaves in Macon, Georgia, and called them the Georgia Minstrels. The next year the troupe came under the management of Sam Hague, also white, who changed its name to Sam Hague's Slave Troupe of Georgia Minstrels, added more men, and took the troupe to England, where he settled permanently. Over the years Hague gradually replaced his ex-slaves with white men performing in blackface makeup.

Another black minstrel troupe that appeared in 1865 was more important to the history of American music. Formed by black showman Charles "Barney" Hicks (ca. 1840–1902) in Indianapolis, the troupe was also called the Georgia Minstrels, but it is doubtful that the men came from Georgia. Perhaps Hicks had heard of the success of Hague's Georgia Minstrels and decided the name might bring good luck to his group, or perhaps he remembered the popularity among black people of an old, old folksong *Sold Off to Georgy*. It was this troupe that the world came to know as the celebrated Georgia Minstrels, although other groups borrowed the name in the ensuing years. Hicks toured widely with his troupe for five years, increasing its numbers and developing its collective skills; by 1868 he could boast of a company of fifteen or more that was notable for its exotic specialty acts and a thirteen-piece brass band. In 1870 he toured in Germany and Great Britain with a few of his minstrels, and during the summer of that year he joined forces with Hague's group to produce shows in the British Isles.

In 1872 Hicks sold his rights to white entrepreneur Charles Callender, and the troupe became known as Callender's Georgia Minstrels. In later years, they came under the management of other white minstrel managers, among them, J. H. Haverly and Charles and Gustave Frohman, but the group remained remarkably cohesive. Some of its members remained Georgia Minstrels for twelve or more years. It is hardly an exaggeration to observe that most of the leading black minstrels of the era were associated at one time or another in their careers with this popular troupe.

There were other troupes owned and managed by black showmen. Lew Johnson, who organized his first permanent group in 1869 at St. Louis, Missouri, was regarded by his contemporaries as the most successful man-

---

[7]This account of the early history of black minstrelsy is based on information culled from the pages of the New York *Clipper* and the *Freeman* (Indianapolis); see further on p. 234. See also Robert Toll, *Blacking Up* (New York, 1974). Also, Eileen Southern, "The Georgia Minstrels: The Early Years," *Inter-American Music Review* 10 (Spring–Summer 1989): 157–67.

Playbill for a Glasgow performance by Haverly's Genuine Colored Minstrels, 1882. *(Courtesy of the author)*

ager of the period. His long career lasted into the twentieth century (he died in 1910), and he managed some of the top stars in the field. Barney Hicks combined with other black entrepreneurs from time to time to form troupes and, as well, managed his own. There were the Hicks–(A. D.) Sawyer's Colored Minstrels and the Hicks–(Tom) McIntosh Minstrels. Other black-owned troupes included M. B. Curtis All-Stars Afro-American Minstrels, McCabe and Young's Minstrels, and groups called by the names of their celebrity owners, such as Billy Kersands, Ernest Hogan, Henry Hart, and the Bohee Brothers. Then there were the giant companies owned by whites, among them, Sprague's Georgia Minstrels, W. S. Cleveland's Big Colored Minstrels, Lew Dockstader's Minstrels, Richard's and Pringle's Minstrels, the troupes of the three Mahara brothers (Frank, Jack, and William), and Al G. Field's Negro Minstrels.

Minstrel Traditions

Since three black minstrels wrote books about their experiences, we know a great deal about black minstrel traditions of the late nineteenth century. Ike Simond (1847–ca. 1892/1905) includes details about both individuals and troupes in his tiny book, *Old Slack's Reminiscence and Pocket History of the Colored Profession from 1865 to 1891*. Tom Fletcher (1873–1958), author of *100 Years of the Negro in Show Business* (1954), and William Christopher Handy (1873–1954, better known as W. C. Handy), who wrote *Father of the Blues* (1941), both began their careers as minstrels; Handy was later associated with Mahara minstrel companies. Both books offer valuable insight into the lifestyles of black minstrels.

Life in a small company was pretty rough! There might not even be a band, just two or three musicians playing on banjos and guitars. On the day of a show, the manager would take his musicians to the site of the town's factories or mines to play during the workers' lunch hour in order to advertise the evening's show. In small towns the troupe frequently had to clean the rented hall or schoolhouse or "opera house" where the show was to be presented and to make its own scenery and footlights. After the show, the troupe might have difficulty in finding a place which would accommodate them overnight, particularly in small towns where there were few African Americans. Often there were signs in southern towns that warned, "Nigger Don't Let the Sun Go Down on You!" or "Nigger, Read and Run!" Old showmen avowed that frequently the latter had an additional message, "If you can't read, run anyway!"[8] Even in places where there were black residents, it was not easy to obtain lodging, for they were often too poor to provide it. Consequently, the minstrels sometimes found themselves sleeping in the unheated hall where the show had been presented, or in a railroad station.

With one of the well-established giant companies, life was quite different. The management provided private Pullman cars for traveling, which were used as a hotel when the troupe stopped overnight in a town to put on a show. The day of a minstrel company typically began at 11:45 A.M. with the conventional parade through the principal streets of the town or city. Sometimes the parade began at the railroad tracks, where the Pullman cars were put on a siding off the regular tracks. The procession started off with the managers in their carriages. Then, also in carriages, followed the stars of the show in their tall silk hats and scarlet or plum-colored long-tailed coats. Next in line was the "walking company" dressed in brilliant coats with brass buttons—the singers, comedians, acrobats and dancers, and instrumentalists—accompanied by local boys who had begged for the opportunity to carry the banners that advertised special features of the show. The bandsmen marched in pairs, maintaining a distance of from ten to twelve feet between pairs so that the parade might stretch out as long as possible.

According to old-timers, bandsmen rarely made concessions to "low-brow taste" in their choice of music for the parades. Only when their lips

---

[8]Tom Fletcher, *100 Years of the Negro in Show Business* (New York, 1954), p. 57.

"The Largest and Best Minstrel Parade." *(Courtesy of Josephine Wright)*

grew weary would they "ease off" into the light marches of John Philip
Sousa or R. B. Hall. Typically a band was composed of twelve or fourteen
men, who played clarinets, cornets, trombones, the tuba, percussion, and
occasionally flutes or piccolos. (For the show concert at night, some players
had to "double," exchanging their wind instruments for fiddles, guitars,
banjos, mandolins, and percussion.)

The parade would come to a halt on the public square, and there the
band would present a concert consisting of classical overtures and of popu-
lar-tune medleys, with a few clarinet, cornet, or trombone solos. At the close
of the concert there was another parade to the hall or opera house, after
which the company was free until show time. Before the evening performance, the band played once more in front of the hall in order to draw a
crowd. This accomplished, the ticket seller would go to work on the people
in much the same manner as a circus or carnival barker. The combination
of the band's "sizzling" music and the barker's hocus-pocus rarely failed to
round up a full house for the evening show.

A minstrel show lasted for an hour and forty-five minutes. The bandsmen sat on an elevated platform on the stage. In front of them were the
performers in the traditional semicircle formations, soloists in front and
supporting company behind. Immediately after the curtain rose, the company burst into song. Then the interlocutor, dressed in silk and lace, came
to the front of the stage to introduce the stars:

> Ladies and gentlemen! We have come out tonight to give you a pleasing enter-
> tainment. With bones on the right and tambourines on the left, we shall now
> proceed with the overture. Gentlemen, be seated!

The first part of the show generally was followed by an *olio,* a kind of
variety show which featured one or more specialty acts. At the end of the
second part, the entire company came on for the *afterpiece* or finale.

Black minstrelsy had its own established traditions. It was traditional, for example, that a would-be minstrel should join the company as a young boy and serve a period of apprenticeship, learning the tricks of the trade from the older men. Typically, the troupes of the nineteenth century were composed only of males; in addition to the tenors with extraordinary ranges, there were male sopranos and altos who could soar to high C as easily as any woman. Moreover, male singers freely used falsetto to obtain desired effects. In later years the ban against women was lowered and women took their places on the stage alongside men. Indeed, Handy notes that a "lady trombonist" played in the Mahara minstrel band as early as the 1890s.

Minstrel songs generally fell into three categories: ballads, comic songs, and specialties. The songs of three black songwriters, James Bland, Gussie Davis, and Samuel Lucas, and of the white writer Stephen Foster, were most popular among black minstrels. In addition, spirituals and other religious songs as well as operatic airs were used. The roles of the singers were fixed by tradition. It was the task of the tenor, for example, to sing ballads that "jerked the tears"; to the comedians were given comic songs; to the rich, deep bassos, specialty numbers.

While minstrel bands generally were small and composed of versatile musicians who were expected to play more than one instrument, some companies did have big bands. At one time the W. A. Mahara Minstrels had a thirty-piece band for day parades and a forty-two-piece band for night shows. The bandleader was an important member of the company; his status was reflected in his attire, consisting of a brightly colored uniform with golden epaulettes and a high silk hat. He was expected to rehearse the band, train those men who needed it, train the vocal ensembles, coach soloists, and make orchestrations if necessary. If he was a composer, he seized the opportunity to write music and hear it performed by a professional company. Ideally, bandsmen were supposed to be music readers. But since many black instrumentalists could play the traditional repertory as proficiently "by ear" as trained musicians, it was frequently difficult for the bandmaster to distinguish the musically literate from the illiterate. Sometimes leaders resorted to ingenious methods to discover the fakes. Fletcher tells us, for example, that in his company:

> There was never any band rehearsal. The band leader . . . would pass out the books that had all of the tunes, but with the names of the tunes cut off. . . . [Then] the leader would give the signal to start playing the march.[9]

Naturally, those who could not read music would be unable to play.

The minstrel repertory included a wide variety of works then in vogue. For the parades the band played marches by such composers as W. P. Chambers, C. W. Dalbey, and C. L. Barnhouse—all of them forgotten today but

---

[9]Fletcher, *100 Years*, p. 59.

well known in their time. According to Handy, one of the most popular medleys for featuring at the outdoor concerts was *Brudder Gardner's Picnic,* a selection of Stephen Foster tunes. In the South, the bands always played *Dixie,* the favorite tune of all southern audiences.

For the evening show, the minstrels preferred to use new music or unusual arrangements of familiar pieces. Many singers wrote their own songs or paid a songwriter to compose special songs for them; the songs then "belonged" to the minstrel who had introduced them to the public. In a similar way, specialty dances became associated with individual minstrels. A composer-bandmaster such as Handy was always on the alert for a novel way to present familiar material. On one occasion, for example, he used *The Holy City* as a "religioso," featuring a cornet solo against a saxophone quartet accompaniment.

Minstrel Stars

Minstrelsy became a way of life for hundreds of black entertainers in the post–Civil War period. The federal census of 1890 counted 1,490 Negro actors and showmen, and that does not include the part-time minstrels who may have earned a livelihood in less glamorous occupations but nevertheless frequently performed on the stage alongside professionals. Nor does the count include the hundreds who identified themselves simply as musicians to the census takers, although they may have been minstrels as was, for example, W. C. Handy in the 1890s.

Just as the white theatrical world had its trade papers in the *Clipper* and the *Dramatic Mirror* (both of New York), so African-American show business had its weekly source of theatrical news in the *Freeman* of Indianapolis, which began publication in 1883. In its columns, particularly "The Stage" by "Trage," one could always find out who was playing where and read the latest gossip. The *Freeman* frequently published pictures of entertainers, and its Christmas issues included a special supplement replete with illustrations, biographical sketches, and anecdotes. Showmen also used the newspaper as a way of corresponding with each other; rare was the week when some minstrel was not replying to another minstrel's letter or writing a letter to the editor about a "happening." Other black newspapers of the period that regularly carried news about the entertainment world were the *Cleveland Gazette* (1883–1940s) and three New York papers, the *New York Globe* (1880–84), the *Freeman* (1884–87), and the *New York Age* (1887–1960s).

The best talent of the race found its way to the minstrel stage, not only because it offered a measure of financial security but also because that was the sole route to the theater and concert world for the majority of the professional entertainers. During the several decades when African-American minstrelsy was in its heyday, the brightest stars were James Bland, Billy Kersands, Sam Lucas, and Horace Weston. There were literally dozens of lesser luminaries who perhaps were equally well known in their time although forgotten today; for example, the Bohee Brothers (James and George), who toured widely with their own troupe and other companies and finally settled in London in 1882, where they conducted a banjo studio and entertained in royal circles. The men mentioned above as owner-managers were also superb performers—Barney Hicks, Henry Hart, Lew Johnson, Dan W. McCabe, Tom McIntosh, and A. D. Sawyer.

Other first-rate minstrels who became famous because of their worldwide travels were Aaron Banks, Japanese Tommy (né Thomas Dilworth), Bob Height, Jim Grace, Jake Hamilton, Billy McClain, and Billy Windom, to name a few.

At the height of his fame, James Bland (1854–1911) was advertised as "The World's Greatest Minstrel Man" and "The Idol of the Music Halls." His songs were sung by all the minstrels—black and white—by college students, and by the American people in their homes and on the streets. Most of them did not even know that they were singing songs written by a black man. The white stars of minstrelsy for whom he wrote often published the songs under their own names. To be sure, this was rather a common practice; some of Stephen Foster's songs were expropriated in the same way. Songwriters often sold their pieces outright for ten or fifteen dollars each. This practice continued into the twentieth century.

Bland attended high school in Washington, D.C., and Howard University as a pre-law student, but the entertainment world lured him away from his studies. He taught himself to play banjo and began performing at private social entertainments, often singing songs he himself had written. In 1875 he left home to become a professional minstrel, touring first with the Black Diamond troupe of Boston, then later with the Bohee Brothers, Sprague's Georgia Minstrels, and Haverly's Genuine Colored Minstrels. Bland went to Europe with Haverly's in 1881, and remained there when the troupe returned to the United States.

During the next decade, Bland toured the music halls and theaters of Europe, dispensing with the blackface makeup he had worn as a minstrel and performing as an elegantly dressed singer-banjoist. It was during this time that he became an international figure in the world of entertainment. But by the mid-1890s life had begun to change for him. The variety show and vaudeville gradually began to replace the minstrel show on the musical stage, and Bland was left behind.

Of the approximately seven hundred songs written by James Bland, the best remembered are *In the Evening by the Moonlight; In the Morning by the Bright Light; Oh, Dem Golden Slippers;* and *Carry Me Back to Old Virginny.* The last-named song was published by Bland in 1878, when he was twenty-four years old. Sixty-two years later (in 1940) the state of Virginia adopted it as the official state song. Few realized that it was the composition of a black minstrel who sang his way into the hearts of the public during the turn of the century.

Sheet music cover for songs by James Bland, 1879. *(Courtesy Harvard Theatre Collection)*

Oh, Dem Golden Slippers was used as the theme song for the Mummers' Annual New Year's Day parade in Philadelphia for over fifty years. Other melodies have been used over the years as campaign songs (*The Missouri Hound Dog*), marching songs (*Dandy Black Brigade*), and in background music for movies, radio, and television shows.

His unpretentious sentimental songs were lightly syncopated and reflected the influence of the folksongs he heard sung by ex-slaves in Washington, D.C., during his youth. A good minstrel was expected to bring tears to the eyes as well as laughter to the lips, and James Bland was one of the best.

In the nineteenth century Sam Lucas (né Milady, 1840–1916) was the most celebrated minstrel in the United States during his time. Self-taught on the guitar, he performed with the major minstrel troupes in his early career, then with touring plays and concert companies, then vaudeville companies, and finally in musical comedies. His first important experience was with Lew Johnson's Plantation Minstrels in the 1870s. In 1873 he joined Callender's Georgia Minstrels as a ballad singer. Beginning in 1876 he toured recurrently with the Hyers Sisters Comic Opera company as the leading man for more than a decade. In 1878 he became the first black man to play the role of Uncle Tom in *Uncle Tom's Cabin*.[10]

When vaudeville began to replace minstrelsy, Lucas found his niche again—as a leading performer—sometimes starring in a special act with his wife, violinist Carrie Melvin Lucas. In the first decade of the twentieth century, he played leading roles in Broadway musicals written by Bob Cole and the Johnson brothers (J. Rosamond and James Weldon). Then, in 1912 he turned to the movies and starred in an early film version of *Uncle Tom's Cabin*. His talent and versatility won him accolades from his contemporaries, who called him "Grand Old Man of the Stage" and "Dean of the Theatrical World."

Despite his very full career, Lucas took time to tour with his own concert company, The Jubilee Songsters, and to write songs, of which many were published in collections, the *Sam Lucas Plantation Songster* (ca. 1875) and the *Sam Lucas Careful Man Songster* (1881). Although his songs appear rather trite in comparison with those of James Bland, they were very popular in the seventies and eighties and were published in music periodicals like *The Folio* of Boston. As a performer, Lucas was celebrated particularly for his singing of *Grandfather's Clock* and *Carve Dat Possum*.

William "Billy" Kersands (1842–1915) was an early member of Barney Hicks's Georgia Minstrels and during his career played with most of the important troupes. He made several worldwide tours, some with his own troupes. Like Sam Lucas, he toured intermittently with the Hyers Sisters Comic Opera troupe and in other road shows with Lucas. Kersands was immensely popular with the public as a singer and comedian. It was said in

---

[10]Harry Birdoff, *The World's Greatest Hit—Uncle Tom's Cabin* (New York, 1947), p. 225.

Sheet music cover for songs by Sam Lucas. *(Courtesy Harvard Theatre Collection)*

the South that a minstrel show without Kersands was like a circus without an elephant. But his specialty was dancing—the old Negro folk dance "buck and wing" and a soft-shoe dance called "the Virginia essence" to the music of Stephen Foster's *The Old Folks at Home.*

Wallace King (ca. 1840–1903) first attracted attention as "the silver-voiced tenor" of the Hyers Sisters Concert company. He remained in the company when it changed over into an "opera bouffe" company in 1876. Later he toured with Callender's Georgia Minstrels in the United States and abroad, and in Australia and Southeast Asia with the Hicks-Sawyer Minstrels.

Horace Weston (ca. 1825–1890) won glory as a minstrel banjoist. Although he began his professional life with Buckley's Serenaders in 1863, he spent the better part of his career with the Georgia Minstrels. In 1873 he made stage history when he toured abroad in an *Uncle Tom's Cabin* company as the first black performer to be featured in a special role.[11] Late in his career, Weston played with the Barnum and Bailey Greatest Show on Earth. His fame among banjoists lasted into the twentieth century.

One of the favorite songwriters of black minstrels was Gussie Lord Davis (1863–1899), who was the first black songwriter to succeed on Tin Pan Alley, New York's commercial-music district. He obtained his musical education at the Nelson Musical College in Cincinnati, Ohio; his application for admission was rejected because of his color, but he arranged to give janitorial services at a low salary in return for private lessons. His first hit was *We Sat Beneath the Maple on the Hill* (1880), written when he was only eighteen. A succession of even more successful songs brought him a contract from George Propheter, who took Davis to New York—and Tin Pan Alley—in 1886.

Within a few years Davis had climbed high on the ladder to success, and his songs were being published by leading companies of the Alley. In 1895 he won second place in a contest sponsored by the *New York World* to find the ten best songwriters in the nation; his song *Send Back the Picture and the Ring* won him $500 in gold. His best-known songs included *The Fatal Wedding* (1894), *Down in Poverty Row* (1896), and *In the Baggage Coach Ahead* (1896). The last-named was popularized by white "female baritone" Imogene Comer and sold thousands of copies within a short time after publication. It was this kind of sentimental ballad that led contemporaries to state that Davis "did more than his share to open up the tear ducts of America."[12]

---

[11]Maxwell F. Marcuse, *Tin Pan Alley in Gaslight* (Watkins Glen, NY, 1959), p. 151. Two Weston pieces are published in Eileen Southern, *African-American [Musical] Theater* (New York, 1994), pp. 65, 147.

[12]A selected list of his published songs appears in Josephine Wright, "In Retrospect: Gussie Lord Davis (1863–1899)," BPIM 6 (Fall 1978): 194–99.

Chorus of **In the Baggage Coach Ahead,** Gussie L. Davis

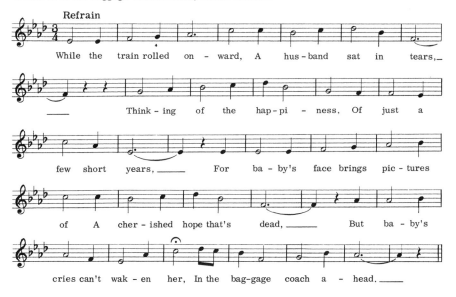

While the train rolled on - ward, A hus - band sat in tears,__ ____ Think - ing of the hap - pi - ness, Of just a few short years, _____ For ba - by's face brings pic - tures of A cher - ished hope that's dead, _____ But ba - by's cries can't wak - en her, In the bag-gage coach a - head. _____

Sheet music cover for a song by Gussie L. Davis. *(Courtesy Library of Congress)*

Davis published more than two hundred songs and undoubtedly left that number or more in manuscript at his death. He wrote a variety of songs, comic and religious as well as ballads, and also experimented with larger vocal and choral forms. One of his musicals, *A Hot Old Time in Dixie,* was on the road at the time of his death. Also a performer, he played piano on Bergen Star Concerts and toured with his Davis Operatic and Plantation Minstrels.

THE CONCERT STAGE

Prima Donnas

Among the first to enter the concert world after the war were the Hyers sisters, soprano Anna Madah (ca. 1855–1925) and contralto Emma Louise (ca. 1853–189?), who gave their joint debut recital in 1867 to critical acclaim in Sacramento, California, their native home. After further study, they set off on a transcontinental tour in 1871, assisted by baritone Joseph LeCount; their father, tenor Sam B. Hyers; and an accompanist. The group was well received by the public at each stop, and finally settled in Boston. The next year they sang in Gilmore's World Peace Jubilee on the same program as the Fisk Jubilee Singers, where they created quite a sensation.

Over the years the Hyers Sisters Concert Company included at one time or another the two Luca brothers, [John] baritone and [Alex] tenor; tenor Wallace King and baritone Sam Lucas, both of minstrel fame; piano accompanists A. C. Taylor and Jacob Sawyer; and violinist Claudio José Brindis de Salas. When the company gave concerts, talented local artists frequently made guest appearances. In 1876, the Hyers changed their concert company into a comic opera troupe, but periodically returned to the concert stage. On occasion they appeared on the minstrel stage, for example, participating in Callender's Mammoth Consolidated Minstrel Festival of 1883, which toured as far west as California after a grand opening in New York in July.

The last quarter of the century saw the rise of no fewer than five black "prima donnas," as they were called by the press, who won international renown, and an additional dozen or more of lesser repute. Nellie Brown Mitchell (1845–1924) studied privately and at the New England Conservatory of Music in Boston; in 1874 she made her New York debut and, in 1882, concertized in Philadelphia. During the 1880s she was the prima donna soprano of the Bergen Star Concert Company, one of the leading promoters of black artists; later she toured with her own concert company. In 1886 the *Cleveland Gazette* called her "America's greatest singer of African descent," but by the mid-1890s she had left the concert stage to conduct a music studio.

Marie Selika Williams (née Smith, ca. 1849–1937) was called "Queen of Staccato" by the press and her fans. Born in Natchez, Mississippi, she

Cover page of music dedicated to Selika Williams. *(Courtesy Library of Congress)*

was taken to Cincinnati as an infant and there began music study at an early age under the patronage of a wealthy white family. During the early 1870s she studied voice in San Francisco and made her debut there in 1876 as a concert soprano. She moved to the East in 1878, where, particularly in Boston and Philadelphia, her voice attracted attention for its brilliance. In 1882 she went to England to study further. An appearance before Queen Victoria in October 1883 added luster to her growing reputation and marked the beginning of a career that lasted about two decades. She toured widely in the United States, generally with her husband Sampson Williams, who was advertised as Signor Veloski, the Hawaiian tenor. She concertized in Europe during the years 1887–92 and in the West Indies several times.

A younger contemporary of Selika's, Flora Batson Bergen (1864–1906), was called the "Double-Voiced Queen of Song" because of her phenomenal range. A native of Washington, D.C., she was taken by her family to Providence, Rhode Island, as a child and began singing locally before she was twenty. In 1885 she became the leading soprano of the Bergen Star Concert Company and thereafter toured extensively throughout the world. Her career included three worldwide tours, with command performances for Queen Victoria, Pope Leo XIII, Queen Lil of Hawaii, the royal family of New Zealand, and other crowned heads of state.

Rachel Walker (1873–194?) began her career in Cleveland but won her laurels primarily in Europe, where she settled about 1897 and toured as Lucie Lenoir, the "Creole Nightingale." But World War I cut short her career, forcing her to return to the United States in 1915. After concertizing nationally for a few years, she resettled in Cleveland, where she conducted a music studio and worked with church choirs.

The most celebrated of the prima donnas was soprano Matilda Sisieretta Jones (1869–1933), who was born in Portsmouth, Virginia, but moved to Providence with her family in about 1876. She studied privately and with teachers at the Providence Academy of Music and the New England Conservatory. Although she began singing locally at an early age, her first professional appearance was in April 1888 at a Bergen Star Concert in New York, where Flora Batson was the prima donna soprano. By that time, however, she had developed a small following as "Mme. M. S. Jones, New England's Rising Soprano Star."

When she made her debut a month later in Philadelphia's Academy of Music, she conquered both the public and the press. For the next eight years she toured extensively in the United States and abroad, at first as Matilda S. Joyner, then later as Madame M. Sissieretta Jones, the "Black Patti"—having been given the sobriquet because her voice compared in richness and musicality to that of the reigning prima donna of the period, Adelina Patti.

Jones first attracted wide attention in February 1892, when she sang at the White House for President Benjamin Harrison. In April of that year she was the featured singer at a concert in New York's Madison Square Garden that was so successful it had to be repeated at the Academy of Music. In 1895 she made her debut to critical acclaim at the Wintergarden Theatre in Berlin, then moved from one triumph to another in Europe, Asia, and Africa, singing before crowned heads and huge audiences at public recitals. Her managers (Voelckel and Nolan) abruptly launched her into a new career, however, in 1896, when she became the featured artist in a touring vaudeville company called Black Patti's Troubadours.

Black Patti (Sissieretta Jones). *(Courtesy of the author)*

In addition to these major figures, there were others who concertized in the United States but not abroad. In 1891 Desseria Plato (d. 1907) attracted attention as Azucena in Verdi's *Il trovatore* in a production staged by A. Farini's Grand Creole and Colored Opera Company in New York. Annie Pindell (ca. 1834–1901), called the "Black Nightingale," was best known in the Far West as a concert soprano and songwriter. Her touring included a recital in Hawaii as well as the United States. Amelia Tilghman (fl. late nineteenth century) made her debut in New York as a soprano in 1880, and the next year sang a leading role in the June Sangerfest held at the Grand Opera House in Louisville, Kentucky. Although active as a concert singer and choral conductor, she is best remembered as the first black publisher / editor of a music magazine, *The Musical Messenger* (1886–90s).

New England produced more than its share of African-American concert artists, undoubtedly because of the opportunity for study at the conservatories in Boston and Providence, where students were admitted without discrimination. In addition to those artists discussed above, others worthy of note were the De Wolf sisters (Rosa and Sadie), Ednah E. Brown (sister of Nellie Brown Mitchell), the Smith sisters (Adelaide and Georgina), and Inez Clough and Estelle Pickney Clough, both of Providence.

The public soon tired of black prima donnas. Although the singers were gifted, well trained, and fortunate in obtaining good management, their careers on the concert stage were relatively short, ranging from three or four

Announcement of a gala concert, 1894. *(Courtesy Philadelphia Historical Society)*

years to a dozen or so in most instances. Their white impresarios staged concerts in the prestigious halls of the United States and Europe and arranged for command performances before important persons, but to no avail. By the mid-1890s the black prima donna had almost disappeared from the nation's concert halls because of lack of public interest. Some of the artists opened music studios and took over direction of church and community choirs.

Male Vocalists and Ensembles

Several male artists won critical acclaim during this period. Sidney Woodward (1860–1924), a concert tenor, began singing professionally in 1890 and made his debut in 1893 at Chickering Hall in Boston. When he sang at the Chicago World's Fair in August 1893, the *Chicago Tribune* lauded his "tenor that for sweetness and purity of tone has rarely been equalled at the Exposition" (August 25, p. 3). Others who won recognition include baritone William I. Powell of Philadelphia, who toured with the

Grand Star and the Bergen Star Concert companies; tenor Harry Williams of Cleveland, who went abroad in 1886 and remained there through the 1890s, giving recitals and studying; and baritone Theodore Drury, who organized an opera company in 1889.

Male singers generally found it more difficult to succeed in the concert world than did the prima donnas. For that reason, they were more likely to join ensembles, minstrel troupes, or touring concert companies. Wallace King, for example, had a voice of concert quality, as did Sam Lucas, but both found it more profitable to tour with groups. Male quartets became very popular. In New England the Lew Male Quartet toured with considerable success in the 1880s under the management of the Redpath Lyceum Bureau and included appearances before assemblies in Chautauqua, New York, in 1887. The quartet's manager and second tenor, William Lew (1865–1949), belonged to the Lew musical dynasty, which stretched back into the eighteenth century with musicians Barzillai and Primus Lew. M. Hamilton Hodges (ca. 1869–1928) sang baritone in Lew's Male Quintette during the 1880s, then toured with McAdoo's Jubilee Singers and settled at Auckland, New Zealand, in 1896. One of the most popular quartets of the time was the Golden Gate Quartet, organized in Baltimore, Maryland, in 1892. For the next sixty and more years, black quartets would use that name through the period of jubilee songs and into the era of gospel.

Concert Instrumental Artists

If the black prima donna reigned in the field of vocal music, it was the black male who dominated the concert stage as instrumentalist. Most celebrated of the early black pianists was Thomas Green Bethune (1849–1909), popularly known as "Blind Tom." Born a blind slave in Columbus, Georgia, he early revealed an aptitude for music, and his slave master, James M. Bethune, allowed the toddler free access to the piano. After Tom had developed his skills to the level that he could play by ear any piece he heard, Mrs. Bethune and the daughters gave him informal lessons by allowing him to listen to music and build up a repertory.

From the time Tom was five or six, the Bethunes began displaying his talent in private circles; in October 1857, he made his formal debut at Temperance Hall in Columbus. Thereafter Bethune "hired out" Tom for a period of three years to Perry Oliver, a Georgia planter, who toured widely with the blind prodigy in the North and South. Although Tom should have become free in 1863, when the Emancipation brought freedom to slaves in states that had seceded from the Union, the Bethunes retained control over him throughout his life, at first through an indenture contract (1864), then later through airtight conventional contracts. Upon Bethune's death in 1883, his son John took over Blind Tom's guardianship; and after John's death, his widow and her second husband, Albert Lerché, became Tom's manager-owners.

Sheet music cover featuring a portrait of Blind Tom, 1860. *(Courtesy Library of Congress)*

Blind Tom's career lasted almost thirty years and took him throughout the United States and into Europe and South America. His managers engaged music teachers and professionals to perform for him so that his repertory was continually growing. Everywhere he played he was subjected to rigorous tests of his talent and extraordinary memory. In 1866 he made his European debut in London, and thereafter collected letters attesting to his genius from established musicians such as Ignaz Moscheles and Charles Halle. By the end of the nineteenth century there were few places where Blind Tom had not played; he had become an American institution.

It was reputed that he could play as many as seven thousand pieces upon request, and he is credited with having composed more than one hundred pieces. His recitals typically consisted of eight parts, each with a title, e.g., *Classical Selections, Piano-Forte Solos, Fantasias and Caprices, Marches, Imitations, Descriptive Music, Songs,* and *Parlor Selections.* Audiences were given a list of the pieces in his repertory and allowed to select the ones they wished to hear.

Another blind pianist who attracted attention during the late nineteenth century was John William Boone (1864–1927), called "Blind Boone."[13] He began playing professionally at the age of fourteen, giving his debut recital in 1878 in Columbus, Missouri, under management of black impresario John Lange. Undoubtedly it was the success of Blind Tom that inspired Boone and other unsighted black pianists to seek careers on the concert stage. Boone never attained the fame of Blind Tom, but he toured with his Blind Boone Concert Company for forty-eight years in the United States and concertized twice in Europe. For his time, he composed many works of considerable variety, including salon and concert pieces, some with African-American themes, such as, *Caprice de concert,* No. 1: *Melodies des negres;* No. 2: *Melodies* . . . and No. 3: *Melodies.* . . . Also *Southern Rag Medley,* Nos. 1 and 2. Some of his piano compositions display a use of ragtime materials, but not consistently enough to classify him as a ragtime composer.

Samuel Jamieson (1855–1930) was active as a concert pianist in Boston, where he studied privately and in 1876 was one of the early black graduates of the Boston Conservatory. Although he eventually had to conduct a music studio in order to earn a livelihood, he gave recitals periodically throughout his career, sometimes with others—as in the 1880s, for example, with baritone George L. Ruffin.

In New York two young men carved out careers for themselves as concert violinists. Little is known of the early life of John Thomas Douglass (1847–1886); it was reputed that a wealthy patron sent him abroad to study. By the late 1860s he had settled in New York, and during the next decade he concertized extensively enough to win a reputation as "the master violinist" and "one of the greatest musicians of the race."[14]

Like most concert artists of his time, Douglass could not earn a living solely with his violin. During the 1870s he toured with the Hyers Sisters and the Georgia Minstrels, and during the eighties he conducted a music studio in New York and led a string ensemble that played for society dances and other kinds of entertainments. Douglass is notable as the first black composer to write an opera; his three-act *Virginia's Ball* was registered with the United States Copyright Office in 1868 (the music is now lost) and performed at the Stuyvesant Institute on Broadway the same year.

The other young violinist, Walter Craig (1854–192?), made his debut in 1870 at Cooper Hall in New York. Although he later became better known for his society dance orchestra, he concertized frequently enough to win critical acclaim. In 1886 Craig became the first black musician to be admitted to the Musician's Mutual Protective Union. The New York *Freeman*

[13]See further in Ann Sears, "Keyboard Music" in *Feel the Spirit* (Westport, CT, 1988) pp. 135–55.

[14]See further in "Black-Music Concerts in Carnegie Hall, 1912–1915," BPIM 6 (Spring 1978): 72–73.

called him "the Prince of Negro Violinists," and in 1887 New York's *Herald Tribune* reported him "a perfect master of his instrument."

Concert Musicians Abroad

New Orleans contributed several reputable musicians to the concert stage. Pianist-composer Victor Eugene McCarty (1821–1881) was one of the first "men of color" to study abroad; in the 1840s he enrolled at the Paris Conservatory, then returned home to build a reputation as a fine singer and pianist. During the 1850s Lucien Lambert (ca. 1828–after 1878) went to Paris and earned critical approval for his piano skills; he remained abroad, however, and so cannot be counted among musicians of New Orleans.

After beginning his studies with local violinist Constantin Deburque, Edmond Dédé (1827–1903) studied at the Paris Conservatory with Jacques-François Halévy and Jean-Delphin Alard. Dédé settled permanently in Bordeaux, France, about 1868 and became director of the L'Alcazar Theater orchestra, but he returned to New Orleans during the year 1893–94 and gave concerts in several places.

Pianist-composer Basile Barés (1846–1902) studied privately with Eugene Provost, director of the French Opera Company orchestra, at the beginning of his career and later, in Paris. Samuel Snaër (ca. 1832–1880s) was active as both a concert pianist and violoncellist. Also a composer and music teacher, he directed the orchestra at the Theatre D'Orleans during the 1860s. Among other notable musicians of New Orleans was Thomas Martin, who conducted a large music studio for many years.

For each of the dozen or so black concert artists who earned a measure of success in their careers during the late nineteenth century, there were hundreds of local artists who could be depended upon to perform the requisite piano or vocal solos on community concerts, accompany singers, and direct church and community choirs, in addition to teaching pupils in their studios. Their names appeared frequently in local newspapers and periodicals—as, for example, pianist-organist Rachel Washington, the first black graduate of the Boston Conservatory. In 1884 she published a teaching manual, *Musical Truth; The Rudiments of Music.*

The black musicians discussed above, and many others as well, seemed determined to pursue careers in music, no matter how arduous the life or how poorly they were paid. It was difficult enough for a white American to earn a livelihood as a concert artist in the nineteenth century; with the exception of Louis Gottschalk, the brilliant pianist-composer of New Orleans, the concert field was dominated entirely by European artists—for example, Ole Bull, the Norwegian violinist; Jenny Lind, the "Swedish Nightingale"; Maria Malibran and Adelina Patti, operatic prima donnas;

the sensational soprano Henriette Sontag; and Sigismund Thalberg, virtuoso pianist.

During this period, America generally ignored its classical musicians, white as well as black (but not its vernacular ones), preferring to import its musical culture from Europe. Black musicians were further handicapped by racial prejudice, especially when they attempted to perform anything other than spirituals or minstrel songs. Even the most gifted black soloists of this period were forced to turn to ensemble singing in order to continue their musical activities.

Black instrumentalists in the United States were greatly inspired by the accomplishments of two violinists of African descent who were active in the European musical world. George Polgreen Bridgetower (1779–1860), son of an African father and a Polish mother, was recognized as a violin prodigy at the age of ten and later became known as "the Abyssinian Prince." A student of Haydn and friend of Beethoven, the violinist enjoyed a short but highly successful concert career in Europe and composed a sizable quantity of music. Beethoven's Violin Sonata, Op. 47, the "Kreutzer Sonata," was originally written for Bridgetower, who gave its first performance at Vienna in 1803.

The other artist, José (Joseph) White (1833–1920), was a native of Cuba. At an early age he entered the Conservatory at Paris where he repeatedly won prizes for his skill in violin playing. In Europe, White was reported to be "one of the most distinguished violinists of the French school" and also "a composer of note." In 1876 White visited the United States where he impressed critics and audiences with his mastery of the violin. In New York he appeared with the Philharmonic and also the orchestra of Theodore Thomas, playing the Mendelssohn Concerto in E minor, among other works.

TRAVELING ROAD SHOWS

It was in 1876 that the Hyers Sisters Concert Company, under the management of Sam Hyers, changed its format to become a musical-comedy company. Its first production, titled *Out of Bondage* and written especially for the company by the white writer Joseph Bradford, premiered in Lynn, Massachusetts, on March 20, 1876. The production's success encouraged the Hyers to produce more musicals; over a period of a dozen or so years, they staged no fewer than seven musicals in repertory. These included *Out of Bondage* (1876), a three-act musical adaptation of the Bradford play; *Urlina; or, The African Princess* (1877; copyright notice filed in 1872 by E. S. Getchell); *Colored Aristocracy* (1877), a musical drama in three acts written by black novelist Pauline Hopkins with the original title of *Aristocracy;* and *The Underground Railroad* (1879), a four-act musical drama also written by Hopkins, but with the title *Peculiar Sam; or, The Underground Railroad.*[15]

During the early 1880s, the Hyers sisters returned to the concert stage and, for a short period, performed on the minstrel stage. Then they resumed touring with their comic opera troupe, producing *The Blackville Twins* (copyright notice filed in 1883 but not staged until 1887), a three-act musical drama adapted by Sam Hyers from the musical comedy by Scott Marble, with music by Fred V. Jones; and *Plum Pudding* (1887), a three-act comedy by G. M. Spence.

All the Hyers' productions had racial themes: generally, the musicals began with slavery scenes, then traced the characters' adventures as they moved to freedom and a more rewarding life. The performers sang authentic plantation songs as well as ballads and operatic numbers, and the dances also were genuine folk dances.

The press acclaimed the Hyers troupe as "one of the best opera bouffe troupes in America"; certainly it was the first black repertory company, and the only one for more than a decade. Until the 1890s, it offered the sole avenue to a stage career for those musician-actors who wished to bypass the minstrel circuit, if only temporarily. Over the years its leading performers included, in addition to the sisters, Sam Lucas, Wallace King, Billy Kersands, and the Luca brothers (John and Alexander), among many others.

Whereas white road shows discriminated against black actor-musicians as individuals, they sometimes provided open doors of opportunity to black choral groups and dancers. The first show to use black performers was an *Uncle Tom's Cabin* company. Its dramatization of Harriet Beecher Stowe's popular novel was staged on January 1852, even before the book was published (it had been serialized in the *National Era* magazine). Enormously successful with audiences at home and abroad, the play generally had several companies on the road at the same time. White actors in blackface handled black roles until 1876, when an enterprising producer conceived the idea of using "real Negroes" in the plantation scenes.

Slavin's Original Georgia Jubilee Singers was one of the first groups to perform in the play. These singers set such a vogue for the use of genuine plantation music that "it became almost fatal for anyone to stage the play without colored singers."[16] Many a black showman began his professional career as a pickaninny or plantation singer in an *Uncle Tom's Cabin* company, among them, Ernest Hogan and Horace Weston.

Another road show that included plantation scenes was Charles Turner Dazey's *In Old Kentucky*, first staged in St. Paul, Minnesota, in 1892. From the beginning, black singers and dancers were used both in minor acting roles and in ensembles. A special feature of the drama was the twenty-four piece "boys' band," called The Whangdoodles, a Pickaninny Brass Band.

---

[15]See further in Southern, *African American [Musical] Theater* (New York, 1994).
[16]Birdoff, *Uncle Tom's Cabin*, p. 235.

The black musician who produced "the colored part" of the play, John M. Powell, maintained such high standards of performance that it became a mark of status to be accepted into "Mistah Powell's band of Ol' Kentucky." Like the *Uncle Tom's Cabin* companies, the *In Old Kentucky* companies served as a training ground for black entertainers over a long period of time. Tom Fletcher, for example, played in the boys' band when he was a child.

Black "boys' brass bands" were very popular during the 1890s. According to Fletcher, one of the first of these was organized in Cincinnati, by John Brister, who toured widely with his Brister's Boy's Band. This may well have been the band that so impressed the producer of *In Old Kentucky* that he put a similar group in his show.

Another celebrated boys' band of the decade was the Jenkins Orphanage Band, which toured from its home site in Charleston, South Carolina. The Reverend Daniel Joseph Jenkins founded his orphanage in 1892 and within a few years conceived the idea of teaching his young charges to play musical instruments, then traveling with them to raise money for the orphanage. The Orphanage Band first toured in the North in 1895 and later the same year in England. Thereafter the band toured extensively for many years; a large number of its members "graduated" in the twentieth century into jazz bands.

A third important road show of the 1890s was *The South Before the War,* produced by Whallen and Martell, which made its New York debut in January 1893 at the London Theatre. Its integrated cast was predominantly black, and the show relied primarily upon black folk materials, for it had the flimsiest of plots. The special features included a plantation scene with the slaves singing spirituals in a cotton field as they worked, a camp-meeting scene, a levee scene on the Mississippi, and a mammoth cakewalk. Players often used the production as a showcase for introducing new songs and dances to the public, as in 1895, for example, when Billy Williams introduced the "possum-ma-la dance." In the early years of the play, the leading actors included Cordelia and Billy McClain and Kate Carter.

While the four companies discussed above were the most celebrated, there were also minor companies that employed black performers, particularly for plantation scenes. Typically, a big show opened each year in New York, or some other large city, then went out on the road to play cities, towns, villages, and hamlets all over the nation in the same way as the minstrel troupes, medicine shows, and circuses. Most places, no matter how small, had an opera house where productions could be staged and a village square for the concerts that advertised the show.

Smaller companies followed the same grueling schedules as the large ones, but were rarely able to tour on big-city circuits. Black showmen, particularly musicians, frequently traveled with medicine shows, but generally were excluded from the circus tent. One of the first circuses to lower the bars of racial discrimination was the Sells Brothers and Forepaugh's Circus, which employed Billy McClain as early as 1886.

FESTIVALS AND EXTRAVAGANZAS

The last three decades of the nineteenth century witnessed one spectacular event after another, all of them providing African-American entertainers the opportunity to appear before the American public, either in white shows or in all-black extravaganzas. The first of these was P. S. Gilmore's World Peace Jubilee, as we have seen, which was produced in Boston in 1872.

In 1876 the celebration of the Centennial of American Independence at Philadelphia was attended by crowned heads of Europe, presidents, and common people of three continents. Among the exhibits was a plantation scene featuring the singing of Negro folksongs by ex-slaves and free-born blacks. A special attraction was the performance of an old folk dance dating back to antebellum times, called "chalk-line walk" or "cakewalk." Originally, the dance had been performed on the plantation by slave couples who competed for a prize, generally a cake, awarded to the pair that pranced around with the proudest, high-kicking steps. On some plantations the dancers moved with pails of water on their heads. Those who spilled the least water and yet maintained erect posture were declared the winners.

In Chicago, in 1893, a celebration was held in honor of the four-hundredth anniversary of the discovery of America (a year late, to be sure). Called the World's Columbian Exposition, it attracted more than 27,500,000 visitors. One of the exhibits consisted of the reproduction of a tiny African village, where Dahomans performed dances several times a day to the music of drums, bells, and singing.

On August 25th, designated as "Colored American Day," the musical performances included singing by tenor Sidney Woodward and mezzo Desseria Plato; the reading of poems by Paul Laurence Dunbar; and violin playing by Joseph Douglass, a grandson of the fiery old abolitionist Frederick Douglass. The amusements of the exposition were centered along a road called the Midway Plaisance. Entertainers from all over the land, black and white, flocked to the Midway seeking employment in the night spots and dance halls.

It was inevitable that eventually an all-black extravaganza should be produced. The idea was conceived by Billy McClain, an old-time minstrel man, who already had helped launch the *South Before the War* company. About 1893 he found a promoter for his show in Nate Salsbury, a white impresario of Buffalo Bill's. The plans called for a big outdoor pageant with a cast of five hundred. Ambrose Park in Brooklyn, New York, and the Huntington Avenue grounds in Boston were selected as sites, and the show, *Black America,* was produced in the summer of 1895. The park grounds were transformed into plantation scenes with real cabins, livestock, cotton fields, and cotton gins, about which people could wander until the show began. The performance itself took place in a huge amphitheater.

The first part of the production was devoted to a re-creation of African episodes in dance and song; the second part consisted of American songs and dances (i.e., in the European and African-American traditions); and for the finale there was a grand cakewalk contest. McClain assembled his cast from all over the nation. Because show people were generally free in the summer, he was able to obtain the best talent of the period. Sixty-three male quartets added their rich voices to the singing of the "field hands" in the plantation scenes and to the operatic choral numbers. One of these was the well-known Golden Gate Quartet. A small company from the United States Ninth Cavalry put on a spectacular drill act, accompanied by costumed girls riding horses. The extravaganza was a success musically and financially. Well attended by blacks and whites, it suggested to white managers the huge reservoir of black talent available for employment in the entertainment world.

BRASS BANDS AND DANCE ORCHESTRAS

Black Americans had established an excellent band tradition during the antebellum period, and they continued to cultivate it after Emancipation. In Philadelphia, for example, the Frank Johnson legacy was handed down to Joseph Anderson (ca. 1816–1873), who had trained regimental bands during the Civil War. In Boston Pedro Tinsley (1856–1921) led his Tinsley's Colored Cornet Band during the 1880s. Theodore Finney (1837–1899) was the leader of a brass band in Detroit, Michigan, that dated back to the 1850s, when he had directed groups in partnership with John Bailey.

Although Philadelphia produced the most famous black bandleader of the nineteenth century—Frank Johnson—it was in postwar New Orleans that the largest number of fine brass bands were to be found. Among the most popular were the Excelsior, Kelly's, the Onward, and the St. Bernard brass bands, all of these organized in the 1870s and '80s. A number of the bandsmen in these groups would later be important in the emergence of jazz in New Orleans.

It is probable that in some places black instrumentalists "passing" for white, played in white bands, despite the rigid segregational practices of the period. Henderson Smith, for example, was reputed to have played cornet in Patrick Gilmore's Famous Cornet Band. Smith, like other black showmen of the period, sometimes passed for white, so Gilmore may not have known that he had a black instrumentalist. He did know, however, that Henry Williams and Frederick Lewis, who performed at the World Peace Jubilee, were black. After one performance, a member of the audience wrote a letter to the *Progressive American*:

> Having occasion to visit Boston, I attended one of the unrivalled concerts at the Coliseum, where to my great astonishment, I saw undoubtedly the greatest assemblage of human beings ever congregated under one roof, and heard a

chorus of nearly or quite twenty thousand voices, accompanied by the powerful organ and an orchestra of two thousand musicians. I was highly delighted. But what gave me the most pleasure was to see among some of the most eminent artists of the world two colored artists performing their parts in common with the others; viz, Henry F. Williams and F. E. Lewis. Each of these was competent to play his part, or he could not have occupied a place in the orchestra. I was informed by the superintendent of the orchestra that both these men were subjected to a very rigid examination prior to the commencement of the concerts.

[July 17, 1872][17]

Frequently, first-rate bands toured with minstrel troupes and vaudeville companies. One such case was Preston T. Wright's Nashville Students and Colored Concert Company, which employed a band that produced several famous bandmasters, among them Dan Desdunes and P. G. Lowery. The Georgia Minstrels always carried superior bands, and W. C. Handy's bands for Mahara minstrel troupes had a wide reputation for excellence.

U.S. Army Bands

Each of the black regiments that fought in the Civil War had its own band, of which several developed into top-notch groups. With the end of the war, however, these well-trained bandsmen scattered; many attached themselves to town bands or toured with minstrel troupes and road shows, and others went into nonmusical occupations. But not all left the armed services. For the first time, black units were organized in the United States Regular Army. A Congressional Act of July 28, 1866, established two cavalry regiments and four infantry regiments (later merged into two), and more than likely the members of these units included ex-bandsmen of the Civil War. The Ninth and Tenth Cavalry and the Twenty-Fourth and Twenty-Fifth Infantry served on America's frontiers for more than twenty years—in Texas, Louisiana, Arkansas, and the Dakotas. During these years their regimental bands won wide recognition for producing good music; they toured the small frontier towns and villages much as brass bands did "back East," and provided music for civilian as well as army functions. In 1895 the Ninth Cavalry band made the long journey to New York City to participate in Billy McClain's *Black America* show.

Society Dance Orchestras

Society dance orchestras were perhaps more common than brass bands in the postwar years. Although these orchestras no longer had a monopoly on providing dance music for the aristocracy as in antebellum days, they remained in demand to the extent that the players could earn a livelihood. The groups not only played for the assemblies and fancy balls of the rich

[17]Quoted in Trotter, *Music,* p. 106.

but also staged concerts and accompanied choral groups on Sacred Music programs, thus serving both black and white communities. As in the prewar years, the leader of a brass band was often the director of a dance orchestra as well. Such was the case with "Old Man" Finney of Detroit, whose Quadrille Orchestra, and later Finney's Famous Orchestra, were celebrated throughout the Midwest. In other places too, there was a tradition for brass-band members setting aside their brass instruments and picking up strings and woodwinds to play for social entertainments.

Walter Craig became a legend in New York. His group, called Craig's Celebrated Orchestra and organized in 1872, played for white society balls up and down the eastern seaboard. Ten years later Craig began the practice of holding an annual Christmas Reception for the black community, which he continued for more than twenty-five years. In 1905 he inaugurated the tradition of sponsoring an Annual Pre-Lenten Recital and Assembly, which lasted until 1915. On these two occasions people came from as far away as Washington, D.C., to the south, and Boston to the north, to hear black artists performing the music of black composers, and, as well, standard repertory items. Thus Craig offered young black musicians an auspicious start in their professional careers. Craig also sponsored chamber music concerts with his Schumann Quintet, beginning in 1889. Another highly regarded orchestra leader in New York was Alfred Mando (1846–1912), who toured widely with both his society dance orchestra and his Mozart Conservatory Concert Orchestra.

OTHER MUSICAL ORGANIZATIONS

Various kinds of musical groups were formed in urban centers—philharmonic societies, musical associations, chamber ensembles, choral groups, Mozart and Schumann Circles—but with one or two exceptions, these groups were active only locally or were short-lived. The Original Colored America Opera Troupe of Washington, D.C. was an exception: in 1873 the troupe produced an opera, *The Doctor of Alcantara* by Julius Eichberg (a German composer who settled in Boston in 1859) that received critical acclaim both in Washington and Philadelphia. A second company, which had a longer life span, was the Theodore Drury Colored Opera Company, which made its debut at Brooklyn, New York, in 1889.

ITINERANT AND COMMUNITY MUSICIANS

The postwar years saw the emergence of a class of black musicians who, though humble and without public recognition, nevertheless contributed their share to the musical traditions of black folk in the United States. They provided essential music services for the newly established ex-slave communities, playing organ or piano in the churches, playing in the opera houses for musical events staged by local groups, playing in the dance halls, beer parlors, and saloons. Sometimes these men were professionals who had been traveling with a minstrel troupe or a circus or medicine show that was left stranded in a town. Frequently the musicians were self-taught drifters who were never to settle down permanently. Then there were those who were natives of the towns where they assumed the roles of community musicians. Perhaps they had studied music with a local white musician or, like the drifters, had taught themselves and developed some degree of skill by virtue of continuous practicing. In addition to providing service music, these men often organized bands and orchestras or vocal and choral ensembles, infusing new spirit into community life during their temporary or permanent sojourns.

In the larger towns and cities, wandering musicians staged impromptu song recitals on street corners or in eating places and saloons, passing around a hat afterward to collect coins from listeners. Sometimes they boarded the riverboats and played for passengers in the staterooms, or they sang and played on trains and in railroad stations. Youngsters formed quartets that serenaded the neighbors, sang on street corners in cheap restaurants, and performed for community dances and picnics.

The part-time musician was as common in black communities as in white communities of the period. When Handy went to Bessemer, Alabama, in the 1890s, for example, he worked at the Howard and Harrison Pipe Works during days and engaged in musical activities during his free time. He organized a brass band, led a string orchestra and taught its members to read music, played trumpet with the choir in one of the churches, and sang to his own guitar accompaniment on social occasions. Waiter-musicians frequently provided entertainment for patrons in the places where they worked, particularly on the packet boats that ran the Ohio, Missouri, and Mississippi Rivers. Tom Fletcher tells of boarding one of the riverboats on the Ohio to join with the boat's barber and a waiter in forming a vocal trio, accompanied by guitar and jew's-harp, to serenade the passengers.

The barber and his shop played an important part in the musical life of early black rural and small-town communities. Owned and operated by black men, open from early morn until late at night, barbershops provided congenial meeting places where the musically inclined could discourse on music or practice in a back room without interruption. It was no accident that many of the early musicians were barbers, some of whom became famous—such as Richard Milburn, the guitarist-whistler; Sam Lucas, the minstrel king; and Buddy Bolden, the famous trumpeter of New Orleans. Barbers could not leave their shops during the day, yet there were periods when no patrons came in and time hung heavy on their hands. If they had musical skills, there was unlimited time to practice and develop those skills, and many musicians frequently received their first lessons in the community barbershop.

COMPOSERS AND WRITERS

In comparison to performers, black composers seem to have been inactive during the postwar years, except for the songwriters already discussed who wrote for Tin Pan Alley or the minstrel stage. If composers wrote other kinds of music, they failed to find publishers for it. The *Complete Catalogue of Sheet Music and Musical Works Published by the Board of Music Trade of the United States of America, 1870* lists hundreds of pieces published by the leading firms of the nation, but with one or two exceptions, the black composers represented, such as Frank Johnson, Isaac Hazzard, James Hemmenway, Henry F. Williams, etc., all belong to the antebellum era. The only postwar pieces are Annie Pindell's song, *Seek the Lodge Where the Red Men Dwell,* some piano pieces by Blind Tom (who was still a youth in 1870), and compositions by Justin Holland.

Despite the scarcity of black composers on the national scene, they were well represented at the Nashville (Tennessee) Exposition in 1897. Charles Anderson, in charge of the New York City exhibitions, was able to collect 450 compositions written by African-Americans for exhibition at the Negro Booth in the New York building. A pianist, E. C. Brown, gave daily recitals of this music in that booth; one of the most popular pieces was the *Tennessee Centennial March* by William J. Accooe.[18]

It remained for a nonprofessional to produce the historical landmark of the period: in 1878 James Monroe Trotter (1842–1892) published a general survey of black American music entitled *Music and Some Highly Musical People.* This was the first time in the history of the nation that anyone, black or white, had attempted to assess a body of American music that cut across genres and styles. It was not until 1883 that a writer ventured to publish a similar book about American music as a whole, *Music in America* by the white composer Frédérick Louis Ritter. Although not a professional, Trotter studied music as a child and was a musical amateur for most of his life. Beginning about 1883 he was active as an impresario, along with his friend William DuPree, another amateur musician, for the dramatic artist Henrietta Vinson Davis, concert singer Marie Selika, and others.

His book is invaluable today for the unique information it provides about black musicians of the nineteenth century, both as individual artists and as members of groups. His coverage extended from the Georgia Minstrels on the one hand to symphony orchestras in New Orleans on the other; he quoted extensively from critical press notices and reproduced recital programs and advertisements. Moreover, he published the works of twelve composers in his appendix. The book was a landmark in the field of writings about black American music, not to be matched for more than fifty years.

---

[18]Entered in the *Allen A. Brown Scrapbooks: Musical Topics,* v. 2, p. 136 (Boston Public Library); John Edward Bruce, "Negro Song Writers," *The Transcript* (July 14, 1899).

MUSIC OF THE BLACK CHURCH, III

After the war, the black church expanded its membership rolls and its activities to an enormous degree. At last the ex-slaves were freed from white supervision over their religious services, and they set up hundreds of churches, some under the denominational shelter of AME (African Methodist Episcopal) and AMEZ (African Methodist Episcopal Zion) churches and others, as independent congregations of the various white Protestant churches. Moreover, new denominations came into being, for example, the Colored Methodist Episcopal Church in 1870 in an amiable separation from the white Methodist Church South. (In 1954 the church changed its name to Christian Methodist Episcopal Church.)

Since Baptist churches were independent entities, black Baptist churches had never been subjected to authoritative structure from above. However, feeling a need for cooperation in meeting common concerns, they began to organize on a national level: in 1865 the black members of the Primitive Baptist Church set up the Colored Primitive Baptist Church, and in 1895 three large black-Baptist organizations merged to form the National Baptist Convention, U.S.A. They held annual meetings, which as we shall see, were to be important in the development of black gospel music.

The most striking religious development, however, was the emergence of holiness and sanctified churches during the 1890s, of which the Church of God in Christ developed into the largest organization. The founder of that church, Charles Henry Mason, left a Baptist church in Lexington, Mississippi, to establish his new denomination at Memphis, Tennessee. The next year dissidents left his congregation to found their own churches: William Matthew Roberts settling in Chicago; Ozra Thurston Jones, in Philadelphia; E. R. Drivers, in California; and E. M. Page, in Texas. Charles Price Jones (1865–1949) left his Baptist ministry in the 1890s to found the Church of Christ (Holiness) U.S.A., which held its first holiness convention at Jackson, Mississippi, in 1897. Perhaps the earliest of all the holiness black churches was the Church of the Living God, founded in 1889 by William Christian at Wrightsville, Arkansas, but that church has remained relatively small in comparison to those mentioned above.

Many holiness church fathers participated in the Azusa Street Revival, 1906–9 held at Los Angeles under the leadership of William J. Seymour. There they "received the gift of the Holy Spirit," and their congregations (and later ones) became a part of the general pentecostal movement established by Seymour, who was formerly a minister of the AME church.[19]

---

[19]Minor discrepancies exist among the various published accounts of the origin of the black holiness churches. The facts outlined above are based on Barbara Baker, "Black Gospel Music Styles, 1942–1975" (Ph.D. diss., University of Maryland, 1978), p. 2. Dr. Baker interviewed the oldest daughter of founder W. M. Roberts; she was an eyewitness to the events

The influence of African traditions upon religious ritual was more in evidence in the holiness churches than in any of the other churches of the period—the spirit possession, holy dancing, speaking in tongues, improvisatory singing, and use of drums and other percussive instruments. Obviously the pentecostal churches fell direct heir to the shouts, hand-clapping and foot-stomping, jubilee songs, and ecstatic seizures of the plantation "praise houses."

Hymn Writers and Collectors

The first new hymnal published for black congregations after Emancipation—and the only one for many years—was *A Collection of Revival Hymns and Plantation Melodies* (1882) by black Methodist minister Marshall W. Taylor (1846–1887) for his church's use in the Lexington (Kentucky) Conference of the white Methodist Episcopal Church. According to all evidence, Taylor was the first African American to publish a collection of slave songs and hymns. His collection of 150 songs (plus seven with texts only) includes gospel hymns written by whites, gospel songs of black songwriters, and a large number of arranged Negro spirituals. In addition, Taylor includes commentary on the origin of the plantation songs and how they should be sung. The hymnal was so popular that Taylor published an enlarged, second edition in 1883.[20]

The AME Church continued to publish periodically new editions of its official hymnal. As stated earlier, the eleventh edition in 1897 included hymn tunes for the first time. John Turner Layton (ca. 1841–1916), who was responsible for compiling the hymns and editing the music, was a notable composer of sacred music; he contributed several hymns and an anthem to the AME hymnal. Several other black hymnists also are represented in the hymnbook.

Pentecostal minister Charles Jones also was a hymnwriter. According to his autobiography, he studied music while matriculating at Arkansas Baptist College and began writing gospel hymns as a youth. His first collection, *The Jesus Only Standard Hymnal,* was published in 1899 and followed the next

---

associated with the founding of COGIC. See also the *Yearbook of American and Canadian Churches* (Nashville: Abingdon Press), which is published annually; *The Negro Almanac,* ed. by Harry Ploski and Ernest Kaiser, 2nd rev. ed. (New York: Bellwether Co., 1971). In regard to the Azusa Street Revival see James A. Tinney, "William Joseph Seymour: Father of Sixty Million Pentecostals" (Paper delivered at the Sixty-Sixth Annual Meeting of the Association for the Study of Afro-American Life and History, Philadelphia, October 1981). Dr. Tinney is founder/editor of *Spirit: A Journal of Issues Incident to Black Pentecostalism.*

Initially, the Azusa Street Revival was interracial, but whites chafed under black leadership and began to withdraw. By the mid-1920s the churches were totally segregated. In 1994, the various groups decided to unite, and formed the Pentecostal-Charismatic Churches of North America (composed of about eighteen million Pentecostals, a third of them African American).

[20]Robin Hough, "Choirs of Angels" in *Feel The Spirit* (Westport, CT, 1988), pp. 17–33.

year by the *His Fulness Hymnal*.[21] Another minister-hymnwriter of the period would later exert wide influence upon the development of a new religious genre, gospel music. Charles Albert Tindley (1859–1933) began his career as an itinerant Methodist preacher and camp-meeting singer in Maryland. Some time during the 1870s he settled at Philadelphia and, in about 1902, founded the East Calvary Methodist Episcopal Church (renamed Tindley Temple in 1924). His church early began to attract attention for its exciting music, some of which was written by Tindley. But it was not until 1901 that he began to copyright his church songs.

[21]A small collection of eleven hymns is included in Jones, "The History of My Songs" in Otho Cobbins, *History of the Church of Christ (Holiness) U.S.A.* (New York, 1966), pp. 400–25.

CHAPTER 8

The
New
Century

THE last decade of the nineteenth century brought a period of unprecedented opportunity for black men and women to develop and exercise
their talents, despite the fact that for every new avenue open to them
twice as many barriers were thrown up to prevent their advance. This was
the era that saw the ascendency of such race leaders as educators Booker T.
Washington (1856–1915), John Hope (1864–1936), William E. B. Du Bois
(1868–1963), Carter G. Woodson (1875–1950), and Mary McLeod
Bethune (1875–1955); the surgeon Daniel Hale Williams (1856–1931) and
the scientist George Washington Carver (1864–1943); the business tycoons
Madame C. J. Walker (1869–1919) and Charles Clinton Spaulding (1874–
1952); the sculptor Edmonia Lewis (1845–1890); the historian George
Washington Williams (1849–1891); the novelist Charles Waddell Chesnutt
(1858–1932); the artist Henry Ossawa Tanner (1859–1937); and the poet
Paul Laurence Dunbar (1872–1906). Other names could be added to the
list, names of black pioneers in the fields of politics, religion, business, and
the professions, who were recognized by America for achievement. In the
field of music, perhaps more than in any other field, the preeminence of the
African American was acknowledged by the nation. As we shall see, their
contributions not only made a decisive impact on the existing style of music
in the Western tradition, they also gave birth to a new style of music.

THE GENERAL STATE OF MUSIC

During the last decades of the nineteenth century, the United States entered upon a new era in its musical history. Symphony orchestras and major opera companies were established, an American school of composers emerged, and promising developments took place in the area of music education. The Philharmonic Society of New York, oldest professional orchestra in the country (1842), was reorganized in 1901 and renamed the New York Philharmonic Society. Other permanent major orchestras founded during these years include the Boston Symphony (1881), the Chicago Symphony (1891), the Philadelphia Orchestra (1900), the Minneapolis Symphony (1903), and the Cincinnati Symphony (1909).

With regard to opera, New Orleans continued its dominance until the end of the nineteenth century, importing famous opera stars to sing with its highly trained companies. New York had had impressive opera performances since 1825, but it was not until 1883 that the Metropolitan Opera Company was founded and gave its opening performance in a new Opera House. In Chicago, a new auditorium was provided for the Chicago Opera in 1889, and soon afterward the company was established on a firm basis.

Meanwhile, schools devoted to the training of professional musicians were being established: in 1857, the Peabody Conservatory in Baltimore; in 1865, Oberlin School of Music; in 1867, the New England Conservatory of Music, the Boston Conservatory, the Cincinnati Conservatory, and Chicago Musical College; and in 1870, the Philadelphia Musical Academy. The next two decades saw the founding of the New York College of Music in 1878, the National Conservatory of Music at New York in 1885, and the American Conservatory at Chicago in 1886. The last major music school to be established before World War I was the Institute of Musical Art, founded in New York in 1904.

While black musicians were barred from participation in the activities of the symphony orchestras and opera companies, they were admitted to some of the music schools and conservatories. Moreover, a few black students enjoyed the patronage of such eminent musicians as the Bohemian composer Antonín Dvořák (1841–1904), director of the National Conservatory of Music during the years 1892–95, and the German violinist-composer Julius Eichberg (1824–1893), co-founder and director of the Boston Conservatory. A number of black men and women took advantage of the opportunity to obtain an excellent music education, and some completed their studies by going to Europe to work with musicians there. It was no accident that the most active and most creative colonies of black musicians should develop in those places where musical training—formal or informal—was available to them and where, after they were trained, they found opportunities to employ their talents.

MUSIC NATIONALISM

In the first part of the nineteenth century at least two white composers had shown interest in developing a truly "American" music, inspired by the nation's history and by the Native American and Negro folk music. Anton Philipp Heinrich (1781–1861), a native of Bohemia who came to the United States about 1818, was so impressed by the country's natural scenery, its exciting history, and the music of the Native American, that he was inspired to write a large quantity of music about these things. His publications, which now have little more than historic value, include works with such titles as *The Dawning of Music in Kentucky, Yankee Doodliad, Indian Carnival,* and *Indian Fanfares.*

Louis Moreau Gottschalk (1829–1869), the first American concert artist and composer to achieve international renown, was born in New Orleans and consequently fell heir to the rich music traditions of that colorful city. Three of his most popular compositions, *Bamboula, La Savane* (or *Ballade Créole*), and *Le Bananier* (or *Chanson Nègre*) used Negro folk tunes of New Orleans. He also wrote pieces inspired by Afro-Cuban folk music.

It was not until the decade of the 1890s, however, that a nationalistic school of music actually got under way in the United States. Antonín Dvořák started it all. Soon after he came to America as director of the National Conservatory in New York in 1892, he revealed his enthusiasm for the folk music of the land and called for the formation of an American school of composition. Dvořák became particularly fond of one of his black students, Harry Burleigh, and spent many hours listening to him sing the folksongs of his people and discussing with him the possibilities for utilizing the folk music as the basis for composition. Within three months of his arrival, Dvořák had begun work on a symphony, *From the New World* (No. 9 in E minor), that employed themes invented in the spirit of Negro and Indian folk melodies. Just before its New York premiere in 1893, Dvořák stated:

> I am now satisfied that the future music of this country must be founded upon what are called the negro melodies. This must be the real foundation of any serious and original school of composition to be developed in the United States. . . . These are the folk-songs of America, and your composers must turn to them. All of the great musicians have borrowed from the songs of the common people. . . . In the negro melodies of America I discover all that is needed for a great and noble school of music. They are pathetic, tender, passionate, melancholy, solemn, religious, bold, merry, gay, or what you will.[1]

Dvořák wrote two other works in which he used themes employing the idioms of Negro spirituals, the so-called "American" Quartet (Op. 96) and a quintet (Op. 97). He returned to Bohemia in 1895, leaving behind an

[1] "Dvořák on Negro Melodies," *The Musical Record* (Boston) (July 1893), p. 13.

awakened interest in America's folk music among the composers of the time, which led to the rise of a genuine musical nationalism for the first time.

Two of Dvořák's white students at the conservatory accepted his challenge. William Arms Fisher (1861–1948) made settings of Negro spirituals, publishing one collection as *Seventy Negro Spirituals* (1926). Fisher's arrangement of the second-movement theme of Dvořák's *From the New World* Symphony as a pseudo-spiritual with the text *Goin' Home* was popular at one time. Rubin Goldmark (1872–1936), who became a teacher at the National Conservatory and, later, at the Institute of Musical Art, wrote *A Negro Rhapsody*.

Among other white Americans who were inspired to use black folk materials during this period were Henry F. B. Gilbert (1868–1928) and John Powell (1882–1963), both of them writing Negro rhapsodies and other symphonic works with Negro themes. Daniel Gregory Mason (1873–1953) wrote a string quartet on Negro themes. Arthur Farwell (1872–1952) not only wrote nationalistic music and collected folksongs, but also founded the Wa-Wan Press in 1901 for the express purpose of publishing compositions of American composers and collections of Native-American and African-American folksongs. No black composers however, were represented in the Wa-Wan Press catalogue.

Nationalistic Music of Black Composers

Almost the entire first generation of post-slavery black composers—i.e., those born after 1863—may be regarded as nationalists in the sense that they consciously turned to the folk music of their people as a source of inspiration for their compositions, whether in the fields of concert music, show music, or dance and entertainment music. Most of those who achieved distinction, and some of lesser stature as well, were excellently trained; they had studied at Oberlin, the New England Conservatory, and the National Conservatory in New York, or privately with competent, European-trained white musicians. Consequently, they knew how to write music in traditional European style and, indeed, often did so, because they wanted the music to sell. But they reserved much of their creative energy for Negro-inspired composition.

The songwriters set the poems of black poets and made vocal and choral arrangements of spirituals and other folksong types. The instrumental composers wrote program music, drawing heavily upon characteristic Negro melodic idioms and dance rhythms. All the composers placed special emphasis upon traditional African-American performance practice, and made efforts to reflect the individualities of the practice in their composed music.

The composers who won recognition in the field of concert music generally began to publish late, first pursuing careers as performers or teachers. The composers of show music and entertainment music wrote prolifically

Harry T. Burleigh. *(Courtesy of the author)*

from the beginning, and although much of their music remained unpublished, it was performed widely in the black community and consequently
was known to the appropriate segment of the public.

Harry T. Burleigh (1866–1949) was the first to achieve national distinction as a composer, arranger, and concert artist. He early showed an interest
in music but was unable to study because of his poverty. Although he had
little formal training, Burleigh sang in churches and synagogues in his home
city of Erie, Pennsylvania, whenever the opportunity arose. At the age of
twenty-six he obtained a scholarship with the assistance of friends to attend
at the National Conservatory of Music. During his second year there he
began to study with Dvořák and absorbed the Bohemian master's theories
about Native-American and African-American music as a basis for a nationalistic school of music.

At the Conservatory Burleigh acquired practical experience with both
orchestral and vocal music. He played double bass and later tympani in the
orchestra and, as a senior, was given the opportunity to teach voice. In
1894 he applied for the position of baritone soloist at St. George's Episcopal
Church and was selected over forty-nine other applicants, though not without opposition from some parishioners of the church because of his race.
During his fifty-two-year tenure in the church he established two traditions:
he sang Fauré's *The Palms* every Palm Sunday, and he gave an annual concert of Negro spirituals. In 1900 he took on a second position, soloist at
Temple Emanu-El, and remained there twenty-five years.

Respectfully, dedicated to Miss Mary Jordan

Deep River

Old Negro melody
Arranged by
H. T. BURLEIGH

FCS 1637

He began composing about 1898, at first writing simple ballads in the style of the period, then turning to art songs and instrumental pieces. He left more than three hundred compositions, including arrangements of spirituals, art songs, and other forms. Best known are the *Six Plantation Melodies for Violin and Piano* (1901), *From the Southland* for piano (1914), *Southland Sketches* for violin and piano (1916), and the song cycles *Saracen Songs* (1914) and *Five Songs* (1919, texts by Lawrence Hope). Undoubtedly, his appointment as a music editor for Ricordi and Company in 1911 was helpful to his career.

His songs were popular during the period and widely sung by white artists such as Lucrezia Bori, Ernestine Schumann-Heink, and John McCormack. *I love my Jean* (1914, Robert Burns poem), *Little Mother of Mine* (1917), *Under a Blazing Star* (1918), and *In the Great Somewhere* (1919) were particularly popular. One of his war songs, *The Young Warrior* (1916, poem by James Weldon Johnson) was translated into Italian and sung by Italian troops as a marching song during World War I.

As an arranger of spirituals for the solo voice Burleigh made a unique contribution to the history of American music. Before he published his *Jubilee Songs of the United States of America* in 1916, spirituals were performed on the concert stage only in ensemble or choral arrangements. Burleigh's achievement made available to concert singers for the first time Negro spirituals set in the manner of art songs. The piano accompaniments in his arrangements rarely overpower the simple melodies but rather set and sustain a dominant emotional mood throughout the song. Chromatic harmonies are used within the basically diatonic coloring, but discreetly, so as not to destroy the balance between piano and vocal line. We may find these features illustrated in Burleigh's fine arrangement of *Deep River.*

After Burleigh, many concert singers developed the tradition of closing their recitals with a group of Negro spirituals, sometimes intermixed with other arranged folksongs. One critic wrote about the Burleigh arrangements:

> They are one and all little masterpieces, settings by one of our time's most gifted song-composers of melodies, which he penetrates as probably no other living composer. [*Musical America,* October 17, 1917]

Burleigh himself wrote about his aim:

> My desire was to preserve them [the spirituals] in harmonies that belong to modern methods of tonal progression without robbing the melodies of their racial flavor. [*New York World,* October 25, 1924]

In 1929 Burleigh published the *Old Songs Hymnal,* a collection of very simple arrangements of Negro songs for nonprofessionals "to be used in church and home and school, preserving to us this precious heritage." Finally, it should be noted that baritone Harry T. Burleigh was in great demand as a soloist. He gave recitals periodically, including a performance for President Theodore Roosevelt and a command performance for King Edward VII in London, and sang solos in numerous productions of oratorios and concert operas.

With the exception of Burleigh, most of the composers of this period were involved primarily in theater music. Will Marion Cook (1869–1944), the patriarch of the group, revealed musical talent early and was sent to study violin at Oberlin when he was only fifteen. Later, the black community sponsored benefit recitals to raise money so that he could study abroad. During the years 1887–89 he matriculated at the Berlin Hochschule für Musik, where he worked with Heinrich Jacobson, a former student of the Austrian violinist Josef Joachim. Jacobson also was Chairman of the Orchestral Instruments Department. (There is no evidence for the oft-repeated statement that Cook studied abroad for nine years.)

In later years (1894–95), he attended the National Conservatory of Music, where he studied with Dvořák and John White, among others. Although Cook began playing professionally during his student days at Oberlin and made his debut in 1889 in Washington, D.C., his solo career was short-lived. As early as 1890 he became director of a chamber orchestra, which toured along the eastern seaboard.

Cook's first essay in composition dates from 1893, when he prepared a work, *Scenes from the Opera of Uncle Tom's Cabin*, for performance on Colored American Day (August 25) at the Chicago World's Fair. The performance failed to take place, however, and Cook apparently gave his attention to other matters until 1898. In that year he wrote a musical-comedy sketch, *Clorindy; or, The Origin of the Cakewalk*, in collaboration with poet Paul Laurence Dunbar. Thereafter he was composer-in-chief and musical director for the George Walker–Bert Williams company for several years.

He continued to write his own musicals, some of which were produced, though none seems to have been commercially successful. These works include *The Policy Players* (1900), *Uncle Eph's Christmas* (1901), *The Cannibal King* (1901, with Will Accooe), *The Southerners* (1904, a Broadway musical), *The Ghost Ship* (1907), *The Traitor* (1913), *In Darkeydom* (1914, with James Reese Europe), *The Cannibal King* (1914), and *Swing Along* (1929, with Will Vodery).

Cook was best known for his songs, which represent an original, distinctive handling of black folk elements in song composition. Written for solo voice and choral groups, some first appeared in his musicals, then were published in *A Collection of Negro Songs* (1912), including *Rain Song; Exhortation—A Negro Sermon; My Lady; Wid de Moon, Moon, Moon; Red, Red Rose;* and *Swing Along* (see further, pp. 303–304).

In his later career Cook was active as a choral and orchestral conductor; over the years he organized several choral societies, in both New York and Washington, D.C., and produced numerous concerts. One of his greatest adventures occurred in 1918 when his New York Syncopated Orchestra (also known as the Southern Syncopated Orchestra) toured the nation, then went to England in 1919, where he played a command performance for

Will Marion Cook *(Courtesy New York Public Library, Theatre Collection)*

Beginning of Rain Song, Will Marion Cook

King George V. His company included Abbie Mitchell, Tom Fletcher, Will Tyers (as assistant director), and jazz clarinetist Sidney Bechet, among others. (Cook's Broadway musicals will be discussed later in this chapter.)

J.[ohn] Rosamond Johnson (1873–1954) obtained his musical education at the New England Conservatory and later studied privately in London, England. He began his career as a music teacher in the public schools of Jacksonville, Florida, his home. At the turn of the century he went to New York, where he became involved in show business and in 1901 formed a song-writing team with his brother, James Weldon Johnson (1871–1938), a poet-writer, and the songwriter Robert "Bob" Cole (1868–1911). One of their earliest efforts was a work, *The Evolution of Ragtime* (1903), subtitled "a musical suite of six songs tracing and illustrating Negro music."

The trio produced two successful operettas with all-black casts on Broadway, *The Shoo-Fly Regiment* (1906) and *The Red Moon* (1908), and contributed music to several white musicals, among them *Sleeping Beauty and the Beast* (1901), *In Newport* (1904), and *Humpty Dumpty* (1904). In later years Rosamond Johnson wrote three additional musicals with other collaborators, *Mr. Lode of Koal* (1909), *Hello, Paris* (1911, with J. Leubrie Hill), and *Come Over Here* (1912). Best known of the songs for which Johnson wrote music are *The Maiden with the Dreamy Eyes, Didn't He Ramble* (under pseudonym Will Handy), *Li'l Gal, Since You Went Away,* and *Lift Every Voice and Sing,* written by the Johnsons in 1900 and performed by school children in Jacksonville, Florida, where the Johnsons were teaching. The song became so popular in black communities that people began dubbing it the *Negro National Anthem.* It was almost always sung at large, formal gatherings, such as NAACP banquets and gatherings to honor race heroes. During the 1950s or 60s, African Americans began singing the song in gospel style, renaming it the *Black National Anthem.*

Rosamond Johnson was active in diverse areas of music during his long career. He toured in vaudeville acts with Cole until the latter's death in 1911, then with Charles Hart and Tom Brown, successively. During the years 1912–13 he served a long residency in a London theater revue, for which he wrote music, and after returning to the United States, was appointed the director of the Music School Settlement for Colored in New York (1914–19). After the war, he toured with his own ensembles, The Harlem Rounders and The Inimitable Five, and as well with Taylor Gordon in concerts of Negro spirituals. In 1936 he was musical director of the London production of *Blackbirds of 1936;* he also took roles in dramas during the 1930s and sang in *Porgy and Bess* (1935).

Johnson edited four important song collections, *The Book of American Negro Spirituals* (1925) and *The Second Book of Negro Spirituals* (1926), both with James Weldon Johnson; *Shout Songs* (1936); and *Rolling Along in Song* (1937), an anthology of folksong types. Johnson's best-known choral work was *Walk Together, Children,* for chorus and orchestra (1915).

This group of postwar composers also includes Harry Lawrence Free-

Lift Every Voice and Sing

Lift ev' - ry voice and sing, till earth and heav - en ring, ring with the
har - mo - nies of lib - er - ty; Let our re - joic - ing
rise, high as the list - 'ning skies, let it re - sound loud as the
roll - ing sea. Sing a song full of the faith that the dark past has
taught us; Sing a song full of the hope that the pres-ent has
brought us. Fac-ing the ris - ing sun of our new day be -
gun, let us march on till vic - to - ry is won.

Stony the road we trod, bitter the chastening rod
Felt in the days when hope unborn had died;
Yet with a steady beat, have not our weary feet
Come to the place for which our fathers sighed?
We have come over a way that with tears has been watered;
We have come, treading our path through the blood of
    the slaughtered;
Out from the gloomy past, 'til now we stand at last
Where the white gleam of our bright star is cast.

God of our weary years, God of our silent tears,
Thou who hast brought us thus far on the way;
Thou who hast by Thy might led us into the light,
Keep us forever in the path, we pray.
Lest our feet stray from the places, our God, where we meet Thee,
Lest our hearts, drunk with the wine of the world, we forget Thee;
Shadowed beneath Thy hand, may we forever stand,
True to our God, true to our native land.

man (1869–1954), who won recognition as an opera composer. He produced his first opera, *The Martyr,* in 1893 in Denver, Colorado, and scenes from his second, *Nada* (1898), were performed by the Cleveland Symphony in 1900. Writing opera of course was a luxury for a black composer of that period; to earn his livelihood, Freeman also wrote stage music and served

Sheet music cover of a song from Cole and Johnson's 1906 operetta, *Shoo-Fly Regiment.*
(Courtesy of the author)

as musical director for vaudeville companies, including Rufus Rastus (1905) and the Cole–Johnson brothers company, and for the Pekin Theatre in Chicago.

He continued to write operas, however, and completed fourteen in all, including *The Tryst* (produced in 1911), *Vendetta* (1923), and *Voodoo* (1928), which was produced on stage and in an abridged version on WCBS radio. Freeman's output also included ballets, a symphonic poem *The Slave* (1925), cantatas, songs and instrumental pieces.

A younger generation of composers, born in the 1880s, included several

Clarence Cameron White. *(Courtesy of the author)*

who were both concert artists and college teachers. Clarence Cameron White (1880–1960) obtained his basic musical training in Oberlin, Ohio, and Washington, D.C., where he also attended Howard University for a year (1894–95). He studied violin briefly with Will Marion Cook when he was twelve years old, then with Joseph Douglass when he was fourteen. During the years 1896–1901 he attended the Oberlin Conservatory but left before graduating to accept a teaching position. His later study included a year at the Hartford (Connecticut) School of Music and three periods abroad: in London during the years 1906 and 1908–10 with Samuel Coleridge-Taylor and M. Zacharewitsch, and in Paris during 1930–32 with Raoul Laparra.

White's teaching career included tenures in the public schools of Washington, D.C., and the Washington Conservatory of Music (1903–7), at West Virginia State College (1924–30), and at Hampton Institute (1932–35). He began to publish little pieces in the conventional (neoromantic) style of the period, then turned to Negro folk music as a source of inspiration for his composition. His early output included violin compositions and the spiritual arrangements *Forty Negro Spirituals* (1927) and *Traditional Negro Spirituals* (1940).

White composed in a variety of forms in his mature period. The orchestral works include *Kutamba Rhapsody* (1942) and Concerto in G minor for violin (1945); chamber music, a string quartet using Negro themes, and a *Spiritual Suite* for four clarinets (1956). One orchestral piece, *Elegy,* won the Benjamin Award in 1954. White was best known for his dramatic works—the incidental music for the play *Tambour* (1929), which includes a ballet often performed independently, *A Night in Sans Souci,* and the opera *Ouanga* (1931). Both are based on Haitian themes and had the collabora-

R. Nathaniel Dett. *(Courtesy of the author)*

tion of playwright and librettist John Matheus. White, a protégé of E. Azalia Hackley's, also won critical praise as a concert violinist. It was she who made possible his study abroad in London by raising money for his scholarships. After his return to the United States, he toured extensively, often accompanied by his wife, Beatrice Warrick White, at the piano. For a period in the early decades of the century, White was regarded as the foremost violinist of the race.

Robert Nathaniel Dett (1882–1943) began piano study at an early age in his birthplace, Drummondsville, Ontario; continued his education at the Lockport (New York) Conservatory; and matriculated at Oberlin, where he earned the B.Mus. degree in 1908, majoring in composition and piano. The first black student to complete the five-year course at Oberlin, Dett toured widely as a concert pianist after leaving Oberlin. His early piano compositions were amateurish but suggested future promise.

During this period Dett came under the influence of the soprano E. Azalia Hackley and, because of her, he developed an enduring interest in black folk music. His teaching career included tenures at Lane College in Tennessee (1908–11), Lincoln Institute in Missouri (1911–13), Hampton Institute in Virginia (1913–32) where he was the first black director of music, and Bennett College in North Carolina (1937–42). The early piano suites and choral works were written for practical use—*Magnolia* (1912);

In the Bottoms (1913), with its perennially popular movement *Dance Juba;*
Enchantment (1922); *The Cinnamon Grove* (1928); and the choral *Music*
in the Mine (1916) and *The Chariot Jubilee* (1921).

Dance Juba, R. Nathaniel Dett

Dett continued to study throughout his lifetime, generally spending his
summers at one of the major institutions of the nation. During the year
1920–21 he attended Harvard, where he studied with Arthur Foote and
won two prizes—the Francis Boott Award for his choral composition *Don't*
Be Weary, Traveler and the Bowdoin Prize for his essay "The Emancipation
of Negro Music." In the summer of 1929 he studied in France with Nadia
Boulanger, and during the year 1931–32 he matriculated at the Eastman
School of Music in New York (M.Mus.).

His compositional interests continued to reflect the demands of his
teaching, such as the collections of spiritual arrangements *Religious Folk-*
songs of the Negro (1927) and *The Dett Collection of Negro Spirituals*
(1936). In the late years of his career, he tended to turn away from his basic
neo-romantic style for contemporary idioms, as in the piano suites *Tropic*
Winter (1938) or the *Eight Bible Vignettes* (1941–43) and the *American*
Sampler (1938). Best known of his choral works are the oratorio *The*
Ordering of Moses (1937) and the anthems *Listen to the Lambs* and *I'll*
Never Turn Back No More, in addition to those cited above.

The concert music of the composers we have been discussing was surprisingly successful when one considers how recently the black composer
had emerged upon the American scene. Their songs and piano pieces were
published in such periodicals as *Etude* and *The Ladies' Home Journal* under
the rubric "fascinating pieces for the musical home." Established white artists performed the compositions on their recitals—among them, violinists
Fritz Kreisler, Irma Seydel, and Albert Spaulding; singers Lucrezia Bori,
John McCormack, and Ernestine Schumann-Heink; and pianist Percy
Grainger. And black concert artists made it a tradition to include the music
of black composers on their concerts, the singers always concluding their
recitals with a group of spirituals.

The white music establishment was equally supportive of those few who
wrote for Tin Pan Alley and the stage. Such Broadway stars as Marie Cahill,
Anna Held, May Irwin, Lillian Russell, and Sophie Tucker, in particular,

used the songs of black writers in their musicals and popularized them in other ways. In the world of commercial music, where cheating the composer was a normal practice, the Cole–Johnson brothers team and a few other black songwriters held good contracts with reputable publishers and were commissioned by such exclusive firms as Klaw and Erlanger to write music for special productions.

Whatever opinion critics of the future may have regarding the intrinsic value of the music of the black pioneers just discussed, these men remain historically important as the first composers to truly assimilate the characteristic idioms of Negro folksong into a body of composed music. Unlike the white composers of so-called Negro music who preceded and followed them, these men did not have to understand first the "exotic" music before employing it in their composition; to them this music was not exotic but natural. According to composer Hall Johnson, African Americans were "surrounded by the sound of Negro singing from birth; they absorbed the music with each breath they took."[2]

The challenge, rather, was to pour that music into traditional European forms—the art song, the motet and chorus, the instrumental suite, the music drama, and the operetta or musical comedy—and their training enabled them to do this. Some of the gifted composers of popular music naturally wrote in the Negro style and scored for ensembles in black folk traditions without even being conscious of doing so.

But the trained musicians were fully aware of their aims. Dett, for example, wrote in 1918:

> We have this wonderful store of folk music—the melodies of an enslaved people, who poured out their longings, their griefs and their aspirations in the one great, universal language. But this store will be of no value unless we utilize it, unless we treat it in such manner that it can be presented in choral form, in lyric and operatic works, in concertos and suites and salon music—unless our musical architects take the rough timber of Negro themes and fashion from it music which will prove that we, too, have national feelings and characteristics, as have the European peoples whose forms we have zealously followed for so long.[3]

To be sure, there were times when the composers "quoted" rather than invented melodies in the spirit of Negro folksong—whether consciously or not, we cannot say. It has been pointed out, for example, that Burleigh used the spiritual melody *Somebody's Knocking at Yo' Door* in one of his *Saracen Songs—Ahmed's Farewell.*[4]

---

[2]Hall Johnson, "Notes on the Negro Spiritual," RBAM, pp. 273–80.
[3]May Stanley, "R. N. Dett of Hampton Institute," *Musical America* (July 1918); reprint in BPIM 1 (Spring 1973): 66.
[4]See Margaret Bonds, "A Reminiscence," *The Negro in Music and Art,* ed. Lindsay Patterson (Washington, D.C., 1967), p. 191.

Somebody's Knocking at Yo' Door

Some-bod-y's knock-ing at yo' door, Some-bod-y's knock-ing at yo' door.

Ahmed's Farewell, Harry T. Burleigh

Andantino

mf lamentoso

Nev - er so state - ly a star   Rode the fair man - sions of

etc.

Heav'n;   Gods gather'd beau - ties a - far,

An amusing anecdote related by old-timers indicates that two composers, at least, knew what they were doing when they employed a spiritual melody in a popular tune. It seems that on one occasion when Bob Cole and J. Rosamond Johnson were urgently in need of a good tune, Cole suggested using the old familiar spiritual *Nobody Knows the Trouble I've Seen.* Upon his companion's protest that to use a spiritual would be sacrilegious, Cole is reputed to have said, "What kind of a musician are you, anyway? Been to the Boston Conservatory and can't change a little old tune around."[5] That did it! Johnson and Cole used the melody in an altered form for one of their biggest hits, *Under the Bamboo Tree,* which was featured by Marie Cahill in the Broadway show *Sally in Our Alley.* In the 1940s, film star Judy Garland sang the song in the movie *Meet Me in St. Louis.*

Nobody Knows the Trouble I've Seen

No-bod - y knows the trou-ble I've seen,   No-bod - y knows my sor-row;

Chorus of **Under the Bamboo Tree,** Bob Cole and J. Rosamond Johnson

If you lak-a-me, lak I lak-a-you, And we lak - a both the same,

A professor at Fisk University, John Wesley Work II (1873–1925), was the first black collector of Negro folksongs. Although he taught in the history and Latin departments, his enthusiasm for folk music led him to orga-

---

[5]See further in Jack Burton, *The Blue Book of Tin Pan Alley* (Watkins Glen, NY, 1950), v. 1, p. 109.

nize Fisk student singing groups about 1898 and take them on tour to raise money for the college in emulation of the original Fisk Jubilee Singers back in the 1870s. During the years 1909–16 Work toured extensively with his Fisk Jubilee Singers quartet, composed of Alfred King, Noah Ryder, James Meyers, and himself. The quartet also recorded for the Victor Talking Machine Company. Work published solo songs and choral pieces, but his major contribution to music history was his collecting and arranging Negro folksongs. In 1901 he collaborated with his brother, Frederick Jerome Work, to publish *New Jubilee Songs as Sung by the Fisk Jubilee Singers,* and in 1915 he himself published *Folk Songs of the American Negro.*

IN THE CONCERT WORLD

Concert Singers

The singers who began concert careers in the first years of the twentieth century include sopranos Emma Azalia Hackley (1867–1922) and Anita Patti Brown (1870s–1950). Hackley obtained her basic training in Detroit, and graduated from the University of Denver in 1901. The same year she made her concert debut in Denver. She toured extensively until 1911, the year she gave her "retiring" concert at prestigious Orchestra Hall in Chicago, then founded a Vocal Normal Institute in that city.

Early in her career she was active as a choral director, and during her last years she gave all her time to organizing mammoth community concerts, called Negro Folk Song Festivals, in large cities of the nation. The choruses she trained to sing at these festivals frequently included as many as three hundred or more performers. For her activities, she earned the soubriquet "Our National Voice Teacher" from the black press. Hackley also devoted much time and money to advancing the careers of promising young black musicians; she worked with singers and raised money for scholarships for both singers and instrumentalists by giving recitals.

Little is known about Anita Brown's early career before she settled in Chicago in about 1900, where in 1903 she gave her debut recital. The black press called Brown "our globe-trotting prima donna" because of her extensive touring in the United States, Europe, the West Indies, and South America. She was one of the first black artists to make recordings (in 1916 and 1920 but never released) and among the first of the singers to study voice in Europe.

Two sopranos of a younger generation were protégés of Hackley: Florence Cole Talbert (1890–1961) and Cleota Collins (1893–1976). Talbert made her debut in New York in 1918 after graduating from Chicago Musical College that year. Her concert tours took her across America and to Europe in the 1920s, where she sang the title role of Verdi's *Aïda* in 1927 at Cozenza, Italy. Collins also toured extensively on the concert circuit, sang

Joseph Douglass and his grandfather, Frederick Douglass. *(Courtesy of the author)*

solos in several of Hackley's festivals, and studied voice in Europe. Both
Talbert and Collins taught in black colleges after leaving the concert stage.

Concert Violinists and Pianists

Joseph Douglass (1871–1935) was the first black violinist to make transcontinental tours and was the direct inspiration for several young violinists
who later became professionals. He came from a family of musical amateurs: his paternal grandfather, fiery old abolitionist Frederick Douglass,
played the violin, as did his father. Lauded by the black press in the 1890s
as "the most talented violinist of the race," Douglass toured extensively for
more than three decades. He was credited with having performed at every
black educational institution in the nation and at most of the churches;
often his wife, Fannie Howard Douglass, accompanied him at the piano.

Douglass first attracted wide attention in 1893 when he performed on
Colored American Day at the Chicago World's Fair (August 25). He was the
first violinist to make recordings—in 1914, for the Victor Talking Machine
Company—but the records were never released. His teaching career

included tenures at Howard University in Washington, D.C., and at the Music School Settlement for Colored in New York. Douglass was also active as an orchestra conductor from time to time, and he conducted a music studio.

Several black pianists began concert careers in the early twentieth century, and for the first time, women were among their numbers. Raymond Lawson (1875–1959) obtained his musical education at Fisk University, where in 1895 he was the first student to complete the music degree program, then attended the Hartford School of Music in Connecticut (B.Mus., 1901), and studied in Europe with Ossip Gabrilowitsch (1911). Lawson made his debut in 1895 in Hartford and toured regularly but gave his primary attention to studio teaching. It is probable that he was the first black pianist in the nation to perform concertos with a symphony orchestra; he played with the Hartford Symphony several times, beginning as early as 1911.

Azalia Hackley had yet two other protégés in the concert world: R. Nathaniel Dett and Carl Diton (1886–1962). After leaving Oberlin, Dett performed widely as a concert pianist. Diton first studied with his father, a professional musician, in Philadelphia and graduated from the University of Pennsylvania in 1909. The next year he became the first black pianist to make a transcontinental tour of the nation. This attracted the interest of Hackley, who raised money for a scholarship that permitted Diton to study in Germany during the year 1910–11. After returning home, he continued to play periodically but also began teaching. Within a few years, he turned his attention to composing and, in later years, to singing.

The first black woman to make a stir in the musical world as a pianist was Hazel Harrison (1883–1969), who began piano study at an early age and in 1904 was invited to play at the Royal Theatre in Berlin, Germany, through the influence of her teacher, Victor Heinz. Over the years she spent much time studying in Germany, working with Ferrucio Busoni and Egon Petri; in the United States she studied again with Heinz and, later with Percy Grainger. Some time after returning home from her second period of study abroad (1910–14), she gave debut recitals, the first in Chicago in 1919 and the second in New York in 1922. Thereafter she concertized regularly before returning to Germany in 1926.

Harrison began her teaching career in 1931, with tenures at Tuskegee Institute in Alabama (1931–34), Howard University (1934–59), and Alabama State College (1959–63). But her primary interest was in concertizing, and she successfully combined performance with teaching, at times taking leaves of absence for as much as a year in order to tour. Harrison won critical acclaim from both the white and black press and was rated the most accomplished pianist of the race for several decades.

Like Dett, Helen Hagan (1891–1964) was a musical pioneer in that she was the first black pianist to earn the B.Mus. degree from Yale University (1912) and the first to win Yale's Sanford Fellowship, which permitted her to study abroad for two years with Blanche Selva and Vincent D'Indy in France. She received a diploma from the Schola Cantorum (1914) and later attended Columbia University Teachers' College in New York (M.A.).

During the years 1914–18 Hagan concertized extensively, then returned to France upon invitation of the YWCA to entertain black soldiers during World War I. After returning home, she made her New York debut at Aeolian Hall in 1921. Thereafter she toured regularly, but left the concert stage during the 1930s to teach in black colleges in the South. Resettling in New York about 1935, she conducted a music studio and performed occasionally.

Although Hagan was a gifted pianist, her concert career never got off the ground. Like most black concert artists of the time, she suffered from an inability to obtain good, professional management. The many years these artists spent preparing themselves for concert careers generally were to no avail; established white impresarios simply were not interested, and black artists could not earn a livelihood by performing solely for black audiences. Finally, the most successful artists were those who learned how to manage themselves, using their personal contacts with friends and the community.

It should be observed, however, that various people and institutions in the black community offered supportive services. In New York, for example, Walter Craig sponsored annual Pre-Lenten Recitals during the years 1905–15, at which he presented young black performers and composers. Established artists also performed on Craig concerts and on concerts promoted by black schools of music, such as the Martin–Smith School and Music School Settlement in New York and the Washington Conservatory in Washington, D.C.

There were also concert series promoted by enterprising black impresarios, such as the Clef Club concerts at Carnegie Hall in New York during the years 1912–15,[6] the William Hackney annual "All-Colored Composers" concerts in Chicago's Orchestra Hall during the years 1914–16, and the Atlanta Colored Music Festivals held in Georgia under the leadership of the Reverend Henry Hugh Proctor during the years 1910–15.[7] A later series in New York, the Educational Concert Series (1917–23), was promoted by two singers, Daisy Tapley and Minnie Brown.

In addition to performing in black churches, colleges, and other community institutions, the established artists traveled from one of these "name" concerts to another as "imported guest artists," and consequently became known to each other as well as to the black public all over the nation. In addition to the artists discussed above, there were others who are forgotten today, and some who would later become world renowned, among them Roland Hayes and Marian Anderson.

[6]"Black-Music Concerts in Carnegie Hall, 1912–1915," BPIM 6 (Spring 1978): 71–88.
[7]Altona Trent Johns, "Henry Hugh Proctor," BPIM 3 (Spring 1975): 25–32.

Artist Professors

As we have seen, most concert artists, after meeting little success on the concert stage, eventually entered teaching careers either in music studios or in black colleges in the South. Dett and Talbert pioneered in directing music departments in these institutions, for until the second decade of the century, black colleges typically had white music directors. Some artists began teaching early in their careers, after only a brief period on the concert stage. Violinist Kemper Harreld (1885–1971) was active in music circles of Chicago until 1911, the year he went to Atlanta to take charge of the music program at Atlanta Baptist College (now Morehouse College). He remained there until his retirement in 1956, making a significant contribution to the musical world through his students.

Violinist Louia Vaughn Jones (1895–1965) earned a music degree from the New England Conservatory of Music, then studied abroad for many years, returning home only for a short period after World War I. When he returned to settle permanently in the states in 1930, he was appointed head of the violin department at Howard University and remained there until his retirement in 1960. He continued to give recitals periodically, however, along with his teaching. Pianist Roy Tibbs (1888–1944) earned music degrees from Fisk University (B.Mus.) and Oberlin (M.Mus.); he also studied in Paris with Isadore Philipp in 1914. After his appointment to Howard University in 1912, he combined teaching with occasional piano recitals and appearances on concerts. He was also director of the university choir for many years.

Some artists combined performance with conducting a music studio or serving as a church musician. William H. Bush (1861–1952) won distinction as an organist for the Second Congregational Church in New London, Connecticut, where he played for many years. He also found time to give regular recitals, however, and in 1904 represented his state in a recital at the St. Louis Exposition. Bush was a member of the American Guild of Organists. Kathleen Howard Forbes (1892–1978) also was an associate of the American Guild of Organists. She began her career as a church organist in 1916 in Hamilton, Ontario, her birthplace; in 1923 she settled permanently in Cleveland, where she was active as a church organist and choral director for forty-two years. In her early career she toured in the United States, Canada, and the West Indies, often serving as an accompanist for Roland Hayes and Louia Vaughn Jones, among others.

Melville Charlton (1880–1973), the first black American to pass the examination for admission to the associate rank of the American Guild of Organists, obtained his musical education at the National Conservatory of Music in New York City. In addition to serving as organist with the Jewish Temple of Covenant (1914–24) and the Union Theological Seminary (1911–ca. 1940), he performed regularly and toured as a piano or organ accompanist.

The Negro String Quartet, active in New York in the 1920s: Arthur Boyd and Felix Weir, violins; Hall Johnson, viola; Marion Cumbo, cello. *(Courtesy of the author)*

One of the nation's first black concert cellists was Leonard Jeter (1881–1970), who conducted a studio in addition to performing on concerts and playing in orchestras and ensembles. In the first decades of the century he toured widely with violinist Felix Weir (1884–1978) in a duo, which was later expanded to a trio with the addition of pianist Olyve Jeter, Leonard's sister.

Weir won recognition for his violin skills at an early age. A graduate of Chicago Musical College, he studied at the Conservatory in Leipzig, Germany, for a short while. After returning home, he became active in the concert field, appearing on concerts and performing in ensembles. About 1914 he formed the American String Quartet, consisting of violinist Joseph Lymos, violist Hall Johnson, cellist Jeter, and himself. In the 1920s his quartet, renamed the Negro String Quartet, included two new members, cellist Marion Cumbo and violinist Arthur Boyd. Weir was active also in other fields during his long career: in public school teaching, with Clef Club orchestras, and in the orchestras of Broadway musicals, particularly during the 1920s–30s.

MUSIC EDUCATORS

The colleges and academies set up expressly for black youth by the American Missionary Association after the Civil War provided most of the education for black students in the South through the early part of the twentieth century, and for the most part these institutions maintained excellent music programs. In the North, where racial discrimination was almost as pronounced as in the South, only more subtle, black students in search of musical training generally had to fend for themselves. In response to the needs of these students, several black professional musicians established music schools, particularly in the large cities.

In Washington, D.C., pianist Harriet Gibbs Marshall (1869–1941) founded the Washington Conservatory of Music in 1903 to offer black students the opportunity to obtain training in the conservatory manner. The first black woman to receive a music diploma from Oberlin (1889), she studied further in music conservatories of Boston, Chicago, and Paris, France. She began her teaching career in a small college in Kentucky, then moved to the public schools of Washington.

From the beginning, her conservatory was successful in meeting its goals; some of the most talented artists in the nation went to Washington to teach in the school or sit on its board of trustees, among them Clarence Cameron White and E. Azalia Hackley. An important ancillary activity of the school was its sponsorship of regular concerts, for which guest artists were brought in from other cities. This benefited the community as well as the students, for the laws of the city prohibited the black population from attending musical events offered in the white community.

In New York, David I. Martin (ca. 1880–1923) set up a violin studio about 1907, then in 1912 joined forces with pianist Helen Elise Smith (later,

The Ladies' orchestra. *(Courtesy of the author)*

Mrs. Nathaniel Dett) to form the Martin–Smith School of Music. Within a few years the school had become one of the most important black musical institutions in the country. Not only did it offer excellent training for the young, it also provided a place for beginning teachers to develop their skills and a haven for retired concert artists, among them, Marie Selika Williams and Sidney Woodward.

For a few years (1911–19) there was a Music School Settlement for Colored in the city, founded by white philanthropists under the leadership of David Mannes of the New York Symphony; black students could not attend the white Music School Settlement. Martin was director of the Settlement during the years 1911–14, after which J. Rosamond Johnson served as director. When Johnson resigned in 1919, the activities of the Settlement were transferred to the Martin–Smith School. After Martin's death, his son continued the activities of the school for many years.

While no other private music schools exerted the kind of influence in the black musical world as did the Martin–Smith and the Washington Conservatory, there were smaller institutions that accepted the challenge of offering professional training to black youths. Violinist William Nickerson (1865–1928) operated the Nickerson School of Music in New Orleans, where many future professionals studied. It was a family enterprise: his wife, Julie, who obtained her musical training at the New England Conservatory, gave lessons and conducted a "ladies' orchestra"; daughter Camille taught for ten years after graduating from Oberlin (1916), then went to Howard University and remained there until her retirement in 1962; and sons Henry and Philip were on the Nickerson faculty in addition to playing in local bands and orchestras.

It should be observed that a number of public high-school teachers contributed an enormous amount of time to developing the skills of talented young people. Nathaniel Clark Smith (1877–1933) might be regarded as the pioneer of these "master teachers." He obtained his musical education at Western University in Quindaro, Kansas (now defunct); at Guild Hall in London, England (1899); and at Chicago Musical College (B.Mus.). He also pursued further study privately and at various musical institutions. In his early career he toured with minstrel groups all over the world, then later directed military bands. His teaching career began in 1916 and included tenures in the Lincoln High School in Kansas City, Missouri (1916–22); Wendell Phillips High School in Chicago (1925–26), and Sumner High School in St. Louis (1930–33).

Smith established such high standards for excellence at the schools where he taught that the traditions lasted through many generations of students. The teachers who succeeded him, either directly or later, followed his precedent—William Levi Dawson and Alonzo Lewis at Lincoln High, Walter Dyett at Wendell Phillips, and Stanley Lee Henderson at Sumner. Smith became a legend in his own time for his marching bands, glee clubs, and orchestras, and some of the students who studied with him in school or community groups developed into the leading jazz and concert artists of the mid-twentieth century.

Smith was also a composer and arranger; black college and high-school bands everywhere played his spirited marches, and his arrangements of Negro spirituals were widely performed by choral groups. His best-known works were *Tuskegee Institute March, New Jubilee Songs, Negro Folk Suite,* and the *Negro Choral Symphony* (composed for performance at the Chicago World's Fair in 1933).

The Midwest was further represented by Wendell Phillips Dabney (1865–1952), who studied music at Oberlin College, taught in the public schools of Richmond, Virginia, then settled in Cincinnati, Ohio, where he conducted a music studio. He was well known for two of his publications, *Dabney's Complete Method of Guitar* and *The Dabney and Roach Mandolin and Guitar Method.* His nephew, Ford Dabney, became an important musician in post–World War I dance-music circles of New York City.

Another legendary teacher of the period was Jesse Gerald Tyler (ca. 1879–1938), who obtained his musical education at Oberlin (B.Mus.). He began his teaching career in Harriet Marshall's Washington Conservatory of Music and the public schools of Washington, D.C. (1904–7). He then settled in Missouri, where he taught at Lincoln High in Kansas City (1907–11) and at Sumner in St. Louis (1911–22). He also served as a music supervisor of colored schools in both cities. Like Smith, his influence as a teacher lasted through several generations of students and younger teachers who came under his tutelage. Tyler was also a gifted composer, whose pieces were widely performed during his time. Best known of these were the song *Ships That Pass in the Night* and the anthem *The Magnificat.*

On the East coast it was Francis Eugene Mikell (1885–1932) who earned recognition as a master teacher. A native of South Carolina, he began his career directing boys' bands for the Jenkins Orphanage in Charleston, then taught in black colleges before going to New York in 1917 to become a bandmaster for the Old Fifteenth Infantry Regiment (later named the 369th). Mikell remained in the North after the war, teaching at the Martin–Smith School of Music and, for many years, at the Bordentown Industrial Institute in New Jersey. He was highly regarded for both his original compositions and his arrangements.

In Baltimore, Maryland, W. Llewellyn Wilson (1887–1950) made a significant contribution to black music history through his students. He obtained his musical training in the public schools of Baltimore and the Colored Normal School there (diploma) . After graduation he went to teach at the Douglass High School and remained there forty years. He also conducted a private studio, published a weekly column in the Baltimore *Afro-American,* and directed the city-sponsored Baltimore City Orchestra and Chorus. At one time during the 1920s all the black music teachers in the city public schools were his former students. Others made their marks in jazz, black musical theater, college teaching, and even ragtime—for example, Eubie Blake.

Two teachers of a younger generation are worthy of mention. John T. Whatley (ca. 1896–1971) of Birmingham, Alabama, was a superior instructor, many of whose students later became professionals, particularly in the field of jazz. A graduate of Tuggle Institute in that city, he began teaching at the Industrial High School in 1917 and remained there until his retirement. He organized the first brass band in Birmingham and throughout his career led community bands and dance orchestras in addition to his school groups.

Walter Henri Dyett (1901–1969) was the top bandmaster in Chicago for more than forty years. He obtained his musical education at the University of California, Los Angeles and at several music schools in Chicago, including the Vandercook School of Band Music (B.Mus.) and Chicago Musical College (M.Mus.). In addition to his long tenures of service at the Wendell Phillips High School (1931–35) and DuSable (1935–69), he was a bandmaster in the United States Eighth Infantry band and conducted dance orchestras as well as community bands. Most Chicago jazzpeople came under Dyett's tutelage and a number of concert artists also studied with him or played in his groups.

SYMPHONY ORCHESTRAS, OPERA COMPANIES, AND CHORAL SOCIETIES

Symphony Orchestras

In 1904 a symphony orchestra was founded in Philadelphia, which became, in 1906, the first black orchestra in the nation to be incorporated. Edward Gilbert Anderson (1874–1926) was the conductor from 1905 to about 1917. The People's Choral Society of Philadelphia, organized in 1908, generally cooperated with the orchestra in producing concerts, which featured renowned guest artists such as soprano Anita Patti Brown, violinist Joseph Douglass, tenor Roland Hayes, and baritone Harry T. Burleigh. But the two Philadelphia organizations also encouraged the development of young talent; during the second decade of the century, for example, Marian Anderson was a featured artist many times, although she was only a high-school student.

In New Orleans, the Lyre Club Symphony Orchestra (organized in 1897) gave concerts on a regular basis, and a community orchestra formed by William Nickerson in the 1890s staged concerts in the city and away from home. In 1900, for example, the Nickerson orchestra played at the Great Congress in Atlanta and traveled to Chicago the same year for another performance. Chicago had its own short-lived black symphony orchestra (ca. 1902–5) under the directorship of N. Clark Smith, which made its debut in March 1903 with Anita Patti Brown and William N. P.

James Reese Europe and the Clef Club Orchestra, 1910. *(Courtesy of the author)*

Spiller as soloists. Beginning in 1906 there was an orchestra at the Pekin Theatre under the direction of Joe Jordan, which played concert music as well as theater music. And in 1914 David Peyton presented his Grand Symphony Orchestra to the public for the first time, after having been inspired by Clef Club orchestras of New York.

In New York, concerts sponsored by the Music School Settlement for Colored and the Clef Club were produced at Carnegie Hall during the years 1912–15, provoking emulation by black groups in other cities, as well as much comment from the press. Presented annually for four successive years, these concerts attracted huge audiences of white and black. The novel feature of the first concert in May 1912 was the Clef Club Symphony Orchestra of 125 players, directed by James Reese Europe, with William H. Tyers as assistant conductor. In addition to traditional instruments, the orchestra included mandolins and banjos, and its program consisted entirely of music written by black composers, among them, Will Marion Cook, Harry T. Burleigh, Samuel Coleridge-Taylor, and Europe himself. The soloists, ensembles, and choral groups on the program sang art songs and ballads, arrangements of folksongs, anthems, and a Mass movement. James Weldon Johnson later wrote about the effect of the opening number, Europe's *Clef Club March,* upon the audience, which was composed of the regular patrons of Carnegie Hall in addition to friends of the orchestra and many serious musicians and music critics as well, who had come out of curiosity.

> New York had not yet become accustomed to jazz; so when the Clef Club opened its concert with a syncopated march, playing it with a biting attack and an infectious rhythm, and on the finale bursting into singing, the effect can be imagined. The applause became a tumult![8]

---

[8]James Weldon Johnson, *Black Manhattan* (New York, 1930), pp. 123–24.

The next three annual concerts were also given over entirely to the music of black composers. By 1914 the novelty had worn off; a white critic wrote in *Musical America:*

This concert, the third effort of those who wish the negro to assert his musical individuality, though more creditable than the two previous, fell short once more of the serious purpose to which these talents might be directed. . . . If the Negro Symphony Orchestra will give its attention during the coming year to a movement or two of a Haydn symphony and play it at its next concert, and if the composers, who this year took such obvious pleasure in conducting their marches, tangos, and waltzes, will write short movements for orchestra, basing them on classic models, next year's concert will inaugurate a new era for the Negro musician in New York and will aid him in being appraised at his full value and in being taken seriously.[9]

And a black musician of Philadelphia wrote in an open letter:

All the renditions of the Club were good, spicy and catchy. . . . All races have their folksongs and dances, but all races try to develop their art from examples set by masters of other periods; and if we expect to do anything that is lasting from an artistic standpoint, we, too, must study the classics as a foundation for our work.[10]

But Europe defended his position. He told an interviewer:

You see, we colored people have our own music that is part of us. It's the product of our souls; it's been created by the sufferings and miseries of our race. Some of the melodies we played Wednesday were made up by slaves of the old days, and others were handed down from the days before we left Africa. . . . [Some] would doubtless laugh heartily at the way our Negro Symphony is organized, the distribution of the pieces, and our methods of organization.

Europe pointed out that mandolins and banjos were used in place of second violins, two clarinets instead of an oboe, baritone horns and trombone instead of French horn and bassoon. He felt, however, that it was the "peculiar steady strumming accompaniment" of the mandolins and banjos that made the music distinctive, and that the use of ten pianos in the ensemble gave the background of chords "essentially typical of Negro harmony." He concluded:

We have developed a kind of symphony music that, no matter what else you think, is different and distinctive, and that lends itself to the playing of the peculiar compositions of our race.[11]

[9]A. W. K., "Negroes Perform Their Own Music," *Musical America* (March 21, 1914).
[10]Adolphus Lewis in the *Philadelphia Tribune,* November 21, 1914.
[11]James Reese Europe, "Negro's Place in Music," *New York Evening Post,* March 13, 1914; reprint in Robert Kimball and William Bolcom, *Reminiscing with Sissle and Blake* (New York, 1973), p. 61.

Europe was never to retreat from that stand. Five years later, after extensive touring and service in the United States Army, he stated emphatically:

> I have come back from France more firmly convinced than ever that negroes should write negro music. We have our own racial feeling and if we try to copy whites we will make bad copies. . . . We won France by playing music which was ours and not a pale imitation of others, and if we are to develop in America we must develop along our own lines. . . . Will Marion Cook, William Tires [Tyers], even Harry Burleigh and Coleridge-Taylor are [only] truly themselves in the music which expresses their race. . . . The music of our race springs from the soil, and this is true to-day with no other race, except possibly the Russians. . . .
>
> [Literary Digest, April 26, 1919]

Opera Companies and Choral Societies

In the field of opera the efforts of Theodore Drury (1860s–1940s) are worthy of note. He was one of several black students who studied at the National Conservatory of Music in New York during the 1890s, along with Burleigh, Cook, and Desseria Plato, among others. He first attracted the attention of the press as a concert baritone on Grand Star Concerts. In 1889 his Drury Colored Opera Company began presenting operatic scenes to the public but was short-lived. By 1900, however, Drury had reorganized his forces, and he began producing grand operas, one each year for nine years, at the Lexington Opera House and other halls or theaters in New York.

Generally he employed a white orchestra and occasionally white soloists, but the choruses and most of the leading roles were sung by black singers. His regular soloists included Desseria Plato, Estelle Pickney Clough, George Ruffin, and himself. Over the years (1900–8) the company presented Bizet's *Carmen*, Antonio Carlos Gomez's *Il guarany*, Gounod's *Faust*, Leoncavallo's *I pagliacci*, Mascagni's *Cavalleria rusticana*, and Verdi's *Aïda*.

Drury continued to produce opera and oratorios throughout his career. In 1911, for example, he staged Handel's *Messiah* at Boston, where he settled some time after 1908. After a period of study abroad, he returned to the United States in 1918 and began touring as a concert singer, then returned to Boston, where he established a music studio. Later he moved to Philadelphia, where he also taught music. He did not give up his original love, however; as late as May 1938 he produced *Carmen* in Philadelphia with his Drury Opera Company.

During this period choral societies sprang up in all the places that had large black communities. In Washington, D.C., Henry J. Lewis organized the Amphion Glee Club in 1892, and the group was active into the 1930s. In 1902 the Coleridge-Taylor Choral Society was formed with John Turner Layton as musical director. The society brought the African-English composer for whom it was named to the United States twice to conduct concerts of his music, in November 1904 and again two years later. Samuel Coleridge-Taylor (1875–1912) again returned to the United States in 1910 as a guest of the Litchfield Choral Union Festival at Norfolk, Connecticut, where his music was performed. Regarded as one of England's rising young composers, he made a marked impression upon the American public, particularly in black communities. Best known for his trilogy of cantatas, *Hiawatha's Wedding Feast* (1898), *The Death of Minnehaha* (1899), and *Hiawatha's Departure* (1900), he also composed other choral works, an opera, a symphony, a number of instrumental works, and art songs. In addition to his teaching at the Trinity College of Music, Coleridge-Taylor conducted choral societies in England and organized the Croydon String Orchestra. In 1899, after attending a concert of the Fisk Jubilee Singers in England, he became interested in Negro folksong, and made a collection of piano arrangements of African and African-American melodies, *Twenty-Four Negro Melodies Transcribed for the Piano* (1905). The *Bamboula* from this collection became very popular with pianists; also popular with audiences were his *African Suite* (1898) and his Concerto in G minor (1911).

Chicago had no fewer than four important choral groups. In 1900 Pedro Tinsley founded the Choral Study Club. The Umbrian Glee Club, founded in 1908 by Edward Morris and Arthur Brown, remained active into the 1980s. In addition to singing in community concerts, both groups presented an annual concert and brought in artists from the East coast to sing solos in oratorios and concert operas.

The other two choruses were started by church choral directors James Mundy (1886–1978) and J. Wesley Jones (1884–1961). Mundy began organizing community groups about 1913 and staged mammoth concerts at Orchestra Hall and at the Coliseum. In 1910 he formed a Federal Glee Club consisting of the city's black postal clerks and mail carriers; during the 1920s he directed the South Side Opera Company. Jones also organized community groups and for thirty years was director of the chorus at the annual Chicagoland Music Festivals. Choruses led by either or both of these men sang on all important occasions in Chicago that called for the participation of blacks. During the 1930s Mundy and Jones attracted wide attention for their "Battles of the Choirs."

Philadelphia had its People's Choral Society, as we have seen, and the periodic concerts of the choir of the East Calvary Methodist Episcopal Church. Since the pastor of that church, Charles Tindley, is regarded as the "father of gospel music," it may well be that the choir's performances anticipated the sound of modern gospel. In New York there were Clef Club groups and other community groups, of which the best known were Will Marion Cook's Afro-American Folk Singers and his Negro Choral Society. In Kansas City, Missouri, Gerald Tyler organized his Tyler Choral Society in the first decade of the century. Like other choral directors, Tyler imported guest artists to sing on his concerts; in 1909 he produced the oratorio *Mary Magdalene* with Burleigh, Carl Diton, and Inez Clough as soloists. Tyler continued to conduct community choirs during his years of residence in St. Louis (1911–22).

Finally, there were the Williams Jubilee Singers, a professional group who toured throughout the world much as the Fisk Jubilee Singers had done several decades earlier. Charles Williams organized the sixteen-member group in 1904 in Chicago. For the first five years of its existence, the group toured on the circuits of white lyceum bureaus and Chautauquas; then, beginning in 1915, they began appearing before both black and white audiences. During the next decade the group sang in most of the concert halls of the nation and circled the globe several times. Their repertory was large and varied, ranging from popular ballads and plantation songs to operatic and oratorio arias and ensembles.

THEATERS AND THEATER MUSIC

In the early twentieth century the black theater served as a secular temple for black communities.[12] One went to the theater not only to see the latest musical comedies and the most recent vaudeville acts but also to listen to presentations of local and touring concert companies, choral organizations, orchestral groups, vocal and instrumental recitalists, and dramatic troupes. These programs were produced by black, white, and integrated groups.

Chicago's Pekin Theatre was the first black-owned theater in the nation. Founded in 1905 by Robert Motts (d. 1911), the theater pioneered in bringing black entertainers, actors, playwrights, and composers before the public. Mott organized a Pekin Theatre Stock Company, which not only staged productions at home but also toured in the Midwest and in the East. He brought the leading artists of the race to Chicago to perform on his Professional Matinees and Sacred Concerts. One particularly notable concert was held on December 4, 1906, when the music of Coleridge-Taylor was performed by singers and pianists, with the English composer himself conducting the Pekin Orchestra.

But the main business of the theater was stage entertainment. The Pekin's first production was *The Man from Bam,* written by musical director Joe Jordan and the play's leading men, Flournoy Miller and Aubrey Lyles. During its lifetime (1905–16), the Pekin gave first performances to a number of musicals, including *The Husband, The Ghost Ship,* and *Captain Rufus,* which also played in New York. Even before the demise of the Pekin, other black communities were establishing theaters: in New York, the Lincoln and the Lafayette; in Philadelphia, the New Standard and the Dunbar,

---

[12]This discussion of stage music is based largely on contemporary black newspapers, particularly the *Indianapolis Freeman,* the *New York Age,* the *Cleveland Gazette,* and the *Chicago Defender.*

both owned by John T. Gibson; in St. Louis, the Booker T. Washington, owned by Charles Turpin of ragtime fame; and in Washington, D.C., the Howard.

All these theaters, and others as well, became invaluable institutions of the community, and some were noted for special kinds of activities. The Lafayette, for example, offered playwrights and composers the opportunity to try out new musicals, beginning in 1913—this in addition to the productions staged by its resident company, the Lafayette Players Stock Company. Will Marion Cook was one of the first to take advantage of the opportunity when he staged his musical *The Traitor* in 1913. The composer most closely associated with the Lafayette, however, was John Leubrie Hill (ca. 1869–1916). Hill established a reputation as a songwriter in a team with Alex Rogers as early as 1896 and worked with the Walker–Williams company as both actor and songwriter. When that company was disbanded, Hill played in *Mr. Lode of Koal,* then organized his own company.

His first production, *My Friend from Dixie,* made a big splash in Harlem, where the Lafayette was located. Two years later, he produced another hit, *My Friend from Kentucky;* among those who were impressed was showman Florenz Ziegfeld, who arranged to use some scenes from the musical in his *Ziegfeld Follies of 1913* on Broadway. Hill toured with his musical, but seems to have been successful only in black communities. For a brief period in 1914, the musical in an abbreviated version, *Darktown Follies,* was on Broadway, but it failed and Hill went back to Harlem.

The Howard in Washington, D.C. (opened August 1910) served as a concert hall as well as theater; even during its first year it was the locale of an Artist Recital Series and Commencement Exercises sponsored by the Washington Conservatory. The Howard and the Lafayette regularly exchanged productions and musicians, thus plays produced at one theater generally found their way to the other. The same was true of theater orchestras.

The extensive theatrical activities in black communities provoked considerable comment in the press. The United States census of 1910 listed more than 7,500 blacks involved in show business, of whom 5,606 were musicians and 1,279 were actors. Black theater was big business! In addition to the numerous stock companies that took their productions from one theater to another, there were enterprising individuals who were active as impresarios, such as William "Billy" King, an ex-minstrel, vaudevillian, and songwriter, and Irvin C. Miller, brother of the actor Flournoy Miller and a talented actor in his own right.

It was a musician-actor who first decided to consolidate black theatrical activity. Sherman H. Dudley (1873–1940) began his career traveling with carnivals, then played in the important minstrel troupes of his time before moving into musical comedy.[13] In 1904 he became the leading man of The

---

[13]Athelia Knight, "Sherman H. Dudley," BPIM 15 (Fall 1987): 152–81.

Smart Set after the death of Tom McIntosh, and remained with that company until 1913.

Obviously Dudley had given serious thought to the idea of setting up a black-theater circuit before he wrote to the *Freeman* in January 1912 about his plan, and he had begun purchasing theaters, his first in Baltimore. Correspondence between Dudley and the *Freeman*'s editor continued in the newspaper through February, and in March Dudley announced that he would retire from the stage in 1913 in order to carry out his plans. Within a short time he was publishing a column each week in black newspapers, "What's What on the Dudley Circuit," in which he listed the names of theaters where shows were in production and the names of theater managers. By the end of 1914 his list included twenty-three theaters, all owned or operated by blacks and located as far south as Atlanta.

For the first time, black companies could arrange for contracts through one agency and play in theaters all over the nation throughout the season. For the first time, black actors and musicians had access to professional management. Dudley built up his empire in the succeeding years until economic circumstances beyond his control forced him to sell out. But his concept of a black-theater circuit found favorable acceptance among entertainers, producers, and theater managers. In 1920 some of these persons organized the Theatre Owners Booking Association, which developed to the extent that a survey made in 1924 counted eighty-five participating theaters. The officers of T.O.B.A. were white, but Dudley, Gibson, and Turpin served as district managers in Washington, D.C., Philadelphia, and St. Louis, respectively.

T.O.B.A. was a memorial to the era of the black theater, when hundreds of show people played before black audiences in productions they wrote, directed, and produced themselves. Black entertainers had come a long way since Emancipation! Although the organization had a negative image for entertainers—they asserted that the initials T.O.B.A. stood for Tough On Black Actors (or something worse!)—it served as a showcase for black talent, and many of the important entertainers of the period toured for T.O.B.A. at one time or another in their careers. Best known of them were Butterbeans and Susie (i.e., Jody and Susie Edwards), the Whitman Sisters (Mable, Essie, "Bert," and Alice), Gertrude "Ma" Rainey, Bessie Smith, and Ethel Waters. Some entertainers graduated from the "small time" of T.O.B.A. to such "big time" circuits as the Pantages, Orpheum, Columbia, and Keith Albee.

SHOWS ON THE ROAD

Minstrelsy was still an important form of entertainment for blacks in the 1890s, but during the early twentieth century the picture slowly began to change. Road shows, vaudeville, and finally musical comedies began to replace the once ubiquitous minstrel show. For a period during the turn of the century, show people constantly moved from one entertainment type to another; minstrels toured with road shows and musical comedy companies, and there was active movement in the other direction by singers and actors. Even the celebrated Sissieretta Jones proved unable to resist the minstrel stage when her financial condition so dictated, as in April 1889 when she appeared with the Georgia Minstrels at Dockstaders Theatre in New York.

Black road shows had a long tradition, reaching back at least to 1876 when the Hyers Sisters began touring with *Out of Bondage.* Several road shows were organized at the beginning of the twentieth century, and three would prove to be long-lived. In 1900 Patrick "Pat" Chappelle (1869–1911), an ex-minstrel, organized a touring company to produce musicals, of which the first was *A Rabbit's Foot.* Although the company staged other productions, the first proved to be most popular, and Chappelle repeated it again and again. Eventually, people began referring to his company as Pat Chappelle's Rabbit Foot Company. When Fred S. Walcott took over management of the company after Chappelle's death, he retained the original name for a few years, then changed it to F. S. Walcott's Rabbit Foot Minstrels (or Company). Based in Port Gibson, Mississippi, the show toured widely, particularly in the South, and employed some of the most important blues and vaudeville singers of the race during its early years, beginning in 1915 with "Ma" Rainey and Bessie Smith. The Rabbit Foot Company was still touring as late as the 1950s.

The tent show *Silas Green from New Orleans* was similar in format to the Rabbit Foot Company and, like that company, was active into the 1950s. Its founder, "Professor" Eph Williams (d. 1921), owned a circus during the 1890s; indeed, he was reputed to be the only black circus owner in the United States at that time. About 1910 he began producing a show called *Silas Green from New Orleans* with his Famous Troubadours Concert Company, and eventually the name of the show became the name of the company. After Williams's death, the show foundered for a while, then found new management that prolonged its life for another thirty or more years.

The most remarkable of these shows was The Smart Set, organized in 1902 by minstrels Billy McClain and Ernest Hogan and white producer Gus Hill. Actually, The Smart Set was not a road show but rather a musical comedy company that toured constantly. Hogan and McClain wrote the company's first musical, *Southern Enchantment,* and also took leading roles. During the next few years, the company attracted several of the nation's leading black showmen, among them Tom McIntosh, Tom Logan, and S. H. Dudley, as well as musical directors James Reese Europe and James Vaughn.

About 1909 two brothers, Salem Tutt Whitney and J. Homer Tutt, organized a second company, referred to in the black press as The Smarter Set or The Southern Smart Set. Within a short time Whitney and Tutt merged their company with the original, and the resulting Smart Set toured until 1923. Although in later years other road shows used that name, none was as successful as the original. Whitney and Tutt were highly reputable showmen and songwriters; their experience prior to joining The Smart Set included two years with Black Patti's Troubadours. Over the years they wrote many musicals, along with such composers as Europe, Vaughn, Henry Creamer, Charles Luckeyeth Roberts, and Will Vodery; the most popular were *Dr. Beans from Boston; The Major of Newtown; His Excellency, the President, George Washington Bullion Abroad; My People,* and *Bamboula.* The last named, produced in the 1919–20 season, was advertised as a "jazzonian operetta."

Black Showmen and the Circus

Thanks to Phineas T. Barnum and others, the circus had become an American tradition by the late nineteenth century. The big tent covered several departments—such as circus bands, side shows, vaudeville acts, and even burlesque, in addition to its main features—and like other American institutions of the period, it discriminated against black performers. Band master Perry J. Lowery (ca. 1870–194?) is credited with being the first black musician to take his vaudeville acts into the circus, when his group performed with the Sells and Forepaugh Brothers Circus at New York's Madison Square Garden in 1899. Before that time, blacks were employed only as bandsmen.

Lowery began his career playing in bands that toured with minstrel troupes, concert companies, and road shows, among them, Darkest America (1895), the Mallory Brothers Minstrels, and P. T. Wright's Nashville Students Concert Company. A gifted cornetist as well as bandleader, he traveled with his own groups, P. G. Lowery's Famous Concert Band and P. G. Lowery's Vaudeville Company, from time to time. By 1901, however, he had made a permanent association with the circus and, during the last three decades of his career, toured with all the great ones: Sells and Forepaugh, Wallace and Hagenbeck, Barnum and Bailey, Ringling Brothers, and Cole Brothers. For many years Lowery published a column in the *Freeman,* "The Cornet and Cornetists of Today."

VAUDEVILLE AND MUSICAL COMEDIES

As we have seen, the Hyers Sisters were the first to produce musical comedies, beginning in 1876 with their stage show *Out of Bondage.* But it was some time before anyone emulated them; minstrelsy had too strong a hold on black entertainers. White managers Sam T. Jack and John Isham were

Black Patti Troubadours. *(Courtesy Theatre Collection, Museum of the City of New York)*

the first to produce shows in major music halls that broke away from the minstrel format. Jack's Creole Burlesque Company toured in New England before opening in New York in the fall of 1890. As a show with a black cast, it was a novelty for that time in that it was more a variety show than a minstrel show, and it included both women and men: among them, Tom and Hattie McIntosh, the DeWolfe Sisters, Irving Jones, and Charles S. Johnson. Jack engaged well-known musicians and accented his chorus line of pretty girls; his costumes were smart, and the songs and jokes up-to-date. It worked! The show enjoyed success in New York and later on the road.

Isham began producing shows with his Octoroons Company in 1895, generally following the model established by the Creole Show. In 1896 the management of Sissieretta Jones (Voelckel and Nolan) introduced Black Patti's Troubadours to the public with Jones as the star. In the same year Isham came out with a second company, Oriental America. All these shows employed the most talented black singers, actors, musicians, and writers of the period, and were successful at the box office. Like the minstrel troupes, the companies spent most of the time on the road in the states and Europe. Black Patti's Troubadours began touring abroad in 1897, and during the same year Isham took a new edition of his show, Octoroons, No. 2, to Europe, where they remained for over a year.

As we have noted, the format of the Isham and Jones shows allowed the principal singers to perform scenes from operas in the show finales, with the concert artists singing arias and members of the companies supporting with choruses and ensemble numbers. A typical show of Black Patti's Troubadours offers an example. Like the minstrel show, it consisted of three parts. In December 1896, the Opening Skit (i.e., Part I) was a comedy titled "At Jolly Coon-ey Island." The skit included comedy, songs, and dances, performed by Tom McIntosh, Stella Wiley, Bob Cole, Billy Johnson, and others—all of them well established entertainers. Part II was titled "Vaudeville Olio"; during this section of the performance, actors and singers offered their "specialty acts." Part III was the "Operatic Kaleidoscope," the show's finale. At this point, Sissieretta Jones made her entrance and sang arias in scenes from several of the following—*Carmen, Faust, Il trovatore, Daughter of the Regiment, La bohème, Rigoletto, Lucia da Lammermoor,* among others. She was supported by a quartet of soloists and a chorus of thirty. The full company comprised fifty, including members of the orchestra.

In Isham's Octoroons Show the finale was titled "Thirty Minutes Around the Operas": in his Oriental America, it was "Forty Minutes of Grand and Comic Opera." Those who performed in one or more of these shows included established artists like Belle Davis, Mamie Flowers, Madah Hyers, Sam Lucas, Theodore Pankey, Fred Piper, Desseria Plato, and Sidney Woodward, as well as others who later would become celebrated, among them Bob Cole, Lloyd Gibbs, J. Rosamond Johnson, Abbie Mitchell, and the Golden Gate Quartet.

At the same time as these new companies were attracting wide attention, smaller companies were on the road, some of them under black management. The companies with white management were John Vogel's Darkest America, which began touring in 1895; Hottest Coon in Dixie (1899); and Isham's King Rastus (1904), which featured S. H. Dudley and Billy Kersands. The companies under black management included McAdoo's Original Colored American Minstrel and Vaudeville Company (1897), the Gussie Davis–Tom McIntosh show, A Hot Old Time in Dixie (1899), and Ernest Hogan's Rufus Rastus (1905).

Hogan (1865–1909) was one of the few showmen whose career made him a star on the minstrel stage, on the vaudeville stage, and in musical comedy. He began his career as a "pickaninny" in an Uncle Tom's Cabin Company, then graduated to minstrel companies. During the 1890s he toured widely with his own minstrel company in the United States and as far as Australia. But he left minstrelsy for a few years (1897–99) to play leading roles in Black Patti's Troubadours and in Will Marion Cook's musical sketch, *Clorindy; or the Origin of the Cakewalk,* in 1898.

Back in the United States by 1902, Hogan was one of the principal organizers of The Smart Set, discussed above. In 1905 he produced a vaudeville act that is credited with being the "first syncopated music concert in history." Then followed two musicals, *Rufus Rastus* (1905) and *The Oyster Man* (1909), with himself as the star. Hogan advertised himself as "the Unbleached American," and was reputed to be the highest-paid black vaudevillian of his time. He also was acclaimed for his ragtime songs, particularly *All Coons Look Alike to Me.*

MUSICALS ON AND OFF BROADWAY

In 1897 Bob Cole (1868–1911) and Billy Johnson (ca. 1858–1916) left Black Patti's Troubadours to strike out on their own. They formed a company, which began producing the musical *A Trip to Coontown* the same year. Both men had had years of experience in minstrel and vaudeville troupes and in writing songs. Raiding other companies for talent, they succeeded in securing Sam Lucas, Alice MacKay, and Lloyd Gibbs, among others. Will Accooe, formerly music director for Isham, joined Cole and Johnson in the same position and as a songwriter.

In April 1898 *A Trip to Coontown* made its New York debut to critical approval, and thereafter toured until 1901. This show has been lauded as the first full-length musical play written and produced by blacks on Broadway. Actually, it was "Off Broadway" at a rather obscure theater on Third Avenue, but that was unimportant to the producers. The important thing was that black-produced shows had finally succeeded in New York, the capital of the theater industry, and that this breakthrough would pave the way for others.

Three months after Cole and Johnson opened in New York, Will Marion Cook produced his revue *Clorindy; or, The Origin of the Cakewalk*, in a major house *on* Broadway, the Casino Roof Garden. Cook wrote the music, and Paul Laurence Dunbar, the lyrics. Twenty-six dancers and singers, with Hogan as the star, rehearsed for several weeks, but it was very difficult to find a promoter. One publisher flatly informed him that Broadway audiences would not listen to Negroes singing Negro opera. Finally, after great exertion and many disappointments, he wrangled an audition with John Braham, conductor of the Casino orchestra, and succeeded in obtaining a place in E. E. Rice's "Summer Nights" production. Cook later wrote about the performance:

> When I entered the orchestra pit, there were only about fifty people on the Roof. When we finished the opening chorus, the house was packed to suffocation. What had happened was that the show downstairs in the Casino Theatre was just letting out. The big audience heard those heavenly Negro voices and took to the elevators. At the finish of the opening chorus, the applause and cheering were so tumultuous that I simply stood there transfixed, my hand in the air, unable to move until Hogan rushed down to the footlights and shouted: "What's the matter, son? Let's go!" . . .
>
> The Darktown finale was of complicated rhythm and bold harmonies, and very taxing on the voice. My chorus sang like Russians, dancing meanwhile like Negroes, and cakewalking like angels, black angels! When the last note was sounded, the audience stood and cheered for at least ten minutes. This was the finale which Witmark had said no one would listen to. It was pandemonium, but never was pandemonium dearer to my heart. . . . We went on at 11:45 and finished at 12:45. Boy, oh boy! Maybe, when the pearly gates open wide and a multitude of hosts march in, shouting, laughing, singing, emoting, there will be

a happiness which slightly resembles that of *Clorindy*'s twenty-six participants. I was so delirious that I drank a glass of water, thought it wine and got gloriously drunk. Negroes were at last on Broadway, and there to stay. Gone was the uff-dah of the minstrel! Gone the Massa Linkum stuff! We were artists and we were going a long, long way. We had the world on a string tied to a runnin' red-geared wagon on a down-hill pull. Nothing could stop us, and nothing did for a decade.[14]

The Walker and Williams Company

Black musicals were indeed on Broadway to stay, at least for more than a decade. In the closing years of the nineteenth century, a vaudeville pair appeared on the New York scene who would revolutionize black theater. George Walker (1873–1911) and Egbert "Bert" Williams (1874–1922) first met in 1893 at San Francisco and formed a vaudeville act. After four years of playing with various kinds of road shows, they opened in 1896 on Broadway in a white musical, *The Gold Bug*. The musical was not overly successful, but Walker and Williams were acclaimed for their act, which gained them entry into the theatrical world.

Encouraged by their success, they formed a black company in 1898 to produce shows, and after two or three weak ventures, they came up with three successes in a row: *Walker and Williams in Dahomey* (1903–5), a satire on the American Colonization Society's "back to Africa" movement; *Walker and Williams in Abyssinia* (1906), an extravaganza with an African locale and a huge cast with live camels; and *Walker and Williams in Bandana Land* (1908), a gentle spoof of Negro life in the South.[15]

The plots of the musicals were slight, but Walker and Williams were gifted performers, as were many of the others, the music was excellent, and the dancing, snappy. Over the years Cook served as composer-in-chief and musical director, with the help of such songwriters as J. Leubrie Hill, Alex Rogers, and James Vaughn. Jesse Shipp wrote the books for the musicals; Paul Laurence Dunbar, white lyricist Harry B. Smith, and others contributed lyrics. The shows gave audiences tunes to whistle as they left the theater and songs to try out on their pianos at home. Best known of the songs were *Who Dat Say Chicken in Dis Crowd?, That's How the Cakewalk's Done, Emancipation Day, Darktown's Out Tonight,* and *Swing Along.*

In May 1903 Walker and Williams took *In Dahomey* to England, where the company played in London, including a command performance for King Edward VII, and toured in the provinces for eight months. By the time they

[14]"Clorindy, Or the Origin of the Cakewalk," *Theatre Arts* (September 1947); reprint in RBAM, pp. 227–33.
[15]Ann Charters, *Nobody* . . . (New York, 1970), p. 40.
[16]See further in Ranier Lotz, "Arabella Fields: The Black Nightingale," BPIM 8 (Spring 1980): 5–20; "The Louisiana Troupes in Europe," BPIM 11 (Fall 1983): 133–42.

were ready to return home, the cakewalk had become the fad in England and France that it was in the United States. In 1908 Walker was forced to retire because of illness, and the company disbanded. Bert Williams starred in one more black musical, *Mr. Lode of Koal* (1909), then moved into the white world of entertainment as a featured performer in the *Ziegfeld Follies* (1910–19), and later toured on the vaudeville circuit.

About 1901 Bob Cole joined forces with J. Rosamond Johnson and James Weldon Johnson (not related to Billy Johnson), as we have seen, to write songs and produce musicals. Like the Walker and Williams shows, these musicals—*The Shoo-Fly Regiment* (1906) and *The Red Moon* (1909)—were notable for the sparkling music and spirited dancing, but Cole and the Johnsons gave more attention to plot development and avoided minstrel comedy clichés. There were no more Cole and Johnson musicals, however; the trio was unable to secure the kind of management they wanted, and Cole and J. Rosamond turned to vaudeville.

By 1912 it appeared that the golden age of black theater had come to an end. Three of its principal movers were dead—Cole (d. 1911), Walker (d. 1911), and Hogan (d. 1909)—as were many of its most talented entertainers. After Hogan's death, the *New York Age* lamented, "all has not gone well in the colored theatrical world." Sixty showpeople were "thrown out of work" when Hogan left the stage, and the unemployed numbered in the hundreds after the disbandment of the Walker–Williams and Cole–Johnson Brothers companies. The great African-American minstrel companies were also gradually disappearing; one of the last disappeared after the death of Billy Kersands in 1915. The future seemed bleak for black theater—at least in New York City.

BLACK ENTERTAINERS ABROAD

There are scattered but intriguing references in contemporary literature to black entertainers who toured in Europe at the turn of the century—these do not include members of minstrel and vaudeville companies who remained there when their companies returned to the United States. Among these expatriates were ex-members of the Georgia Minstrels, such as the Bohee Brothers, James Bland, and others; members of such groups as the Fisk Jubilee Singers; and various individuals who toured in Europe with white groups such as Rachel Walker and Harry Williams, both of Cleveland.

As early as 1899, for example, a team called "James and Bella Fields, Negro Duettists" of Philadelphia, was performing in a theater in Prague, Bohemia (now Czech Republic). Bella toured widely during the next two decades, singing German lieder and Swiss yodels as well as English-language songs, and apparently settled permanently in Europe. During the 1920s and '30s, she appeared in various black-American companies that toured

Europe, among them Sam Wooding's Chocolate Kiddies and Louis Doug-las's Black Follies Girls and Negro Revue.[16]

In 1901 a troupe of seven women, called the Louisiana Amazon Guards, went abroad under the management of a German impresario. The singers included Ollie Burgoyne, Emma Harris, Virginia Shepherd, and Coretta Alfred. After three years of touring, the women settled in Russia, where they sang for a year in theaters of Moscow and St. Petersburg, then disbanded in 1905 because of revolutionary activities taking place at that time. Alfred and Harris remained in Russia after the others returned home, Alfred to pursue a musical career. She studied at various conservatories in Russia and made her operatic debut, as Coretti Arle-Titz, in the title role of Verdi's *Aïda* in the 1920s in Kharkov, Russia. Over the years she developed an enviable reputation as a concert and opera singer. In 1905 another women's group, The Creole Belles, a quartet under the leadership of Georgette Harvey (1883–1952), went to Europe, intending to stay only three months. They, too, performed in Russia and broke up because of the revolution in 1905. Harvey, however, remained until 1917, when the outbreak of war forced her to flee. After a few years in Southeast Asia, she returned to the United States in 1921, and thereafter was active in musical and theatrical productions in Harlem and on Broadway.

MILITARY MUSIC

When the Spanish-American War broke out in 1898, black men immediately volunteered for service as they had done in previous wartimes. As before, they met with rebuffs from the War Department. To be sure, there were already four groups of Negro soldiers in the regular army: the Ninth Cavalry, the Tenth Cavalry, the Twenty-fourth Infantry, and the Twenty-fifth Infantry, all stationed in the West. After considerable red tape, four new all-black regiments were organized under a special recruitment act of Congress. In addition, a number of Negro outfits organized on the state level were permitted to fight. One of these groups, Company L of the Sixth Massachusetts Infantry, traced its military lineage back to the all-Negro company, "Bucks of America," that had fought in the Revolutionary War.

The year 1909 was an historical one for black regimental bands; in that year black bandmasters were appointed for the first time. Emmett Scott, secretary to Booker T. Washington, had waged a campaign to accomplish this for several years; finally, in November 1908, President Theodore Roosevelt signed a special order directing that black bandmasters should be assigned to the four regular units as soon as the white bandmasters then serving could be transferred. The four men promoted to the rank of Chief Musician were Wade Hammond (Ninth Cavalry), Alfred Jack Thomas (Tenth Cavalry), William Polk (Twenty-fourth Infantry), and Egbert Thompson (Twenty-fifth Infantry).

Several other military musicians of the period are worthy of note. In Chicago, a Knights of Pythias band led by George Dulf and Alexander Armant was so excellent that the entire band was inducted into the United States Army in 1898, where it became the Eighth Illinois State Militia Band with Armant as bandmaster and Dulf as principal musician.

N. Clark Smith (1877–1933) had a long association with military bands, dating from the years of his service with the Illinois Eighth. In 1907 he was commissioned a captain in the United States Army and in 1913 was promoted to the rank of major. He went to Kansas, where he served as a bandmaster at Western University in Quindaro for two years (1913–15), and thereafter embarked on a teaching career.

Walter H. Loving (1872–1945) won distinction as the director of the Philippines Constabulary Band during the years 1901–23. He began his career in the U.S. Twenty-fourth Infantry, then served as a bandmaster for the Forty-eighth Volunteer Infantry. When that regiment was mustered out of service in 1901, the Governor-General of the Philippines at that time, William Howard Taft (who later became president of the United States), commissioned Loving to organize a Filipino band. Over the years Loving's band toured several times in the United States, performing at the St. Louis World's Fair in 1904, the Seattle Exposition in 1909, and the Panama-Pacific Exposition in San Francisco, in 1915, among other places.

Alton A. Adams (1889–1987) was the first black bandmaster of the United States Navy. A native of the Virgin Islands, he directed bands in St. Thomas from the time he was a youth and enjoyed a wide reputation for the excellence of his groups. After the United States took over the Virgin Islands in 1917, the Governor of the Islands appointed Adams a Chief Musician, and his band entered the navy as a unit. Like Loving, Adams toured in the United States with his bands, but not as extensively. He wrote a quantity of band music, of which the best-known marches were *The Virgin Islands* and *The Governor's Own,* and was a prolific music journalist. He served as a music columnist for *Jacobs Band Monthly* of Boston for several years and published articles in most of the music journals and newspapers of his time.

THE MUSIC BUSINESS

Musicians' Unions

Chicago was the home of the first black unit of the American Federation of Musicians. In 1902 Alexander Armant and George Dulf organized Local 208 after their bid to join the white Local 10 was rejected on racist grounds. In New York a few musicians joined the Musicians Protective Union of the AFM, as we have seen, but the majority elected to go a different route. In 1910, under the leadership of James Reese Europe, they obtained a charter for the Clef Club, an organization that combined the functions of a union with that of music contracting. In its peak years, the Clef Club had more than two hundred men on its roster; Europe boasted that he could furnish a dance group, consisting of as few as three or as many as thirty men, at any time, night or day. The Clef Club also sent performers on the concert circuit at home and abroad. A second group in New York, The New Amsterdam Musical Association, had been established in 1900 when the white Local 310 refused to admit black musicians; that organization was incorporated in 1905.

The black press played an important role in the promotion of black musical activities. Journalists and critics called attention to the new forms of stage entertainment and concert music emerging at the turn of the century just as they had covered minstrelsy in earlier decades. The *Freeman* of Indianapolis retained its position as the leading source of entertainment news for the first two decades of the century, but the *New York Age* and the *Chicago Defender* (est. 1905), moved into competitive positions. Other good sources of information were the *Cleveland Gazette* (est. 1883) and such periodicals as the *Colored American* (Boston, 1900–8), the *Negro Musical Journal* (Washington, D.C., 1902–3), and the *Crisis* (est. 1910).

In the Midwest the notable music and drama critics of the period were Sylvester Russell, Tony Langston, and Nora Holt, among others. I. Corker published insightful articles in the *Cleveland Gazette*, as did Walt Holt occasionally. In New York Lucien White and Lester Walton restored the *New York Age* to the preeminent position it had enjoyed decades earlier when Walton had joined the editorial staff in 1906. Maude Cuney Hare served as music editor for the NAACP's *Crisis* for several years.

Music Publishing

A few black entrepreneurs published their own compositions in the nineteenth century—for example, Joseph Postlewaite—but such ventures were sporadic. At the beginning of the twentieth century, the first relatively permanent music publishing companies came into existence in Chicago in 1903 when N. Clark Smith and J. Berni Barbour set up what was probably the first black-owned music publishing company in history. About 1904 a group under the leadership of Cecil Mack formed the Gotham-Attucks Music Publishing Company in New York.[17] Somewhat later in Chicago, William Foster established his firm. These enterprises were fortunate in obtaining publication rights for some of the most popular pieces of the time, such as Bert Williams's *Nobody* and Shelton Brooks's *Some of These Days*.

The most enduring of the companies was the one W. C. Handy and Harry Pace organized in Memphis, Tennessee, in 1908. The Pace & Handy

---

[17]Wayne D. Shirley, "The House of Melody" BPIM 15 (Spring 1987): 79–112.

Music Company—Publishers moved to New York in 1918 and achieved considerable success considering their size. The partnership was dissolved in 1921, when Pace went into the record business, but Handy turned the company into a family enterprise by including his brother and sons. Even after Handy's death in 1958, the Handy Brothers Music Company continued its publishing activities for many years.

Several other small companies were organized about this period. During the years ca. 1915–17 Clarence Williams joined with Armand Piron (both of New Orleans) to form a music publishing business, and the pair traveled on the vaudeville circuit performing their songs. During the early 1920s Williams founded another music publishing company in New York that lasted until 1943.

EARLY RECORDINGS OF BLACK MUSICIANS

The history of the recording industry in the United States dates back to the summer of 1877 when Thomas Alva Edison first became involved in trying "to store up and reproduce automatically at any future time the human voice perfectly." On July 18 he tried an experiment "with diaphragm having an embossing point and held against paraffin paper moving rapidly" that would have profound implications for the future. Further experimentation resulted in the tin-foil cylinder phonograph, for which he filed a patent application in December 1877. During the next few years other inventors, along with Edison, contributed to the improvement of the new machine, and within a decade commercial recording was under way. The year 1887 brought a second milestone: Emile Berliner invented the gramophone, a talking machine that used lateral-cut discs rather than the vertical-cut cylinders. The two instruments coexisted for some time before the cylinder phonograph lost out.[18]

The earliest recordings of black musicians that can be documented were made in 1901 when the Victor Talking Machine Company recorded Bert Williams and George Walker singing popular songs and songs from black musicals of the period. Reputedly, Victor also recorded bluesman Gus Cannon singing a blues to his own banjo accompaniment, but no proof of it is extant. The next year Victor released records of the Dinwiddie Colored Quartet singing *Genuine Jubilee and Camp-Meeting Shouts* and also the first in its series of Fisk Jubilee Quartet recordings, which continued until 1917. At this time the members of the Dinwiddie quartet were Harry Cryer, Clarence Meredith, Sterling Rex, and James H. Thomas; the members of the Fisk Jubilee Quartet were Alfred King, James Meyer, Noah Ryder, and

---

[18]See further in Roland Gelatt, *The Fabulous Phonograph: 1877–1977* (New York, 1977), 2nd rev. ed. Quotations from p. 19. The next milestone in recording history was of course the release of the first LP record by Columbia Records in June 1948.

John Work, Jr. Finally, the Columbia Phonograph Company engaged an African-American, baritone, C. Carroll Clark (1890?–1933?) of Denver, Colorado, to record ballads and light classical music during the years ca. 1907–16.[19]

From time to time the black press carried notices about the recording activities of other black artists, but none of these can be substantiated. According to the *Philadelphia Tribune,* for example, Joseph Douglass recorded violin solos for Victor in November 1914, and Anita Patti Brown is reputed to have sung for Victor in 1916. But if records were made, they seem not to have been released. We know, however, that in December 1920 Roland Hayes recorded for Victor's English branch in London, His Master's Voice; Hayes himself refused to allow the release of those records.

Much more is known about the early recordings of black dance bands, primarily because of the enormous amount of research that has been invested in the subject. In 1903 Wilbur Sweatman and his band became the first black group to record when the band played Scott Joplin's *Maple Leaf Rag* (for a cylinder phonograph) in a music store in Minneapolis, Minnesota. Sweatman (1882–1961) was the pioneer of his time. In 1916 he began making disc recordings with trios and with five- and six-piece groups. He continued to record extensively, for that time, into the early 1930s—drawing from a repertory of rags, blues, popular and novelty songs, and he achieved wide notoriety for his special vaudeville act—simultaneously playing three clarinets in three-part harmony. Although it is not clear that what Sweatman played was jazz, he early on appropriated the word for his groups: Wilbur Sweatman and his Jass Band in 1917, for example, and Wilbur Sweatman's Original Jazz Band in 1918. During the years 1913–19 the dance bands of Ford Dabney, James Reese Europe, W. C. Handy, and Sweatman recorded with some degree of regularity. In 1917 Noble Sissle recorded popular songs, and Eubie Blake recorded piano rags.

The first piano-roll recordings of black musicians were made in 1912 by the QRS company (Quality Reigns Supreme), a subsidiary of the Melville Clark Piano Company. In that year John "Blind" Boone recorded light classical pieces, such as *Woodland Murmurs* and *Sparkling Spring,* and piano rags, *Rag Medley No. 1* and *Blind Boone's Southern Rag Medley No. 2.* Eubie Blake began recording piano rolls in 1917 and continued through

---

[19]Victor's Record Catalog is the source of information about the early recordings. The Dinwiddie quartet members are listed also in Robert M. Dixon and Jon Godrich, *Blues and Gospel Records, 1902–1942* (London, 1969): See further about Clark in Walter C. Allen, *Hendersonia* (Highland Park, NJ, 1973), p. 576. The standard reference on early jazz recordings is Brian Rust, *Jazz Records, 1897–1942* (New Rochelle, NY, 1978), 4th rev. ed. It is profitable to use along with Rust the series of articles by Harold H. Hartel, "The H³ Chrono-Matrix File," *Record Research* (1980–82), which list chronological jazz recordings made during the years 1897–1942. Many nonjazz performers are included in Rust, *The Complete Entertainment Discography* (New Rochelle, NY, 1973)—for example, Bert Williams and George Walker.

1921, playing rags, blues, and popular songs. Sissle and Blake also recorded as a pair (piano and voice) and with Sissle's Sizzling Syncopators Orchestra.

PROFESSIONAL ORGANIZATIONS

ASCAP

The American Society of Composers, Authors, and Publishers (commonly known as ASCAP) was organized in 1914 for the purpose of protecting the rights of copyright owners whenever their music was "performed publicly for profit." The charter members, which counted 170 writers and twenty-two publishers, included only two African Americans, musician Harry T. Burleigh and writer James Weldon Johnson. Within the next dozen years, eight of the leading black musicians and lyricists had joined ASCAP: Will Marion Cook, Henry Creamer, R. Nathaniel Dett, W. C. Handy, Cecil Mack, Maceo Pinkard, Will Tyers, and Spencer Williams.

The requirements for membership were rigorous, and only established composers could afford to join. By the time ASCAP published its third biographical dictionary in 1966, its black membership had increased to no fewer than 189 composers and writers; by 1980, when the fourth edition of the dictionary was published, there were 259 blacks in the total membership of 8,200 composers and authors. Whereas in the early years of ASCAP, the black members tended to come primarily from the world of show business—for that was the most financially rewarding field of activity—by 1980, black members represented a wide range of musical activities, from religious and classical music to rhythm 'n' blues and disco. We will discuss later a similar association, BMI.

The National Association of Negro Musicians

Black composers, performers, and teachers in the field of classical and religious music began to feel the need to organize themselves during the second decade of the century. In 1916 Clarence Cameron White mailed letters from his home in Boston to black musicians all over the nation, proposing that a National Association of Negro Music Teachers be established in order to "raise the musical standards of the teaching profession of our race throughout this country."[20] Encouraged by the positive response he received, he and R. Nathaniel Dett planned a meeting that would coincide with the celebration of the fiftieth anniversary of Hampton Institute, where Dett was teaching at that time. But the onset of World War I interrupted those plans.

It was not until 1919 that the idea was taken up again, spearheaded this

[20]Nora Holt, "The Chronological History of the NANM," BPIM 2 (Fall 1974): 234–35.

time by Nora Holt in Chicago, music editor of the *Chicago Defender*. With her easy access to publicity, she was able to advance the cause forcefully; a small planning group met in Chicago in the spring of 1919, renamed the organization the National Association of Negro Musicians (NANM), and set the date for the first convention, to be held in Chicago on July 29–31. From the beginning the convention was a success. The next annual meeting was held in New York; the third, in Nashville, Tennessee, and so on. Over the years only one convention was canceled, that in 1942 because of World War II.

The charter members of NANM were among the black elite of the concert world, including artists such as Dett, White, Carl Diton, Cleota Collins, Henry Grant, and T. Theodore Taylor, among others . With one exception, they were concert artists and/or composers. Grant was a teacher of instrumental music at Dunbar High School in Washington, D.C. The members took seriously the charge to improve instruction and encourage the development of talent; from the beginning they held workshops at the annual meetings and gave scholarships to talented youths. In 1921 NANM gave its first scholarship to Marian Anderson. Eventually NANM became a grass-roots organization, with as much or more support coming from small studio teachers as from concert artists and university teachers. The annual meetings met their needs for exchanging ideas, learning about new theories and the latest teaching materials, and improving their skills; they also served as showcases for young and mature artists. During the 1960s NANM established the tradition of honoring prominent artists, composers, teachers, choral and orchestral directors, and historians for achievements and contributions to black culture.

CHAPTER 9

Precursors
of
Jazz

THE GENERAL STATE OF MUSIC

THE beginning of the twentieth century brought the promise of new musical developments both in Europe and in the United States—here, in areas affecting both black people and white people. The century opened auspiciously with the Exposition Universelle in Paris. Those attending heard for the first time a strangely exciting music from America called "ragtime." During the first decade of the century, European composers began to produce works that started a revolution in the art of music. Startled and bewildered audiences reacted violently to the "New Music"—i.e., that of Arnold Schoenberg (1874–1951), Igor Stravinsky (1882–1971), and their contemporaries, which broke away from traditional concepts of melody, rhythm, texture, form, and instrumentation.

Stravinsky was in the forefront of the movement. He came to Paris in 1910 to write ballets for Sergei Diaghilev and his Ballet Russe, which had opened its first season in Paris in 1909. Stravinsky's music for a ballet produced in the spring of 1913, *Le Sacre du printemps* (The Rite of Spring), touched off a near-riot on opening night. Some music historians applied the label "primitivism" to this work and to similar ones—such as, for example, the *Allegro barbaro* (1910) of the Hungarian composer Béla Bartók (1881–1945). In Vienna during the same period, Schoenberg was writing music that was described as "expressionistic." It was an abstract kind of music with highly chromatic melodies and dissonant harmonies. Eventually Schoenberg and his disciples entirely rejected tonality—i.e., the system of tonal relationships underlying music of the eighteenth and nineteenth centuries—and arrived at a music in which a single note no longer functioned as a tonal center; all twelve tones of the octave were of equal importance. The new system of tonal relationships, called the "twelve-tone method" (later, "serial technique"), was developed to take the place of the old system based on major and minor scales.

In the United States most white and black composers continued for many years to write in the tradition of nineteenth-century music. The composer whose music was closest in style to the "New Music" of Europe was Charles Ives (1874–1954) of Danbury, Connecticut, a musician who followed a career in the insurance business. In fact, Ives anticipated many of the European developments, but he did not begin to publish his music until the 1920s. If any twentieth-century European composer was emulated by Americans during this period, it was the Frenchman Claude Debussy (1862–1918), a figure of the late nineteenth century as well as the twentieth. His best-known work, *Prélude à "L'Après-midi d'un faune"* (Prelude to "The Afternoon of a Faun"), was published in 1894. Debussy's music was innovative in its use of scales other than major and minor—the church modes, for example, Oriental scales, and a new whole-tone scale; in its use of parallel chords (which gave the effect of blocks of tones sliding up and down); of vague, restless rhythms; of wispy, indefinite melodies; and of veiled, shimmering orchestra sounds. The critics called his music "impressionistic," but Debussy himself disliked the term.

THE EMERGENCE OF RAGTIME

Not all composers in the United States were writing in the styles of European art music. Large numbers of musically illiterate black music makers were not aware of its existence, and many blacks who could read music were unconcerned about it. One effect of slavery had been to create discrete and separate black communities within the larger white communities of the nation, and the emancipation of the slaves did nothing to change this situation. Black lived, for the most part, in their own world and developed their own institutions and culture. Of particular relevance here is the fact that black music makers developed a distinctive style of entertainment music, fitted to their own personal needs and expressive of their own individuality. It was not intended to be analyzed or even understood by whites. Ragtime was one of the earliest manifestations of this distinctive music. The other was the blues.

From its beginnings, rag music was associated primarily with the piano. As slaves, black musicians had little access to the piano, of course, but after freedom they displayed a marked predilection for keyboard instruments. Families purchased small organs (i.e., Estey organs or harmoniums) for use in the home (pianos were too expensive), often paying fifty cents down and fifty cents per week for a lifetime. In this regard Booker T. Washington recounts an illuminating experience in his autobiography, *Up from Slavery:*

> I remember that on one occasion when I went into one of these cabins [in the plantation districts of Alabama] for dinner, when I sat down to the table for a meal with the four members of the family, I noticed that, while there were five of us at the table, there was but one fork for the five of us to use. Naturally there was an awkward pause on my part. In the opposite corner of that same cabin was an organ for which the people told me they were paying sixty dollars in monthly installments. One fork, and a sixty-dollar organ![1]

Washington was bothered, naturally, that the ex-slaves should be so impractical as to buy an organ when such a necessity as tableware was overlooked. Undoubtedly he was right in one respect; he was wrong, however, in assuming that music was not a necessity to the ex-slaves. One of the first ways they showed their independence was to purchase the musical instruments for which they had earlier longed. If they could not play these instruments, then their children would learn to do so.

Early references to rag-music players cite anonymous drifters in the South and on the eastern seaboard who played the piano in cheap eating-places, honky-tonk spots, saloons, and riverside dives—often for meager wages, sometimes only for tips. It was the job of the lone musician to substitute for an orchestra in providing music for listening or dancing. W. C. Handy remembered having heard one of these "piano thumpers" during a visit to Memphis, Tennessee, in the 1890s:

> As I was walking down Beale Street one night, my attention was caught by the sound of a piano. The insistent Negro rhythms were broken first by a tinkle in the treble, then by a rumble in the bass; then they came together again. I entered the cheap café and found a colored man at the piano, dog tired. He told me he had to play from seven at night until seven in the morning, and [so he] rested himself by playing with alternate hands.[2]

The fact that few of the early ragtime piano players could read music seemed to stimulate rather than to deter them in the production of a novel style of piano music.

The style of piano-rag music—called "jig piano" by some—was a natural outgrowth of dance-music practices among black folk. As we have seen, the slaves danced in antebellum times to the music of fiddles and banjos, the percussive element being provided by the foot stomping of the musicians and the "juba patting" of the bystanders. In piano-rag music, the left hand took over the task of stomping and patting while the right hand performed syncopated melodies, using motives reminiscent of fiddle and banjo tunes.

Just when rag music—this music developed by black music makers for

[1]Booker T. Washington, *Up from Slavery* (Washington, D.C., 1901), p. 113.
[2]W. C. Handy, "The Heart of the Blues," *Etude Music Magazine* (March 1940): 193.

the entertainment of their own people—first emerged on the wider stage of American music is not known. In the South, piano playing among the ex-slaves could have developed only after freedom came, except for profession-als such as Blind Tom and Blind Boone. It is possible, however, that on the East coast, particularly in the New York–Philadelphia–Baltimore area, "jig piano" may have been played much earlier than in the South. As we have seen, middle-class blacks began purchasing pianos for use in the home in the early part of the nineteenth century. And there is evidence suggesting that not only daughters of the middle classes were given piano lessons, but occasionally men also.

A literary reference to "jig piano" associates the term with social gather-ings in the parlors of middle-class African Americans during the last quarter of the nineteenth century. The source of the reference is the ballad opera *Out of Bondage* (1876), in which the last scene shows Jim, a young classical pianist, playing a piano "medley" for old Uncle Eph. "At the end [of the medley] the music becomes very lively—jig time—and Uncle Eph . . . rises from the sofa and begins dancing."[3] "Jig time" refers here to music that is livelier than conventional classical music and may include syncopation. In any event, the term "jig time" is without doubt a forerunner of the term ragtime, which did not gain currency until the 1890s.[4] Journalist Lafcadio Hearn, writing in the 1870s about the dance music he heard in black dance houses of Cincinnati reported that the instruments used were violin, banjo, and bass fiddle.[5] Similarly constituted groups provided dance music in other places, wherever the ubiquitous fiddler was joined by others. It seems clear then that at mid-century, the black fiddler still held sway over community dance places. However, this state of affairs could not have existed too long in the East. According to the evidence, the rag-playing pioneer "Old Man" Sam Moore was "ragging the quadrilles and schottisches" in Philadelphia before 1875. Moore played in dance ensembles of the time, doubling on the bass fiddle and the piano.[6]

At some time during the 1860s or '70s an historic event took place—the piano was brought for the first time into a dance ensemble. And probably it happened in some night spot of a black tenderloin district in the East. It did not take long for canny nightclub owners to discover that piano music could be used as a substitute for the traditional combination of fiddle, wind instru-ment, and bass fiddle and, more important, that it was less expensive.

White America first became aware of the new style because of the nov-elty of its syncopated rhythms in the dance music and "coon songs" of min-strelsy. But it was in partnership with the dance called the cakewalk that syncopated music made its most impressive showing. That dance of planta-

---

[3]Southern, *African-American [Musical] Theater,* p. 62.
[4]See further regarding "jig band" and "jig piano" in H. Wiley Hitchcock, *Music in the United States,* 3rd ed. (Englewood Cliffs, NJ, 1988), pp. 131, 133.
[5]Lafcadio Hearn, "Levee Life," *The Cincinnati Commercial* (March 17, 1876): 2.
[6]Mark Tucker, *Ellington: The Early Years* (Urbana, 1991).

tion origin had been taken up by minstrels and given a special place in their shows, sometimes as a feature entitled "walking for that cake" or "peregrination for the pastry."[7]

The dance took over everywhere—in hamlets, towns, and cities—and with everyone. Throughout the nation contests and jubilees were held where, for substantial prizes, cakewalking couples improvised steps, prances, and kicks to the accompaniment of syncopated music. And the music used for cakewalking shared in its popularity. By the end of the century, the entertainment industry was sponsoring contests that offered two sets of prizes, one set for cakewalkers and the other set for ragtime pianists, who were given an allotted time in which to demonstrate their ability to improvise on select songs in ragtime style.

Ragtime Songs

In the 1890s songwriters began more and more often to use syncopation, particularly in the so-called "coon songs." To be sure, the predecessors of the coon song had been a basic stock in trade of the early minstrel stage, but its importance had diminished considerably by the end of the Civil War. A list of the 130 most successful popular songs of the '80s, as compiled by Edward B. Marks, included only seven coon songs, all written by whites, and of the seven, only one, J. S. Putnam's *New Coon in Town* (1883), employed enough syncopation as "to foreshadow the true, shouting, ragtime school." The others, according to Marks, were "mere blackface numbers . . . no more essentially Negroid than the minstrel men who sang them in their curiously conventional style."[8]

Matters changed in the next decade. Minstrel songwriter Ernest Hogan wrote a song, *All Coons Look Alike to Me,* that contributed to a tremendous vogue for syncopated coon songs, from which both black and white songwriters profited. Published in 1896, the song was an immediate hit and "sold like wildfire all over the United States and abroad." When ragtime pianists from all over the country gathered for the Ragtime Championship of the World Competition held at Tammany Hall in New York on January 23, 1900, it was Ernest Hogan's song that was recommended for the final test. The three pianists who had reached the semifinals were asked to demonstrate their skill in ragging a song by playing *All Coons Look Alike to Me* for two minutes.[9]

Despite its success, the song brought unhappiness to Hogan, its black originator. Although the lyrics were relatively innocuous, black showmen did not like the title, which was derisive when separated from the song's lyrics.[10]

---

[7]Rudi Blesh and Harriet Janis, *They All Played Ragtime* (4th ed., New York, 1971), p. 190.
[8]Edward B. Marks, *They All Sang* (New York, 1935), p. 45.
[9]Ann Charters, ed., *The Ragtime Songbook* (New York, 1955), p. 33.
[10]For a full account of the story see Tom Fletcher, *100 Years* pp. 137 ff.

Second chorus from *All Coons Look Alike to Me,* Ernest Hogan

The ragtime song was characterized by a regular, straightforward bass and a lightly syncopated melody. Frequently the syncopation was confined to the vocal line, the piano providing an "um-pah um-pah" accompaniment based chiefly on simple harmonic progressions. The emergence of piano-rag is illustrated in the second, or "Choice" Chorus of the song (see Chorus of example on p. 318). This is the first published example of what was to develop into a genuine art style.

Like many of the pioneer ragtime pianists, some of the early black song-writers were musically illiterate. They played their songs on the piano for professional arrangers in Tin Pan Alley, who wrote down the notes as fast as the ragtimers played. Inevitably more songs were "lost" by this method than were turned over to publishers. Nevertheless, writers such as Chris Smith (1879–1949) and Irving Jones (ca. 1874–1932) were the acknowledged authors of a large number of the hit songs written in ragtime style that were on everyone's lips around the turn of the century. All the black songwriters of the early twentieth century wrote ragtime songs. At least one, *My Ragtime Baby* (1898) written by Fred Stone, became internationally famous. According to Tom Fletcher, this piece won a prize for John Philip Sousa's band at the Paris Exposition in 1900 and, at the same time, gave Europe its first sound of ragtime music.[11]

A list of the successful syncopated songs by black writers during this period should also include such favorites as *Cuban Cake Walk* (James T. Brymn); *Bon Bon Buddy* (Will Marion Cook); *Under the Bamboo Tree* (Bob Cole and J. Rosamond Johnson); *When the Band Plays Ragtime* (Cole and Johnson); *Didn't He Ramble* (Cole and Johnson, under the nom de plume of Will Handy); *Darktown Is Out Tonight* (Cook); *My Home Ain't Nothing Like This* (Irving Jones); *Possumala* (Jones); *Wouldn't That Be a Dream* (Joe Jordan); *Miss Dora Dean* (Bert Williams); and *Ballin' the Jack* and *Good Morning, Carrie* (Chris Smith).

Instrumental Rags

In the early years of the ragtime era, there was a thin line of demarcation (which often disappeared entirely) between the coon song and ragtime. Indeed, as a modern scholar points out, by the end of the nineteenth century the term *ragtime* was applied to (1) the coon song; (2) arrangements of coon songs for performance by instrumental groups, such as marching bands, dance bands, and other combinations of instruments; (3) dance music and marches with a high level of syncopation; and (4) the piano rag.[12]

The piano rag itself was not a clearly defined type; it might represent a piano arrangement of a coon song or the "ragging" of a nonsyncopated piece (vocal or instrumental), or it might be an original composition. Some

[11]Fletcher, p. 145.
[12]See further in Edward Berlin, *Ragtime. A Musical and Cultural History* (Berkeley, 1980), pp. 5 ff.

black pianists went to great lengths to learn the European classics so that they could add "ragged" versions of such compositions to their repertories; the music of Grieg and Tchaikovsky, for example, was especially valued for that purpose. But patriotic anthems were also ragged, as were popular songs, operatic airs, marches, dances, and other "straight" pieces.

The earliest association of the word *rag* with instrumental music occurred in 1896 in the publication of Ernest Hogan's *All Coons Look Alike to Me;* the second chorus of that song carries the caption "Choice Chorus, with Negro 'Rag' Accompaniment, Arr. by Max Hoffman." (Hoffman was employed by the music publishing firm of Witmark and Son, New York.) As the score indicates, conventional accompaniment for the coon song was a simple um-pah affair; "rag" accompaniment, on the other hand, was marked by pronounced syncopation (see example on p. 318).

In the 1890s the terms *rag* and *dance* were practically synonymous in black communities, and knowledgeable whites were aware of this. In 1899 the novelist Rupert Hughes wrote, "The Negroes call their clog dancing, 'ragging' and the dance, a 'rag,' . . . the rag dance is largely shuffling."[13]

The first published piano piece to include the word *rag* in its title was *Mississippi Rag,* written by white bandmaster William Krell, and copyrighted in January 1897.[14] The captions of the four sections of the piece suggest its character—Cakewalk, Plantation Song, Trio, Buck-and-Wing Dance—to which are added an introduction, coda (using the same music), and interludes. That the composition was originally intended for performance by band is indicated by a statement on its cover sheet, "The First Rag-Time Two-Step Ever Written, and First Played by Krell's Orchestra, Chicago."[15]

The ragtime era was under way. According to some scholars, however, it was not until October 1897 that a genuine piano rag appeared, Theodore Northrup's *Louisiana Rag,*[16] which departed significantly from coon-song conventions.

In December 1897 Thomas Turpin published *Harlem Rag,* the first piano rag published by an African American. At last black composers were involved in writing down the music they had been playing for their own people for many years. With the entrance of ragtime into mainstream music, an improvisational music would be transformed into a notated music; a functional music, intended for dancing and entertainment, into a concert music intended for listening; a folk-style music, into the music of the individual composer, upon which he stamped his unique personality. Scott Joplin represented the peak of the tradition, earning for himself the title "King of Ragtime."

[13]Rupert Hughes, "A Eulogy of Ragtime," *The Musical Record* (April 1, 1899): 158.
[14]Blesh and Janis, *They All Played Ragtime,* p. 101.
[15]Terry Waldo, *This Is Ragtime* (New York, 1976), p. 30.
[16]David Jasen and Trebor Tichenor, *Rags and Ragtime* (New York, 1978), pp. 17 ff.

Joplin's compositions, called "classic ragtime" by some scholars, fused African-American elements with European forms and techniques. The form of the piano rag was multisectional: several sections of music, generally consisting of sixteen measures each and called "strains" or "themes," were joined together in an arrangement similar to that of the march or quadrille. Within the sections, four-measure phrases were the norm. The most common forms were ABAC, ABACB, ABCD, ABACD (each letter stands for a strain); but other combinations were used by composers over the years. Typically, the compositions also included introductions, codas, and interludes (insertions of musical material between the strains; sometimes referred to as "breaks")—these consisting of from four to eight or twelve measures in length. And strains almost always were repeated, thus producing forms such as A A B B A C C D D.

The most significant element of ragtime of course was syncopation. The syncopated patterns might be simple ones, written as ♪ ♩ ♪ or ♩ ♩ ♩ (see example on p. 318); or they might be complex, resulting from the play of additive rhythms in the right hand—such as ♫♩ ♪♩ ♫ = 3 + 3 + 2— against consistent duple meters in the left hand.

Discussion of ragtime in modern literature invariably turns to the question of origins, and there is general agreement in regard to the importance of black folk-dance traditions in the development of the style. It has been suggested that other traditions might also have influenced the evolution of ragtime—that ragtime also points back to dance-music traditions established in the early nineteenth century by Frank Johnson, Isaac Hazzard, Aaron J. R. Conner, Henry Williams and other black composers of society dance music. It will be recalled that as early as 1819 a white observer pointed out Frank Johnson's "remarkable taste in *distorting* a sentimental, simple, and beautiful song into a reel, jig, or country dance" (italics mine). From the vantage point of the present, it appears that Johnson was "ragging" his music or, perhaps, "jazzing" it.[17]

While examination of the thesis is beyond the scope of the present discussion, it may be summarized as follows: There are discernible links between the early black composers named above and composers such as Thomas Turpin, Scott Joplin, and their contemporaries at the end of the century. Joseph Postlewaite of St. Louis might be regarded as a transitional figure, and Blind Boone, as representing the culmination of the black dance-music style before the first publication of rags in 1897. During the years 1885–89 Postlewaite, Boone, and Joplin all were active in St. Louis and undoubtedly came into contact with each other.

[17]See further in Floyd and Reisser, "Social Dance Music" BPIM 8 (Fall 1980): 171.

Scott Joplin. *(Courtesy of the author)*

Composers of Piano Rags

Scott Joplin (1868–1917) was born in Texarkana, Texas. As a child he studied music with a local German music teacher. He left home at an early age and began playing professionally in about 1884; the next year he went to St. Louis, Missouri, and it was there that he first won recognition for his rag piano skills. Ten years later he settled at Sedalia, Missouri, and during the next decade took an active role in the musical life of the city: he conducted a music studio, played cornet in the Queen City Concert Band, and attended the George Smith College for Negroes, where he studied theory and composition. During this period he also toured with a vocal group he organized, the Texas Medley Quartette.[18]

Joplin first published some of his compositions in 1895—two songs and three piano pieces—but they gave scant evidence of the originality that would appear in later pieces. In 1899 he published his first rag pieces. The previous year he had offered several compositions to publisher Carl Hoffman of Kansas City; *Original Rags* was accepted and the *Maple Leaf Rag* was rejected. The latter became very popular in the black community, however, for Joplin played it constantly. Finally, in the summer of 1899, Joplin found a publisher, John Stark, for his *Maple Leaf Rag;* Stark was to publish most of Joplin's music for the next ten years.

The *Maple Leaf Rag* brought unprecedented success, commercially and artistically, to both composer and publisher. The piece sold more than a million copies and is still popular today. More important, it established a

[18]See the Bibliography for biographical studies of Joplin. A complete edition of his music, except for three piano pieces, is in Vera Brodsky Lawrence, *The Complete Works of Scott Joplin* (New York, 1981).

model for classic ragtime that was emulated by all rag composers interested in serious composition. The *Maple Leaf Rag* became a test piece for pianists; it ushered in a new order for showy, virtuoso instrumental pieces that demanded technical brilliance. Concert artists had available to them works, written in a new American musical language, that matched the dances and character pieces of the great romantic composers of Europe. To quote one music historian, "the *Maple Leaf Rag* became an American institution." And another observed:

> [Joplin's piano rags] can only be described as elegant, varied, often subtle, and as sharply incised as a cameo. They are the precise American equivalent, in terms of a native style of dance music, of minuets by Mozart, mazurkas by Chopin, or waltzes by Brahms.[19]

Maple Leaf Rag, Scott Joplin

[19]Hitchcock, *Music*, p. 135.

Joplin wrote many other rags, of which the best known were *The Enter-tainer* (featured in the film *The Sting* in 1974), *Euphonic Sounds, Magnetic Rag, Sunflower Slow Drag,* and *Wall Street Rag.* But he also turned his attention immediately to works in larger forms. In 1899 he completed a folk ballet, *The Ragtime Dance,* which received a single performance in Sedalia's Woods Opera House. By 1903 he had written a rag opera, entitled *A Guest of Honor* (the score now is lost), and staged one performance of it with his Scott Joplin Drama Company. Although Joplin failed to find a publisher for the score, he was apparently undaunted, for he began work soon thereafter on a second opera, *Treemonisha,* which he completed in 1905.

In 1907 Joplin settled at New York. Musically active in several ways, he conducted a music studio, made piano-roll recordings, published a large quantity of his music, including a manual *The School of Ragtime—Six Exercises for Piano* (1908), and even founded his own publishing company. He also toured on the vaudeville circuit. Most of all, he invested his energy in trying to produce his opera. Finally, in May 1911, he published the 230-page manuscript himself; and in 1915, despairing of ever finding a producer, he staged the opera himself in a nondescript hall in Harlem, without benefit of scenery, costumes, or orchestra. Predictably, the production was a failure. Joplin's young friend, ragtimer Sam Patterson, attended the performance:

> Without scenery, costumes, lighting, or orchestral backing, the drama seemed thin and unconvincing, little better than a rehearsal, and its special quality, in any event, would surely have been lost on the typical Harlem audience that attended . . . sophisticated enough to reject their folk past but not sufficiently so to relish a return to it.[20]

Treemonisha was given its world premiere in 1972—some sixty-seven years after Joplin completed it. We will discuss the opera more fully in that context.

When Joplin arrived at St. Louis in 1885, it was a frontier town with a thriving black population and a prosperous sporting-life district. Chestnut and Market Streets were especially notorious for their bawdy houses and saloons, from which came forth the sound of piano thumping day and night. Joplin got a job playing piano in the Silver Dollar, a saloon owned by "Honest" John Turpin, one of the important men of the district. The Turpins—first the father and later the sons—were true patrons of ragtime music; their saloons and clubs provided hospitable centers for local and visiting pianists, places where they could exchange ideas and engage in friendly competition.

Thomas Million Turpin (1873–1922), the "Father of St. Louis Ragtime" and owner of the Rosebud Bar and other places in St. Louis's tenderloin district, wrote and featured most of his piano rags at the café. Like his father's saloon in earlier days, his café became a rendezvous for ragtime

---

[20]Rudi Blesh, "Scott Joplin: Black-American Classicist," *The Collected Works of Scott Joplin* (New York, 1971), p. xxxix.

pianists. Despite Turpin's many business ventures, he found time to publish a number of his piano rags and to encourage the development of a younger generation of ragtime pianists, some of whom became important figures in the diffusion of ragtime. Best known of Turpin's compositions, in addition to the *Harlem Rag,* were the *Bowery Buck* (1899), *A Ragtime Nightmare* (1900), *St. Louis Rag* (1903), and *The Buffalo Rag* (1904).[21]

James Sylvester Scott (1885–1938) is regarded by some scholars as ragtime's second-ranking composer after Joplin. He began his career as a music clerk in Carthage, Missouri, where his chief responsibility was to play the piano for customers to promote the sale of sheet music, and published his first piano rags at the age of seventeen. Although these early pieces reveal the influence of Joplin's *Maple Leaf Rag* (as did, indeed, most rags of the time), the pieces nevertheless reflect the young composer's originality.

In 1914 Scott settled at Kansas City, Missouri, where he established himself as a music teacher and theater musician, playing the organ and working as a music arranger for various theaters in the city. Later he organized an orchestra that played in Kansas City theater pits until about 1930, when the advance of sound films made theater orchestras obsolete all over the country. Best remembered of his pieces are the *Frog Legs Rag* (1906), *Kansas City Rag* (1907), *Quality—A High-Class Rag* (1911), *Climax Rag* (1914), and *Pegasus—A Classic Rag* (1920). Scott's last rag was the *Broadway Rag—A Classic,* published in 1922.

Two composers of the St. Louis group, Scott Hayden and Arthur Marshall, were students of Joplin. Hayden (1882–1915) and Louis Chauvin (1883–1908), wrote piano rags only in collaboration with others. Marshall (1881–1956) left several compositions, two written in collaboration with Joplin, four published by Stark, and three of them unpublished but copyrighted and recorded on Circle Records. Sam Patterson (ca. 1881–1955) published a piano rag and several songs in collaboration with Chauvin, and also a musical show, *Dandy Coon.* In 1906 he left St. Louis to travel with a variety act, the Musical Spillers.

Joe Jordan (1882–1971) was active in ragtime circles of St. Louis during his early career and studied music at the nearby Lincoln Institute (now Lincoln University) in Jefferson City. About 1903 he settled in Chicago, where for the next three and a half decades he was active in black theater as a musical director at Chicago's Pekin Theater and for Broadway shows, and as a composer of musical comedies. In 1905 he directed the historic "jazz" concert of the Memphis Students in New York. *Lovey Joe,* the song he wrote for Fanny Brice to sing in the 1910 Ziegfeld Follies, started her on the road to stardom. Jordan was also a bandleader; he toured and recorded with his Ten Sharps and Flats, directed WPA orchestras during the 1930s and directed army and USO groups during World War II.

---

[21]DeVeaux and Kenny, *The Music of James Scott* (Washington, D.C., 1992), p. 2. Note our correction of the birthdate given in some sources.

Throughout his life Jordan wrote various kinds of music: rags such as *Pekin Rag, J.J.J. Rag,* and *Nappy Lee—A Slow Drag,* and musicals such as *The Man from Bam, Mayor of Dixie,* and *Rufus Rastus.*

Ferdinand Joseph "Jelly Roll" Morton (1890–1941, né La Menthe) was ragtime pianist, composer, bluesman, and jazzman, all in one.[22] He began playing professionally in the tenderloin district of New Orleans, called Storyville, in 1902 when he was only seventeen, and had become an itinerant pianist by 1904. Contemporaries from that period remembered him: "Jelly would sit there and play that barrelhouse music all night . . . he'd play and sing the blues until way up in the day." He wandered throughout the nation, stopping in St. Louis at the time of the World's Fair in 1904, stopping also in Chicago, then moving to the West coast, into Canada and Alaska, and returning to Chicago by 1922, where he made his first recordings in 1923. Morton's best-known rags were *Frog-I-More Rag, The Naked Dance, Kansas City Stomp,* and *King Porter Stomp.* He also was noted for his performance of *Tiger Rag,* although it is doubtful that he wrote it.

James Hubert "Eubie" Blake (1883–1983), the leading exponent of piano rag on the East coast, began playing professionally when he was about sixteen years old. As a child he studied piano; as an adult he studied theory and composition with W. Llewellyn Wilson in Baltimore and, late in life, he studied the Schillinger System of Composition with Rudolph Schramm in New York. He began to write music, however, before beginning formal studies in theory; his first rag piece, *Sounds of Africa* (renamed *Charleston Rag*), was completed in 1898, and he wrote continuously thereafter.

Blake made notable achievements in three areas of musical activities during his long, successful career: as a ragtime pianist, vaudevillian, and composer during his early career as a composer of Broadway musicals and songs and as a dance-band leader in his mid-career period, and as a piano composer to the end.

In 1915 he teamed with singer and lyricist Noble Sissle to write popular music and to tour as a vaudeville act. Their first song, *It's All Your Fault,* introduced by Sophie Tucker, was a hit. In 1921 the collaborators wrote and produced the musical *Shuffle Along,* which marked the beginning of a new career for Blake. Thereafter he wrote several musicals, some with collaborators Andy Razaf and Henry Creamer, and contributed music to shows with white casts, such as *Elsie* (1924) and Cochran's *Revue of 1926* in London.

Throughout his career he recorded periodically, beginning with piano rolls for QRS as early as 1917, and in 1969 released the historic *The Eighty-Six Years of Eubie Blake.* In 1972 he formed his own publishing and recording company, which specialized in piano rags and songs of the twen-

---

[22]Alan Lomax, *Mister Jelly Roll* (Berkeley, 1950).

Jelly Roll Morton. *(Courtesy New York Public Library, Americana Collection of the Music Division)*

ties. In his late career he toured widely throughout the world: lecturing and performing on college campuses, playing in concert halls, at jazz festivals, and on radio and television. As a bandleader he toured widely with USO shows during World War II.

Blake wrote more than 350 piano pieces and songs—waltzes and ballads as well as rags and popular music. His best-known piano pieces are *Chevy Chase, Baltimore Todolo, Troublesome Ivories,* and *Charleston Rag;* his best-known songs, *Memories of You, Loving You the Way I Do, You Were Meant for Me, Love Will Find a Way,* and *I'm Just Wild About Harry.* musicals. His best-known musicals with Razaf as collaborator were *Blackbirds of 1930* and *Tan Manhattan.*

While Noble Sissle (1889–1975) may be best known for his collaboration with Eubie Blake as both a vaudeville performer and as lyricist for songs and Broadway musicals, he also enjoyed an independent career as entertainer, singer with such groups as Hahn's Jubilee Singers in his early career, vaudevillian, and dance-band leader. In later years he led a jazz group, Noble Sissle's Orchestra. During World War II, he played in an army band and toured with his USO Camp Show. Sissle recorded with Blake, singing and writing lyrics, and also independently. In their old age, Sissle and Blake frequently met to perform again, on stage and in the recording studio. Sissle's close relationship with James Reese Europe inspired him to write a biography of Europe, "Memoirs of Lieutenant Jim Europe," completed in 1942.[23]

---

[23]A forthcoming biography of James Reese Europe will use this voluminous manuscript (on deposit at the Library of Congress) as the primary source of information.

Rag Performers

By the end of the nineteenth century there were several important ragtime areas in the United States, each with its own coterie of black players, favorite rendezvous spots, and distinctive style of performance. Generally the gathering places were located in the heart of a sporting-life district, for it was there that black performers of rag music found ready employment and warm acceptance. Among the pianists—many of now legendary fame—who congregated in the back rooms of bars to play for one another and for other connoisseurs of good ragtime were "habitual winners" of contests. Composers as well as performers, few bothered to publish their music—either they were too busy, or they felt that at the going rate of ten or fifteen dollars per piece it was hardly worth the trouble.

The Missouri area, with St. Louis at the core, may not have produced the earliest school of ragtime players, but its composers were the first to be published and to win national recognition. In addition to the men already discussed, other black pianists belonging to the group included Otis Saunders, Bob and John Moore, Charlie Warfield, and a man known as Klondike.[24]

A big ragtime contest, sponsored by the Turpins, was held in St. Louis during the time of the Louisiana Purchase Exposition (the "St. Louis Fair") in 1904. Black pianists came from all over the nation to enter the competition—as much for the thrill of competing with the country's best rag pianists as for the prizes. Top honors were won by a pianist from New Orleans, Alfred Wilson, and second place went to Charlie Warfield. Beginning about 1906 the St. Louis men began to drift away—to Chicago, Kansas City, and New York.

In New Orleans at the turn of the century, the city's best rag pianists were accustomed to gathering in the back room of Frenchman's Saloon after leaving their regular places of employment; among them were Albert Carroll, Anthony Jackson, Alfred Wilson, and the somewhat younger Buddy Carter, Sammy Davis, and "Jelly Roll" Morton. All knew about the legendary rag pianist called John the Baptist who had been active in the '70s and '80s, but none had actually heard him play. Of the group, Anthony "Tony" Jackson was most famous; singer as well as pianist, he became known as the "World's Greatest Single-Handed Entertainer."

Some older ragtimers felt that the rag music played by the New Orleans group was slower, the rhythms more strongly marked, the texture contrapuntal, and the harmonies more chromatic than that of the St. Louis ragtimers. While each player had his or her own distinctive style, they all favored the use of "walking" or "rolling" basses in the left hand.

---

[24]Willie "the Lion" Smith, *Music On My Mind* (New York, 1964), pp. 54–56, 63–69; and the present author's personal interviews with Blake.

A Stride Pattern

A Walking Bass

etc.

First-rate rag pianists were to be found in smaller southern cities, as well as in old, sprawling New Orleans. At one period during 1905, for example, there were four well-known raggers in Mobile, Alabama, at the same time: Porter King, Baby Gryce, Frazier Davis of Florida, and Frank Rachel of Georgia. Louisville, Kentucky, was known for its rag pianists Glover Compton and "Piano" Price Davis. In Memphis, Tennessee, Pee Wee's saloon on Beale Street was the chief headquarters for musicians, but piano thumpers were to be heard all up and down the street. In the northern city of Pittsburgh, the best pianist was a woman known as "Ragtime Mame." Indianapolis was the home of Russell Smith, whose rags were published by a local company.

When the southern pianists began drifting into Chicago during the first decade of the twentieth century, they found there an established tradition for rag music dating back at least to the time of the World's Fair in 1893. The patriarch of the group in Chicago, "Plunk" Henry (1850s-d. before 1906), was one of ragtime's earliest pioneers. One of the younger men, Johnny Seymour, had made a name for himself with his sensational playing at the Chicago Fair. Other important players were Eddie James, Harry "Squirrel" Crosby, Needham Wright, Fred Burke, George "Sparrow" Kimbrough, James "Slap Rags" White, and Ed Hardin, "chief of the ragtime roost." When the newcomers to Chicago—including such men as Charlie Warfield, Tony Jackson, Joe Jordan, and Jelly Roll Morton—added their talents to the existing store, the results were impressive. Chicago became the center of ragtime playing that St. Louis had been a decade earlier.

Ragtime on the eastern seaboard also had its legendary figures. The pioneers included "Old Man" Sam Moore of Philadelphia, Bud Minor of Washington, D.C., and "Old Man Metronome" French of Baltimore (a rag-playing banjoist). Among the members of a later generation born in the 1860s and '70s were Sam Gordon of Trenton, Walter "One-Leg Shadow" Gould of Philadelphia, and John "Jack the Bear" Wilson, originally from Pennsylvania or Ohio.

In 1969 Eubie Blake, reminiscing about the Baltimore of his youth (i.e., in the 1890s), discussed the eastern style of ragtime music and named several "piano sharks" who played this music: Jesse Pickett, "Big-Head" Wilbur, "Big Jimmy" Green, "Shout" Blake (not related to Eubie), William Turk, Sammy Ewell, "Slew-Foot" Nelson, and Willie "Egg Head" Sewell. Shout Blake was the only one of the group who could read music, but "all of the men could play in any key." It was Jesse Pickett ("some say he was from Philadelphia") who taught Eubie Blake how to play ragtime, using the famous Pickett rag *The Dream* as the demonstration piece.[25]

Other members of Blake's generation who were widely known for their ragtime skill were Richard "Abba Labba" McLean of New York, "One-Leg" Willie Joseph of Baltimore (originally from New England and reputedly a graduate of the Boston Conservatory of Music), and "Sticky" Mack and Louis Brown of Washington, D.C. Many of these pianists eventually settled in New York, going there during the opening decade of the twentieth century. There was also a continuous influx into New York of rag pianists from other centers—particularly from Baltimore, Chicago, St. Louis, Memphis, and New Orleans—who stayed there briefly, then moved on to other places.

Since none of the music of the eastern pioneers, except for Eubie Blake's, was published or recorded, it is impossible to know how this music actually sounded. Some insight into the early eastern style is afforded, however, by the playing of Blake, although his personal style undoubtedly underwent many changes over the long span of years from the time of his first job in the Baltimore tenderloin district in 1899 and the release of his album *The Eighty-Six Years of Eubie Blake* in 1969.

The most striking features of Blake's rags were the fast tempos and the powerful pulsating basses. The latter, consisting chiefly of "um-pah" skips from low octaves to mid-keyboard chords and octave passages are generally referred to as "stride basses." But Blake occasionally interrupted the straightforward patterns in his left hand to inject a few measures of stentorian broken octaves, his right hand continuing all the while in its flowing embellishing of the syncopated melody (he called the embellishments "tricks").

Blake's strongest complaint about modern piano playing, which he generally admired, concerned the neglect of the bass—"they don't play a bass!" The old-timers realized that their piano playing served in lieu of an orchestra and compensated for the absence of percussion instruments by emphasizing the left-hand bass. Blake's simple statement, "We had to do it because we had no drums to help us," reflected, perhaps unconsciously so, a basic premise of African American music—there is no music without the drum.[26]

Rag players were called "professors" (generally shortened to "Fess" among black musicians), titles given also to bandmasters and music teachers. By 1910 the rag professors were either writing fewer and fewer rags or moving into other areas of music activity. The publication in 1911 of white songwriter Irving Berlin's *Alexander's Ragtime Band* was in reality the swan song of the ragtime-song period, although it brought about a brief revival

---

[25]Southern, Interviews with Blake. See also BPIM (Spring 1973) and (Fall 1973).
[26]Personal interview of Blake by the author.

of interest in the music. The vogue for instrumental rags in the classic style ended symbolically with the death of Scott Joplin in 1917.[27]

Yet Joplin's music lived on, and some rag pianists continued to compose and publish music in the style and form of *The Maple Leaf Rag*. Joplin's immediate followers, James Scott and white composer Joseph Lamb, won acclaim for the fine quality of their compositional output. But as the public gradually lost interest in classic ragtime, dance musicians transferred their allegiance to jazz, and the ragtime era quietly came to a halt. By the 1940s, however, a ragtime revival was under way, led by white bandleader Lu Watter and his Yerba Buena Jass Band, and by the 1970s the revival was full-blown.

Except for Eubie Blake, black musicians were noticeably absent from ragtime revival activities. That grand old man was giving rag recitals and lectures even as he approached his centennial birthday. The black community paid scant attention: the older members had forgotten Scott Joplin, and the younger generation seemed not to have ever heard of him, or if they recognized the name, they thought Blake was a white composer.

Rag Elements in the Music of White Composers

Of the great European art-music composers, Debussy was the first to take notice of the new music of black folk origin; his *Golliwog's Cakewalk*, a movement of the piano suite *Children's Corner* (1905), bounces along in typical ragtime song style with a syncopated melody in the right hand and "um-pah" accompaniment in the left. Stravinsky wrote *Piano Rag-Music* (1920), *Ragtime* for eleven instruments (1918), and included a ragtime movement in the popular *L'Histoire du soldat* (The Soldier's Tale, 1918). The French composer Erik Satie (1866–1925) wrote a ballet, *Parade* (1917), in which *The American Girl's Dance* is in ragtime style. The German composer Paul Hindemith (1895–1963) inserted a *Ragtime* finale in his piano suite of 1922. There is a report that Brahms had envisioned a ragtime project, which was under way just before his death.[28] In the United States, John Alden Carpenter (1876–1951) seems to have been the first white composer to use ragtime style in art music, in his Concertino for Piano and Orchestra (1916).

Some of this music reflects the captivating but rather vapid style of the ragtime song rather than the essence of serious rag music. But then, few persons outside the black world had the opportunity to hear rag music as played by the legendary figures. The music composed by Joplin, Scott, Turpin, Blake, and others was too difficult to be taken home "and tried out on the piano." The public came to know instead a simplified ragtime song style

[27]The term "classic" is used to denote piano rags written in the style of Scott Joplin.
[28]Cited in Blesh, "Scott Joplin", p. xiii. See further in Robert Haven Schauffler, *The Unknown Brahms* (New York, 1933), p. 176.

popularized by Tin Pan Alley and exemplified in the playing of pianists like the white ragtime composer Mike Bernard.

THE BLUES

We know even less about the origin of the blues than we know about the beginning of ragtime. W. C. Handy, the first man to popularize the blues, was struck with the possibilities of utilizing it in musical composition in 1903 when he heard a man singing a song in a Mississippi train station. The singer was a "lean, loose-jointed Negro" clothed in mere rags, whose face reflected the "sadness of the ages." As he sang, he plunked on a guitar, producing some of the "weirdest music" Handy had ever heard. Handy recognized the song type, an earthy kind of music that he had known as a boy in Alabama.[29]

The earliest professional blues singer, Gertrude "Ma" Rainey (1886–1939), remembered first hearing the blues in 1902.[30] She was touring in Missouri with the Rabbit Foot Minstrels when she heard a local girl sing a song about the man who had deserted her. Its plaintive poignancy haunted Ma, who learned the song and used it in her act, where it became so popular with audiences that Ma began to specialize in the singing of such songs. She claimed that it was she who gave to the songs the name "blues" after being asked time and time again about the kind of song she was singing and having finally answered in an inspired moment, "It's the blues."

But old-timers who sang and played the blues in tenderloin districts across the nation scoffed when asked about its origins. In New Orleans an old fiddler said, "The blues? Ain't no first blues! The blues always been." Eubie Blake answered, "Blues in Baltimore? Why, Baltimore is the blues!" Bunk Johnson, a pioneer bluesman, told an interviewer, "When I was a kid [i.e., in the 1880s] we used to play nothing but the blues." In New Orleans, even the street vendors used the blues, advertising their wares by playing blues on toy horns bought from Kress's dime stores.[31]

The early anonymous singers of the blues often were wanderers, sometimes blind, who carried their plaintive songs from one black community to another, some of them sauntering down the railroad tracks or dropping from freight cars, others coming in with the packet boats, and yet others coming via the dirt road, having caught a ride on a wagon or in a later time, on a truck. They sang their songs in the segregated railroad stations, on the street corners, in eating places, juke joints, honky-tonk night spots, and even on the trains. They also could sing happy blues for community social affairs,

[29]W. C. Handy, *Father of the Blues* (New York, 1941), p. 74.
[30]See further in John W. Work, *American Negro Songs and Spirituals* (New York, 1940), pp. 32–33.
[31]Nat Shapiro and Nat Hentoff, *Hear Me Talkin' to Ya* (New York, 1955), p. 7.

dances, and picnics. From the time of its origin the blues was generally associated with the lowly—received with warmth in the brothels and saloons of the red-light district, but generally rejected by "respectable," church-going people.

Blues and Spirituals

The dividing line between the blues and some kinds of spirituals cannot always be sharply drawn. Blues singers, like the singers of the spirituals, often draw upon songs that belong to the community repertory, borrowing from this one and that one, and refashioning the verses into a new song even as they are singing. Blues scholar David Evans observes that

> the music has a special appeal for the community, but it is usually respected by them as the momentary invention of the song-maker whose job it is (at that particular time, anyway) to give back to the people their own songs in acceptable form and with new, and often topical, flavouring.[32]

Many spirituals convey to listeners the same feeling of rootlessness and misery as do the blues. The spiritual is religious, however, rather than worldly and tends to be more generalized in its expression than specific, more figurative in its language than direct, and more expressive of group feelings than individual ones. Despite these differences it is nevertheless often difficult to distinguish between the two kinds of songs. Some songs have such vague implications that scholars classify them as "blues-spirituals."

Singers of spirituals and jubilee songs wandered from place to place, as did blues singers. Handy describes in his book a scene of Clarksdale, Mississippi, that depicts the "blind singers and the footloose bards" in their natural habitat:

> A favorite hangout with them was the railroad station. There, surrounded by crowds of country folks, they would pour out their hearts in song while the audience ate fish and bread, chewed sugar cane, [and] dipped snuff while waiting for trains to carry them down the line.
>
> They earned their living by selling their own songs—"ballets," as they called them. . . . Some of these country boys hustled on trains. Others visited churches. I remember buying such a ballet entitled *I've Heard of a City Called Heaven*. It was printed on a slip of paper about the size of a postcard. Fifty years later . . . I heard the number sung with great success by the Hall Johnson singers in *The Green Pastures* [a Broadway show first produced in the 1930s].[33]

Characteristics of the Blues

As an aural music, the blues has few absolute features; it is intended to take on its shape and style during the performance. Generally, but not

---

[32]David Evans, *Big Road Blues* (Berkeley, 1982), p. 96.
[33]Handy, *Father of the Blues,* pp. 87–88.

always, the blues reflects the personal response of its inventor to a specific occurrence or situation. By singing about their misery, blues singers achieve a kind of catharsis and life becomes bearable again. Most often they bemoan the fickleness or departure of a loved one. They don't need an audience for their singing, although others may listen if they wish. When others do listen to the blues singer, they frequently find that they have shared experiences in one way or another.

The antecedents of the blues were the mournful songs of the stevedores and roustabouts, the field hollers of the slaves, and the sorrow songs among the spirituals. Such spirituals as *Lay This Body Down,* for example, would probably have been called blues had the term been in use at the time. Other early blues types are to be found in the collections of secular folksongs that began to appear in print during the first decade of the twentieth century, of which many obviously dated back into the nineteenth.

In 1901, for example, an archaeologist engaged in field work in Mississippi noted that the texts of the songs he heard sung by black laborers dealt with "hard luck tales" and "love themes," the subject matter of blues although that term was not used.[34] Moreover, some of the songs had guitar accompaniment that used primarily "inversions of the three chords of a few major or minor keys." He wrote down several texts and melodies of the blues types:

Four Mississippi blues

In other early collections the term *blues* actually appears in a few texts:[35]

[34]Charles Peabody, "Notes on Negro Music," *Journal of American Folklore* 16 (July 1903): 148–52.

[35]Eber C. Perrow, "Songs and Rhymes from the South," *Journal of American Folklore* 28 (1915): 190; Howard Odum, "Folk-Song and Folk Poetry as Found in the Secular Songs of the Southern Negroes," *Journal of American Folklore* 24 (1911): 272.

I laid in jail, back to the wall;
Brown skin gal cause of it all.

I've got the blues; I'm too damn mean to talk
A brown-skin woman make a bull-dog break his chain.

Look'd down de road jes' as far as I could
Well, the band did play "Nearer, my God, to Thee."

I got the blues, but too damn mean to cry,
I got the blues, but too damn mean to cry.

Although the blues typically concerns itself with the problems and / or experiences of the individual, it is impossible to convey precisely the sentiments of the blues. As Handy observed, the blues, like all Negro folksong, was drawn from a "well of sorrow." But it was not a well of despair! Almost always there is a note of irony or humor in the blues, as if the blues singer is audaciously challenging fate to mete out further blows. Sure, he has lost his job, and his woman has left him, and he has the blues; but he will go out the next morning to look for another job, and perhaps his woman will return, or perhaps another will come into his life. Like other black folksong, blues texts are rich in imagery—generally of a very earthy quality.

In addition to its lyrics, the blues is distinctive for its three-line stanza, which perhaps is a throwback to African origins, for the three-line stanza is uncommon in European folksong repertories.

In the early blues, the three lines often had identical texts (see Example 1); in later forms two identical (or similar) lines are followed by a contrasting statement (see Example 2). Typically, the third line answers a question raised in the first two lines or offers a philosophical comment upon the situation:

EXAMPLE 1. I thought I heard that K.C. whistle blow,
I thought I heard that K.C. whistle blow,
Oh, I thought I heard that K.C. whistle blow.

Blow lak' she never blow befo',
Blow lak' she never blow befo',
Lawd, she blow lak' she never blow befo'.

Wish to God some ole train would run,
Wish to God some ole train would run,
Carry me back where I come frum. *etc.*

EXAMPLE 2. Woke up this morning, feeling sad and blue,
Woke up this morning, feeling sad and blue,
Didn't have nobody to tell my troubles to.

or

I've got the blues, but I'm too darn mean to cry,
I've got the blues, but I'm too darn mean to cry,
Before I'd cry I'd rather lay down and die.

or

> When a woman gets the blues she hangs her head and cries,
> When a woman gets the blues she hangs her head and cries,
> But when a man gets the blues, he grabs a train and flies.

Like most black folk music, the blues tends to move in duple rhythms and uses marked syncopated patterns. Its musical form parallels the poetic form, generally with an *a a' b* arrangement for the three-line text, each line composed of four bars and the entire song of twelve bars. To be sure, a blues form may consist of eight measures or bars of sixteen. The melody for each line is typically condensed into a little more than two measures of the four-measure phrase (see example on p. 337); this allows for a pause or "break" at the end of each vocal line of three measures, during which the accompanying instrument (guitar, piano, or instrumental ensemble) improvises, or "fills in the breaks." The singer may interject spoken asides, such as "Oh, Lordy," "Yes, man," "Oh, play it," etc. The resulting effect is that of call-and-response, the instrumental improvisation representing the "response" to the voice's "call."

The blues melody derives from an altered scale in which the third, fifth, seventh, and occasionally the sixth degrees are treated ambiguously, sometimes being lowered and at other times sung at the natural pitch levels of the major scale. At these points in the scale the singer is apt to "scoop," "swoop," or "slur." The altered tones are commonly called "blue notes," or "bent" tones. Freely using such vocal devices as falsetto, shouting, whining, moaning, speaking, or growling, the blues singer gives vent to pain—or happiness. Because of the performance practice associated with the singing of blues, it is almost impossible to notate a blues melody accurately on a staff. The notated melody can only approximate the melodic outline of the actual blues.

According to some bluesmen and scholars, the tune associated with the *Joe Turner* blues was the prototype for all folk blues. As one writer pointed out, "the old *Joe Turner* and almost any other blues of an unsophisticated type may actually be played or sung together without any serious difficulties being encountered"—this, because there is so little difference between the tunes.[36] The *Joe Turner* tune was used all over the South for a number of texts, among them *Goin' Down the River 'Fore Long* in Kentucky and *Goin' Down That Lonesome Road* in Georgia.[37]

The story behind the original text referred to a prison officer, Joe Turney, brother of Tennessee governor Pete Turney.

> . . . Joe had the responsibility of taking Negro prisoners from Memphis to the penitentiary at Nashville [in the early 1890s]. Sometimes he took them to the "farms" along the Mississippi. Their crimes, when indeed there were any crimes,

---

[36]Quoted from Abbe Niles in W. C. Handy, ed., *Blues: An Anthology* (New York, 1949), p. 210.

[37]See also in regard to Joe Turner in Evans, *Big Road Blues*, pp. 46–47.

Joe Turner

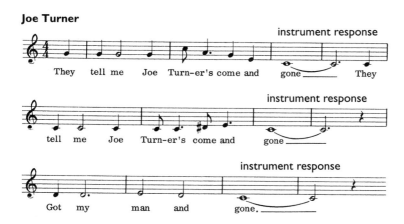

were usually very minor, the object of the arrests being to provide needed labor for spots along the river. As usual, the method was to set a stool-pigeon where he could start a game of craps. The bones would roll blissfully till the required number of laborers had been drawn into the circle. At that point the law would fall upon the poor devils, arrest as many as were needed for work, try them for gambling in a kangaroo court, and then turn the culprits over to Joe Turney. That night, perhaps, there would be weeping and wailing among the dusky belles. If one of them chanced to ask a neighbor what had become of the sweet good man, she was likely to receive the pat reply, "They tell me Joe Turner's come and gone."[38]

The accompaniment most often draws on the three primary chords of the key—tonic, dominant, and subdominant—in a prescribed way: the first line of the blues is supported by the tonic chord; the second line uses the subdominant in the fifth and sixth measures, then returns to the tonic; and the third line begins with the dominant, often progresses to the subdominant, then concludes with the tonic. In the following diagram the roman numerals represent the primary chords and each vertical stroke represents a barline.

Line 1	I	I	I	I
Line 2	IV	IV	I	I
Line 3	V	V or IV	I	I

While an individual blues singer, guitarist, or banjoist might deviate from this harmonic structure in actual performance, the diagram represents the customary procedures.

[38] W. C. Handy, *Father of the Blues*, p. 147.

The foregoing discussion serves as an introduction to the blues. Its history, however, cannot properly begin until 1920, the year of the first recorded blues, for phonograph records are the chief sources of blues history. We can surmise how the blues sounded before that date, but critical discussion must be concerned with the music itself. The blues performer is at the same time its composer.

Father of the Blues

When William Christopher Handy (1873–1958) published his first blues composition, the *Memphis Blues,* in 1912, he created an unprecedented vogue for that kind of music.[39] Originally written in 1909 as a campaign song for one of the mayoral candidates in a Memphis election, Edward H. Crump, it was an immediate success upon its first performance. Handy's bandsmen became "intoxicated" with the melody and rhythm of the piece even during the rehearsal. Once the playing began, both the crowd and the band went wild! People danced on the streets; in the office buildings the "white folks pricked up their ears" and "stenographers danced with their bosses."

As a result of this performance Handy's band jumped to the top spot among Memphis bands. Two years later Handy published the famous *St. Louis Blues,* a composition that carried the blues all over the world.

Handy was well equipped for his role as a musical pioneer. He played in a minstrel band at an early age, later was a bandmaster at the A & M College in Huntsville, Alabama, then returned to minstrel life—this time as director of brass bands for Mahara's Minstrels. About 1903 he left minstrelsy and for the next five years was active in the Mississippi Delta region as a bandmaster and director of dance orchestras. He then settled at Memphis, Tennessee, where he continued his band activities and also founded a music publishing company with Harry Pace, a businessman and lyricist.

In 1918 Handy and Pace moved their company to New York, where they soon became important figures in black New York music circles. The company published popular music that was sung by the leading entertainers of the period—for example, *A Good Man is Hard to Find,* featured by white "torch singer" Sophie Tucker—and pamphlets and small books from time to time. Handy also toured with his blues bands and other music groups, made recordings, played trumpet with various groups, and staged concerts. Through the years he continued to write music, arranging spirituals and blues, and composing marches, hymns, and miscellaneous songs. His best-known collections were *Blues: An Anthology* (1926) and *Book of Negro Spirituals* (1938). His autobiography, *Father of the Blues* (1941), is an invaluable contribution to black-music history.

[39]Handy, *Father of the Blues,* p. 100.

W. C. Handy. *(Courtesy World Wide Photos)*

Although Handy was the first man to popularize the blues, two blues appeared in print prior to his *Memphis Blues*. *Baby Seals Blues*, written by black rag pianist Artie Matthews, was published in August 1912; *Dallas Blues*, written by the white songwriter Hart A. Wand, appeared the following month. Handy's blues piece came out three weeks later, followed by his *Jogo Blues* in 1913, *St. Louis Blues* in 1914, and *Joe Turner Blues* in 1915. Matthews wrote another blues in 1915, the *Weary Blues*, that became popular. In the same year, Morton published his *Original Jelly Roll Blues*. These early pieces, along with some traditional folk-blues melodies, provide a basic repertory of stock melodies, which jazz composers have used time and again.

BRASS BANDS AND STRING BANDS

By the end of the nineteenth century, black brass bands and dance orchestras were flourishing all over the country, particularly in the large cities of the nation. The society dance-orchestra tradition on the eastern seaboard reached back to the beginning of the century, as we have seen, with the orchestras of: Frank Johnson of Philadelphia; Peter O'Fake of Newark, New Jersey; and Joseph Postlewaite, among others.

Even in sparsely populated areas of the country there were opportunities for black "string bands" to find employment. George Morrison, a bandleader of Denver, Colorado, recalled that as a boy during the early 1900s in Boulder, Colorado, he organized a boys' string band that played for all the dances held in the mining camps and in the mountain towns.[40] There simply was no other music group available to the mountain people. Morrison and other old-timers give the reason for this state of affairs: throughout the nineteenth century and on into the twentieth, white youths were discouraged from preparing for careers as dance musicians. We know that since colonial times black men had traditionally provided music for the dancing of whites. In many places the profession of dance musician was reserved by custom for African-Americans, just as was, for example, the occupation of barber.

The town brass band was a traditional American institution, and every village aspired to have its own band to provide Sunday afternoon concerts in the village square and to play for parades on civic occasions and holidays. Although some towns hired their own bandmasters to organize town bands and to train the bandsmen, black bands generally were independently sponsored by fraternal and benevolent societies, or social clubs, or by the bandsmen themselves. In the latter instance the black bandsmen could often depend upon the patronage of wealthy white townspeople in helping with the purchase of uniforms and instruments.

A good band found itself in great demand by both whites and blacks for all kinds of occasions. The opening of a country store, for example, called for brass-band music after the ceremonies. Band music was demanded for political rallies and Election Day ceremonies. Some large cities in the South maintained amusement parks for blacks, where dances were among the chief attractions and brass bands provided the dance music in open-air

---

[40]An interview with George Morrison by Gunther Schuller, *Early Jazz* (New York, 1968), pp. 359–72.

pavillions. The dance floor in Memphis's Dixie Park could, and often did, accommodate a thousand dancers at a time; at Lincoln Park in New Orleans there were two dance places—an open-air pavillion and a dance hall. The bands in towns and cities located along the Mississippi or its main tributaries, the Ohio and the Missouri, found opportunities to play on excursion boats and packet boats that plied up and down the rivers.

Typically, a brass band was composed of twelve to fourteen men and used the following instruments: trumpets or cornets, trombones, horns, clarinets, and drums. To this basic ensemble might be added melophones, tubas, flutes, piccolos, and other instruments, depending upon the place and the availability of players. In Maryland, Virginia, and the Carolinas, for example, the euphonium was a popular band instrument. In most places, bandsmen were expected to read music and to play the music as written. Undoubtedly there was some "ragging" of the music, but according to all evidence there was very little improvisation or embellishing of melodies.

Brass-band repertories included marches of all kinds, hymns, overtures, medleys of popular songs or operatic arias, and "light classics." Bands were frequently called upon to play for funerals, particularly in southern cities. On the way to the cemetery it was customary for the band to play a dirge very slowly and mournfully, or a Protestant hymn such as *Nearer My God to Thee,* but on the way back the band would strike up a lively spiritual such as *When the Saints Go Marching In,* or a ragtime song such as *Didn't He Ramble,* or a syncopated march.

Generally, brass bands had their own little satellite dance orchestras, composed of seven or eight bandsmen who could double on other instruments. For dances, the bandsmen added violins, guitars, banjos, mandolins, and basses to a few winds and the drums. They were expected to provide music for the popular dances of the period: waltzes, schottisches, polkas, quadrilles, and two-steps. By the turn of the century, one-steps and "slow drags," as well as the cakewalk, were becoming popular.

An integral part of life for black bandsmen was the band competition. Just as ragtime pianists and cakewalkers competed in regional and national contests, so did brass bands. A town or city expected its brass band to bring back honors from a competition, as did its baseball team. In some places, particularly in New Orleans, brass bands engaged in local battles. One band would literally play another off the streets by playing louder or more brilliantly or with sweeter tones, much to the delight of the hundreds of band watchers on the streets who would assemble at the first sounds of a *ta-ta-ta-ta ta-ta* from the trumpets calling the bandsmen together. These contests were called "cutting" or "bucking" contests.

When on parade, bands were generally accompanied by a grand marshal, his aides, and a host of nonmusicians, chiefly children who danced along in time to the music, called the "second line." For an important occa-

342 BLOW YE THE TRUMPET

sion the fraternal organization or benevolent society sponsoring the parade might hire three or four bands to participate, the members themselves also parading in fancy uniforms.

Brass Bands and Dance Orchestras in New Orleans

At the turn of the century, New Orleans had dozens of African-American brass bands, dance orchestras, and strolling groups of players. The leading brass bands included the Eagle, Eureka, Excelsior, Imperial, Onward, Peerless, and Superior. Some of these bands dated back to the 1880s–90s; others were formed during the first decade of the twentieth century. As described above, their instrumentation consisted of twelve to fourteen musicians. Like their predecessors in the early nineteenth century, some bandsmen studied with members of the French Opera Company orchestra and other important white musical organizations of the city. The Tio brothers had studied at the Mexican Conservatory of Music before coming to New Orleans in 1885.[41]

The six- and seven-piece "string bands" that played for dances generally included cornet, trombone, string bass, guitar, drums, and one or two clarinets or violins. Among the principal dance groups were the Silver Leaf, the Olympia, and Adam Olivier's band; sometimes brass bands such as the Excelsior also played for dances. But the top dance bands of the years ca. 1893–1906 were the society dance band of John Robichaux (1866–1937) and the "hot" band of Charles "Buddy" Bolden (1877–1931).[42]

Robichaux, a talented, well-trained violinist, began his career in Theogene Baquet's Excelsior Cornet Band about 1891, but organized his own band a short time afterward. "Buddy" Bolden was chiefly self-taught, although in about 1894 he studied music basics and cornet briefly with Manual Hall, who was not a professional musician. Bolden first played professionally in a band led by Charles Galloway, but struck out on his own very soon.

Bolden and Robichaux frequently competed with each other, not only in regard to securing engagements in the dance halls and parks where the unending dances of the black community took place, but also in live "cutting contests." Eventually Bolden began to win out over the smooth, sophisticated band of Robichaux. The two bands often played in adjacent Johnson and Lincoln Parks; Bolden would play his cornet so "powerfully" that dancers would leave Lincoln to join him. Contemporaries referred to this as

[41]This discussion of musicians of New Orleans is based largely on Al Rose and Edmond Souchon, *New Orleans Jazz: A Family Album*, rev. ed. (Baton Rouge, 1978), which corrects some of the data found in earlier sources.

[42]See further in Donald M. Marquis, *In Search of Buddy Bolden* (Baton Rouge, 1978), which effectively dispels the myths that have surrounded Bolden as the "first man of jazz," uncovering the facts of his pioneering role in the history of jazz.

"calling" the dancers. Perhaps even more important than Bolden's powerful tones was the exotic sound of his music for that period, for it incorporated blues and ragtime and his men improvised as they played.

Bolden is generally regarded as the patriarch of jazz, although the term *jazz* had not at that time been invented. He was as celebrated for his "sweet" music as for his "driving, ragged" music; he became "King Bolden," the cornetist to be emulated by Freddie Keppard, Joseph Oliver, Louis Armstrong, and others who came after him. The songs he made famous included *Make Me a Pallet on the Floor, The House Got Ready,* and *Bucket's Got a Hole in It. Buddy Bolden's Blues* was written by Jelly Roll Morton.

Bandsmen in New Orleans fell into two groups—the "creoles of color," who lived in the so-called downtown district, and the black folk, who lived in the uptown district. During the 1890s two events occurred that deeply affected the development of entertainment music in New Orleans. In 1894, the city enacted a segregation code that forced colored creoles to live in the uptown district and consequently brought them into closer contact with black folk. In 1897, the city passed a resolution that instituted vice segregation, setting up a tenderloin district, later called Storyville after the resolution's sponsor, Alderman Sidney Story.

Eventually the best musicians, colored creole and black, found their way to Storyville, where the wages were good and the work was regular. They played together in bands, exchanging musical ideas and teaching each other the things they knew best. Basin Street was the important street of the district; the Tuxedo, one of the large dance halls in the area. They later were immortalized in the two songs *Basin Street Blues* and *Tuxedo Junction.*

In 1910 Oscar "Papa" Celestin (1884–1954) organized two groups in association with the Tuxedo Hall, his Original Tuxedo Orchestra and Tuxedo Brass Band, that soon rivaled older bands in popularity. An important cornetist of the period, William Geary "Bunk" Johnson (1879–1949), played with several of the leading bands, among them, the Superior, but his significance as a participant in the developmental stages of jazz became clear only in the 1940s with the revival of public interest in Dixieland jazz. There were other bands, too, that began to attract attention for their "hot" music; the best places to hear the music were in Storyville at such cafés as Pete Lala's and in dance halls, such as the Odd Fellows and Masonic Hall, the Globe Hall, and Perserverance Hall.

Cornetists and clarinetists forced their instruments to sing the blues. They stretched the ranges of the instruments, ascending to dizzy heights and descending to incredible depths. In order to get the "dirty" tones they wanted, they used a wide variety of mutes—plungers, cups, drinking glasses, and small bottles. Trombonists came up with a distinctive style called "tailgate," which developed because, in order to have room to work the trombone slide, they had to sit to the rear of the band wagons that carried music groups through the streets during parades. This seating position allowed them sufficient space in which to play, and they made a speciality of contributing glissando runs to the ensemble sound.

These pioneers passed on the traditions of their music to the youngsters who idolized them, who followed after them in the street parades, who took music lessons from them, who watched them perform from the swinging doors of the saloons, and who finally took places beside them in the endless parades and in the dance halls, "parlors," and saloons of Storyville.

The legendary figures of the pioneering generations included (in addition to those named above) the celebrated clarinetists Frank Lewis (1870–1924), Alphonse Picou (1879–1961), Lorenzo Tio, Sr. (ca. 1865–1920), and his brother Louis Tio (1863–1927). The important cornetists were Henry Allen, Sr. (1877–1952), Theogene Baquet (1858–1920), James "Jim" Humphrey (1861–1937), and Manuel Perez (1879–1946). The notable trombonists were Frank Dusen (1881–1936), Willie Cornish (1875–1942), and "Buddy" Johnson (1875–1927). The important bassists were Jimmy Johnson (1884–1937), William Manuel "Bill" Johnson (1872–1972) and Henry Kimball, Sr. (1878–1931). Outstanding among the guitarists were Charles "Happy" Galloway (ca. 1865–1921) and Jefferson "Brock" Mumford (1873–1927) and the leading drummers were Edward "Dee Dee" Chandler (1870–1925), and Henry Zeno (1870–1917).

Chandler is credited with having been the first dance drummer to use the foot pedal; Picou later became famous for his solo on *High Society*. But all the musicians contributed greatly to the development of jazz, either as leaders or sidemen, and there were others, half-forgotten now. Despite their range in age these performers may be regarded as contemporaries, for they played alongside each other in the musical groups of the period.

To be sure, the same statement could be made about musicians of the next generation, of whom two were sons of the older men and several, students; among them, clarinetists George Baquet (1883–1949), Louis "Big Eye" Nelson (1885–1949), and Lorenzo Tio, Jr. (1884–1933); cornetists Peter Bocage (1887–1967), Freddie Keppard (1889–1933), and Joseph Oliver (1885–1938); trombonist "Fess" Manuel Manetta (1889–1969), who also played other instruments; and drummer Louis Cottrell, Sr. (ca. 1875–1927).

The exodus of black bandsmen from New Orleans began in the first decade of the century. One of the first to leave was Bill Johnson, a bassist who began playing professionally in 1900 and who had toured with a small group called the Original Creole Orchestra about 1908 (also known as the Original Creole Jass Band).[43] In 1911 he went to California; two years later

---

[43]According to the evidence, it was Bill Johnson, not Freddie Keppard, who was the leader of the Original Creole Band in its historic transcontinental tours. See further on the stage-news pages of the *Chicago Defender,* July 15, 1916; the *Freeman* of Indianapolis, February 13, 1915 and May 22, 1915; Rose and Souchon, *New Orleans Jazz,* p. 64.

he sent for some of his bandsmen, putting them in the charge of Freddie Keppard, founder-leader of the Olympia Orchestra. During the years 1913–17 this band toured widely on the vaudeville circuit. It was the first black dance band to make transcontinental tours. It was this band that carried the jazz of New Orleans to the rest of the nation.

Syncopated Orchestras in New York

In 1900 the center of African-American fashionable life at New York was an area on the West Side of Manhattan known as Black Bohemia, and the headquarters of black artistic talent in the area were the Marshall Hotel on West Fifty-third Street and Barron Wilkins's Cafe on West Thirty-fifth Street. Here were to be found the actors, performers, artists, composers, writers, and poets who were the celebrities of the time. Here also came white actors, musicians, and composers from the nearby Broadway theater district, to see and be seen. Black entertainers would gather in the bar, waiting for calls to go out on private engagements, for it was known all over the city that one could always find dance musicians and singers at the Marshall. The musicians, in particular, were caught up in the exciting lifestyle of Black Bohemia, and their activities represent a considerable contribution to the development of jazz.

James Reese Europe (1881–1919), a leading figure in black musical circles, along with Bob Cole, J. Rosamond Johnson, and Will Marion Cook, arrived in New York about 1905 and almost immediately become involved in musical activities. He had obtained his musical education in the public schools of Washington, D.C., and had studied piano and violin privately, the latter with Enrico Hurlei, assistant director of the United States Marine Band. First, he served as a musical director for the George Walker and Bert Williams company, then for the Cole–Johnson musical, *The Shoo-Fly Regiment,* beginning in 1906. But he first attracted attention because of his association with Ernest Hogan in producing a show that has been called the first public concert of syncopated music in history.[44]

Hogan organized a group of about twenty experienced entertainers (singers, dancers, and instrumentalists); called them the Memphis Students, although none was from Memphis and none was a student; brought in Joe Jordan and Jim Europe to write music and help with the rehearsing; then took his show to Hammerstein's Victoria Theatre on Broadway in May 1905, for a two-week engagement. The show was so successful that it was held over for five months. In the fall of 1905 Will Marion Cook took over

---

[44]See further about the concert in Fletcher, *100 Years,* pp. 129–31 (Fletcher errs, however, in calling the group the Nashville Students); James Weldon Johnson, *Black Manhattan,* pp. 120–22. The black press also carried stories about the concert; for example, the *New York Age,* August 24, 1905, and October 26, 1905.

leadership of the group and toured with it in Europe for several months, appearing at the Palace Theatre in London, the Olympia in Paris, and the Schumann Circus in Berlin, among other places.

The Memphis Students' show was highly innovative. In addition to the syncopated music—which in itself was a novelty in New York at that time—there was a "dancing conductor," Will Dixon:

> All through a number he would keep his men together by dancing out the rhythm, generally in graceful, sometimes in grotesque, steps. Often an easy shuffle would take him across the whole front of the band. This style of directing not only got the fullest possible response from the men, but kept them in just the right humour for the sort of music they were playing.

The drummer, Buddy Gilmore, contributed to the excitement by performing juggling and acrobatic stunts while drumming. His use of other noisemaking devices in addition to the drums—unusual at that time—emphasized the rhythms of the music. And the unorthodox combination of instruments called further attention to the novel sound. The traditional dance orchestra's violin-dominated ensemble of strings and woodwinds was replaced almost entirely by instruments formerly associated with folk music—mandolins, guitars, and banjos—or with symphonic music, such as the saxophone. (Up to this time, the saxophone had been used primarily by Europeans for special effects in their symphonic music and operas.) A final novelty was that the instrumentalists, except for those playing wind instruments, sang as they played. First to introduce the concept of the "singing band" to the entertainment world, the Students provided four-part harmony (now known as "barbershop harmony") for several of the musical numbers.[45]

Jim Europe left the musical theater about 1910, after completing his tenure as musical director for *Mr. Lode of Koal.* He turned his attention to organizing black musicians of New York into the Clef Club (1910) and to producing concerts at Carnegie Hall in the ensuing years. In 1913 he resigned from the Clef Club and formed the Tempo Club, an organization that also combined the functions of a musician's union and a contracting service.

In 1914 Jim Europe began an association with Vernon and Irene Castle, a white dance team, that brought fame to all three. The Castles popularized several ballroom dances; notably the turkey trot, the fox-trot, the one-step, and the Castle walk. Europe produced the kind of music for the Castles with his Tempo Club Band that helped them to become an institution in New York. He composed special music for their dances and directed the resident orchestra at their dance salon, the Castle House or "Castles-in-the-

---

[45]To be sure, members of Frank Johnson's band of the 1830s–40s sang as they played, much to the annoyance of some of the dancers.

Air," as it was called. Europe even invented several of the dances featured by the Castles; for example, the fox-trot and the turkey trot. His eleven-piece orchestra consisted of violins, cornets, clarinets, mandolins, drum, and piano. By 1914 Europe had become so important musically that the Victor Record Company signed him to a recording contract. It was the first time an African-American band had been so recognized.

A dance craze swept over the United States beginning in the second decade of the century and nowhere was it more obvious than in New York. In the 1890s the public had wanted songs to sing and to try out on the piano at home; after 1910 they wanted only dance music. Clef Club and Tempo Club men profited from the new fad. Their orchestras played in the big hotels, theaters, restaurants, clubs, and in private homes, on yachts, and at resorts. A tiny item appeared in *Variety* magazine in 1915: "Since the tur-key-trot craze, the colored musicians in New York have been busy dispensing syncopated music for the 400" (i.e., the cream of white society).[46]

The orchestra leaders who "dispensed" syncopated music for New York society were well trained, experienced, and ambitious. Like Jim Europe, they wrote much of the music that they played, and they arranged the rest of it. According to one publisher, Jim Europe and Ford Dabney wrote so many songs and marches that their names were spelled backwards on some sheet music in order to "lend an appearance of variety."[47] The music they played may not have been genuine ragtime, but it was nevertheless a lusty, joyful music, full of zest. Its distinctive sound derived not so much from syncopation as from the instrumentation (such as the use of saxophones), the way the men handled their instruments, and the way they produced their tones. It was an indoor music: the ensembles generally were small, with the violin, clarinet, or flute playing the lead.

James "Tim" Brymn (1881–1946), who led a twenty-piece band at the New York Roof Garden in 1915, was a musical director for Walker and William shows—he went to England with the show *In Dahomey* in 1904—and for The Smart Set for many years. He also wrote musical scores for Smart Set productions, including *The Black Politician* and *His Honor, the Barber*. During World War I the press cited his 350th Field Artillery Regiment band as having "introduced jazz into France."

Ford Dabney (1883–1958), who was the official court musician to the president of Haiti during the years 1904–7, settled at New York about 1913 and soon allied himself with the Clef Club and, later, the Tempo Club. He also was associated with Irene and Vernon Castle, along with Jim Europe, and wrote music for their dances. During the years 1913–21 his orchestra played regularly at the New Amsterdam Theatre on Broadway in the Zeigfeld Midnight Frolic Show—the first black orchestra to fill such a long

---

[46]Quoted in Samuel B. Charters and Leonard Kunstadt, *Jazz: A History of the New York Scene* (New York, 1962), p. 32.
[47]Marks, *They All Sang*, p. 158.

engagement. In later years Dabney continued his activities as a dance-band leader and composer; his best-known works included the Broadway musical *Rang Tang* (1927) and the song *That's Why They Call Me Shine* (1910, with Cecil Mack).

William H. Tyers (1876–1924), who conducted an orchestra at the Strand Roof Garden, was a close associate of Jim Europe's with both Clef Club and Tempo Club groups, and in 1919 he toured as an associate conductor with Will Marion Cook's New York Syncopated Orchestra. Tyers's songs were very popular with black bands, particularly *Panama, Maori* and *Trocha*.

Will Vodery (1885–1951), who conducted for the Coconut Grove at the Century Theatre Roof Garden in 1915, also was active as a musical director in the early years of his career. He settled at New York in about 1907, and soon attracted attention as a songwriter, arranger, musical director, and composer of scores for musicals. His early works included the musicals *The Time, the Place, and the Girl* (1907) and *The Oyster Man* (1909), a vehicle for Ernest Hogan. His association with Ziegfeld Follies as an arranger began in 1913 and lasted for twenty years.

During World War I, Vodery, along with Alfred Jack Thomas (1884–1962), attended the Bandmaster's School at Chaumont, France. After the war, Vodery returned to conducting orchestras, both theater and dance, and choral groups; and he arranged music for leading entertainers of the period, white and black. During the years 1929–33 he served as arranger and musical director for Fox Films in Hollywood, the first black musician to fill such a post. Vodery was revered by his contemporaries for his great arranging skills and his willingness to help advance the careers of black musicians.

During the crowded years in the African-American world of New York before World War I, several important events took place. About 1910 black folk began moving north into the area called Harlem; within a few years, Harlem would become the intellectual, artistic, and cultural capital of black America. In 1913 J. Leubrie Hill produced his musical *My Friend from Kentucky,* at Harlem's Lafayette Theatre, and Broadway audiences thronged to Harlem to see it. And, as we have seen, Florenz Ziegfeld was so impressed by what he heard that he bought numbers from it to use in his Follies of 1913, including "At the Ball," which featured a dance called "Ballin' the Jack." Once whites in search of entertainment had found their way to Harlem, the nightly migrations would continue for more than twenty years.

W. C. Handy's *Memphis Blues* made a big impact on New York in 1912, but the *St. Louis Blues* in 1914 made an even greater impression, especially on Harlem. Everyone began to sing blues, and all the songwriters began to write blues. In response to the public's interest in dancing, composers such as James P. Johnson and Luckey Roberts published dance rags and other kinds of dance music. Marks wrote that his publishing company fell back on its "corps of colored writers":

The new dancing rhythm, almost bare of melody, and Luckey Roberts, one of the hardest-pounding colored piano players of any weight, gave us *Pork and Beans* [1913], a perfect example of the genre. An Englishman once asked the Castle House orchestra for "that song without any tune," and they immediately responded with Luckey's composition.[48]

Willie "the Lion" Smith, who was playing rag music in Harlem clubs during this period, said that Clef Club musicians were "not allowed to rag it [their music] or beautify the melody [by] using their own ideas—they had to read those fly-spots [the music notes] closely and truly."[49] This was not the case in the dance halls and night clubs of Harlem. There, dance music was furnished by a three-man combination—consisting of piano, drummer, and banjoist or harmonica player—that poured out hot, raggy, improvised music for the patrons. At that time, Chicago was reputed to have the best black bands, but it was admitted that New York had the best pianists and drummers.

It was during this period that the so-called Ladies Orchestra became established in the entertainment world of black communities.[50] Although such groups dated back to the early twentieth century, they were generally directed by male musicians, and their repertories consisted primarily of concert music. Perhaps the first woman conductor to attract wide attention was Hallie Anderson (1885–1927), who directed a society dance orchestra in New York for many years and, beginning in 1905, promoted an Annual Reception and Ball for some seven or eight years.

Best known of the female leaders of syncopated orchestras was Marie Lucas (1880s–1947), daughter of the celebrated minstrel and vaudeville figure Sam Lucas. Beginning in 1915 her Famous Ladies Orchestra was one of the resident groups at the Lafayette and New Lincoln Theatres in Harlem; her groups also played regularly at theaters in Baltimore, Philadelphia, and Washington, D.C.

Like the male musicians, the women moved from one group to another. The most active women on the East Coast during this period included, in addition to Anderson and Lucas, Alice Calloway (drums), Mildred Franklin (violin), Pearl Gison (cornet), Leora Meaux (cornet), Mamie Mullen (piano), Olivia Porter (string bass), Ruth Reed (cornet), Maud Shelton (violin), Nellie Shelton (string bass), Eva Sinton (violin), Della Sutton (trombone), and Florence Washington (drums). Trombonist Mazie Mullins played with both male and female bands. In Chicago there was a female

---

[48]Marks, *They All Sang,* p. 158.
[49]Smith, *Music On My Mind,* p. 90.
[50]See further in Fletcher, *100 Years,* p. 76; the *Freeman,* August 19, 1916; the *Chicago Defender,* March 27, 1915; also D. Antoinette Handy, *Black Women in American Bands and Orchestras* (Metuchen, NJ, 1981).

"syncopated" group composed of Eddie Lange (cornet), Ethel Minor (piano), Gertrude Palmer (violin), and Marion Pankey (drums).

Syncopated Orchestras in Chicago and Other Cities

Chicago's Pekin Theatre became the center of musical activities in the black community early in the twentieth century. As we have already seen, Joe Jordan directed the music there and brought to the public a variety of dramatic and musical performances. By the second decade of the century, other places were beginning to compete with the Pekin—for example, the Royal Gardens (later called the Lincoln Gardens), the DeLuxe Café, and the Dreamland Café—all these located in the heart of Chicago's so-called Black Belt. Small dance ensembles played in the nightclubs, and in the theaters there were larger syncopated orchestras.

Shelton Brooks and Dave Peyton led orchestras at the Grand Theatre; Will Dorsey, Clarence Jones, and Wilbur Sweatman directed at the Monogram; and Erskine Tate held forth at the Vendome. In the nightclubs were entertainers such as rag pianist Tony Jackson, singer and songwriter Clarence Williams, and a women's group, the Panama Trio, composed of Cora Green, Ada "Bricktop" Smith, and Florence Mills.

Mills was later to become a celebrated figure in black theater. Jackson (1876–1921) had written a number of songs since leaving New Orleans in 1905, but he chose not to publish until about 1915. His first two publications, *Pretty Baby* and *You're Such a Pretty Thing,* were immediate hits. Later songs, among them, *Some Sweet Day,* were equally popular. Clarence Williams (1893–1965), also a native of New Orleans, was to make his mark later as a music publisher. But during these years, he was known for such songs as *Baby, Won't You Please Come Home, 'Tain't Nobody's Business If I Do,* and *West End Blues.*

Chicago, like New York and other urban centers, received thousands of black migrants from southern farms and plantations during World War I. Naturally the migrants included musicians, many of whom came directly to Chicago via Mississippi River boats or the railroads. By the summer of 1916 "the migration had reached flood tide"; in 1920 the Bureau of the Census report indicated that the black population of the North and West had increased by 330,000 persons since the last census count in 1910.[51] By 1918 the Chicago nightclubs were featuring newcomers to the city, particularly from New Orleans, as band musicians and singers. The Royal Gardens, for example, advertised that its resident band was the New Orleans Jazz Band. It was this band that Joe Oliver joined in 1918.

The leading exponents of Chicago's syncopated music during the early decades of the century were Dave Peyton (ca. 1885–1956) and Erskine Tate (1895–1978), not only because they directed the best orchestras over a long

[51]Franklin, *From Slavery to Freedom* p. 472.

number of years, but also because they nurtured the development of many young jazzmen, among them Louis Armstrong, Darnell Howard, Earl Hines, Milt Hinton, Eddie South, and "Fats" Waller. Both Peyton and Tate were highly versatile; their orchestras played theater and concert music, as well as dance music. For a period, beginning in 1914, Peyton also conducted a small symphony orchestra that gave concerts regularly.

Wilbur Sweatman (1882–1961) conducted theater orchestras in Chicago during the years 1910–13, then moved into the world of vaudeville. Shelton Brooks (1886–1975) played piano and sang in nightclubs and theaters; he received much attention for two songs he wrote, *Some of These Days* (1910) and *Darktown Strutter's Ball* (1917). In 1919 Will Marion Cook brought his New York Syncopated Orchestra into town to give concerts at Chicago's Orchestra Hall, thus acquainting audiences with the sound of New York's style of syncopated music. When he left, he took with him the young clarinetist Sidney Bechet, a native of New Orleans, who had been playing in a Chicago nightclub.

Syncopated orchestras flourished in other midwestern cities and in the West as well. In Detroit, for example, Benjamin Shook continued the traditions established by Old Man Finney's dance orchestras in the nineteenth century; based on the evidence, it is obvious that his orchestra was playing syncopated music during the war years. In Denver, Colorado, George Morrison (1891–1974) was an important dance-orchestra leader for many years. During the years 1917–19, he lived in Chicago, where he studied violin at the Columbia Conservatory of Music and played in nightclubs and in Dave Peyton's orchestra. The dance orchestra he formed upon his return to Denver undoubtedly reflected the influence of Chicago's syncopated style. Later, Morrison employed such jazzmen as Andy Kirk and Jimmie Lunceford. In San Francisco, it was D. W. McDonald and his La Estrella Mandolin Club that played for the social entertainments of the "Nob Hill" society set.

WORLD WAR I

The First World War began on July 28, 1914; nearly three years later, on April 6, 1917, the United States joined the struggle in declaring war on Germany. At this time there were about 20,000 blacks in the United States Army—10,000 in the four units of the regular army and 10,000 in various units of the National Guard. Upon the declaration of war, black men immediately began volunteering, to such an extent that the quota for black volunteers was filled within a week. Others entered the service as draftees. By the end of the war, more than 200,000 black men had served with the United States Army, in ranks from lowly private to captain and in all kinds of units except pilot sections of the aviation corps. They were not accepted into the Marines or Coast Guard, however, and were generally confined to menial duties in the Navy.

An unidentified army band on parade during World War I. *(Courtesy New York Public Library, Schomburg Center for Research in Black Culture)*

Most of the black units maintained their own bands, with black bandmasters, and some of the bands won distinction overseas for their exciting music and for their efforts to raise the morale of the soldiers on the front and in hospitals. Among such bands were the 349th Infantry under Norman Scott; the 351st under Dorsey Rhodes; the 367th, the so-called "Buffaloes," under Egbert Thompson; the 368th under Jack Thomas; and the 370th under George Dulf.

The most important bands were those under the direction of Clef Club New York's musicians: the 350th Infantry (formerly the Eighth Illinois) under Tim Brymn, the 807th under Will Vodery, and the 369th (formerly the Fifteenth New York) under Jim Europe. Brymn's band was known as the Seventy Black Devils of the U.S. 350th; rag pianist Willie "the Lion" Smith was a drum major in the band, which was as well known for its "jam sessions" (i.e., impromptu, informal gatherings of musicians to play dance music) as for its formal military concerts.

But it was the 369th Band, under the direction of Jim Europe, that won the most honors abroad for the United States. From the beginning of its organization, the band was marked for distinction. Europe, who had enlisted in the Fifteenth New York, was asked by the colonel in charge, William Hayward, to organize an army band that would measure up to his Clef Club and Tempo Club groups. Europe accepted the charge and, within a few months, had recruited a large number of men from all over the country, some coming from as far away as Puerto Rico. Egbert Thompson worked with Europe in training the band; Noble Sissle was a drum major.[52]

[52]James Reese Europe, "A Negro Explains Jazz," RBAM, p. 238. See further in regard to regimental bands in Emmett J. Scott, *Scott's Official History of the American Negro in the World War* (Washington, D.C., 1919), pp. 300–14.

An account of the war experiences of Europe's band is contained in the book *From Harlem to the Rhine* by Arthur Little, one of the officers of the regiment. Some of the band's experiences may be cited as generally illustrative of the activity of black bands in the armed services. When the band played for its first parade up Fifth Avenue in New York, the newly recruited soldiers of the regiment had had no official drill practice. But, as Little points out, the men were

> . . . natural born marchers and cadence observers. With a band playing, or with spectators cheering, they just couldn't be held from keeping step. That bright, sunny, Sunday morning we had both—the playing band and the cheering spectators. The churches had just concluded their services; and the crowds . . . were strolling along New York's wonderful promenade avenue as our picturesque organization swung up the line, to the brass toned expression of *Onward Christian Soldiers*.[53]

Once in France, Jim Europe's band became unique because of its excellent performance; Europeans were not accustomed to seeing and hearing black men on the concert stage. Although several of the Negro bands overseas spent some time in entertaining soldiers in hospitals and rest camps as well as those of their own units, Europe's band was the only one sent on a special mission to Aix-les-Bains (during the period February 12 to March 20, 1918) to play for the soldiers there on "rest and recreation" leave. En route, the band gave concerts in public squares of the towns and villages through which the army train passed. Its concerts were attended by thousands who crowded into the squares, maintaining perfect silence during the playing but after each number applauding wildly and giving out shrill whistles or catcalls.

In August 1918, Jim Europe was sent by Colonel Hayward to Paris to give only a "single concert." The band played in the Théâtre des Champs-Elysées. Europe recalled the occasion for a reporter:

> Before we had played two numbers the audience went wild. We had conquered Paris. General Bliss and French high officers who had heard us insisted that we should stay in Paris, and there we stayed for eight weeks. Everywhere we gave a concert it was a riot, but the supreme moment came in the Tuileries Gardens when we gave a concert in conjunction with the greatest bands in the world— the British Grenadiers' Band, the band of the Garde Républicain [sic], and the Royal Italian Band. My band, of course, could not compare with any of these, yet the crowd, and it was such a crowd as I never saw anywhere else in the world, deserted them for us. We played to 50,000 people at least, and, had we wished it, we might be playing yet.[54]

Later the music of Jim Europe's band would be called jazz. But it was not actually jazz for, as Europe stated, his men played the music strictly as it was written—that is, with regard for accuracy of pitch and note values. But Europe admitted to introducing certain innovations:

[53]Arthur Little, *From Harlem to the Rhine* (New York, 1936), p. 9.
[54]Europe, "A Negro Explains Jazz," p. 226.

With the brass instruments we put in mutes and make a whirling motion with the tongue, at the same time blowing full pressure. With wind instruments we pinch the mouthpiece and blow hard. This produces the peculiar sound which you all know. To us it is not discordant . . . we accent strongly in this manner the notes which originally would be without accent. It is natural for us to do this; it is, indeed, a racial musical characteristic. I have to call a daily rehearsal of my band to prevent the musicians from adding to their music more than I wish them to. Whenever possible they all embroider their parts in order to produce new, peculiar sounds.[55]

The bandsmen of the French Garde Républicaine were so impressed that they borrowed Europe's orchestrations in order to try to duplicate the sound. When their efforts were unsuccessful, they insisted upon examining the musical instruments of the black bandsmen, thinking perhaps that the instruments were different. So Paris came to know the sound of the African-American music that would later develop into jazz. The United States was immensely proud of Europe's band. A newspaper reporter for the *New York Times* wrote that Jim Europe produced an organization that "all Americans swore, and some Frenchmen admitted, was the best military band in the world."[56]

Songs of the War

Inevitably the war produced special war songs and a large amount of impromptu singing around campfires. Black and white soldiers sang such songs as *Over There, Keep the Home Fires Burning, There's a Long, Long Trail a-Winding, My Buddy,* and *Tipperary.* The Cole–Johnson trio made a contribution to war-song literature with *The Old Flag Never Touched the Ground.*[57] And Harry Burleigh wrote several war songs, among them *The Young Warrior* (poem by James Weldon Johnson, 1916), which was translated into Italian and used as a marching song by Italian regiments in World War I, and *Ethiopia Saluting the Colors* (1916, poem by Walt Whitman).

Overseas, white entertainers generally bypassed black army units, and there were no black entertainers available as there would be in later wars. But a small enterprising group, which included the Reverend Henry Hugh Proctor, song leader Joshua Blanton, and pianist Helen Hagan, traveled through France under the sponsorship of the War Camp Community Service and staged entertainment for black troops. One of Blanton's aims was to lead the soldiers in singing spirituals and to teach them new Negro folksongs.[58] Baritone William H. Richardson was active also in the "community sing" movement in the States during the war years.

A white pilot, John Jacob Niles, made a collection of the songs he heard

---

[55]Europe, p. 225.

[56]Editorial in the *New York Times,* May 12, 1919.

[57]Though composed in 1907 for the Cole–Johnson *Shoo-Fly Regiment* musical, *The Old Flag never Touched the Ground* was revived and performed again during the war.

[58]See further in Altona Trent Johns, "Henry Hugh Proctor," BPIM 3 (Spring 1975): 32; Henry

sung by black soldiers abroad and later published it in a book, *Singing Soldiers*. He avoided the music-hall ditties and Tin Pan Alley ballads, preferring to write down the songs of

> . . . the natural-born singers, usually from rural districts, who, prompted by hunger, wounds, homesickness, and the reaction to so many generations of suppression, sang the legend of the black man to tunes and harmonies they *made up* as they went along.[59]

Of the total number of twenty-nine melodies and many more song texts in the Niles collection, a considerable number are worksongs and blues. The soldiers sang parodies of ancient spirituals such as *Roll, Jordan, Roll* or *The Old Ark's a-Movering*. They contracted all kinds of blues: "the awful, deep-sea blues," "the holy hell, soldier-man blues," and "the jail-house blues." They sang about their labors, "diggin' in France," and how the

> Black man fights with the shovel and the pick . . .
> Never gets no rest 'cause he never gets sick . . .

and complained about their mode of life, "it's a hell of a life aboard of a destroyer." And there were the inevitable "lonesome songs":

> Oh, we're long gone from Alabama . . . from Georgia . . .
> And we may never see home again.
>
> I don't want anymore France,
> Jesus I want to go home.
>
> Oh, my, I'm too young to die—
> I want to go home.

At one performance of a traveling army show, Niles heard ten black soldiers sing a song in the ubiquitous call-and-response form, one man singing the innumerable verses and the others coming in on the refrain:

> My mama told me not to come over here
> But I did, did, did.

Niles was apparently unaware that in collecting songs of black soldiers he was following in the tradition established by the Civil War collectors Higginson, Ware, and Allen; at any rate, he does not mention the earlier collectors in his book.

After the War

The various black army bands that had "filled France with jazz" returned in triumph to proud, welcoming crowds in the United States. Jim Europe soon embarked on a nationwide tour with his sixty-five musicians,

---

Hugh Proctor, *Between Black and White* (Boston, 1925), p. 157; Scott, *The American Negro*, pp. 300–14.

[59]See further in John Jacob Niles, *Singing Soldiers* (Detroit, 1926).

the "best band the war produced." A critic reported on one of the concerts staged at the Manhattan Opera House in New York on March 16, 1919:

> There was a flood of good music, a gorgeous racket of syncopation and jazzing, extraordinarily-pleasing violin and cornet solos, and many other features that bands seldom offer.[60]

The band's repertory included all kinds of music, from medleys of operatic arias and overtures to blues. The former were frequently identified on the printed program as "highbrow" selections. In one of the band's favorite featured numbers, the *St. Louis Blues,* one player after another would play a solo (consisting of a variation on the blues melody), then the entire band would join in a rousing finale. According to contemporaneous reports, this performance never failed to bring audiences to their feet, "applauding and cheering." Invariably programs listed syncopated versions of standard works—such as Grieg's *Peer Gynt* Suite, for example, to which would be added the phrase "with respectful apologies to Mr. Grieg."

The world was shocked to learn of Jim Europe's murder by one of his bandsmen on May 10, 1919, during a band concert held at Mechanic's Hall in Boston. A *New York Times* editorial stated the sentiments felt by Americans in mourning the "untimely death of a man who ranked as one of the greatest ragtime conductors, perhaps the greatest, we ever had" and one who had enhanced American prestige overseas.[61]

In December 1918, Will Marion Cook organized the New York Syncopated Orchestra. He had scoured the country to find the best musicians possible for his group. In Chicago, as we have seen, he engaged Sidney Bechet (1897–1949), who would later win international fame as a jazz clarinetist and soprano saxist. One of his drummers was Buddy Gilmore, known widely for his role in the Memphis Students orchestra of 1905. Will Tyers served as Cook's assistant conductor; George Lattimore, as his business manager; and Tom Fletcher, as an assistant manager, advance agent, and performer.

After completing a four-month tour of the United States, Cook took his forty-one piece ensemble, now called the American Syncopated Orchestra, or the Southern Syncopated Orchestra, and nine singers to London and Paris. At the Royal Philharmonic Hall in London the group picked up a loyal fan, Swiss conductor Ernest Ansermet, who attended every performance and plied the performers with questions backstage after performances. Ansermet wrote a newspaper article praising the orchestra, "the astonishing perfection, the superb taste, and the fervour of its playing," Ansermet stated further:

> There is in the Southern Syncopated Orchestra an extraordinary clarinet virtuoso who is, it seems, the first of his race to have composed perfectly finished

---

[60]The *New York Sun*, March 17, 1919. Reproduced in the James Reese Europe Clipping Files at the Schomburg Center for Research in Black Culture in New York.

[61]Editorial in the *New York Times*, May 12, 1919.

blues for the clarinet. I have heard two of them [i.e., blues] that he has elaborated at length, then played to his fellows so that they might devise an accompaniment. Extremely different from each other, they were equally good in their rich invention, communicative power, and bold use of the new and unexpected. . . . I want to pass on the name of this artist of genius. For my part, I will never forget it. It is Sidney Bechet.[62]

On all his programs, Cook featured African-American folk music and the music of black composers as well as standard concert works; in a single evening, for example, his group might perform Brahms's Waltzes, Cook's own *Rain Song* or *Exhortation,* R. Nathaniel Dett's *Listen to the Lambs,* W. C. Handy's *Memphis Blues* or *St. Louis Blues,* and spirituals sung *a cappella.* The orchestra's makeup was somewhat unorthodox but in the tradition of Clef Club groups, consisting of violins, mandolins, banjos, guitars, saxophones, trumpets, trombones, French horns, timpani, pianos, and drums.

A highlight of Cook's stay in London was the command performance at Buckingham Palace in August 1919. Cook took about a quarter of his players to the Palace and arranged special numbers that featured Bechet as a soloist supported by a wind quartet. When King George V was asked which numbers he had liked best, his choice was Bechet's playing of *The Characteristic Blues.* In Paris, the Syncopated Orchestra performed at the Théâtre des Champs-Elysées and the Apollo Theatre in Montmartre, and toured in the provinces.

Back in the United States in 1922, Cook organized a Clef Club Orchestra that served as the core of a touring musical-show company. Two members of the company, singer-actor Paul Robeson and actor-orator Richard B. Harrison, were destined to become famous in the concert world and on the stage.

SUMMARY

The several decades between the end of the Civil War and the beginning of World War I represent an important era in the history of black music—an era which might be regarded as one of transition. Slavery had forced black Americans to center all their creative energy and collective will upon obtaining the rights promised in the Declaration of Independence—life, liberty, and the pursuit of happiness. With the Emancipation came freedom not only in regard to civil rights, but in other respects as well—for example, mobility. It was as if black musicians were caught up in a huge cultural whirlwind that scattered them in a thousand directions.

They were free to go as they pleased, so they traversed the globe many times over with their jubilee singers, concert companies, minstrel groups,

[62]Quoted in Howard Rye, "The Southern Syncopated Orchestra," in *Under the Imperial Carpet* (Crawley, England, 1986), pp. 220–21.

and vaudeville troupes. They were free to sing whatever they pleased, and they brought into existence new song genres, such as the blues and early gospel. After years of confinement primarily to the fiddle and banjo, they were free to play any instrument they wished, and they invented piano ragtime. Above all, they gave full range to their propensity for improvisation in whatever they sang or played.

It was a time of musical beginnings. In the manner of African-American composers everywhere and at all times, they drew upon the repertory already in their possession—that is, the slave songs—in fashioning the new music. But it *was* a new music!

PART FOUR

LIFT
EVERY
VOICE

1920–1996

Lift every voice and sing,
Till earth and heaven ring,
Ring with the harmonies of liberty; . . .
Facing the rising sun
Of our new day begun,
Let us march on till victory is won.

—JAMES WELDON JOHNSON AND
J. ROSAMOND JOHNSON

IMPORTANT EVENTS

1920 Beginning of regularly scheduled programs on radio: Pittsburgh, PA., station KDKA.

Beginning of "race records" series: recording of Mamie Smith at New York.

1921 Return of black musicals to Broadway, beginning with Sissle and Blake's *Shuffle Along*.

Publication of *Gospel Pearls* by the Baptist National Convention, U.S.A.

Founding of the first black record company: Pace Phonograph Company with the Black Swan label.

Opening of the Eastman School of Music at Rochester, NY.

1923 Opening of the Juilliard School of Music at New York (merged with the Institute of Musical Art in 1926).

Founding of the League of Composers.

1925 Institution of the John Simon Guggenheim Foundation fellowships for improvement in the arts and education for all Americans, regardless of color.

1926 Establishment of the Schomburg Collection of Literature and History at New York (as part of the public library system; name changed to Schomburg Center for Research in Black Culture in 1980).

Institution of the William E. Harmon Foundation awards for achievement by an individual black artist.

1927 Institution of the Rodman Wanamaker Musical Composition Prizes for black composers.

1928 First "black-music survey" concert at Carnegie Hall in New York, including music from spirituals to jazz and symphonic music: W. C. Handy's Orchestra and Jubilee Singers.

1929 Beginning of the Great Depression.

First major film musical with black cast, *Hallelujah*, directed by King Vidor.

1930 First public endorsement of gospel at the Jubilee annual meeting of the National Baptist Convention, U.S.A., at Chicago.

Establishment of first chair of musicology in the United States at Cornell University.

1931 First performance by a major orchestra of a black composer's symphony: the *Afro-American Symphony* by William Grant Still; Rochester (New York) Philharmonic Symphony Orchestra.

Organizing of the first gospel choirs, by Thomas A. Dorsey and Theodore Frye at Chicago.

1932 Founding of the National Convention of Gospel Choirs and Choruses by Dorsey at Chicago.

Sound of "new music" predicted in *It Don't Mean a Thing If It Ain't Got That Swing* by Duke Ellington.

1933 Century of Progress Exposition at Chicago; Chicago Symphony performs Florence Price's Symphony in E minor at an Exposition concert.

First production on Broadway of a Negro folk opera written by a black composer: *Run Little Chillun* by Hall Johnson.

1934 First production on Broadway of an opera with black cast: *Four Saints in Three Acts* by Virgil Thomson.

Founding of the American Musicological Society.

The Philadelphia Orchestra performs William Dawson's *Negro Folk Symphony*.

1935 Establishment of the Federal Arts Projects of the Works Progress Administration; provided work for unemployed creative artists and performers.

Production on Broadway of second opera with a black cast: *Porgy and Bess*, by George Gershwin.

Inauguration of the annual Berkshire Music Festivals at Stockbridge, MA.

1936 Organization of the National Negro Congress, including more than 500 black organizations.

1937 Founding of the Southern Youth Negro Congress.

Founding of the American Composers Alliance, Inc.

IMPORTANT EVENTS

1938 Production of a "black-music survey" concert, From Spirituals to Swing, at Carnegie Hall by John Hammond.

Rosetta Tharpe takes gospel out of the church into the Cotton Club, a nightclub in Harlem.

1939 Golden Gate International Exposition at San Francisco.

New York World's Fair; music of William Grant Still played continuously at the Perisphere for the Theme Exhibit.

Ferdinand "Jelly Roll" Morton records a *History of Jazz* for the Archive of American Folksong at the Library of Congress.

John Hammond produces a second concert, From Spirituals to Swing, at Carnegie Hall in New York.

1940 Founding of BMI (Broadcast Music, Incorporated).

1941 World War II (1941–45).

Huge migration of black Americans out of the South into the North and West during the war years.

Emergence of bebop at jazz sessions in Harlem.

Debut of first permanent black opera company, the National Negro Opera Company (1941–62), in Pittsburgh, organized by black musician Mary Cardwell Dawson.

1942 Founding of the Congress of Racial Equality.

1945 First performance by a black singer with a major opera company: Todd Duncan with the New York City Opera; followed by Camilla Williams in 1946.

1948 Beginning of regular appearances of black entertainers on television variety shows, particularly on the Ed Sullivan Show.

1949 First production of an opera written by a black composer, *Troubled Island* (1941) by William Grant Still, by a major opera company, the New York City Opera.

Popular music industry uses the term *rhythm 'n' blues* for the first time,

replacing the older term *race records*.

1950 First mammoth all-gospel concert: at Carnegie Hall in New York, featuring Mahalia Jackson.

1951 First appearance of black concert artists on television shows: William Warfield and Muriel Rahn on the Ed Sullivan Show, followed by Marian Anderson in 1952.

1954 Supreme Court decision overturns legal segregation of public schools in the South.

First Newport Jazz Festival at Newport, RI.

First recording of a rock 'n' roll song: *Sh-Boom,* by the Chords.

1955 Beginning of the Montgomery, Alabama boycott of public buses; beginning of the black Civil Rights revolution.

First performance by a black singer with the Metropolitan Opera Company: Marian Anderson in Verdi's *Un ballo in maschera* (A Masked Ball); followed by Robert McFerrin in 1955 and Mattiwilda Dobbs in 1956.

First appearance of a black singer in a television opera: Leontyne Price in Puccini's *Tosca* on NBC.

1958 Founding of the Monterey Jazz Festivals at Monterey, CA.

The legendary Savoy Ballroom (opened in 1926), which was called the "home of the happy feet" and "cradle of stars," closes its doors.

1960 First "sit-ins" of black college students protesting discrimination in places of public accommodation at Greensboro, NC.

1962 Founding of the American Folk Blues Festival by bluesmen Willie Dixon and "Memphis Slim" Peter Chatman.

1963 Mammoth March on Washington for "jobs and freedom" for all, regardless of race and color, at Washington, D.C.

Century of Negro Progress Exhibition (1863–1963) at Chicago.

1964 Enactment of the Civil Rights Act by Congress, the first to bring about significant progress in the area of civil rights; included the establishment of the Equal Employment Opportunity Commission.

First tours of important English rock groups in the United States, beginning with the Beatles, following by the Rolling Stones and others.

1965 First jazz concert in a major church: Duke Ellington's sacred-music concert at Grace Cathedral Church in San Francisco.

Debut concert of the Symphony of the New World (1965–76) at Carnegie Hall in New York.

Establishment of the National Endowment for the Arts and the National Endowment for the Humanities by the federal government.

1966 Black Americans perform at the First World Festival of Negro Arts at Dakar, Senegal.

1967 John Hammond produces a third concert, From Spirituals to Swing, at Carnegie Hall in New York.

1968 Organization of the Society of Black Composers at New York.

Composer Olly Wilson wins first place with his *Cetus* in the First International Electronic Music Competition at Dartmouth, NH.

1969 Founding of AAMOA (Afro-American Music Opportunities Association) by C. Edward Thomas at Minneapolis, MN: AAMOA promoted Black Composer Symposia and the Black Composer Series (in collaboration with Columbia Records).

Sound of "jazz in the seventies" predicted in the Miles Davis album *Bitches Brew.*

1970 Founding of Opera / South at Jackson, MS.

1972 World premiere of Scott Joplin's opera *Treemonisha* at Atlanta.

1974 Founding of Opera Ebony at Philadelphia.

1976 United States celebrates its Bicentennial Birthday.

1977 Black-American artists perform and

scholars present papers at the Second World Black and African Festival of Arts and Culture (called FESTAC) at Lagos, Nigeria.

Celebration of Black Composers, a week-long series of concerts, at New York.

1979 National Black Music Colloquium and Competition (1979–80) sponsored by the John F. Kennedy Center for the Performing Arts at Washington, D.C.

Smithsonian Institution inaugurates a Black Gospel Music Concert Series at Washington, D.C.

Kennedy Center for the Performing Arts, Washington, D.C., establishes its Honor Awards, to be given in recognition of artists who have made distinguished contributions to the performing arts over a lifetime. Each year's awardees include African-American artists.

Sugar Hill Records, NY, an independent African-American label, releases first rap single, "Rapper's Delight," which quickly sold 500,000 copies.

1980 The Schomburg Center for Research in Black Culture (of the New York Public Library), which houses the world's largest collection of materials about peoples of African descent, moves into a new multi-million-dollar facility.

Black Entertainment Television (BET cable) founded by Robert L. Johnson.

1981 Publication of a pioneering collection of hymns, spirituals, and gospel songs, *Songs of Zion,* as a supplement to the official hymnal of the United Methodist Church.

The National Endowment for the Arts establishes a National Heritage Fellowship Program through its Folk Arts Program.

1982 The Church of God in Christ (COGIC) publishes an official hymnal for the first time in its history. *Yes Lord! The Church of God in Christ Hymnal.*

IMPORTANT EVENTS

Congress votes to extend the Civil Rights Act of 1965 (also known as the Voting Rights Act) despite strong opposition of some Congressmen. Affirmative Rights program especially benefits African-American students and faculty in white academe.

1984 Michael Jackson's record album "Thriller" becomes the best-selling album in pop-music history.

The first annual nationwide telethon of the United Negro College Fund raises more than $14 million for its historically black college and university members.

1987 Congress passes a resolution declaring jazz "a rare and valuable national American treasure."

1990 U.S. Census Bureau reports black population in the U.S. includes 14.7 million men and 16.8 million women; New York state has nation's largest, with 2.7 million. California is second, with 2.1 million.

1992 Awadagin Pratt becomes the first African American to win the Walter W. Naumburg International Piano Competition.

1995 The Million Man March on Washington, D.C. takes place on October 16. Hundreds of thousands of African-American men (and some women) rally behind Minister Louis Farrakhan in search of spiritual renewal and atonement.

Lincoln Center for the Performing Arts in New York City establishes a jazz department on equal terms with opera and symphony orchestra.

1996 Pianist George Walker becomes first African American to win a Pulitzer Prize in Music (Composition).

Black and white congregations of the Pentecostal Church unite, forming the Pentecostal-Charismatic Churches of North America. Of the 18 million members, a third are African Americans.

CHAPTER 10

The
Jazz
Age

F ROM the fusion of blues, ragtime, brass-band music, and syncopated dance music came jazz, a genre that developed its own style and reper- tory.

Regarding the origin of the word jazz, various theories have been advanced over the years. James Europe denied, for example, having given an explanation that was attributed to him in the press—that the word *jazz* represented a corruption of "razz," the name of a Negro band active in New Orleans about 1905. It is noteworthy, however, that all of the theories suggest that the word is to be associated in one way or another with the folk music of African Americans, either in the United States or in Africa.[1]

Undoubtedly, the word jazz had circulated orally for some time before anyone found a need to see it in print. Some historians trace its origin back to about 1912, when the press began referring to the white dance bands that flourished in the larger cities as "Jazz Bands."[2]

The trade-journal *Variety* identified Chicago as the most innovative in its support of the new dance music, but New York City, too, had a contribu- tion to make, and it came not from musicians but from painters. In 1913 the city was host to the International Exhibition of Modern Art, better known as the Armory Show, where Americans were exposed for the first

---

[1]See, for example, James Reese Europe, "A Negro Explains Jazz," RBAM, p. 238.
[2]John Tasker Howard and George Bellows, *A Short History of Music in America* (New York, 1957), p. 215. See also Southern and Wright, *African American Traditions*, pp. 265–66.

time to Europe's most avant-garde paintings and sculptures, and some Europeans were exposed for the first time to African-American cultures.

Francis Picabia and Albert Gleizes were so inspired by their contacts with black culture that they produced paintings on the subject: Picabia called his two paintings *Chanson negre 1* and *2* (both 1913) and Gleizes named his paintings *Composition for Jazz* (1915). Based on available evidence, the catalogue for the exhibition contains the earliest reference in print to jazz as a musical genre. It was the American painter Charles Demuth, however, who made the definitive contribution to the early history of jazz: his watercolors, which date from 1915 to 1919, depict jazz trios (piano, drums, banjo) and singers (male, female) and carry such titles as "Negro Jazz Band" and "Cabaret."

Ironically, the first groups to formally introduce the music called jass or jazz to the public were white dance orchestras from New Orleans. In 1915 the Lamb's Club of Chicago hired a white band, under the direction of Tom Brown, that was billed as "Brown's Dixieland Jass Band, Direct from New Orleans, Best Dance Music in Chicago." Two years later an orchestra led by Nick LaRocca, the Original Dixieland Jazz Band, opened at the Reisenweber Café in New York and made musical history, for during the same year LaRocca's band made the first recordings of jazz music. According to legend, the Victor Recording Company offered a contract to Freddie Keppard and his Original Creole Band, but Keppard refused it for fear that other trumpet players might steal his musical ideas. But Victor did make a test recording of a black band, the Creole Jass Band playing *Tack 'em Down,* on December 2, 1918. Presumably this was the group managed by William "Bill" Johnson.

In the black tenderloin districts of villages and large cities throughout the nation, black ensembles (or "combos") continued to play the kind of music they had been playing for many years, a blues-rag kind of music, most frequently performed by a pianist, drummer, and banjoist or harmonica player or by a lone pianist. Few of the black players were aware that their kind of music was invading the dance spots of white America, and there is no evidence that they consistently used the word "jazz" in reference to their music before the 1920s. The leaders of large black dance orchestras in such places as New York, Chicago, Denver, Memphis, St. Louis, and Kansas City must have known that the term *jazz* was being applied to dance orchestras, but they did not make immediate changes in the names of their groups. They were doing quite well, after all, as "syncopated orchestras."

There were, however, a few exceptions; as early as 1916 pianist-songwriter W. Benton Overstreet used the term *jass* in reference to back-up groups he directed for the vaudeville acts of Estelle Harris at the Grand Theatre in Chicago. And the songs that Harris featured in her act included two with the word *jazz* in their titles—*Jazz Dance* (copyrighted 1917) and *That Alabama Jazbo Band* (1918). According to the black press, *Jazz Dance* was used by more black vaudeville acts than any other song ever published.

In September 1917 W. C. Handy recorded a song titled *The Jazz Dance,* which may have been the Overstreet song; and in March 1919 James Reese Europe recorded the song with his Hell-Fighter's Band.[3]

By 1918 the term *jazz* had moved into common usage. Black regimental bands fighting overseas in World War I were identified as jazz bands, and both black and white newspapers published articles about the new music. In April 1918 W. C. Handy staged a "jass and blues concert" at the Selwyn Theatre in New York, assisted by Fred Bryan, "the Jazz Sousa." And The Smart Set toured with a musical comedy, *Bamboula,* that was described as a jazzonian opera.

During the last half of the second decade, two phenomena occurred that greatly affected the development of jazz. As we have seen, there was a wholesale migration of blacks out of the South beginning about 1915. They left not only because of the depressed economic conditions in the South, but also because they were beginning to feel that there would never be relief from the unrelenting pressures of discrimination and disfranchisement and from the terrors of lynching. Since the end of the Civil War there had been more than 3,600 lynchings, most of them in southern states, but some also in the Midwest. Then, with the beginning of the twentieth century, a succession of race riots had swept over the country, and again these were concentrated for the most part in the South.

Northern industry accepted the migrants; black men were able to obtain good jobs, many for the first time, in factories and shipbuilding yards and on the railroads. In the ghettos of the northern cities, nightclubs and eating places flourished as never before, and the newcomers demanded "their kind of music" from the entertainers—that is, the blues. The second phenomenon was the exodus of tenderloin musicians from New Orleans because of the closing down of Storyville in 1917 by order of the United States Navy. The displaced music makers went "up the river," to Memphis and other river towns, and continued north to Chicago.

CHARACTERISTICS OF JAZZ

The most distinctive features of jazz derive directly from the blues. Jazz is a vocally oriented music; its players replace the voice with their instruments, but try to recreate the voice's singing style and blue notes by using scooping, sliding, whining, growling, falsetto, and the like. Jazz, like the blues, emphasizes individualism. The performer is at the same time the composer, shaping the music into style and form. A traditional melody or harmonic

[3]Early uses of the terms *jass* or *jazz* by black musicians are found on the stage-news pages of the *Chicago Defender,* September 30, 1916, October 14, 1916. See also Harold H. Hartel, "The H³ Chrono-Matrix File," *Record Research,* Issue 175 (September 1980): 5–9, which is Part I of a chronological listing of jazz or jazz-related recordings made during the years 1897–1942.

framework may serve as the takeoff point for improvisation, but it is the personality of the player and the way he or she improvises that produces the music. Like the blues tune, the preexistent core of musical material used by jazz players is generally short. The length of the jazz piece derives from repetition of the basic material.

Jazz is primarily an aural music: its written score represents but a skeleton of what actually takes place during a performance. Performances of the same work differ from player to player, for each one recreates the music in his or her own individual way. Jazz is learned through oral tradition, as is folksong, and those who would learn to play it do so by listening to others playing jazz. Finally, jazz uses the call-and-response style of the blues, by employing an antiphonal relationship between two solo instruments or between solo and ensemble.

The influence of ragtime is represented in jazz by the emphasis on syncopation and the presence of the piano in the ensemble. The influence of the brass band reveals itself in the jazz instrumentation, in the roles assigned to each instrument, and in the resulting musical texture. In the classic New Orleans band, for example, the "front line" consisted of three instruments that were given melodic roles; the cornet typically played the lead, the clarinet played a countermelody, and the trombone played the lower voice of the trio. The "back line" instruments—the drums, banjos, guitars, and basses—functioned as the rhythm section. Although pianos were added to jazz bands from the beginning, and often a second cornet as well, the instrumentation remained basically the same as in brass bands. Later, trumpets began to replace cornets, and saxophones were added or used in place of clarinets. The addition of saxophones suggests the influence of the syncopated dance orchestra which, as we have seen, used saxophones early in its development.

The brass band emphasized the ensemble sound, as distinguished from solo music, and this tradition, too, passed over into the performances of the early jazz bands. In many jazz performances of the early 1920s, for example, all of the instruments play throughout the piece, the cornet always retaining the lead melody. In performances that include solo passages, the other instruments typically give firm support, particularly the rhythm section. The ensemble sound of the band was basically polyphonic in nature, not chordal. As many as two or three clearly defined melodic lines dominated the texture, and frequently the rhythm instruments furnished little countermelodies.

To summarize, jazz was a new music created from the synthesis of certain elements in the style of its precursors. Its most striking feature was the exotic sound, which was produced not only by the kinds of instruments used in the orchestra, but also from the manner in which these instruments were played. Little attention was paid to "correct" intonation (i.e., playing strictly in tune), for example, or to obtaining exact pitches. Instead, the players glided freely from one tone to another (or through long series of tones in glissandos) and frequently fluctuated the pitches of sustained tones (i.e., used a wide vibrato). Equally striking was the rhythmic intensity of the early jazz music, derived from solid, driving, four-beats-to-the-measure rhythms coupled with strong accents on beats one and three.

The polyphonic texture of the music was a result of "collective improvisation," with each melody player improvising his or her part in such a way that the parts combined into a balanced, integrated whole. The concept of jazz improvisation was to change its implications over the years. In this early period, the performer *embellished* the melody, adding extra tones and altering rhythmic patterns, but in such a manner as to retain the essential shape of the original melody. Similar techniques were applied to choral improvisation. The sound of jazz was in the same tradition as the slaves' singing of spirituals, which produced the effect of "a marvellous complication and variety" of sounds "sung in perfect time."

Jazz developed its own special repertory of melodies and compositions that served as bases for improvisatory elaborations. Among the popular staples of the 1920s were pieces by black composers, such as *Panama* (Will Tyers), *Didn't He Ramble* (pseud. Will Handy for Bob Cole and the Johnson brothers), *Original Rags* and *Maple Leaf Rag* (Joplin), the *Beale Street Blues* and the *St. Louis Blues* (Handy); marches and dance pieces, such as drags, stomps, and shuffles; some traditional worksongs, such as *John Henry*, and spirituals like *Down by the Riverside* (or, *Ain't Goin' to Study War no More*); and above all, blues melodies of all kinds, traditional and composed.

Jazz also had its own special vocabulary: a *break,* for example, was a brief flurry of notes played by the soloist during a pause in the ensemble playing; a *riff* was a short phrase repeated over and over again by the ensemble; *scat singing* meant singing nonsense vocables instead of words; a *sideman* was any member of the orchestra other than the leader.

The main materials of early jazz history are phonograph records. It was in April 1923 that the Paramount Company began to record extensively King Oliver's Creole Jazz Band in Chicago. The history may quite properly begin, however, three years earlier, when the recording of blues and jazz first got underway.

RACE RECORDS

The earliest documented recording of a black female singer took place on February 14, 1920, at New York in the studio of the General Phonograph Corporation, which issued the OKeh label (but see p. 309 in regard to male singers and bands). The singer was Mamie Smith (1883–1946), a vaudeville and cabaret singer; her manager was Perry Bradford, a black songwriter, who wrote the two "character songs" she sang—*You Can't Keep a Good Man Down* and *This Thing Called Love*. Encouraged by the public response to this record, OKeh recorded her again on August 10, singing two more Bradford songs, *Crazy Blues* and *It's Right Here for You*.[4]

The demand for this record in black communities was so enormous that OKeh realized for the first time the vast potential market among blacks for blues and blues-jazz. In the summer of 1921 the company established its OKeh "Original Race Records," starting with the series number 8001. A black musical director, Clarence Williams (1893–1965), was hired who aggressively sought the best blues and jazz people of the time. Mamie Smith made more recordings with her Jazz Hounds; those who followed her included jazzmen Louis Armstrong, King Oliver, and Williams himself; blues singers Lonnie Johnson, Sara Martin, Victoria Spivey, and Sippie Wallace, among others; and preachers J. M. Gates and Elder Richard Bryant. For almost fifteen years OKeh was the leading label in the race-records market—recordings of black dance bands were also released in its 40000 series; in later years Columbia acquired the label, but made few releases until the 1950s, when it was reactivated for the rhythm 'n' blues market.

The race-record industry was off with a bang! Other companies soon pushed into the market: Columbia, during the years 1923–33, with its 14000-D series featuring stars such as Bessie Smith, Ethel Waters, and Clara Smith; Paramount (1922–32) with its 12000 series, called "The Popular Race Records," and such singers as Alberta Hunter, Ida Cox, Charley Patton, and "Blind" Lemon Jefferson. The several smaller companies that entered the market included Vocalion in 1926 (merged with Brunswick in 1931), Victor in 1927, Gennett, Emerson, Arto, and Pathé Actuelle, among others. Black songwriter J. Mayo "Ink" Williams (1894–1980) was a recording director and talent scout for Paramount, Gennett, Vocalion and, later, Decca. In 1927, he launched his own label, Black Patti, which was short-lived.

Early Black Recording Companies

Harry Pace (1884–1943) settled in New York in 1918 when the music publishing company he owned with W. C. Handy (1873–1958) moved there from Memphis, Tennessee. In January 1921, however, Pace and Handy dissolved their partnership, and Pace set up the Pace Phonograph Company, which pressed records on the Black Swan label. Obviously, Pace chose the name in memory of Elizabeth Taylor Greenfield, the nation's first black concert singer. Like Greenfield, Pace made his mark on music history; his company is credited with being the first recording company to be owned and operated by African Americans.[5]

---

[4]See further in regard to the development of race records in Brian Rust, *The American Record Label Book* (New Rochelle, NY, 1978).

[5]The story of the Pace Phonograph Company and its recording artists is told in detail in Walter C. Allen, *Hendersonia*.

Pace brought in Fletcher Henderson (1897–1952) as recording manager and William Grant Still (1895–1978) as arranger (later, musical director), both of them former employees of the Pace–Handy music publishing company. Within a period of three months, Pace's first releases were available. The first record featured baritone C. Carroll Clark. During those early months, Pace recorded concert sopranos Revella Hughes and Florence Cole Talbert; blues singers Alberta Hunter and Ethel Waters; the vaudeville duo Henry Creamer and J. Turner Layton and vaudevillians Essie Whitman and Katie Crippen; violinist Kemper Harreld; the Four Harmony Kings quartet; and dance bands, including Fletcher Henderson's Novelty Orchestra. The Black Swan's repertory consisted of light classical pieces, spirituals, blues, ballads, piano and violin solos, and character songs.

Ethel Waters (1896–1977) made Black Swan's first big successful records, *Down Home Blues* and *Oh, Daddy,* in the spring of 1921. She had come to New York in 1919 and established herself as one of Harlem's leading entertainers, billed as "Sweet Mama Stringbean." In the fall of 1921 Pace sent her on the road with the Black Swan Troubadours, directed by Henderson, to advertise his records, and started her on the road to stardom. She won wide recognition for her blues singing, particularly on the vaudeville circuit.

Although Pace engaged some of the best artists of his time, the competition from the white record companies proved to be overwhelming. In 1923 his business began to falter; he declared bankruptcy in December of that year, and, in March 1924, sold the Black Swan label to Paramount Records, which set aside its race series numbers 12100–12189 for Black Swan reissues. The *Chicago Defender* noted Pace's failure, but pointed out that he nevertheless had accomplished three things: (1) he had forced white record companies to recognize the large market for recordings by black performers; (2) he had forced the companies to publish race-music catalogues; and (3) he had forced them to advertise in black newspapers.

Women and Blues

The early 1920s was the golden era of the black female blues singer.[6] Talent scouts scoured the South and black communities in the North, looking for singers to equal Mamie Smith. Before the end of 1920, Lucille Hegamin had been signed up to make records, and the next year brought into the fold Alberta Hunter, Trixie Smith, Edith Wilson, and, as we have seen, Ethel Waters.

[6]Daphe Duval Harrison, *Black Pearls: Blues Queens of the 1920s* (New Brunswick, NJ, 1988), p. 45. See the Bibliography for sources of information about early blues and jazz people. In addition to the titles of biographies and surveys listed there are periodicals that regularly publish interviews with these musicians, such as *Living Blues* and *Cadence.*

Bessie Smith. *(Courtesy Corbis-Bettman)*

The list of important blueswomen is long, and the regal titles given them by their fans and the public suggest the high regard in which they were held. Gertrude "Ma" Rainey (1886–1939) was the oldest. Called "Mother of the Blues," she forged a link between the rural blues of the South and the sophisticated blues of urban centers. She sang blues on her tent-show programs as early as 1902 and was a celebrity long before she began to record in 1923.

"Empress of the Blues" Bessie Smith (1894–1937) became the most famous of the women. By 1912 she was touring professionally with a troupe, which also featured "Ma" Rainey, and by 1914 she was on the road to stardom. Her first recordings in 1923, *Down Hearted Blues* (written by Alberta Hunter and Lovie Austin) and *Gulf Coast Blues,* sold a million copies within the first year. Her blues had the earthiness and raw intensity of country blues despite her sophistication. She recorded prolifically during the years 1923–31 and toured extensively, both with her own shows, such as the Harlem Frolics, and with other shows. She was the featured performer in 1929 in the two-reel film *St. Louis Blues.*

Lucille Hegamin (1894–1970), "The Cameo Girl," toured on the vaudeville circuit for many years with her husband, Bill Hegamin, and their Flame Syncopators. In later years she was active in musical revues and comedies. Ida Cox (1896–1967) was the "Uncrowned Queen of the Blues," Clara Smith (ca. 1894–1935) was "Queen of the Moaners," and Edith Wilson (1896–1981) was also called "Queen of the Blues." Wilson toured on the vaudeville circuit and played in musicals both on Broadway and on the road, including Sam Wooding's *Chocolate Kiddies* in Europe (1925). She was best known as the Aunt Jemima who promoted Quaker Oats through musical performance for more than twenty years on radio and television and in personal appearances at schools and other community institutions.

Alberta Hunter (1895–1984), called "Prima Donna of Blues Singers," went to Chicago after recording with the Black Swan in New York, and picked up her recording career there; she sang in nightclubs, toured on the vaudeville circuit, and took part in revues. About 1927 she went to Europe, where she sang in musicals—including *Show Boat* in the London production that featured Paul Robeson—and in nightclubs over all the continent. After World War II she returned home, prepared for a nursing career, and worked in a New York hospital for twenty years (1957–77). At the age of eighty-one she successfully picked up her entertainment career once again and enjoyed a revival of public interest until her death. Hunter is credited with having introduced the female blues singer to Europe.

Victoria "Queen" Spivey (1906–1976) enjoyed the longest career of any of the celebrated blueswomen. Although she left the blues clubs in the 1950s to work in the church, she returned to her career in the sixties, established her own recording company, and sang in clubs up to the time of her death.

Beulah "Sippie" Wallace (1898–1986) was active in church music longer than most of her blues contemporaries, but she too returned to blues singing in her old age, and made a successful career of it. The women listed above represent only a few of the female blues singers that made the 1920s and '30s such important periods in the history of blues. Some went on to longer and more prosperous careers; others are unknown today. Oddly, the singer who started it all, Mamie Smith with her historic recordings of the *Crazy Blues* and the other first race records in 1920, did not pick up a sobriquet, yet everyone knew about Mamie Smith and her Jazz Hounds.

Blues scholars have found it difficult to describe adequately the quality and style of the blueswomen's voices, which ranged from lilting soprano to deep contralto, from expressive, soulful wails to abrasive, gut-bucket groans and moans. Since most of the women were vaudeville artists, their singing inevitably reflected a sophisticated approach to the song material. The vaudeville-blues often were written expressly for the singers, who sang them in "artificial" surroundings—the cabaret, the stage, or the recording studio—not in the cotton fields or on the dusty roads.

Some of the leading black songwriters of the time wrote for the blues queens, among them Clarence Williams, Thomas "Fats" Waller, Charles Warfield, Alex Hill, Perry Bradford, and Chris Smith. Some of the queens, including Ida Cox, "Ma" Rainey, Victoria Spivey, and Bessie Smith, wrote their own songs. Typically, the blueswomen sang to the accompaniment of a piano or a trio consisting of piano, cornet or clarinet, and rhythm instruments. On some of Mamie Smith's recordings, she was accompanied by James P. Johnson (piano), Ward Andrews (trombone), Ernest Elliott (clarinet), and Leroy Parker (violin).

The blueswomen were consummate entertainers who knew how to put over a song. They sang of love, jealousy, sweet revenge, bad luck, and the other hundreds of things that were important in the lives of city women. In the following lament, with words and music by Bessie Smith, the singer's depression is palpable, though she cannot adequately express her feelings:

> Settin' in the house with ev'rything on my mind,
> Settin' in the house with ev'rything on my mind.
> Lookin' at the clock an' can't even tell the time.
>
> Walkin' to my window, and lookin' out of my door.
> Walkin' to my window, and lookin' out of my door.
> Wishin' that my man would come home once more.
>
> Can't eat, can't sleep, so weak I can't walk my floor.
> Can't eat, can't sleep, so weak I can't walk my floor.
> Feel like hollerin' let the Police Squad get me once more. Etc.

Downhome Blues

Beginning about 1924 recording companies shifted their interest in blues from the sophisticated ballads of the blues queens to the rural, "downhome" blues,[7] which was performed by males to the accompaniment of a guitar or a banjo, the string band or jug band. The former band consisted of fiddles, banjos, guitars, mandolins, and string basses; the latter, of ordinary crockery jugs, banjos, harmonicas, mandolins, toy instruments called kazoos, and household washboards. As in the early 1920s, talent scouts again scoured the country looking for genuine folk bluesmen; after finding them, some companies took them North to be recorded in studios, while others recorded them "in the field"—in southern cities near the homes of the bluesmen. The race-records market reflected the change in emphasis; the

---

[7]See further about the term "downhome" blues in Jeff Titon, *Early Downhome Blues: A Musical and Cultural Analysis* (Urbana, IL, 1977), p. xiii. I accept Titon's use of the term "downhome" to refer to what is generally called "country blues," for the reason he gives: " 'Downhome' refers not to a place but to a spirit, a sense of place evoked in singer and listener by a style of music. The term 'country' is troublesome because downhome blues songs were performed regularly in towns and cities and by people who grew up there."

Gus Cannon at home, 1971. *(Photo by Val Wilmer / Format Photographers)*

number of recordings made of the classic blues dropped after 1926, while recordings of folk blues increased markedly.

The first male to record the blues guitar, either as a solo or accompaniment instrument, was Sylvester Weaver (1897–1960) in October 1923, with his *Guitar Blues* and *Guitar Rag*. But it was "Papa" Charlie Jackson (d. 1938) who really opened the market with his *Lawdy, Lawdy Blues* and *Airy Man Blues* released in August 1924. Within the next five years, most of the bluesmen who later became famous had been given contracts; outstanding among them were "Texas" Alger Alexander (ca. 1880–ca. 1955), Gus Cannon (1883–1979) and his Jug Stompers, "Sleepy" John Estes (1899–1977), "Mississippi" John Hurt (1893–1966), Alonzo "Lonnie" Johnson (1889–1970), "Blind" Lemon Jefferson (1897–1929), Tommy Johnson (ca. 1896–1956), "Furry" Walter Lewis (1893–1981), Charlie Patton (1881?–1934), and "Son Brimmer" Will Shade (1898–1966) and his Memphis Jug Band.

The blues pianists who began recording during this period included Jimmy Blythe (1899–ca. 1936), Charles "Cow Cow" Davenport (1894–1955), Thomas "Georgia Tom" Dorsey (1899–1993), "Blind" Arthur Blake Phelps (ca. 1890–ca. 1933), and "Tampa Red" Hudson Whittaker (1904–1981).

Bluesmen passed repertory items and techniques from one to the other in genuine folk practice. Charlie Patton, for example, reputedly learned his style from Henry Sloan, a bluesman of the Mississippi Delta region who was identified as a blues singer as early as 1897. In due course, Patton passed on his lore to those who came after him and is credited with being one of the most influential bluesmen of the times.

Bluesmen sang of themselves, of their personal problems, and of their experiences—*I'm a Po' Boy 'Long Way from Home* or *Hitch Up My Pony, Saddle Up My Black Mare.* They sang of nature's disasters—the *Boll Weevil Blues* and *Lord, the Whole Roun' Country, Lord, River Is Overflowed*—or about a favorite train in *Goin' Where the Southern Cross the Dog.* They sang of anything within their perceptions or those of their listeners. Most of all they sang of love and / or sex. Some songs were mournful laments, others lively dance tunes that set the feet to stomping and seemed to go on forever.

Blues styles differed from place to place; bluesmen of Texas, for example, had different traditions than those of the Mississippi Delta or the Carolina Piedmont, but all styles reflected the black folksong heritage of the nineteenth century. The voice quality was strained, raspy, abrasive, nasal, fierce; there was a great deal of falsetto, humming, growling—whatever it took to sing the lament or tell the story. The melodies and harmonies were full of "bent" tones or were strangely without tone graduations in the manner of field hollers. The men slapped their instruments, stomped their feet, and beat the strings of the guitar, producing percussive effects. And they worked out special devices—drawing the blade of a knife across the strings of the guitar as they played, or using a broken bottleneck or a brass ring or a piece of polished bone slipped over the finger—to produce whining tones reminiscent of the human voice, so that their instrument could "talk" to them. As we have seen, this practice of treating the string instrument as a partner in the music making dates back into the nineteenth century.

It was common practice to retune the strings of the guitar or banjo so that the open strings formed the notes of a chord or some other combination of tones specially favored by the bluesman. The harmonica player, or harpist, imitated trains and the howling and wailing of animals; a favorite imitation was the "fox chase." Special effects were obtained by fluttering the fingers, cupping the hands over the instrument and opening and closing them to vary the sound, and by controlling the flow of breath into the instrument. The harpist often played "crossed" harmonica, playing in a key different from the one in which the instrument was tuned so that he could more easily "bend" the tones by drawing in rather than blowing out the tones.

Blind Lemon Jefferson was perhaps the most famous of these early bluesman. His singing,

> close to the holler, did not have an insistent beat; instead he would suspend the rhythm or hold a note to emphasize a word or line. By hammering on the strings—using a quick release which produced a succession of open and fretted notes—by choking the strings and by dextrously picked arpeggios, Lemon used rapid phrases which extended the vocal line. For him the guitar was another voice, and he frequently used imitative phrases. . . . Each line of Lemon's vocal would be answered by a fragment on the guitar—a simple phrase or a rapid arpeggio.[8]

In composing his song, the bluesman typically drew upon phrases, verses, even full stanzas from a traditional blues repertory, which he combined with his original material in making the new song, and he introduced such changes as necessary to fit the context in which the song was being sung. Naturally this led to variants of a number of songs in the repertory. Once the blues was recorded, of course, it was relatively easy to identify at least one of the definitive versions.

The year 1929 ushered in severe problems for the recording industry, not only because of the Great Depression but also because of the competition offered by radio broadcasting; as a result, recording activities were cut back severely. The number of records sold in 1932 represented less than 6 percent of the total record sales in 1927. Blues and jazz people were especially hard hit. Nevertheless, some bluesmen continued to make records during the 1930s, and some even made their recording debuts during that decade.

The second wave of influential bluesmen who migrated in the late 1920s into urban areas, particularly Chicago, and into recording studios included Francis "Scrapper" Blackwell (1903–1962), William Lee "Big Bill" Conley Broonzy (1893–1958), Leroy Carr (1905–1935), "Memphis Minnie" Douglas (1897–1973), Amos "Bumble Bee" Easton (b. 1905), Eddie "Son" House (1902–1988), Robert Lee McCoy (1909–1967, also known as Robert Nighthawk), "Big Joe Slim" Joseph Turner (1911–1985), "Big Joe" Lee Williams (1903–1982), and John Lee "Sonny Boy, No. 1" Williamson (1914–1948), among others.

Memphis Minnie, best known of the early female singers of downhome blues, recorded guitar duos extensively with her husband, "Kansas Joe" McCoy, in the 1930s. Guitarist Blackwell and pianist Carr also performed as a team.

A significant number of bluesmen of this period concentrated on piano blues or boogie-woogie, among them Albert Ammons (1907–1949), "Memphis Slim" Peter Chatman (1915–1988), Pete Johnson (1904–1967), Meade Lux Lewis (1905–1964), Clarence "Cripple" Lofton (1887–1957), "Little Brother" Eurreal Montgomery (1915–1985), Rufus "Speckled Red" Perry-

---

[8]Paul Oliver, *The Story of the Blues* (Philadelphia, 1969), pp. 37–38.

man (1892–1973), Clarence "Pine Top" Smith (1904–1929), Roosevelt Sykes (1906–1983), and "Papa" James Edward Yancey (1898–1951). In 1927 Lewis recorded his *Honky-tonk Train Blues,* which proved to be a classic of the piano blues genre. A year later Smith recorded the second boogie-woogie, which he called *Pine Top's Boogie Woogie,* and thereby pin-pointed the origin of that style.

Boogie-woogie pianists held forth at social entertainments, particularly "rent parties," in urban black communities, where they took on the function of an entire dance ensemble—in terms of volume as well as musical density. They preferred a piano that was out of tune in order to get the effects they wanted. Generally they used an old upright, from which they removed the front cover and put newspapers behind the hammers and tin on the felts.[9] Then the pianist set to work, and the dancing began, often to last the entire night. The left hand played an ostinato figure that replicated the chord changes of the blues and moved in eighth notes, eight to the measure, often with dotted rhythms and emphasizing open fifths and octaves in the broken-chord patterns. The right hand played a highly embellished melody that set up cross rhythms against the left hand and was distinctive for its tremolos. To obtain the effect of the essential "bent tones," the pianist struck harsh, dissonant intervals, such as minor seconds and major sevenths, simultaneously. The driving rhythms of the music derived from the walking or rolling basses, as they were called, and the performance was loud! The object was to play so loudly that customers were attracted to the apartment where the rent party was in full swing.

JAZZ BAND RECORDING

Although the recording of jazz bands dates from the beginning of the race-records era in 1920, the year Mamie Smith first recorded with her Jazz Hounds, it was not until 1922 that the record industry began to focus on the instrumental ensemble as a source of entertainment in its own right rather than as accompaniment for singers. The first instrumental jazz records of a black group were made by Edward "Kid" Ory (1886–1973) and his Sunshine Orchestra in Los Angeles; the band played *Ory's Creole Trombone* and *Society Blues* for the Nordskog label in June 1922. Predictably, the repertory of the early jazz recordings consisted primarily of blues and rags.

The jazzmen from New Orleans who migrated to Chicago during World War I made that city a capital of classic jazz in the New Orleans tradition. One year a waggish reporter of the *Chicago Defender* observed, "The fire department is thinking of lining 35th Street with asbestos to keep those bands from scorching passers-by with their red-hot jazz music." Among the

[9]Smith, *Music on My Mind,* p. 157.

early arrivals was William Manuel "Bill" Johnson (1872–1972), organizer and first manager of the Original Creole Band, who arrived in Chicago about 1917 and within the year was directing a jazz band, called the New Orleans Original Band, at the Royal Gardens Café.

In 1918 Joseph "King" Oliver (1885–1938) left New Orleans to join Johnson's band in Chicago; after settling there he played also with the band of Lawrence Duhé at the Dreamland Café. By 1920 Oliver was leading his own group, the Creole Jazz Band. He was famous by this time and with good cause, for he was a skilled, gifted, and experienced cornetist. He began playing cornet as a child in a boys' brass band, and as an adult he played at one time or another with most of the famed brass bands of New Orleans, including the Olympia, Eagle, Onward, and Magnolia, and, as well, Kid Ory's band. It was Ory who named Oliver "the King."

Oliver, in turn, sent for Louis Armstrong in 1922, thus adding a second cornet to his six-piece band, which included clarinet, cornet, trombone, banjo, piano, and drums. He made his recording debut on April 6, 1923, and thereafter recorded regularly until 1931. There were changes in personnel, however, over the years, and in 1926 he began calling his band King Oliver and His Dixie Syncopators. Oliver also toured widely with his groups, but his career declined in the 1930s and he was unable to hold together a permanent band for his recordings and engagements. Several times he made poor business decisions, as in 1927 when he turned down

King Oliver's Creole Jazz Band, ca. 1923. (Left to right) Baby Dodds, drums; Honoré Dutrey, trombone; King Oliver, cornet; Louis Armstrong, trumpet; Bill Johnson, bass; Johnny Dodds, clarinet; and Lil Hardin (later Armstrong), piano.

an offer to play at the newly opened Cotton Club in Harlem. (A young man from Washington, D.C., Edward Kennedy Ellington, accepted the job.)

Those who played with Oliver over the years included in addition to Armstrong, clarinetist Albany "Barney" Bigard, clarinetist Johnny Dodds, drummer Warren "Baby" Dodds, trombonist Honoré Dutrey, banjoist Bill Johnson, pianist Lillian "Lil" Hardin Armstrong, clarinetist Albert Nicholas, and guitarist John "Johnny" St. Cyr. In its peak period, Oliver's band was at the top of the jazz world. He is credited with having defined jazz cornet / trumpet style, particularly through his practice of using a wide variety of mutes for expressive purposes—inserting mutes, cups, bottles, water glasses, sink plungers, derby hats, and even buckets into the bell of his instrument in order to obtain expressive tones from his horn.

When Daniel Louis "Satchmo" Armstrong (1901–1971) arrived at Chicago in 1922 to play second cornet in Oliver's Creole Jazz Band, he was already an accomplished cornetist and fully capable of taking over the solo slot. His musical career began when, as a child, he sang for pennies on the streets of New Orleans. Later he studied music with Peter Davis at the Colored Waifs' Home for Boys, where he lived during the years 1913 and 1914, and learned to play several instruments, moving up from the tambourine to the lead-instrument cornet. Eventually he became leader of the Home's brass band, which often played for private social gatherings in the city and frequently joined parades through the city's streets.

After leaving the Home, Armstrong found ample opportunities to blow his cornet in nightclubs and bars. His talent brought him to the attention of Oliver, who befriended him, helping him to improve his playing and to obtain work. In 1918 Armstrong took Oliver's place in Kid Ory's band when Oliver went to Chicago. For a short time during this period Armstrong played in Fate Marable's band on the excursion steamer *Sydney,* which cruised up and down the Mississippi, and he improved his music-reading skills with the help of David Jones, the band's mellophone player.

By the time Armstrong reached his maturity, Storyville had closed down, but he never forgot its music. In his autobiography, *Satchmo,* he wrote:

> On every corner I could hear music . . . the music I wanted to hear. . . . It was worth my salary—the little I did get—just to go into Storyville. . . . And that man Joe Oliver . . . kept me spellbound with that horn of his. Storyville! With all those glorious trumpets—Joe Oliver, Bunk Johnson—he was in his prime then—Emmanuel Perez, Buddy Petit, Joe Johnson. . . .[10]

To Armstrong, Joe Oliver's playing was the strongest and most creative, but Bunk Johnson's tone was the sweetest. In Armstrong's playing is reflected the best of the great trumpeters who had preceded him and who were his spiritual or actual mentors—Buddy Bolden's fiery, powerful tone, Bunk

---

[10]Louis Armstrong, *Satchmo: My Life in New Orleans* (New York, 1954), pp. 148–49.

Louis Armstrong, ca. 1946. (© *William P. Gottlieb. Courtesy of the Artist and the Stephen Cohen Gallery*)

Johnson's lighter, sweet tone and imaginative phrasing, and King Oliver's delicate but firm style with its inventiveness and wide variety of tone.

Armstrong was the first great jazz soloist and one of jazz's most creative innovators. Over the long years of his career, his genius remained immune to the onslaught of commercialism and to the ascendency of other popular music styles. Hundreds of jazz people were inspired by his playing and tried to emulate it—not only trumpeters, but other instrumentalists who tried to adapt aspects of that style to their own instruments. His special style of singing also attracted imitators. Armstrong emerged as a soloist when he left Oliver's band in 1924 to join a New York band under the leadership of Fletcher Henderson. He returned to Chicago in 1925, played with a succession of bands, including Erskine Tate's Vendome Theater "Symphony Orchestra," and made recordings with his own Hot Five and Hot Seven groups (1925–27). It was during these years that Armstrong began to earn his worldwide reputation. His sidemen for the recordings included Lil Armstrong, Pete Briggs, the Dodds brothers, Kid Ory, Johnny St. Cyr, and John Thomas in the early years. Later he was joined by Earl Hines, Fred Robinson, and Arthur "Zutty" Singleton, among others.

Armstrong also recorded extensively with his Savoy Ballroom Five and his Orchestra, but in later years he generally "fronted" the bands of others rather than organize his own. He toured widely throughout the world, making his first European tour in 1932. Increasingly he came to represent to the world the spirit of American jazz and its international appeal; in 1960 he made two goodwill tours, one to Africa under private-industry sponsorship, and the second to other parts of the world under the auspices of the U.S. State Department. He appeared in Broadway musicals, films, on radio and television, and in concert halls, theaters, and jazz festivals. He exerted enormous influence on the development of jazz trumpet and on jazz improvisation as a whole. No other jazzman in history was as influential.

Some of Armstrong's most memorable recordings were made before he organized his own groups. Among them are *Dipper Mouth Blues* with King Oliver, *Copenhagen* with Fletcher Henderson, and *Cake Walkin' Babies from Home* with Clarence Williams. Other well-known Armstrong recordings included *West End Blues, Weather Bird, Mahogany Hall Stomp, When the Saints Go Marching In, Savoy Blues, Hotter than That,* and *Heebie Jeebies.*

Jelly Roll Morton is regarded by some scholars as the first true jazz composer in that he was probably the first to write down his jazz arrangements in musical notation.[11] Also, he was the originator of a large number of pieces that became staples in the jazz repertory. Morton's arrangement of his own *Jelly Roll Blues* was the first published jazz arrangement in history (1915). In preparing for the Red Hot Peppers' recordings in 1926, Morton carefully planned how each piece would be played, either by writing out the arrangement in advance or by discussing his ideas with the bandsmen so that each would know how his playing should fit into the ensemble (this is called a "head arrangement"). Morton's sidemen included Barney Bigard (clarinet), the Dodds brothers (drums, clarinet), André Hilaire (drums), Darnell Howard (clarinet), John Lindsay (double bass), George Mitchell (cornet), Kid Ory (trombone), Omer Simeon (clarinet), and Johnny St. Cyr (guitar).

Earlier, Morton made recordings of his piano jazz, for example, the *Kansas City Stomp, King Porter Stomp,* and *Wolverine Blues,* which are equally valued by jazz connoisseurs. He capped his eventful career with a massive recording adventure at the Library of Congress (May–July 1938), where he related his version of the history of jazz and illustrated it with piano solos and song—making fifty-two records with more than one hundred pieces. Alan Lomax interviewed Morton and supervised the recording sessions.[12]

Jazz specialists generally use the term *classic jazz* in referring to the music produced by the small orchestras of Oliver, Morton, Armstrong, and

[11]Gunther Schuller, *Early Jazz: Its Roots and Musical Development* (New York, 1968), p. 137.
[12]Alan Lomax, *Mister Jelly Roll* (Berkeley, 1973), pp. 239–51; 307–18.

other black contemporaries. We have discussed the basic features of classic jazz: the small ensembles, consisting of a trumpet-clarinet-trombone trio and a piano-bass-drum rhythm section; the emphasis on collective improvisation and polyphonic texture; and the preference for an individualized, expressive approach to the making of music rather than a "correct," intellectual approach.

But jazz proved to be ever changing, and even during the 1920s it began to take on a new aspect. Orchestras grew in size, and new instruments were added to the ensemble. With fourteen or more performers in a band, it was no longer possible to have collective improvisation or head arrangements. The younger black jazz musicians coming on the scene were more likely to have received their musical training in a college or conservatory than "in the field," as had the pioneers. Entertainment music became for many a full-time profession that brought both financial rewards and social prestige.

THE BIG BANDS

As the nation's music center, New York had attracted black musicians in all fields even in the nineteenth century, and it began to play an increasingly important role in the history of jazz. It was in New York in 1923 that the nation's first "big band" was organized. The musicians credited with starting the big-band movement were pianist Fletcher Henderson (1897–1952) a graduate of Atlanta University, (but not a music major) and saxophonist Donald "Don" Redman (1900–1964) a graduate of Storer College (West Virginia) in music. In New York, Henderson fell heir to the tradition established by James Reese Europe, which included exciting music and unorthodox instrumentation, as we have seen, but little of the blues in its style. Henderson came into close contact with the blues, however, during his first year in New York (1920), when he worked as a house pianist for Handy and Pace's music publishing company, and the next year when his Black Swan Dance Masters went on tour with blues singer Ethel Waters.[13] Waters recalled her experiences with Henderson and his music:

> I kept having arguments with Fletcher Henderson about the way he was playing my accompaniments. Fletcher, though a fine arranger and a brilliant bandleader, leans more to the classical side. On that tour Fletcher wouldn't give me what I call "the damn-it-to-hell bass," that chump-chump stuff that real jazz needs. . . . When we reached Chicago I got some piano rolls that Jimmy Johnson had made and pounded out each passage to Henderson. To prove to me he could do it, Fletch began to practice. He got so perfect, listening to James P. Johnson play on the player piano, that he could press down the keys as the roll played, never missing a note.[14]

[13]In regard to the early black big bands, see further in Allen, *Hendersonia*.
[14]Ethel Waters, *His Eye Is on the Sparrow* (New York, 1978), p. 147.

By the time Henderson began an engagement at the exclusive white Club Alabam on Forty-fourth Street in 1923, his ten-piece orchestra was playing jazz. Its composition was that of the classic jazz group of the 1920s, except for its size and the addition of saxophones, reflecting the influence of Clef Club and Harlem honky-tonk ensembles and combos. Obviously, such a large group could not improvise in the New Orleans style. Henderson and Redman wrote arrangements for the band that alternated solo and ensemble sections, and allowed for soloist improvisation. Not all of the arrangements were written; often the band used "head arrangements," and sometimes there was sectional improvisation in the finales. Among the special features of the Henderson style were the three-clarinet ensemble (used as a single instrument in counterpoint with a trumpet) and the call-and-response byplay between brasses and reeds. During the period 1924–36 Henderson's band, enlarged to sixteen players, was the dance band "in residence" at the big Roseland Ballroom in New York. In its creation of an original style, this band led the way for the big bands that followed, both black and white.

The next few years saw the emergence of a number of African-American big bands led by black jazzmen. The bandleaders who played in New York or used the city as a base from which they toured included, in addition to Henderson and Redman, Edward "Duke" Ellington (1899–1974), Erskine Hawkins (1914–1993), James "Jimmie" Lunceford (1902–1947), Lucius ("Lucky") Millinder (1900–1966), Luis Russell (1902–1963), and William "Chick" Webb (1909–1939). Cabell "Cab" Calloway (1907–1994), Hawkins, and Lunceford came to New York during the 1930s with college groups they were leading, Hawkins with the Alabama State Collegians and Lunceford with a Fisk University group, some of whom were his former students. Lunceford's band was especially noted for its precision and showmanship, to which arranger Melvin "Sy" Oliver (1910–1988) contributed.

Chick Webb's band was one of the first to play at the new Savoy Ballroom in Harlem (opened 1926)—"the home of happy feet"—and he reigned over the birth of such dances as the lindy hop and the Susie Q. It was at the Savoy that Webb introduced his protégé, singer Ella Fitzgerald (1918–1996), to the world of entertainment. Erskine Hawkins also built his reputation at the Savoy, as did Stanley "Fess" Williams (1894–1975) with his Royal Flush Orchestra. Redman's band was the first (and only black band during this period) to have a sponsored radio series (by the Chipso Soap Company in 1932).

In Chicago the important big bands included those of Charles "Doc" Cooke (1891–1958) and his 14 Doctors of Syncopation, Earl "Fatha" Hines (1905–1983), David "Dave" Peyton (1885–1956), and Erskine Tate (1895–1978). Hines settled at Chicago in 1924 and for a short while played piano in nightclubs and dance halls. He then played with various groups, including Louis Armstrong, Carroll Dickerson, and James "Jimmie" Noone. During the years 1928–48 Hines led his own big band, which included a women's group in 1943; next he toured with the Louis Armstrong All-Stars (1948–51), and after that with small groups.

In the Midwest and Southwest Territories the big-band movement flourished as elsewhere. Clarence Love led bands in Tulsa, Omaha, Dallas, and Kansas City; the Jeter-Pillars Orchestra was active primarily in Kansas City. Other bandleaders associated with Kansas City were Andy Kirk (1898–1992) George E. Lee (1896–1958), Bennie Moten (1894–1935), and Jay McShann (b. 1909). Many of the young jazzmen who played in these groups later became important contributors to the development of jazz; for example, James "Jimmy" Blanton, Albert "Budd" Johnson, "J. J." Johnson, Charlie Parker, Jesse Stone, and Clark Terry, to mention only a few. The most celebrated Kansas City group was, of course, William "Count" Basie's band.

On the West coast, Les Hite led the top band of the region; frequently Louis Armstrong fronted Hite's band and, beginning about 1929, Lionel Hampton played drums in the band. Hampton (b. 1909) organized his own group in 1934, then played in the Benny Goodman quartet with Theodore "Teddy" Wilson (1912–1986) and white drummer Gene Krupa during the years 1936–40 before returning to his big band.

Hampton's long career took him through all the style periods of black music, from swing to avant-garde, but he adapted to the changing styles and remained an important figure in the jazz world into the 1990s. He introduced important innovations into jazz: he was the first to establish the vibraharp as a regular member of the band, rather than a novelty instrument, and the first to add electric organ and electric bass to the ensemble. His encouragement of young, untried talent brought large numbers of performers to his groups over the years, singers as well as instrumentalists; consequently, his groups served as a veritable training ground for jazzmen and women who later became famous in their own right.

THE SWING ERA

In 1932 Duke Ellington offered a harbinger of things to come with his song *It Don't Mean a Thing If It Ain't Got That Swing,* which provided a label for a new style of jazz developing among big bands during the 1930s. Duke was no newcomer to the field of jazz, having written his first song, *Soda Fountain Rag,* at the age of fourteen and organized his first band not too many years later.

He obtained his musical training in the public schools of Washington, D.C., studied piano as a child, and basic theory privately with well-established musicians in the community, among them, Henry Lee Grant, a music teacher at the Dunbar High School who taught him harmony, Oliver "Doc" Perry, and Louis N. Brown. His musical development was influenced by the

Lionel Hampton. *(Courtesy Raymond Ross)*

pianists he heard in Washington and New York City, and by the piano rolls
to which he listened, particularly those of James P. Johnson. In later years
Ellington had discussions about compositional techniques with composer /
arranger Will Vodery and composer Will Marion Cook, both of whom he
regarded as mentors.

> Several times, after I had played some tune I had written but not really com-
> pleted, I would say, "Now, Dad [Cook], what is the logical way to develop this
> theme? What direction should I take?"
>
> "You know you should go to the conservatory," he would answer, "but since
> you won't, I'll tell you. First you find the logical way, and when you find it,
> avoid it, and let your inner self break through and guide you. Don't try to be

Duke Ellington. *(Courtesy CBS Records)*

anybody else but yourself." That time with him was one of the best semesters I ever had in music.[15]

But Ellington's ideas were his own and his genius led him to create an orchestra style marked by rich and daring harmonies, by subtle contrastings of colors and timbres, and by an ingenious handling of solo and ensemble relationships. The orchestra became the vehicle through which Ellington expressed his creativity; it came to represent the ideal big "swinging band."

When Ellington's band began its memorable engagement in December

[15]Edward Kennedy Ellington, *Music is My Mistress* (New York, 1973), p. 97.

1927 at the famed Cotton Club in Harlem, it included two trumpets, trombone, alto saxophone, baritone saxophone, tenor saxophone (doubling with clarinet), guitar (doubling with banjo), bass, drums, and piano. Later it was enlarged to include three trumpets and two trombones, and in 1932 a third trombone and a fourth saxophone were added. It was during the Cotton Club years that Duke's orchestra began to win distinction for its thorough musicianship and homogeneity.

Duke, as the leader, could accept the credit for this, but the contributions of his sidemen were significant. Some were brilliant soloists in their own rights; they fitted in well with Duke's temperament and they remained with him over long periods of time. William Alexander "Sonny" Greer (drums) and Otto "Toby" Hardwicke (alto and bass saxophone) were charter members of the Washingtonians, Duke's first band. Other long-timers included Fred Guy (banjo, guitar), Johnny Hodges (alto saxophone), Charles "Cootie" Williams (trumpet, and Harry Carner (baritone saxophone). Trumpeter James "Bubber" Miley, with his "growling" solos, was largely responsible for the "jungle effects" in the orchestra's performances, one of the most distinctive features of the early style. He and trombonist Joseph "Tricky Sam" Nanton became experts in the use of the rubber-plunger mute to give an almost vocal sound to their playing of trumpet and trombone.

Many of Duke's arrangements were worked out with his sidemen in the tradition of collective improvisation. Duke would bring to the band meeting his musical ideas, and one or another of the bandsmen would make suggestions for changes or additions. Things were tried out on the spot in order to find out whether they worked. Often a composition was changed after it had been performed three or four times, sometimes resulting in an entirely new work. Duke's constantly reiterated statement was, "Good music is music that sounds good." Sometimes other musicians of the orchestra would bring their compositions to "creating sessions" to be worked out by the entire group. In 1939 Billy Strayhorn (1915–1967), pianist-composer, joined Duke's orchestra as an arranger and over the years developed into Duke's musical alter ego. The collaboration between the two men was so close that sometimes neither could identify which part of a musical work was his. Duke's son Mercer (1919–96), bandleader, composer, arranger, trumpeter, was best known as manager of the Duke Ellington Orchestra, and, after Duke's death, as the musical director.

Although Duke Ellington was not the first to carry jazz into the church, his sacred jazz concerts (beginning in 1965) contributed largely to the growing movement for making the music of the worship service more relevant to the times. He produced three Concerts of Sacred Music: at Grace Cathedral Church in San Francisco on September 16, 1965; at the Cathedral of St. John the Divine in New York on January 19, 1968; and at Westminister Abbey in London on United Nations Day, October 24, 1973.

The first of these concerts was repeated and recorded at New York's

Fifth Avenue Presbyterian Church on December 26, 1965. The entire performance consisted of one work divided into several movements, much like a Mass. Ellington composed some of the numbers especially for the occasion and drew upon earlier works for others. The opening piece, *In the Beginning God*, employs full orchestra, choir, and solo voice. Then follow gospel and spiritual songs *Tell Me It's the Truth; Come Sunday; The Lord's Prayer;* a saxophone version of *Come Sunday;* two more spirituals, *Will You Be There* and *Ain't But the One;* a piano solo, *New World a-Coming;* and the finale, *David Danced Before the Lord with All His Might,* for orchestra and tap dancer. *Come Sunday* and the piano solo were originally performed at Ellington's 1943 concert; the second pair of spirituals belonged to his music for the pageant *My People.*

Ellington left more than three-thousand compositions, an impressive record equaled by few composers in the history of American music.[16] His extended works include the symphonic suites *Creole Rhapsody* (1931), *Black, Brown, and Beige* (1943), *Deep South Suite* (1947), *Liberian Suite* (1947), *Such Sweet Thunder* (1957), and *Far East Suite* (1970); the ballet *The River* (1970); the pageant *My People* (1963); the television musical *A Drum Is a Woman* (CBS, 1957); and the musicals *Jump for Joy* (1941; 1959) and *Beggar's Holiday* (1946). Best known of the hundreds of songs he wrote were *Sophisticated Lady, In a Sentimental Mood, I Let a Song Go Out of My Heart, Mood Indigo,* and *I Got It Bad and That Ain't Good.* His popular instrumental pieces include *East St. Louis Toodle-Oo, Ko-Ko, Cotton Tail,* and *Take the A Train.*

Ellington made enormous contributions to the development of jazz and, indeed, to American music in general. His innovations, unusual at the time, passed into the sounds of jazz so quickly that the jazz world accepted them as if always there; for example, the use of the voice as an instrument in Adelaide Hall's wordless solo on *Creole Love Call* (1928), or the employment of Cuban elements in *Caravan* (1937), or the use of extended form in *Concerto for Cootie* (1939). The first jazzman to write concert jazz in extended forms, (1943–50) he presented annual concerts at Carnegie Hall in New York for seven years.

KANSAS CITY JAZZ

William "Count" Basie (1904–1984), a native of Red Bank (New Jersey), began his professional career while still in his teens, touring on the vaudeville circuit as pianist, accompanist, and musical director. As a child he first

---

[16]In 1988 the Smithsonian Institution acquired the Duke Ellington Collection and installed it at the National Museum of American History. The archives contain more than 3,000 original and orchestrated pieces of music, many in Ellington's handwriting, as well as tape recordings, concert programs, correspondence, and other documents.

Count Basie.

studied piano with his mother, then piano and basic theory with a local German music teacher. Inevitably, his travels took him to Harlem, where he came under the influence of the "stride pianists" James P. Johnson, Willie "the Lion" Smith, and Thomas "Fats" Waller. Basie studied informally with Waller and also learned by listening to Waller play both piano and organ.

In 1936 Basie was playing in Kansas City, where he had been active since 1927. When John Hammond, white jazz enthusiast and record producer, heard Basie's nine-piece band that was broadcasting from the Reno Club in Kansas City, Missouri, he became so excited that he arranged for the Music Corporation of America (MCA) to take over its management. A show with which Basie was touring became stranded there, and he found himself without a job. For a year he played piano in a movie-theater pit, then joined Walter Page's Blue Devils orchestra. Upon the disbanding of Page's band in 1929, Basie joined the orchestra of Bennie Moten, where he remained until Moten's death and the orchestra's demise in 1935. Soon thereafter Basie formed his own band, taking over some of Moten's personnel, and featuring the blues singer Jimmy Rushing; it was this group that Hammond heard playing on a local radio station.

Kansas City in the early 1930s occupied a position in the Southwest similar to that of St. Louis in the 1890s. It had grown wealthy as a trading center, largely because its location at the junction of the Kansas and Missouri Rivers allowed it to serve as a port of call for riverboat traffic, and because it became an important railway junction (connecting East to West, and with direct links to Chicago and St. Louis) and highway intersection point. Money flowed in the city's tenderloin districts, and entertainers flocked there to work. (To be sure, the influence of the so-called Pendergast political machine and gangsterdom also contributed to the generally "relaxed" atmosphere of the city.)

The city became a magnet for black musicians: for members of touring bands from the East, Chicago, and the West with a few hours to spare between the changing of trains; for itinerant jazzmen from the South, particularly New Orleans; and for blues singers from urban areas, the Delta regions of Mississippi, and the wide open spaces of Texas, Arkansas, and Oklahoma. Jazzmen met together to match their skills in cutting contests or in interminable jam sessions.

A set of standardized procedures evolved naturally out of the practical demands of the situation in which the musicians found themselves. All would join in the playing at the beginning of a number, then each would take his or her turn at improvising on the chorus, and finally they would all play together again to bring the piece of music to a close. The procedure allowed for any number of visitors to participate, and at the same time allowed the musicians to display their improvisatory skills.

Inevitably the blues became the basic material used in this kind of performance. Its structure was fixed—the conventional twelve-bar form and prescribed harmonic patterns—and it was familiar to all jazz musicians. Moreover, the basic simplicity of the blues lent itself well to reshaping and elaboration. Blues could be handled to fit any mood; played fast, it generated excitement, and played slowly, it could be as melancholy as desired. The Kansas City music makers adopted the plan of using riffs as the basis for the opening chorus. The use of these short melodic ideas—repeated again and again by the full ensemble, often in unison by the brasses and sometimes by the rhythm section to support solo improvisation—became a distinctive feature of the style. Another innovation emphasized a different approach to the basic beat than had been employed by the jazz musicians of New Orleans. Instead of accenting the strong beats of the measure, the first and third as in a march, the Kansas City players stressed all four beats equally, though lightly, thus producing a smoothly flowing beat-rhythm—a "swinging" rhythm.

Blues singers, too, found themselves changing some of their practices in conformity with the Kansas City style. Under the pressure of the driving beat of jazz, the blues became lustier and more powerful. Blues singers did not limit themselves to singing laments with guitar accompaniment; they could use the same form and text to sing joyfully and with a jazz-orchestra or jazz-piano accompaniment. The "Kaycee" school (K. C., for Kansas City) produced leadership for the new jazz movement in its pianists (Sammy Price, Mary Lou Williams); in its band instrumentalists (trumpeter Oran "Hot Lips" Page and tenor sax man Lester "Prez" Young); in its singers (Jimmy Rushing, "Big" Joe Turner, Billie Holiday, and Helen Humes); and its bandleaders (Bennie Moten, Jesse Stone, Jay McShann, Walter Page, Andy Kirk). Basie's band stood at the peak of the tradition. Jazz personnel of course came and went; the 1950s, for example, brought in singer Joe Williams.

MCA took the Basie band first to Chicago's Grand Terrace Ballroom, then to New York's Roseland Ballroom, and finally to the Famous Door Club on West Fifty-second Street. The place was a little small for Basie's big band, but this did not prevent musicians and jazz connoisseurs from flocking there to listen to its exciting music. At that time the band was composed of three trumpets, two trombones, two alto saxes, two tenor saxes, piano, guitar, bass, and drums. By 1939 a fourth trumpet and a third trombone had been added. But Basie worked hard to keep the same swinging sound he had developed with the smaller group:

> I wanted my fifteen-piece band to work together just like those nine pieces did. I wanted fifteen men to think and play the same way. I wanted those four trumpets and three trombones to bite with real guts. But I wanted that bite to be just as tasty and subtle as if it were the three brass I used to use. . . . My piano? . . . I fed dancers my piano in short doses, and when I came in for a solo, I did it unexpectedly, using a strong rhythm background behind me.[17]

Predictably, Basie used riffs in the Kansas City style for full ensemble playing, for antiphonal play between brasses and reeds, and for sectional support of soloists. Head arrangements were more favored than written-out arrangements and as a consequence there was often a great deal of collective improvisation on the spot. The soloists, of course, always improvised. Another innovation of Basie's was to begin the performance of a piece with himself at the piano playing the first chorus (instead of using the full orchestra); this enabled him to set just the right tempo and mood for the music.

The Basie band early established itself as an innovative group from which other bands borrowed ideas heavily. Drummer Jo Jones, (1911–1985) for example, helped to popularize the use of the "high hat" cymbal (i.e., two small cymbals operated by a foot pedal) as a way to maintain the swinging beat. No other orchestra could play the blues as well as Basie's, nor had as good blues singers. The sidemen included some of the chief

---

[17]Shapiro and Hentoff, *Hear Me Talkin' to Ya,* p. 304.

instrumentalists of the time; among them, Big Ed Lewis (lead trumpet), Walter Page (bass), Freddie Green (guitar), Lester "Prez" Young (alto sax), Dicky Wells (trombone), and Wilbur "Buck" Clayton (trumpet).

Basie's band began to achieve nationwide fame soon after its move to Fifty-second Street. In 1950 Basie found it necessary for economic reasons to disband the large group and tour with a sextet, but he soon organized another big band. Its tours abroad were successful from the beginning (in 1954), as were also its appearances at jazz festivals and in large concert halls of the States. Among the best-known recordings of Basie's works are *One O'Clock Jump, April in Paris, Jumping at the Woodside, Blues by Basie, A Night at the Apollo,* and *Lester Leaps In.*

The golden age of big bands came to an end about 1946, brought about by the emergence of new forms of entertainment that replaced dancing (such as bowling and watching television), the gradual disappearance of big ballrooms, and the changing taste of the public. Undoubtedly, many other factors were involved as well—World War II, for example, and the changing attitude of the jazz musicians themselves toward their patrons, as well as the increasing invasion of commercialism into the world of jazz.

The jazz age had produced an imposing array of talent, not only among bandleaders, but also among singers, instrumentalists, songwriters, composers, and writer-critics. As early as the 1920s, articles and books began to appear in Europe that seriously explored the nature of the new music being created by African Americans in the United States. The origin of jazz was examined, its development discussed, and the contributions of its major figures evaluated. Later would come special magazines devoted to jazz, popularity polls, and jazz festivals. A London magazine, *Melody Maker,* began publishing articles on jazz as early as 1926. In 1934 a publication devoted entirely to jazz, *Down Beat,* was established in the United States.

By 1938 recording companies specializing in jazz had begun to appear on the scene; among them, the Commodore HRS and the Blue Note label. About the same time the first of a steady stream of American books on jazz were published: *So This Is Jazz* by Henry Osgood, *American Jazz Music* by Wilder Hobson, and *Jazzman* by Frederic Ramsey and Charles E. Smith. By the end of the 1920s jazz was increasingly being acknowledged as a vital and valid music by American intellectuals—Europeans had accepted jazz much earlier—and jazz critics were ready to single out the "great" leaders, performers, and composers. Basie was one of the leading figures of the Swing Era: his piano style has been called the greatest single influence on jazz band piano.

PRINCIPAL JAZZ INSTRUMENTALISTS

With few exceptions, there was a great deal of mobility among black jazz performers during the three decades following World War I. Instrumentalists moved from one band to another, soloists organized or "fronted" bands, and some ensemble men moved into the area of solo performance. In discussing performers it is more convenient to associate persons with their instruments than with the orchestras in which they played. Among the most highly regarded trumpeters, after the legendary Oliver, Keppard, and Armstrong, were Henry "Red" Allen (1908–1967), Adolphus "Doc" Cheatham (b. 1905), Wilbur "Buck" Clayton (1911–1991), Johnny Dunn (1900–1938), Roy Eldridge (1911–1989), Robert "Jonah" Jones (b. 1908), Thomas "Tommy" Ladnier (1900–1939), Oran "Hot Lips" Page (1908–1954), Cladys "Jabbo" Smith (1908–1991), Joe Smith (1902–1937), and Charles Melvin "Cootie" Williams (1908–1985). Willis "Ray" Nance (1913–1976), and James "Bubber" Miley (1903–1932) were noted for their contributions to the Ellington band sound.

The great trombonists were Kid Ory (1886–1973), and James "Jimmy" Harrison (1900–1931). Those in a somewhat younger generation included Victor "Vic" Dickenson (1906–1984), J. C. Higginbotham (1906–1973), Henry "Benny" Morton (1907–1985), Joseph "Tricky Sam" Nanton (1904–1946), Juan Tizol (1900–1984), William "Dicky" Wells (1909–1985), Albert Wynn (1907–1973), and James "Trummy" Young (1912–1984).

We have already mentioned the celebrated clarinetists Jimmie Noone (1895–1944), Johnny Dodds (1892–1940), and Sidney Bechet (1897–1959)—all three players in the New Orleans tradition. Both Noone and Bechet acquired distinguished European fans: Noone's playing was acclaimed by the French composer Maurice Ravel, who listened to jazz during his visit to Chicago in 1928; and Bechet's performance was lauded, as we have mentioned, by the conductor Ansermet.

All three men greatly influenced the playing of the jazz clarinetists who followed them, white and black. Other important clarinetists from New Orleans included Leon "Barney" Bigard (1902–1967), Edmond Hall (1901–1967), George Lewis (1900–1968), Albert Nicholas (1900–1973), and Omer Victor Simeon (1902–1959). To this list of top clarinetists should be added the name of William "Buster" Bailey (1902–1967).

Rated as the three greatest alto saxophonists of the jazz era were Benny Carter (b. 1907), Johnny Hodges (1906–1970), and Willie Smith (1910–1967). Another highly rated sax man was Hilton Jefferson (1903–1968). To critics, the tenor saxophonist Coleman "Bean" Hawkins (1904–1969) was in a class by himself; his style was imitated by most tenors who followed him. Other tenors highly regarded during the time were Leon "Chu" Berry (1910–1941), Herschel Evans (1909–1939), and Lester "Prez" Young (1909–1959). It was Sidney Bechet who revealed most thoroughly the resources of the soprano saxophone, although he had developed his style on the clarinet.

The jazz-band drummer was one of the most important members of the group, but often the least conspicuous. Among the best of the great drummers were three from New Orleans: Warren "Baby" Dodds (1898–1959), Alfred "Tubby" Hall (1895–1946), and Arthur "Zutty" Singleton (1898–1975). No less important were Sidney "Big Sid" Catlett (1910–1951), William "Cozy" Cole (1909–1981), William "Sonny" Greer (1903–1982), Jonathan "Jo" Jones (1911–1985), and bandleader Chick Webb (1909–1939).

Among the guitar and banjo players rated as superior were several from New Orleans: Alonzo "Lonnie" Johnson, Johnny St. Cyr (1890–1966), and Arthur "Bud" Scott (ca. 1890–1949). Other important players were Bernard Addison (b. 1905), Theodore "Teddy" Bunn (1909–1978), Frederick "Freddie" Green (1911–1987), Daniel "Danny" Barker (1909–1994), Fred Guy (1899–1971), and Leonard Ware (b. 1909).

The best bassists of the period were James "Jimmie" Blanton (1918–1942), Wellman Braud (1891–1966), George "Pops" Foster (1892–1969), William Manuel "Bill" Johnson (1872–1972), John Kirby (1908–1952), Milton Hinton (b. 1910), Albert Morgan (1908–1974), and Walter Page (1900–1957). Although jazz bands rarely used violins, the period nevertheless produced some fine jazz violinists. Eddie South (1904–1962) was regarded as a man of extraordinary talent. His gifted contemporaries included Darnell Howard (1895–1966), Hezekiah Leroy "Stuff" Smith (1909–1967), and Robert "Juice" Wilson (1904–1962).

JAZZ SINGERS

With regard to singers, it was difficult to distinguish among blues, jazz, and popular-music singers. Certainly the best of those who moved in the jazz orbit included Ivie Anderson (1905–1949), Ella Fitzgerald (1918–1996), Adelaide Hall (1910–1993), Billie "Lady Day" Holiday (1915–1959), Helen Humes (1913–1981), and Maxine Sullivan (1911–1987). Although Bessie Smith and Ethel Waters were blues singers, they also frequently sang jazz. Of the male jazz singers, William "Billy" Eckstine (1914–1993) was the most famous; to be sure, there were celebrated singers among the jazz bandleaders—Louis Armstrong, for example, and "Hot Lips" Page.

JAZZ PIANISTS

The pianists fall into two categories: those who played with orchestras and those who were soloists or who played with small combos (i.e., instrumental trios or quartets). The leading figures of the first group were of course Count Basie, Duke Ellington, and Earl Hines, who had their own bands. Others who won recognition as pianists in orchestras included Lillian (Lil) Hardin Armstrong (1898–1971) and Luis Russell, both of whom played with Oliver and Armstrong; Mary Lou Williams (1910–1981), who came to the public's attention with Andy Kirk's band; Theodore "Teddy" Wilson (1912–1986), who first won wide recognition in Benny Goodman's interracial units; and Theodore "Teddy" Weatherford (1903–1945), who spent the last twenty years of his life as a pianist-bandleader in Southeast Asia.

Jelly Roll Morton was the father of solo jazz piano. His piano style represented a synthesis of the chief elements of the blues, of piano ragtime, and of orchestral jazz. After World War I, Harlem became the center of piano activity and Harlem pianists were the direct inheritors of the eastern ragtime tradition. They had learned to play by standing at the elbows of legendary "sharks"; their more recent mentors were Eubie Blake and Abba Labba McLean. Indeed, several of the most noted pianists began their careers as rag pianists in the first part of the twentieth century and only gradually changed their style to adapt to the changing times. The Harlem jazz pianists filled the functions of orchestras until about the mid-1920s, at which time the night spots began struggling to obtain a three- or four-piece ensemble to support the piano.

Frequently the label "orchestral style" has been applied to the Harlem piano music of this period: the pianist made the instrument literally roar, using full, fat harmonies in the right hand and a powerful bass in the left hand that emphasized the strong beats with low-register octaves or tenths and the weak beats with mid-keyboard chords ("stride piano"). The music reflected the influence of the blues scale in the pianist's use of "blues clusters" (the striking of major and minor thirds or sevenths simultaneously). The pianists' aim was to improvise, to vary and embellish the basic musical material, for which they drew upon several sources—blues, rags, concert piano music, popular songs, instrumental dances and marches, or their own compositions.

Charles Luckeyeth "Luckey" Roberts (1895–1968) entered the entertainment world at the age of three, when he took a part in *Uncle Tom's Cabin*. His very full career included touring as a singer, dancer, and pianist in vaudeville companies in the United States and in Europe. From time to time he organized and conducted his own ensembles; he also maintained a music studio, and played background music for radio shows.

Roberts was regarded as the founder of the Harlem piano school. His early rags, which served as models for the later piano pieces called "shouts," called for great technical skill. In addition to a large number of popular songs and dance pieces, Roberts wrote fourteen musical-comedy scores, and composed several concert works, including *Ripples of the Nile* (renamed *Moonlight Cocktail*) and *Whistlin' Pete—Miniature Syncopated Rhapsody,* which was played at a Robin Hood Dell concert at Philadelphia.

James Price Johnson (1891–1955) began playing rag piano professionally in 1904. The competitive spirit that existed among black pianists of the period led them to practice constantly in order to excel in the frequent cutting contests. Johnson once told an interviewer that he used to practice in the dark in order to develop a firm feeling for the keyboard. During a contest, each pianist would be given a stated number of minutes to demonstrate

James P. Johnson. *(Courtesy New York Public Library, Americana Collection of the Music Division)*

his or her skill at improvising on a given theme. Johnson's method for "carving" his rivals (i.e., winning a contest) was to "put tricks in on the breaks" (i.e., to fill in all the pauses of the original melody with elaborate embellishments). Johnson boasted, "I could think of a trick a minute: double glissandos, straight and backhand; glissandos in sixths, and double tremolos."

As an adult, Johnson spent many hours listening to recordings of European piano compositions, so that not only could he use "concert effects" in his playing of jazz piano but also "rag" such classics as Grieg's *Peer Gynt* Suite and Rachmaninoff's Prelude in C♯ minor.[18]

Like many pianists of the period, Johnson composed most of the music he played but published comparatively little. Nevertheless, his publications include a large number of rags, stomps, blues, and popular songs as well as a body of serious works. His first piece was a a piano blues, *Mama and*

[18]See further in Tom Davin, "Conversations with James P. Johnson," *Jazz Review* (June 1959): 14–17; (July 1959): 10–13.

Willie "the Lion" Smith at home, 1946. *(© William P. Gottlieb. Courtesy of the Artist and the Stephen Cohen Gallery)*

Papa Blues (1914). His *Carolina Shout* became a "test piece" for would-be jazz pianists in the same way that Joplin's *Maple Leaf Rag* had been for ragtimers. Best known of the many popular songs he wrote were *If I Could Be with You, Old-Fashioned Love,* and the *Charleston.*

In later years Johnson gave much time to composing extended works in the tradition of Negro music. Included among his works were *Symphonic Harlem, Yamekraw, Symphony in Brown,* Piano Concerto in A♭, and *Symphonic Suite on the "St. Louis Blues."*

William Henry Joseph Berthol Bonaparte Berthloff Smith (1897–1973) acquired his nickname, "the Lion," because of his bravery during World War I. His published memoir, *Music on My Mind* (1964), includes rare, firsthand information about the music of Harlem (and, indeed, of the African-American world) during the first half of the century. His career followed the typical pattern of black jazz pianists: he began playing professionally at the early age of seventeen in Newark, New Jersey, and worked at various entertainment spots in Atlantic City (a mecca for black entertainers in the East before World War I) and New York before going to Europe in 1917, where he served with the 350th Infantry.

After the war he picked up his career, touring as a soloist, making recordings (sometimes with combos), playing in nightclubs in Harlem, on Fifty-second Street, and, during the 1940s, in Greenwich Village. His tours carried him to Europe several times, to Canada, and to Africa during the 1949–50 season. Smith is best known for his piano style, which has been described as having an extraordinary mixture of power and delicacy. The titles of his pieces *(Echoes of Spring, Morning Air, Fingerbuster)* suggest his concern for expressive melody ("charming with graceful contours") and harmony ("rich and unusual"), but fail to reflect his equal concern for powerful and supple basses.

For some jazz specialists Thomas "Fats" Waller (1904–1943) represented the summation of the Harlem style and the link between it and modern jazz pianism. According to one scholar:

> His real service lay in taking the still somewhat disjunct elements of Johnson's style and unifying them into a single, cohesive jazz conception in which ragtime was still discernible underneath the surface as a source, but no longer overtly active as a separate formative element.[19]

Waller made yet another contribution to the history of jazz: he was the first person to successfully adapt the style of jazz pianism to the pipe organ and the Hammond organ.

Best known of the Harlem pianists, Waller toured the United States and Europe as piano soloist, accompanist, singer, and orchestra pianist (often with his own band). His fame spread through a long series of radio broadcasts ("Fats Waller's Rhythm Club") over station WLW in Cincinnati in 1932, and he began to record as a pianist, singer, organist, and with his ensembles. Waller was a prolific composer of jazz and popular songs. His first composition, which he called *Boston Blues,* was published as *Squeeze Me* in 1925 (with lyrics by Spencer Williams). Other well-known songs included *Honeysuckle Rose, Ain't Misbehaving, Keeping Out of Mischief,* and *I'm Gonna Sit Right Down and Write Myself a Letter.*

The Harlem pianists with their stride piano influenced not only contemporaries but also jazz musicians of later generations. Both Ellington and Basie, for example, developed their early piano styles by emulating the Harlem pianists, and Basie studied organ informally with Waller for a period at the Lincoln Theatre. Aspects of the Waller sound could be heard in Basie's playing, despite his later absorption of blues and boogie. Other pianists in the stride tradition included Clifton "Cliff" Luther Jackson (1902–1970) and Joe Turner (1907–1990), the latter settling in Paris during the 1960s.

In the Midwest during the 1920s and '30s Earl Hines (1905–1983) was laying the foundation for a different kind of jazz piano. His pianism first attracted attention when he played in Chicago with Louis Armstrong's Hot Five. Inspired by Armstrong's trumpet playing, Hines developed a piano style in which his right hand played melodic figures similar to those of a

---

[19]Schuller, *Early Jazz,* p. 225.

trumpet, but *in octaves,* while his left hand provided the firm bass of an orchestral rhythm section. Hines's so-called "trumpet piano" style was imitated widely by other pianists, black and white, of the period. The Hines style has been described as "tormented and passionate," primarily because of his predilection for suddenly introducing passages marked by great melodic and rhythmic complexity into the playing of pieces in conventional jazz style.

Theodore "Teddy" Wilson (1912–1986) studied music for a short while at Talladega College in Alabama, then left for Chicago where he began his professional career and played with bands led by Louis Armstrong and Benny Carter, among others. During the years 1936–39 he toured with white bandleader Benny Goodman in small, interracial groups along with vibraphonist Lionel Hampton, guitarist Charlie Christian, and white drummer Gene Krupa. Except for the years 1939–40, when Wilson led his big band, he played and recorded with his own small ensembles. Wilson was regarded as heir to Hines in his penchant for using tenths in the left hand against short melodic fragments outlined in octaves in the right, and in creating elegant, "swinging" improvisatory textures.

The partially blind Arthur "Art" Tatum (1909–1956) studied piano in his youth at the Toledo School of Music, where he learned how to read music. He developed his personal style, however, by listening to piano rolls, particularly those of Fats Waller, to recordings, radio broadcasts, and live performance.

His style synthesized the "horn" piano of Hines, the delicacy of Wilson, and the stride piano of Harlem and, at the same time, embraced originality and a virtuosity previously unknown in jazz piano. He was primarily a soloist, although early in his career he played with groups and accompanied both jazz and blues singers. Tatum proved to be one of the most influential jazz pianists in history, particularly for solo pianists.

JAZZ WOMEN AS BANDLEADERS

Although most of the important jazz women of this period are forgotten today, they were highly regarded during their careers, and served as mentors and sidewomen, as well as bandleaders, for a large number of jazz men who later became celebrated. Olivia Porter Shipp (1880–1980), a contemporary of Marie Lucas and Hallie Anderson and their "ladies" dance orchestras, may well have been the most active of all the women of this period. She played several instruments, but it was as bassist that she built a solid reputation for herself in New York City, playing in several bands and orchestras and leading the Negro Women's Orchestral and Civic Association. Julia Lee (1902–1958), pianist and singer, played for many years in various bands led by her brother George Lee (1896–1958). She also performed and recorded with her own band, Julia Lee and Her Boy Friends. Her contribution to the Kansas City jazz community influenced such jazzmen as Count Basie, Ben Webster, Bennie Moten, and Lester Young.

Cab Calloway credits his sister, Blanche Calloway Jones (1903?–1978), with having inducted him into the world of show business. Early in her career she toured on the revue circuit, but by the 1930s had begun to form her own groups, some of which were otherwise all male. Blanche Calloway and Her Joy Boys included such sidemen as Vic Dickenson, Ben Webster, and William "Cozy" Cole.

Mary Lou Williams (1910–1981) has been called the First Lady of Jazz because of her significance as composer, arranger, and sidewoman for major black bands. She began her professional career as a child and toured on the T.O.B.A circuit while still in her teens. She played with several groups, including the Syncopators led by her husband, John Williams, before joining Andy Kirk and His Clouds of Joy (1930–41). After her long stint with Kirk, she toured widely as a soloist and with a trio, recorded extensively, and provided arrangements for Benny Goodman, Cab Calloway, and Louis Armstrong, among others. Her religious works, including *The Zodiac Suite* (1970) and three jazz Masses, attracted special attention. The third, *Mary Lou's Mass,* was premiered in 1971 by the Alvin Ailey Dance troupe.

JAZZ COMPOSER-ARRANGERS

In one sense all the leading jazz performers were composers as well as soloists; with their improvisations they shaped the basic themes into musical compositions. But some of the jazzmen were responsible also for a large number of the original themes used as basic material, among them Louis Armstrong, Earl Hines, Richard Myknee Jones (1889–1945), King Oliver, and Spencer Williams (1889–1965). In a more conventional sense, the jazz composer was the jazz arranger, who built the original theme into a musical composition before bringing it to the band rehearsal. The talent lay in writing music that fitted in with the style of the band and of the individual soloists. The first bands to use written arrangements were those of Fletcher Henderson, Don Redman (leader of McKinney's Cotton Pickers), and Duke Ellington. The most eminent composer-arrangers were, in addition to those just cited, Benny Carter (b. 1907), Horace Henderson (1904–1988, brother of Fletcher), Alex Hill (1907–1937), James "Jimmy" Mundy (1907–1983), Fred Norman (b. 1910), Sy Oliver (1910–1988), Edgar Melvin Sampson (1907–1973), and Mary Lou Williams. Several of these arrangers also composed symphonic music—notably, Duke Ellington.

WHITE MUSICIANS AND JAZZ

Along with the emergence of the African-Americans big bands, a comparable development took place in the world of mainstream jazz. Among the white bands most highly regarded by jazz experts were those of Benny Goodman, Tommy Dorsey, Jimmy Dorsey, Bob Crosby, Glenn Miller, Artie Shaw, and Glen Gray (Casa Loma Orchestra). Paul Whiteman, originally of Denver, was the leader of the best-known "symphonic jazz" orchestra in New York. Several of the big bands used arrangements written by blacks: Sy Oliver arranged for the Dorsey band; Jimmy Mundy wrote for Paul Whiteman; Horace Henderson, for Charlie Barnet. Benny Goodman probably used arrangements of black musicians to a greater extent than anyone; at one time or another he employed as arrangers Fletcher Henderson, Horace Henderson, Benny Carter, Edgar Sampson, Fred Norman, and Jimmy Mundy. Bob Crosby occasionally played arrangements adapted from interpretations of major jazz figures such as Louis Armstrong.

Some white bandleaders, such as Dorsey, Charlie Barnet, and Gene Krupa, consistently used black singers or instrumentalists. Benny Goodman, however, was the first to use black jazzmen on a regular basis when Teddy Wilson and Lionel Hampton joined him in 1936. Goodman is credited with being the first white bandleader to break racial taboos in the music industry when he hired black musicians as regular, integrated members of his band. Several of the African-American big bands, Duke Ellington's and Count Basie's, began to include whites in the 1950s. To be sure, integrated music ensembles became more common during the 1940s, and in the following decades some of the small combos were mixed racially. On the other hand, the mixing of black and white jazz musicians in recording studios began in the 1920s. Jelly Roll Morton undoubtedly was the first to record with a white band, when he played piano with the New Orleans Rhythm Kings in 1923. Among the black recording groups of the '20s and '30s that included white musicians were those of Louis Armstrong and Fats Waller.

After World War I, leading European composers began to realize the rich promise and vitality of jazz and to incorporate some aspects of the style in their works. The list of these composers is long and includes the names of such eminent figures as Alban Berg, Frederick Delius, Paul Hindemith, Ernst Krenek, Darius Milhaud, Francis Poulenc, Maurice Ravel, Arnold Schoenberg, Igor Stravinsky, Kurt Weill, and William Walton.

These men heard authentic jazz when touring ensembles played in Europe or when they visited the United States; for example, Milhaud, when he visited Harlem in 1920, and Ravel, when he went to Chicago in 1928. Several of these men, of course, eventually settled permanently in the United States. Best known of the works inspired by jazz were Krenek's opera *Jonny spielt auf* (Johnny Strikes Up the Band, 1927), Milhaud's ballet *La Création du monde* (The Creation of the World, 1923), Ravel's Piano Concerto in D (1931), and William Walton's *Façade* (1922). In Krenek's opera, the hero Johnny is a black bandleader from Alabama. Although Stravinsky was among the first of the major composers to use ragtime idioms and to employ elements of jazz in his compositions, it was not until 1945 that he wrote a work entirely in the jazz style, the *Ebony Concerto for Dance Orchestra*.

The Jazz Age also inspired a number of white American composers to write works employing elements of jazz style. Among the most enduring of the symphonic works have been Aaron Copland's *Music for the Theater* (1925) and Concerto for Piano and Orchestra (1927); John Alden Carpenter's ballets *Krazy Kat* (1921) and *Skyscrapers* (1926); and George Gershwin's *Rhapsody in Blue* (1924), Concerto in F (1925), and *An American in Paris* (1928). Among Gershwin's piano compositions, the three Preludes in jazz style won lasting popularity. Finally, there is Ferde Grofé's *Grand Canyon Suite* (1931).

THE END OF AN ERA

Although the Great Depression, with its attendant economic distress for all levels of the population, had caused record companies to cut their production activities sharply, by the mid-1930s the record industry was on its way up again, aided immensely by the jukebox, a commercial record player that blared out the latest popular songs in luncheonettes, diners, drugstores, ice-cream parlors, bars, and cabarets all over the nation. In black communities, the jukebox also promoted race music—the blues, jazz, popular music, and swing of black performers. All this activity came to a slowdown, however, when the United States was plunged into war on December 7, 1941.

The next year the government cut the use of shellac for nonmilitary purposes by 70 per cent; with this basic ingredient of records in such short supply, the record industry had no choice but to cut back production. Another contributing factor in the decline of the record industry was an action taken by the American Federation of Musicians, which had become more and more apprehensive about the competition offered to live musical performance by the jukebox. In July 1942 the AF of M ordered a ban on commercial recording that lasted for two years.

CHAPTER 11

The Harlem Renaissance and Beyond

D URING the post–World War I period there developed in the United States a new interest in the so-called "Negro problem." White sociologists began investigating the plight of black people in the South and in the ghettos of the North; white novelists and dramatists became interested in the possibilities of utilizing Negro themes in their works; and, as we have seen, white composers experimented with employing Negro folk music and jazz in composition. Moreover, the white public in general displayed a growing interest in learning more about black Americans and particularly about their arts. Black folk, too, were becoming more interested in learning about themselves. They were becoming increasingly aware that the democracy for which they had fought in Europe did not exist for them in the United States. Furthermore, they were becoming more militant and more articulate in expressing their concern.

On various levels and in diverse ways the black population made known its discontent. There were so many race riots during the summer of 1919 that writer James Weldon Johnson named it "The Red Summer." The various national Negro organizations embarked on more vigorous programs of action to obtain the rights of citizenship for the black population—such groups, for example, as the NAACP (the National Association for the Advancement of Colored People, organized 1909), the Urban League (the National League on Urban Conditions, established 1911), the National Race Congress, and the National Baptist Convention. In New York the magnetic activist Marcus Garvey succeeded in gaining the support of hundreds of thousands of disenchanted black folk from all over the country for his "back to Africa" movement. A general feeling of unrest, defiance, impatience, and even bitterness swept over black communities; few were unaffected.

In New York, the nation's business, cultural, and intellectual center—and particularly in Harlem, the undeclared capital of black intellectual life—black artists began to rally their forces. Writers, poets, painters, and musicians joined together to protest in their own way against the quality of life for black folk in the United States. Out of this grew what has been called "The Harlem Renaissance" or "The Black Renaissance" or "The New Negro Movement." It manifested itself primarily in literature. James Weldon Johnson informally inaugurated the movement with his publication of *Fifty Years and Other Poems* in 1917. (The title poem of the collection referred to the fifty years that had elapsed since the signing of the Emancipation Proclamation, which was supposed to bring first-class citizenship to Negroes.) Other books soon followed—collections of poems, novels, prose—written by Claude McKay, Jean Toomer, Countee Cullen, William S. Braithwaite, Langston Hughes, Jessie Redmond Fauset, Walter White, Johnson, and others. In national periodicals could be found articles about the renaissance by such writers as W. E. B. Du Bois, George Schuyler, E. Franklin Frazier, Benjamin Brawley, Joel A. Rogers, Arthur Schomburg, and Alain Leroy Locke. Two Negro periodicals, *Crisis* (organ of the NAACP) and *Opportunity,* offered prizes to stimulate literary production among black writers and to encourage the younger ones.

Black musicians participated in the movement by turning to the folk music of the race as a source of materials in composition and performance. Some black composers had been drawing on such materials for a number of years—particularly those who had been associated with the musical nationalism advocated by Dvořák in 1895—but now they became more race conscious than ever. Composers used poems by black poets in their art songs; they exploited the rhythms of Negro dances and the harmonies and melodies of blues, spirituals, and the newer music called jazz in their composed concert music. Almost without exception black concert artists began to include on their programs the folk and composed music of black musicians, and some artists staged recitals consisting exclusively of black music.

Various organizations and individuals offered awards and prizes to black musicians who made significant achievements. In 1914 the NAACP instituted the Spingarn Medal for a Negro who during the period of any one year made the highest achievement in a field of human endeavor. Beginning in 1920 the National Association of Negro Musicians gave scholarships to talented singers, held workshops and seminars for professional musicians, and provided occasions for the performance of works composed by black musicians.

In 1925 a black New York businessman, Casper Holstein, donated substantial sums of money for annual prizes to be given to composers who competed successfully in contests set up by the magazine *Opportunity.* The

Rodman Wanamaker Musical Composition Contests for black musicians, established in 1927, offered prizes in several categories: songs, choral works, symphonic works, and solo instrumental pieces. The Harmon Foundation gave awards for both composition and performance. Finally, ambitious musicians could compete, as we shall see, for prizes offered by some white organizations and institutions without regard for race or color.

For black concert musicians and composers of art music, the decades of the '20s and '30s were full of paradoxes. Because of the barriers of discrimination, performers generally found it very difficult to launch a career, regardless of how well qualified they were—and yet by 1941 there were three blacks among the ten most highly paid concert artists in the United States, and a fourth was near the top. Black composers generally found that the doors of publishing houses were closed to them, and that leading music organizations would not perform their music—but it was during this period that, for the first time in history, major symphony orchestras performed works written by black composers, major opera companies used black singers in leading roles, black musicians conducted symphony orchestras and radio orchestras, wrote scores for full-length movie films, and appeared in drama and ballet productions on Broadway.

More than ever before, individual black artists received recognition for achievement. Some composers, for example, were given commissions to write works and gained opportunities for performances. Talented students were given fellowships for further study after graduating from the nation's conservatories, often for study abroad. It is noteworthy that young white Americans struggling to get started in musical careers frequently met with some of the same obstacles that black Americans faced—except, of course, for racial discrimination. For them, also, the postwar decades were a time of both uncertainty and promise, primarily because of the changing attitude of the nation toward the arts.

THE GENERAL STATE OF MUSIC IN THE NATION

Since the beginning of the twentieth century, various European schools of music had begun to challenge the domination of German romanticism and to strike out in new directions toward the establishment either of national schools or of more international music. The United States, at the end of the war, was on the brink of a period of extraordinary musical development and expansion. The movement to increase music-training opportunities for young people, which had begun after the Civil War, gained momentum. Between the years 1921 and 1923, three of the world's finest music schools were established in the East, schools that offered to Americans for the first time the opportunity to study music under the same ideal conditions as in Europe. All three institutions—the Eastman School of Music in Rochester, New York (1921); the Juilliard Graduate School in New York City (1923);

and the Curtis Institute of Music in Philadelphia (1923)—opened with generous endowments that allowed them to gather the finest artist-teachers from all over the world for their faculties. Eastman, under the direction of the composer Howard Hanson, became famous for its emphasis on composition and for its sponsorship of concerts featuring the works of American composers. Juilliard (which combined with the Institute of Musical Art in 1926) and Curtis became noted for the training of concert and opera performers. From these schools would come the most celebrated black musicians of the mid-century period.

A second interest among musicians of progressive outlook was the improvement of the status of American composers. In 1919 the Society for the Publication of American Music was established. In 1921 two organizations were set up with the primary purpose of providing for the performance of American works and the commissioning of new works: the International Composers' Guild and the League of Composers. The latter soon began the publication of a periodical, *Modern Music,* and arranged for exchange concerts with European organizations. (In 1954 this organization merged with the American section of the International Society for Contemporary Music.)

Not to be overlooked in the drive for bettering the condition of the American composer were the established concert artists and the directors of leading symphonies and opera companies, whose responsibility it was to ensure that the new works of American composers received not only a first performance, but also a second and a third. Fortunately, during this period some of the world's most illustrious musicians assumed the leadership of the prominent orchestras. Leopold Stokowski had gone to the Philadelphia Orchestra in 1912; Serge Koussevitsky became conductor of the Boston Symphony in 1924; and Arturo Toscanini took over the New York Philharmonic in 1926.

There were yet other sources of encouragement to promising young black musicians; for example, the Walter Naumburg Musical Foundation Award in New York, the Guggenheim Foundation Fellowships, and the Metropolitan Opera Auditions. When the Great Depression came at the end of the 1920s, the federal government's WPA (Works Progress Administration) came to the rescue of American musicians, especially benefiting black Americans by providing jobs for them in community music projects and setting up orchestras, choral groups, and chamber music groups that not only employed musicians but also performed works of American composers.

Black Americans continued to go abroad for additional study—the composers going now more often to France than to Germany, particularly to the composer-teacher Nadia Boulanger, who had a reputation for developing craftsmanship in students without destroying their individuality. Well-trained singers found opportunities for advancement more plentiful in Europe than in America, especially in opera. Consequently, many began their careers over there. And when they returned to the United States with European credentials, they found it easier to launch American careers.

Black music students and established musicians were greatly affected by the developments taking place in the field of music on both the national level and in the smaller black world. The musicians who won distinction during the period spent long years of study and sacrifice in preparation for their careers. They availed themselves of every opportunity for study and for gaining experience, in order to develop poise and self-assurance. The concert artists participated in competitions, sang in church choirs and in local choral organizations, and gave recitals in churches and schools. The composers played in musical-comedy and jazz orchestras, wrote music for radio programs and film shorts, and, like the performers, entered all of the competitions that were open to them.

In addition to the organizations and institutions discussed above that helped struggling black artists to move ahead, there were always the black church and the black college. The church discovered black talent, fostered its growth by sponsoring recitals, and often paid for advanced study by the talented through fund-raising among the members of the congregation. The school, and particularly the college, played a similar role. In several instances, members of college communities raised funds to send a gifted student away for advanced study.

Established musicians found employment in the black colleges, which allowed them to combine concertizing or composing with teaching, and assisted them in obtaining grants for study or for composing. The choruses and orchestras of these colleges were invaluable to composer-teachers, of course, as media for testing the effectiveness of their compositions. To a limited extent, the black-owned theater also assisted the development of concert musicians, although its greatest contribution was in the field of entertainment music and jazz.

The leading musical figures of the Black Renaissance displayed their race consciousness in a number of ways. As we have noted, they chose to work with Negro materials in their singing, playing, or composing. Some spoke out publicly against discrimination and other social evils; one or two refused to perform for segregated audiences. The important black artists of the time helped the younger artists by counseling them, sponsoring recitals for them, and giving them letters of introduction to white organizations and private individuals who could further their careers.

IN THE CONCERT WORLD

To the black communities that helped them to rise, the black concert artists who achieved distinction during the Harlem Renaissance were more than just talented and successful individuals. They became race symbols, whose successes were shared vicariously by the great mass of black Americans that

A poster for Roland Hayes's concert tour in Russia, 1928. *(Photo by F. W. Woolsey of the Louisville Times. Courtesy of the author)*

could never hope to attain similar distinction. Any artist who succeeded in breaking down a color barrier inspired other talented black men and women to overcome almost insurmountable difficulties. In a very real sense, the artist was a trail-blazer, proving to white America that given the chance, black artists could sing, play, and compose. The artists made it easier for those who followed after them to obtain concert management or to get a symphony performed, to enter a career in opera, or to become a symphony conductor or instrumentalist. Predictably, it was the black singer who led the way to the international concert stage; over the years black singers had met with less discrimination than instrumentalists, and the post–World War I years proved to be no different in that regard.

Roland Hayes (1887–1976) was the first black male to win wide acclaim at home and abroad as a concert artist. He obtained his basic musical training in Chattanooga with Arthur Calhoun and at Fisk University in Nashville. Later he studied with Arthur Hubbard in Boston and with George Henschel and Amanda Ira Aldridge in London, England. Hayes began singing in public even during his student days and in 1911 toured with the Fisk Jubilee Singers. Thereafter he settled down for serious study with Hubbard, supporting himself by working as a messenger at the Hancock Life Insurance Company.

He seized every opportunity to sing before the public; he arranged his own recitals, which included several coast-to-coast tours during the years 1916–19, and accepted invitations to sing on all the important concerts of the decade—Craig's Pre-Lenten Recitals and, later, the Carnegie Hall concerts in New York; the concerts of the Philadelphia Concert Orchestra; William Hackney's Orchestra Hall concerts in Chicago; the Atlanta Colored Music Festivals; and the Washington Conservatory concerts in Washington, D.C. In 1917 Hayes toured with his Hayes Trio, composed of baritone William Richardson (1869–1930s) pianist William Lawrence (1895–1981) (his regular accompanist), and himself. Later that year he made his debut in Boston's Symphony Hall, but attracted little public support despite critical acclaim. After a second, more successful recital, he left in 1920 for London, with plans to study further and concertize.

In April 1920 Hayes made his debut at London's Aeolian Hall, with Lawrence Brown (1893–1972) at the piano. This led to more engagements, of which the highlight was a command performance before King George V in 1921. Within a relatively short period, Hayes was singing in the major capitals of Europe, and in 1923 he returned home a celebrity. For the first time he was able to secure professional management, the Boston Symphony Orchestra Concert Company.

The recital given by Hayes on December 2, 1923, at Boston in Symphony Hall marked the beginning of a long, illustrious career on the concert stages of the world. Sometime later a notice about Hayes would carry the headline, "From Stove Molder to $100,000 a Year,"[1] and a critic could observe:

> [He] is an artist primarily, and a Negro incidentally . . . the essentially racial quality of his singing is something that exists chiefly in the imaginations of his more romantic hearers. . . . [He] has a beautiful tenor voice, silken smooth in mezzo forte, ringingly vibrant in fortes, and trained to perfect evenness of production in all of its registers.[2]

Other critics wrote about his "meticulous phrasing," "lyric tone," and "mastery of fine nuances in expressive and musical color." He was acclaimed for his perfect command of language in his singing of French, German, and Italian songs, and for his catholic taste in selecting song materials. A 1953 program included, for example, two songs from a fifteenth-century source, the *Lochamer Liederbuch;* songs by a white contemporary composer, Germaine Tailleferre; and spirituals arranged by black composers William Grant Still and Edward Boatner.

[1]Mary Mullett, "From Stove Molder to $100,000 a Year," *The American Magazine* (June 1925): 26 ff.
[2]Quotation reproduced in Vertical Files for Roland Hayes at the Schomburg Center for Research in Black Culture, New York. Deems Taylor, music review in the *New York World,* October 24, 1924.

Marian Anderson. *(Courtesy of the author)*

Hayes had very positive ideas regarding the importance of Negro folk music. He once said to an interviewer:

> My people have been very shy about singing their crude little songs before white folks. They thought they would be laughed at—and they were! And so they came to despise their own heritage. . . . If, as I truly believe, there is purpose and plan in my life, it is this: that I shall have my share in rediscovering the qualities we have almost let slip away from us; and that we shall make our special contribution—only a humble one perhaps, but our very own—to human experience.[3]

Hayes performed throughout the Western world during his long career, appearing with major symphony orchestras as well as in solo recitals, and enjoyed an international reputation during the 1920s–40s as one of the world's leading concert tenors. His interest in black folksongs led him to publish a collection of his favorites, *My Songs; Aframerican Religious Folk Songs* (1948).

Marian Anderson (1902–1993) was destined to climb even higher on the ladder of fame than Hayes. As a child she sang in church choirs of Philadelphia, her home, and first appeared in public at the age of ten as "the

[3]Vertical Files for Roland Hayes, Schomburg.

baby contralto." She began serious voice study as a high-school junior with local teacher Mary Patterson, who refused to accept payment for the lessons. Encouraged by her family, her church, and the community, she sang constantly on local concerts and even traveled as far as New York to perform. Then her church, the Union Baptist, set up a trust fund for her that enabled her to extend her studies; she later worked with Agnes Reifsyner, Guiseppe Boghetti, and Frank La Forge, among others.

In 1922 she made her debut at Town Hall in New York, but the reviews were less than enthusiastic, as they were again after her New York recital in 1924. But in 1925 she won first place in a singing competition held by the New York Philharmonic at Lewisohn Stadium. The critical acclaim she received led to more engagements, and in 1929 she went abroad to study further, having received a Rosenwald Fellowship.

During the 1930s Anderson acquired European management and toured widely in Europe; in 1935 she made her debut in Paris and further enhanced her growing reputation as a gifted artist. Later that year impresario Sol Hurok, the giant in the concert-management field, heard her perform and offered her a contract. In August 1935, she sang in Salzburg, Austria; it was her usual program of lieder ending with a group of spirituals. Afterwards a listener wrote about the audience's response:

> At the end of the [last] spiritual, there was no applause at all—a silence instinctive, natural, and intense, so that you were afraid to breathe. What Anderson had done was something outside the limits of classical or romantic music: she frightened us with the conception, in musical terms, of course, but outside the normal limits, of a mighty suffering.[4]

And conductor Arturo Toscanini, who was in the audience, told her, "Yours is a voice such as one hears once in a hundred years."[5] By 1941 Anderson was one of the ten highest-paid concert artists in the United States.

She continued to grow as a musician. In 1952 she made her television debut, singing a program of sacred music on the Ed Sullivan Show. Three years later, in January 1955, Anderson made history when she sang the role of Ulrica in Verdi's *Un ballo in maschera* at the Metropolitan Opera, the first black artist to sing with the Metropolitan. In 1957 she toured in Southeast Asia as a goodwill ambassador for the U.S. State Department and ANTA (American National Theater and Academy). The next year she was appointed a member of the U.S. delegation to the United Nations.

During the season of 1964–65 Anderson gave fifty-one farewell concerts across the nation, climaxing her thirty-one-year career as "the world's greatest living contralto" with a final concert at Carnegie Hall in New York on Easter Sunday. She sang before audiences all over the world during her long

---

[4]Vincent Sheean, *Between the Thunder and the Sun* (New York, 1943); reprinted in Lindsay Patterson, ed., *The Negro in Music and Art* (Washington, D.C., 1967), p. 158.
[5]Quotation from Marian Anderson, *My Lord, What a Morning* (New York, 1956), p. 158.

Paul Robeson in the movie "Big Fella." *(Courtesy New York Public Library. Schomburg Center for Research in Black Culture)*

career, and her achievements were both numerous and impressive. The Marian Anderson Fellowships she established in 1942 served as a lasting memorial to her accomplishments as a concert singer; many of the fellowship recipients became renowned concert and opera singers.

During this period Paul Robeson (1898–1976) was as celebrated as Hayes and Anderson, although he did not have comparable musical training. In fact, he began his professional career as an actor, and for most of his life was active in the theater or in films. In 1925 he made his debut, to critical acclaim, as a bass-baritone in New York's Greenwich Village Theatre, singing a program consisting solely of Negro spirituals. This was the first all-spirituals concert in history. The next year he repeated the concert in Town Hall with equally successful results, and for thirty-five years thereafter toured throughout the world singing the folksongs of his people and of other ethnic groups, accompanied at the piano by Lawrence Brown, who had played for Roland Hayes in the early 1920s.

Robeson also was active in musical theater: in 1928 he sang the role of Joe in the London production of *Show Boat,* in 1932 he sang in the Broadway revival of that musical, and in 1936 he sang in the second filming of *Show Boat.* He also sang in other film musicals. During the 1940s Robeson was counted among the top ten concert artists in the United States. Some of his performances were associated with political activism, for example, the *Ballad for Americans,* which was given its premiere via radio broadcast in 1939, and his folksong recitals in later years.

Another renowned concert artist of the period was Dorothy Maynor (1910–1996), a soprano who was encouraged to embark on a concert career by R. Nathaniel Dett at Hampton Institute, from which she graduated in 1933. She studied further at the Westminster Choir School in Princeton, New Jersey, and privately in New York with William Klamroth and John Alan Haughton. Conductor Serge Koussevitsky aided her career development after she auditioned for him in 1939 at the Berkshire Music Festival in Massachusetts. She made her debut in November of that year at Town Hall in New York, and soon after made her recording debut.

Maynor established herself as one of the leading concert artists of the nation and as a member of the select circle of celebrated black artists, along with Anderson, Hayes, and Robeson. She toured widely throughout the world, appearing with major symphony orchestras and giving recitals. After retiring from the concert stage in 1965, she founded the Harlem School of the Arts and served as its first director until 1980. Thus she shared her talent and experience with the children and youth of Harlem.

Concert / Opera Singers

Hayes, Anderson, Robeson, and Maynor were the first black Americans to win secure places in the galaxy of concert stars; their accomplishments not only inspired others to emulate them but also lowered the barriers of race discrimination. On a less lofty plane other black singers of the 1920s–30s also were taking giant steps. Some began to sing with established opera companies for the first time; predictably, most entered through the doorway of Verdi's *Aïda,* where color was to their advantage. Two operas of the 1930s, Thomson's *Four Saints in Three Acts* (1934) and Gershwin's *Porgy and Bess* (1935), also served as points of entry for African Americans hopeful of careers in opera, as did, to a lesser extent, the drama *The Green Pastures* (1930) and the several films with all-black casts that were released during the decade, including *Hallelujah* and *The Green Pastures.* Finally, a small number of singers began their careers in Broadway musicals and from there moved into opera.

Efforts of African Americans to produce grand opera date back to the late nineteenth century, as we have seen, with the productions of Theodore Drury. In later years there were sporadic attempts made to organize black opera companies, but it was not until 1941 that the first permanent one came into existence. Mary Cardwell Dawson (1894–1962), who founded the National Negro Opera Company in 1941 at Pittsburgh, Pennsylvania, prepared for a career in music with studies at the New England Conservatory and Chicago Musical College. In 1927 she set up the Cardwell School of Music in Pittsburgh and thereafter toured frequently with its resident Cardwell–Dawson Chorus.

Her continuous contacts with singers made her aware of the difficulties that confronted black voice students who wanted to sing opera. Consequently, she founded her company with a twofold purpose: to inspire black students to study opera, and to provide a training ground for those students aspiring to become opera singers. (We shall return to the discussion of black opera companies.)

Lillian Evanti (1890–1967) was one of the first black Americans to sing in opera abroad; in 1927 she made her debut in the title role of Delibes's *Lakmé* at Nice, France. A graduate of Howard University (B. Mus.) she studied further in France and Italy during the 1920s. As both concert soprano and opera singer she toured widely in Europe and South America as well as at home. In 1943 she attracted special attention for her performance as Violetta in Verdi's *La traviata* in a production of the National Negro Opera Company.

Todd Duncan (b. 1903) was the first black male to sing with a major opera company. He came to the experience with excellent credentials; after obtaining his musical education at Butler University in Indianapolis (B.A.) and Columbia University Teachers College (M.A.) he studied privately. Thereafter he toured as a concert baritone, sang in several Broadway musicals, and sang in films. In 1934 he made his debut in Mascagni's *Cavalleria rusticana* at the Mecca Temple in New York; in 1935 he created the role of Porgy in *Porgy and Bess* in New York; and in 1944 he made his concert debut at New York's Town Hall.

It was in 1945, however, that he made history when he sang the role of Tonio in Leoncavallo's *I pagliacci* with the New York City Opera Company, thereby becoming the first of his race to sing with a major American company. Later the same year he sang the role of Escamillo in Bizet's *Carmen*.

Duncan successfully combined a teaching career at Howard University with extensive concert touring throughout the world, accompanied by concert pianist William Allen. After retiring Duncan opened a voice studio and continued to give recitals periodically. In 1978 the Washington Performing Arts Society held a gala celebration of his seventy-fifth birthday.

Another pioneering opera singer was Caterina Jarboro (1903–1986), who received her basic training in her native North Carolina, then went to New York for further study. She became involved with theater musicals and sang in Blake and Sissle's *Shuffle Along* (1921) and James P. Johnson's *Running Wild* (1923), among others. About 1926 she went abroad to study and to sing; in 1930 she made her operatic debut in the title role of Verdi's *Aïda* at the Puccini Theater in Milan. Thereafter she sang with several opera companies in Europe and the United States, making her American debut in 1933 with Salmaggi's Chicago Opera Company at the Hippodrome in New York.[6]

Baritone Jules Bledsoe (1898–1943) graduated from Bishop College in

---

[6]See further in regard to black singers with Salmaggi's opera company in Cardell Bishop, *Opera at the Hippodrome in New York City* (Santa Monica, CA, 1979).

Texas (A.B.) and studied further at Virginia Union College and Columbia University. He went to New York to prepare for a career in medicine, but was persuaded by admiring friends to continue his vocal studies. His debut recital at Aeolian Hall in 1924 was impressive enough to obtain for him the management of impresario Sol Hurok; thereafter he toured at home and abroad as a concert singer. Beginning in 1926 he turned to the stage, singing in Frank Harling's opera *Deep River* and, the next year, creating the role of Joe in Jerome Kern's *Show Boat.*

Bledsoe sang several "big" opera roles: Amonasro in Verdi's *Aïda* with Salmaggi's Chicago Opera at the Hippodrome, the title role of Gruenberg's *The Emperor Jones,* also at the Hippodrome, and the title role of Mussorgsky's *Boris Godunov* with the Italian Opera in Holland. During these years he also toured on the concert circuit and served on the music staff of the Roxy Theatre on Broadway as a member of Roxy's Gang. He was the first black artist to be employed continuously by a Broadway theater. In 1935 he programmed a series for the British Broadcasting Company, "Songs of the Negro", and the following year he sang in the London production of *Blackbirds of 1936*. A versatile and gifted musician, Bledsoe made several recordings of his songs and compositions, of which the best known is the *African Suite for Violin and Orchestra.*

Chicago had its pioneering black opera singers in La Julia Rhea (1908–1992) and William Franklin (b. 1906). Rhea obtained her musical education in Louisville, Kentucky, and in Chicago. In 1929 she made her concert debut as a soprano at Kimball Hall in Chicago and during the next decade sang regularly on concerts, studied operatic roles, and in 1931 took a leading role in the Broadway musical *Rhapsody in Black*. It was in 1937 that she made her operatic debut with the Chicago City Opera Company in the title role of Verdi's *Aïda,* with Franklin as Amonasro.

Franklin was also making his operatic debut. Both he and Rhea sang later in other operas, including productions of the National Negro Opera Company, and in Gilbert and Sullivan operettas, in addition to touring as concert artists. Franklin attracted special attention for his many performances of the title role in the Gilbert and Sullivan operetta *The Mikado*. He also sang the male lead in a revival of *Porgy and Bess* in 1944, and during the late 1940s he sang with the Southernaires.

Porgy and Bess served as a showcase for talented singers from the time of its first production in 1935 through its numerous revivals in later years. Soprano Anne Brown (b. 1915) created the role of Bess in the 1935 production. She obtained her musical training at Morgan College in Baltimore and at the Institute of Musical Art in New York (now the Juilliard School of Music). After her debut in *Porgy and Bess* she sang in Broadway musicals and, later, in revivals of *Porgy*. During the years 1942–48 she toured extensively as a concert artist, then settled in Norway in 1948, where she continued activity as a professional musician. In 1950 she sang in Norwegian productions of Menotti's *The Medium* and *The Telephone*.

Etta Moten (b. 1901) attracted wide attention when she sang the role of Bess in a revival of *Porgy and Bess* (1943–44). Her professional career, however, began much earlier. She received her musical education at Western University in Quindaro, Kansas, and at the University of Kansas (B.A.). After graduation from college she went to New York, where she was a soloist with the Eva Jessye Choir. Thereafter she sang in musicals, both stage and film, including *Golddiggers of 1933* and *Flying Down to Rio* (1934). During the 1940s–60s she toured widely as a concert contralto on the college-concert and lecture circuits.

The New York City Opera was responsible for the debuts of two other black singers in the 1940s, along with that of Todd Duncan. Baritone Lawrence Winters (1915–1965) was a graduate of Howard University (B.Mus), where he studied with Duncan, and later began his career singing in the Eva Jessye Choir. In 1941 he sang the leading role in a concert production of the opera *Ouanga,* written by Clarence Cameron White, then entered the U.S. Armed Forces, where he served as a music director in the Special Services Division at Fort Huachuca, Arizona. In 1947 he made his concert debut at Town Hall in New York, and it was the following year, 1948, that he made his debut with the New York City Opera as Amonasro in Verdi's *Aïda.* Like many of his contemporaries, Winter also toured on the concert circuit and sang in musicals; he attracted special attention for his performance in *Call Me Mister* (1946). In 1952 he made his European operatic debut in *Aïda* with the Hamburg (Germany) State Opera; in 1961 he became principal baritone with the company and remained there until his death in 1965.

Soprano Camilla Williams (b. 1922), the first African-American woman to sing with the New York City Opera, obtained her musical education at Virginia State College (B.S.) and studied privately in New York. In 1943 and 1944 she won Marian Anderson Fellowships and her career was off to a fine start. During the next few years she won honors in vocal competitions, performed on a RCA coast-to-coast radio network, and recorded. In 1946 she made her debut with the New York City Opera singing the title role in Puccini's *Madama Butterfly.* Thereafter she sang with opera companies in the United States and in Europe, and also toured as a concert artist. In 1977 she was appointed to the music faculty at Indiana University. In 1951, baritone Fred Thomas (b. 1914) became the first African-American artist to appear on a Metropolitan Auditions of the Air progam, tying for second place in the annual competitions. His honors included cash prizes and a Metropolitan Opera scholarship—but no contract!

Concert Artists in Mid-Career

Several artists who began their careers in an earlier period continued to perform during the 1920s–40s, among them pianist Hazel Harrison and sopranos Florence Talbert and Abbie Mitchell. Mitchell (1884–1960) came late to the concert stage, having begun her career in musical comedy in 1898 in Will Marion Cook's *Clorindy; or, The Origin of the Cakewalk*. Thereafter she sang with Black Patti's Troubadours, the Walker and Williams companies, and in the Cole–Johnson operetta, *The Red Moon*. She was a member of both "editions" of the Memphis Students (1905, 1908) and went to Europe with Cook's Southern Syncopated Orchestra in 1919. She then turned to the concert stage, opera, and teaching. She was active in New York during her later career, except during the years 1932–34, when she taught at Tuskegee Institute in Alabama. Her last stage appearance was in the role of Clara in *Porgy and Bess* (1935). Hazel Harrison combined college teaching with concertizing beginning in 1931; she taught at Tuskegee Institute, then Howard University, and finally at Alabama State College.

MUSICAL ORGANIZATIONS

New York was the musical center of the nation for black concert artists—as indeed it was also for the mainstream music establishment—and many of them eventually settled there at some point in their careers.[7] Musicians could always find some kind of employment in New York—in the churches, music schools, cabarets, dancing schools, Broadway theaters, Harlem theaters, and other urban institutions. Moreover, the city could be used as a base from which to tour on the concert circuit. Harlem was a city within the city for black musicians; every conceivable kind of musical activity could be found within its boundaries.

During the 1920s–40s New York was an active dispenser of culture. There was the Negro String Quartet; Will Marion Cook staged concerts, such as Negro Nuances in 1924 or Virginia Nights in 1925, with one or the other of his choral groups; a Young Woman's Orchestra gave regular concerts; and the Monarch Symphonic Band, led by Fred Simpson, sponsored a regular concert series for more than a dozen years, beginning in the early 1930s. In addition, there were the annual concerts given by various music schools. All these organizations called upon established concert performers (black and white) to serve as guest artists on the programs.

Adding to the constant flow of concerts were the individual recitals given in large numbers. Every week there was someone, it seems, making a debut or pulling off a "first" that called for a musical celebration—as in 1923, for example, when David I. Martin, Jr., became the first black violinist to graduate from the Institute of Musical Art, or in 1924 when Rudolph Dunbar received a diploma in clarinet, piano, and composition from that prestigious institution. Some twenty years later Dunbar would win renown in Europe as a symphony orchestra conductor.

[7]This discussion is based largely upon my systematic examination of the music and stage-news pages of the *New York Age* and the *Chicago Defender* during the years ca. 1905–40.

It was inevitable that Harlem instrumentalists should attempt to organize another symphony orchestra after the demise of James Reese Europe's Clef Club Symphony and Negro Symphony Orchestra. About 1917 Edward Gilbert Anderson, formerly director of the Philadelphia Concert Orchestra, had left Philadelphia to settle in New York, and within a few years had organized the Harlem Symphony Orchestra and the Renaissance Theatre Orchestra. The idea that Harlem should maintain a symphony orchestra seems to have disappeared after Anderson's death in 1926, but in the 1930s others made attempts to revive the idea. Dean Dixon (1915–1976), who later would become an eminent symphony conductor, organized two groups in 1932, the Dean Dixon Symphony Orchestra and the Dean Dixon Choral Society. He was still a student at Juilliard at that time.

And in 1938 a white conductor, Ignatz Waghalter, organized the Negro Symphony Orchestra and appointed Alfred Jack Thomas of Baltimore as the associate conductor. Thomas (1884–1962) had had many years of experience in conducting instrumental groups. The Negro Symphony Orchestra proved to be short-lived, however, and Thomas returned to Baltimore in 1946, where he established his Baltimore Institute of Musical Arts.

Although preeminent in the field of music, New York was not the only urban community to support black musical organizations during the 1920s–40s. In Chicago, for example, Pauline James Lee founded the Chicago University of Music in 1920 and succeeded in attracting to her faculty some of the finest black musicians in the nation. In 1925, opera singer Ernestine Schumann-Heink gave Lee a fine building in which to house the music school. Other Chicago musicians who contributed to maintaining the city's lively music schedule were pianist Tom Theodore Taylor and singers George Williams and John Greene. In 1923 violinist Harrison Ferrell (ca. 1901–1976) organized the Ferrell Symphony Orchestra. Although a well trained musician, Ferrell earned his Ph.D. in Romance languages and left the city in 1928 to teach at West Virginia State College. But he did not disband the orchestra; instead he put assistant conductor Owen Lawson in charge of the orchestra, and returned to Chicago each summer to conduct it.

In 1929 W. Llewellyn Wilson founded the Baltimore City Colored Orchestra, which gave frequent concerts during the 1930s–40s. In Philadelphia Raymond Lowden Smith, formerly a member of the old Philadelphia Concert Orchestra, formed a new orchestra in 1930, calling it the E. Gilbert Anderson Memorial Symphony in honor of the old orchestra's first conductor. The orchestra's name was changed to Philadelphia Concert Orchestra in 1944. In Boston there was the Victorian Concert Orchestra, founded in 1906 by Charles Sullivan, who remained its manager until his death in 1933. During the years 1914–20 Clarence Cameron White conducted the orchestra, which continued to give concerts through the 1930s. And far off in Nebraska, a military-symphonic band led by Dan Desdunes developed such a good reputation that it won national attention.

Professional Choruses

It was during the 1920s that professional black choruses began to appear regularly on the concert and theater stage and in films. Before that period the black singing groups that toured throughout the world were more ensembles than choruses—except for the Williams Jubilee Singers—who modeled themselves after the Fisk Jubilee Singers and the Hampton Students. Rarely did these groups include more than ten or twelve members. Hall Johnson and Eva Jessye were pioneers in the new movement to develop concert choral groups.

Johnson (1888–1970) acquired his musical training at the University of Pennsylvania (B.A.) and the Institute of Musical Art in New York. About 1914 he settled in New York and became active as a violinist and violist in Harlem: he played in the groups led by James Reese Europe that toured with dancers Vernon and Irene Castle; he also played in the Negro String Quartet, in Cook's Southern Syncopated Orchestra, and in the orchestras of Broadway musicals. All the while Johnson knew, however, that his interests lay elsewhere.

He possessed strong opinions about how Negro folksongs should be sung. He always retained in his memory how the blacks (many of them ex-slaves) sang during his childhood in Athens, Georgia—in his father's Methodist church, in the fields, along the road, and in the homes as they went about their work. As he recalled it, they "sang with every breath!" It was this kind of sound that he wanted to recreate with his professional group, before the world would have forgotten what a glorious sound it had been. He knew exactly what he wanted to preserve:

> . . . The conscious and intentional *alterations* of *pitch* often made. . . . The unconscious, but amazing and bewildering *counterpoint* produced by so many voices in *individual improvisation*. . . . The *absolute insistence* upon the pulsing, *overall rhythm,* combining many varying subordinate rhythms.[8]

By 1925, he had gathered together a small band of eight singers who believed, like him, in the necessity for preserving the integrity of the Negro spiritual. By the time of its first recital, the group had increased its membership to twenty. In February 1928 the Hall Johnson Choir made its formal debut at the Pythian Temple in New York City and repeated the concert in March at New York's Town Hall.

Warmly received by the public and by critics, the group found itself in great demand for concerts and for theater and radio appearances. In 1928 the choir recorded for the RCA Victor Company. Two years later Hall Johnson was appointed choral director for the production of *The Green Pas-*

---

[8]Personal interview of Johnson by the author. Quotation from Hall Johnson, "Notes on the Negro Spiritual," RBAM, pp. 273–80.

The Hall Johnson Choir in the mid–1950s. *(Courtesy of the author)*

tures, a drama written by white playwright Marc Connelly and produced on Broadway. Hailed by a New York critic as "one of the loftiest achievements of the American Theater," the play nevertheless presented rather primitive conceptions about the black man's views of the Book of Genesis in the Bible. But it provided jobs for ninety-five black actors and singers and included some challenging roles and much glorious singing. Under Johnson's direction the "Celestial Choir" sang spirituals he had arranged continuously throughout the play, both off stage and in the orchestra pit.

In 1933 Hall Johnson's folk play, *Run Little Chillun,* had a run of 126 performances on Broadway. The outstanding quality of the play was its music, particularly in two spectacular scenes—a revival meeting and a pagan religious orgy. *Run Little Chillun* was revived in 1935 at Los Angeles with notable success. In 1936 Johnson took his chorus to Hollywood to sing in the film production of *The Green Pastures* and remained there many years, directing choruses in such films as *Lost Horizon, Way Down South,* and *Cabin in the Sky.* He also organized community groups, including a 200-voice Festival Choir in Los Angeles.

In 1946 Johnson resettled in New York, where he organized the Festival Negro Chorus of New York, which gave concerts on a regular basis. In 1951 the U.S. State Department sent his group to perform at the International Festival of Fine Arts in Berlin, Germany, and they remained to tour in Europe for several months. Johnson arranged spirituals and other black folksongs, as well as larger works, for his groups. His Easter cantata, *Son of Man* (1946), was widely performed.

Concert artists liked Johnson's spiritual arrangements and popularized especially *Honor, Honor, His Name So Sweet, I've Been 'Buked,* and *Scandalize My Name.* His art song *The Courtship* and the operetta *Fi-yer* were

Eva Jessye. *(Courtesy of the author)*

equally popular among singers. Johnson's publications included *The Green Pastures Spirituals* (1930) and *Thirty Negro Spirituals* (1949).

Eva Jessye (1895–1992) was a pioneer among women choral conductors, black or white; she was the first black woman to win international distinction as a professional choral conductor. She obtained her basic musical training in Kansas, her native state, and later studied privately in New York with Will Marion Cook and the music theorist Percy Goetschius. She began her musical career as a teacher, then decided in 1922 to go to New York to further her musical career. There she found it difficult, as a newcomer, to gain a place in the music world.

But she persevered, and by 1926 she was actively involved in the musical life of the city, appearing regularly with her singers (first named the Original Dixie Jubilee Singers, then the Eva Jessye Choir) on the "Major Bowes Family Radio Hour," the "General Motors Hour," and other radio programs. Her growing reputation led to commissions for organizing ensembles and quartets to sing on special radio programs in New York and in London and in the field of commercial advertisement. In 1929 Jessye was called to Hollywood to train a choir to sing in the King Vidor film *Hallelujah;* four years later she was asked to be the choral director for the production of Thomson's *Four Saints in Three Acts;* and the next year Gershwin chose her as his choral director for *Porgy and Bess* (1935). Jessye toured with the opera through several revivals in the United States and abroad during the next three decades.

Jessye also wrote and conducted her own works, including the folk oratorios *Paradise Lost and Regained* (1934), *The Life of Christ in Negro Spirituals* (1931), and *The Chronicle of Job* (1936). She exerted considerable influence indirectly upon the black concert world in that many concert artists began their careers as members of one of her choral groups. Shortly before her death she established the Eva Jessye African-American Music Collection at the University of Michigan.

Wings Over Jordan, while not a professional chorus, won wide recognition during the 1930s–40s as a broadcasting church choir. Founded by Glenn T. Settle, pastor of the Gethsemane Church in Cleveland, Ohio, the choir made its radio debut in July 1937, over local station WGAR. In less than two years the choir was broadcasting "Wings Over Jordan" on the CBS national network every Sunday morning, singing a program of religious music in the black tradition that was "dedicated to the heart of the Americas." Over the ten years of its existence as a broadcasting choir, Wings Over Jordan had various directors, including Thomas King. In 1945 the choir toured with USO (United Services Organization) units in the European Theater, entertaining soldiers in the army camps of World War II. After returning to the United States, Wings Over Jordan returned to radio broadcasting; in about 1949 the national program came to an end, and thereafter the choir toured on the concert circuit for several years.

Professional choirs and ensembles dominated the concert world, although concerts by some of the established community organizations were not infrequent. There was a third kind of choral group, however, that more and more became an important part of the concert world beginning in the 1920s: the Negro college choir. The Hampton Institute Choir under R. Nathaniel Dett, its first black director, gave concerts in the major churches and concert halls of the nation and toured Europe in 1930. Upon Dett's resignation in 1933, Clarence Cameron White took over direction of the choir, and the group continued its vigorous concert activity.

The sixty-voice Fisk University Choir (directed by white musician Ray Francis Brown during the '30s) made national tours annually, as did the Tuskegee Institute Choir. In 1932 Tuskegee's one-hundred-voice chorus, under the direction of William Levi Dawson, was invited to sing at the opening of Radio City Music Hall in New York City; the chorus made six appearances daily for the full week of the festivities. Among the other black institutions that sent out touring choral groups were Morehouse College (Georgia), Howard University (Washington, D.C.), Wilberforce University (Ohio), Virginia State College, Shaw University (North Carolina), and Claflin University (South Carolina). The musical activities of the college groups generally included radio broadcasts as well as recitals, and frequently included appearances at the White House. The Hampton Choir's activity in Paris in 1930 included making recordings for the Pathé Talking-Picture Company.

Beginning about 1950 the black college choirs of the nation were featured on a regular Sunday morning broadcast, "Negro College Choirs," on the ABC network. The idea of programming black college choirs on the radio undoubtedly originated in 1945, when a replacement had to be found for the touring Wings Over Jordan, and the Fisk University Choir filled in. When the older group left the air permanently, the Sunday morning spot was filled by the college choirs in rotation.

COMPOSERS AND COMPOSER / EDUCATORS

After World War I the black composers began to come into their own. Through the 1920s and the Depression of the '30s, established composers continued to write music, and new composers appeared on the scene. Most of the music written was performed at least once, and a surprising amount was published, in view of the fact that a large part of it was written upon commission to be performed on a specific occasion.

Directors of professional choruses and college choirs often wrote choral works in order to have something "new" to present to their audiences or to use in conjunction with a stage work. Singers arranged spirituals for their own recitals or asked composer-friends to write settings of admired poems for particular concerts. We have already observed how prolific were the composers who directed orchestras and jazz bands. Even the composers of instrumental concert works wrote, to some degree, for the use of their students or friends or themselves.

Black performers frequently found it important to have black-music pieces in their repertories—because of segregation, they were performing primarily for black audiences, and they wanted to be able to communicate with their listeners. Thus the singer sang spirituals or Negro folksongs or settings of poems about Negro life. The pianist or violinist played program music with titles that suggested Negro life and that made obvious use of folklike melodies and rhythms. The dance-music composer utilized boogie-woogie rhythms, the blues, and jazz because black dancers demanded these musical styles. All this of course did not excuse black performers from developing classical music repertories. They simply had to learn both—the African American and the European.

It was during the 1920s–30s that foundations for the first time began to give awards and fellowships in any significant numbers to black musicians. Generally, the Rockefeller and Rosenwald fellowships went to performers, although there were exceptions. The Holstein, Harmon, and Wanamaker awards went solely to composers, some of whom had previously won recognition for their skills, others of whom were newcomers to the field. Those who won frequently over the seven years that the awards were offered included Harry Burleigh, R. Nathaniel Dett, Carl Diton, Lawrence Freeman, N. Clark Smith, and Clarence Cameron White among the older composers, and Edward Boatner, J. Harold Brown, William L. Dawson, Hall Johnson, and Florence Price among the newcomers. Two others are worthy of mention, although they each won only one prize—Margaret Bonds and Edmund Jenkins.

The award-winning composers included both neophytes and established composers; the latter have been discussed previously. Florence Price (1888–1953) was the first black woman to achieve distinction as a composer.[9] A recipient of diplomas in piano and organ from the New England Conservatory where she studied with George Chadwick and Frederick Converse, she continued her work at the Chicago Musical College and the American Conservatory of Music. Price began composing as a child and had published small pieces even before entering the Conservatory. After a brief teaching career—at Shorter College in her home town, Little Rock, Arkansas, and at Clark College in Atlanta—she settled in Chicago in 1927, all the while continuing with her composing.

In 1925, and again in 1927, she won prizes in Holstein competitions. In Chicago she found publishers for her teaching pieces, which became a speciality for her, and she wrote radio commercials in addition to serious compositions. Her works are in a variety of forms: three symphonies, two violin concertos, concert overtures, a piano concerto, chamber music, organ and piano pieces, teaching pieces, and arrangements of spirituals and other Negro folksongs.

Some of her compositions were frequently performed—the Piano Concerto in One Movement, the organ pieces, the spiritual arrangement *My Soul's Been Anchored in the Lord*, and the *Three Little Negro Dances*. Her Symphony in E minor, which won a Wanamaker prize in 1932, was given a first performance by the Chicago Symphony Orchestra, conducted by Frederick Stock, at the Chicago World's Fair in 1933, and repeated several times by the orchestra. Although Price's music became known only in the postwar world, she belonged to an older generation in terms of her training and experience, and her style is best defined as neoromantic, which was rather conservative for her time. She was also a black nationalist in that she drew freely upon folk idioms in her compositions.

Edmund Jenkins (1894–1926) had his first musical experiences playing in the boys' bands of the orphanage his father founded and directed, and went to England with a Jenkins band in 1914. When the band returned home, he remained in England, becoming essentially an expatriate, for he spent the rest of his life abroad. Before leaving the United States he had studied with Kemper Harreld at the Atlanta Baptist College (now More-

[9]See further in articles in the Biography by Barbara Garvey Jackson and dissertations by Rae Linda Brown and Mildred Denby Green.

Margaret Bonds, pianist, plays Florence Price's Piano Concerto with the Women's Symphony Orchestra of Chicago, 1934. Composer Price is the conductor. (From Margaret Bonds, "A Reminiscence," in *The Negro in Music and Art*, Lindsay Patterson, ed., New York, 1968. *Courtesy of the author*)

house College), and in London he attended the Royal Academy of Music for seven years. He won several prizes for composition at the Academy; in 1925 he received Holstein prizes for his *African War Dance* for orchestra and his Sonata in A minor for violoncello. His *Charlestonia*, a rhapsody for orchestra using Negro themes, was performed in Belgium in 1926, and his *Negro Symphony* was performed in London. Death cut short a promising career.

Edward Boatner (1898–1981) obtained his musical education at Western University in Quindaro, Kansas, the Boston Conservatory, Chicago Musical College (B.Mus.), and through private study. In his early career he was a concert singer—encouraged and aided by Roland Hayes and R. Nathaniel Dett—and choral director; during the years 1925–31 he was director of music for the National Baptist Convention.

During the 1930s he taught at Samuel Huston College (now Huston-Tillotson) and Wiley College (both in Texas), then settled permanently in New York. Thereafter he conducted a studio, directed church and community choirs, and gave time to composing, particularly arrangements of Negro spirituals, which were widely sung by concert artists. His best-known arrangements included *Oh, What a Beautiful City, Let Us Break Bread Together, Soon I Will Be Done,* and *Tramping.* In addition to spirituals, Boatner published a *Freedom Suite* for chorus, narrator, and orchestra; a "spiritual musical," *The Man from Nazareth;* and the musical comedy *Julius Sees Her.*

Another composer in the Chicago orbit during the 1920s–30s was William Levi Dawson (1899–1990), who attended Tuskegee Institute as a youth, graduated from the Horner Institute of Fine Arts in Kansas City, Missouri (B.Mus.), studied at Chicago Musical College with Felix Borowski and others, and at the American Conservatory of Music (M.Mus.). In his early career he played trombone with the Redpath Chautauqua (summer 1921) and first trombone in the Chicago Civic Symphony Orchestra.

He then embarked on a teaching career, first in public schools of Topeka, Kansas, and Kansas City, Missouri, then at Tuskegee Institute (1931–56). Dawson established a superior music program at Tuskegee, appointing the leading artists of the race to serve on his faculty, and developed a choir of international renown.

He began composing as a youth. One of his early compositions, a Trio for Violin, Cello, and Piano, was performed by members of the Kansas City Symphony Orchestra on the occasion of his graduation from Horner. Dawson wrote in a variety of forms—chamber music, orchestral compositions, and a sonata for violin and piano—but was best known for his arrangements of spirituals and his *Negro Folk Symphony* (1934). His spirituals were sung widely, especially *King Jesus Is a-Listening, Talk about a Child That Do Love Jesus,* and *Jesus Walked This Lonesome Valley.*

His major orchestral works, the *Negro Folk Symphony,* attracted national attention upon its world premiere in 1934 by the Philadelphia Orchestra under the direction of Leopold Stokowski. A critic of the *New York Times* observed that the Dawson work had "dramatic feeling, a racial sensuousness and directness of melodic speech, and a barbaric turbulence." The *New York World Telegram* commented upon its "imagination, warmth, drama . . . [and] sumptuous orchestration."

After returning from a visit to West Africa in 1952, Dawson revised his symphony, infusing it with the spirit of the African rhythms he had heard there. The three-movement work includes subtitles for each movement: I, *The Bond of Africa;* II, *Hope in the Night;* III, *O Let Me Shine!* According to the composer's program notes, "a link was taken out of a human chain when the first African was taken from the shores of his native land and sent to slavery."

Dawson was directly inspired by Dvořák's views on nationalism in music. His aim was "to write a symphony in the Negro folk idiom, based on authentic folk music but in the same symphonic form used by the composers of the [European] romantic-nationalist school."

John Harold Brown (1902–197?) was trained at Fisk University (B.A.), the Horner Institute of Fine Arts in Kansas City (M.Mus.), Indiana University (M.A.) and through private study with Virgil Thomson, Arthur Shepard, and others. His teaching career included tenures in the public schools of Kansas City (Kansas), Indianapolis, and Cleveland; and at colleges in the South, including Florida A & M in Tallahasee and Southern University in Louisiana. In 1946 he settled at Cleveland, where he was appointed music director at Karamu House and the Huntington Playhouse.

Publishing under the name J. Harl Brown, he won distinction especially for his vocal and choral works. He began composing early in his career, and several of his pieces won prizes in the competitions discussed above, including a String Quartet, the *Negro Rhapsody,* and the cantata *The African Chief* for female voices and concert band. Other works were the oratorio *Job,* a choral work, *The Saga of Rip Van Winkle,* and his many arrangements of spirituals.

At least three college educators of this period gave considerable attention to research in Negro folklore, collecting songs and tales, and disseminating their findings to the public through lectures, publications, and recitals. Camille Nickerson (1888–1982), a professor at Howard University during the years 1926–62, was particularly interested in the Creole folksongs of her native Louisiana. John Wesley Work, III (1901–1967) taught at Fisk University from 1927 to 1966, following in the footsteps of his father, who also was a pioneering black folklorist. Willis Lawrence James (1900–1966) set out to collect folksongs in the early 1920s in Louisiana, where he first began to teach. The work of these scholars was important not only because of the new information they uncovered, but also because they provided a "black perspective" for the extensive research under way on black folkways by white scholars of the period.

Nickerson came from a musical family in New Orleans and was educated at Oberlin (B.A., M.A.), Juilliard, and Columbia University Teachers College. A Rosenwald Fellowship made it possible for her to pursue graduate studies, and she developed her longtime interest in folksong. She collected the songs of Louisiana creoles, made arrangements suitable for the concert stage, and published many of the arrangements, of which the best known were *Michieu banjo,* and *Lizette, to quitté la plaine.* During the 1930s–50s she toured as "The Louisiana Lady," singing creole songs and wearing creole dress; in 1954 she toured in France under the sponsorship of the U.S. State Department.

James obtained his musical education at Morehouse College in Atlanta (B.A.) and through private study. His teaching career included tenures at Leland College in Louisiana, Alabama State Teachers College, and Spelman College in Atlanta. In 1927 he collaborated with white folklorist James Edward Halligan in making recordings (now lost) of folksongs collected in Louisiana; he transcribed the music and sang, while Halligan transcribed the texts. During the 1940s James was a Recording Fellow for the Library of Congress and spent much time producing both field and studio recordings of black folk singers. On some projects he collaborated with John Work.

James toured extensively as a lecturer on Negro folksong, appearing on college campuses, before professional societies, and at such festivals as the Newport Jazz and Folk Festivals. The article he published in *Phylon* (1955), "The Romance of the Negro Folk Cry in America," attracted wide attention. At his death he left a complete manuscript, "Stars in the Elements," which consists of a collection of songs with analysis. James was also noted for his arrangements of folksongs.

Work was educated at Fisk (A.B.) the Institute of Musical Art (now Juilliard), Columbia University Teachers College (M.A.), and Yale University (B.Mus.), where he studied with David Stanley Smith. Like his father and grandfather before him, he was intensely interested in Negro folksong; he toured with Fisk student singing groups, lectured on black folklore, published articles in music journals, and published the collection *American Negro Songs and Spirituals* (1940).

Work wrote for a variety of media—orchestra, piano, chamber ensemble, violin, and organ—but his largest output was for solo voice and for chorus. His best-known works were *Yenvalou* for orchestra (1946); the piano pieces *Sassafras* (1946), *Scuppernong* (1951), and *Appalachia* (1954); the organ suite *From the Deep South* (1936); and the cantatas *The Singers* (1941) and *Isaac Watts Contemplates the Cross* (1962). Rosenwald Fellowships received in 1931 and 1932 permitted Work to further develop his compositional skills and his research interests.

The importance of choral singing in the black tradition, and the concern among black educators in particular for preserving the Negro folkmusic repertory, combined to give choirs at black colleges a rather exalted position—this, in addition to the realization that touring college music groups could raise money for their institutions. That the historic tours of the Fisk Jubilee Singers in the 1870s had brought in large sums of money for Fisk was as firmly embedded in black legend as the fact that the Fisk singers had acquainted the world with Negro folksongs. As we have seen, the black college choir was as important an institution in the concert world as was the professional chorus.

Several of the educators of this period who earned recognition as composers and arrangers of folksong undoubtedly wrote music in order to increase the repertories of their choral groups. Certainly they were renowned choral directors, and their choirs were regarded as among the best in the nation. Frederick Douglass Hall (1898–1982) organist and choral director, developed choirs in Mississippi, Louisiana, and Alabama. Warner Lawson (1903–1971), a concert pianist in his early career, was at Howard University for most of his teaching career from 1942 to 1971. Oscar Anderson Fuller (1904–1989), a singer and composer, is credited with being the first African-American to earn the Ph.D. degree in music.

Hall obtained his musical education at Morehouse College (A.B.), Chicago Musical College (B.Mus.), Columbia University Teachers College (M.A.; D. Mus. Ed.), the Royal Academy of Music in London, and through private study. He taught at Jackson College in Mississippi, Dillard University in New Orleans, Alabama State College, and Southern University in Louisiana. He was a prolific composer of choral music, and his spiritual arrangements were performed widely, for example, *Dry Bones, The Crucifixion,* and *Every Time I Feel the Spirit,* as well as his folk pageants and the oratorio *Deliverance* (1963).

Hall also had ethnomusicological interests; during his two-year sojourn in Great Britain, he studied the folk music of several countries, and later toured in West Africa investigating the folk traditions of that area. Noted for the excellence of his choirs in all four of the institutions where he taught, he sent one of his quartets, the Delta Rhythm Boys, into the world of popular music as professionals.

Warner Lawson received his musical training at Fisk (B.A.), Yale (B.Mus.), Harvard (M.A.), and through private study with Artur Schnabel in Berlin, Germany. Before going to Howard University in 1942, he taught at Fisk and North Carolina A & T College. During his early career he combined teaching with touring as a concert pianist, then later devoted more attention to choral directing. His choirs won national distinction for their excellence; indeed, they sang so regularly with the National Symphony Orchestra in Washington, D.C., that they were called "the unofficial chorus" of that orchestra.

Fuller, who was active primarily in the Southwest and Midwest, obtained his basic musical training at Bishop College in Texas (A.B.), and the New England Conservatory of Music, and his advanced degrees at the University of Iowa (M.A., Ph.D.). His teaching career included tenures at North Carolina A & T College, Prairie View College in Texas, and Lincoln University in Missouri. In addition to producing fine choirs, Fuller also was in great demand as a choral clinician.

It is of interest that some of the composers associated with theater music and other kinds of nonconcert music were inspired to write symphonic music during this period, perhaps in emulation of the composers discussed above. Maceo Pinkard and W. C. Handy, for example, entered the Harmon competitions, but failed—along with other jazz and popular music composers—to win prizes.

Jazz musicians were not discouraged by the obvious preference for art music in the competitions, however, for several succeeded in securing performances for their works. The orchestral rhapsody *Yamekraw* (1927) of James P. Johnson, for example, which was orchestrated by William Grant Still, was performed several times, and his *Symphonic Harlem* also received performances. Johnson also tried his hand at folk operas, among them, *De Organizer* with a libretto by Langston Hughes. Charles L. Cooke, another jazz and theater-music man, wrote an orchestral suite, *Sketches from the Deep South,* that was performed on at least one important occasion.

Dean of Afro-American Composers

In 1945 Leopold Stokowski wrote of William Grant Still (1895–1978), "Still is one of our greatest American composers." And ten years later, in 1955, a writer observed in *Micro Magazine* (Brussels, Belgium):

> This American composer shows remarkable qualities which place him as one of the very greatest living composers of the New World: a sense of immediate observation; the taste for a rigorous and brilliant orchestration; spontaneity and sincerity characterize his compositions.[10]

In 1970 musical organizations across the country celebrated the diamond anniversary of a man whose composing had earned him a secure niche among American composers. His music had truly become a music of the people. It was performed widely by college groups and civic organizations as well as by professional orchestras; it was heard on college campuses, in community-concert series, on radio and television programs, at festivals, and in the leading concert halls of the nation.

In observance of the centennial anniversary of Still's birth in 1995, universities and community organizations across the nation sponsored performances of his music in all-Still concerts and recitals, and held symposia, workshops, film festivals, exhibits and touring exhibitions, and other similar activities. Some celebrations lasted the full year, such as the William Grant Still Centenary Project set up by the Joint Planning Committee at the New England Conservatory and Northeastern University. Still had studied composition with faculty member George Chadwick at the Conservatory in 1922. Most programs lasted from two or three days to a week, and in some places the Still festival was linked to observances of Black History Month. The most gala celebration of all was held at the University of Arkansas, where the William Grant Still–Verna Arvey Papers are deposited.

Still obtained his education at Wilberforce University in Ohio (1911–14); at Oberlin (1917, 1919), where he studied with Friedrich Lehmann and George Andrews; and through private study with George Whitefield Chadwick (1922) and Edgard Varèse (1923–25). He began playing violin during his high-school years. At Wilberforce he joined the string quartet, conducted the college band, and arranged music for that organization and other groups.

In 1914 he left college before completing the music degree program to play professionally with a dance orchestra. During the summer of 1916 he worked for W. C. Handy in Memphis, Tennessee, where he made the first arrangements for band of Handy's historic *Beale Street Blues* and *St. Louis Blues*. Still served in the U.S. Navy (1918), then, in 1919 settled in New York where he worked again for Handy's music publishing company. Two

---

[10]Both quotations reprinted in a publicity brochure for Still: Stokowski is dated April 21, 1945; *Micro Magazine*, dated November 6, 1955.

William Grant Still. *(Courtesy of the author)*

years later he became musical director of Harry Pace's Phonograph Company. He was active musically in other ways: he played in the pit orchestra of *Shuffle Along* and other shows; he made arrangements and orchestrations for bandleaders and show people in New York, continuing all the while to write in the art-music tradition.

His first serious works included *Darker America* (1924), *From the Land of Dreams* (1925), and *From the Journal of a Wanderer* (1925). Notwithstanding Still's reservations, his work was being noticed by critics and New York composers, and in 1925 *From the Land of Dreams* (for three voices and chamber orchestra) received a first performance at a concert of the International Composers' Guild. In January 1926, his *Levee Land,* a three-movement suite for orchestra with soloist Florence Mills, was performed to critical acclaim on a concert of the Guild. The work, which blended jazz elements with European-tradition elements suggested the direction in which Still would be moving in the future.

For a period of about fifteen years, Still wrote primarily black nationalistic music in a variety of forms, such as *From the Black Belt* (1926), a suite for small orchestra; *La Guiablesse* (1927), a ballet with a West Indian plot; *Sahdji* (1930), a ballet with chorus and a narrator who recited African proverbs; and three symphonies that formed a trilogy—*Africa* (1930), the *Afro-American Symphony* (1931), and the Symphony in G minor (1937), subtitled *Song of a New Race.*

But it was the performance of his *Afro-American Symphony* in 1931 by the Rochester Philharmonic Symphony under Howard Hanson that brought wide recognition to Still. This was a milestone in African-American music—the first time in history that a major American symphony orchestra had played a symphonic work written by a black composer, and it established a vogue of sorts. (As we have seen, the Chicago Symphony played Price's symphony in 1933, and the Philadelphia Orchestra played Dawson's in 1934.) In 1935 the New York Philharmonic gave the New York premiere of Still's symphony at Carnegie Hall. This became Still's most consistently played work over the next sixty years, receiving hundreds of performances both in the United States and abroad.

A Guggenheim fellowship in 1934 (later twice renewed) had enabled Still to give full attention to composing for the first time in his life. He moved to Los Angeles and turned to opera, his favorite genre; over the years he wrote six, of which three were performed during his lifetime. The first one, *Troubled Island* (1941), an opera about Haiti with a libretto by black poet Langston Hughes, was produced in 1949 by the New York City Opera under the direction of László Halász. The opera, like Still's *Afro-American Symphony,* established a milestone: for the first time in history a major opera company performed an opera written by an African-American composer. Still's wife, Verna Arvey, wrote the libretto for his other five operas. In 1963 *Highway I, U.S.A.* (1962) was staged at the University of Miami under the direction of Fabien Sevitsky, and performed again several times, most notably in 1972 by Opera / South. *A Bayou Legend* (1941, libretto by Arvey) made its debut in 1974 with Opera / South in Mississippi. This opera about black folkways in the Bayou country of Mississippi in the nineteenth century was produced nationwide on Public Television in June 1981, and thereby made history as the first opera written by a black composer to be telecast on a national network.

Still was a prolific composer and wrote in all the forms. Best known of his works, in addition to those named above, were the piano suite *Seven Traceries* (1939); the Sonata for Violin and Piano (1943); the song suite *Songs of Separation* (1949, texts by Langston Hughes, Countee Cullen, Arna Bontemps, and others); and the orchestral *Festive Overture* (1944), *Old California* (1941), and *Danzas de Panama* (1948). Also important were two works for orchestra and vocal forces, *And They Lynched Him on a Tree* (1940) and *Plainchant for America* (1941).

Although he wrote in a neoromantic style, Still resists neat classification as a nationalist and traditionalist. His two piano suites, for example, reflect the avant-garde influence of Varèse. Much of his music, however, draws heavily upon folk idioms—Negro, Native American, Hispanic, and Anglo-American. One reason for listeners' initial and continued attraction to the *Afro-American Symphony* was its modern "American" sound. Still was the first African American to employ the blues and jazz in a symphonic work; previously, black composers had confined their use of Negro folk idioms in concert works to spirituals, worksongs, and dance songs. Still explained his aim as follows:

Like so many works which are important to their creators, *The Afro-American Symphony* was forming over a period of years. [It was completed in 1930.] Themes were occurring to me, were duly noted, and an overall form was slowly growing. I knew I wanted to write a symphony; I knew that it had to be an American work; and I wanted to demonstrate how the blues, so often considered a lowly expression, could be elevated to the highest musical level.[11]

Still has given to each of the symphony's four movements a subtitle (Moderato assai, *Longings;* Adagio, *Sorrows;* Scherzo, *Humor;* Lento con Risoluzione, *Aspirations*) and a brief program based on an excerpt from a poem by Paul Laurence Dunbar. A theme invented in the spirit of a blues melody, first presented after the introduction in the first movement, dominates the entire work.

Blues theme, **Afro-American Symphony**

The blues theme is used in later movements in various ways: sometimes a secondary theme derives from it, as in the introduction to the scherzo and in the finale; sometimes the theme itself is stated in a transformed version, as just before the coda in the third movement. The other themes of the symphony are reminiscent of spirituals, shout songs, ragtime (with banjolike accompaniment), and jazz tunes. Critics found the work to be "straightforward, with no pretense of profundity," and effectively scored. And this is what Still had intended. He wrote, "The harmonies employed in the Symphony are quite conventional except in a few places. The use of this style of harmonization was necessary in order to attain simplicity and to intensify in the music those qualities which enable the hearers to recognize it as Negro music."[12]

[11]Quotes from program notes for the *Afro-American Symphony* score.
[12]Robert Haas, *William Grant Still and the Fusion of Cultures in American Music* (Los Angeles, 1972), p. 11.

BLACK MUSICALS ON BROADWAY

The decade of the 1920s–30s was an exhilarating time for black musical theater. The first musical of the period, *Shuffle Along,* established a model for plot and material that would affect the format of those to follow for the next sixty and more years. Moreover, its success inspired a number of black composers and writers to produce musicals who otherwise might have moved in a different direction. They invaded the Great White Way year after year for more than a dozen years. The onslaught of their productions, in addition to those with all-black casts that were staged by whites, would prove to be overwhelming for some of Broadway's clientele; in 1922 a singer in the Ziegfeld Follies, Gilda Gray, prophetically complained, *It's Getting Dark on Old Broadway,* and she was not referring to the absence of street lights.[13]

Few of the shows written and produced by African Americans on Broadway prior to the 1920s had been successful. The last one, Bert Williams's vehicle, *Mr. Lode of Koal,* closed in December 1909, then went on the road to tour the following year. It would be more than ten years before another black musical would have a successful run on Broadway. During these years, black composers and writers worked at developing, then refining their crafts; they wrote dozens of musicals for production at the Pekin, Lafayette, Howard, and other black theaters of the nation or to be taken on the road by companies such as The Smart Set.

As we have seen, the blazing stars of the old world of black theater had died or retired or, in the case of Bert Williams, moved into the white theatrical world. During this period new talent was being discovered and trained. By 1921 black showmen were ready: on May 23, 1921, *Shuffle Along* opened at the Sixty-third Street Theatre and made theatrical history.

Eubie Blake and Noble Sissle wrote the music and lyrics; Flournoy Miller and Aubrey Lyles wrote the libretto or "book," basing it on one of their old productions at the Pekin Theatre back in 1907, *The Mayor of Dixie.* It was no easy matter preparing the show for its debut on Broadway. The limited funds of the producers barely allowed for the requisite pre-runs at the Howard Theater in Washington, D.C., and the Dunbar in Philadelphia before the producers opened at the dilapidated and previously empty Broadway house. But once open,

> Within a few weeks *Shuffle Along* made the 63rd Street Theatre one of the best-known houses in town and made it necessary for the Traffic Department to declare 63rd Street a one-way thoroughfare.[14]

[13]Roger D. Kinkle, *The Complete Encyclopedia of Popular Music and Jazz* (New Rochelle, NY, 1974), v. 1, p. 131.
[14]Johnson, *Black Manhattan,* p. 188.

Noble Sissle (right) and Eubie Blake in 1969. *(Courtesy of the author)*

The glorious singing and exhilarating dancing delighted both critics and audiences. Blake led the orchestra in the pit, which included among its players Hall Johnson and the oboist William Grant Still (not yet famous at that time). The hit songs of the show set all of New York to humming, then went around the world: *Shuffle Along, Love Will Find a Way, In Honeysuckle Time, Bandana Days, The Gypsy Blues,* and *I'm Just Wild About Harry.* (The last-named was revived to become a campaign song for Harry Truman in the 1948 presidential election.)

Shuffle Along brought a "different" kind of musical to Broadway, a Harlem folk show in which few concessions were made to white taste or to theater clichés. It was funny (and sometimes sentimental), fast-moving, and melodious. In addition to the future stars in the pit, many members of the cast later won stardom and fame, among them, Josephine Baker, Caterina Jarboro, Florence Mills, and Paul Robeson. After a record 504 performances on Broadway, *Shuffle Along* went on the road to play for two more years.

Shuffle Along created a vogue for the black musical on Broadway—Broadway actually "got darker" every year! None of the musicals that followed it achieved such phenomenal success, and most were not as good, but Broadway gave both writers and performers the kind of experience necessary if black artists were to develop their potential in the realm of theater.

The original *Shuffle Along* orchestra, 1921. Among the players are Leonard Jeter, cello; William Grant Still, oboe; Hall Johnson, viola; and Eubie Blake, piano. *(Courtesy of the author)*

It was a heady freedom. Fewer than sixty years earlier they had been slaves on the plantation, compelled to entertain their masters by clowning and dancing; and the post-emancipation years of minstrelsy and vaudeville did little to excise the derogatory stereotypes of black entertainers that had developed over a century. Now they were free to develop their own ideas of what black musical theater should be—or, at least, relatively free. The box office made the final decision, and Broadway audiences tightly specified the roles that African Americans could play on the stage. But within those constraints, all was possible, so black show people invaded Broadway again and again with revues and musical comedies. Wisely, they drew upon their folk roots for materials and, in the process, put an indelible stamp upon the development of American musical theater.

A selected list of the most enduring black musicals on or off Broadway over a twenty-seven year period and the names of their chief composers provides a glimpse into this rich repertory.[15]

1921   *Shuffle Along* (Eubie Blake, Noble Sissle)
1921   *Put and Take* (Perry Bradford, Tim Brymn, Spencer Williams)
1922   *Liza* (Maceo Pinkard)
1922   *Strut Miss Lizzie* (J. Turner Layton)
1923   *Runnin' Wild* (James P. Johnson)
1924   *Chocolate Dandies* (Eubie Blake, Spencer Williams)
1925   *Lucky Sambo* (Porter Grainger, Fred Johnson)

---

[15]A number of fine books on black musical theater have been published in recent years; see especially entries in the Bibliography under Gerald Bordman, Bernard L. Peterson, and Allen Woll.

1926   *My Magnolia* (Charles Luckey Roberts)
1927   *Bottomland* (Clarence Williams)
1927   *Rang Tang* (Ford Dabney)
1927   *Africanna* (Donald Heywood)
1928   *Keep Shuffling* (Thomas "Fats" Waller, J. C. Johnson)
1929   *Deep Harlem* (Joe Jordan)
1929   *Hot Chocolates* (Waller, Harry Brooks)
1929   *Messin' Around* (James P. Johnson)
1930   *Change Your Luck* (J. C. Johnson)
1930   *Blackbirds of 1930* (Blake)
1930   *Brown Buddies* (Joe Jordan)
1930   *Hot Rhythm* (Porter Grainger)
1931   *Sugar Hill* (James P. Johnson)
1932   *Shuffle Along of 1932* (Blake)
1932   *Tom-Tom* (Opera, Shirley G. Du Bois)
1933   *Run, Little Chillun* (Hall Johnson)
1934   *Kykuntor* (Dance Opera, Margaret Kennerly Upshur)
1937   *Swing It* (Blake)
1938   *The Organizer* (James P. Johnson)
1939   *The Hot Mikado* (jazz version of the Gilbert and Sullivan operetta, *The Mikado,* with orchestrations by Charles L. Cooke)
1941   *Jump for Joy* (dance, Duke Ellington)
1941   *A Bayou Legend* (opera, William Grant Still)
1941   *Troubled Island* (opera, William Grant Still)
1944   *Miller's Brownskin Models* (Irene Higginbothan)
1947   *Meet Miss Jones* (James P. Johnson)

Several gospel musicals toured in Europe after successful Broadway runs, among them *Black Nativity* (1962), which went to the Festival of Two Worlds at Spoleto, Italy (1962) and thereafter toured for many months abroad in Europe, Australia, and New Zealand.

In addition to these works by black composers and librettists, there were the musicals written by whites that had all-black casts; for example, *Plantation Revue* (1922), *Dixie to Broadway* (1924), *Africana* (1927), *Bamboola* (1929), *Rhapsody in Black* (1931), five of the Lew Leslie *Blackbird* revues (1928, 1932, 1933, 1934, 1939), *Swingin' the Dream* (1939), and *The Swing Mikado* (1939). A few stage works of this period with white casts included important roles for black musicians, which gave them wide exposure; for example, Jules Bledsoe in *Deep River* (1926) and *Show Boat* (1926), Paul Robeson in a revival of *Show Boat* (1927), and Ethel Waters in *As Thousands Cheer* (1933) and *At Home Abroad* (1935). Several black composers wrote music for white shows, among them, Eubie Blake, Luckey Roberts, and Fats Waller.

A number of shows with black casts—some written by black composers and some by whites—opened in Harlem or other places away from Broadway. A representative sampling includes the 1920 edition of Leubrie Hill's *The Darktown Follies;* Will Vodery's *Blue Monday* (1922) and *Kykuntor* (1934), a ballet-opera produced by the African composer Asadata Dafora. The musical *Dinah* (1923) with music by Tim Brymn, which opened at the Lafayette in Harlem, featured the dance called the "blackbottom," which became almost as celebrated as the "Charleston" dance in *Runnin' Wild.* Lew Leslie's *Blackbirds of 1926* opened at the Alhambra in Harlem; after a six-week run the show went directly to Paris for five months, then to London for another six months—thus totally bypassing Broadway. And Fats Waller's *Hot Chocolates* began its existence as a musical revue for Connie's Inn in Harlem, then later was expanded to become a Broadway musical.

All these theater pieces established a number of black performers as stars and sent some into a glorious future. We mentioned earlier those people associated with *Shuffle Along* who were destined for fame. Florence Mills (1895–1927) began her professional career as a four-year-old child in a walk-on performance with the Cole–Johnson musical *A Trip to Coontown,* in 1899. As a teenager she sang in a sister act and, later, in the Panama Trio in Chicago nightclubs. After attracting wide attention in *Shuffle Along,* she moved to stardom in the *Plantation Revue, Dover Street to London* (produced in London), *Dixie to Broadway,* and *Blackbirds of 1926,* which opened in Harlem and toured widely in Europe. She was one of the most popular stage entertainers of her time, and especially celebrated for her singing of *I'm Just a Little Blackbird Looking for a Bluebird.*

Josephine Baker (1906–1975) was only a chorus girl in *Shuffle Along* and *Chocolate Dandies,* but she left for France in 1926 with *Le Revue Nègre* and landed on the other side of the ocean a featured performer. A replacement for Ethel Waters at the last moment, she was rehearsed on board ship by musical director Claude Hopkins (1903–1984), who presented her to Paris in an explosive scene that got her career off to a glowing start.[16] Over the years she was a star at the Folies-Bergère and the Casino de Paris; she performed in films, stage shows, and on radio and television, and she made records. She returned to the United States several times to appear in the Ziegfeld Follies and other revues.

For Eubie Blake and Noble Sissle, *Shuffle Along* marked the beginning of a new career. They had toured as a vaudeville team for several years and had written a few songs, with one success—*It's All Your Fault,* popularized by Sophie Tucker. Now the success of *Shuffle Along* encouraged them to give attention to writing as well as performing. Blake had aspired to write operettas ever since he first heard those of Franz Léhar and Victor Herbert in the early part of the century, and Leslie Stuart was his special idol. Moreover, he and Sissle had shared a dream with James Reese Europe that the three of them would write for Broadway. In addition to writing the musicals

---

[16]Warren Vaché, *Crazy Fingers* (Washington, D.C., 1992), pp. 14–15.

cited above, Sissle and Blake wrote scores for or contributed music to *Elsie* (1923), Charles Cochran's *Revue* of 1926 (in London), and *Shuffle Along of 1952*.

After returning from London in 1926, they dissolved the partnership; Sissle moved into the field of jazz and led an orchestra for many years, while Blake began to collaborate with other lyricists, although he too was active as a performer on the vaudeville stage and as conductor of a USO orchestra during World War II. He and Andy Razaf wrote a host of songs and the musicals *Blackbirds of 1930* and *Tan Manhattan* (1940); with Flournoy Miller he wrote songs for Irwin C. Miller's *Brown-Skin Models* (1954) and *Hit the Stride* (1955); and he wrote with others for musicals that were never produced.

Among the other Broadway performers who began their stage careers during this period were Minto Cato (1900–1979), Adelaide Hall (1910–1993), Bill "Bojangles" Robinson (1878–1949), Valaida Snow (1900–1956), Edith Wilson (1896–1981), and Buck and Bubbles (né Ford Lee Washington and John Sublett). Cato sang in both musicals and opera; Blake wrote the ballad *Memories of You* especially for her to sing in his *Blackbirds of 1930*. Hall (c. 1904–1983) attracted wide attention for her wordless solo in *Creole Love Song* with Duke Ellington's orchestra; in addition to singing in musicals, after 1938 she operated nightclubs in Paris and in London for many years. Snow was noted as a jazz trumpeter as well as actress-singer. And John Sublett created the role of Sporting Life in Gershwin's opera *Porgy and Bess* in 1935.

During this period the black musical on Broadway developed an "image" that proved to be long lasting. Typically, its strong components were the dancing and singing, both solo and chorus numbers. Above all, there was jazz, jazz, jazz! The vivacious dances included folk types, such as the buck-and-wing; carryovers from minstrelsy and vaudeville, such as the soft shoe; and contemporary types, particularly precision tap dancing. New dances frequently made their initial bows on the stage and from there went into dance halls—as had happened with the cakewalk at the turn of the century. In 1924 the Charleston was such a dance; it came to the stage in James P. Johnson's *Runnin' Wild*. According to one theater historian, the play brought some "real" life back into the season. As usual, in the case of black-cast plays, the critics were condescending:

> [But] in this instance the critics turned out to be remarkably myopic, for there was one number in the show, a dance that ultimately expressed and symbolized the whole gaudy era about to explode. It pronounced the beat for the "lost generation" and liberated the whole jazz movement. The dance song was of course, "The Charleston." The dance typified the black-inspired, high-stepping of the era. It was gawky, zesty, and, obviously, irresistible.[17]

[17]Bordman, *American Musical Theatre*, p. 382.

The ballads and songs of the black musical were written in conformity with Broadway convention, which, at this time, called for the thirty-two-bar song with an a-a-b-a (b is "the bridge") structure (each section consisting of eight measures). In addition to that song type, the black musical included, of course, the eight-bar spiritual, the sixteen-bar rag strain, and the twelve-bar blues types. The lively, folklike tunes were likely to start audiences tapping their toes; the poignant blues, to draw tears; and the captivating melodies of the ballads, to send them home humming. To the sparkling solos and rousing choral numbers was added the piquancy of barbershop-harmonizing quartet singing. The Harmony Four, for example, appeared in many of the musicals of the 1920s. Some of the popular stage songs of the era were *Ain't Misbehavin', Dear Old Southland, Memories of You, Love Will Find a Way*, and *Way Down Yonder in New Orleans*.

The plot of the black musical generally was its weakest element. The model of the comedy pair set by George Walker and Bert Williams in the early part of the century—the swindler interacting with the dupe—reappeared in several musicals of this period. And inevitably, a musical's scenes would include a Harlem rent party, plantation scene, jungle scene, religious scene (camp meeting or church service), if it were at all possible to slip them into the action.

It was during this era that the first freelance black arrangers of theater music began to appear on Broadway. To be sure, black arrangers dated back to the early twentieth century, but they generally had worked for specific individuals or organizations. Charles L. Cooke (1891–1958) one of the very active ones, settled in New York about 1930 and thereafter was a staff arranger for RKO and Radio City Music Hall. He also wrote arrangements and / or served as a musical director for several musicals, including *The Hot Mikado* (1939) and *Cabin in the Sky* (1940).

Other important arrangers for musicals were Will Vodery, Joe Jordan, and William Grant Still. Vodery maintained his position as one of the foremost black arrangers of the period; he also conducted groups on Broadway: his Plantation Orchestra played for all the Florence Mills musicals, and his choral groups sang in *Show Girl* (1929) and *Strike Me Pink* (1933).

With Vodery's help, William Grant Still entered the business of arranging and orchestration.[18] He made arrangements for shows like Paul Whiteman's *Old Gold Show* (1929), Willard Robison's *Deep River Hour* (1930s), and for individual performers like Donald Vorhees, Artie Shaw, Earl Carroll, and Sophie Tucker. After he moved to Hollywood in 1934, he wrote orchestrations for films, including *Lost Horizon* (1937), *Pennies from Heaven* (1936), and *Stormy Weather* (1943). Joe Jordan, too, was active on Broadway as a musical director and arranger, in addition to writing and producing musicals.

[18]Personal interview with Still by the author.

HARLEM AND THE NEW NEGRO

Although the renaissance movement was national in its scope, its center was Harlem. The area was both populous and prosperous. The heavy migration of black folk from the South during World War I had brought thousands into Harlem, and this population was augmented by a large influx of black people from the West Indies. The war industries had provided Harlemites with good jobs, so people had money to spend. Musicians fared well under the circumstances, particularly entertainers, but also concert artists. As in the larger world, the smaller world of Harlem maintained a color line. Such exclusive night clubs as the Cotton Club on Lenox Avenue and Connie's Inn on 135th Street catered to whites, although the performers in the shows were black, and among the special attractions were the jazz bands of Duke Ellington and Cab Calloway. Most of the small nightclubs that were frequented by both whites and blacks, or blacks only, were concentrated on 133rd Street between Lenox and Seventh Avenues and nearby.

Edmond's Cellar, where blues singer Ethel Waters obtained her first Harlem club job ca. 1919, was typical of the small clubs patronized by black people. Its band consisted of a drummer, pianist, and guitarist. The entertainers included singers and dancer-singers, who worked long hours—from nine at night until eight or nine the next morning. Although the entertainers appeared only three or four times during these hours, each appearance lasted for as long as the singer or dancer could keep the attention of the patrons. The patrons in places like Edmond's listened politely to the popular ballads of the day, but most of all they wanted to hear the blues. And for music to dance to, they wanted either lively "hot" music or the slow "gut bucket" kind.

Larger clubs maintained four- or five-piece bands, entertainers, and often singing-and-dancing waiters. The bands, which included saxophones, clarinets, and basses along with the ubiquitous piano, drum, and guitar or banjo, played improvised jazz for the patrons' dancing (few of the players were music readers) and, for the singers, mostly blues, but also ballads requested by patrons. But it was in the small Harlem clubs that white and black jazz musicians could play together in jam sessions. Whites and blacks also mixed at rent parties, where music was furnished by a drum-piano-saxophone trio, or most often simply by a pianist. The most exotic attraction in Harlem was the Savoy Ballroom, built in 1926, where white and black danced to the music of the best jazz bands of the nation. There, one Negro dance after the other was invented—the lindy hop, black bottom, shimmy, truckin', snake hips, Susie Q—some of which later moved downtown into the white world.

Books such as Carl Van Vechten's *Nigger Heaven* (1926) and James Weldon Johnson's *Black Manhattan* (1930) contributed to the growing interest in Harlem by whites. To them it was an exotic place where gaiety and the sound of good jazz were all around. A small section of Harlem became "a vivid and glorified night spot." Harlem was also, however, the gathering place of the intellectuals, white and black, who sparked the renaissance movement. Some of their adventures were as exotic, in effect, as was the entertainment of Harlem. The black millionairess A'Lelia Walker gave soirées, for example, in her mansion on 136th Street, where African-American artists, writers and intellectuals mixed with white society and came into contact with publishers, critics, and others who helped them advance their careers.

It is significant that the Walker mansion, enlarged by the addition of a back-adjoining brownstone building on 135th Street, later became the site of a branch of the New York Public Library that houses the most famous collection of books on black culture in the world. The circulating library of the branch was named the Countee Cullen Branch after the black-renaissance poet; the reference library was named the Schomburg Collection of Negro Literature and History after Arthur Schomburg, who came to New York from Puerto Rico in 1891 at the age of seventeen and amassed a huge collection of books on African Americans for his own pleasure. In 1926 the Carnegie Corporation of New York purchased Schomburg's rare collection and presented it to the New York Public Library. Schomburg was appointed the first curator of the collection.

THE FEDERAL ARTS PROJECTS

Despite these events the 1930s ushered in a period of gloom for the majority of black entertainers in the United States. Not all of the blame could be placed on the Great Depression. Two of the most important factors in the gradual disappearance of the once ubiquitous black entertainer were the movie and radio industries. Before the rise of the movie, and the sound film in particular, Americans depended upon the theater for entertainment—there they went to see operas, plays, vaudeville shows, or burlesque, depending upon their tastes. In 1900 there were approximately five thousand theaters in the nation; by 1940 there were fewer than two hundred theaters. Negroes owned or operated a sizable number of theaters—there were two or more Negro theaters in such places as New York, Chicago, Philadelphia, Atlanta, and Washington, D.C. Negro stock companies such as the Pekin and Lafayette companies, T.O.B.A., and similar agencies assured black entertainers steady employment as long as theaters provided the chief source of entertainment for people.

In addition to the vaudeville circuit for touring performers, there were jobs available for local black musicians as theater musicians accompanying acts of the touring companies and playing during the showing of the silent movie films. Moreover, the revival of the old minstrel tradition of singing spirituals in the theater created even more employment. In this period, however, the singers sat in the orchestra pit along with the players and sang their spirituals between the acts of the shows or plays. But T.O.B.A. could not compete with the Depression and the growing popularity of the "talkie" movie; it was destroyed by forces beyond the theaters' control. With it went the black entertainer industry.

During the years 1935–39 the government supported the Federal Arts Projects of the WPA (Works Progress Administration) to provide employment for the unemployed in the fields of music, writing, the theater, and the fine arts. One of the special aims of the music unit was to give trained musicians assignments that would allow them to preserve their skills. Instrumentalists were employed in bands and orchestras, singers were placed in choruses and opera groups, teachers were given classes of children and adults to train. Musicians were also involved in the theater units. And composers of all kinds of music profited—first, because their assignments allowed them the hours necessary for composing; and second, because after their works were completed there were groups available to perform them. There were even jobs for the folksong collectors and persons interested in music research.

The WPA Negro Theatre Project was especially beneficial to African Americans. For the first time they were able to participate in all of the complex activities involved in stage productions—as actors, writers, directors, technicians, adapters, and producers. In essence, they were provided with the finest kind of apprenticeship for working in the theater arts, and many good things resulted from the program. The theater unit in Chicago produced two works, Margaret Bonds's *Romey and Julie* and the *Swing Mikado* (a jazz version of the Gilbert and Sullivan operetta *The Mikado*), which created a vogue for "swinging the classics." This led to such later commercial productions as *The Hot Mikado* and *Carmen Jones* (based on Bizet's *Carmen*).

The unit in Seattle produced a folk opera, *Natural Man*, based on the legend of John Henry, the "steel drivin' " railroad folk hero. The Los Angeles unit revived Hall Johnson's *Run Little Chillun,* and it played for almost a year to enthusiastic audiences. At New York, the WPA Theater produced a musical about John Henry and Eubie Blake's *Swing It.*

THE MEDIA: FILMS AND RADIO

In 1929 the first full-length Hollywood musical films with all-black casts, *Hearts in Dixie* and *Hallelujah*, were released. The same year saw the release of the first African-American film short, which featured blues singer Bessie Smith in her only film appearance, W. C. Handy as musical director, pianist James P. Johnson, the W. C. Handy Choir, and members of the Fletcher Henderson Band. While *The Green Pastures* film (1936) was not a musical, there was a lot of music in it, particularly choral singing directed by Hall Johnson. On the other hand, *St. Louis Blues* (retitled *Best of the Blues* in

1939) was a genuine musical that featured Maxine Sullivan and the Hall Johnson Choir.

The Emperor Jones (1933) was a film version of the opera by Gruenberg with Paul Robeson in the title role. The heyday of film musicals with black casts was to come in the mid-century years rather than the 1920s–30s. But there were several white film musicals that featured black singers; among them, Jules Bledsoe and Paul Robeson in *Show Boat* (1929 and 1936, respectively), Ethel Waters and Duke Ellington and his orchestra in *Check and Double Check* (1930), and the Hall Johnson Choir in several films.

The first steady representation of black musicians on radio came from jazz bands that were playing in the dance halls and cabarets of large cities across the nation. Among the pioneers were Fletcher Henderson and Ethel Waters from New Orleans in April 1922; and later Henderson from Club Alabam and the Roseland Ballroom in New York; Edward "Kid" Ory from the Plantation Club in Los Angeles; and Duke Ellington from the Cotton Club in New York. After its opening in 1926 the Savoy Ballroom in Harlem sent out broadcasts regularly. Many black performers appeared on radio programs during the 1920s, including among others, Florence Mills, Sissle and Blake, Paul Robeson, Revella Hughes, Antoinette Garnes, LeRoy Smith, and Clarence Williams and his wife Eva Taylor. Singer Eva Taylor, who began broadcasting as early as 1922, had her own show in 1932–33 on station WJZ in New York, and later (1938–40) Alberta Hunter had her own show on the same station. In 1930 Fats Waller began his radio broadcasting career on station WLW in Cincinnati, and by 1934 he had his own series on CBS.

CONCERTS, FESTIVALS, AND OPERAS

The period of the Harlem Renaissance witnessed a number of notable concerts in New York, some of which featured concert music of black composers or performers and some, entertainment music. In 1926, for example, the League of Composers presented a concert at Town Hall that included Jules Bledsoe singing the leading role in a first performance of the Gruenberg setting of James Weldon Johnson's *The Creation*. That same weekend, the International Composers' Guild included in a concert at Aeolian Hall the premiere of William Grant Still's symphonic work, *Darker America*. In 1928 a black opera composer, Lawrence Freeman, produced his opera *Voodoo* at the Fifty-second Street Theatre.

W. C. Handy started a vogue for the "historical survey" concert in 1928 when he took his orchestra and chorus to Carnegie Hall in New York to perform black music of the nineteenth and twentieth centuries. His aim was twofold: to begin with folk music of the slave era and move through the years to the music of his time, and to demonstrate the variety of black music, from folk to symphonic.

During the decade of the '30s white critic John Hammond produced two concerts at Carnegie Hall, both entitled From Spirituals to Swing. Hammond's first concert, which took place on December 23, 1938, was dedicated to Bessie Smith, who had died the previous year. It consisted of seven sections: *Spirituals and Holy Roller Hymns, Soft Swing, Harmonica Playing, Blues, Boogie-Woogie Piano Playing, Early New Orleans Jazz,* and *Swing.* Recordings of African tribal music, made by the H. E. Tracy Expedition to the west coast of Africa, were played as an introduction to the program. The performers included Mitchell's Christian Singers and Sister Rosetta Tharpe singing gospel songs; boogie-woogie pianists Albert Ammons, Meade Lux Lewis, and Pete Johnson; clarinetist Sidney Bechet with his New Orleans Feetwarmers; blind blues-singer Sonny Terry and his harmonica; and Count Basie with a number of his Kansas City bandsmen and blues singers.

For the second concert, staged in December 1939, Hammond brought to New York the Golden Gate Quartet, a spiritual-singing male group; blueswoman Ida Cox; and Basie's Kansas City Six, which included Charlie Christian, Buck Clayton, and Lester Young. Poet Sterling Brown, a professor at Howard University, served as master of ceremonies, and Benny Goodman closed the show with jazz played by his interracial Sextet, which included Christian, Lionel Hampton, and Teddy Wilson.

At the mammoth ASCAP Silver Jubilee Festival held at Carnegie Hall in October 1939, which lasted a week, the second night's concert was given over to Negro music, "from symphony to swing." W. C. Handy wrote in his autobiography about the elaborate preparations made for the performance and the eventful night. Handy, Harry T. Burleigh, and Rosamond Johnson were appointed to work on securing the best Negro talent of the nation. The concert opened with the singing of Johnson's *Lift Every Voice and Sing* by a 350-voice chorus, accompanied by a symphony orchestra of seventy-five players under the direction of Joe Jordan. The next three numbers on the program were excerpts from symphonies conducted by their composers: *From Harlem* by James P. Johnson, *Sketches of the Deep South* by Charles L. Cooke, and *Afro-American Symphony* by William Grant Still.

The second half of the program began with a minstrel show, which featured the popular songs of black composers from the days of the minstrel shows to the present, songwriters presenting their own famous compositions to the audience. The finale of the evening offered the chorus and orchestra in Creamer and Layton's song, *Way Down Yonder in New Orleans,* followed by a jazz medley played by the bands of Cab Calloway, Noble Sissle, Louis Armstrong, and Claude Hopkins.[19]

Three great "world's fairs" took place during the period in Chicago, San Francisco, and New York. The Century of Progress International Exposition was held at Chicago (1933–34); the Golden Gate International Exposition,

[19]Handy, *Father of the Blues,* pp. 274–77, 282–89.

at San Francisco (1939–40); and in New York, the fair was named The World of Tomorrow (1939–40). All three events involved black musicians— as consultants for the preparation of special programs, as composers, and as performers. Among the established musicians called upon to contribute either as consultants or composers were Will Marion Cook, Lawrence Freeman, Noble Sissle, Will Vodery, William Grant Still, and W. C. Handy. The list indicates the elite of black musicians during the time.

The Chicago committees gave special emphasis to the Negro pageant *O Sing a New Song* held at Soldiers Field in September 1934. At San Francisco, the ASCAP-sponsored Festival of American Music held at Treasure Island in September 1940, included the music of Shelton Brooks, W. C. Handy, and William Grant Still. During the New York World's Fair, Still's music quite literally permeated the air in the area of the main exhibit since it was played continuously in the Perisphere for the Theme Exhibit.

Two works of the 1930s, Virgil Thomson's *Four Saints in Three Acts* and George Gershwin's *Porgy and Bess,* were more than merely operas for black performers—they were milestones in the history of black music. Thomson's opera was staged first, on February 20, 1934; for its time it was electrifying, even shocking, because it flouted so many opera traditions. In the first place, there was no real plot. Gertrude Stein, author of the libretto, was noted for her disdain of logic, being more interested in the sounds of words than in their meanings. One music historian has described the libretto as "an unlogical landscape of words and images."[20]

The story of the opera is about two Spanish saints in the sixteenth century, St. Ignatius Loyola and St. Teresa of Avila, and their followers, St. Settlement, St. Chavez, and other saints. In addition, St. Teresa has an alter ego, St. Teresa II, and two performers, the Compère and Commère, serve as master and mistress of ceremonies. The action centers on scenes from the lives of the saints, showing them "doing all the things that saints do, such as praying, singing hymns, seeing visions, performing miracles, traveling, and organizing." Act I takes place in front of the cathedral in Avila; Act II, at a picnic; and Act III, in a monastery garden. There is a fourth act (despite the title of the opera) which takes place in heaven.

A second source of surprise was Thomson's music, which sounded not at all like conventional grand opera; it was deceptively simple—charming, imaginative, melodious, and sophisticated, drawing upon Protestant hymnody and other religious traditions, dance rhythms, and even quotation of familiar melodies. Then there was the startling effect of the sets and costumes, which were made primarily of cellophane and glass beads; the costumes emphasized brilliant colors—red, purple, green, yellow, white, and black—in silks, taffetas, and lace.

But the biggest shock of all was the idea that an all-black cast should perform an opera about European saints. Black singers in an opera that was

[20]Chase, *America's Music,* p. 647.

A scene from the original 1934 production of Virgil Thomson's *Four Saints in Three Acts.* *(Courtesy New York Public Library, Schomburg Center for Research in Black Culture)*

not about black folk life had no precedent in the history of stage works. The production was immensely successful, artistically and musically; audiences were lifted into a world of fantasy and enchantment; the singers "moved, sang, spoke with grace, and with alacrity took on roles without self-consciousness as if they were the saints they said they were. . . [They] gave meaning to both words and music by making the Stein text easy to accept."[21] Although the critical reviews were mixed, *Four Saints* had a run of forty-eight performances, an impressive record at the time for an American opera.

The original company of eighteen principals and six dancers included Edward Matthews and Beatrice Robinson-Wayne in the principal roles, Abner Dorsey and Altonnell Hines as the Compère and Commère, and among the others, Ruby Greene, Inez Matthews, and Charles Holland. Eva Jessye was placed in charge of the chorus. Over the years the opera would have several revivals in concert version, including radio broadcasts in 1942 and 1947, and stage revivals in 1952 and 1973. A gala celebration in New York of Thomson's eighty-fifth birthday in 1981 was the occasion for another concert production of *Four Saints*. The principal roles were sung by Betty Allen, Gwendolyn Bradley, William Brown, Clamma Dale, Benjamin Matthews, Florence Quivar, and Arthur Thompson.

George Gershwin's opera, advertised as "An American Folk Opera,"

[21]Virgil Thomson, *Virgil Thomson* (New York, 1967), p. 239.

received its premiere in Boston in September 1935 and opened in New York on October 10, 1935. DuBose and Dorothy Heywood wrote the libretto, basing it on Heywood's novel *Porgy* and the later play of the same title; Ira Gershwin, George's brother, contributed most of the lyrics. Gershwin had spent the summer of 1934 in Charleston, South Carolina, working on his opera about black folk life on that city's imaginary Catfish Row and absorbing the musical sounds. He paid particular attention to the Gullahs on James Island, whose folkways seemed close to the African tradition, and the Holy Roller prayer meeting that he attended left an indelible impression upon him. The summer's experiences enabled him to give the music of his opera an authenticity that helped make it an American masterpiece.

The music of *Porgy and Bess* reflects the jazz milieu of New York in the 1930s, but at the same time portrays the musical habits of black folk in the South. All the folksong types Gershwin could have known about appear in the score: spirituals, worksongs, street cries, praying songs, mournful blues-types, and jubilees—this in addition to conventional arias and recitatives. Gershwin did not actually quote folk melodies but rather invented melodies in the spirit of folk music.

The essential outlines of the story are as follows: Porgy, a crippled beggar who moves about in a goat cart, falls in love with Bess, who is Crown's girl. After a series of adventures and misadventures, Bess returns his love, but Crown refuses to release her. More misadventures. In an altercation, Porgy fatally stabs Crown and is sent to prison, whereupon Sportin' Life

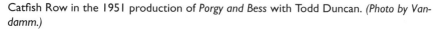

Catfish Row in the 1951 production of *Porgy and Bess* with Todd Duncan. *(Photo by Vandamm.)*

persuades Bess to go off with him to New York. When Porgy is released from jail and finds Bess gone, he sets off in his goat cart for New York to find her. This brief summary in no way conveys the dramatic intensity of the work, nor its zest, vivacity, poignancy, and real sense of tragedy.

The original cast included Todd Duncan as Porgy, Anne Brown as Bess, Warren Coleman as Crown, Henry Davis as Robbins, Ruby Elzy as Robbins's wife Serena, John Bubbles (né Sublett) as Sportin' Life, Abbie Mitchell as Clara, Edward Matthews as Clara's husband Jake, Helen Dowdy as the Strawberry Woman, J. Rosamond Johnson as the lawyer, and Georgette Harvey as Maria. It is of interest that three of the principals of the opera had been associated the previous year with *Four Saints*—Matthews, Eva Jessye, and the white musical director, Alexander Smallens.

The opera produced several memorable songs, among them, *Summertime,* Clara's lullaby that opens the opera; *My Man's Gone Now,* Serena's lament for her husband murdered by Crown; Porgy's *I Got Plenty of Nuttin';* the ensemble's *Oh, I Can't Sit Down;* Porgy and Bess's moving love duet, *Bess, You Is My Woman Now;* Sportin' Life's humorous *It Ain't Necessarily So;* and *Oh, Doctor Jesus,* sung by the ensemble in the haunting prayer scene. From one scene to the next, the singers evoke the sounds of genuine black folk music.

From the outset, *Porgy and Bess* captured the interest of the public, although the first production was not a financial success. As early as 1938 the opera was mounted in a revival on the West coast with most of the original cast, except that Avon Long replaced John Bubbles. The next revival in 1942 was a streamlined edition, with a smaller cast and forty-five minutes of music eliminated. Financially successful this time, the opera toured for many months, then returned to New York for another run on Broadway in 1943. It was during this period that new singers began to replace the original cast and that the opera made its European debut at Copenhagen in March 1943.

A revival in 1952 was notable for its new cast of principals, which included Leontyne Price as Bess, William Warfield as Porgy, and Cab Calloway as Sportin' Life. This company toured for more than four years, with singers alternating in roles and new ones coming in as old ones left the company. A 1959 film version has Robert McFerrin and Adele Addison dubbing the voices of the title roles. The New York City Center staged revivals in 1961 and 1964. The most important revival of all was the bicentennial production, which opened on Broadway in September 25, 1976, mounted by the Houston Grand Opera Company. Later productions followed in 1983 on Broadway, in 1985 at the Metropolitan Opera, and in 1987 in Houston. A centennial celebration of the Gershwin brothers planned for 1996–98 includes a new production of *Porgy and Bess.*

For the first time in its history, the opera was performed in 1976 as Gershwin had written it—in an uncut version based on the full score; even in the first production, compromises had been made for financial reasons.

Music previously omitted was returned to the opera, and the previously spoken dialogue was changed back to the original recitative.

Over the years the leading concert artists of the race sang in one or both of the two operas under discussion, and some became very closely identified with these works. Edward Matthews (1907–1954) created the roles of St. Ignatius in *Four Saints* and Jake in *Porgy,* as we have seen, then began singing the role of Porgy in 1943. His sister Inez (b. 1917) sang St. Teresa and Serena, and his wife Altonnell Hines (1905–1977) was the Commère in *Four Saints* and a chorus member in *Porgy.* Avon Long 1910–1984), who joined the cast in 1938, may have held the record for the number of times he sang the role of Sportin' Life, but Helen Dowdy (d. 1971) undoubtedly was a close runner up as the Strawberry Woman, for she sang in the 1935, 1942, 1952, and 1964 productions. Ruby Elzy (ca. 1910–1943) sang the role of Serena more than eight hundred times during her relatively short tenure with the opera.

Since the operas were revived every decade, there were always experienced singers working alongside the novices. Thus traditions established with the first productions were passed on from one generation to the next. It is of interest that three old troupers from the George Walker and Bert Williams era sang in the original *Porgy:* Georgette Harvey, Abbie Mitchell, and J. Rosamond Johnson. Other singers associated with the principal roles of *Porgy and Bess* or *Four Saints* over the long years of its history included, in addition to those named above, Joyce Byrant, Carol Brice, Georgia Burke, Clamma Dale, Billie Lynn Daniel, Gloria Davy, Martha Flowers, Urylee Leonidas, Margaret Tynes, Veronica Tyler, Irving Barnes, Andrew Frierson, William Franklin, Andrew Smith, and Donnie Ray Albert, among others.

WRITINGS ABOUT MUSIC

For the first time since Trotter's survey of black music in the nineteenth century, *Music and Some Highly Musical People* (1878), there were efforts made by black writers during this period to document the history of their music. Two modest pamphlets, Penman Lovinggood's *Famous Modern Negro Musicians* (1921) and W. C. Handy's *Negro Authors and Composers of the United States* (1938), offer brief biographical coverage of the most important musicians of the time, Handy's including both jazz and concert musicians. Both authors were performers, not writers, and the booklets plainly reveal their lack of writing skills, but are historically important.

More informative are books written by two scholars who were not musicians, *The Negro and His Music* (1936), a text by Alain Locke, and *The New Genius* by Benjamin Brawley (1935). The one publication produced by a musician who was also an experienced writer was Maude Cuney Hare's

Negro Musicians and Their Music (1936), which attempts to explore the whole sweep of black musical activity, from its folk to art traditions, and to trace its development from the African roots to the present (that is, the 1930s). It should be noted, however, that black musicians regularly published articles in the press, black and white, about the history of their music, the relationship between folk and composed music, and other philosophical matters—this in addition to the writings of black music journalists and critics.

Hare (1874–1936) obtained her musical education at the New England Conservatory and through private study. A teacher in her early career, she settled in Boston about 1906. Thereafter she conducted a studio, collected folk materials, and toured widely as a lecturer / concert pianist, in later years with baritone William Richardson. She also was a leader in promoting cultural activities in Boston, particularly through the Allied Arts Center she established. Hare published articles about black music in the leading musical journals of her time, including *The Musical Quarterly* and *Musical America,* and was for many years the music editor of the *Crisis.* In addition to her music history, she published *Six Creole Folk Songs* (1921).

THE EMERGENCE OF GOSPEL

White Gospel Hymnody

Just as the Protestant "Second Awakening" movement at the beginning of the nineteenth century had produced its distinctive song, the spiritual, so the Protestant City-Revival Movement of the 1850s created gospel hymnody, a new song genre that was more relevant to the needs of the common people in the rapidly growing cities. The spiritual was born in the rural setting of the camp meeting, where thousands assembled under the stars amid the blaze of campfires and torch lights to listen to itinerant preachers. The gospel song evolved in urban settings, in temporary tents erected for revival meetings by touring evangelists, in football stadiums, and in mammoth tabernacles. The gospel hymnwriters incorporated the traditions of the early nineteenth-century camp-meeting songs in their hymns, using stanza-chorus forms and hymns with refrains; they also borrowed forms and melodies from popular songs, the songs of Tin Pan Alley, just as their hymnwriting predecessors had borrowed contemporaneous folksongs and popular tunes for religious songs many decades earlier.

Dwight Lyman Moody and Ira David Sankey were important figures in the evangelistic crusades; in 1870 they joined forces, Moody to "preach the gospel," and Sankey "to sing the gospel." Their evangelical travels in the United States and Great Britain during the years 1872–75 firmly established the gospel hymn as an effective song genre for use in Sunday Schools and revival meetings and resulted in the publication of *Gospel Hymns and*

Sacred Songs (1875), to which Sankey, Philip P. Bliss, and Philip Phillips among others, contributed.

More important to the history of black gospel hymnody is the white musical evangelist Homer A. Rodeheaver, who began traveling as a song leader with Billy Sunday in 1909. The next year Rodeheaver published the first of his long series of gospel-music collections which, over the years, included many hymns that gained popularity among black congregations. *Brighten the Corner Where You Are* (Charles Gabriel), *His Eye Is on the Sparrow* (Gabriel), *Let the Lower Lights Be Burning* (Bliss), Since Jesus Came into My Heart (Gabriel), *Yield Not to Temptation* (Sankey) and *The Old Rugged Cross* (George Bernard). In 1911 a young black boy, Thomas Andrew Dorsey, attended a Sunday, Rodeheaver, revival meeting on the "Colored Night" and sang in the hastily assembled choir. The experience made a lasting impression upon him (a point to which we shall return).

Music in the Black Folk Church

As we have seen, during the post–Civil War period new denominations, founded by Baptists and Methodists who had left the traditional churches, began to appear among the ex-slaves. In regard to musical performance, these denominations fall loosely into two groups: those that followed, more or less, the conventions and procedures of the mother churches, black or white, and those that struck out in new directions reflecting the strength of African traditions. An example of the former was the Colored Methodist Episcopal Church; examples of the latter were the various holiness and sanctified sects, which some scholars call the "folk church."

In the early twentieth century Baptist and AME as well as pentecostal churches, were to be counted among the folk churches. The most enduring of the early sanctified churches were the Church of the Living God, the Church of God in Christ, and the Church of Christ, Holiness; but other durable sects were founded in later years. The Baptist folk churches included the Primitive Baptists—also called "Old Baptist" or "Hard Shell Baptist"—Free Will Baptists, and individual congregations of the Missionary Baptist Church. Some congregations of AME and CME churches also fell into the category of folk churches.

As in the established churches, the song repertories of folk churches might include one or more of the following types: Protestant hymns by such writers as Isaac Watts, John Newton, and Charles Wesley; spirituals and jubilee songs; and the Sunday School or gospel hymns of such writers and Sankey and Gabriel. But the way these songs were performed in folk churches was highly unorthodox. According to the evidence, the musical practices of the slave "invisible church" were passed on to the post-emancipation folk churches with full vigor: the hand clapping, foot stomping, call-and-response performance, rhythmic complexities, persistent beat, melodic improvisation, heterophonic textures, percussive accompaniments, and ring shouts.

Lining-out and Dr. Watts

Some congregations, particularly the Primitive Baptists, banned the use of instruments in the church, primarily because they associated the easily accessible instruments, such as guitars, banjos, harmonicas, and piano, with a "worldly" lifestyle. They also conducted services without hymnbooks, relying upon the deacon or precentor who, in lining-out or "raising" the hymns, set the pitch and reminded them of the words in half-singing, half-chanting stentorian tones. The people called their hymns "long-meter hymns," not in reference to metrical patterns but because of the very slow tempos. The hymns also were referred to as "Dr. Watts," although not all the texts in common use were written by that clergyman.

Example of a lined hymn:**Father, I Stretch My Hand to Thee** (Transcribed by Ben E. Bailey)

This kind of singing was distinctive for its surging, melismatic melody, punctuated after each praise by the leader's intoning of the next line of the hymns, and its heterophonic texture, with the male voices doubling the female voices an octave below and with thirds and fifths occurring when individuals left the melody to sing in a more comfortable range or to improvise. The imprecise way in which phrases were attacked and released also contributed to the heterophony.

After chanting his line the leader may begin singing before the congregation staggers in after a beat or more. Individual singers drop out in the middle of a phrase, only to surge back in before the phrase is ended. A few singers might prolong the final tones of a phrase after the majority have finished it. In some instances, such a prolongation may last well into the leader's next chanted line.[22]

The combination of the very slow tempo and surging melismatic melody gave the impression of a music without rhythmic patterns, but underlying the whole was a steady relentless pulse, emphasized by the foot-patting of the singers. The quality of the singing was distinctive for its shrill, hard, full-throated, strained, raspy, and / or nasal tones, with frequent exploitation of falsetto, growling, and moaning.

Clearly this was in the tradition of plantation "praise house" singing as described in nineteenth-century literature. And it was not confined to Primitive Baptist churches; other folk churches also practiced it, if not throughout the worship service, then in devotional periods preceding the service, after the sermon, or during the minister's call to join the church. Other occasions that draw upon the lining-out tradition were the mid-week prayers services and revival meetings. It should be observed that the practice continues today, not only in folk churches but in large urban churches as well, without regard for denomination or socio-economic status of the congregation. Hymns conventionally associated with lining-out practices include *I Heard the Voice of Jesus Say* (Bonar); *Amazing Grace, How Sweet the Sound* (Newton); *Must Jesus Bear the Cross Alone* (Shepherd); *I Love the Lord, He Heard My Cries* and *Am I a Soldier of the Cross* (Watts); and *Father, I Stretch My Hands to Thee, A Charge to Keep I Have,* and *O, for a Thousand Tongues to Sing* (Wesley).

Shape-note Singing and *The Sacred Harp*

Another tradition of the black folk church during this period was that of shape-note singing. An observer writing in 1938 noted that the tradition in some communities of Alabama dated back at least fifty years and that it was a permanent feature of community life.[23] The sound of the singing was similar to that of lining-out; practices also were similar in that a "tuner" set the pitch and tempo, and no instrumental accompaniment was used. There the similarities ended, for the singers sang "by note" rather than "by rote." They read music from a favorite hymnbook, *The Sacred Harp,* collected and edited by W. M. Cooper, singing the hymn first with use of sol-fa-syllables, then singing the words. Only four symbols were used to represent pitches: ◢ fa, ◗ sol, ◻ la, ◆ mi; hence the participants were called Four-Shape Note Singers.

They participated in their special kind of singing when they gathered together for social events—the county festivals, where singers met for ses-

---

[22]Ben E. Bailey, "The Lined-Hymn Tradition in Black Mississippi Churches," BPIM 6 (Spring 1978): 9.

[23]John W. Work, "Plantation Meistersinger," *The Musical Quarterly* 27 (1941): 97–106.

sions lasting one or two days, and the annual statewide conventions. A typical singing group might include as many as five hundred people, who sat in a semicircle with the leader in the center. In addition to singing sessions, the activities of Shape-Note singers included classes conducted by teachers who received licenses to teach after passing examinations administered by the convention.

Often black communities had their own *Colored Sacred Harp,* which they used in addition to or in place of Cooper's. It contained the old favorite hymns found in the white *Sacred Harp* but also hymns written by members of the community.[24] The repertory of the Four-Shape Note Singers did not include spirituals or other kinds of black folksongs. A related tradition, called Seven-Shape Note Singing, was prevalent throughout the South, but according to contemporary reports, it differed significantly from Four-Shape Note singing, belonging rather to the black gospel tradition.

Black Church Songs

A different kind of music developed once musical instruments were brought into the folk church. Although these churches may have previously used traditional hymnody and spirituals, they added a new dimension to that musical repertory in supporting the singing by using a piano or melodeon and tambourines. Frequently there might also be a guitar, and sometimes the saxophone, trombone, and / or violin, as well as drums and other percussion. Thus an instrumental ensemble was incorporated into the worship service, particularly in the larger churches—poor churches might have only the piano and percussion—and the kind of rhythmic intensity formerly associated with dance music passed over into church music.

The pentecostal church called for full participation of the congregation in all its worship activities; as a contemporary observer pointed out, "Music [was and] is [today] exploited to a degree that probably is not attained in any other denomination."[25] One of the patriarchs of the holiness church is reputed to have said, "The devil should not be allowed to keep all this good rhythm,"[26] and pentecostal congregations followed his dictum to the letter. During the musical performances of the worship service, members of the congregation clapped their hands (typically on off-beats of the music), stomped their feet, and, if so moved, played their own tambourines and joined the choir in singing. Moreover, the holy dance was an integral part of the worship ceremonies.

[24]A hymnal in my possession is the publication of J. Jackson, "Author and Publisher," *The Colored Sacred Harp* (Ozark, Alabama, 1931). The book contains seventy-seven hymns, but no spirituals.

[25]John Work, "Changing Patterns in Negro Folk Songs," *Journal of American Folklore* 62 (1949): 140; reprint in RBAM, p. 286.

[26]Work, "Changing Patterns," reprint in RBAM, p. 287.

One striking aspect of the performance was the role of the keyboard instrument, called the "rhythmic piano," although it might be a pump organ. It was hardly an accompanying instrument but rather a full partner in the music making and was expected to fill in pauses in the singing with improvisation—broken chords, arpeggios, runs, glissandos, and other kinds of embellishment—although occasionally pauses might be used for special effects. Thus improvisation took place on two levels, the melodic and the harmonic. A third level was represented by text improvisation: performers were free to add words to the original text or to omit them, to reiterate single words or phrases, or to interject exclamatory words. Members of the congregation, too, might toss words or snatches of phrases into the musical performance in call-and-response fashion.

The song repertory included spirituals, often embellished to such an extent that original melodic and rhythmic patterns were obscured and the results sounded like newly invented songs. In true folk tradition, the person who wrote the text typically was the same person who composed the music. In the early years, songs were disseminated orally. For a long time black folk had no name for their accompanied religious songs; they called the songs spirituals or jubilees or "church songs." Persons outside the church might refer to them as "holy roller" songs. During the 1930s–40s the songs were sometimes called "Dorseys," after Thomas Dorsey, the most prolific church-song writer of the period.

Pentecostal churches expanded rapidly in the rural South. When black folk began pouring into the nation's cities during the second decade of the twentieth century, they took their joyful church songs with them into the urban ghettos, into the storefront churches, some of which developed into large temples within a few years. Very little documentation of this music in its early stages is extant. By the 1920s it had developed into a distinctive genre, displaying features of both the historical sacred black music and the secular. Observers perceived that this expressive church music was essentially the sacred counterpart of the blues, frequently the sacred text being the only distinguishing element. The call-and-response, rhythmic vitality, musical density, predilection for duple meters, syncopation, improvisation, and "bent note" scale were all present. The harmonic patterns of the music were chiefly diatonic—that is, based on tonic, dominant, and subdominant chords as in the blues—but the scalar "bent tones" changed some of the chords to secondary dominant and diminished seventh chords.

The first important gospel-hymn writer, the Reverend Charles A. Tindley (1851?–1933), sponsored periodic concerts of church songs beginning as early as 1901, some of which he himself wrote. Tindley began to copyright his music in the early 1900s and in 1916 published a collection, *New Songs of Paradise,* which comprised thirty-seven works, including those copyrighted earlier.[27] The collection was immensely popular and had gone

---

[27] A copy of this rare publication may be consulted at the Library of Congress.

into a seventh edition by 1941. Best known of his songs are *A Better Home, Leave It There, Stand by Me, What Are They Doing in Heaven Tonight, We'll Understand It Better By and By,* and *I'll Overcome Some Day.*

Significantly, Tindley pointed out that his songs were "popular and religious songs for Sunday Schools, Prayer Meetings, Epworth League Meetings, and Social Gatherings." Clearly he did not intend that the songs should be sung in the formal worship services of his Methodist Episcopal Church, but rather on informal occasions in the same way as Sankey's gospel hymns were used. It would be some time before the "new," black church songs would be accepted into the formal worship services of middle-class churches.

Fortunately, Tindley was able to promote and publish his songs, undoubtedly supported by his church. Other church-song writers of the period sought the help of the National Baptist Convention, U.S.A., in getting their songs before the public. Founded in 1880, the Convention had established a music department by 1900 (later called the National Baptist Music Convention), and singers not only were permitted but encouraged to perform church songs at the annual meetings. Songwriters also used revival meetings as a platform from which to introduce their music. By the 1920s a number of religious singers had developed wide reputations among black communities, among them the preachers A. W. Nix and J. M. Gates; "Professors" Britt, J. H. Smiley, and Stringfield; and Mrs. J. D. Bushell and Geneva Williams.

In 1921 the Sunday School Publishing Board of the National Baptist Convention produced a small landmark in the history of black church music, a collection of 165 songs called *Gospel Pearls.* The title page stated that this "First Edition of a Song Book [was] born in due time out of an urgent demand for real inspiring and adaptable music in all of [their] Sunday Schools, Churches, Conventions, and other religious gatherings." The hymnal, which seems to have been intended for any denomination, contains "pearls of song" for use in the worship service as well as "Evangelistic services, Funeral, Patriotic, and other special occasions."

Section 1, entitled "Worship and Devotion," consists primarily of standard Protestant hymns and gospel hymns of white writers, but includes two Tindley songs. Section 2, "Revival," consists chiefly of gospel hymns and songs but includes one or two standards, such as Wesley's *Father, I Stretch My Hands to Thee,* apparently because of the association of the hymns with lining-out traditions. Tindley is well represented in this section, as are also other black songwriters. Section 3, "Spirituals," comprises a mixture of black gospel songs and arranged spirituals, chiefly by John W. Work II and his brother, Frederick J. Work.

Like Richard Allen's hymnal of 1801, *Gospel Pearls* is a folk-selected anthology in that it contains song favorites of black churches in the 1920s, without regard for denomination. Moreover, the collection provides examples of the various religious song-types in current usage and documents the history of the black gospel song. Indeed, as the editors point out, the hymnal was intended as "a boon to Gospel singers, for it contains the songs that have been sung most effectively by . . . prominent singers."

Other than the hymnals cited above, there are few records of this early church music, for it existed primarily in oral tradition. Curiously, the first people to bring the music to the attention of the church-going public were not members of the pentecostal churches, but Baptist and Methodist preachers and evangelists. On the surface it might appear that the early writers of black-church music took the gospel hymnody of the white evangelists as a starting point, from which they moved in a different direction. But the evidence is that these writers used their own religious songs as the starting point; they were nourished in black folk churches and were inheritors of the same musical conventions as the pentecostal folk. It is not surprising, therefore, that their music should share the same folk elements.

To black folk, the white gospel hymns belonged to the same class as the standard Protestant hymns; but the spirituals, jubilees, and "holy rollers" were products of their own creativity. Although pentecostal churches rarely had middle-class congregations in the early years, their worship services attracted black folk from all socio-economic ranks in the same way that concerts did; people often went simply to "listen to the music" and to enjoy the glorious sounds of the instrumental ensembles. For many years, ministers of mainline churches strongly opposed bringing that kind of music into their churches.

Just as we have compared the spiritual and the blues, we pause here to comment on this new, black-song genre that was in the making in the 1920s–30s. Scholars, collectors, and enthusiasts—particularly whites— were well aware that the old-time spiritual was disappearing, and greatly bemoaned its loss. But as black scholar John W. Work points out, "the style of singing spirituals and the type of song have not disappeared. . . . only passed into another type of singing and song."[28]

The differences and similarities between gospel and spiritual may be summarized:

1. Gospel texts are subjective and hortative. The poems generally center on a single theme, which is stressed through the repetition of phrases. The subjects are wide ranging, such as conversion, salvation, yearning for spirituality, etc. Spiritual texts are group-oriented and tend to tell stories about Biblical events and figures, especially of the four Gospel books of the Bible and the old Testament. Its themes and subjects are similar to those of the spiritual.
2. Gospel songs have instrumental accompaniment, which is as "integral part of the performance as is the singing, and in like manner equally an expression of the folk." The spiritual is sung *a capella*.
3. Gospel has a characteristic rhythmic intensity because of its marked syncopation and percussive instrumental rhythms.

[28]Quotations are from Work, "Changing Patterns," reprint in RBAM, pp. 281–90. See also Boyer, *How Sweet the Sound* (1995).

4. Gospel uses strophic forms, with verses and refrains, and, like white gospel, its songs tend to be sixteen or thirty-two measures in length. Spirituals typically consist of one strain repeated again and again, as a, a, a, a etc; or of two strains as in a b patterns.
5. Gospel melody, with its flatted thirds and sevenths, is related to blues; the spiritual uses "bent tones" only occasionally.

The foregoing statements apply primarily to gospel in the decades of the 1920s and '30s, as it was beginning to emerge in the community and in the black church. Over the years, gospel would change faster and to a greater extent than any other black-song genre in history.

Father of Gospel Music

Chicago is regarded as the birthplace of black gospel, for its churches produced the most celebrated of the pioneering writers and singers and established the most enduring traditions. The decade of the 1920s begins the era of Chicago gospel and Thomas Dorsey (1899–1993), called the "Father of Gospel Music," who settled in Chicago about 1916. Born in rural Georgia, he often traveled as a child with his father, an itinerant Baptist preacher, to rural churches, where he played the pump organ. When he was about eleven, his family moved to Atlanta, where he came into contact with important stars of vaudeville, several of whom assisted his musical development.

By the time Dorsey left Atlanta in 1916 he was an experienced dance pianist and had earned the nickname "Barrelhouse Tom." During the years 1923–26 he toured with blues singer "Ma" Rainey on the T.O.B.A. circuit, accompanying her with his Wildcats Jazz Band and writing and arranging music for her shows. During the off-seasons he played with other groups, recorded with his Famous Hokum Boys and others, formed a songwriting team with Tampa Red (né Hudson Whittaker), and wrote dozens of songs with him and other lyricists.

As "Georgia Tom" he became noted for his blues, but he also was writing religious music. He had never forgotten the power and excitement of the gospel hymns he sang as a child at the "Colored Night" service in 1911. When he attended a meeting of the National Baptist Convention in 1921 and heard the Reverend A. W. Nix electrify the congregation with the hymn *I Do, Don't You* (written by Excell), Dorsey decided he would be a gospel singer, and he wrote his first song, *If I Don't Get There*. Dorsey is credited with being the first person to use the term "gospel song" to apply to the church songs of the black folk, but the term did not come into common usage until much later.

Dorsey continued to write gospel songs at the same time as he was active as a blues pianist and writer, and some of the songs were successful. He said, "If I could get into the gospel songs the feeling and the pathos and the moans and the blues, that [would get] me over." About 1927 he began "peddling" his songs from church to church in Chicago and through the Midwest and South. Ministers would not allow him to sing the songs during the worship service, but he could do so after its conclusion. He printed only the texts on small sheets, called "ballets" by some black folk, which he sold for a few cents, and hired a singer to perform the songs to his piano accompaniments. This use of the piano was unique for that period. The singers who toured the country singing church songs and spirituals generally were male groups who sang *a capella*. A few years later Dorsey took another innovative step when he organized a female group to sing his songs, at first as a backup for himself, then later (enlarged) as an independent group. This was the first appearance of a female gospel quartet in history.

Beginning in 1929 the Great Depression brought chaos to the lives of blues and jazz people, as we have seen, and within a year or two Dorsey moved into the field of religious music exclusively, where he could earn a livelihood as a singer and songwriter. In 1930 he became a minor celebrity when one of his songs, *If You See My Saviour,* was performed at the National Baptist Convention in Chicago, and "took the audience by storm." In 1931 he organized, with Theodore Frye (1899–1963) the world's first gospel chorus at the Ebenezer Baptist Church, and the same year he formed, with Frye and Magnolia Lewis Butts, the Chicago Gospel Choral Union, Inc. In 1932 he was a co-founder, with gospel singer Sallie Martin, of the National Convention of Gospel Choirs and Choruses, Inc., which met annually to offer workshops to and provide a showcase for gospel singers. Also in 1932 Dorsey opened the Dorsey House of Music, the first music publishing company founded for the sole purpose of selling the music of black gospel composers.

A prolific composer, Dorsey wrote nearly a thousand songs and published more than half of them. Although he was inspired by Tindley's songs, he wrote in a different style. To the religious intensity of the Tindley song he added the melodic and harmonic patterns of the blues, and his experience as a blues-jazz pianist was reflected in the musical density and improvisatory nature of his accompaniments. Dorsey's best known songs were *Precious Lord, Take My Hand* (which was translated into more than fifty languages), *When I've Done My Best, Hide Me in Thy Bosom, Search Me, Lord,* and *There'll Be Peace in the Valley.*

Other Gospel Composers

Lucie Campbell (1885–1963) obtained her first copyright for a gospel song as early as 1905, but most of her songs were written during her mature years. A public school teacher in Memphis for her entire career, she was active for many years, beginning in 1916, with the National Baptist Convention, the National Baptist Music Convention, and the Convention Choral Society. She first attracted wide attention as a composer when her song,

Something Within, was sung at the Convention in 1919. Her best-known songs were *I Need Thee Every Hour, The Lord Is My Shepherd,* and *He Understands, He'll Say Well Done.*

Sallie Martin (1896–1988), a native of Georgia, settled in Chicago in 1919 and immediately began singing in church choirs. In 1932 she auditioned to sing in Dorsey's chorus at the Pilgrim Baptist Church, was accepted, and began a long professional association with him. During the 1930s she toured extensively with him as a song demonstrator. Thereafter she traveled the gospel concert circuit as a soloist and with her own groups. In 1940 she founded a gospel-music publishing company with jazz pianist and gospel composer Kenneth Morris (1917–1988), which released such successful songs as *Just a Closer Walk with Thee.* Martin retired in 1970 but continued to sing on special occasions as, for example, in 1979 when she took a leading role in the French production of *Gospel Caravan* in Paris. Sallie Martin exerted wide influence on gospel music developments through her performance, her original songs, and the achievements of her students.

[W]illiam Herbert Brewster, Sr. (1897–1987), minister of a Baptist church in Memphis and an officer of the National Baptist Convention for many years, is credited with being the first to popularize the use of triplets in gospel songs, of which an early example was *Surely God Is Able* (see example on page 463). His songs were distinctive for their melismatic cadenzas, vivid biblical images, and sharp tempo changes, and were immensely popular. The well-known songs include *How I Got Over, Just over the Hill,* and *Move on up a Little Higher.* Like Tindley, he used his church as a showcase for his songs, plays, and pageants; choristers of his church sang his songs, particularly "Queen Candace" Anderson, in addition to such professionals as Mahalia Jackson and the Ward Sisters.

Roberta Martin (1907–1969) began her career in 1931 as an accompanist for the Dorsey–Frye gospel choir at Ebenezer Baptist Church, and the two men contributed much to her musical development. In 1933 she was co-founder of a five-member male group, the Martin–Frye Quartet, which in 1936 became her own Roberta Martin Singers. In the 1940s she added women to the group and toured widely for a decade or so. She then devoted most of her time to working with choirs and writing and arranging gospel music; by 1939 she had founded her own publishing company, the Roberta Martin Studio of Music. Her great contribution to the history of gospel was her development of a distinctive gospel-piano style and the special sound of her groups, which integrated for the first time men and women into the gospel chorus. Like Sallie Martin (not related), she exerted enormous influence on gospel through her students.

Gospel Traditions

The years 1920s–30s saw the establishment of certain traditions of gospel that served to define it as a distinctive genre. First, it was treated as a

Surely God Is Able

W. Herbert Brewster

Arr. by Virginia Davis

liturgical music, despite its secular undertones, intended for performance in the church during the various kinds of worship services, formal and informal. Second, it was performed by members of the church, although guest artists might be invited to sing solos on special occasions or give recitals. Church-related activities also might include the performance of gospel music, such as sacred-music concerts, mid-week devotional services, Sunday afternoon entertainments, and revivals. In some instances singing evangelists and groups toured on the church-concert circuit (as distinguished from the revival circuit), among them, the blind Arizona Dranes and "Sister" Sallie Sanders, both of whom were recording by 1926, and the Dixie Hummingbirds, a male quartet of Greenville, South Carolina, which was organized in 1929. Although this published song, *Surely God Is Able,* uses the 6/4 time signature, it was performed in 12/8 when it was first recorded.

By the end of the period two kinds of gospel groups had emerged: the all-male "gospel quartet" consisted of four or five singers who dressed in business suits, sang *a capella* in barbershop "harmonizing" style, and added percussive effects to their singing by snapping their fingers and slapping their thighs in the tradition of juba pattin'. The "gospel chorus" was composed of females who wore choir robes and sang music with piano accompaniment, accenting the rhythmic patterns of the music by clapping their hands. The music performed by these two groups, which was in the style discussed earlier, was called either "quartet singing" or "gospel singing."[29]

By the mid-1930s changes were beginning to creep into gospel traditions. Dorsey reputedly was responsible for one of the first: in 1936 he promoted a "battle of song" between the Martins—Roberta and Sallie—at Chicago's DuSable High School and charged fifteen cents admission. "Cutting contests" have a long lineage in the black music tradition, but this apparently was the first time anyone had asked for an admission fee for a sacred-music concert. Church music was supposed to be free of charge for those who wanted to listen to it, although voluntary offerings were "acceptable." The success of the concert created a vogue for the gospel-music concert with paid admission, which has lasted to the present time, and gospel began to produce professional singers who received compensation for their singing, although they sang only in churches or for church groups.

Three other events of the period portended the direction in which gospel was to move in the future. First, in 1938, gospel songs were taken into a secular setting for the first time when "Sister" Rosetta Tharpe (1921–1973) sang on a Cab Calloway show at the Cotton Club in New York, accompanying herself on the guitar. The same year she signed a recording contract with Decca Records, thus becoming the first gospel singer to record for a major commercial company. And finally, in December 1938, gospel music

---

[29]See further in Horace C. Boyer, "Contemporary Gospel Music," BPIM 7 (Spring 1979): 5–58. Boyer's recent publication, *How Sweet the Sound* (1995), is a history of *The Golden Age of Gospel.*

again appeared in a secular setting, although it was labeled "Spirituals and Holy Roller Hymns." The occasion was John Hammond's concert entitled From Spirituals to Swing at Carnegie Hall, which presented the black tradition from African tribal music to Kansas City jazz. The gospel singers were Sister Tharpe with her guitar and Mitchell's Christian Singers, a male quartet from Kinston, North Carolina. The 1940s presaged a new era of gospel music history.

CHAPTER 12

The Mid-Century Decades

A s the United States slowly moved toward its two-hundredth birthday, and the black population, toward the celebration of its one hundred years of freedom, there was yet little progress being made with regard to the integration of black Americans into the mainstream of American life. Blacks generally lived in their own communities and continued to develop their own institutions to serve their cultural and social needs. Of these, religious institutions remained the most powerful; by mid-century, more than five million blacks belonged to all-black denominations. A number of new denominations began to rival the supremacy of the Baptists, Methodists and pentecostals among the common people; for example, the Church of God, Seventh-Day Adventist groups, and Jehovah's Witnesses, as well as smaller independent black sects.

Some African Americans turned away altogether from Christianity to the new Nation of Islam, called the Black Muslims, under the leadership of Elijah Muhammad (formerly Elijah Poole). One of the early dynamic leaders in the Black Muslim movement was Malcolm X, who later broke with the movement and was assassinated in 1965 while presiding over a meeting of his new organization. Ostensibly a religious group, the Black Muslim movement had political and social undertones and attracted thousands of blacks who were alienated from the American way of life. Its members took Muslim names and observed strict laws in diet, dress, and conduct. Many jazz artists, in particular, began to embrace orthodox Islam.

The church continued to support black artists in their music projects, whether they concerned concerts, dramas, workshops, or music education.

Other institutions that helped in the sponsoring of music activities were local libraries, YM and YWCA establishments, settlement houses—all of these groups operating under black directors, although receiving some financial support from the white parent organizations. Finally, the black fraternal groups began to take a more active part in promoting cultural activities—the Greek-letter organizations and other fraternal groups, lodges, social clubs, and benevolent societies.

The black press, which included more than three hundred newspapers and periodicals by the 1960s, assumed the responsibility for keeping its readership informed of events and people, a task of vital importance since few white newspapers included news about blacks. A few of the large cities, however, maintained special radio and television stations that programmed news and music solely for black listeners. Thus, during the mid-century years the African-American world became smaller and more self-contained than ever before.

Beginning in the 1940s barely perceptible changes began to take place with regard to integration. The music called jazz, which had been created by African Americans, was gradually coming to represent the true American music to the world; moreover, it had penetrated the fields of mainstream dance and entertainment music; each new idea that came out of black jazz groups was emulated by whites and snatched up by the powerful music industry. Eventually, black and white jazz artists began to play together, thus facilitating the exchange of musical ideas. In the concert world and in opera, too, change began to take place slowly. It was during the 1940s, as we have seen, that African Americans sang with major opera companies for the first time and that the opera of a black composer was first produced by a major company.

WORLD WAR II

The fifth decade of the century brought World War II. Approximately one million black men and women served in the armed forces, including the newly established WAACs (Women's Army Auxiliary Corps, later Women's Army Corps) and WAVES (Women Accepted for Volunteer Service in the Navy). Although the predictable discrimination occurred, it was not as rampant as during previous wars, and blacks served in sectors of the armed services from which they had been excluded in the past, notably the Air Force and the Marine Corps. Moreover, in many places blacks were trained in officer-candidate schools along with whites.

With regard to musical activities, life was different for both black and white servicemen—and servicewomen—than it had been in the past. The establishment of the selective-service system obliterated the need for recruiting songs, an important category of music in previous wars. Servicemen and women had access to so many outlets for their musical needs that old-fashioned group singing played a relatively minor role. Established concert artists and popular singers as well as musical groups of all types were assembled to tour the United States and overseas, providing entertainment for all units. Moreover, the armed services organized its own bands and glee clubs to entertain at-home bases and to tour.

Nevertheless, servicemen and women did participate in some group singing and professional songwriters turned out a large number of war songs, many of doubtful quality. Among the most popular songs were *White Christmas, The White Cliffs of Dover, The Last Time I Saw Paris, Coming In on a Wing and a Prayer, Praise the Lord and Pass the Ammunition, Rodger Young, We Did It Before,* and *This Is the Army, Mister Jones.* Duke Ellington made his contributions with *Don't Get Around Much Anymore* and *Do Nothing Till You Hear from Me.* The songwriters of the nation organized a Music Committee that contacted various branches of the armed services asking what kinds of songs were needed. As a result, each branch had its own songs (some of which became official), as did also the Red Cross, the USO, and the Treasury Department (which used songs in selling war bonds).

The Great Lakes Experience

Prior to 1942 black men were excluded from service in the navy, except as mess attendants and stewards. In World War II the armed services generally promoted an antidiscriminatory policy, however, and the navy had to fall in line; beginning in 1942 it actively recruited black men and trained them—but kept them in segregated units. Insofar as black-music history is concerned, this segregation turned out to have positive aspects, as we shall see. The navy readied a special camp, Camp Robert Smalls, at the Great Lakes base, for its black recruits and selected Leonard Bowden, an experienced bandmaster and jazzman from St. Louis, to take charge of music. Later, two additional locations were designated "black camps," Camps Lawrence and Moffett.[1]

During the years 1942–45 more than five thousand black bandsmen went through music training at the three camps; many were sent out in units of twenty-five men to other bases of the navy, where they had to serve as military, concert, and dance bands. They performed so ably that the Great Lakes camps earned a well-deserved reputation for producing some of the finest musicians in the armed services. Camp Smalls' A Band, the best at Great Lakes, was Ship's Company Band; it performed regularly in Chicago's

[1]See further in Samuel A. Floyd, "The Great Lakes Experience: 1942–45," BPIM 3 (Spring 1975): 17–24.

Marine Corps jam session, World War II. *(Courtesy New York Public Library, Schomburg Center for Research in Black Culture)*

Grant Park concert series. In 1943 they participated in Chicago's fund-raising campaign, "Forty Million in Forty Days," to replace the sunken American cruiser, the *Chicago*. The next best group, B Band, was in residence at Camp Lawrence, and C Band, at Camp Moffett.

The best men in the three groups were formed into a Radio Band that presented a "Men O' War Radio Show" every Saturday night on the CBS network from station WBBM in Chicago. Also appearing on the show were a 200-voice chorus, an octet, and a quartet, all directed by Wayman Hathcock. Thomas Anderson served as scriptwriter and announcer.

The men who went through Great Lakes included some of the leading jazzmen and concert artists of the race; before joining the navy, they had played with Duke Ellington, Earl Hines, Fletcher Henderson, and Jay McShann, among others; they had sung on the concert stage and in the choruses of Hall Johnson and Eva Jessye; they had performed in operas, Broadway musicals, and in films. At Great Lakes they rubbed shoulders with each other and with the untrained, but often gifted, recruits, teaching as well as performing with the younger men.

Many of the bandsmen continued their involvement with performance or composition after being discharged—among them Clark Terry, Major Holley, Luther Henderson, Gerald Wilson, Donald White, and Ulysses Kay, to cite a few—and others, such as Huel Perkins and Thomas Bridge, went into music teaching or administration. One observer pointed out, "There have never been so many good musicians in any one place, at any one time, as there were at Great Lakes."[2]

The USO Camp Shows

The USO (United Service Organization) early determined that entertaining the troops would be one of its top priorities. In the fall of 1943 the first Negro Units of the USO Camp Shows went abroad to tour in the European Theater under the direction of Willie Bryant (1908–1964), an ex-vaudeville and jazzman, who later would become celebrated as a jazz disc jockey in New York. With him went concert singer Kenneth Spencer (1913–1964), as well as Julie Gardner, Betty Logan, and Ram Ramirez. The next year the USO sent over a *Porgy and Bess* Unit, and the year after that, the church choral group Wings Over Jordan.

Other groups that toured abroad on the USO Negro Overseas Circuit were the Deep River Boys, International Sweethearts of Rhythm, Noble Sissle and his band, opera singer Caterina Jarboro with her USO Negro Concert Unit, concert singer Jules Bledsoe, and many others. According to the black press, the USO had more than two hundred acts among its Negro units.

Regimental Bands and Choruses

The navy bands at the Great Lakes base attracted wide attention, but there also were excellent army bands, as there had been during World War I. The 369th Regiment, which won fame during World War I under James Reese Europe's direction, had been mustered out of service in 1919. In 1924 it was brought back into the New York National Guards as the Fifteenth Regiment (its prewar designation), then reactivated into the regular army during World War II, where again it produced fine regimental bands. Opera singer Lawrence Winters was a music director in the army's Special Services Division at Fort Huachuca, Arizona, and composer Joe Jordan was a music officer at the same base. The air force had Rutherford Strider, who directed a chorus at the air force's Basic Flying School in Courtland, Alabama.

One of the all-black music groups organized during the war years later won fame as De Paur's Infantry Chorus. The group's conductor Leonard De Paur (b. 1915), a native of Summit, New Jersey, served as a choral director for fifteen months in the Air Force's *Winged Victory* show before being assigned to organize a glee club in the 372nd Infantry Regiment. De Paur, a graduate of the University of Colorado, had studied at Juilliard and had served as the associate choral director of the Hall Johnson Choir in civilian life. His fifty-voice infantry glee club so impressed officialdom that it was detached and sent around to battle areas as a morale booster. De Paur made

[2]Floyd, p. 24.

a point of singing Negro folksongs on his programs as well as the traditional concert works of European and American composers. After the war, the De Paur chorus toured widely until 1956 under management of Columbia Artists.

THE BLACK REVOLUTION

On December 1, 1955, a black seamstress in Montgomery, Alabama, refused to move to the rear of a bus in order to make available a seat for a white man when ordered to do so by the white bus driver. The seamstress, Rosa Parks, was arrested, for in Alabama the law stated that blacks should sit in the back part of a bus. Local leaders called a one-day boycott to protest the arrest and to demand improvement in the conditions for black Americans with regard to seating regulations on the city buses and employment of African Americans as bus drivers. The boycott extended to 369 days; it produced a world-renowned leader, the Reverend Dr. Martin Luther King, Jr., who helped to shape a new philosophy for black Americans, that of non-violent resistance, which eventually spread its influence over the entire nation.

World War II, with its emphasis on fighting for "the four freedoms," had created a climate for change to which the growing militancy of blacks made further contribution. Political, civic, social, and religious organizations—the NAACP (National Association for the Advancement of Colored People) in particular—began to press harder for full equality for the black population. The Korean War, beginning in 1950, brought further progress toward integration, at least for black servicemen and servicewomen. In 1954 the Supreme Court outlawed segregation in the public schools. In 1957 a Civil Rights Act was passed by Congress, the first since 1875. But massive, wide-spread resistance on the part of whites to the extension of civil liberties to blacks—including not only intimidation and persecution, but also murder—convinced many black Americans that more drastic steps would have to be taken if the move toward freedom were ever to succeed. At first there was little coordination, however, among the various groups that pressed for change.

On February 1, 1960, four students attending the Agricultural and Technical College of North Carolina, in Greensboro, sat down at the lunch counter of a variety store after completing their shopping. Because they were black, the waitress refused to serve them, but the students sat at the counter until the store closed and returned the next day to repeat the action. Thus began the sit-in movement. Before it was over, blacks and whites had participated in the demonstrations against segregation and discrimination that swept the country and that effected a basic change in the availability of public accommodation to blacks for the first time in history.

To be sure, the sit-in movement marked only the beginning of a period of great turmoil and violence for Americans. The national government took a positive stand in the fight to obtain civil rights for blacks. More civil-rights laws were passed and laws already passed were enforced. When some aroused whites took a firm stand against freedom and equality for Negroes, black organizations closed ranks to fight together in a common cause. A vast army of nonviolent black and white crusaders attacked racism in the United States under the leadership of Martin Luther King and SCLC (the Southern Christian Leadership Conference), John Lewis and SNCC (the Student Nonviolent Coordinating Committee), James Farmer and CORE (the Congress of Racial Equality), the NAACP, and the Urban League. There were mammoth "marches": from Selma, Alabama, to Montgomery, the capital of the state; on the streets of the nation's capital, Washington, D.C.; through the state of Mississippi; through the streets of Detroit and Chicago. There were bombings and murders—first of ordinary, humble persons, then of student and adult workers in the movement, and finally of leaders in the movement. The hatred and violence reached even into the White House with the assassination of the young president, John F. Kennedy, in November, 1963.

We Shall Overcome became the theme song of the movement in the early days.

We Shall Overcome, traditional

On the morning when 10,000 started out from Selma, the people sang about "that great gettin' up morning." There were songfests at night when they camped along the roadside; there were songfests in Washington while the crowds waited for speeches to begin. They sang Oh, Freedom and various folksongs, but again and again they came back to We Shall Overcome, making up hundreds of verses to fit the simple melody.

The origin of the freedom song is obscure. Its opening and closing phrases point back to the old spiritual No More Auction Block for Me—indeed, Martin Luther King, among others, commonly referred to We Shall Overcome as a spiritual in his speeches and sermons, obviously because of its strong resemblances to the nineteenth-century slave song. The middle section of the freedom song seems to be a contemporary insertion. The text of the song apparently derived from Charles Tindley's gospel song *I'll Overcome Some Day* (1900), and there are musical similarities as well between the gospel and freedom songs.[3]

I'll Overcome Some Day, Tindley

As the black masses began to realize that nonviolence was powerless against the entrenched racism in the United States, the singing stopped. Instead, there were angry slogans and riots. Only for one day was there singing again—on April 9, 1968, the day of the funeral of the martyred Martin Luther King. The crowds marched through the streets of Atlanta, Georgia, behind the mule-drawn funeral caisson, blacks and whites holding hands and singing *We Shall Overcome.* It was almost as if they thought King's death would set things right. Many songs were heard during the open-air service held after the funeral procession on the grounds of Morehouse College, but the most moving of them was Mahalia Jackson's singing of King's favorite, the gospel song *Precious Lord, Take My Hand.*

King's death left black Americans numb. The different segments of the black population gave vent to their feelings of desolation in varied ways. In the music written by black composers in response to the tragedy there seemed to be an emphasis on the discordant sounds of jazz twelve-tone, and electronic music. David Baker wrote a jazz cantata, *Black America,* for jazz orchestra, vocal and instrumental ensembles, solo voices, and narrator. Its four movements were named *The Wretched of the Earth* (Machinations, Missionaries, Money, Marines); Kaleidoscope; 125th Street (a reference to Harlem in New York); and *Martyrs: Malcolm, Medgar, Martin.* Olly Wilson wrote *In Memoriam: Martin Luther King, Jr.,* for chorus and electronic sounds. From Frederick Tillis came *Freedom: Memorial to Dr. Martin Luther King,* for chorus. A work written in memory of Dr. King by Carman Moore, *Drum Major,* used sections of King's last speech along with trumpets, trombone, tuba, percussions, and tape.

[3]See further about the history of the song in James J. Fuld, *The Book of World-Famous Music* (New York, 1966), pp. 510–14.

EDUCATING THE BLACK COMMUNITY

Despite the inevitable waning of the revolutionary spirit, black musicians renewed their resolve to develop the talent of their children, to acquaint the public with black music, and, even more important, to rediscover their own black-music heritage. Across the nation, enterprising music educators founded "schools of the arts," which functioned not only as teaching institutions, but also as national platforms for young artists.

Best known of these institutions was the Afro-American Music Opportunities Association (AAMOA), founded by Edward C. Thomas in 1969 at Minneapolis. AAMOA, a nonprofit organization, hoped to "contribute to the enrichment of the total musical life of America" by finding a way to cut through the social and economic obstacles that prevented black musicians from participating in the musical life of the nation. Among its activities, AAMOA published a newsletter, sponsored lecture-concert series, and maintained a placement service.

Best known of AAMOA's projects was the Black Composer Series, produced in collaboration with Columbia Records during the years 1974–78, which resulted in a recorded anthology of twenty-four major works of black composers, with Paul Freeman as artistic director and Dominique-René de Lerma as chief consultant. Closely related in purpose was the Black Composer Symposia series, week-long conventions which featured concerts, solo recitals, workshops, and panel discussions in various cities of the nation, among them: Baltimore in 1973; Houston in 1974; Minneapolis in 1975, and Detroit in 1976. AAMOA had foundered by 1977, but its efforts to promote the performance of black music and to document black-music history were not wasted: various organizations, institutions, and individuals picked up the challenge to continue AAMOA's work.

Community education also took place through the broadening of music coverage in the black press and the ever-increasing number of publications about black music that began to appear in the 1970s. The major black newspapers employed knowledgeable journalists or critics, of whom some worked for more than one press. Nora Holt, at first critic for the *Chicago Defender* from 1918 to about 1944, then the *Amsterdam News* until she retired in 1964, was the first black journalist to be elected to the New York Music Critic's Circle. Holt also produced classical-music radio programs. A later generation of influential music journalists included Raoul Abdul of New York, Charles Theodore Stone and Earl Calloway of Chicago, Robert Nolan of Detroit, William Duncan Allen of San Francisco, and Gladys Graham (for the Negro Associated Press).

The decade of the 1970s also saw the publication for the first time of African-American academic music journals, of which the best known were *The Black Perspective in Music* (1973–90) and the *Black Music Research Journal* (1978–)—the first founded and edited by Eileen and Joseph Southern with the support of their family foundation, Foundation for Research in the Afro-American Creative Arts; and the latter, founded in 1978 and edited by Samuel Floyd, Jr., which later came under the aegis of Columbia College/Chicago, where Floyd established and directed the Center for Black Music Research. In addition to the magazines published by black musicians, there were publications by white writers that gave all or most of their attention to black music; for example, *Living Blues,* which identified itself as "A Journal of the Black American Blues Tradition."

Whereas in the past, black musicians generally had appeared to be content in letting others define their music and recount their history, they now began to publish their own autobiographies or to supervise closely the writers who wrote their biographies. Black musicians wrote genre studies, teaching manuals, collective biographies, sociological studies, historical surveys, and the like. In essence, the decade of the 1970s opened the floodgates for publications about black music, and about the men and women who made the music. Literally hundreds of books and articles were published by black and white musicians, and, as well, Europeans. It became fashionable to include discussion of the subject—if given only a few lines—in general surveys of American music, whereas formerly the subject practically had been ignored.

THE GOSPEL SOUND

Gospel in the mid-century years retained its vibrant, stirring, deeply emotional appeal, but became more sophisticated as it developed in an urban environment. One gospel researcher has suggested that the changes in gospel style over the 1940s–70s might be ascribed to three factors: (1) the change in the composition of the performance forces; (2) the change in the nature of the keyboard accompaniment; and (3) the impact of individual styles upon the music as a genre.[4]

In the early years the accompaniment for the gospel choir might have consisted solely of a piano and small percussion. During the 1950s the electric organ, amplified guitars, and drums were added to the standard gospel ensemble and by the 1970s the performance forces frequently included strings, brasses, and additional percussion, including bongo and congo drums. For a mammoth concert in a large hall or for a recording engagement in the studio a full orchestra might be used or an entire battery of synthesizers and electronic instruments. The modern gospel choir added male voices to the previously female group, and the male quartet added guitar, sometimes a bass, and occasionally the piano.

The gospel pianist in the 1940s used primarily diatonic and blues harmonies, rarely modulated, and embellished moderately the basic material.

[4]See Baker, "Black Gospel Music Styles, 1942–1975," p. 159.

Forty years later a hymnal of black music included these suggestions for the pianist and organist:

> There are very few moments of silence in instrumental improvisation of black music, and when they do occur, they are generally for special effects. Fill in all measures of rests (or open spaces) with chords duplicated at the upper or lower octave, broken chords (arpeggios), passing tones either as single notes or in octaves, passing tone chords, upper and lower neighboring tones, runs, turns, glissandi, chromatic motives or phrases, and so on. Remember, however, that all these "extras" must be utilized with taste and discretion. Whatever the nature of your improvisation *do not* leave open spaces.
>
> The changing of keys (modulation) is very common in black music performance. It adds variety and often heightens the emotional effect of the composition. In most instances, a half or whole step change of key or a series (succession) of half or whole step changes will suffice.[5]

Beginning in the 1960s or earlier the chordal piano style became more common, with its emphasis on the polarization between low-pitched chords in the left hand played simultaneously with high-pitched chords in the right hand.

Over the years the diatonic and blues harmonies gave way to more complex chord usage. In the hymnal cited above, the gospel pianist was reminded that since most compositions are based on a I-IV-V-I structure, it is important to apply embellishment:

> Use augmented tonic and dominant chords; dominant chords; secondary dominant chords; diminished triads; dominant, augmented, and diminished seventh chords; ninth, eleventh, and thirteenth chords; chordal inversions; and altered chords. Flatted thirds, sixths, and sevenths are common. Use them. The common cadences appear in black music, but deceptive ones are also frequently used. V-vi, V-IV, and V-V^7 / ii-V^7-I are common. Delayed chordal resolutions and chord-pedals are also very common.[6]

Obviously, the role of gospel pianists is strenuous and technically demanding. It is of interest that while they are expected to improvise on the spot, they are reminded: "Spontaneity does not necessarily mean lack of rehearsal." Most often gospel pianists play "by ear," developing their skills by attending concerts of the celebrated pianists they want to emulate and / or by listening to their recordings. Thus they received training in the same way as jazz pianists did. Those who rose to the top, however, generally had closer contact with the notable pianists—either in an apprentice relationship or as a member of a leading performing group.

The black hymnist also has suggestions for the gospel soloist, who is encouraged to use "slurs, runs, shouts, extra-held long notes, turns, chromaticisms, flatted thirds, sixths, sevenths, and so forth." All singers should

[5] *Songs of Zion,* ed. by J. Jefferson Cleveland and Verolga Nix (Nashville, 1981), p. xiv.
[6] *Songs of Zion,* p. xiii.

sing with wide, open mouths, making their consonant sounds "short and distinct," and their vowel sounds "long and intense." Above all, the vocal forces and the instrumental forces should be sensitive to each other: when there is elaborate vocal embellishment, the instrumental embellishment should be restrained.

Gospel repertories in the 1980s often were enlarged by the addition of nongospel music performed in gospel style, particularly spirituals but also other musical types. According to current recommended practice, hymns and Negro spirituals may be embellished if desired, but to a limited degree; improvisation should never be used for music in the European art tradition; compositions written in the black tradition, excluding art music, may employ improvisation, if desired. An example of this occurs when *Lift Every Voice and Sing* by J. Rosamond Johnson and James Weldon Johnson, earlier called the *Negro National Anthem,* is renamed *Black National Anthem* by the black community and sung in gospel style. Finally, gospel should always employ unrestricted improvisation. Gospel scores generally were written as simply as possible, with only the bare essentials of vocal and piano notation, in order to allow opportunity for extensive improvisation by the performer.

The vocal quality of modern gospel is fully in the black tradition as described previously. The full-throated, strained, raspy sound is sought after; special effects are practically obligatory—the growl, falsetto, humming, moaning, and similar kinds of sounds. It is common for singers to change voice quality within the course of a song, sometimes for expressive reasons, sometimes in conformity with tempo changes, or for other reasons. Male singers often emphasize their falsetto tones; female singers, their low-register tones. Talking through parts of the text—phrases, or full stanzas—is a common procedure.

Gospel improvisation involves embellishment not only in terms of pitch, but also in terms of rhythm and text. The kind of rhythmic improvisation occurring in gospel has been described as that which "emphasizes accents *between* the strong and weak pulse, rather than on the strong and weak pulse, in producing syncopation. The result is a subtle syncopation that is difficult to describe and even more difficult to notate, but is apparent to the careful listener."

Embellishment of the text takes the form of interpolating extra words between the phrases or at the end of lines of texts or wherever the singer can fit words in. Such phrases as "Yes, Lord," "Help me, Jesus," "Oh, yes," and "Hallelujah" are commonly used interpolations. Another form is the commentary on the text as, for example, in the song *If You Ask Him,* when the choir is responding to the soloist by reiterating, "Ask Him, Ask Him, Ask Him," then interpolates the phrase "[All you have to do is] Ask Him." A more elaborate interpolation is this one: "[And sometimes, when I'm tired and lonely, I just say, to myself] What a friend we have in Jesus."

By the mid-century years one could divide black churches into two classes in terms of musical repertories. The established Protestant churches used a variety of musical materials—standard hymns, anthems, lined-out hymns, folk spirituals, arranged spirituals, Moody-Sankey gospel hymns, and black gospel. Large churches generally maintained two choirs, the "senior choir," and the gospel choir. Frequently there also was a junior choir and / or a young peoples' chorus. In the smaller churches, one choir sang everything. Churches in the second category, which cuts across denominational lines, primarily used music in the African-American tradition, folk spirituals, gospel, and perhaps Moody-Sankey hymns. In these churches it was assumed that one could worship through music as well as through the spoken word and, as one scholar pointed out, music "often consumes as much as fifty percent of the time allotted to services."

The gospel concert—which might take place in the church, a hall, a public-school auditorium, or any similar place—often included preaching as well as singing. Willie Mae Ford Smith (1906–1994) is credited with having established the tradition of introducing each song with a little sermonette consisting of explications of the text. Another common practice was the performance of a reprise either following immediately after the song or after a sermonette.

> This practice was introduced into gospel music by Clara Ward, who, [in the mid-fifties] . . . sang only six songs at each concert—four of them before the intermission, each of which was immediately followed by a reprise which was often longer than the initial performance. After the intermission came the two additional songs, each of them reprised, which brought the concert to a close.[7]

Some soloists left the stage to walk among the audience, shaking hands or "acting-out" the song, while the chorus continued to sing the response sections. Julius "June" Cheeks (1929–1981), who sang with most of the celebrated gospel quartets of his time, was one of the first to move into the audience during a performance.

Gospel Composers / Performers

As in the black folk tradition, gospel songwriters typically combined the functions of poet, composer, and performer in one person, and their songs were disseminated orally or by recording. They concerned themselves not only with musical elements but even more so with the "message" of the song, which, according to some, drew upon the four gospels of the New Testament—Matthew, Mark, Luke, and John. But the sources drawn upon obviously were more varied than that, including personal experiences as well as scriptural verses in the same way as did the spirituals of the slave era.

The strength of the gospel personality and the vibrancy of its many individual styles brought traditional gospel into the mainstream of American

---

[7]Boyer, "Contemporary Gospel," p. 31.

Amazing Grace[8]

Transcribed by Horace Boyer

[8]The notes encircled in the voice part represent the tones of the original melody; the other notes represent embellishment.

Mahalia Jackson. *(Photo by Frank Donato. Courtesy New York Public Library, Schomburg Center for Research in Black Culture)*

music. The most celebrated gospel figures of the mid-century years came out of the Chicago tradition established by Thomas Dorsey, Sallie Martin, and Roberta Martin.[9] Chicago, of course, was not the only place where gospel thrived in the early days. Philadelphia had been an important center from the time of Charles Tindley, and Memphis flourished under the influence of Lucie Campbell and W. Herbert Brewster. Also, it must be remembered that thousands of black folk churches throughout the South kept alive the traditions of gospel as handed down from slavery.

Mahalia Jackson (1912–1972) settled in Chicago in 1927 and soon became active in church circles, singing in church choirs and in a spiritual quintet, the Johnson Singers. She first became associated with Dorsey in 1929. Jackson perhaps was responsible more than any other single person for bringing gospel to the attention of the world; as we shall see, she established many milestones in its history.

She recorded regularly from 1946 on and toured extensively at home

[9]In addition to the sources listed in the Bibliography, see further about the careers of the major gospel figures in Tony Heilbut, *The Gospel Sound: Good News and Bad Times* (New York, 1971); *Sepia* magazine (1953–); *Ebony* magazine (1946–).

and abroad, making her first European trip in 1952. During the last two decades of her career, she was practically an American institution. Her style was distinctive for its rich, contralto voice quality, wide range, and expressiveness. Since almost every song Jackson sang was enthusiastically received by audiences, it is difficult to single out the most favored. Her performance of Brewster's *Move On Up a Little Higher,* for example, was one of the first two gospel recordings to sell over a million copies.

Clara Ward (1924–1973) sang in a trio that included her mother Gertrude and her sister Willa, after the family settled in Philadelphia in the 1920s. The Wards Singers' link to the Chicago school of gospel was through Dorsey, who, during a visit to Philadelphia, heard the women sing on a concert and persuaded them to develop a gospel repertory. The trio first began attracting wide attention at annual meetings of the National Baptist Convention during the 1940s. In 1947 the group was enlarged to include Marion Williams and Henrietta Waddy, and its name was changed to the Famous Ward Singers. Thereafter they recorded more extensively and toured widely; they also took the initiative among gospel groups in making rather controversial moves.

In 1957, for example, the Ward Singers was the first gospel group to sing at the Newport Jazz Festival; in 1961, the first group to move into

The Clara Ward Singers (Clara Ward in center). *(Courtesy James Boyer)*

nightclubs; in 1963, the first to sing at Radio City Music Hall in New York; and among the first to appear in films and gospel musicals, Clara taking a leading role in Hughes's *Tambourines to Glory* in 1963.

The style of the Ward Singers has been described as pop-gospel, of which they were among the earliest representatives. They emphasized showmanship in their concerts and discarded the traditional choir gowns for elaborate dress and hairstyles. Their best-known performances included *Surely, God Is Able,* with Clara as soloist (which, like *Move on Up,* sold over a million copies), and *How I Got Over,* with Marion Williams as soloist.

Alex Bradford (1926–1978) settled in Chicago after World War II, and there came into close contact with Dorsey, Roberta Martin, Sallie Martin, and Mahalia Jackson. He sang with various groups before organizing his own Bradford Specials, an all-male chorus, in 1954. Beginning in the 1960s he became involved with gospel theater; Langston Hughes wrote *Black Nativity* (1961) especially for him, Marion Williams, and Princess Stewart. Bradford sang in several other musicals and collaborated with Vinette Carroll and Micki Grant in writing music for and directing *Don't Bother Me, I Can't Cope* (1972) and *Your Arm's Too Short to Box With God* (1976). Although a minister, Bradford nevertheless took gospel out of the church; in addition to performing on stage, he founded a Creative Movement Repertory Company during the 1970s. His best-known song was perhaps *Too Close to Heaven.*

James Cleveland (1931–1991), a native of Chicago, became a protégé of Roberta Martin at an early age; she influenced the development of his piano style and encouraged his early efforts to write songs. At the beginning of his career he sang with such groups as the Caravans and the Gospelaires, among others; about 1959 he formed the first of his own groups, the Gospel Chimes. In the 1960s he achieved wide recognition and established himself as one of the leading gospel figures of the period with recordings such as *The Love of God* with the Voices of Tabernacle of Detroit and *Peace, Be Still* with the Angelic Choir of Nutley, New Jersey.

During the sixties Cleveland became a minister and later founded the Cornerstone Institutional Baptist Church in Los Angeles. The most prolific and one of the most gifted composers of his generation, Cleveland earned the title "Crown Prince of Gospel." His style influenced the musical development of many gospel figures, particularly William "Billy" Preston, Aretha Franklin, and Jessy Dixon.

Several other gospel figures of the 1930s and '40s contributed to the development of the genre in Chicago; only a few will be cited here. Gospel had received its second infusion of jazz in 1935 when jazz pianist Kenneth Morris (1917–1988), who went to Chicago in 1934, became an arranger for the gospel publishing company of Lillian E. Bowles (Dorsey had provided the first jazz infusion). Later Morris founded his own company, which by 1980 was the world's largest publisher of gospel music. A songwriter as well as arranger, Morris's best-known song was *Yes, God Is Real.* Another important Chicago figure was Delois Barrett Campbell (b. 1926), who sang with the Roberta Martin singers for eighteen years before organizing her Barrett Sisters Trio. Their best-known songs were *Climb Every Mountain* and *I'll Fly Away.*

Marion Williams (1927–1994) toured first with the Ward Singers, then formed her own Stars of Faith; as we have seen, she sang a leading role in *Black Nativity.* Another East coast group was that of Clinton Utterbach (b. 1931), who organized the Utterbach Concert Ensemble in 1961; its repertory ran the gamut—gospel, spirituals, folk music, and popular music. Shirley Caesar (b. 1938), who became a full-time evangelist in 1958, sang with the Caravans of Chicago, at that time under the direction of Albertina Walker (b. 1930), before forming the Shirley Caesar Singers. Although her style has been described as rock-gospel, she has limited her repertory to sacred music and her appearances to church-sponsored concerts. Inez Andrews, much sought after as a lead singer, sang with the Gospel Harmonettes before joining the Caravans in Chicago.

Gospel Quartets

A number of gospel singers won recognition as members of the dozens of gospel quartets that thrived during the mid-century years. In 1980 the oldest of the permanent groups was the Dixie Hummingbirds (organized in 1928); its repertory and style changed over the years from spirituals, jubilees, and hymns sung in close-harmony, *a capella* style to gospel that reflected the influence of rock with guitar accompaniment. Ira Tucker and James Walker wrote much of the music that "The Birds" sang.

The Soul Stirrers (org. 1935) are credited with establishing most of the practices of modern gospel quartet style: they were the first to add a fifth man to the quartet, thus providing four-part harmony support for the lead singer; the first to use guitar accompaniment; and the first to give concerts consisting solely of gospel music.[10] Their most celebrated members were Rebert Harris and Sam Cooke.

The Swan Silvertones (org. 1938), like "The Birds," changed styles over the years, moving from traditional quartet style with barbership harmonies to the sophisticated, modern style. The most celebrated member of the group, Claude Jeter, was noted for his falsetto. A contemporaneous quartet was the Sensational Nightingales (org. 1940s), of whom Julius Cheeks was best known. The Staples Singers (org. 1948), a family group, eventually moved over into the field of popular music; its founder, "Pops" Staples, is credited with being the first major gospel figure to use the electronic guitar.

---

[10]Two Soul Stirrers quartets are touring today: The Original Soul Stirrers and The Soul Stirrers. See Roy Funk, "The Soul Stirrers," *Rejoice* (Winter 1987): 12–20.

And finally there was the Mighty, Mighty Clouds of Joy (org. ca. 1959), who used amplified instruments and sang in a style that blended rhythm 'n' blues elements with traditional gospel.

The discussion above refers to only the most celebrated of the gospel groups active in the mid-century years. Many groups were known primarily to black audiences or were recorded less extensively than those discussed above. Certainly the choir of Clarence Cobb's First Church of Deliverance in Chicago was widely known in the Midwest for its superior music. In the South there were the Five Blind Boys of Alabama, the Five Blind Boys of Mississippi, the Heavenly Gospel Singers of Spartanburg, (South Carolina), the Norfolk (Virginia) Jubilee Singers, the Selah Jubilee Singers of Texas, and the ubiquitous Golden Jubilee Singers, among others.

Prominent female groups in the South included the Original Gospel Harmonettes of Birmingham, whose most celebrated member was Dorothy Love Coates (b. 1930s), a songwriter as well as singer. A noted group of New Orleans was the Southern Harps Spiritual Singers, from whose ranks came Linda Hopkins (b. 1925, known as "Baby Helen" in her early career) and Bessie Griffin (1927–1989), who later toured with her own Gospel Pearls.

Milestones in Gospel History

From the present vantage point it is obvious that gospel had shaken itself loose from its original pentecostal moorings to establish itself in the majority of black churches across the nation. At least three factors contributed to the phenomenon: first, the huge migrations of southern, rural blacks to the urban North and Far West during World War II, who took their gospel music with them; second, the National Baptist Convention, which gave its public endorsement of gospel; (indeed, many of the leading gospel figures were first "discovered" at an annual meeting of the Convention); finally, the organizing and publishing activities of Dorsey and his contemporaries, particularly through his National Convention of Gospel Choirs and Choruses.

As we have noted, the year the music was first publicly endorsed at the National Baptist Convention's Jubilee Meeting—1930—is generally considered the beginning of the history of gospel music, and Chicago, its birthplace. For the first time, the Convention's music directors allowed the promotion of gospel songs during the meeting; the performance of Dorsey's *If You See My Saviour* drew a wildly enthusiastic response from the audience. After that endorsement, the prime movers of gospel moved forward, organizing the first choruses, the first publishing houses, the first professional organizations, and the first paid gospel concerts.

In the 1940s, some gospel singers began to take their music into the secular world, thus raising the question as to whether gospel was religious or entertainment music. Actually, this movement away from the church began in 1938 with "Sister" Rosetta Tharpe and was highlighted in 1943 when Tharpe made her debut at the Apollo Theatre in Harlem. In 1946 Tharpe introduced another innovation into gospel tradition when she formed a duo with Marie Knight (b. ca. 1924), which was immensely successful. Roberta Martin was the first to organize a mixed gospel choir when during the mid-1940s she brought female voices into her all-male group. Up to that time, choirs were female and quartets (with four or five members) were male.

By the early 1940s gospel was popular enough to command its own radio program, "Gospel train," produced by Joe Bostic (1909–1988) on Sunday mornings for station WLIB in New York. Although major companies had indicated some interest in recording gospel singers since the historic Tharpe recordings in 1938, it was not until gospel won the interest of Savoy Records in 1942 that its recording future seemed secure. And its "legitimacy" received a push forward in 1948 when Mahalia Jackson and Theodore Fry organized the National Baptist Music Convention as an auxilliary to the National Baptist Convention.

The decade of the fifties began auspiciously with the first big all-gospel concert in history: in 1950 Joe Bostic produced the Negro Gospel and Religious Music Festival at Carnegie Hall in New York with Mahalia Jackson as the star attraction. Its success was overwhelming, and the next year Bostic returned with the Second Festival and more leading gospel figures, among them James Cleveland, J. Earle Hines, and Norsalus McKissick. Thereafter this was an annual affair. In 1959 Bostic opted for even larger concerts, moving into Madison Square Garden for his mammoth First Annual Gospel, Spiritual, and Folk Music Festival. His activities earned him the title "Dean of Gospel Disc Jockeys."

In the 1950s, gospel singers began to appear on television, led first by Mahalia Jackson on the Ed Sullivan Show, then with her own Mahalia Jackson Show in September 1954 on CBS. In 1954 Alex Bradford made history when he organized the first all-male gospel choir in history (as distinguished from the male quartet). And in the South, female quartets began to attract attention, most notably the Southern Harps Spirituals Singers and the Original Gospel Harmonettes. In 1957 the Newport Jazz Festival enticed the Ward Singers to move outside the church and sing at the festival, and the next year the festival organizers persuaded Mahalia Jackson to sing. Thereafter gospel took its place alongside jazz and blues at Newport Jazz Festivals.

Bessie Griffin is credited with being the first gospel singer to invade the cabaret; in 1959 she sang a leading role in a show, *Portraits in Bronze,* produced by Robert "Bumps" Blackwell at the Cabaret Concert Theatre in New Orleans. That show was reputed to be the first gospel musical in history. After Griffin, other gospel singers began appearing in coffee houses and nightclubs, among them, as we have seen, the Ward Singers. Some enterprising men even organized a chain of gospel nightclubs, called the Sweet Chariot Clubs; but these were not successful and had disappeared by 1964.

Gospel singer Bessie Jones, 1966. *(Photo by Rick Stafford. Courtesy of the author)*

In 1961 gospel reached the pinnacle of "respectability" when Mahalia Jackson was invited to sing at an inauguration party for President John F. Kennedy. Gospel had come a long way from the time when ministers refused to let Dorsey sing in their churches, and people ridiculed the Holy Rollers. By 1963 gospel had acquired its own television show, "TV Gospel Time," which was broadcast every Sunday morning to sixty major cities of the nation. About this time, gospel musicals and gospel singing in films became very popular. *Black Nativity* (1961) was the first of several gospel musicals to tour on both sides of the Atlantic. The final event of the decade came in

1969 when Cleveland organized the Gospel Music Workshop of America. Like Dorsey's earlier organization, this one brought together thousands of singers and songwriters each year to be trained in the black gospel tradition.

With the decade of the seventies, it would seem that gospel milestones no longer were needed. Gospel had firmly established itself over the land; its sound was heard in churches of all denominations; on college campuses wherever there was a sizable black-student population; in concert halls, theaters, and movie houses; and on radio and television. The gospel industry was flourishing: recordings both of the famous and the unknown were being produced in quantity; gospel literature no longer confined itself to the anecdotal but included solidly researched articles and books, bibliographies and discographies, and doctoral dissertations of quality. Moreover, the periodic workshops and conventions held nationwide assured the founding elders that acceptable standards of performance would be maintained and important black traditions preserved.

NEW DEVELOPMENTS IN JAZZ

Bebop

During the early 1940s several black jazzmen developed the habit of dropping into a Harlem night club, Minton's Playhouse on West 118th Street, after their working hours to play together in jam sessions. Sometimes they met at Clark Monroe's Uptown House nearby. Usually the group included pianist Thelonious Monk, drummer Kenny Clarke, guitarist Charlie Christian, and trumpeter Dizzy Gillespie. The musicians generally experimented with creating something more challenging and exhilarating than the jazz currently in vogue. Eventually news of the experimentation drifted throughout the jazz world, and jazz artists began going to Minton's to listen and to "sit in" with the group—some from as far away as Chicago.

Each of the jazzmen in the early Minton group had something special to offer. Charlie Christian (1919–1942), who had played in Benny Goodman's orchestra (1939–41), played his electric guitar as if it were a horn, producing long, flowing melodies that were suitable for solos or for melodic lines in ensemble passages. The piano style of Thelonious Sphere Monk (1917–1982) was somber and marked by a subtle use of dynamics; his improvised melodies were highly original, stark, and angular in shape. Kenneth "Kenny" Clarke (1914–1985) had played with Teddy Hill's band in 1939–40, then had taken a part of the band to play at Minton's under his leadership. His style of drumming, inspired by the playing of Jo Jones, gave the maintenance of the steady beat to the top cymbal, while using the bass drum to play rhythm patterns or sudden punctuations. At the time of the Minton gatherings, John Birks "Dizzy" Gillespie (1917–1993) was playing in Cab

Outside Minton's Playhouse, ca. 1947. (Left to right) Thelonious Monk, Howard McGhee, Roy Eldridge, and Teddy Hill. (© *William P. Gottlieb. Courtesy of the Artist and the Stephen Cohen Gallery*)

Calloway's orchestra, having previously played with Teddy Hill and Mercer Ellington. Influenced by the style of Roy Eldridge, Gillespie's trumpet playing was driving, powerful, and biting, with short, choppy phrases.

Other influential figures in the development of the new music were bass player Jimmy Blanton (1918–1942) and tenor saxophone player Lester "Prez" Young (1909–1959). Blanton had played with Duke Ellington's band during the years 1939–41. His innovation was to transform the string bass from an instrument that played chiefly notes on the four beats of a measure to a solo instrument that played fluent melodies, with fast running notes, sharply defined phrases, and ingenious melodic turns. Young instituted the light, "cool" approach to saxophone playing, using a pure tone that avoided vibrato and giving his melodies irregular phrases.

In 1942 Charles Christopher "Bird" or "Yardbird" Parker (1920–1955) joined the Minton sessions. Parker's saxophone style derived from the blues, but he freely juxtaposed full, rich tones and thin, shrill ones; smooth, flowing phrases and staccato short motives; on-beat and off-beat accents. Two other frequent visitors to Minton's were Earl "Bud" Powell (1924–1966), whose fast, highly individual piano style laid its stamp upon the new music, and drummer Max Roach (b. 1924), whose legato, but strongly rhythmical style was imitated widely.

In 1943, several of the leaders in the "new-music" movement played in the band of Earl Hines, but because of the nationwide ban on recording, little of the music was preserved for history. The next year a group orga-

Dizzy Gillespie and Louis Armstrong at a dress rehearsal for a television show. *(Photo by Irving Haberman. © 1996 Three Trees Entertainment)*

nized by Billy Eckstine became the first big band to feature publicly the new music and to record it.

Gillespie was the musical director of the band as well as trumpeter. The sidemen included (at one time or another) trumpeters Theodore "Fats" Navarro, Miles Davis, and Kenny Dorham; tenor saxophonists Gene Ammons, Dexter Gordon, and Eli "Lucky" Thompson; alto saxophonist Charlie Parker; baritone Leo Parker; pianist John Malachi; bassist Tommy Potter; drummer Art Blakey; and vocalists Sarah Vaughan and Eckstine, who also played trombone. About the mid-1940s the new music moved down to West Fifty-second Street between Fifth and Sixth Avenues, where a string of tiny nightclubs welcomed both black and white jazzmen.

Gillespie went to the Onyx Club on Fifty-second Street in 1943, where he formed a quintet that included Max Roach, white pianist George Wallington, bassist Oscar Pettiford as co-leader, and, within a short while, Carlos "Don" Byas on tenor saxophone. Also performing at the Onyx at that time were Billie Holiday and the Al Casey Trio. But Gillespie's most exciting quintet was formed a year later with Roach, Parker, Powell, and bassist Dillon "Curley" Russell (later there were changes in personnel).

Dizzy regarded the opening of the first quintet at the Onyx as the "birth of the bebop era." He explained later how the name originated:

> We played a lot of original tunes that didn't have titles. We just wrote an introduction and a first chorus. I'd say, "Dee-da-pa-da-n-de-bop . . ." and we'd go into it. People, when they'd wanna ask for one of those numbers and didn't know the name, would ask for bebop. And the press picked it up and started calling it bebop. The first time the term bebop appeared in print was while we played at the Onyx Club.
>
> The tune *Bebop* was written around the same time. We thought we needed a tune to go with the name. I'd composed a fast thing, and just named it *Bebop* later on the record date. I've written two more tunes, stolen from myself, *Things To Come* and *Things Are Here,* which both came from the chord changes of *Bebop,* the same changes.[11]

Gillespie became a legend in his own time as he toured extensively throughout the world during the next fifty years. In 1956 he made history when he toured abroad as a goodwill ambassador for the U.S. State Department; it was the first time the United States had given official recognition to a jazz orchestra. Not only was he one of the major architects of bop, he also was credited with being the first to bring Afro-Cuban rhythms into jazz and the first to use the electric string bass in a jazz group. He made a smooth transition from bop to contemporary music, and until his death in 1993 remained the trumpeter without peer in the world of jazz. Like Armstrong, he contributed original tunes to the jazz repertory that became standards over the years, such as *Salt Peanuts, A Night in Tunisia,* and *Woody 'n You.*

Bop developed into a music that was characterized by complex polyrhythms, shifting accents, exciting dissonant harmonies, new tone colors, and irregular phrasing. A melodic signpost of the new music was the flatted fifth of the scale, which thereafter joined the other "blue notes" or "bent tones" of black music. And bebop had its own distinctive format: typically two horns—trumpet and saxophone—announced the theme in unison; a series of improvisations followed; and the piece concluded with a repeat of the unison theme-statement by the horns.

The old "standards" were used as bases for improvisations—such as *Cherokee* or *Stomping at the Savoy*—but generally the melodies of these

---

[11]Dizzy Gillespie with Al Fraser, *To Be or Not to Bop* (New York, 1979), p. 207.

pieces were discarded and entirely new melodies created over the old harmonic progressions. Gillespie explained it as follows:

> We'd take the chord structures [i.e., progressions] of various standard and pop tunes and create new chords, melodies, and songs from them. We found out what the composers were doing by analyzing these things, and then added substitute chords to songs like *Night and Day, How High the Moon, Lover, What is This Thing Called Love?* and *Whispering.* When we borrowed from a standard, we added and substituted so many chords that most people didn't know what song we really were playing. *How High the Moon* became *Ornithology* and *What Is This Thing Called Love* was *Hothouse.*[12]

Other bop transformations based on chord changes of well-known popular songs included *Cherokee,* which became *Ko-Ko* and *Marshmallow; I Got Rhythm* became *Thriving from a Riff; Embraceable You, Meandering;* and *Honeysuckle Rose, Marmaduke*—to cite a few.

Opening bars of **Cherokee,** Ray Noble

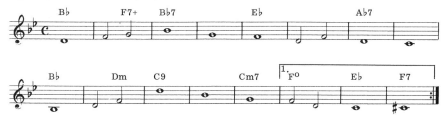

Marshmallow, Warne Marsh. Transcribed by Frank Tirro

---

[12]Gillespie, *To Be,* p. 208.

Charley "Bird" Parker had come to New York in 1942 deeply rooted in the jazz-blues tradition, having played in Kansas City bands from the time he was seventeen years old. In December of that year he joined Earl Hines's orchestra, in 1943 he played in Billy Eckstine's big band, and in 1944 joined the Dizzy Gillespie Quintet. Later he toured with Gillespie's big band, then in 1947 formed his Charlie Parker Quintet with Roach, Miles Davis, pianist Irving "Duke" Jordan, and bassist Charles "Tommy" Potter (changes in personnel came later).

Parker's quintet established him as one of the true geniuses of jazz, particularly in the performances of *Now's the Time, Ko-Ko, Billie's Bounce,* and *Parker's Mood.* His saxophone style influenced not only his contemporaries but many who came after him, not only in jazz but also in popular music. As a co-architect of bop, along with Gillespie, he helped to change jazz from a dance music into a chamber music that demanded serious listening.

But the average listener lost his bearings with bop; it was difficult to follow the melody or anticipate what was to come. Bop players performed brilliantly, eliciting admiration for the display of technical skill and the originality of the improvisations, but it was not primarily a dance music. Eventually, it became so esoteric that it lost the audience who wanted to dance. Inevitably, there was a reaction against bop from the musicians themselves.

So-called "cool jazz" came into vogue, undoubtedly inspired by the saxophone playing of Prez Young, but epitomized in the music of a nine-piece group led by trumpeter Miles Davis (1926–1991) during the years 1948–49. Examples of the style were recorded in Davis's album *Birth of the Cool.* The "West Coast Jazz" school that developed during this period, composed of white jazzmen, emphasized the cool style.

Davis had settled in New York in 1945 and played with many of the groups on Fifty-second Street as well as some of the leading big bands of the time. By 1948 he was leading his own groups and attracting attention for his unorthodoxies, such as using the French horn and the tuba. By the mid-1960s he had explored other frontiers in jazz; he used modal melodies and harmonies, blended elements of jazz, soul, rock, and rhythm 'n' blues in his music, and employed electronic instruments. His album *Bitches Brew* (1970) best represented his new style. Into the 1990s, Davis retained his musical leadership as an innovator and influential jazz trumpeter.

Various styles developed in reaction to cool jazz. Generally there was a "back to the roots" movement (i.e., to blues, spirituals, and gospel songs). Some black jazz performers felt that jazz had been drained of its vigor and emotion by an overuse of superficial effects, that jazz should move back to

Miles Davis, Berlin, 1926–1991. *(Photo by Val Wilmer)*

its primary function of communicating directly with listeners. According to Gillespie, "the movement . . . was tagged 'hard bop' because it reasserted the primacy of rhythm and the blues in our music and made you funky with sweat to play it."[13]

The leaders of the new movement included bop artists, among them Dexter Gordon (1923–1990), Thelonious Monk (1917–1982), Theodore Navarro (1923–1950), and Max Roach (b. 1924); as well as pianist Horace Silver (b. 1928); drummer Art Blakey (1919–1990); alto saxophonists Julian "Cannonball" Adderley (1928–1975) and Jackie McLean (b. 1931); tenor saxophonists Henry "Hank" Mobley (1930–1986) and Theodore "Sonny" Rollins (b. 1930); trumpeters Nathaniel "Nat" Adderley (b. 1931), Clifford Brown (1930–1956), Donald Byrd (b. 1932), and Lee Morgan (1938–1972); and organist James "Jimmy" Smith (b. 1928).[13]

Documentation for the new music is found in such albums as Blakey's *Hard Bop* (1956) and *Buhaina's Delight* (1961), Byrd's *The Cat Walk* (1961), McLean's *Bluesnik* (1961), and Silver's *Finger Poppin'* (1959), to cite a few. Roach and Blakey established models for drummers with their insistent, relentless beats, use of the sock cymbal to give punch to syncopated patterns, and penchant for setting up polyrhythmic interplay among the percussions. Silver and the other pianists played blues in the "funky" style—that is, slowly, expressively, and "hard on the beat." The horn players

[13]Gillespie, *To Be*, p. 369.

blew aggressively, in flowing lines or angular ones, but with great emotional intensity and with freedom in phrasing and melodic improvisation.

Free Jazz

With the 1960s came more changes in jazz, a movement generally referred to as avant-garde or "free jazz." The leading figures were Ornette Coleman (b. 1930) and John Coltrane (1927–1967). Other innovators included pianist Cecil Taylor (b. 1933), tenor saxophonist Archie Shepp (b. 1937), and bassist Charles Mingus (1922–1979), who linked the older jazz with the new avant-garde. Eric Dolphy (1928–1964), who played in groups with Coleman, Coltrane, and Mingus, was important in defining the roles of the bass clarinet and the flute in the new jazz.

Alto-saxophonist Coleman was both jazzman and composer in the traditional sense—he was the first jazz performer to receive Guggenheim fellowships—and his techniques and ideas exerted great influence upon his contemporaries. Representative are his albums *The Shape of Jazz to Come* (1959) and *Free Jazz* (1960). While he promoted the concepts of harmonic freedom—even to the extent of developing a "harmolodic theory" to explain his ideas—rhythmic freedom, and emotional intensity, his music nevertheless reflected his roots in the blues. His best-known work in the European art tradition was *Skies of America* (1972) for quartet and symphony orchestra.

Tenor-saxophonist Coltrane played with most of the leading bands and small groups of his time, first attracting wide attention in the 1950s as a member of Miles Davis's quintet with his solo on *Round Midnight*. About 1959 he began leading his own small groups, and although he played at times with larger groups, it was his quartet and quintet music that contributed enormously to music history. He was notable for his innovative approach to improvisation, his unorthodox handling of rhythms and form, his use of African, Arabic, Indian, and other nonwestern elements in his music, and his deep spirituality. The albums *Giant Steps* (1959), *A Love Supreme* (1964), and *Meditation* (1965) represent three levels of his development.

A major contribution of Charles Mingus to jazz history was his effort to bring back the importance of collective improvisation, which largely had given way to an emphasis on solo improvisation with the development of the big band. His music, too, reflected the freedom that was in the air, but also drew upon older styles, sometimes bop, even swing. The most important of the early albums documenting his individual style was *Pithecantropus Erectus* (1956).

We can do no more than single out a few of the other jazz musicians active in the 1960s and '70s, to whom the essence of free jazz meant breaking many of the old rules—particularly those having to do with tonality and meter. Some historians, as well as jazz performers, felt that the atonality of free jazz pointed back to the nontonal music of the nineteenth-century field hollers, street cries, and jubilees in a return-to-the-roots movement, rather than to a conscious attempt to devise a formal, atonal system in the European sense. The free-jazz musician's search for and use of elements from exotic musics, particularly African, Arabic, and Indian, also contributed to the breakdown of tonality and to the freeing of metrical constraints as well.

Improvisation became truly "free" by ridding itself of dependence upon fixed, preexistent chord progressions, as in the earlier styles. A broader approach to rhythm led to polytempic as well as polyrhythmic textures. And finally, it was during the 1960s that the concept of "soul" came into jazz, represented most concretely by the use of gospel idioms and elements, and most strikingly in the music of Horace Silver and Milton "Milt" Jackson, among others.

Sun Ra (1914–1993) and his Solar Arkestra played music steeped in a new black mysticism, as depicted in *The Heliocentric Worlds of Sun Ra* (1965), as did also saxophonist Albert Ayler (1936–1970) and his brother, trumpeter Don Ayler (b. 1942). Their style also reflected a black folk-style primitiveness, as in the album *Spirits Rejoice* (1965). Other examples of the new music were Cecil Taylor's *Unit Structures* (1966), Archie Shepp's *Things Have Got to Change* (1971), and Marion Brown's *Afternoon of a Georgia Faun* (1970) and *Geechee Recollections* (1973). Sam Rivers, composer-in-residence for the short-lived Harlem Opera Company, wrote the jazz-improvisational opera *Solomon and Sheba* (1973).

Some jazz artists of this period combined college teaching with jazz performance, among them Roach and Shepp, both of whom taught at the University of Massachusetts in Amherst (Roach later returned to full-time performance). Byrd earned a doctorate from Columbia University Teachers College (1971) and taught at Howard University for several years before returning to the jazz arena with his Black Byrds, a group that included some of his former students.

Pianist William "Billy" Taylor (b. 1921), who earned his doctorate at the University of Massachusetts, combined teaching at the C. W. Post College in Long Island with his many other musical activities, including Harlem's Jazzmobile, of which he was a co-founder in 1965. For several years he was bandleader for the David Frost Show, then returned to television in 1981 as a music commentator for the CBS "Sunday Morning" show. His publications include *Jazz Piano: A Jazz History* (1983) and a number of compositions.

George Russell (b. 1923), on the faculty of the New England Conservatory, was regarded as "the great pathbreaker" for his promoting the use of modes by free-jazz composers / performers. His novel theory about the "organization of tonal resources from which the jazz musician may draw to create his improvised lines," is explained in his book *The Lydian Chromatic Concept of Tonal Organization* (1959). His best-known works were

Billy Taylor. (© William P. Gottlieb. Courtesy of the Artist and the Stephen Cohen Gallery)

Othello Ballet Suite (1967), *Listen to the Silence* (1971), and *Living Time* (1975).

David Baker (b. 1931) taught at Indiana University in Bloomington, his alma mater (B.Mus); M.Mus.). He also was an active performer, playing 'cello and double bass with chamber ensembles and symphony orchestras and touring widely with his college jazz groups. One such group in 1982 was called the 21st-Century Bebop Band. Baker wrote music in a variety of forms such as *Levels* for flutes, horns, strings, solo contrabass, and jazz band (1973); Concerto for Cello and Chamber Orchestra (1975); and *Contrasts* for violin, cello, and piano (1976). He also published manuals on jazz improvisation, including a four-volume set titled *Jazz Improvisation* (1969–76); a four-volume set *Techniques of Improvisation* (1971); and *Jazz Styles and Analysis: Trombone* (1973).

Innovations of the Seventies

Beginning in the decade of the 1970s it seemed that old and new styles were existing contemporaneously and, moreover, that there were as many "old" styles as "new" ones. A revival of interest in New Orleans jazz, which began as early as the 1940s, reached a high point in 1961 when jazz enthusiast Allan Jaffre founded Preservation Hall in New Orleans. Thereafter, in a small bare room, seven or eight old-time musicians gathered together almost every evening to play for tourists and jazz connoisseurs in the tradition of the Storyville jazz performers. By 1980 most of the musicians were in their seventies, all black, and all male except for the leader, pianist "Sweet Emma [Barrett] the Bell Gal," but the music they played was not "museum" music. Possessing all the excitement and gusto of the original tradition, it nevertheless had subtly incorporated later jazz elements and, consequently, sounded as fresh as any modern music. White groups playing in the New Orleans tradition, however, constituted the major part of the New Orleans revival.

A second return to the past was represented by the revival of interest in swing. To be sure, Count Basie, Lionel Hampton, and other immortals of an earlier period had continued to play through the years—always to enthusiastic and packed houses—but gradually it became evident that large portions of those audiences consisted of young people, who could not have come to listen for nostalgic reasons. Moreover, young jazz people were taking an interest in emulating the great swing artists of the past and learning the intricacies of the style.

Third, there was a return to bebop. Some jazz commentators date the beginning of the neobop period with the return of tenor saxophonist Dexter Gordon (1923–1990) in late 1976 to play in New York and New Orleans; almost singlehandedly, he initiated a revival of interest in bop because of his exciting performances, and the excitement was infectious.

All these revivals were stimulated by the recording industry, which reissued old jazz classics in each of the styles. These new recordings invariably included jazz elements that had been absorbed since the emergence of the various styles; for example, the neobop of the late '70s encompassed elements of the free jazz of the '60s. The jazz associated with one or more of these styles constituted the "mainstream" of the period, whether its origin was in classic jazz, swing, or bop. In addition to those discussed previously, there were trumpeters Thaddeus "Thad" Jones (1923–1986) and Clark Terry (b. 1920); saxophonists Arnett Cobb (b. 1918), Eddie "Lockjaw"

Davis (1921–1986), Illinois Jacquet (b. 1922), and Roland Rahsaan Kirk (1936–1977); trombonist James Louis "J.J." Johnson (b. 1924); bassists Raymond "Ray" Brown (b. 1926) and Richard Davis (b. 1930); and drummers Elvin Jones (b. 1927) and Joseph "Philly Joe" Jones (1923–1985).

Third-stream music, representing a fusion of jazz and Western art music, found its best representative in pianist John Lewis (b. 1920) as composer and director of the Modern Jazz Quartet, which had the longest life of any jazz ensemble in history (1951–74). The term "third-stream" music, invented in the 1950s by white composer and jazz historian Gunther Schuller, implies the recognition of classical music as the first stream, jazz as the second stream, and the fusion of classical and jazz as the third. The members included vibraharpist Milt Jackson (b. 1923), bassist Percy Heath (b. 1923), and drummer Kenny Clarke (1914–1985), along with Lewis; in 1955 Connie Kay (1927–1994) took Clarke's place. The men frequently reunited to perform in concerts, and finally, in 1982, they reorganized the MJQ.

The group was noted for its highly integrated collective improvisation and, particularly in its early years, for the performance in jazz style of classical forms with contrapuntal textures, largely compositions of Lewis such as the jazz fugues *Concorde, Vendome,* and *Versailles,* and the suite *Fontessa.* The MJQ pioneered in opening up the concert stage to the jazz ensemble, and its performance in 1961 with the Cincinnati Symphony was an event without precedent at that time. MJQ toured widely, appeared on television, and in films, including *Monterey Jazz* (1973).

AACM (the Association for the Advancement of Creative Musicians) was founded in 1965 by Muhal Richard Abrams (b. 1930) for the purpose of promoting the music of black musicians, but it became well known only after its members had won recognition in Europe during the late '60s and had returned to the United States in the '70s. Those associated with AACM included Lester Bowie (b. 1941), Anthony Braxton (b. 1945), Malachi Favors (b. 1937), Joseph Jarman (b. 1937), Leroy Jenkins (b. 1932), Roscoe Mitchell (b. 1940), and Leo Smith (b. 1941), among many others.

AACM was an umbrella for several small groups: the Art Ensemble, Air, Creative Construction Company, and the Revolutionary Ensemble, which included along with violinist Jenkins, drummer Jerome Cooper and bassist Sirone (né Norris Jones). Similar groups of the period were BAG (Black Artist Group), with saxophonist Oliver Lake (b. 1942) as leader, and the World Saxophone Quartet, of which Lake was a co-founder with Julius Hemphill and included Hamiel Bluiett and David Murray. The music of these men epitomized the free-jazz style; most were multi-instrumentalists, and they preferred to be called "improvisers" rather than jazzmen or composers. A distinctive feature of the music was its enormous variety of instrumental color, which derived from the varied forces used in performance. The music was also characterized by the kind of free improvisation previously described. Braxton attracted wide attention as a composer as well

Illinois Jacquet. (Courtesy of the author)

as performer; his best-known works were *Three Compositions of New Jazz* (1968), *Five Pieces 1975,* and *Duets 1979.*

The "new" styles of the '70s actually were continuations of developments in the '60s and earlier as, for example, the free jazz of the AACM "improvisers." Miles Davis's *Bitches Brew* (1970) was the starting point for the style labeled "jazz-rock," which used electronic instruments and synthesizers, placed emphasis on collective improvisation, a free handling of forms and rhythm, and the unaccompanied solo on wind instruments. The leaders in this style included saxophonist Wayne Shorter (b. 1933), particularly with his tone poem *Odyssey of Iska* (1970), and pianist Herbert Hancock (b. 1940), with *Sextant* (1973), but most of its adherants were white Americans and Europeans.

In the prevalent "fusion" style, composers felt even freer than in the earlier decade to combine disparate elements in their music—jazz in any style, popular music, folk musics, conventional melody, rhythm 'n' blues, whatever. Weather Report, of which Shorter was a co-founder with white keyboardist Joe Zawinul, was the most important group representing that fusion.

Jazz at the Keyboard

As always, jazz pianists fell into two classes during the mid-century years: those who played with music groups and those who were soloists. In a literal sense, however, there were few soloists, for most pianists used at least the support of a bassist, and many added a drummer to form a trio. Several celebrated pianists of an earlier era were still performing at the beginning of the eighties, or had left the field and had returned, among them Eubie Blake, Earl Hines, Mary Lou Williams, and Teddy Wilson. "Grand old man" Blake continued to play on television programs and at jazz festivals into his ninety-ninth year, playing without accompanying instruments, and using his powerful left hand to do the work of a bassist.

Hines made his debut as a soloist in 1964 at the Little Theatre in New York, thereby entering a second career as he approached his sixtieth birthday. His venture proved a success, and thereafter he toured widely as a concert pianist (generally supported by drums and bass). Williams absorbed all the styles and techniques of each passing era, and long before her death in 1981 had earned the title "First Lady of Jazz Piano." She also composed works in the larger forms; in 1946 she played her *Zodiac Suite* with the New York Philharmonic. Wilson, too, accommodated elements of the new styles in his always elegant piano playing, but so subtly that his swinging, exquisite runs and turns seemed a continuation of what he had been doing for the previous fifty years. His popularity remained as high as ever.

The younger pianists active during the mid-century years included the virtuosos Errol Garner (1921–1977) and Oscar Peterson (b. 1925); the modernists John "Jaki" Byard (b. 1922) and Randolph "Randy" Weston (b. 1926); and the Detroit pianists Tommy Flanagan (b. 1930), Barry Harris (b. 1929), and Henry "Hank" Jones (b. 1918).

The '70s saw the rise of the "keyboardist," for almost without exception, pianists now played a variety of both acoustic and electronic instruments—electric pianos and organs, synthesizers, and, in some instances, specially constructed keyboards, such as George Duke's portable Clavator. Some of the most prominent of these performers were Anthony Davis (b. 1951), George Duke (b. 1946), Andrew Hill (b. 1937), Ahmad Jamal (b. 1930, né Fritz Jones), Ramsey Lewis (b. 1935), and Alfred McCoy Tyner (b. 1938).

Generally the music produced by these men was regarded as "fusion," because of the freedom with which they drew upon a number of resources—Southeast Asian and African, for example, or classical procedures or gospel

Mary Lou Williams. *(Courtesy New York Public Library, Otto Hess Collection)*

elements. Perhaps the best known of the fusion pieces was Hancock's *Chameleon* (1973), which fused elements of "funk" with jazz. In this piece Hancock gives funk's "rhythm guitar" part to electronic keyboards and puts both an electronic keyboard and an electric bass guitar on the part normally played by the bass in funk. Fusion style was also represented in works as far apart as Davis's *Episteme* (1981) for violin, 'cello, flute, bass clarinet, piano, trombone, and three percussion, which included sounds reminiscent of gamelan orchestras; and Duke's *Reach for It* (1977), in which the conventional rhythm group is augmented by electronic guitar, electronic keyboard, and *finger-snapping;* another keyboard offers jazz improvisation; and the ever-present vocal activity includes singing with "soul" intonation and males speaking in a rhythmic rap.

As mentioned earlier, Fats Waller was the first to use the organ for jazz, utilizing both the Hammond electric and pipe organs for that purpose. Those who helped to define jazz organ style after Waller, played the Hammond exclusively, obviously for practical reasons. These organists included Count Basie, William "Wild Bill" Davis (b. 1918–1995), and Milton "Milt" Buckner (b. 1915). The 1950s brought in the innovator James "Jimmy" Smith (b. 1928), who developed a virtuoso, highly original style; he is credited with revolutionizing jazz organ in the same way as Charlie Christian gave new directions to jazz electric guitar. In recent decades jazz pianists simply were expected to know how to play keyboard instruments as a part of their normal preparation for professional performance.

Jazz Singers

Many of the pre-World War II singers were still active in the mid-century years—Jimmy Rushing, for example, and Billie Holiday until her death in 1959. Others, like Adelaide Hall, had left the field, then later turned to the musical theater and nightclub entertaining. Singers, like instrumentalists, reflected the style period in which they lived, and the style of the 1940s was bop. The great singers of that decade were Billy Eckstine (1914–1993) and Sarah "Sassy" Vaughan (1924–1990). To be sure, Eckstine's roots were in the swing era—he first won recognition as a singer with Earl Hines's band—but he was such an enthusiastic convert to bop, as we have seen, that he organized a big band to play the new music.

Through the years the ideal jazz singer was one who used the voice like an instrument, blending it with the other instruments of the jazz ensemble. Perhaps that was one reason why scat singing and wordless vocals were so popular among black jazz groups. Bop singers were very conscious of this; Eckstine said,

> You know, they always say an instrumentalist tries for perfection by imitating the human voice. But by the same token, the singer can use what he learns technically about an instrument in developing his style. . . . You can sing . . . just as if you were playing an instrument . . . taking a vocal solo like you would an instrumental solo.[14]

Both Eckstine and Vaughan improvised melodic lines based on the chord progressions of standard songs in the same way as did bop instrumentalists.

The roster of bop singers included Oscar Brown, Jr., Betty Carter, Carmen McRae, and Babs Gonzales (1919–1980, né Lee Brown), who is credited with having invented much of bop's vocabulary—for example, the word "expubidence" to refer to the joy of life.

It was in the 1940s that Edgar "Eddie" Jefferson (1918–1979) invented the "jazz vocalese" when he wrote lyrics to the melodies of improvised solos, of which the best known were sets of lyrics for James Moody's saxophone solo on *I'm in the Mood for Love* and Charlie Parker's *Now's the Time*. Among those who later popularized the concept were King Pleasure (1922–1981, né Clarence Beeks) and John "Jon" Hendricks (b. 1921), who by 1960 was called the "poet of the jazz solo."

During the next two decades, black singers moved freely among jazz, theater music, gospel, pop, and rhythm 'n' blues. Among those who sang

[14]Eileen Southern, "Conversation with William Clarence ("Billy") Eckstine," BPIM 8 (Spring 1980): 56.

Ella Fitzgerald. *(© William P. Gottlieb. Courtesy of the Artist and the Stephen Cohen Gallery)*

jazz at one time or another were Ernestine Anderson, Lena Horne, Cleo Laine, Abbey Lincoln, Lou Rawls, Nina Simone, Dakota Staton, and Dinah Washington. Among the younger singers were Dee Dee Bridgewater, Roberta Flack, Al Jarreau, Gil Scott-Heron, and Leon Thomas.

Ella Fitzgerald, who began her career in the swing era, moved through the years with supreme success. In the bop era she improvised scat vocals on the standard songs; in later years her singing moved in the mainstream jazz tradition, but subtly absorbed and reflected the new sounds.

Public interest in jazz increased greatly during the mid-century years, not only in the United States but all over the world. White promoter Norman Granz successfully instituted his "Jazz at the Philharmonic" concerts, which were first held at the Los Angeles Philharmonic Auditorium in 1944, sent JATP units on tour throughout the world, and sponsored the touring of other groups as well. The recordings that resulted from these performances had distinctive and innovative feature because they were made in the concert hall rather than in studios.

Jazz Festivals

Another innovation arising from the increasing popularity of jazz was the jazz festival. The first one took place in July 1954 in Newport, Rhode Island, sponsored by wealthy residents of the city, who engaged white promoter George Wein to produce the show. For two days people gathered on the grassy tennis courts of the Newport Casino, listening to jazz groups and soloists, among them Ella Fitzgerald, Dizzy Gillespie, the Oscar Peterson Trio, and the Modern Jazz Quartet. On the third day, a panel of scholars discussed "The Place of Jazz in American Culture"; one of the speakers was black folklorist Willis Lawrence James.[15]

In 1978 the Newport Jazz Festival–New York (the site was changed in 1972) celebrated its twenty-fifth anniversary; during the ten-day celebration, musical events were staged all over the city, in neighboring New Jersey, and at Saratoga Springs, New York. President and Mrs. Jimmy Carter gave a jazz reception at the White House in honor of the anniversary. The format of the festival was well established by that time: concerts in all the styles and genres were performed by celebrated jazz people representing all the generations. Almost from the beginning the Festival embraced all kinds of black music: gospel made its first appearance at the 1957 Festival; blues came in in 1960; and popular music was always there. In 1979 producer Wein brought to the Festival the music of "Black Broadway," thereby closing the gap in regard to jazz-related black music.

The success of the Newport Jazz Festivals paved the way for others, such as the Monterey (California) Festival, organized in 1958 under the leadership of John Lewis. In 1957 Lewis and some of his colleagues opened the nation's first summer jazz school at Music Inn in Lenox, Massachusetts, where students could enroll for a three-week course. Some time earlier, in 1945, Lawrence Berk had founded Berklee College of Music in Boston for the purpose of training jazz musicians. For many years it was the only institution of its kind in the world; 20 percent of the student population was foreign. The black jazz artists who had been trained there included Quincy Jones, among others.

Jazz in the Church

As we have seen, Duke Ellington was the first notable composer to write jazz works for performance in the church in lieu of the worship service, or as an essential part of the service. The Catholic Church, however, was in the vanguard of the movement to bring jazz and other folk music elements into the liturgical music, and Clarence Rivers (b. 1931), an ordained Catho-

---

[15]The history of the Newport Jazz Festival is given in Lillian Ross, "Profile of the Newport Jazz Festival," *Program for the Twenty-Fifth Anniversary of the Newport Jazz Festival* (June 1978): n.p.

lic priest, composed some of the first jazz Masses. His Mass, *Brother of Man (1967),* was performed at the Newport Jazz Festival in 1967 with the assistance of the Billy Taylor (Jazz) Trio; a later work, *Resurrection,* for gospel and jazz soloists, gospel chorus, and piano or chamber orchestra, also was widely performed.

The first jazz Mass to be performed in a Roman Catholic church as part of a traditional service was the *Missa Hodierna* (1966) by Catholic layman and practicing jazzman Edward V. Bonnemère (1921–96). Bonnemère also introduced jazz into the Luthern Church with his *Missa A Nuestro Dio* (1971), which included references to Latin-American rhythms.

Composer David Baker (b. 1931) has written music for both Catholic and Lutheran services, among them, *The Beatitudes,* (1968) for chorus, narrator, dancers, and string orchestra, and *Lutheran Mass* (1968) for chorus and jazz sextet. Jazz pianist Mary Lou Williams (1910–1981) was another composer active in the religious jazz movement. Among her compositions were *Black Christ of the Andes* (1963), a hymn in honor of the St. Martin de Porres; two short works, *Anima Christi* and *Praise the Lord;* and three jazz Masses (1970–72), including *Mary Lou's Mass.*

THE URBAN BLUES

Performers of the blues formed a part of the huge migrations of black folk into the North and Far West during World War II and immediately afterwards; along with the other migrants they took the most direct routes from their homes. Those from the eastern seaboard went to New York; those from Mississippi, Arkansas, and other states of the deep South took the trains and followed the highways to Chicago and Detroit; those from Texas and the Territories (that is, sections of Arkansas, Oklahoma, and Missouri) ended up primarily in San Francisco and Los Angeles.

As we have seen, there was a slowdown in the recording industry because of the wartime rationing of shellac and the American Federation of Musicians ban on commercial recording. After the war small independent companies, called "indies," entered the industry to compete with the major companies for the newly expanding market. Since the leading bluesmen were under contract to the giants, the indies had to seek new talent, who brought new sounds into the recording studios and, as well, into the blues bars and nightclubs. The blues music of this period has been labeled "urban blues"; its distinctive features were the use of amplified guitars and harmonicas and a blues band, which added drums, piano, and winds to the traditional blues accompaniment.[16]

[16]See further in Oliver, *The Story of the Blues;* Charles Keil, *Urban Blues* (Chicago, 1966); Mike Rowe, *Chicago Blues* (New York, 1975); Robert Palmer, *Deep Blues* (New York, 1981); and the magazines *Living Blues* and *Cadence.*

The Mississippi Delta Blues

The radio was an important avenue of dissemination for race music; all over the South and in large cities of the North stations continuously beamed programs of blues and gospel, both live and recorded, from several hours to as many as twenty-four hours a day, from one or two days to seven days a week. One of the longest-lived and most celebrated of these programs came from station KFFA in Helena, Arkansas; in 1941 it began broadcasting a live, country-blues program—King Biscuit Time, Mondays through Fridays, 12:15–12:30 P.M.—that continued without interruption until 1981 (although it did include recorded blues during the more than forty years of its existence).

Harmonica-player Willie "Rice" Miller, also known as "Sonny Boy" Williamson, No. 2 (1897–1965), and guitarist Robert "Junior" Lockwood (b. 1915) inaugurated the program in November 1941; within a year they had enlarged the two-man King Biscuit Entertainers into a blues band. The show advertised King Biscuit Flour and, in homage to Miller, Sonny Boy Corn Meal. Helena's central location in the Mississippi Delta region insured a large listening audience and, for a period of time, the show was broadcasted simultaneously from Clarksdale, Mississippi, on station WROX.

Many of the important post-World War II blues artists appeared on King Biscuit Time or similar shows on KFFA over the years; among them, James "Peck" Curtis (1912–1970), David "Honeyboy" Edwards (b. 1915), "Little" Walter Jacobs (1930–1968), Elmore James (b. 1918), Willie Love (1911–1957), "Muddy Waters" (1915–1983, né McKinley Morganfield), Robert Nighthawk (1909–1967), James "Jimmy" Rogers (b. 1924), Houston Stackhouse (1910–1981), and Joe Willie Wilkins (1923–1979), among others. Miller, Lockwood, and Robert Johnson (1911–1938) exerted wide influence upon the style development of Delta bluesmen, either directly as teachers or indirectly as models whose style was imitated, techniques adopted, and repertory taken over.

Miller had a unique "orchestral harmonica style":

> He alternated quavering, vocally inflected melodies and rich chords, sometimes thickened with his humming, and he alternated them so skillfully the music took on an almost hypnotic ebb and flow. . . . He seemed to mould the notes through the long fingers of his hand, which were laid palm in palm as if he were to take a long drink of water from them. He would utter the words of his blues from the side of his mouth, slipping the harp between his lips as he finished a vocal phrase so that the melody was sustained on the instrument.[17]

By the late 1940s other cities in the area had begun to broadcast blues programs, particularly West Memphis with KWEM and Memphis with sta-

[17]Palmer, *Deep Blues*, p. 185.

tion WDIA. In 1948 "Howlin' Wolf" (1910–1976, né Chester Burnett) began broadcasting on KWEM with an electric blues band; a year later Riley "Blues Boy" King (b. 1925, later called "B.B.") became a blues disc jockey on WDIA and within a short time was broadcasting with his own band. By 1951 Ike Turner (b. 1932) was a disc jockey on station WROX in Clarksdale, leading a band called the Kings of Rhythm. During the 1950s these leaders and many of their sidemen settled in Chicago, where they contributed to the development of urban blues, as did also the bluesmen mentioned above.

Others from the Delta region and other parts of Mississippi who began recording careers in the 1940s and '50s included "Johnny Ace" (1929–1954, né John Alexander), "Bobby Blue" Bland (b. 1924, né Robert Calvin), Arthur "Big Boy" Crudup (1905–1974), Willie James Dixon (1915–1992), George "Buddy" Guy (b. 1936), John Lee Hooker (b. 1917), "Big" Walter Horton (1918–1981), "Sunnyland Slim" Andrew Luandrew (1907–1995), "Magic Sam" Maghett (1937–1969), Herman "Little Junior" Parker (1932–1971), James "Jimmy" Reed (1925–1976), Otis Rush (b. 1934), Johnny Shines (b. 1915), Otis Spann (1930–1970), Theodore Roosevelt "Hound Dog" Taylor (1915–1975), and Amos "Junior" Wells (b. 1934), among others. Son Seals (b. 1942), belonging to a younger group, was perhaps the last of the Delta bluesmen to arrive in Chicago.

Chicago Blues

As we have seen, many of the blues people who established themselves in Chicago from the 1920s on were from the Mississippi Delta. A seminal figure in the transformation of Delta country blues into Chicago urban blues was Sonny Boy Williamson, No. 1, who went to Chicago in 1937 and thereafter defined the solo blues harmonica. By 1940 he was recording with a drummer, and his music, influenced by the jazz all around him, was distinctive for its heavy, relentless beat—called by some "jump blues." Williamson's laurel wreath passed to Little Walter Jacobs, who went to Chicago in 1947 and was the first bluesman to play amplified harmonica. In adding a rhythm section—bass, drums, piano, and / or guitar—to his harmonic blues, Sonny Boy had moved into the field of rhythm 'n' blues by 1948, the year of his untimely death.

The king of Chicago blues was Muddy Waters, who arrived in the city in 1943, began playing electric guitar soon thereafter, and by 1948 was recording with his electric blues band, composed primarily of blues performances from the Delta region. He attracted the most talented men in the city; some of them later formed their own bands which became celebrated. Waters, B. B. King, Big Bill Broonzy, and Howlin' Wolf were the dominant influences in developing the distinctive Chicago blues, which was widely imitated all over the world, particularly by rock 'n' roll groups. Willie James Dixon (1915–1992) is credited as the architect of the "Chicago blues" sound. As an arranger he infused the old downhome blues with elements of jazz, pop, spirituals, and gospel, producing a new modern sound. As a composer he wrote songs for the important blues singers—Muddy Waters, Otis Rush, Little Walter, Bo Diddley, Rolling Stones, and others—which turned their rural impulses into an urban sophisticated music.

Bluesmen born in Chicago, such as Amos "Junior" Wells, or taken there as children, joined with the Delta men in creating the gospel-tinged, jazz-inflected, Delta-derived Chicago blues. It was during the 1950s that the 12/8 patterns of gospel were integrated into blues style.

Blues Styles in Other Places

The blues of Texas and the Territories has been described as less harsh, more sophisticated, and of lighter texture than that of the Delta. During and after World War II, many Texas blues artists migrated to the West coast, where they fused their style with that of blues performers from Kansas City and the Southwest; among them Lowell Fulson (b. 1921), "Ivory" Joe Hunter (1911–1974), and Aaron "T-Bone" Walker (1910–1975). The blues bands that toured in the South and Southwest during the 1940s were already rhythm 'n' blues bands, complete with rhythm sections, electric guitars, and saxophones. The Kansas City "shouting" blues style was essentially a jazz-blues style from the beginning; some of its important figures remained entirely within the jazz orbit, and others won recognition in the field of rhythm 'n' blues.

The Carolinas Piedmont region generally sent bluesmen to New York, although some made recordings also in Chicago. Best known of these men was Joshua "Josh" White (1908–1969), who sang both gospel and blues and later sang in nightclubs and musical theater. Others from the region included "Blind" Gary Davis (1896–1972), "Blind Boy" Fuller (1908–1941, né Fulton Allen), Walter "Brownie" McGhee (1915–1996), and "Sonny Terry" (1911–1986, né Saunders Terrell).

Blues in Europe and Festivals

"Big Bill" Broonzy was the first to take the Chicago-Delta blues to Europe, and it was this style that exerted wide influence upon the development of rock groups in England. He made his first trip in 1951, and toured several times after that, taking Blind John Davis with him in 1952. In 1958 the ailing Broonzy recommended Muddy Waters to his fans, and Waters began touring overseas. Among the others who crossed the Atlantic in the 1950s were Sonny Terry and Brownie McGhee as a team and Memphis Slim. In 1961 Memphis Slim and Willie Dixon organized the American Folk Blues Festival, which made the first of its many European tours in 1962. The Rolling Stones and other English groups began recording the blues of

Muddy Waters and other Chicago blues singers in 1964, thereby launching the blues revival of the 1960s.

In the United States there were major blues festivals and folk festivals every year in various parts of the country; moreover, blues performers appeared at all the jazz festivals. In 1980 the newly organized Blues Foundation inaugurated the W. C. Handy Blues Awards, with ceremonies at Memphis on November 16th. The polling process selected fifty-nine winners, including twenty inductees into the Blues Hall of Fame. Predictably, established bluesmen and women walked off with honors in most classes; but the "contemporary male" and "contemporary female" winners called attention to lesser-known performers—Albert Collins (b. 1932) and Cora "Koko" Taylor (b. 1938). Other winners were James "Jimmy" Johnson (b. 1928), Professor Longhair (1918–1980, né Henry Byrd), Esther Phillips (1935–1984), and Willie Mae "Big Mama" Thornton (1926–1984).

Johnson and Taylor settled at Chicago during the 1950s and both became important figures in the Chicago blues scene. The other three winners developed careers away from Chicago—Thornton in Houston, Texas, and Phillips on the West coast, where she was billed as "Little Esther." Professor Longhair was a celebrity in New Orleans long before the blues establishment recognized him as the seminal figure in the unfolding of New Orleans piano blues and as the inventor of the rhumba blues.

Blues Repertories

When blues performers adopted songs as their own, they invariably altered them, as we have seen. Nevertheless, many of these songs became staple items in the blues repertory, and, in some instances, were carried over into rock 'n' roll. Typically, the bluesmen and women revised lyrics, changed the accompaniment both in style and presentation, and often changed the title when they took over a song. One of the piano blues standards was the *Vicksburg Blues,* also known as the *44 Blues* and by any number of other titles. The standards among vocal blues include *Catfish Blues* or *Rollin' Stone, Big Road Blues, I'm Your Hoochie Coochie Man, Dust My Broom, Hellbound on My Trail, How Long Blues, Rollin' and Tumblin', Got My Mojo Working, Everyday I Get the Blues,* and *Stormy Monday.*

Library of Congress Recordings

During the mid-century years the Library of Congress sent out folklorists to make recordings of blues and jazz, some of them even going inside prison walls to do so. In 1932, Huddie "Leadbelly" Ledbetter (1889–1932) became the first of the blues singers to record for the Archive of Folk Song at the Library of Congress. The pioneering collectors of the movement, white folklorists John A. Lomax and his son Alan, later were joined by others, including black folklorists John W. Work and Willis Laurence James, as we

Bunk Johnson and Leadbelly playing at the Stuyvesant Casino in New York, 1946. (© William P. Gottlieb. Courtesy of the Artist and the Stephen Cohen Gallery)

have seen. A significant number of bluesmen were involved in these recordings, among them Willie Brown, Son House, Ivory Joe Hunter (who recorded as Ivory Joe White), Blind Willie McTell, "Fiddling" Joe Martin, Muddy Waters, and Booker T. "Bukka" Washington.

POPULAR MUSIC

In black communities popular music had embraced two styles since the nineteenth century—the one firmly rooted in folk tradition, and the other, in the style of the sentimental ballad and, later, of Tin Pan Alley. Examples of the former were the minstrel and novelty songs of writers such as Sam Lucas or Ernest Hogan, while the ballads of Gussie Davis would typify the Tin Pan Alley style. In the early twentieth century Bob Cole and J. Rosamond Johnson wrote in the ballad style, and such songwriters as Chris Smith or Shelton Brooks wrote songs that pointed to black folk styles. Although there were no terms in common use to distinguish between the two styles, those who sang the songs or listened to the singing were clearly aware of the distinctions; they also were aware of the differences between popular music and genuine folk music—the worksongs, spirituals and blues.

When the industry began to record black singers in 1920, it was popular music in the form of so-called "character songs," not genuine blues, that opened up the market for the race-records series. Recordings made this music more accessible to the black public than in the past, and it began to produce its stars in the same way as did blues and jazz. Mamie Smith might

Billy Eckstine with Bobby Tucker at the piano. *(Courtesy of the author)*

be regarded as the first "pop" singer, with her recordings of *You Can't Keep a Good Man Down* and *Crazy Blues*. Similarly, several of the other women who recorded in the early 1920s sang popular songs or vaudeville songs rather than genuine blues.

Pop Soloists

The first male to become a "pop" idol was Billy Eckstine (1914–1993), who began his career singing with jazz orchestras; his recording of *Skylark* in 1942 with Earl Hines's band attracted wide attention to his successful handling of ballads. After he left Hines in 1944, Eckstine toured as an independent soloist for a brief period before he organized his own big band. His career as a "solo attraction" really began in 1948, however, when he signed a contract with MGM to tour and record with the backing of a studio band. Thereafter he recorded such pop songs as *I Apologize* and *My Foolish Heart* in a deep-voice vibrato that set teenagers to swooning. Eckstine is credited with being the first black ballad singer to succeed as a soloist independently of a dance band.

Nat King Cole (1919–1965, né Nathaniel Coles) was the second. Like Eckstine, he began his career in jazz, forming his King Cole Trio with guitarist Oscar Moore and bassist Wesley Prince in 1939. By 1948 his jazz combo was so popular that it had its own sponsored series on the radio—the first black jazz group to achieve that distinction. Gradually Cole gave more and

Nat King Cole. (© William P. Gottlieb. Courtesy of the Artist and the Stephen Cohen Gallery)

more attention to singing, recording such songs as *Nature Boy*, *Mona Lisa*, and *Too Young* in a warm, clear voice with precise diction. By 1952 he was one of the leading balladeers of the popular music world.

The 1950s brought new black balladeers before the public: Harry Belafonte, Brook Benton, Leon Bibb, Sam Cooke, Al Hibbler, Herb Jeffries, Johnny Mathis, Joe Williams (né Joseph Goreed; also an important jazz-blues singer), and Jackie Wilson. The most popular female pop singers included Lena Horne, Damita Jo, Della Reese, and Dinah Washington. In the best-seller charts published by trade magazines, the recordings of these singers were listed in both the Pop and Race Records categories.

Pop Quartets

Quartet singing of popular music had a long history in the black tradition, beginning with minstrel and vaudeville quartets, of which the Harmonizing Four in the early twentieth century was perhaps best known. The longest-lived quartet of modern times was the Mills Brothers, which began singing about 1922 and was still active in 1982. The four brothers—first tenor Herbert, second tenor Donald, baritone Harry, and bass John, Jr.—received their first contract in 1925. They began their professional careers as a broadcasting group on station WLW in Cincinnati and in 1929 became the first black music group to have commercial sponsorship on a national network, CBS. The quartet was distinctive for its close smooth harmonies and vocal imitations of instruments; only a guitar was used as accompaniment. When the bass singer died in 1936, his father replaced him; when the father retired in 1957, the Mills Brothers became a trio, then a duo when Herbert died in 1989.

A second quartet, the Ink Spots, appeared on the scene in the 1930s. Although formed in 1934, the quartet did not receive wide recognition until it returned from touring in England in 1939 and began to record such songs as *If I Didn't Care, Glow Worm,* and *It's Funny to Everyone But Me.* The Ink Spots were celebrated for high falsettos and deep-voiced "talking" choruses. Both quartets toured worldwide, recorded extensively, and appeared on radio, on television, and in films. Both quartets sang wholly within the black tradition, despite the smooth harmonies that contributed to their popularity with white listeners.

Dozens of quartets added to the sounds of black music in the mid-century years, some singing in the jubilee spirituals / gospel tradition, some in the popular music style, and others singing a varied repertory. Two college groups that became professional quartets were aided by appearances on the Major Bowes Family Amateur Hour radio show: the Deep River Boys, who began singing during their college years as the Hampton Institute Quartet, turned professional in 1936. The Delta Rhythm Boys, which began as the Dillard University Quartet, first toured in 1937 and became professional after the men had graduated from college. These two quartets developed mixed repertories of spirituals, popular songs, and light classical songs; as did also the Southernaires, organized in 1929; the Golden Gate Quartet, which flourished during the 1940s; and several other quartets of the period.

Rhythm 'n' Blues

On June 25, 1949, the trade magazine *Billboard* introduced a new term, *rhythm 'n' blues,* in referring to the popular music of African Americans on records intended for distribution in black communities. As we have seen, the term *race records* had been used by the music industry since the 1920s for recordings of black performers, no matter how diverse the musical styles. *Billboard*'s other categories were Pop (for popular music) and Country and Western. The year 1949 is as convenient a time as any for marking the beginning of the rhythm 'n' blues also known as R&B era, although the music actually had been evolving over a period of several years from the folk blues and other black-music styles.[18]

By the late forties, rhythm 'n' blues was perceived as a genre with its own distinctive features: it was an ensemble music, consisting of a vocal unit (solo or group), a rhythm unit (electric guitar and / or string bass, piano, drums), and a supplementary unit (generally the saxophone and sometimes other winds). The music generally used twelve-bar structure of the blues and its harmonic patterns; it emphasized propulsive duple meters with heavy stress on the strong beats of the measure. In regard to performance style, rhythm 'n' blues followed in the tradition of urban blues and gospel, with much use of special vocal effects for expressive purposes; melodic, rhythmic, and text improvisation; and call-and-response between soloist(s) and group. R&B lyrics were earthy and realistic, and the singers typically wrote their own songs, both music and lyrics.

The small independent companies that had taken the lead in recording downhome urban blues and gospel in the early 1940s also moved ahead with recording rhythm 'n' blues. Several of these enterprises were owned by blacks: in Los Angeles as early as the 1930s, the René brothers, Otis and Leon, formed their own companies, which recorded popular music for the most part in the early days. They were the first, for example, to record Nat King Cole. Two of their own songs were great successes: *When It's Sleepy Time Down South* (1931, with Clarence Muse as collaborator) and *When the Swallows Come Back to Capistrano* (1940). René's Exclusive Records label released its first rhythm 'n' blues hits in 1945, *Honeydripper* and *I've Got a Right to Cry,* sung by Joe Liggins. Later hit songs included *Little Bitty Pretty One* (1957) and *Rockin' Robin* (1958), both sung by Bobby Day (né Robert Byrd).

Vee Jay Records was founded in Chicago about 1953 by Vivian Carter Bracken, her husband James Bracken, and her brother Calvin Carter. Vee Jay was very successful for most of the dozen or so years of its existence—the company declared bankruptcy in 1966. Its roster included blues, pop, gospel, and rock 'n' roll singers, but its chief interest was in rhythm 'n' blues. Vee Jay first reached the Top Ten charts in 1954 with a recording by The Spaniels, *Goodnight, Well It's Time to Go.* Thereafter its best sellers came from male rhythm 'n' blues groups such as the Dells, El Dorados, and the Impressions; rhythm 'n' blues soloists such as Jerry Butler and Dee Clark; bluesmen Jimmy Reed and John Lee Hooker; and the gospel group, the Staple Singers.

[18]See further in Carl Belz, *The Story of Rock* (New York, 1972); Arnold Shaw, *Honkers and Shouters* (New York, 1978); Shaw, *The Rockin' '50s* (New York, 1974); Shaw, *The World of Soul* (New York, 1970); *Sepia* and other black magazines.

It is of interest that Vee Jay also won laurels in the field of rock 'n' roll: one of its white groups, the Four Seasons, earned best-seller ratings in 1962 with recordings of *Sherry* and *Big Girls Don't Cry;* and Vee Jay was the first company to introduce the celebrated English group, the Beatles, to American audiences in 1964. Another black-owned company in Chicago during the period was J.O.B. Records, formed by Joseph Brown, which flourished from 1949 into the 1960s but released few best sellers.

In 1949 at Houston, Texas, Don Robey organized Peacock Records and remained in business until 1973, at which time he reputedly sold his business for a million dollars. His special interest in gospel led him to engage such groups as the Five Blind Boys of Mississippi with lead-singer Archie Brownlee, the Dixie Hummingbirds with Ira Tucker, and the Sensational Nightingales with Julius Cheeks. But Robey also produced blues records, and his roster included leading figures in the field: Johnny Ace, Bobby Blue Bland, Little Junior Parker, and "Big" Mama Thornton.

Finally, there was Robert "Bobby" Robinson, who founded a New York record company in 1953, which used a number of labels over the years, such as Red Robin, Fury, and Everlast. His major artists were Gladys Knight and the Pips (for a period), who produced an early best seller in *Letter Full of Tears* (1961), and King Curtis (1934–1971, né Curtis Ousley), whose most successful song was *Soul Twist* (1962).

In 1959 an enterprising record-shop owner and songwriter, Berry Gordy, founded Motown Records, with the Tamla label, in Detroit. But the company hardly remained an "indie" very long; within a few years it had mushroomed into a huge conglomerate with a publishing arm, a management company, and recording studios, in addition to the record company. Gordy's first priority seems to have been to establish the unique "Detroit Sound," a music combining elements of rhythm 'n' blues, pop, gospel, and big band. Promoting unknowns, he soon began to collect top ratings on the charts, at first with rhythm 'n' blues, then with songs that crossed over to the Pop charts.

The first hit song came from William "Smokey" Robinson and the Miracles in 1960, *Shop Around*. Others followed in rapid succession: the Marvelettes in 1961 with *Please, Mr. Postman;* Mary Wells with *You Beat Me to the Punch* and the Contours with *Do You Love Me,* both in 1962; Stevie Wonder with *Fingertips* and Martha Reeves and the Vandellas with *Heat Wave,* both in 1963: the Supremes (later billed as Diana Ross and the Supremes) with *Where Did Our Love Go* and the Tops with *Baby, I Need Your Loving,* both in 1964. The list of winners through the years seemed to be unending. Gordy hired songwriters, choreographers, and other kinds of support personnel to insure that his singers remained on top.

"Little Stevie Wonder" (b. 1950, né Stevland Judkins) first attracted wide attention in 1963 when he performed in a Motown Revue at the Apollo Theatre in Harlem. He began writing his own music while still in his teens, and as an adult was counted among the leading entertainers of the

Stevie Wonder. *(Courtesy Motown Records)*

times. His style, rooted in rhythm 'n' blues, attuned itself to "soul" in the mid-1960s and, with the arrival of "disco" in the seventies, earned him the title "Godfather of Disco-Soul." His best-known song was *You Are the Sunshine of My Life;* his best-known albums, *Music of the Mind* and *Talking Book.*

The "Memphis Sound," which reflected greater influence of the blues and country music than did Motown songs, was promoted by Stax Records, a racially integrated company with white owners and black executive-vice-president Al Bell. Its first successes came in 1962 with *Green Onions,* sung by Booker T and the M.G.'s (i.e., Booker T. Jones and the Memphis Group singers), which was also integrated. Other black Stax musicians were Isaac Hayes, Eddie Floyd, Albert King, Otis Redding, Johnny Taylor, and Rufus Thomas and his daughter Carla.

There were other "sounds" in the mid-century years: the West coast, the Harlem, the Philadelphia—the last-named promoted by black musicians Kenneth Gamble, Leon Huff, and Thom Bell in the 1970s. New York was a recording mecca for rhythm 'n' blues groups, many of whom came out of Harlem. There were groups named after birds, such as the Crows, Flamingos, Orioles, and Ravens, and after cars, such as the Cadillacs, Impalas, and Imperials—to cite a few. In 1956 a group of school boys, Frankie Lymon and the Teenagers, reached the Top Ten on both Rhythm 'n' Blues and Pop charts with *Why Do Fools Fall in Love,* written by Lymon when he was only thirteen. The five-voice Chantels was a pioneering woman's group in 1958 in a field dominated by men and undoubtedly smoothed the way for later female groups such as the Supremes, Vandellas, and Chiffons.

No fine lines of distinction existed between blues or jazz singers and those singing rhythm 'n' blues in the early years of the genre. Such singers as the following sang both genres with equal effectiveness: Benjamin "Bull Moose" Jackson (b. 1919) with his ballads *I Love You, Yes I Do* (1947) and *Little Girl, Don't Cry* (1949); Dinah Washington (1924–1963, née Ruth Jones) and *Baby, Get Lost* (1949); Wynonie "Mr. Blues" Harris (1915–1969) with his *Good Rockin' Tonight* (1949); and Mabel "Big Maybelle" Smith (1924–1972) with *Candy* (1956) bringing into rhythm 'n' blues the techniques they had used in singing other kinds of black music, particularly gospel.

Louis Jordan (1908–1975), who formed his Tympany Five in 1938, was a pioneering rhythm 'n' blues bandleader, who contributed a number of songs to the repertory, including *Saturday Night Fish Fry* and *Choo, Choo, Ch-boogie*. Jazzman Illinois Jacquet was credited with starting the vogue for the "honking" tenor-saxophone style of rhythm 'n' blues with his solo on *Flying Home* as a member of Lionel Hampton's band. Later "honking" saxists were Eddie "Lockjaw" Davis, "Bull Moose" Jackson, Clifford Scott, and Eddie "Cleanhead" Vinson. In 1956 William "Bill" Doggett recorded one of rhythm 'n' blues' most popular instrumental pieces, *Honky Tonk*.

Soul Music

It appeared that no sooner had rhythm 'n' blues won recognition as a distinctive black music than it began to give rise to new styles—rock 'n' roll in the 1950s, "soul" in the 1960s, "disco" and "funk" in the 1970s. From November 1963 to January 1965 *Billboard* did not publish Rhythm 'n' Blues best-seller charts; there were so many crossovers from Rhythm 'n' Blues to Pop and vice versa, that two lists seemed superfluous. A rhythm 'n' blues revival in the sixties brought back the charts, which thereafter included "soul" and other black-music styles.

Whereas the predominant theme of rhythm 'n' blues was love and other kinds of human relationships, soul singers voiced concern about social injustice, racial pride, black militancy, and forms of protest; their music was correspondingly harsher, more intense, and more explosive than rhythm 'n' blues, with more emphasis upon traditional black-music elements—such as gospel, for example—and performance practices. Like other black-music styles, soul music resists precise definition; most of its leading figures were also claimed by the gospel or blues worlds, or by rock. Certainly a list would include, in addition to those already named, James Brown, Ray Charles, Sam Cooke, Aretha Franklin, and Nina Simone.

Brown, whose first hit song was *Please, Please, Please* in 1956, had earned the titles "Godfather of Soul" and "Soul Brother, No. 1" by the late sixties, and was especially well known for his vocal manifesto *Black Is Beautiful: Say It Loud: I'm Black and I'm Proud* (1968). Aretha Franklin, who regularly placed first in gospels, blues, and rhythm 'n' blues polls, was

James Brown. *(Photo by Val Wilmer)*

called the "Queen of Soul": Nina Simone was the "High Priestess of Soul." Sam Cooke (1935–1964) moved from the position of highly praised lead-singer of the gospel group the Soul Stirrers to an equally high position in the rhythm 'n' blues and soul orbit; he exerted wide influence on such singers as Marvin Gaye (1939–1984), Al Green, Otis Redding (1941–1967), and Robert "Bobby" Womack. Other important figures include "Little" Anthony and the Imperials, Roy Hamilton, Clyde McPhatter, Jackie Wilson, and a female group, The Shirelles.

Rock 'n' Roll

The first rock 'n' roll record was *Sh-Boom,* recorded in 1954 by the Chords, a black, male rhythm 'n' blues group. The record quickly made the best-selling charts of rhythm 'n' blues and, within a period of three weeks, sold enough copies to climb to the Top Ten list on Pop charts. It was the first time in history that a rhythm 'n' blues recording had made the top of the Pop charts; although earlier rhythm 'n' blues records had crossed over into Pop, none previously had done as well. The popularity of *Sh-Boom* effected the release of "covers" almost immediately by both black and white groups and soloists; the best-selling cover was made by a Canadian group, the Crew Cuts. It quickly outsold the original and finished the year as one of the Top Five of 1954.

This phenomenon presaged a practice that was to last for some time: a blues or rhythm 'n' blues group relatively unknown (that is, outside black communities) released a best-selling record; established white pop singers covered it; and the cover outsold the original, aided by the powerful promotion and distribution facilities of the music industry. Thus white Bill Haley and his Comets covered Joe Turner's *Shake, Rattle, and Roll* in 1954 and produced a best seller; Pat Boone became a winner with covers of Fats Domino's *Ain't That a Shame* and Little Richard Penniman's *Tutti-Frutti;* Georgia Gibbs, with Etta James's recording of *Roll with Me, Henry* (title changed by Gibbs to *Dance with Me, Henry*) and LaVern Baker's *Tweedle Dee;* Gale Storm, with Smiley Lewis's *I Hear You Knocking.* The list of covers was long!

Naturally, black performers suffered from these practices, but since recording arrangements were not protected by copyright laws, nothing could be done. Eventually consumers began to search out the original versions, and market demand brought relief to black artists—and, as well, the blues and rhythm 'n' blues revivals of the 1960s. Although covers frankly and openly imitated the originals, there were nevertheless subtle differences; rock historian Carl Belz discussed a few in comparing the black *Sh-Boom* with its white cover:[19]

> This distinction in musical styles is apparent immediately in a comparison of the Chords' version of *Sh-Boom* with that of the Crew Cuts—as it is apparent in a comparison of nearly all of the early rock originals with their covers by Pop musicians. The Chords' version contains a rich blend between the vocal and instrumental portions of the song. In the Crew Cuts' version, the instrumental background is clearly separated from the lyrics. . . . The Chords put everything together, and they used fragmentary words or words which had no logical relation to the literary content of the song . . . they used the voice like an additional musical instrument . . . the lyrics often consisted of oohs and aahs, dip-dips, and dom-be-do-bes. And there was the suggestion that the singers were creating lines as they went along and using them to express immediate feelings.

Belz continues by pointing out why covers outsold the originals. While the source of *Sh-Boom*'s appeal to the largely white audience for Pop records was its new exotic sound, at the same time that audience felt more comfortable with the familiar sound of the white cover.

> [The Chords' record] projected a fabric of sound in which everything struck the listener at once—instrumental sound, lyrics, fragmentary or improvised lyrics, and all with a powerful incessant beat. . . . This immediate totality of impact . . . probably . . . sounded strange to many listeners. . . . They were accustomed to a cleaner kind of music in which the separate parts were more easily perceptible, where lyrics were distinctly enunciated, where voices were either individualized or precisely unified, and where vocal and instrumental sections did not impose on one another. The Crew Cuts "cleaned up" *Sh-Boom.* . . .

Belz's comparison sets forth dramatically the essential differences between black-music styles and white styles—not only with regard to rock but also to other styles.

Because of the growing importance of radio and recordings in the dis-

---

[19]Belz, *Story of Rock,* pp. 29–30.

semination of popular and folk musics during the mid-century years, the disc jockey assumed an increasingly important role, for he could make the difference between success and failure of a recording by the way he promoted it. In 1951 white disc jockey Alan Freed used the term *rock and roll* for the first time. He furthered his identity with the music by promoting large rock concerts, recording rock music with his band, writing songs, publishing articles in its favor, and otherwise contributing to its development. As we have seen, Joe Bostic played a similar role in the development of commercial gospel. Typically, the "dee jays" (for disc jockeys) associated with black music, whether they were black or white, seemed to feel a responsibility for entertaining their listeners as well as playing records, and some of them were professional musicians—like, for example, B. B. King.

Rock 'n' roll was a fusion of rhythm 'n' blues, pop, and country-western elements. From the beginning, rhythmic intensity was a distinctive feature along with a realistic approach to the subject matter of the lyrics—at least, in comparison to the romanticism of pop lyrics. Although rock 'n' roll developed into a largely white-artist music later called rock, a few black artists contributed to its early development (in addition to providing songs to be covered). Like rhythm 'n' blues singers, black rock 'n' roll singers typically wrote their own material, either alone or in collaboration with others.

Charles "Chuck" Berry early appeared on the scene with his guitar and such top-selling records as *Maybellene* (1955) and *Roll Over, Beethoven* (1956); he continued to produce best sellers regularly for more than two decades, including *My Ding-a Ling* in 1972. Blues pianist Antoine "Fats" Domino, who wrote songs in collaboration with Dave Bartholomew, attracted wide attention with his *Blueberry Hill* (1955) and *Walking to New Orleans* (1960). Both Berry and Domino were acclaimed as rock 'n' roll poets. "Little" Richard Penniman first won recognition with his *Tutti-Frutti* (1955), then later with *Long Tall Sally* (1956) and *Good Golly, Miss Molly* (1958). Jimi Hendrix (1942–1970), who began his career in London, was a virtuoso guitarist and the most exotic of the black rock 'n' roll stars. Chubby Checker (né Ernest Evans) came to fame with his recording of *The Twist* (1960) and other dance songs. The music of Ray Charles defied neat categorization; he wrote, played piano, and sang in all the styles, from blues and jazz to soul. Perhaps his most original contribution to the history of popular music was his fusion of gospel with country-western, as in his album *Modern Sounds in Country and Western Music* (1962).

Bill Haley, generally regarded as the first important white rock 'n' roll figure, attracted international attention in 1955, the year his recording *Dim, Dim the Lights* crossed over to the best-seller list of rhythm 'n' blues and his song *Rock Around the Clock* (1954) was reissued in connection with the film *Blackboard Jungle,* for which it was the theme song. The major figure of the 1950s—indeed, of early rock 'n' roll history—was Elvis Presley (1935–1977). His songs drew upon a wide variety of sources in the fields

Ray Charles (b. 1930). *(Courtesy of the author)*

of pop, country-western, gospel, blues, and rhythm 'n' blues—such as, for example, his covers of "Big Mama" Thornton's *Hound Dog,* Arthur "Big Boy" Crudup's *That's All Right,* and Thomas Dorsey's *Peace in the Valley.*

The year 1964 brought a wave of English groups to the United States, first the Beatles, then the Rolling Stones, and others who made a tremendous impact upon rock 'n' roll and all of whom warmly acknowledged their indebtedness to black blues artists, rhythm 'n' blues figures, and rock 'n' roll stars, whose songs they covered and whose styles they emulated. Those most frequently imitated were bluesmen Muddy Waters and Bo Diddley (né Ellas McDaniel); rhythm 'n' blues singers Marvin Gaye, the Isley Brothers, Otis Redding, and Wilson Pickett; and singers Chuck Berry and Little Richard. The Beatles developed a highly original style, which exerted its influence upon the music in general. The Rolling Stones, on the other hand, retained a kind of fidelity to black-music traditions, as evidenced by their repertory, which helped to bring about the blues and rhythm 'n' blues revivals of the late 1960s.

An outgrowth of rhythm 'n' blues was "funk," developed in live shows that combined music distinctive for heavy rhythms and dense textures with extravagant costumes and staging. Its chief representative was James Brown, the founder and perpetrator of the style. Other groups included George Clinton with the Funkadelics, the Ohio Players, and the Commodores.

New Dance Music

In the decade of the seventies there emerged a new black-music style called "disco." Freddie Perren, one of its songwriters, defined it as

> music made primarily for dancing. This is not to say that music before 1974 or '75 was not danceable. There has been, however, a change in lifestyle. Disco is music for people who are going out, dressing up, putting themselves on display. Pre-disco dance records were short. . . . Now we have longer records because we're trying to fill massive spaces with dancers. That's one of the reasons we use such long intros. An eight-second intro is not enough time to get those people out on the dance floor to be ready when the real goods start to happen, when the tune actually begins. . . . The music is dramatic. There are more swirls of notes, more effects, more Syndrums [drum synthesizer].[20]

The insistent pounding rhythms of disco pushed conventional melody and harmonies into subordinate positions. Indeed, some pieces had no melody at all; but rather, consisted of a sing-song reciting of the lyrics to the accompaniment of a rhythm track; this, in a manner that recalled descriptions of juba reciting to accompany dancing on the plantations in the nineteenth century. Like the juba rhymes, the pieces were intended solely for dancing.

Performers and songs associated with disco included, among others, Donna Summer, called the Disco Sex Goddess, with her albums *Love to Love You, Baby* (1975); and *Bad Girls* (1979); Gloria Gaynor, with her song *I Will Survive* (1977); and Peaches and Herb (Linda Green and Herb Feemster) with the song *Reunited* (1978).

---

[20] Allen Levy, "Disco Wiz," *ASCAP in Action* (Fall 1979): 29–30.

CHAPTER 13

Singers,
Instrumentalists,
and Composers

Singers at Mid-Century

RELATIVELY few black singers began concert careers in the 1940s, undoubtedly because of the general moratorium on cultural activities after the United States' entrance into the war in December 1941. Earlier that year, Kenneth Spencer (1913–1964) made his debut as a concert baritone at Town Hall in New York; thereafter he toured widely, singing with symphony orchestras and giving solo recitals at home and in Europe, where he lived during the years 1950–63. He also sang in stage musicals and films.

Contralto Portia White (1917–1968), a Canadian, made her debut in 1941 in Toronto and her New York debut at Town Hall in 1944. The next year she was featured in a documentary film, *This Is Canada*. She also toured widely as a concert singer. Other singers active during the 1940s included Anne Brown, Louise Burge, June McMechen, Aubrey Pankey, and Helen Thigpen.

Soprano Muriel Rahn (1911–1961) began her professional career in Eve Jessye's Dixie Jubilee Singers, then moved into musical theater, where she attracted wide attention in 1943 in the title role of *Carmen Jones* (which she sang in alternation with Muriel Smith). Later Rahn performed in grand opera and, as a member of the National Orchestral Association, sang in several of its productions. Rahn also created roles in American operas, including Harry Freeman's *The Martyr* in 1947 and the Jan Meyerowitz–Langston Hughes opera *The Barrier* in 1950.

One of the leading black concert singers in the 1940s was soprano Ella-belle Davis (1907–1960). Although she began her professional career in the 1920s, it was not until 1942 that she felt herself ready for a recital at Town Hall. In 1946 she made her operatic debut as Aïda at the Opera Nacionale in Mexico City, and she sang the role again in 1949 at La Scala in Milan, Italy. In 1947 the League of Composers singled Davis out as the outstanding American singer of the 1946–47 season and commissioned Lukas Foss to write a work especially for her. The composition, a cantata *The Song of Songs,* was performed by the Boston Symphony with Davis as soloist.

Pianists and Other Instrumentalists

The important concert pianists of the 1940s included Marc D'Albert (1908–1975), who began to tour in the 1930s and settled at New York during the '40s, and Roy Eaton (b. 1930), who made his debut with the Chicago Symphony Orchestra in 1951, and his debut at Town Hall in 1952. He was active as a concert pianist during the 1950s, touring extensively at home and in Europe and appearing with symphony orchestras; thereafter he combined concertizing with his activities as a music producer and director.

The towering figure among concert instrumentalists in the 1960s was pianist André Watts (b. 1946). His family moved from Nuremburg, Germany, his place of birth, to Philadelphia when he was eight years old, and he obtained his musical education at the Philadelphia Musical Academy. Later he studied at the Peabody Conservatory. Even as a child he won prizes in music competitions; at sixteen he played the Liszt Piano Concerto in E-flat with the New York Philharmonic on a CBS national network. The orchestra's director, Leonard Bernstein, was so impressed that when the soloist, Glenn Gould, fell ill, Bernstein called upon Watts to fill in. From that time on, his career soared. Since the late 1970s, he has been regarded as one of the world's leading pianists.

Other prominent pianists of the nation included Armenta Adams, Leon Bates, Eugene Haynes, Natalie Hinderas (1927–1987), Raymond Jackson, Robert Jordan, Cecil Lytle, Roosevelt Newsome, Philippa Duke Schuyler (1931–1967), Frances Walker, and George Walker. Wilfred Delphin and Edwin Romain won acclaim as a duo-piano team, and Frances Cole (1937–1983) attracted attention as a harpsichordist. Herndon Spillman, concert organist, specialized in performing and recording the works of Maurice Duruflé.

A number of other instrumentalists were active in the concert world, among them, violinists Elwyn Adams, Sanford Allen (formerly a member of the New York Philharmonic), and Darwyn Apple; violist Marcus Thompson; and cellists Ronald Lipscomb, Earl Madison, Kermit Moore, Eugene Moye, and Donald White. Flutist Harold Jones also gave recitals regularly. Ortiz Montaigne Walton was one of the few double-bass concert artists in the United States during this period. And symphonic-harpist Ann Hobson

André Watts. *(Photo by Christian Steiner. Courtesy of the author)*

was rare as a woman harp-recitalist. Most of these artists toured widely in the United States and in Europe; many performed in Africa, the Caribbean, and South America; and several toured in Southeast Asia, particularly Japan.

Symphony Orchestra Players and Conductors

Black instrumentalists who wanted to play in symphony or opera orchestras met with markedly less success during the mid-century years than did their colleagues who were seeking employment as opera singers. A list of those who played with major orchestras is short: New York Philharmonic— violinist Sanford Allen; Boston Symphony—harpist Ann Hobson; Cleveland Symphony—cellist Donald White; Philadelphia Orchestra—violinist Renard Edwards and Henry Scott; Pittsburgh Symphony—keyboardist Patricia Prattis, violinist Paul Ross, cellist Earl Madison; Baltimore Symphony—trumpeters Langston Fitzgerald and Wilmer Wise; San Francisco Symphony—tympanist Elayne Jones; Milwaukee Symphony—tympanist Laura Synder; and St. Louis Symphony—violinists Darwyn Apple and Charlene Clark. There may have been a few others in large orchestras over

Philippa Duke Schuyler. *(Courtesy Kathryn Talalay)*

the nation, but by the end of the 1970s several artists were missing from the scene.

At the beginning of the 1980s few black players were to be found in the major symphony orchestras. Moreover, there were no reasons for optimism about the future. Many orchestras had phased out or deemphasized training programs for minorities, and the Symphony of the New World, an orchestra founded at New York in 1964 to provide the symphonic experience for professional musicians, black and white, gave its final concert in 1976. During its twelve years of existence, the orchestra not only had performed the traditional symphonic repertory but also had given premiere performances to works of black composers such as Ulysses Kay, Coleridge Perkinson, Hale Smith, Howard Swanson, and William Grant Still.

America's leading black concert artists, both classical and jazz, appeared with the Symphony of the New World at one time or another—among them, Duke Ellington and the Modern Jazz Quartet—and several young artists made their debuts with the orchestra. Benjamin Steinberg, one of the white founding members, was musical director from 1965 to 1973; Everett Lee was director for the remaining years. The guest conductors over the years included Denis de Coteau, James DePreist, Paul Freeman, Kermit Moore, and Leon Thompson. Symphony orchestras had been organized in various places during this period, such as the National Afro-American Philharmonic in 1978 at Philadelphia by James Frazier, but none made the impact on the national scene as did the Symphony of the New World.

Black conductors seemed to have less difficulty in finding positions than black instrumentalists, but generally they had to leave the country in order to do so. Dean Dixon (1915–1976), one of the first African Americans to prepare himself as a symphony conductor, obtained his musical education at Juilliard (B.S.) and Columbia University Teachers College (M.A.). He began to conduct orchestras during his college years and in 1948 made his debut with the New York Philharmonic. Unable to find a permanent position, he settled in Europe (1949–70), where he served as musical director with the Göteborg Symphony in Sweden, the Hesse Radio Symphony in Frankfurt, Germany, and the Sydney Symphony in Australia. In 1970 he returned to the United States and filled guest-conductor slots with various orchestras until 1974, when he retired because of ill health.

Another conductor who first won critical acclaim during the 1940s was Everett Lee (b. ca. 1919). A graduate of the Cleveland Institute of Music (B.Mus.) he studied further at the Berkshire Music School in Massachusetts, the Saint Cecilia Academy in Rome, and privately with Dimitri Mitropoulos, Max Rudolph, and Bruno Walter. Lee first attracted attention in 1944 as a substitute conductor for the Broadway musical *Carmen Jones;* later he founded and directed the Cosmopolitan Little Symphony. Unable to find a permanent position at home, like Dixon he emigrated to Europe, where he lived during the years 1956–73, serving as a musical director for the Munich Traveling Orchestra of Germany, the Norrkoping Symphony in Sweden, and other orchestras. In 1973 he returned to the United States to direct the Symphony of the New World. After its demise in 1976 he accepted the directorship of the Bogota (Columbia) Symphony.

Paul Freeman (b. 1936) studied at the Eastman School of Music (B.Mus.; Ph.D.) and the Hochschule für Musik in Berlin; he also studied privately with Ewald Lindemann and Pierre Monteux, among others. He conducted several smaller orchestras before going to the Dallas (Texas) Symphony in 1968 as an associate conductor, and then to the Detroit Symphony (1970–79) in the same position. During these years he also was principal guest conductor for the Helsinki (Finland) Symphony, other orchestras, and music festivals. In 1979 he was appointed musical director of the Victoria (British Columbia) Symphony.

James DePreist (b. 1936) attended the University of Pennsylvania (B.S. and M.A.) and the Philadelphia Conservatory of Music. In his early career he led a jazz group called the Jimmy DePreist Quintet. In 1963 he made his debut as a conductor with the Bangkok Symphony of Thailand during a period when he was serving the U.S. State Department as a specialist in American Music. He conducted other orchestras, including the National Symphony in Washington, D.C., as an associate, before he went to the Quebec Symphony in 1976 as musical director.

Isaiah Jackson (b. 1945) received his musical education at Harvard University (B.A.), Stanford University (M.A.), and the Julliard School of Music (M.Mus.; D.M.A.). His conducting experience included tenures as associate conductor with the American Ballet Company and the Rochester Symphony in New York before he became musical director in 1982 of the Anchorage (Alaska) Symphony and the Flint Symphony in Michigan. In his later career he was music director of the Royal Ballet in London, then accepted that position at the Queensland (Australia) Ballet.

Jon Robertson (b. 1941) obtained his musical training at the Juilliard School of Music (now The Juilliard School), where he earned three degrees (B.Mus., M.S., and D.M.A.), then studied conducting further with Richard Pittman and Herbert Blomstedt, among others. In his early career he toured widely as a concert pianist before turning his attention to conducting. He was appointed music director of the Kristiansand Symphony Orchestra (Norway) in 1979 and three years later also accepted appointment to the Redlands (California) Symphony Orchestra.

Denis Montague de Coteau (b. 1937) obtained his musical training at New York University (B.A., M.A.) and Stanford University (D.M.A.), and studied further with Heinrich Goldsmith, among others. He taught at Grinnell College in Iowa and California State University at San Francisco before beginning his professional career as music director of the Oakland Symphony Youth Orchestra. In addition to touring as a guest conductor, he gained accolades for his work with the Youth Orchestra, which won medals at the Van Karajan International Competitions in Germany (1972, 1974). In 1974 he was appointed music director of the San Francisco Conservatory of Music Orchestra.

James Frazier, Jr., (1941–1985), obtained degrees in music from the University of Michigan. His talent attracted the attention of Eugene Ormandy, director of the Philadelphia Orchestra, who was influential in his development. Some of the world's leading orchestras engaged him as a guest conductor, including the orchestra at La Scala in Milan, Italy, in 1964; the Leningrad Philharmonic in Russia in 1971; and the Philadelphia Orchestra in 1973, among many others. In 1978 he organized the short-lived National Afro-American Philharmonic Orchestra, which made its debut concert at the Philadelphia Academy of Music.

Other notable conductors of the mid-century years included Henry Lewis (1932–1996), who was founder-director of the Los Angeles Chamber Players and musical director of the Los Angeles Opera Company before he became musical director of the New Jersey Symphony, where he remained for eight years. Darrold Hunt (b. 1941) organized and conducted community orchestras, including the Urban Philharmonic Society, as did also Karl Porter (b. 1939), who served as a director for the Harlem Philharmonic, the New York City Housing Authority Orchestra, and the Massapequa (New York) Symphony, beginning in 1974. Only one woman was active as a conductor during the mid-century years—composer Julia Perry, who in 1957 conducted a series of orchestral concerts in Europe under the auspices of the U.S. Information Service.

One of the youngest conductors in the nation in the 1970s was Calvin Simmons (1950–82), who received his musical training at the Cincinnati College Conservatory of Music and the Curtis Institute of Music; he also studied privately with Max Rudolf and Rudolf Serkin. In 1975 he made his American conducting debut with the Los Angeles Symphony and his European debut with the Glydenbourne Festival Opera in London. In 1979 he became musical director of the Oakland (California) Symphony. Thereafter he conducted performances of the San Francisco Opera, the Metropolitan Opera, the St. Louis Opera, and the New York City Opera, before his untimely death in a boating accident ended a spectacularly promising career.[1]

THE WORLD OF OPERA

The decade of the 1940s inaugurated a new era for black singers in the field of opera. In August 1941 Mary Cardwell Dawson's National Negro Opera Company made its debut at the annual meeting of the National Association of Negro Musicians in Pittsburgh; the opera was Verdi's *Aïda* with La Julia Rhea in the title role, William Franklin as Amonasro, and Napoleon Reed as Radames. Dawson organized National Negro Opera Company (NNOC) Guilds in several large cities to provide support services when she brought her opera to New York, Washington, D.C., Chicago, and Philadelphia. Among the other productions of the company during its twenty-one years of existence were Verdi's *La traviata,* R. Nathaniel Dett's oratorio *The Ordering of Moses* in 1951, and Clarence Cameron White's opera *Ouanga* in 1956.

The Harry T. Burleigh Music Association staged the world premiere of White's opera in June 1949, at South Bend, Indiana. Dawson's production of the opera in May 1956, at the Metropolitan Opera House, was a concert version with ballet; the performance was repeated in September 1956, at Carnegie Hall in New York. Others who sang leading roles with the National Negro Opera Company over the years included Edward Boatner, Minto Cato, Maurice Cooper, Lillian Evanti, Omega King, Joseph Lipscomb, Robert McFerrin, Nellie Dobson Plants, Jackson Smith, and Bettye Vorhis.

In Cleveland, the Karamu Theatre encouraged the staging of operas and plays that provided opportunities for blacks to perform on stage. In 1949

---

[1]See further in D. Antoinette Handy, *Black Conductors* (Metuchen, NJ, 1994); K. Robert Schwarz, "Black Maestros On the Podiums, But No Pedestal." *New York Times,* October 11, 1992; and Anne Lundy, "Conversations with Three Symphonic Conductors: Denis de Coteau, Tania Léon, Jon Robertson." BPIM 16 (Fall 1988): 13–26.

Zelma George (1903–1994) attracted national attention in the title role of *The Medium,* a work of the white composer Gian Carlo Menotti. In 1950 George appeared to critical acclaim in the role on Broadway. She also starred in Menotti's *The Consul,* produced at the Cleveland Playhouse, and in Kurt Weill's *Threepenny Opera.*

All these productions provided stage experience—not only before the footlights, but also in the orchestra pit and backstage—for hundreds of talented African Americans who would not have been able to obtain the experience in any other way. As we have seen, the periodic revivals of Gershwin's *Porgy and Bess* and Thomson's *Four Saints in Three Acts* served in a similar way as a training ground for black operatic talent.

In 1945, the New York City Opera became the first major company to employ black singers in principal roles, and in 1955 the Metropolitan Opera engaged its first black artist, Marian Anderson (1902–1993). Robert McFerrin (b. 1921) and Mattiwilda Dobbs (b. 1925) followed in her footsteps, McFerrin in 1955 and Dobbs in 1956. Both had impressive credentials before joining the Metropolitan Opera.

McFerrin was a graduate of Chicago Musical College (B.Mus.), where he studied with George Graham. In 1942 he won first place in a national voice competition held by the *Chicago Tribune,* and thereafter sang leading roles in the National Negro Opera during the years 1949–52. He appeared in the production of William Grant Still's opera *Troubled Island* in 1949, sang with the New England Opera in 1950, and in several Broadway musicals. In 1954 he won first place in the Metropolitan Auditions of the Air, which led to his appointment by the Met (1955–57).

Dobbs was educated at Spelman College in Atlanta (B.A.) and Columbia University Teachers College (M.A.), and studied privately with Lotte Leonard in New York and Pierre Bernac in Paris, among others. She began singing professionally in 1952, made her operatic debut at La Scala in Milan in 1953, and her American debut with the San Francisco Opera in 1954.

While it appeared that black singers at last had been admitted into the world of grand opera, the fact was that these appointments proved to be transitory. It was not until the 1970s that black artists began to sing regularly with the major companies. By 1980 the color bar seemed no longer operative in the field of opera—at least, not in regard to female singers; they sang principal roles in all operas on both sides of the Atlantic, particularly at the Metropolitan and the San Francisco Opera companies, and won critical and audience approval.

A list of those most active during the 1960s–80s includes: sopranos Martina Arroyo, Carmen Balthrop, Kathleen Battle, Grace Bumbry, Clamma Dale, Gloria Davy, Christiane Eda-Pierre, Reri Grist, Hilda Harris, Barbara Hendricks, Leona Mitchell, Leontyne Price, Faye Robinson, Veronica Tyler, Margaret Tynes, Shirley Verrett (also a mezzo-soprano), and Felicia Weathers; the mezzo-sopranos include Betty Allen, Maria Ewing, Isola

Robert McFerrin as Amonasro in the Metropolitan Opera production of Verdi's *Aïda,* 1955. *(Photo by Sedge LeBlang. Courtesy Metropolitan Opera)*

Jones, Gwendolyn Killebrew, and Florence Quivar; among the tenors are Vinson Cole, Philip Creech, Seth McCoy, George Shirley, and James Wagner; the baritones include Andrew Frierson, Eugene Holmes, Edward Pierson, and Arthur Thompson; and the bass-baritones include Simon Estes, Andrew Smith, and Willard White.

Leontyne Price (b. 1927) was one of the world's leading prima donnas during this period. Educated at Central State College in Ohio (B.S.) and at Juilliard, where she studied with Florence Kimball, she first attracted attention for her roles in Thomson's *Four Saints in Three Acts* (1952 revival) and *Porgy and Bess* (1952 revival). Thereafter the honors came swiftly. In 1955 she sang the title role in Puccini's *Tosca* on NBC television, the first black artist to sing in an opera telecast, and later she sang in other television operas.

She made her American operatic debut with the San Francisco Opera in

Leontyne Price as Leonora in Verdi's *Il trovatore. (Photo by Louis Melançon. Courtesy Metropolitan Opera)*

1957, her European debut with the Vienna Staatsoper in 1958, and her debut at the Metropolitan Opera in 1961. For the next two years she was chosen to open the season at the Met, and when the Met moved to its new home at Lincoln Center in 1966, she again opened the season, appearing as Cleopatra in an opera especially written for her, *Anthony and Cleopatra* by Samuel Barber.

After Price the leading black opera divas were Grace Bumbry and Shirley Verrett. Bumbry (b. 1937) studied at Northwestern University and the Music Academy of the West in Santa Barbara, California; her teachers included Lotte Lehmann and Pierre Bernac. She made her operatic debut with the Paris Opera in 1960, singing the role of Venus in Wagner's *Tannhäuser* at the Bayreuth (Germany) Festival in 1961—the first of her race to sing a principal role there—and sang the same role in her American operatic debut with the Chicago Lyric Opera in 1963. Two years later she made her debut with the Metropolitan Opera as Princess Eboli in Verdi's *Don Carlo.* Beginning in the 1970s she sang soprano roles in the standard operas, ranging from Donizetti to Janáček.

Verrett (b. 1931) obtained her musical education at Ventura Junior College near Los Angeles and at Juilliard, where she studied with Anna Fitziu and Marian Székely-Fresche. She first attracted wide attention in 1967 when she made her debut at Covent Garden in London as Queen Elizabeth in Donizetti's *Maria Stuarda;* the next year she made her debut at the Metropolitan Opera in the title role of Bizet's *Carmen.* She won critical acclaim for singing both soprano and mezzo-soprano roles in the standard operas.

Almost without exception the leading opera singers of the 1960s had first to win laurels with European opera companies before they were invited to join the important American companies. Some of those who sang with European companies abroad did not return to the United States, for example, Therman Bailey, Annabelle Bernard, Kathleen Crawford, Allan Evans, Howard Haskins, Charles Holland, Charlotte Holloman, Rhea Jackson, Leonora Lafayette, Vera Little, Beryl McDaniel, Olive Moorefield, William Ray, Daniel Washington, and Arthur Woodley.

With the decade of the seventies, it became easier for black singers to enter opera without first having to obtain European credentials. One route was to win first place in the Metropolitan Auditions of the Air. Generally those who followed this route, however, had previously won other awards in various voice competitions and had sung with small regional opera companies or with national black companies (a point to which we shall return). Sometimes it was superior performance in a single production, such as *Porgy and Bess,* that brought singers to the attention of opera directors.

As is obvious in the above list, the number of black males who succeeded in opera was far smaller than the number of women. The leading singer of the 1960s was George Shirley (b. 1934), who graduated from Wayne State University in Detroit (B.A.) and studied with Themy Georgi and Cornelius Reid, among others. He made his American debut with the Turnau Opera Players in 1959, his European debut in 1960 at the Teatro Nuova in Milan, and his Metropolitan Opera debut in 1961, after winning first place in the Metropolitan Auditions of the Air. His tenure with the Met (1961–73) was longer than that of any other black male, before or after his time. He sang a wide variety of roles but was perhaps best known for the role of Rodolfo in Puccini's *La bohème,* Pelleas in Debussy's *Pelléas et Mélisande,* Don Ottavio in Mozart's *Don Giovanni,* and MacDuff in Verdi's *Macbeth.*

Another important opera singer of the 1980s was Simon Estes (b. 1938), who had won an international reputation before he began singing with an American opera company. He attended the University of Iowa (obtaining degrees in psychology and theology), where he studied with Charles Kellis. Estes began his career with German opera companies, and during the 1960s won prizes in international vocal competitions.

In 1978 he attracted wide attention when he sang the title role in

George Shirley. (*Courtesy of the author*)

Wagner's *The Flying Dutchman* at the Bayreuth Festival in Germany—the first male of his race to sing there. Two African-American women had preceded him, Grace Bumbry in 1961, and Luranah Aldridge, who reputedly sang a small role at the Festival at the end of the nineteenth century. Estes made his debut with the Metropolitan Opera in January 1982 in the role of The Landgrave in Wagner's *Tannhäuser.*

The Concert / Opera Singers

The same people who sang in grand opera during the 1960s–80s also gave recitals and sang with symphony orchestras in oratorio and other large choral productions. The reverse, however, was not always true; some concert singers rarely appeared in opera, and others not at all. Those best known for their concert work were Adele Addison, Carol Brice, McHenry Boatwright, Thomas Carey, Joyce Mathis, Jessye Norman, Louise Parker, Willis Patterson, Elwood Peterson, Rawn Spearman, and William Warfield, among others.

Norman (b. 1945), one of the world's great sopranos, obtained her musical education at Howard University (B.Mus.), the Peabody Conservatory of Music in Baltimore, and the University of Michigan in Ann Arbor; she studied privately with Alice Duschak and Pierre Bernac. Norman began

Jessye Norman. *(Courtesy New York Public Library at Lincoln Center)*

her professional career in opera, singing for several years with the Deutsche Oper in Berlin and other European companies as well, but by the mid-1970s she had begun to give most of her attention to the concert stage. She is particularly celebrated for her lieder recitals and solo work with symphony orchestras in the great choral and vocal masterpieces.

Bass-baritone William Warfield (b. 1920) studied piano as a child and, as a boy soprano, sang in his father's church. He obtained his musical education at the Eastman School of Music (B.Mus.), studied further at Eastman, and privately with Otto Herz, Yves Tinayre, and Rosa Ponselle. In 1950 he made his debut in New York's Town Hall. He concertized extensively throughout the world, giving recitals and singing with symphony orchestras and in oratorios. From time to time he also sang small roles in such musicals as Rome's *Call Me Mister* and Blitzstein's *Regina*. In 1951 he stepped into major leading roles when he sang the role of Joe in Jerome Kern's *Showboat* and, in 1952, joined the production of Gershwin's *Porgy and Bess* to sing Porgy. He also sang in several revivals of the two works.

Contralto Carol Brice (1918–1985) received her musical education at Palmer Memorial Institute in North Carolina, Talladega College in Alabama (B.Mus.) and the Juilliard School of Music (prof. diploma in voice), where she studied with Francis Rogers. In 1944 she made her debut in New York's Town Hall; the same year she won first prize in the Walter W. Naumburg International Voice Competition, the first African-American to be so honored. She toured extensively often accompanied by her brother, concert pianist Jonathan Brice; recorded regularly; and performed in opera and oratorio, Broadway musicals, and on television shows.

Most of the singers, opera and concert, recorded regularly, particularly with European companies, and a few recorded extensively. The instrumentalists met with less success, except for André Watts, in developing recording careers. Natalie Hinderas, however, gained a unique reputation by recording the piano music of black composers in addition to the usual piano literature, and also commissioning piano music from black composers.

New Opera Companies

The 1970s saw the founding of two black opera companies, of which the prime mover was a white nun, Sister Elise of the Catholic order the Sisters of the Blessed Sacrament. A voice teacher for many years at Xavier University in New Orleans, she came out of retirement in 1970 to work with Opera / South, which she founded along with three black-college members of the Mississippi Inter-Collegiate Opera Guild—Jackson State University, Utica Junior College, and Tougaloo College. The company used students in the choruses and ballet ensembles and imported professionals to sing the principal roles. Opera / South made a significant contribution to the world of opera by serving as a kind of display case for talented and experienced black singers, several of whom went directly to major American and European companies. Moreover, in addition to staging grand opera, the company mounted operas by black composers, as we have seen, among them, William Grant Still's *Highway No. 1, U.S.A.* and *A Bayou Legend*, and Ulysses Kay's *The Juggler of Our Lady* and *Jubilee*.

In 1974 Sister Elise and three African-American musicians—Margaret Harris, Benjamin Matthews, and Wayne Sanders—organized Opera Ebony in the North, with Philadelphia as the home site. Like the southern company, Opera Ebony used nonprofessionals in the choruses, generally composed of community groups in the cities where the operas were staged, and professionals in the leading roles. Both companies offered opportunities not only to black singers but also to stage directors, technicians, and other kinds of opera personnel to become fully involved in operatic production.

Those who performed with one or both of the companies included conductors Leonard De Paur, Margaret Harris, and Everett Lee; pianist Wayne

Sanders; and singers Donnie Ray Albert, William Brown, Alpha Floyd, Esther Hinds, Robert Mosley, Wilma Shakesnider, and Walter Turnbull. To these names should be added several of singers who were members of other opera companies.

A New Old Opera

The Houston Grand Opera Company's production in 1975 of the opera *Treemonisha* (1911) by Scott Joplin had an impact on the operatic world as great as that of Opera / South and Opera Ebony productions in that it served as a showcase for black talent and sent some of its featured artists to major opera companies. Singers of the leading roles in the Houston productions included Carmen Balthrop, Betty Allen, Curtis Rayam, Willard White, and Edward Pierson, among others.[2]

The first staged performance of *Treemonisha* had taken place at the Atlanta Memorial Arts Center on January 28 1972, under the sponsorship of Morehouse College. Critics were highly laudatory and the audience response was exuberant. Robert Shaw conducted the orchestra, assisted by Wendell Whalum, choral director and chairman of the Department of Music; Katherine Dunham was the stage director and choreographer; and T. J. Anderson, Visiting Professor for 1972, orchestrated the musical score. The principal roles were sung by professional artists: Alpha Floyd, Louise Parker, Seth McCoy, and Simon Estes, and the Morehouse students furnished the dancing and choral work.

The theme of the opera, education as the salvation of the race, was important to black folk; Joplin chose an eighteen-year-old girl, Treemonisha, as the heroine—a symbol of the teacher of the race. The work uses all the elements of grand opera; its twenty-seven numbers include an overture, prelude, recitatives, arias, small ensembles, choruses, and ballet. The composer furnished a preface to the opera score in order to help audiences "better comprehend the story." The setting was a remote plantation in Arkansas; the time was 1884.

The plot is a simple one, almost naive. Black Americans living on the plantation, having had no access to education, were caught up in superstitious ways and conjuring—all except Ned, leader of the group; his wife Monisha; and their adopted daughter, Treemonisha, the only one on the plantation with education. At considerable peril to herself, Treemonisha foils the evil plans of the conjurors, Zodzetrick and Luddud; Remus, the hero, rescues her; and the people choose her as their leader.

Treemonisha's music, written in the romantic style current during the period, is utterly charming and piquant and, in many places, deeply moving. Folk dances and folksongs appear in operatic disguise, along with such contemporary dances as the Slow Drag (see example), the Dude Walk, and the

---

[2]The Houston Opera Company production of *Treemonisha* was recorded in 1976.

TREEMONISHA.

No. 27.   A REAL SLOW DRAG.

By SCOTT JOPLIN.

Directions for The Slow Drag.

1. The Slow Drag must begin on the first beat of each measure.
2. When moving forward, drag the left foot; when moving backward, drag the right foot.
3. When moving sideways to right, drag left foot; when moving sideways to left, drag right foot.
4. When prancing, your steps must come on each beat of the measure.
5. When marching and when sliding, your steps must come on the first and the third beat of each measure.
6. Hop and skip on second beat of measure. Double the Schottische step to fit the slow music.   SCOTT JOPLIN.

INTRO. Larghetto. ♩=100

(Treemonisha and Lucy stand on bench in rear of room.)

(Salute partners.)
Treemonisha.

Sa – lute your part – ner, do the drag,   drag,

(Slow Drag forward.)

drag......... Stop and move back – ward, do the drag.

(All stop.)

(Slow Drag backward.)

The Finale of *Treemonisha* in the Houston Grand Opera 1982 production. *(Photo by Jim Caldwell. Courtesy of the author)*

Schottische. Scenes traditionally associated with black musical theater are present—all this before such models as the operettas of Bob Cole and the Johnson brothers or the Blake and Sissle *Shuffle Along* were available to Joplin. There is a preacher scene, for example, with the congregation offering choral responses in the traditional way; a spirituals-singing scene; even a blues scene, although the opera was completed before W. C. Handy had begun to popularize the blues. To be sure, Joplin does not identify the singing as blues, but the sound of the blues is present.

Neither does Joplin identify the opera as a ragtime opera, but ragtime harmonies and rhythms infuse the whole and give the finale a special snap and effervescence. His accomplishment is incredible, all the more so when it is remembered that he probably never saw grand opera or heard recordings of opera. The only explanation for his great achievement is that he was a man of genius. He was the first American to write American folk operas and ballets. More than any other single person, he made possible with his composition "the first widespread acceptance of a black cultural influence into the mainstream of American life."[3]

COMPOSERS

Music historians generally use the term *eclectic* in reference to a composer who draws upon several sources and different styles for his compositional

[3]Berlin, *Ragtime*, p. 196.

materials and techniques. In the broad sense of the term, William Grant Still was an eclectic, for his music included many styles and types, although it emphasized folklorism and the traditional. In a narrower sense, however, the young black composers who emerged during the mid-century years were more eclectic; they refused to be tied down by racial self-consciousness and drew freely upon widely divergent styles and sources in their writing. Some wrote conservatively in the classic forms; others experimented with free forms and exotic materials. The one quality they shared in common was that each believed it important to chart his or her own course.

Most of these composers, though not all, grew up in black communities and came to know intimately the music of their people, which was now broadened to include orchestral and piano jazz, along with the traditional spirituals and other folksongs, gospel songs, and the ubiquitous blues. The younger musicians also came into contact with bop, rock 'n' roll, and finally soul music—in some instances, participating in the creating of this music. All encountered, sooner or later, the "black experience"—that is, the understanding of what it meant to be a creative black artist in a basically hostile white society—and each coped with it as best he or she could. Some exploited more thoroughly African traditions with their emphasis on functionalism, communication, and purpose; others made the effort to combine African and European traditions into an integrated whole; a few ignored the problem and wrote wholly in the European tradition.

After World War II the social status of the African American in the United States gradually improved, and that of the black composer as well, but only to a certain extent. By the 1970s composers born in the North no longer had to go south in search of college teaching positions or other music occupations, as black musicians often had been forced to do in earlier years because of raw discrimination. Nevertheless, the black college, along with the black church, continued to nurture the creative artists in addition to serving as their chief patron, providing teaching and church positions for them and performing their music.

Beginning in the 1950s the federal government became the most supportive patron of all musicians—black and white; performer, composer, and researcher; jazz, folk, and classical. In 1965 the government established the National Endowment for the Humanities and the National Endowment for the Arts, which gave fellowships over the years to many musicians regardless of race. Moreover, the U.S. State Department sent musicians on worldwide tours, and such organizations as the U.S. Information Services sponsored concerts for them in Europe, Africa, and other parts of the world.

The position of the black composer in the total picture of American music remained relatively the same as it had in previous periods of music history. Two or three composers of concert music in each generation achieved national distinction, following in the course set by Burleigh, Cook, Dett, and White at the beginning of the century; by Dawson, Still, and

Swanson in a later period; and by Ulysses Kay and George Walker still later. At the same time a number of black composers not as well known were active, producing works of merit and contributing to the total creativity of the musical world. In the field of jazz and jazz-related music black composers dominated, as they had from its beginning. Most jazz composers continued to function primarily as performer-composers, but some also composed in the more conventional sense, particularly the younger jazz artists.

In 1940 a number of music enterprises formed Broadcast Music, Inc. (hereafter, BMI), a nonprofit, music-licensing organization, designed to compete with ASCAP. Before that year, ASCAP controlled the performance of live music—at least, that performed on the nation's four major radio networks in the evening hours—and distributed the performing-rights income it received among fewer than 150 music publishers and slightly more than 1,000 songwriters and composers. ASCAP did not monitor recorded music or music performed on independent stations. In regard to the recording industry, it was dominated by three companies, who controlled virtually all records produced for individual consumption or for performance on radio and in jukebox machines.[4]

The number of persons belonging to ASCAP represented but a small proportion of the nation's composers and music publishers, for only the well established could meet their membership standards and afford their initiation fees. Certainly, few black musicians belonged to ASCAP. Those who were not members of ASCAP, white and black, were unable for the most part to negotiate individually with the thousands of business enterprises that used their music commercially.

BMI changed the situation dramatically. It welcomed all kinds of composers and worked out ways to compensate them for recorded-music performance as well as live performance. This opened the doors to blues, gospel, rhythm 'n' blues, and other kinds of black music, as well as jazz, theater, popular, and concert music. By 1980 more than 21,000 publishers licensed their music through BMI, and 37,346 writers were members of the organization—including hundreds of black musicians. To be sure, the number of black men and women belonging to ASCAP increased over the years, and by 1980 they represented a greater diversity of musical genres than was true in the 1920s. But black-composer membership in ASCAP remained small in comparison to BMI membership. Both ASCAP and BMI offered awards to musicians in various classes—students, established songwriters and composers, writers, film composers, and other kinds—and black musicians were represented among the recipients.

[4]*The Many Worlds of Music*, BMI Issue 4 (1980): 29–35. Both ASCAP and Broadcast Music, Inc., publish trade journals, and since 1948 ASCAP has published four editions of its biographical dictionary.

Howard Swanson. *(Courtesy of the author)*

Composers After the War

With few exceptions, the composers whose music was being performed in the mid-century years were university professors, some at the most prestigious institutions in the nation. Howard Swanson (1907–1978), however, was one of the exceptions. He obtained his early musical training in Cleveland, attended the Cleveland Institute of Music (B. Mus.) where he studied with Ward Lewis and Herbert Elwell; then won a Rosenwald fellowship that enabled him to study with Nadia Boulanger at the American Academy in Fontainebleau, France, in 1938. He remained in Europe until 1941, when the onset of World War II forced him to return home. In 1952 he received a Guggenheim fellowship, and he returned to Europe to study and travel, this time remaining until 1966. Thereafter he settled in New York and gave full time to composing (made possible by a small pension and personal sacrifice).

Swanson began composing while in college, encouraged by his teachers, and when he was a senior the Institute's symphony orchestra played one of his pieces. Beginning about 1946 his songs were being performed more and more frequently, and in 1949 he attracted wide attention when Marian Anderson sang *The Negro Speaks of Rivers* (text by Langston Hughes) in a recital at Carnegie Hall in New York. Three years later his *Short Symphony* won the New York Critic's Circle Award as the best work performed during the 1950–51 concert season. Thereafter this work was widely performed in the United States and abroad.

The *Short Symphony,* in three movements, is scored for two flutes, two oboes, two clarinets, two bassoons, two horns, two trumpets, trombone, timpani, and strings. The composer's aim was to achieve in the work the "depth, seriousness, and intensity inherent in a large work." The first movement, Allegro moderato, has the outer structure of a sonata-allegro form with exposition, development, and recapitulation (restatement of the exposition material), but deviates from the conventional in its use of a little fugato for the first theme-group. The brief fugato theme is tossed back and forth from winds to strings to brasses:

Fugato theme, **Short Symphony,** Swanson

The second movement, Andante, is in three-part song form (a-b-a), again with an emphasis on call-and-response play between instruments of contrasting timbres.

Beginning of the second movement, **Short Symphony,** Swanson

The final movement, *Allegro giocoso—Andante con moto,* is a sonata-rondo. Contrasting sections are different in tempo as well as in musical material. The impudent rondo theme is given to the bassoons for the most part.

Rondo theme of the last movement, **Short Symphony,** Swanson

Although not a prolific composer, Swanson wrote in a variety of forms: three symphonies, a piano concerto, a concerto for orchestra, chamber music, two piano sonatas, some character pieces for piano, and about three dozen songs. His basically neoclassical style was distinctive for its intense lyricism, contrapuntal textures, and dissonant harmonies. Critics commented upon the fusion of power and delicacy in his music; one wrote that his songs "have a delicate elaboration of thought and intensity of feeling that recall Fauré." Swanson's best-known works, in addition to those named above, were the Piano Sonata No. 2 (1972), *The Cuckoo* for piano (1948), the Trio for Flute, Oboe, and Piano (1976), the *Fantasy Piece* for saxophone and string orchestra, and many songs.

Margaret Bonds (1913–1972) was another of the few composers of this period who had no university affiliation. A native of Chicago, she attended Northwestern University (B.Mus., M.Mus.) and the Juilliard School of Music, where she studied with Roy Harris and Robert Starer, among others.

She wrote in a neoromantic style that was subtly infused with jazz and

Negro folksong elements. Her compositions most frequently performed were the cantata *Ballad of the Brown King* (1961, text by Langston Hughes); the songs *The Negro Speaks of Rivers* and *Three Dream Portraits* (both texts by Hughes) and song arrangements *Five Spirituals;* and the *Spiritual Suite for Piano.*

Composers teaching at black colleges in the South tended to write music using black folk idioms, and, frequently, made arrangements of spirituals and other folksong types. The composers could be sure that their works would be performed by the college groups where they taught, not only on the campus but also when the groups went on tours. In this way, the music became known away from the campus where it originated, even though much of it might not have been published.

When the music was published, of course, it reached a larger audience. Among the composers who published fairly regularly during the 1940s–60s were John Duncan (1913–1975), Mark Fax (1911–1974), Thomas Kerr (1915–1988), and Noah Ryder (1914–1964). Since Undine Smith Moore (1904–1989) began publishing late in her career, she too belongs in this group. All these composers had long tenures at the institutions where they taught, going there early in their careers and remaining there until retirement. Duncan taught at Alabama State College in Montgomery; Fax and Kerr, at Howard University; Ryder, at Norfolk State College; and Moore, at Virginia State College.

Duncan obtained his musical education at Temple University in Philadelphia (B.Mus.; M.Mus.) and New York University. Although few of his compositions were published, they were performed widely on black and white college campuses in the South. Best known of his works were *Three Proclamations for Trombone and String Quartet,* Concerto for Trombone and Orchestra, the string quartet *Atavistic,* the opera *Gideon and Eliza,* and the choral piece *An Easter Canticle.* His published music included the trombone concerto and a song, *You're Tired, Chile.*

Mark Fax and Thomas Kerr both came from Baltimore, where their early musical development was encouraged by W. Llewellyn Wilson, teacher in the "colored high school" there. Fax attended Syracuse University (B.Mus.), the Eastman School of Music (M.Mus.), and New York University. He wrote in a variety of forms—choral works, songs, piano and organ pieces, operas, and symphonic works, of which the best known were the operas *A Christmas Miracle* (1958) and *Till Victory is Won* (1967) and the piano pieces *Toccatina* and *Three Piano Pieces.* Kerr, who also attended Eastman (B.Mus.), was best known for his organ piece *Anguished American Easter* (1968) and the piano composition *Easter Monday Swagger, Scherzino* (1970).

Noah Ryder attended Hampton Institute (B.A.) and the University of Michigan (M.Mus.). During his college years he organized singing groups and wrote arrangements for them; one of his groups later entered the professional world as the Deep River Boys. During World War II Ryder was a director of music in the U.S. Navy, and in 1946 his composition *Sea Suite for Male Voices* won a navy prize in a competition. His numerous spiritual arrangements and piano compositions included the *Five Sketches for Piano* (1947).

Undine Smith Moore, who received her musical training at Fisk University (B.A., B.Mus.) and Columbia University Teachers College (M.A., professional diploma), taught at Virginia State College for forty-five years. Her music was performed in many places, particularly the *Afro-American Suite* for flute, cello, and piano; her choral works *The Lamb* and *Lord, We Give Thanks to Thee*; many spiritual arrangements; and the oratorio *Scenes from the Life of a Martyr*. Moore also lectured widely on black music and was co-founder / co-director with Altona Trent Johns of the Black Music Center at Virginia State, which brought the leading black artists and composers of the nation to the campus during the years 1969–72.

Black composers coming to musical maturity during the 1940s–50s found that the curtain of racial discrimination was beginning to lift ever so slightly. Fellowships became more accessible, opportunities for performance came more frequently, and music critics and publishers less often insisted that "black music" had to be jazzy or folksy in order to be acceptable. Then too, the composers themselves were becoming more independent, having gained a measure of economic stability by securing positions as music editors and / or university professors. Freed of the necessity to write "race music" in order to secure performances, they began to reach out to larger audiences, writing music that carried no identifiable clues as to the origins of its composers.

Perhaps the first composers to benefit from the more liberal atmosphere of the post–World War II period in the United States were Ulysses Kay (1917–1996) and George Walker (b. 1922). Kay came from a musical family; his maternal uncle was the celebrated jazzman Joe "King" Oliver. After graduating from the University of Arizona (B.S.), Kay obtained scholarships that enabled him to attend the Eastman School of Music (M.Mus.), where he studied with Bernard Rogers and Howard Hanson, and later Paul Hindemith and Otto Luening. Then he won fellowships for study abroad during the years 1949–52.

After returning to the United States, he was an editorial adviser for Broadcast Music, Inc., and a college lecturer before his appointment as a Distinguished Professor at Lehman College of the City University of New York in 1968. First performances of Kay's music by university groups and the Rochester Civic Orchestra came during his years at Eastman. During the 1940s his music was heard increasingly on concerts offered by chamber groups, choruses, and soloists, and in 1944 his overture *Of New Horizons* attracted wide attention when it was performed by the New York Philharmonic at the Lewisohn Stadium. Later the piece won a prize from the American Broadcasting Company (1946), which led to more performances. In 1947 *A Short Overture* (1946) won the George Gershwin Award, and this

Ulysses Kay (1917–1995). *(Photo by Mary Gail Walker. Courtesy of the author)*

was only the beginning of a series of honors and awards that included the Prix de Rome (1949, 1951) and election to the Academy of Arts and Letters (1979).

Kay's style represents a kind of contemporary traditionalism; his lyricism points to neoromantic roots, while his crisp, dissonant, contrapuntal textures reflect his interest in mid-twentieth-century techniques. A prolific composer, by the time he moved into his sixties, he had completed eighteen or twenty works for symphony orchestra, four operas, some half-dozen or more works for band, about twenty compositions for chamber ensembles, and numerous pieces for solo instruments and songs.

In addition to those named above, there are his orchestral works *Portrait Suite* (1948), *Serenade for Orchestra* (1954), *Markings* (1966), *Theater Set* (1968), and *Southern Harmony* (1975), the last-named based on themes from William Walker's hymnal, *The Southern Harmony,* of 1835). His songs were popular with concert singers, particularly the *Fugitive Songs* (1950) and the *Triptych on Texts of Blake* (1962). Performers also showed special liking for his *Song of Jeremiah* (1945) for solo, chorus, and orchestra; *A Covenant for Our Time* (1969) for chorus and chamber orchestra; and *Parables* (1970) for chorus and orchestra.

Three of his operas—*The Boor* (1955, text adapted from Chekov), *The Juggler of Our Lady* (1956, libretto by Alexander King), and *The Capitoline Venus* (1970, text after Mark Twain)—were given first performances by American universities. The fourth opera *Jubilee* (1976, text after Margaret

George Walker *(Courtesy of the author)*

Walker's novel of the same title), was commissioned for the bicentennial, most received a premiere from Opera / South.

On the occasion of Kay's retirement from Lehman in 1989, the college staged a gala concert of his music, which included a concert version of his opera *Jubilee* and other large-form works. In 1991 the New Jersey State Opera produced his opera *Frederick Douglass* (libretto by Donald Dorr) in its world premiere.

One of Kay's popular works has been the "symphonic essay" *Markings* (1966), which was dedicated to the memory of Dag Hammarskjold, the second person to serve as Secretary General of the United Nations.

After the Detroit premiere, music critic Howard Klein wrote:

> A meditative sadness pervades Mr. Kay's 20-minute orchestral essay. Moments of conflict break out in grinding dissonances but are resolved finally in the pianissimo string ending. . . . a feeling of hope arises in this emotionally touching work that lends a rightness. One is tempted to call Mr. Kay's *Markings* a masterpiece of conservative modern orchestral writing.
>
> [*New York Times*, August 20, 1966]

George Walker (b. 1922) began his professional career as a concert pianist. He obtained his musical education at Oberlin (B.Mus.); the Curtis Institute of Music in Philadelphia (artist diploma), where he studied with Rudolf

Serkin and Rosario Scalero; the American Academy at Fontainebleau, France, where he studied with Nadia Boulanger (artist diploma) and at the Eastman School of Music (D.M.A.). In 1945 he made his debut at Town Hall in New York, and thereafter toured extensively as a concert pianist under management of National Concert Artists and Columbia Artists, giving recitals and playing with major symphony orchestras.

During the 1950s–60s Walker received scholarships and awards that enabled him to study in Europe and to compose. He began his teaching career in the '60s, serving tenures at Smith College in Massachusetts the University of Colorado and beginning in 1969, at Rutgers University at Newark, in New Jersey. Walker began composing soon after leaving college and published his first serious piece, *Lament for Strings* (later renamed *Lyric for Strings*), in 1946.

His mature style was distinctive for its fusion of contemporary elements, including serialism, with a predilection for classical forms—this in combination with rhythmic complexities and concern for melodic expressiveness. His music reflects the influence of jazz and black folk idioms, sometimes obviously, sometimes subtly. His Sonata for Cello and Piano (1957), for example, used a boogie-woogie bass; his Piano Concerto (1976) evoked the spirit of Duke Ellington. Included among his works performed most often were the *Address for Orchestra* (1959), Trombone Concerto (1957), *Music for Brass—Sacred and Profane* (1976), Concerto for Cello and Orchestra (1981), *In Praise of Folly* (1981), and the piano pieces, particularly the Piano Concerto (1975) and the three sonatas.

Concert pianists especially found his music attractive, for as a pianist himself, he wrote idiomatically for the instrument. Those seeking the music of black composers to perform on recitals were especially grateful; before Walker and Swanson, black composers typically wrote character pieces, which were acceptable for the second, lighter half of a program, but hardly suitable for the more weighty opening section. In 1979 Walter Hautzig included some Walker piano music on a recital in the People's Republic of China, undoubtedly giving China its first exposure to the non-jazz music of a black composer. In 1996 Walker received a Pulitzer Prize for his symphonic work *Lilacs,* based on a poem by Walt Whitman. He was the first African American in history to win the Prize for music.

By the decade of the 1950s works of other composers were attracting attention among them, Thomas Jefferson Anderson (b. 1928), Arthur Cunningham (b. 1928), Noel DaCosta (b. 1930), Coleridge Taylor Perkinson (b. 1932), Julia Perry (1924–1979), Hale Smith (b. 1925), and Frederick Tillis (b. 1930). The males of this group shared in a common background, although one was born in the South, another in Nigeria, and the others, in the North: they began studying instruments as children and played in jazz groups during their high-school years. They also began arranging for jazz groups at a young age, and in some instances wrote music for their groups. Anderson toured with a professional jazz group in the summers during his high-school years.

Julia Perry was unique in this generation of black composers, not only because of her sex and her lack of firsthand experience with jazz, but also because she spent many years abroad in study. She received her basic musical training at the Westminster Choir College in New Jersey (B.Mus.; M.Mus.) and at the Juilliard School of Music; she then lived in Europe during the years 1951–59, where she studied with Nadia Boulanger, Luigi Dallapiccola, Henry Switten, and others.

Her basically neoclassical style was distinctive for an intense lyricism and penchant for contrapuntal textures. She wrote in all the forms: symphonies, operas, concertos, band works, chamber ensembles, piano pieces, and songs. Several of her works were published, and two or three recorded—this, despite the large musical forces demanded by the works. Her best-known compositions were *Stabat Mater* (1951) for contralto and string orchestra; *Homunculus C.F.* (1960) for piano, harp, and percussion; *Homage to Vivaldi* for symphony orchestra; and the opera *The Cask of Amontillado,* which was first staged at Columbia University in 1954.

Like white composers of their generation, these composers learned to use twelve-tone techniques in their composition classes, but their later employment of the twelve-tone method varied from one to the other. Smith did not regard himself as a classic twelve-tone composer, despite such labeling given him by music critics; rather, he felt that he tended "to work with a few, key motivic ideas. . . ."[5] Anderson, too, protested at being labeled a serialist, saying, "I have my own method of organizing music . . . not even vaguely related to the twelve-tone system." And Cunningham stressed his independence of conventional modes of composition, while Tillis, although admitting his reliance upon twelve-tone method in his early years, pointed out that he had moved into a period of "free composition" in the 1960s.

All of these men drew freely upon black-music elements, using jazz as well as folk idioms; all felt the importance of the black aesthetic, whether or not it was obvious in their composition. They also freely combined the African-American tradition with European techniques and forms, such as using improvisation and aleatoric devices in their classical composition and using serial devices, tone clusters, and timbral manipulations in their jazz pieces for "expressive purposes."

T. J. Anderson was educated at West Virginia State College (B.Mus.), Pennsylvania State University (M.Mus. Ed.), and the University of Iowa (Ph.D.) He taught in African-American public schools and colleges in the South before he was appointed as professor of music at Tufts University in Massachusetts in 1972. He began publishing his music in 1959, and composed slowly but steadily thereafter. His mature style was distinctive for his use of melodic fragments in ever-shifting melodic and rhythmic patterns and intense instrumental coloring. His works include *Squares* (1965) and

---

[5]This quotation and much of the information that follows is drawn from Baker et al., *Black Composer* (Metuchen, N.J., 1978) and from Eileen Southern, "America's Black Composers of Classical Music," *Music Educators Journal* (November 1975): 46–59.

Transitions (1971) for orchestra; *Swing Set* (1972) for clarinet and piano, *Variations on a Theme by Alban Berg* for viola and piano (1978), and *Minstrel Man* for bass trombone and percussion; the liturgical music-drama *Re-Creation* (1978) and the opera *Soldier Boy, Soldier* (1982). His interests in African-American music led him to orchestrate Scott Joplin's score of *Treemonisha* for the world premiere of the opera in 1972 at Atlanta.

Frederick Tillis, a graduate of Wiley College in Texas (B.A.) and the University of Iowa at Iowa City (M.A.; Ph.D.), also taught in black colleges before his appointment to the faculty of the University of Massachusetts at Amherst in 1970. His mature style was eclectic in that he drew upon black-American, African, and Southeast Asian idioms and freely used European styles and forms. Although he wrote for a variety of media, his instrumental works and vocal-instrumental works predominate: *Ring Shout Concerto* for percussion and brass (1973), *Spiritual Cycle* for soprano and orchestra (1978), and *Concerto for Pro Viva Trio* (flute, cello, piano) and symphony orchestra (1980).

Born in Nigeria, Noel DaCosta moved with his family to New York when he was eleven. He received his musical training at Queens College of the City University of New York (B.A.) and Columbia University Teachers College (M.A.) and studied further with Luigi Dallapiccola in Italy. He taught at Hampton Institute in Virginia and at City University of New York before joining the Music faculty at Rutgers University in 1970. He was best known for his choral and vocal works: the song cycle *The Confession Stone* (1970), *Ceremony of Spirituals* for soprano, saxophone, chorus, and orchestra (1976), and *The Singing Tortoise*, a theater piece for children. His *Blue Mix* for bassist and instruments and *Spiritual Set* for organ also were frequently performed.

Hale Smith obtained his musical education at the Cleveland Institute of Music (B.Mus.; M.Mus.), where he studied with Marcel Dick. He settled in New York in 1958, served as a music editor and advisor for various music publishing companies, then began a teaching career with his appointment to C. W. Post College of Long Island University. In 1970 he joined the music faculty of the University of Connecticut at Storrs. Of the composers under discussion for this period, Smith probably had more continuing contacts with jazz than any; during the 1950s–60s he was an arranger and musical director for several of the celebrated jazz figures, and he wrote music for films, radio, and television.

Smith freely used the compositional techniques of his time, except electronic devices, and wrote for a variety of media. Most frequently performed are *Music for Harp and Orchestra* (1967); *Ritual and Incantations* (1974) and *Innerflexions* (1977) for orchestra; the jazz cantata *Comes Tomorrow* (1972; revised 1976); and *Meditations in Passage* (1980) for soprano, tenor, and piano. His *Contours for Orchestra,* (1962) recorded by the Louisville Symphony, is perhaps his best-known work.

A twelve-tone composition, *Contours* employs serial techniques, that is,

Hale Smith in 1994. *(Photo by Marcel H. Smith. Courtesy of the author)*

instead of using the major-minor system of keys and scales as a basis for composition, the serial composer uses a *twelve-tone row,* a specific arrangement of the twelve pitches of the octave, as the source for the melodic and harmonic patterns in his musical composition. (For each work, he devises a different row.) If the composer strictly adheres to his method, he will use the twelve tones always in the same order throughout the composition (except for immediate repetitions), but the tones may be used in any octave, high or low. The tone row may be used in four forms: the original; backward (retrograde); upside down (inversion); or upside down and backward simultaneously (retrograde of the inversion). The following example shows Smith's tone row for *Contours* in the four forms:

Tone row, **Contours,** Smith

Some of the important motives of the work are presented below:

Motives, from **Contours,** Smith

To be sure, *Contours* hardly impresses upon its listeners that its composer employed certain kinds of compositional techniques. It has the typical sound of some contemporary music: it is dissonant and contrapuntal, with unconventional orchestral combinations of sounds; and it emphasizes imitation among the various instruments. A critic writing in the *Courier-Journal* of Louisville, Kentucky, noted:

> *Contours* opens and closes on a note of protest. The piece makes versatile use of orchestral sonorities, pitting raucous cries from the brass against suave strings, quieting clamorous outbursts from the percussion with the sweet sound of woodwinds. It is a delicately balanced score, virile and persuasive.

Smith himself said of his work:

> Everything derives from a basic tone row and its variants and, though certain rhythmic proportions also derive from it, the idea of this being a serial "sounding" piece was perhaps the farthest thing from my mind.[6]

The title of another piece, *Innerflexions,* suggests a similar abstraction in the sound of the music, but that does not follow. Smith points out:

> Its title refers to the bending (or *flexing*) of its motives which appear as a twelve-tone set from which the melodic, harmonic, and structural materials derive.
>
> The piece, however, should be listened to as *music,* not as a technical exercise, because the "innerflexions" or inner bendings may also apply to the changes of moods or emotional responses of each listener.[7]

Arthur Cunningham earned degrees from Fisk University (B.A.) and Columbia University Teachers College (M.A.). He studied further with Wallingford Riegger, Peter Mennin, and Norman Lloyd. Cunningham orga-

[6]Letter to author from Hale Smith.
[7]Letter to author from Hale Smith.

nized a jazz group when he was twelve years old and wrote for such groups through his high-school years. He began composing concert music in 1951. His output includes compositions in all the forms: such as his *Perimeters* for flute, clarinet, vibraharp, and double bass (1965), *Lullabye for a Jazz Baby* for trumpet and orchestra (1970), *Concentrics* for orchestra (1968, nominated for a Pulitzer Prize), *Harlem Suite Ballet* (1971), and *Jubilee Songs* (1971).

Coleridge Taylor Perkinson (b. 1932) studied at New York University and the Manhattan School of Music (B.Mus.; M.Mus.), and also at the Mozarteum in Salzburg, Austria, and the Netherlands Radio Union in Hilversum, where he studied conducting with Dean Dixon. He was the first composer-in-residence for the Negro Ensemble Company (founded 1967) and wrote music for several of its productions, including *Song of the Lusitanian Bogey* (1967) and *Ceremonies in Dark Old Men* (1974). He also wrote extensively for films—among them, *A Warm December* (1962), *Amazing Grace* (1974), and *The Education of Sonny Carson* (1974)—television, radio, and ballet. His vocal works include *Nine Elizabethan Love Lyrics* (1952) and *Attitudes* (1962, written for George Shirley); his instrumental works, *Concerto for Viola and Orchestra* (1954) and *Sinfonietta for Strings* (1953).

The Society of Black Composers

In 1968 twenty-five or so young black composers met in New York to organize the Society of Black Composers, whose aims were "to provide a permanent forum for the works and thoughts of black composers, to collect and disseminate information about black composers and their activities, and to enrich the cultural life of the community at large." Their numbers included established jazz artists, composers of concert music who were beginning to build their reputations, and composers entering careers in composition. With the help of grants from various foundations, the society presented a number of concerts of contemporary black American music over the three-year period of its existence as well as colloquia and lecture tours.

That the experience was valuable for both the young and the established composers is evident in a newsletter of May 1969:

> And while a common vocabulary or grammar is not even desirable among black composers, a new and highly desirable consensus of positive and assertive attitudes is clearly emerging. The questions of a year ago—most often concerning which specific musical sounds and materials would be necessary to make black music—are no longer necessary. We know that because we are black, we are making black music. And we hear it, too![8]

In addition to some of the composers discussed above, the society's membership included Talib Rasul Hakim (1940–1988, né Stephen Cham-

---

[8]Also quoted in Southern, "America's Black Composers of Classical Music," p. 56.

bers), William Fischer (b. 1935), Carman Moore (b. 1936), Dorothy Rudd Moore (b. 1940), John Price (b. 1935–1996), and Alvin Singleton (b. 1940). Also Roger Dickerson (b. 1934), Primous Fountain (b. 1949), James Furman (b. 1937), Adolphus Hailstork (b. 1941), Wendell Logan (b. 1940), and Olly Wilson (b. 1937).

These were the persons who received Ford, Fulbright, Guggenheim, and Whitney fellowships and, later, grants from the National Endowment for the Arts and the National Endowment for the Humanities that enabled them to study in Europe with such teachers as Nadia Boulanger and Luigi Dallapiccola. Some used their awards to travel in Africa or to study traditional African music in Ghana and Nigeria. Several entered teaching careers during the 1960s–70s and had become university professors by the decade of the 1980s: James Furman at Western Connecticut State College, Adolphus Hailstork at Norfolk State University, Wendell Logan at the Oberlin School of Music, John Price at Tuskegee Institute, and Olly Wilson at the University of California, Berkeley.

Like black composers of an earlier generation, most of the men were closely involved with black music in their youth, except that it was rhythm 'n' blues instead of, or in addition to, bop; Miles Davis as well as Charlie Parker; gospel rather than spirituals. Some of them began playing in jazz groups even before reaching high school, and they also played in high school and college marching and symphonic bands. And several sang in church choirs or played for church choirs in their youth.

They were eclectic writers; they used the twelve-tone method in their formative years, then moved into avant-garde styles and, in some instances, electronic music. As high-school students they listened avidly to Stravinsky, Bartók, and Webern, and were impressed. Later they worked with "chance music" and improvisatory techniques, but their essays were rooted in jazz practices rather than the "experimental" music theories of John Cage and his followers.

During the 1970s there seemed to be increasing interest among the composers in vocal music—for the solo voice with conventional piano accompaniment or voice with chamber ensembles or orchestra or tape. Wilson's *Sometimes* for tenor and electronic tape (1976) referred to an old spiritual, *Sometimes I Feel Like a Motherless Child*. Other songs used poems by black poets or folk-music idioms, as Logan's *Dream Boogie* for voice and piano (1979). This generation of composers was well represented in Willis Patterson's *Anthology of Art Songs by Black American Composers* (1977), which was released in a record-album edition in 1982.

Generally they tended to fuse European styles and techniques with elements of black music, or the spirit of black music, to produce their own personal modes of expression. But there was little interest in the neoromantic style, in actually quoting folk tunes or inventing melodies in the spirit of folksong or depicting folk-life scenes in music, as had been the case with some black composers in earlier generations. Wilson, for example, pointed out, "I have always thought of [composing] in terms of abstract expression, of musical ideas—never in terms of imagery or anything like that. Also, I was somewhat turned off by much nineteenth-century composing."[9]

Above all, the composers believed in music as a way of communicating with others. Hakim said, "I am most concerned . . . that the materials I have chosen and the manner in which I choose to make use of them result in touching and moving the inner spirit of both audience and performer." And Wilson stated emphatically:

> I have never agreed with those who say that contemporary music is the expression of the composer working in a very sophisticated way in the twentieth century, and "Who cares whether or not people relate to it"; that is, that no one should expect people to understand what the composer is doing anymore than it is understood what a nuclear physicist is doing. I'm very much concerned about communication—and inspiration.[10]

Generally the composers wrote upon commission or wrote for the college and / or community groups they directed. Their economic security allowed them to reject commissions that had no appeal for them and to avoid hack writing if they wished. The commissions came from diverse sources in addition to the conventional ones—symphony orchestras and chamber groups, opera and ballet companies, educational and community institutions, and individual artists. The nation's bicentennial celebration in 1976, for example, was a source of commissions for many black composers, as were other kinds of anniversary celebrations—for example, Wilson's commission to write a piece for the Boston Symphony Orchestra's observance of its centennial anniversary in 1981.

Roger Dickerson, educated at Dillard University in New Orleans (B.A.) and Indiana University (M.Mus.), studied with Bernard Heiden; and with Karl-Schiske at the Akademie für Musik in Vienna, Austria. He began composing concert music at an early age, but also toured professionally with musicians such as bluesmen Joe Turner and "Guitar Slim" Eddie Jones during summer vacations. His works include *A Musical Service for Louis* (1972, with reference to Louis Armstrong), *Orpheus an' His Slide Trombone* (1975), and *New Orleans Concerto* (1977).

William Fischer attended Xavier University in New Orleans (B.S.), Colorado College in Colorado Springs (M.Mus.) and the Adademie für Musik in Vienna, where he studied with Gottfried von Einem. Like Dickerson, he was active in the world of jazz and blues, touring with such figures as Muddy Waters and Ray Charles. During the 1970s he was a musical director and record producer for film and stage artists. His works include *The Rise and Fall of the Third Stream, Experience in E* for jazz quintet and orchestra, *Quiet Movement for Orchestra,* and the opera *Jesse.*

---

[9]Eileen Southern, "Conversation with Olly Wilson," BPIM 6 (Spring 1978): 58.
[10]Southern, "Conversation with Wilson," p. 58.

Primous Fountain obtained his musical training in the public schools and junior colleges of Chicago and at DePaul University in Chicago. He began writing for jazz groups during his high-school years, and later turned to the writing of concert music. When he was eighteen, he won an award for composition from BMI and the next year received a Guggenheim fellowship—the youngest person ever to receive that award for musical composition. Fountain's most frequently performed works included the *Ritual Dance of the Amaks for Orchestra* (1973), *Duet for Flute and Bassoon* (1974), Concerto for Cello and Orchestra (1976), and *Caprice for Orchestra* (1980).

Adolphus Hailstork studied with Mark Fax at Howard University (B.Mus.) and with Nadia Boulanger in France. He also attended the Manhattan School of Music (B.Mus.; M.Mus.), where he studied with Vittorio Giannini and David Diamond, and at Michigan State University (Ph.D.). His best-known works were *Mourn Not the Dead* for mixed chorus (1968), *Celebration* for orchestra (1975), *American Landscape No. 1* for band (1976), and *The Pied Piper of Harlem* for unaccompanied flute (1980).

Talib Hakim obtained his musical education at the Manhattan School of Music, the New York College of Music, Adelphi University, and the Mannes College of Music; his teachers included Margaret Bonds, Robert Starer, Chou Wen-chung, and Ornette Coleman. He employed avant-garde techniques and displayed a penchant for using non-western instruments or unorthodox performance on traditional instruments. His best-known works included *Sound Gone* for piano (1967), *Visions of Ishwara* for orchestra (1970), *Shapes* for chamber orchestra (1965), and *Recurrences* for orchestra (1977).

Wendell Logan studied at Florida A & M University (B.S.), Southern Illinois University (M.Mus.), and the University of Iowa (Ph.D.). He composed in a variety of forms, often using electronic techniques and freely drawing upon jazz idioms in some works. Most frequently performed of his compositions were *Song of Our Time* for choir and instrumental ensemble (1970), *Three Fragments* for soprano, clarinet, piano, and percussion (1974), *Five Pieces for Piano* (1977), and *Dance of the Moors* (1980) for jazz group, drummers, and chorus.

Carman Moore attended Ohio State University (B.Mus.) and the Juilliard School of Music (M.Mus.); his teachers were Luciano Berio, Hall Overton, Vincent Persichetti, and Stefan Wolpe. His best-known works were *Gospel Fuse* (1975) and *Wild Fires and Field Songs* (1975) for orchestra, *Dawn of the Solar Age* for brass, percussion, and synthesizer (1978); and Quartet for Saxophones and Echoplex (1978).

Dorothy Rudd Moore, like Hailstork, studied at Howard University (B.A.) with Mark Fax; she also studied privately with Chou Wen-chung in New York and Nadia Boulanger in Fontainebleau, France. Her compositions display special concern for color and melodic expressiveness: *Dirge and Deliverance* for cello and piano (1971), *Dream and Variations* for piano

Olly Wilson in 1995. *(Courtesy Ed Kirwan Graphic Arts)*

(1974), and the song cycles *Twelve Quatrains from the Rubaiyat* (1962) and *Songs from the Dark Tower* (1970).

Olly Wilson was educated at Washington University in St. Louis (B.Mus.), the University of Illinois at Urbana (M.Mus.), and the University of Iowa (Ph.D.), where he studied with Robert Kelley and Phillip Bezanson. Before his appointment to the University of California, Berkeley, in 1970, he had taught at Florida A & M University and Oberlin. Although Wilson wrote almost exclusively in avant-garde styles, he feels that his music reflects his wide experiences with black music in his formative years, whether or not that quality is obvious to listeners.

In addition to his exposure to the music heard in most black communities in the 1940s–50s, Wilson heard a large amount of spiritual singing, for his father sang in a community chorus, the Harry T. Burleigh Society, that sang a spirituals repertory. Wilson began playing for church choirs at an early age, and during his high-school years he often earned money by playing the blues all night long in tiny blues clubs—really "little holes in the wall . . . [where] that's all they would listen to."[11]

His best-known works included *Piece for Four* (1966); *SpiritSong* for mezzo soprano, women's chorus, orchestra (with some amplified instruments), and gospel chorus (1973); *The Eighteen Hands of Jerome Harris* (1971), an electronic ballet; *Akwan* (1974) for piano and orchestra; *Reflec-*

[11]Southern, "Conversation with Wilson," p. 58.

tions for symphony orchestra (1978), and *Expansions* for organ (1979). He first attracted wide attention in 1968 as the winner in the first competition devoted to electronic music, The International Electronic Music Competition, held at Dartmouth College in New Hampshire. Over one hundred entries from all over the world were received and judged anonymously by established electronic-music composers Milton Babbitt, Vladimir Ussachevsky, and George Balch Wilson. Olly Wilson's prize-winning work was entitled *Cetus* (1967).

Composers and Synthesizers

Electronic music had begun to attract more and more composers during the 1950s, although it was really not an entirely new development. Actually, the French-born composer Varèse, a pioneer in the field in the United States, had experimented with sounds as early as 1934. In Europe after the Second World War, much work was done in France and Germany. To the composer, electronic music offers unlimited resources of pitch, dynamics, texture, and rhythms. A discussion of electronic music is beyond the scope of this book, but a few generalizations may be made at this point.

Sounds, natural or electronic, are recorded on magnetic tape and then transformed electronically into "new" sounds. This may be done in a number of ways—the simplest involving a splicing of the tape, speeding it up or slowing it down, and reversing its direction. In working with the new sounds, the composer manipulates them in much the same way as he or she does conventional sounds; some sounds are used to provide background accompaniment, and some to function as solo "instruments." A common practice is to combine in a single work both electronically produced sounds and the sounds derived from conventional musical sources. (The electronically produced sound may itself have been derived from either a musical instrument or from a nonmusical source.) The completed work is then taped for performance.

Not only does electronic music expand composers' tonal vocabulary; it also allows them to present their work directly to the listener, bypassing an intermediary, the performer. The composer thus becomes identical with the performer, a typical occurrence in the fields of jazz and folksong. Wilson provided the following comment on his *Sometimes:*

> It is based on a contemporary interpretation of the Black spiritual *Sometimes I Feel Like a Motherless Child.* In this work, I attempted to recreate within my own musical language, not only the profound expression of human hopelessness and desolation that characterizes the traditional spiritual, but simultaneously on another level, a reaction to that desolation which transcends hopelessness. It is for this reason that musical events associated with the original spiritual appear in this work in a number of different ways—sometimes straight forward, sometimes fragmentized or extended, and sometimes in completely new relationships with one another, both on the immediate as well as the large scale formal level.

The relationship between the tenor soloist and the electronic tape also reflects a multitude of shifting roles. They frequently exchange solo and complementary functions in varying degrees at different times in the course of the piece. Following an opening section by the tape alone, the tenor gradually enters, eventually becoming the focal point. A series of interrelated sections ensues in which the interplay between tape and singer becomes increasingly complex. The tenor then states a cadenza, followed by the tape reentry and, eventually, a buildup to the climactic point of the piece. The composition closes with a "moan-like" postlude.[12]

BLACK MUSICALS ON BROADWAY

The decade of the 1930s brought bleak times to black musical theater, both on and off Broadway, not only because of the Great Depression but also because of the growth of the "talkies" movie industry. The black theater managed to limp along, however, as we have seen, helped by genuine audience interest on Broadway and by the WPA Federal Negro Theater. Films gradually replaced the old vaudeville and road shows in black communities, although for a long period the two genres existed compatibly. People went to the theater to see the latest film, then stayed another hour or two to watch their favorite comedians or listen to their favorite performers and jazz big bands. Such theaters as the Apollo in New York, the Regal in Chicago, the Paradise in Detroit, and the Howard in Washington, D.C., were more than simply places that offered live entertainment; they were community institutions.

If the 1930s were bleak, the 1940s–60s were disastrous for black stage people. For more than twenty years, few black composers essayed to produce musicals on Broadway—at least, not with black casts. Then came a period that might be called the gospel period: beginning in the '60s a succession of black musicals appeared on Broadway, using music that was drawn primarily from gospel and folk repertories, the librettists sometimes replacing old texts with new texts. Some of these musicals were more concerts than plays. Melvin Van Peebles broke the gospel spell in the 1970s when he produced two musicals on Broadway for which he wrote both words and music, plays which some white critics found to be "hostile" in the way the racism was handled on the stage.

But the decade of the seventies was notable also for bringing back to Broadway some black composers of charming but exciting musicals. One could echo the old song again, *It's Getting Dark on Old Broadway*. Soon it became evident that a trend was in motion—all these musicals looked to the past, if not in the "book," then in the music and dances. Black musical theater seemed to have run out of things to say. It could only repeat its

[12]Quotation from program notes to the score.

history, bringing back in one nostalgic wave after another, the old masters—Eubie Blake, Fats Waller, and finally Duke Ellington. A musical that opened off Broadway in May 1980 seemed to sum it all up. Titled *Black Broadway,* it brought back not only the music of the 1920s–30s but also many of the performers singing the songs they originally had introduced, among them Adelaide Hall, Edith Wilson, and John W. Bubbles, as well as tap dancers Charles ("Cookie") Cook and Lester ("Bubba") Gaines of the Three Dukes and, later, the Copasetics.

The following is a selective list of the most enduring of the Broadway musicals written by black composers during this period:

1960	*Ballad of the Brown King* (Margaret Bonds)
1962	*Highway I, U. S. A.* (William Grant Still)
1963	*Tambourines to Glory* (gospel and spirituals)
1963	*Trumpets of the Lord* (gospel)
1963	*Ballad for Bimshire* (Irving Burgie); title changed to *Calalou* in 1973 revival.
1967	*The Prodigal Son* (gospel)
1968	*The Believers* (Josephine Jackson)
1970	*Don't Bother Me, I Can't Cope* (gospel, Micki Grant)
1970	*Don't Play Us Cheap* (Melvin Van Peebles)
1971	*Ain't Supposed to Die a Natural Death* (Melvin Van Peebles)
1972	*Treemonisha* (opera [premiere] Scott Joplin)
1975	*The Wiz* (Charles Smalls)
1975	*Treemonisha* (opera, Joplin)
1975	*Me and Bessie* (Songs of Bessie Smith)
1975	*Bubbling Brown Sugar* (Eubie Blake, Fats Waller)
1976	*Your Arm's Too Short to Box with God* (Alex Bradford, Micki Grant)
1976	*Jubilee* (opera, Ulysses Kay)
1978	*Ain't Misbehavin'* (Waller)
1979	*Eubie* (Eubie Blake)
1979	*One Mo' Time* (New Orleans jazz, folksong)
1980	*Black Broadway* (vaudeville music)
1980	*Mama, I Want to Sing* (Grenoldo)
1981	*Satchmo* (Louis Armstrong)
1981	*Sophisticated Ladies* (Ellington)
1981	*The Lady [Lena Horne] and Her Music*
1982	*Waltz of the Stork* (Van Peebles)
1983	*Frederick Douglass* (opera, Ulysses Kay)
1983	*Amen Corner* (Garry Sherman)
1983	*The Gospel at Colonus*
1986	*"X"; The Life and Times of Malcolm X* (opera, Anthony Davis)
1986	*Queenie* (Ellington)

1990   *Once on This Island* (Stephen Flaherty)
1991   *The Mother of Three Sons* (dance opera, Leroy Jenkins)
1991   *Long Tongues: A Saxophone Opera* (Julius Hemphill)
1992   *Jelly's Last Jam* (Luther Henderson, Jelly Roll Morton)
1994   *Jelly Roll! The Music and the Man* (Jelly Roll Morton)

Several gospel musicals were successful off Broadway, among them *Black Nativity*, which opened at Lincoln Center in New York at Christmas time, 1962, then went to the Festival of Two Worlds at Spoleto, Italy, the following summer and thereafter toured for many months in Europe, Australia, and New Zealand. *Trumpets of the Lord* (1963) and *The Prodigal Son* (1967) also toured in Europe after runs in New York. Langston Hughes wrote texts for several of the gospel musicals of this period.

If black composers showed little interest in Broadway, it does not follow that Broadway showed no interest in black shows. At least one theater historian gives the black-cast musical credit for lifting Broadway out of its doldrums in the 1970s because of the exuberance and zest of the black performers.[13] Here is a list of the important black-cast shows and those with predominantly black casts that were big hits at the box office:

1940   *Cabin in the Sky*
1942   *Carmen Jones*
1945   *Memphis Bound*
1946   *St. Louis Woman*
1949   *Lost in the Stars*
1954   *House of Flowers*
1956   *Mr. Wonderful*
1963   *Hello Dolly* with black cast
1964   *Golden Boy*
1970   *Purlie*
1973   *Raisin*
1975   *Hello Dolly* revival
1976   *Guys and Dolls* with black cast
1978   *Timbuktu*
1982   *Dream Girls*

To this list should be added the many revivals of *Porgy and Bess* and *Four Saints in Three Acts*.

Several reasons can be advanced for the black composer's lack of interest in the musical theater. For one thing, black composers began to gravitate toward Hollywood, where they wrote a different kind of theater music. Then too, the stock companies that had flourished so vigorously in black communities in the early twentieth century had disappeared by the mid-century years, and sporadic attempts to establish Negro Theater groups

---

[13]Bordman, *American Musical Theatre*, p. 643.

over the years were unsuccessful until the late 1960s. Moreover, once established and thriving, these groups tended to prefer straight drama to the musical. Of the groups established in the '60s that proved to be permanent, the Negro Ensemble Theater of New York was one of the most highly respected. Founded in 1967, this repertory company had a composer-in-residence, Coleridge Taylor Perkinson, during its early years, and made it a practice to include musicals among its productions.

OTHER FORMS OF THEATER MUSIC

As stated above, some composers were drawn into the Hollywood orbit, where they wrote scores for or contributed music to soundtracks for films and television shows. Black composers or arrangers contributed to the several Broadway musicals, for example, that were remade as films, including *Cabin in the Sky* (1943), *Carmen Jones* (1954), *The Wiz* (1978), and others. As we have seen, Will Vodery and William Grant Still were the pioneering black writers of music for films and television. Ulysses Kay wrote his first film score, *The Quiet One,* in 1948 and thereafter wrote much music for films and television. Among others who wrote for Hollywood were James Mundy, Fred Norman, and Hale Smith. Robert Holmes specialized in the documentary film; his best-known scores included music for *The Gift of Black Folk, Two Centuries of Black American Art,* and *Drawings from Life* (about artist Charles White).

It was in the 1960s that the black film-television music writer began to come into prominence. The giants in the field were few but gifted; they had to be, for the competition was formidable. Benny Golson (b. 1929), whose first full-length score was *Where It's At* (1969), contributed music to such television shows as *Room 222, The Partridge Family, Mission: Impossible,* and others, in addition to writing for such films as the box-office winner *Cheech and Chong's Next Movie* (1980). "J. J." (né James Louis) Johnson (b. 1924) was singled out in June 1981 for special recognition by BMI as one of its pioneers who had completed twenty-five years of association with BMI. He settled in Los Angeles in 1970 and thereafter wrote prolifically for the film industry, including *Across 110th Street* (1972) and *Cleopatra Jones* (1973).

Quincy Jones (b. 1933), who wrote his first full-length score for a Swedish film, *Boy in the Tree* (1961), settled in Hollywood, where he produced music for *In Cold Blood* (1967), *For the Love of Ivy* (1968), *The Anderson Tapes* (1971), *The Getaway* (1972), and many others. He also wrote music for the television soundtracks of such shows as *Ironside, Sanford and Son,* and *Roots.* Oliver Nelson (1932–1975) also began his film-score career in the sixties and wrote the film scores for *Istanbul Express* (1968), *Last Tango in Paris* (1972), and *Inside Job* (1973). His television music was heard on

Six Million Dollar Man, It Takes a Thief, The Name of the Game, and other shows.

With the ascendancy of the rhythm 'n' blues era, a younger generation of composers found opportunities in Hollywood, among them, Curtis Mayfield (b. 1942), who was a newcomer in 1972 when his music was used on the soundtrack of *Superfly.* Once involved, he continued to write for television and films, including *Claudine* (1974) and *Let's Do It Again* (1975). Issac Hayes (b. 1942) wrote only one notable film score, *Shaft* (1971), but it was good enough to win the Academy Award for him in 1972 and several other major awards. Donny Hathaway (1945–1979) contributed music to the score for *Come Back, Charleston Blue* (1972) and the theme for the television show *Maude.*

All these men were active in jazz or rhythm 'n' blues as arrangers, songwriters, musical directors, and producers, and they continued their involvement with performance at the same time as they wrote for films and television. Nelson and Jones, in particular, wrote concert music in traditional art forms, which received repeat performances. In 1971 Jones's *Black Requiem* was performed by the Houston Symphony with an eighty-voice choir and his friend, Ray Charles, as soloist. Nelson's best-known works in the larger forms were *Soundpiece* for Jazz Orchestra (1964), *Dialogues for Orchestra* (1970), and *Suite for Narrator, String Quartet and Jazz Orchestra* (1970).

Music for the Dance

The dance has always been important to black Americans, whether folk, popular, jazz, or concert, and black composers have written for all kinds of dance, including ballets for occasional performance, such as the ballets of Harry Lawrence Freeman and William Grant Still. The black concert dance troupe is a relatively new phenomenon, however, whose roots lie in the 1930s—perhaps with the first troupes of Katherine Dunham (b. 1910). Also in that decade, the nation saw its first African ballet-opera, *Kykuntor,* produced by Asadata Dafora (1889–1965) in May 1934 in New York. Thereafter Dafora staged African folk musicals and dance festivals regularly until 1960, when he returned to his home country, Sierra Leone.

Dunham is regarded as the founder of the black-American concert dance company as an institution. She established a dance troupe, the Ballet Nègre, as early as 1931 and had shaped her permanent touring company by the 1940s. Like Dafora, she drew primarily upon folk-music repertories for her dances, or music invented in the spirit of folk music, some of which she herself wrote. Another pioneering dance leader was Pearl Primus (b. 1919), who toured as a soloist and with her own companies, and who explored ethnic dances as did her predecessors.

There were other pioneering dancers and choreographers, some of whom worked with white companies or integrated ones, and others, with black companies, but there were no black resident companies in the United States—at least, none with a national reputation—until 1958. In March of that year Alvin Ailey (1931–1989) launched his Alvin Ailey American Dance Theater in a New York performance. This modern-dance company glorified black dance and used the music of black writers for many ballets; for example, Duke Ellington, Alice Coltrane, gospel, folk blues and blues arrangements by "Brother" John Sellers, and traditional spirituals and spiritual arrangements by Hall Johnson.

For the most part, Ailey used preexistent music for his dances, but on at least one occasion, there may have been collaboration between composer and choreographer—the premiere in 1971 of *Mary Lou's Mass,* written by jazz pianist Mary Lou Williams. By 1980 Ailey's company was no longer black but interracial; he continued, however, to emphasize dance in the black tradition, accompanied by traditional or composed black music.

America's first black classical ballet company was formed in 1966 by Arthur Mitchell, a former principal dancer of the New York City Ballet. He started out with a ballet school in Harlem, out of which came the Dance Theatre of Harlem. In its early years the Dance Theatre of Harlem danced in the classical ballet tradition; then as the company matured, the director began to explore black traditions, combining elements of ballet with elements of ethnic dancing. The music used included compositions by Geoffrey Holder (arranged by Tania León); Primous Fountain, *Manifestation* (1969); and Quincy Jones, *Every Now and Then* (1975), in addition to folk materials. It appears that as the public's interest in ballet and ethnic dancing increases, and as black companies proliferate, there will be increased opportunity for black composers to write music for ballet and modern dancing.

CHAPTER 14

Currents
In Contemporary
Arenas

D URING the years after World War II, the demography of the African-American population changed character dramatically. Over a span of four short decades (1950–90), more than five million African Americans left the South to pour into northern and far western cities, and in the process a rural people became an urban people. It was the greatest mass migration in the nation's history. In search of economic opportunities unavailable to them in the South, African Americans settled primarily in seven urban centers: New York, Philadelphia, Baltimore, Washington, Detroit, Chicago, and Los Angeles. By 1980 more than 34 percent of the nation's African-American population (26,489,000) lived in these cities alone, and 81 percent of the total black population lived in metropolitan areas of varying smaller sizes.[1]

African-American culture thrived in the heady life of the city; its presence made all Americans more aware than ever before of its creativity and ingenuity, and the African-American influence on national life greatly expanded. This was particularly true of music. Inevitably, new styles of popular music, such as soul and rap, appeared on the scene and old genres, such as the blues, were revitalized. Black concert artists—jazz, classical, gospel—increasingly found ways to participate in the cultural life of the cities, as recitalists, as members of their own professional groups, or, in some instances, as performers with long-established, white music organizations. The generally good employment conditions for many African Americans

[1]Franklin, *From Slavery to Freedom* (New York, 1994), 7th ed., p. 470.

ensured that they could afford to attend performances by their favorite jazz, blues, and pop artists, and to purchase large numbers of their recordings.

One of the most striking changes of this period took place in the area of education, undergraduate and graduate. The enrollment of black students in white educational institutions increased steadily each year; by 1970, for example, more than 375,000 black students were enrolled in white colleges.

For the first time in history, large numbers of black and white Americans found themselves contending with each other as equals in political, educational, and occupational settings.[2] The problems of adjustment were eased somewhat by new government programs instituted during the decade, such as affirmative action, federal grants, and various other policies accompanying and resulting from the Civil Rights movement.[3] The response of African-American students and, at times, faculty, was to devise various means of affirming their racial identity while at the same time adjusting to the demands of white society and culture. How this has been achieved varies from campus to campus, but almost always it is the gospel choir that serves as the preeminent symbol of African-American culture on white college campuses. At the end of the twentieth century, the sounds of gospel were to be heard over all the land.

JAZZ IMPROVISERS AND COMPOSERS

The last quarter of the twentieth century saw some extraordinary developments in African-American music, particularly in jazz composition and improvisation, but also in performance—classical, gospel, and popular music. For some of the young composers and improvisers who came of age in the 1980s and '90s, eager to begin their professional careers, the jazz scene was incredibly rich. Despite its youth—as a genre it has hardly reached the century mark—jazz offered a variety of styles to choose from. Moreover, many of the founding elders of African-American music still walked the streets and were accessible to "Young Lions" seeking to learn more about the history of their black music: "gospel king" Thomas A. Dorsey, "blues king" "Sunnyland Slim" (b. Andrew Luandrew), and "swing kings" Lionel Hampton, Count Basie, and Earl Hines, to name just a few. These celebrated figures and their equally celebrated colleagues still practiced their arts, playing in nightclubs, in concert halls, and at festivals. Although octogenarians, some were still concertizing as they moved into their ninth decades—rag pianist-composer Eubie Blake and "blues queen" Alberta Hunter are two remarkable examples.

---

[2] *Blacks on the Move: A Decade of Demographic Change,* The Joint Center for Political Studies (Washington, D.C., 1982), p. 6.
[3] Richard Merelman, *Representing Black Culture* (New York, 1995), p. 34.

A NEW GENERATION

The new generation of aspiring black musicians was unlike any previous one in the history of African-American music. First, and perhaps the most striking feature of the group as a whole, was their youth at the time they became "superstars": many were in their early twenties (some, barely there), and long committed to, and involved in, jazz, or gospel, or whatever their chosen genre. Second, they came well prepared: they had begun their musical studies as children, had played in grade-school and high-school bands, attended summer music camps, studied music at college, and "sat in" with mainstream jazz groups at every opportunity. Having studied both jazz and classical music in school, they felt comfortable with both genres, whether as composer, improviser, or instrumentalist.

Guitarist Stanley Jordan, for example, graduated from Princeton, where he studied composition with Milton Babbitt, composition for digital computer with Paul Lansky, and jazz composition with Kenny Barron. Anthony Davis earned his B.A. at Yale, then played with "free-jazz" groups before organizing his own octet Episteme. Wynton Marsalis was attending the Juilliard School of Music when he left to join Art Blakey's Jazz Messengers. Pianist Geri Allen earned an M.A. in ethnomusicology at the University of Pittsburgh. And several completed the jazz program at the Berklee College of Music, among them, saxophonist Branford Marsalis and trumpeter Roy Hargrove. There is a long list of musicians who attended college to obtain the kind of maturation formerly available only to those who had played in big bands and ensembles as apprentices over a period of time, who had learned by listening to records and live performances.

Inevitably, the question arose whether the training offered by mainstream academic institutions (black or white) was adequate for persons planning careers in jazz, a music so deeply rooted in the African-American experience. Joshua Redman (tenor saxophonist), who chose to bypass college, expressed his own views and those of some of his counterparts:

> Graduates of the academy may be more accomplished technically, but they are more orthodox in the way they solo. . . . My attitude is that race means nothing. . . . If you can play, you can play, period. . . . It means that you may have to immerse yourself in the jazz tradition. . . . It means you have to learn the jazz idiom, which is by and large an African-American idiom. . . . It means you have to work at all the nuances that have developed from that tradition.[4]

For jazz students eager to work at catching all the "nuances" and immersing themselves in the jazz tradition—preferably as a sideman in one of the important ensembles of the period—the person to get to know was drummer Art Blakey (1919–1990).

[4]Peter Watrous, "Is Josh Redman a New Archetype?" *New York Times* (November 20, 1994), p. 38.

Blakey studied piano as a child and, self-taught on the drums, he began playing professionally while still in his teens. During the early 1940s he played with several important groups before joining Billy Eckstine's band (fl. 1944–47), where he first came in contact with bebop, the "new music" of the period. For more than forty years, from 1947 on, he led his own groups, and thereby exerted enormous influence on the jazz scene, particularly as a bandleader, as provider of a training ground for neophytes, and, informally, as a teacher—whom the jazz community called the "godfather of jazz." He gave to all his groups, no matter their size, the same name: The Jazz Messengers. Over the years, hundreds of young musicians received their basic training in jazz as performers in his groups, and nearly all those who later became the superstars of the 1980s and '90s had been trained by Blakey. As we have seen, Blakey's style associates him with the driving, aggressive school of "hard bop."

Blakey's sphere of influence spanned several generations of bop players. The first included fellow bandmembers in Eckstine's orchestra, among them Charlie Parker, Dizzy Gillespie, and Dexter Gordon. The last generation is represented by Marsalis and his followers. A list of the hard-bop musicians who played in Jazz Messenger groups during the intervening years would read like a Who's Who in Jazz. Certainly it would include the Adderley brothers—Cannonball and Nat—Donald Byrd, John Coltrane, Charles Mingus, and Herbie Hancock, to name only a few.

Under the influence of Blakey and Horace Silver, in particular, many young improvisers of the 1980s avoided the experimentation of the previous decades, turning instead back to bop of the 1950s and '60s, where they found models in the performances of Clifford Brown, Wayne Shorter, Jackie McLean, Joe Henderson, Andrew Hill, Mal Waldron, and Miles Davis's Quintets of the mid-1950s.

BLAKEY'S KIDS

In the 1980s and '90s, a representative list of "Blakey's Kids" (as they were called in the jazz community) includes trumpeters Terence Blanchard (b. 1962), Roy Hargrove (b. 1970), Marlon Jordan (b. 1971); guitarists Ronny Jordan (b. 1966), Stanley Jordan (b. 1959), and Mark Whitfield (b. 1967); saxophonists Steve Coleman (b. 1967), Donald Harrison (b. 1960) and Joshua Redman (b. 1969); percussionist Thelonious Monk, Jr., (b. 1951); pianists Geri Allen (b. 1957), Marcus Roberts (b. 1964), and Jacky Terrasson (b. 1966); and, best known of all, the Marsalis brothers, Branford and Wynton.

The Marsalises are a virtual First Family of jazz. Wynton (b. 1961) plays trumpet, his brother Branford (b. 1960) play tenor and soprano saxophone, another brother, Delfeayo, plays trombone, the youngest brother *Jason* plays drums, and the patriarch, Ellis Marsalis, is a professional pianist and

Wynton Marsalis in 1995. (Frank Stewart)

music teacher. Wynton studied both classical music and jazz as a child, and at fourteen played Haydn's Trumpet Concerto with the New Orleans Symphony. He attended the Juilliard School of Music, but left to play in Art Blakey's Jazz Messengers (1979–82). In 1984 he attracted international attention when he won Grammy awards in both classical (trumpet concertos by Haydn and Hummel) and jazz categories (*Think Of One*, 1982).

Branford studied music at Southern University (Louisiana) and graduated from the Berklee College of Music (Boston), then joined Blakey's Jazz Messengers, playing tenor and soprano saxophone (1981–82). In addition to touring in a quintet with his brother Wynton for three years, he toured, performed, and recorded with groups—Clark Terry and Miles Davis—and in 1985 toured with the rock musician Sting and with his own quartet. In May 1992 a small milestone in the history of black music was reached when Branford was appointed leader of the band for NBC's "The Tonight Show" with Jay Leno. It was the first time a black musician had occupied a major spot on mainstream nighttime television. Branford, however, had other plans for his future, and returned to his jazz activities in January 1995.

ASPECTS OF THE NEW MUSIC

By the 1980s it was apparent that a revival of interest in pre-bop jazz was under way, led by jazz musicians belonging to Blakey's younger generations; indeed, it also was apparent that in many respects the new movement represented a jazz renaissance, which embraced traditional jazz styles as far back as Louis Armstrong, Joe King Oliver, and Duke Ellington, and reflected the existence and importance of a jazz canon.

As we have seen, the 1970s were transitional years, with jazz artists moving away from the hard bop of the fifties into a future dominated by experimentation that took several different directions. Various terms were used to describe the "new thing": "free jazz," "avant-garde jazz," and "fusion," among others. Some improvisers sought to achieve freedom by avoiding tonality, conventional song structure, the steady pulse, and predetermined chord changes in order to allow the artist to concentrate on melodic improvisation, which generally was unstructured and often seemed to make few, if any, references to other elements of the music.

But the lines separating the various jazz styles were blurred. While some musicians were extending the frontiers of jazz by borrowing elements and techniques from gospel, blues, non-Western folk music (particularly African), and earlier jazz styles, others were exploiting the possibilities of fusing jazz with rock—thus creating "jazz-rock," with its emphasis on heavy amplification, electronic keyboards, and driving aggressive rhythms. Still other groups were extending the frontiers of sound, pushing the outer range limits of traditional instruments and bringing into the ensemble various kinds of non-Western instruments and objects made to function as instruments.

Long-lived groups, like the Modern Jazz Quartet (fl. 1951–92), continued into the 1990s to explore ways of combining jazz and classical music into a "third-stream" music. Similarly, Richard Muhal Abrams's AACM (Association for the Advancement of Creative Musicians, founded 1965) continued to flourish as an experimental movement into the 1990s. Based in New York from the 1980s on, AACM encouraged both individuals and groups under its umbrella to extend their horizons as far as possible. In 1990, a concert celebrating its twenty-fifth anniversary featured one piece that called for trumpet, thumb piano, wooden flute, koto, and Indonesian xylophone. Following that, Abrams's thirteen-member ensemble performed a set that alluded to European classical and avant-garde music, to modal jazz, to the textures of gongs and bells, and to big-band blues.

The World Saxophone Quartet—founded in 1976 and composed of Hamiet Bluiett (b. 1940), baritone; Julius Hemphill (1938–1995), alto; Oliver Lake (b. 1942), alto; and David Murray (b. 1955), tenor—moved in quite an opposite direction in expressing its concept of how jazz should be freed of its shackles. Using no supporting rhythm section, the group depended upon the individuals to improvise solos or serve as sidemen, as necessary; to merge avant-garde techniques with rhythm 'n' blues and other black-music idioms; to improvise or to play notated music or combine the two; and to perform original works or interpret jazz classics, as on the album *The World Saxophone Quartet Plays Duke Ellington* (1986).

Free jazz, of course, provoked reactions from individuals as well as group members, some of whom were at the midlife peaks of their careers. It has been suggested, for example, that saxophonists Ornette Coleman and Jackie McLean, on their recordings of the 1980s–90s, were both "running away from the baroque complexities of bebop," but that they "landed in different places."[5] Coleman borrows from jazz, non-Western, gospel, and blues, blending all genres freely with his special interest in melodic manipulation. McLean's music reflects his sophisticated abstraction and also shows that he is not wholly free of bop influences. Pianist Cecil Taylor, of the same generation, also improvised a sophisticated music, one that makes great demands on audiences while it reflects his debt to the African-American experience lying at the roots of his style.

THE YOUNG LIONS

A group of young musicians, led by Wynton Marsalis, revolted against the excesses of the free-jazz period. Their style, rooted in hard bop, has been defined as the most complex of all the jazz musical languages, but developing the technical skills necessary to master hard bop was only the beginning for these "Young Lions." The styles of the great masters—King Oliver, Louis Armstrong, Duke Ellington, Charlie Parker, John Coltrane, and Miles Davis—were studied, analyzed, interpreted or reinterpreted, and revitalized. Above all, the masters were to be revered and their traditions preserved.

The players' control of the musical material reflected itself in the way they referred to the masters by quoting or suggesting a melody, rephrasing an idea, or seamlessly blending-in elements from other jazz styles or classical genres. Musicians paid homage to their musical ancestors but did not slavishly imitate them. Most important, jazz musicians worked at trying to develop a personal creative voice, as Blakey and other elders constantly reminded them. "You have to figure out a way to get beyond [Art] Tatum," said Blakey. "You have to try, for better or worse, to get individuality."[6] Models were offered by albums such as Joe Henderson's *Lush Life: The Music of Billy Strayhorn* (1992).

There were, of course, those who wanted to introduce the new and novel

[5]John Rockwell, "The Cecil Taylor Enigma Is Intact. . . ." *New York Times* (1988); Peter Watrous, "Two Paths Taken in the Flight from Bebop," *New York Times* (February 13, 1994), p. 30.
[6]Peter Watrous, "The Youth Movement Puts Jazz Back in JVC," *New York Times* (June 16, 1991).

or "the more widely familiar" into their music and thereby broaden their audiences. Guitarist Ronny Jordan, for instance, mixed elements of pop, jazz, and hip-hop in *The Antidote* (1992), thus producing a hybrid "new jazz swing."

Under the leadership of Wynton Marsalis, the "Young Lions" informally worked out a program indicating where they wanted to go and what they wanted to accomplish, although, to be sure, there was no formal organization such as the Society of Black Composers that thrived in the 1960s. Jazz critics expressed views that were shared by many in the jazz community:[7]

> To some, the young musicians have seemed the product of hype, gaining exposure that should have gone to older musicians. Others see the youngsters' attention to what has been called the jazz canon as an attempt to halt the gears of artistic progress.

Both critics and musicians, however, recognized that a new era was beginning:

> In a sense, what the jazz world has been experiencing—the controversy over the direction a new generation is taking, the anxiety over what to make of the past, the re-examination of values—is a collective midlife crisis. How, the implicit question seems to run, should this art form negotiate the passage, begun in the 1960s around the time that rock-and-roll became a major industry, from being the coolest new kid on the esthetic and commercial block to a role as a mature, though still evolving, music with a body of recognized, classic work behind it?

THE PROFESSORS

As in the mid-century years, most African-American professional musicians in the classical sphere were associated with academic institutions, which permitted them to combine teaching with their professional activities—concertizing or composing. The ranks of black classical composers had always been small, however, and during the last two decades of the twentieth century, several of the preeminent ones died, among them, William Grant Still, William Levi Dawson, Howard Swanson, Undine Smith Moore, and Ulysses Kay. The period also saw retirements, though most retirees, especially the composers, continued their musical activities. Finally, the nation's desegregation policies brought changes in the academic world that directly affected African-American musicians. No longer were qualified black musicians assured of finding employment in the historically black colleges, for they had to compete with white musicians for the few available positions in black colleges, yet few were invited to join the music faculties of white institutions.

[7]Tom Piazza, "Keepers of the Flame, and Hot," *New York Times* (March 12, 1995), p. 32.

Nevertheless, beginning in the 1970s a small number of highly regarded jazz musicians were appointed to professorial positions at academic institutions, allowing them to combine teaching with touring, recording, and lecturing. They filled positions as guest lecturers, composers-in-residence, artists-in-residence, visiting professors, and tenured professors. One fascinating byproduct of this development was that aspiring jazz artists could study with black jazz masters at prestigious white institutions, an impossibility in earlier years because of institutional discrimination.

By the 1980s some sixty or more academic institutions had established programs that offered jazz students the choice of majoring in jazz, in classical music, or, indeed, in fields unrelated to music. However, the Berklee College of Music was the only *conservatory* devoted expressly to jazz studies until the 1991 opening of the Thelonious Monk Center for Jazz Studies in Washington, D.C. Under the direction of drummer Thelonious Monk, Jr., son of pianist Monk (1917–1982), for whom the Center is named, the Monk Center soon began offering annual awards of $10,000 to pianists and trumpeters. Beginning in 1982, the National Endowment for the Arts has made available several American Jazz Masters Awards each year. But the number of awards available to jazz and folk musicians is pitifully small, compared with those available to students of mainstream faculty and institutions.

There were signs, however, that the nation's cultural establishment was taking jazz more seriously than at any time in the past. In 1991 the Lincoln Center for the Performing Arts in New York announced the establishment of a jazz department that would function like the other Lincoln Center departments, producing its own concerts, lectures, films, and young people's concerts, and performing with its own repertory company and Classical Jazz Orchestra. The program actually had begun in August 1987 with a weeklong classical jazz series. Beginning July 1, 1996, Jazz at Lincoln Center became a fully independent constituent organization, with its own board of directors and management. Wynton Marsalis, who had been artistic director of the Jazz Department since its inception, said, "We are proud to take our place among the other outstanding organizations in the Lincoln Center family. The action places the uniquely American legacy of swing and blues as a history to be valued, an artistic achievement that is on par with the most magnificent works of Western classical music."[8] Lincoln Center president Nathan Leventhal said, "From the beginning we strongly believed that jazz richly deserved a home here at Lincoln Center. . . . we congratulate the directors and the entire jazz staff." And executive director Rob Gibson said, "We look forward . . . to showcasing the rich canon of jazz masterworks in every corner of the world."

---

[8]This quote and the two following are from the *Amsterdam News,* April 1996. See also Peter Watrous, "Finally, a Lincoln Center for American Music," *New York Times* (January 20, 1991), p. 2.

The early '90s also saw the Lila Wallace / Reader's Digest Fund establish a $3.4 million endowment project to support the promotion of jazz activities throughout the nation. Like the Lincoln Center project, the Digest Fund would sponsor all kinds of jazz activities, including research into jazz history and publication.

If there was little support for jazz in the United States, the same could not be said about jazz in Europe. There, the great enthusiasm for both avant-garde and "neotraditionalist" American jazz led an Italian jazz fan, Giovanni Bonandrini, to establish the Black Saint Records label in Milan, Italy. Beginning in 1977 Bonandrini has been recording the full spectrum of contemporary jazz. On its roster are such black artists as Max Roach, George Lewis, John Carter, and Anthony Braxton, and groups including George Russell's New York (big) Band, David Murray's Octet, and the Muhal Richard Abrams Orchestra. Another example of the support given to jazz abroad is an award established by the Danish Music Center in Copenhagen. Called The Jazzpar, the $30,000 award seeks to recognize great talent and encourage its further development. The first two awards went to African Americans, pianist Muhal Richard Abrams (1989) and saxophonist David Murray (1990).

"CLASSICAL" COMPOSERS AND IMPROVISERS

With a few exceptions, the eminent black composers of the mid-century years continued to contribute in the 1980s and '90s to a cadre of concert music that can be classified as African-American. This genre is not to be equated solely with jazz or spirituals or other black-music genres and styles, although it may include elements of any or all of these styles. Most black classical composers were practicing jazz musicians at some point in their careers and found it natural to utilize their experience with jazz when writing, say, programmatic music, just as they might employ some jazz techniques when writing avant-garde music. Composer Alvin Singleton explains:

> From the point of view of the composer, we draw upon it [black music], whether consciously or subconsciously, because it works musically. You don't sit there and say "this is black"—you simply draw upon it because it works for you at that particular moment. Drawing upon these experiences is what makes your work or that particular piece unique, and it becomes part of the organization of the material that goes into making a new piece.[9]

Though publishing less than they had in earlier times, the concert composers produced a wider variety of music during the last decades of the century than previously, primarily because of commissions they received to

[9] Alvin Singleton, "Programming African-American Music," *Chorus* (May 1991).

write pieces for recitalists and performance groups and to compose music for special occasions and special projects. Frequently, for example, they wrote music to be performed at the many festivals promoted by the black community, such as the Atlanta Black National Arts Festival or for the commemoration of special events, such as the nationwide centennial observance in 1995 of the birth of composer William Grant Still.

To the lay listener the avant-garde music of the classical composers was sometimes barely distinguishable from the free jazz of the jazz composers. While the former used serial techniques and other art-music procedures and forms, they also brought black-music elements into their composition. The free-jazz improvisers, meanwhile, drew upon classical elements at will, blending them with their natural repertory of jazz and other black-music elements. Both groups of composers revealed a penchant for including sections of improvised and notated (or arranged) music within the same work. The players appreciated the importance of the delicate relationship between the ensemble, playing arranged or notated music, and the improvising soloist, who plays both *with* the ensemble and *against* it. Wynton Marsalis, among others, commented upon this connection:

> Jazz is the primary art form. . . . When it's played properly, it shows you how the individual can negotiate the greatest amount of personal freedom and put it humbly at the service of a group conception.[10]

Composer Alvin Singleton (b. 1940), a native New Yorker, obtained degrees from New York University (B.A.) and the Yale School of Music (M. Mus.). During the years 1971–85 he lived abroad, then returned to the United States after receiving an appointment as a composer-in-residence with the Atlanta Symphony Orchestra. He has also served as artist-in-residence at Spelman College in Atlanta and as a Rockefeller Foundation grantee in its Meet-the-Composer series.

Anthony Davis (b. 1951), pianist and composer, received his music education at Yale (B.A.). He first attracted attention as a jazz pianist playing with free-jazz groups as a co-leader or sideman and in 1979 founded the octet Episteme. He was influenced by the principles of AACM and played with some of its groups, including those of Leo Smith during the years 1974–77 and Leroy Jenkins in 1977–79. Davis's musical language represents a fusion of several styles and techniques—the European classical and avant-garde, improvisation and notated music, African, non-Western, gospel, rhythm 'n' blues, and jazz.

Edward Bland (b. 1926), composer, producer, and musical director, studied at the American Conservatory of Music in Chicago. His compositions include a concerto for electric violin and chamber orchestra; *Sketches Set Seven* (for piano); and film scores for *A Raisin in the Sun* and *A Soldier's Story*.

Luther Henderson (b. 1919), arranger, composer, and orchestrator,

[10]Thomas Sancton, "Horns of Plenty," *Time* (22 October 1990): 70.

obtained his musical education at the Juilliard School of Music (B.S.) and New York University. He has produced and directed more than fifty Broadway musicals, including *Ain't Misbehavin'* and *Jelly's Last Jam.*

CONCERT ARTISTS

André Watts, now at the peak of his career, has maintained his position in the final decades of this century as one of the world's leading concert pianists, but there seem to be few young black pianists "waiting in the wings." It is not clear why so few young artists were embarking upon concert careers in the 1980s–90s. Certainly, the black community was concerned, and it stood prepared to give assistance as best it could. Moreover, there were mainstream institutions like the prestigious Naumburg Foundations and a number of lesser-known organizations, that offered awards and fellowships to talented young artists.

One such institution, the John F. Kennedy Center for the Performing Arts in Washington, D.C., sponsored the National Black Music Colloquium and Competition during the 1979–80 season as a "means of fulfilling its commitment as the National Cultural Center to expanding minority participation in the performing arts." Young people from all over the nation competed in the finals in the required categories of piano or strings after winning regional honors. Each finalist was presented in a recital at the Kennedy Center, and the two winners received additional monetary prizes. The project was a grand success, not only because of the gifted performers brought before the public, but also because the weeklong event gave exposure to the music of black composers.

Certainly, the National Commission on Blacks in the Performing Arts achieved its goals: to assist young black artists in furthering the development of their talents and to encourage the writing and performance of the music of black composers. Twenty-seven composers were represented on the programs, some by several compositions. Predictably, the black-music establishment was well represented—by T. J. Anderson, David Baker, Roque Cordero, Arthur Cunningham, and Noel DaCosta, among others— but there were also new names, many of which, regrettably, have not reappeared. The competition also showcased fourteen performers—seven pianists and seven string players—who seriously aspire to careers on the concert stage. Some, such as pianists Alison Deane and Cecil Lytle, violinist Darwyn Apple, violist Marcus Thompson, and cellist Ronald Lipscomb, were already known to concert-goers.

Alison Deane (b. 1962) earned degrees at the Manhattan School of Music (B. Mus., M. Mus.) and studied piano further with Robert Goldsand. She attracted wide attention when she won the piano competition sponsored by the National Black Music Colloquiom and Competition.

Pianist Althea Waites (b. 1939) attended Xavier University in New

Orleans (B.A.) and Yale University (M. Mus.), and studied further with Donal Currier, Russell Sherman, and Alice Shapiro. Since her 1987 debut in New York, she has toured extensively in the United States and abroad. She has been specially commended for her commitment to performing and recording the music of women composers, black and white.

Pianist Leon Edward Bates (b. 1949), was graduated from Temple University (B. Mus.) and studied further with Cristofor Sinjani, Natalie Hinderas, and Leon Fleisher. He made his debut with the Philadelphia Orchestra in 1979 and since then has concertized widely, appearing as soloist with major orchestras and presenting solo recitals.

Awadagin Pratt (b. 1966) attended the University of Illinois at Normal and the Peabody Conservatory in Baltimore, earning diplomas in conducting, violin, and piano. In 1992 he won first prize in the prestigious Walter W. Naumburg International Piano Competition, the first African American to win the piano award (in 1944 Carol Brice was the first African-American artist to win first prize in the Naumberg competition for voice). Following his 1993 debut at Alice Tully Hall in New York City, Pratt has performed in many cities throughout the United States.

Ben Holt (1955–1990) matriculated at the Oberlin Conservatory of Music and the Juilliard School of Music. He toured the nation extensively in 1983 under the auspices of the young Concert Artists International Auditions. His Metropolitan Opera debut in 1985 as Schaunard in *La bohème* was followed a year later by his New York City Opera debut in the title role of Anthony Davis's *X*.

COMMUNITY-BASED MUSIC GROUPS

While it may appear that gospel groups have taken over the nation's listening spaces, secular as well as sacred, there are still community-based groups that have maintained their individuality and, consequently, developed an appreciative following in the United States and abroad. One such group is The Boys Choir of Harlem. Founded in 1968 as a small church choir and incorporated in 1975, it is known today all over the world. The Choir sings from a repertory that ranges in style from Gregorian chant to contemporary songs, gospel, and spirituals. The group travels extensively and records prolifically, often together with music celebrities.

Founder / director Walter J. Turnbull, a graduate of Tougaloo College (B. Mus.) and the Manhattan School of Music (M. Mus., D.M.A.), has also concertized and performed operatic roles. Although Turnbull continues his recital work, he now devotes most of his time to his Boys Choir (which also includes girls-in-training).

Sweet Honey in the Rock, an all-women *a cappella* quintet, was founded in 1973 by Bernice Johnson Reagon, who has also been directing the group. The ensemble advertises itself as "a community-based political institution

The Boys Choir of Harlem. *(Courtesy Columbia Artists Management, Inc.)*

that recognizes its responsibility to preserve and perpetuate cultural struggles, and serves as a voice for the voiceless in this society." The group has won international acclaim for its challenging song material and its intense performance style. Reagon writes much of the music and many of the lyrics.

Academic-Based Groups

The longstanding practice of African-American college groups touring on the concert-hall and church circuits to raise money for their institutions continues to the present time. Some of these groups have enjoyed a measure of the success and celebrity that attended the Fisk Jubilee and Hampton Institute Singers during their concertizing in the 1870s. Among the best known in the 1990s are the Morgan State University Chorus (Baltimore, Maryland) under the direction of Nathan Carter; the Hampton Institute Choir (Hampton, Virginia), directed by Roland Carter; and the Spelman College Jazz Ensemble (Atlanta, Georgia), directed by Joseph W. Jennings.

The Black Music Repertory Ensemble, a performance arm of the Center for Black Music Research at Columbia College (Chicago), is devoted to exploring the music written for small ensemble during the past 250 years by African-American and African-European composers. The Ensemble is unique in its dedication to enlarging its repertory by searching out the published music of African-American composers that has not been performed previously or that is newly composed. Samuel A. Floyd, Jr., artistic director of the Ensemble, draws upon the talents of an active advisory board, includ-

Sweet Honey in the Rock. *(Photographer, Deborah J. Crable, 1980. Courtesy Bernice Johnson Reagon Archives)*

ing composers T. J. Anderson and Hale Smith, and guest soloists and conductors.

Here and there across the nation enterprising musicians have formed community groups chiefly for the purpose of giving aspiring young instrumentalists an opportunity to learn the standard orchestral literature. Few of these groups have attracted national attention except, perhaps, on special occasions, as when Anne Lundy and her Scott Joplin Chamber Orchestra gave a concert at Houston, Texas, in July 1989 honoring the ninetieth birthday of composer William Levi Dawson. Co-founder and musical director of the group, Lundy regularly produced concerts for the community, often including members of the Houston Symphony.

Professional Groups

Two string quartets based in New York City have won high praise from critics and enthusiastic receptions from concert-goers. The Uptown String Quartet, a women's group formed in 1980 by drummer Max Roach to work occasionally with his regular jazz quartet in a double-quartet format, includes his daughter Maxine (viola), Lesa Terry (violin), Diane Monroe (violin), and Eileen Folson (cello). Later the group became independent, but still plays with Roach's quartet on occasion. Although all four women have had classical training and all play both classical and jazz repertory, they specialize in playing music written for them by black composers and have delved into all forms of black music.

The unorthodox instrumental composition of The Black Swan Quartet—Akbar Ali, founder and violin, Eileen Folson, cello, Abdul Wadedud, cello, and Reggie Workman, double bass—gives the group a deep, rich tone quality. Ali writes most of the music, which generally follows classical rules for structure but allows ample space for extensive improvisation in jazz style. He explains his ambition to form a link between classical chamber music and jazz:

> I want to bring these two worlds into one performing hall. . . . The bass is the backbone of black music. The cello is just too light. It wouldn't have the same force; it couldn't swing.

The Bridgetower String Quartet, formed in 1973 at Boston, has toured widely throughout the nation and has spent a year concertizing in Brazil. At present, the Quartet is based in Washington, D.C.

OPERA OLD AND NEW

We have discussed the nostalgia that swept over the African-American community in the 1980s, bringing with it revivals of interest in such genres as the downhome blues, certain jazz styles, and reanimated popular-music forms. These genres had enjoyed popularity in the 1960s, and their return to public consciousness reflected the never-ending search by black composers for something new. The "old," of course, becomes the "new," under some circumstances. The interest in opera writing, for example, held by both classical and jazz composers of this period is not easily explained, although it may become clearer after the following brief survey of African-American opera in the United States.

It began with Scott Joplin, this obsession to write and produce an opera no matter what the cost, although it is doubtful that Joplin ever saw an opera. The story of Joplin's experience with his opera *Treemonisha* has been told more than twice: to summarize, its performance in 1915 was a dismal failure, and it was not until 1972 that *Treemonisha* was given the kind of reception it deserved. At least one critic, however, perceived Joplin's genius after reading a score of the opera (which Joplin had published in 1911), and asserted that Joplin "has created an entirely new phase of musical art and has produced a thoroughly American opera."

Another composer obsessed with the idea of writing operas, Harry Lawrence Freeman, wrote fourteen, none of which gained much more than local recognition, although three were produced. Clarence Cameron White's single opera, *Ouanga*, was produced in concert versions. William Grant Still's passion for opera led him to write six, of which three were staged during his lifetime. Julia Perry left four operas, of which only one was staged. Of the five operas Ulysses Kay wrote on various subjects over a span of about twenty years, the fourth, *Jubilee* (1976), had an indelible impact on the history of black-American music because of its sensitive treatment of the slavery theme.

Up to the mid–1970s, when the nation began to celebrate its bicentennial anniversary, black composers of opera drew their materials from a variety of sources, but none had dealt with the tragedy of slavery and its impact on them personally as African Americans and on American culture and history. Kay's *Jubilee,* with a libretto by Margaret Walker, was based on the true story of a slave girl in Mississippi. Commissioned by Opera / South, the opera was highly successful and offered a model for similar works in the future. In 1983, Kay came forward with another "slave" opera, this one based on the life and struggles of the fiery abolitionist *Frederick Douglass.* Produced by the New Jersey State Opera Company, the work won more critical acclaim for its composer.

Other operas by black composers that treat the subject of slavery include Dorothy Rudd Moore's *Frederick Douglass,* premiered in 1985 by Opera Ebony in New York City, and Leslie Adams's *Blake,* about a slave uprising, based on an 1859 novel *Blake: Or the Huts of America* by black activist Martin Delany.

This brief summary reflects the newly awakened interest in the past on the part of black opera composers and their willingness to tackle such controversial subjects as slavery and race relations. Certainly Anthony Davis's opera *"X"; The Life and Times of Malcolm X,* with a libretto by Thulani Davis, offers much opportunity for handling controversy. Since Malcolm X was a hero to many in the black community, the opera makes political as well as musical statements. The composer felt that the issues facing Malcolm continue to confront African Americans, and Davis took every precaution to insure that the opera be perceived as a serious undertaking that observed the conventional procedures of opera composition.

Davis's opera was first developed in a series of workshops supported by Opera Ebony and the African-American Historical and Cultural Museum in Philadelphia. In 1985 the American Music Theater Festival at Philadelphia gave the opera a first presentation; the following year the New York City Opera gave the world premiere. As the first example of an avant-garde opera written by a black composer, the opera received a great deal of attention and gave promise of stimulating other black composers to try their hand at writing operas. The musical language of the work reflects a synthesis of several styles that contrast in various ways: jazz is juxtaposed with classical, notated music with improvisation, non-Western with swing, and European avant-garde with free jazz. Davis's own octet Episteme formed the core of the orchestra.

A second contemporary opera that attracted much attention was produced in 1988 when the Munich Biennial Festival commissioned choreographer Bill T. Jones to create a stage work—specifically, a *black* "blues opera" that would deal with contemporary conflicts in a mythological context. Jones instead worked out a dance opera, *The Mother of Three Sons* (libretto by Ann T. Greene), with jazz violinist Leroy Jenkins as musical director and composer. Jones offered the conflict between man and woman, and the myths were derived from sub-Saharan folklore. In 1991, the New York City Opera Company presented its world premiere. Unconventional in several ways, the opera requires minimal musical forces—solo violin, solo alto and soprano saxophone, solo African percussion, synthesizer, and drums—and improvisation pervades the work from beginning to end. Among the other operas by black composers premiered in the 1980s–90s are Julius Hemphill's *Long Tongues: A Saxophone Opera*, Duke Ellington's *Queenie Pie*, and Tania León's *Scourge of Hyacinths*.

OPERA COMPANIES

Opera Ebony (founded in 1974), like Mary Cardwell Dawson's National Negro Opera Company (fl. 1941–62), had as its main objective the professional advancement of gifted black artists, but the company made it clear in its promotional literature that talent was welcomed "whatever its skin color or ethnic mix." Two of the founders of Opera Ebony, bass-baritone Benjamin Matthews, the artistic director, and pianist Wayne Sanders, the music director, were still guiding the company in the mid-1990s. Through the decades Opera Ebony continued to serve as a showcase for musicians aspiring to careers in opera and to create performance opportunities for beginners—singers and instrumentalists as well as managers, conductors, and technicians—in all phases of opera production. Although Opera Ebony has always focused upon the traditional repertory, special attention is given to other kinds of extended works written by black composers. Observing its tenth anniversary in 1984, for example, Opera Ebony staged "A Salute to Black Broadway," with singer / pianist Emmy Kemp, singer / composer Valerie Capers, and the John Motley Singers.

Three other Opera Ebony productions of the 1980s looked back to the past, as indeed did many of the theater works staged by African Americans during this period. *Journeyin' on the Underground Railroad* (1988), drew its materials largely from Negro spirituals and called for minimal musical forces: saxophone, piano, percussion, trap drum, and electric bass. Composer Valerie Capers took an avant-garde approach to *Sojourner*, a work she called an "operatorio," in both her musical language and her borrowings from other musical and literary genres.

BLACK SINGERS ON STAGE

There were few black singers on opera stages in New York City during the last decades of the twentieth century, which were relatively barren years, even as compared to the 1960s–70s. With Leontyne Price retired, Jessye Norman spending more and more time in European opera companies and Kathleen Battle singing away from the Metropolitan Opera, there were no African-American prima donnas immediately at hand to take their places.

Among members of a younger generation who revealed promise were Carmen Balthrop, Priscilla Baskerville, Harolyn Blackwell, Gwendolyn Bradley, Maria Ewing, Denyce Graves, Barbara Hendricks, and Florence Quivar. Black male singers who were becoming more visible included Donnie Rae Albert, Philip Creech, Mark S. Doss, Gordon Hawkins, Eugene Perry, Ben Holt, Herbert Perry, Mark Rucker, Kevin Short, and Thomas Young.

In 1994, Dominique-René de Lerma founded the Ben Holt Memorial Concert Series (based in Chicago), and now serves as its director. The stated purpose of the series, established in memory of the baritone whose untimely death cut short a brilliant career, is to present promising young black artists to the public.

Three operas associated with black folk seem destined to live forever:

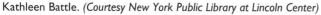

Kathleen Battle. *(Courtesy New York Public Library at Lincoln Center)*

Joplin's *Treemonisha,* Gershwin's *Porgy and Bess,* and Thomson's *Four Saints in Three Acts.* Every decade or so, there has been a revival of one or more of the three in a theater, film, or television production. In 1985, *Porgy* was taken into the repertory of the Metropolitan Opera Company, after the Houston Grand Opera had presented important revivals. Since all three operas require black casts, African-American opera singers found increased employment opportunities when revivals were mounted.

SYMPHONY ORCHESTRAS: THE CONDUCTORS

Black conductors are gaining increasing visibility on the symphony-orchestra scene, and their conducting skills suggest that even more will be heard from in the future. The aspiring conductors are well prepared: most began by performing orchestral or band music in public schools and continued their studies at the leading conservatories. Many served apprenticeships in the various ranks of conductors, and some have won conducting awards and competitions. But the numbers are deceiving; the positions made available to young black conductors are rarely those of principal conductor or music director.

Some of the older "young conductors" who have served as music directors of community, metropolitan, or regional orchestras look forward to directing larger and more prestigious orchestras. Among those who have taken the initial steps toward realizing their ambitions are Isaiah Jackson (b. 1945), director of the Dayton (Ohio) Symphony and the Queensland (Australia) Symphony, and Tania León (b. 1944), a composer who is also staff conductor at the Brooklyn Philharmonic.

Those who have appointments as assistant or associate conductors include William Henry Curry (b. 1954), with the New Orleans Philharmonic; Leslie Byron Dunner (b. 1956), with the Detroit Symphony, also serving as principal conductor of the Dance Theatre of Harlem; Harvey Felder (b. 1955), with the Tacoma (Washington) Symphony; Raymond Curtis Harvey (b. 1950), with the Fresno (California) Philharmonic; Michael DeVard Morgan (b. 1957), with the Oakland East Bay Symphony; Kay George Roberts (b. 1950), with the University Orchestra at the University of Massachusetts at Lowell; Willie Anthony Waters (b. 1951), with the Chautauqua Opera Company at Miami; Andre Raphel Smith (b. 1962), with the Philadelphia Orchestra; and Thomas Alphonso Wilkins (b. 1956), with the Florida Orchestra. All have been active on the guest-conductor circuit. Generally, young conductors are offered two- or three-year appointments, but many leave for greener pastures before the apprentice period has come to an end, particularly if the move involves a promotion to a music directorship.

Tania León in 1995. *(Photo by Marbeth)*

SYMPHONY INSTRUMENTALISTS

In the last decades of the century, black members of symphony orchestras were even less visible than black conductors, although the situation was not as bleak as in previous years. Some artists were at mid-career points in their professional lives, having performed with their (white) orchestras for ten, fifteen, or twenty years. However, few young African Americans were beginning careers in the field of symphonic music, even though some of the nation's leading orchestras were actively recruiting minorities. According to a report of the American Symphony Orchestra League, in the early 1990s black instrumentalists in the nation's symphony orchestras constituted much less than 2 percent of the total number of players. And the representation of African Americans in the audiences at symphony concerts was abysmally low. Critics noted that minorities were absent not only from the stage but also from the ranks of audiences.

SYMPHONY OF THE NEW WORLD

Over the years, black cultural activists mounted protests again and again in opposition to the racism and discrimination in the symphonic world but met with little success. Excluded then from the mainstream, they moved within the black community to organize their own symphony orchestras. Various such attempts have been noted above, including the Negro Philharmonic Society of New Orleans in 1830, the Philadelphia Concert Orchestra in 1904, and the several groups founded in places where the black community was large and supportive, such as Harlem in 1912 for James Reese Europe's Negro Symphony Orchestra and in the 1930s for Dean Dixon's symphonic groups.

In 1964 several music and community groups in New York City joined forces to take the decisive step of organizing a symphony orchestra that would be integrated by race and gender, maintain high artistic standards, and vigorously reach out to the community, enriching its cultural life while gaining—indeed requiring—its support.

Such an orchestra, named the Symphony of the New World, made its debut in May 1965 at Carnegie Hall in New York City. From the outset, the orchestra won critical respect for the high quality of its programming, and the community gave proof of its support by filling the hall for concerts. The orchestra was well integrated: of the eighty-five to ninety instrumentalists on stage for a concert, typically more than 40 percent would be members of minority groups. Finally, the orchestra gave promise of becoming a contributor to the musical development of young aspiring musicians by sponsoring performance debuts and commissioning works from the composers.

The agenda of the Symphony of the New World was shaped largely by two of its music directors, co-founder Benjamin Steinberg and conductor Everett Lee. The orchestra was not formed in order to shock or impress audiences by its being integrated. Nor was most of its repertory unusual—indeed, it was conservative by normal standards. The novel aspects related to the programming of extended works written by mainstream black composers—William Grant Still, and Howard Swanson, among others—alongside works of the European masters. True, the bop performances of jazzmen Dizzy Gillespie and Yusef Lateef might have prompted some raised eyebrows—though Duke Ellington and the Modern Jazz Quartet were welcomed as "high" classical—but no one showed any uneasiness. And the many debuts over the twelve years brought gifted young artists, such as pianists Natalie Hinderas and her concert-pianist student, Leon Bates, to the stages along with seasoned ones.

During the twelve years of its existence, from 1964 to 1976, the Symphony of the New World served as a model that other African-American groups—or white groups—could emulate. When the orchestra disappeared from the scene, the public was not given a reason for its demise, but it was generally understood that poor management was to blame.

FESTIVALS

Black musicians participated in the many music festivals held in the United States and abroad during the mid-century years, such as, for example, the Berkshire Music Festival in Massachusetts (established in 1937) and the Festival of Two Worlds at Spoleto, Italy (1958). An American branch of Spoleto was founded at Charleston, South Carolina, in 1977. As we have seen, black artists performed at jazz and folk festivals and at the prestigious opera and concert music festivals, such as the Glyndebourne, Salzburg, and Bayreuth.

FESTAC in Nigeria

Twice musicians and scholars went to Africa to participate in festivals: the first time to the First World Festival of Negro Arts in Dakar, Senegal, in 1966; then to the Second World Black and African Festival of Arts and Culture (called FESTAC) in Lagos, Nigeria, January 15–February 12, 1977. Some forty-eight nations were represented by more than 17,000 musicians, dancers, and artists; 60,000 spectators crowded into the national stadium to watch the activities on the opening and closing days. A Nigerian musician, Bayo Martins, was heard speaking to a friend:

> For the first time, it dawned on me that all black people have one thing in common, a culture and a heritage. I believe in the spirit of FESTAC, the need for black people to get together and rekindle their consciousness and confidence.[11]

Celebration at Lincoln Center

The year 1977 was also a lively one for black artists of the concert world in the United States: from August 29 to September 2 the Celebration of Black Composers took place at Lincoln Center under the sponsorship of the New York Philharmonic Orchestra, with two black guest conductors, Leon Thompson and Paul Freeman. The major black composers of the time were represented by their chamber music, art songs, choral works, piano pieces,

---

[11]Bayo Martins; quoted in the *New York Times* (February 13, 1977).

Blues Singer at a Folk Festival. *(Photo by Rick Stafford. Courtesy of the author)*

electronic music, and orchestral works, including several premieres. These established musicians heard their music played by gifted performers and conducted by established conductors, although the press severely criticized the Philharmonic and its members for the sloppy and generally mediocre quality of the performances. Nevertheless, New Yorkers filled the concert halls to hear a wide variety of music written and performed by black artists. One afternoon was devoted to a workshop, "The Afro-American Influence in Music," which included participants such as music critic Raoul Abdul, composers Undine Smith Moore and Roque Cordero, and jazz composer / saxophonist "Budd" Johnson.

Despite its shortcomings, the Celebration of Black Composers marked a milestone in the history of African-American music: for the first time, a principal American orchestra had presented a music festival wholly devoted to music written by black composers and performed by black artists.

A Symposium in Michigan

The Black American Music Symposium was held at the University of Michigan School of Music, August 9–15, 1985. For a week, from 9:00 A.M. to as late as 11:00 P.M., musicians from across the nation listened to music, exchanged ideas in symposia, participated in workshops as teacher or student, and greeted old friends at gala luncheons and banquets. Every genre of black music was represented, from the nineteenth-century Negro spiritual to contemporary electronic works, and in a variety of forms, such as jazz anthems, symphonic works, chamber music, and gospel. For orchestral music, the symposium drew upon the services of the Detroit Symphony Orchestra.

The Symposium marked the first time that the younger generations had met together with the "elders," such as nonagenarians Eva Jessye and Jester Hairston. For the young people—many preparing for their debut concerts or putting the last touches on their dissertations—meeting their musical ancestors was inspiring. The Symposium also marked the first time that the jazz, gospel, and classical music of black musicians had been given equal time on the concert stage. Finally, it represented the first time that black musicians of all types—composers, concert artists, academicians, folk artists, and community groups—had an opportunity to meet each other and discuss issues of common interest. The driving force behind the Symposium, Willis Patterson, Associate Dean at the University of Michigan's School of Music, obtained the cooperation of many leading black musicians to insure the success of the Festival.

The Atlanta Festivals

It appeared that African Americans were indeed becoming more conscious of their shared culture, judging by the occasions they found for meeting in large numbers. Atlanta, Georgia, was the site of numerous prestigious gatherings of African-American artists. The Inaugural Black Arts Festival 1988 offered a showcase for black artists in eight major disciplines: music, dance, theater, film, visual arts, performance arts, literature, and folk art. The Atlanta Jazz Festival was held during the same period. More than 500,000 persons attended the 124 events that were offered during the ten-day period.

Composer Alvin Singleton observed in 1988 that Atlanta's National Black Arts Festival offered no concert music of black composers, and proposed to the Festival's executive director that the 1990 Festival include a series of chamber music concerts in its ten-day program. Singleton and an appointed committee examined more than sixty scores, from which fourteen were selected for performance in a three-concert series titled Music Alive 1990! Not surprisingly, the eleven musicians whose works were chosen for performance included some of the nation's foremost black composers representing a span of three generations, from "Young Lions" like David Sorley (b. 1962) to mid-career composers like Wendell Logan (b. 1940) to the "elders" Hale Smith (b. 1925) and T. J. Anderson (b. 1928). And their works represented a wide variety of styles and genres. Those entering their peak-career years included John E. Price, David Baker, Tania León, Noel DaCosta, Adolphus Hailstock, Alvin Singleton, Jalalu-Kalvert Nelson, Dwight Andrews, and Olly Wilson. The performers were established musicians, some of them well known for their association with jazz groups, for example, trumpeter Leo Smith and violinist Leroy Jenkins. The works reflected the composers' predilection for fusing African-American elements with those of European, African, and Caribbean music, and the importance given to instrumental color as, for example, in Sorley's *Linea* for solo viola and electronic tape.

The producers of the Atlanta festivals developed a theme for each alternate year: in 1994 the National Black Arts Festival offered ten days of "exhibitions, symposia, concerts, and theater . . . in an exploration and celebration of traditional and contemporary life on the continent and throughout the African Diaspora." At every turn, visitors and participants were admonished to "celebrate Africa."

Summer Festivals

By the late 1950s, the concept of a jazz festival was well established throughout the United States and the Newport Jazz festival (first held in Rhode Island and later based in New York City) was flourishing. From the beginning, African Americans were lively contributors and participants, not only in jazz, but also in gospel, blues, pop, and stage music. The sponsorship of the Newport Festival changed from time to time, and in some years black jazz people rebelled against official procedures and held their own festivals in large cities, including Chicago, Washington, D.C., Atlanta, and Los Angeles.

In addition to performing at mainstream festivals at home and touring abroad on the festival circuits, African Americans also organized their own festivals. In Texas, for example, there was Juneteenth or Emancipation Day, which commemorates June 19, 1865, the day Texas slaves finally were freed—two and a half years after President Lincoln issued the Emancipation Proclamation.

The Cincinnati Festival

Another festive event is the Annual American Negro Spiritual Festival (based in Cincinnati), founded in 1982 with the aim of reminding students at historically black colleges of their rich musical heritage of Negro spirituals. Student choirs learn the required repertory and the three regional winners are brought to Cincinnati to compete in the finals. The two-day festival includes a symposium on the spiritual and concludes with a concert of spirituals by the combined choruses.

Carnegie Hall Concerts

Festivals were not the only kinds of events that occasioned large gatherings of black musicians. People decended on New York City, for example, from all parts of the land to pay homage to Howard Swanson at an all-Swanson concert held at Alice Tully Hall in celebration of the composer's seventieth birthday. Also, the black music establishment honored composer / educator Undine Smith Moore with a concert of her music at Carnegie Hall in 1988. Then there were the periodic concerts titled The Art of the Spiritual, which were presented at Carnegie Hall by Today's Artists Concerts, an organization based in San Francisco.

Among black artists as among white, New York City was favored for a debut recital or concert; Merkin Concert Hall or Carnegie Recital Hall for the small ones, Alice Tully Hall for chamber music, and Avery Fisher Hall or Carnegie Hall for the big recitals. A black artist, or group, who could fill one of the large halls enjoyed great prestige among friends and the public.

Carnegie Hall holds special memories for African Americans because of its important role in the history of black music, and as early as the 1960s, music promoters, impresarios, and community groups began looking to the past with a view of recreating some of its landmark events. Black concert music first filled the hallowed Carnegie Hall on May 2, 1912, when the Music School Settlement for Colored People presented a Concert of Negro Music. Included among the performers were the most celebrated of the race at that time: the Clef Club Orchestra (also referred to by the press as the Negro Symphony Orchestra) with James Reese Europe, conductor, and William H. Tyers, assistant conductor; the Clef Club Male Chorus, Will Marion Cook, leader; St. Philip's Church Choir, Paul C. Bohlen, organist; the Royal Poinciana Quartette; and the Versatile Entertainers Quintette. The concert included J. Rosamond Johnson as pianist and Elizabeth Payne as contralto soloist.

White New Yorkers hardly knew how to respond to the exotic sounds they heard, particularly the syncopation, but they were impressed, and that encouraged black musicians to continue their concert activities. For four consecutive years, 1912–15, an overflow audience filled Carnegie Hall each spring to hear black musicians perform both the classics and their own "syncopated" music. All four concerts were promoted by the Music School Settlement for Colored People, with James Reese Europe serving as chief conductor of the orchestra for the four concerts; in 1915, J. Rosamond Johnson was musical director for the 1915 performances.

In July 1989, Maurice Peress, a white conductor and musical director, presented to the public his Landmark Jazz Concerts series at Carnegie Hall, reconstructing two concerts of black music that had taken place there in the past. Peress's first historic reenactment was the James Reese Europe concert discussed above. Among the performers were William Warfield, Barbara Conrad, pianist Leon Bates, the Harlem Boys Choir, directed by Walter Turnbull. Next Peress recreated a concert by Duke Ellington and His Orchestra, originally performed on January 23, 1943. The program, titled *Black, Brown and Beige to Mood Indigo: An Evening of Duke Ellington,* featured guest artists Jimmy Hamilton and Milt Hinton. It was at this concert that Ellington had made his debut as a composer of "extended works" with his *Black, Brown and Beige: A Tone Parallel to the History of the Negro in*

America. In all, Ellington presented seven Carnegie Hall concerts of his own music between 1943 and 1950.

Another historic concert at Carnegie Hall, staged by W. C. Handy on April 27, 1928, was recreated in 1981 under the auspices of the Hall and impresario George Wein. It was Handy's ambition in 1928 to give an historic survey of African-American music in all its many forms, from spirituals and blues to jazz and light classics. He formed an orchestra, organized a sixty-voice chorus, and recruited the finest talent he could find to sing his songs. One of the high points of the original event was Fats Waller's premiere performance of James P. Johnson's piano rhapsody *Yamekraw.* A high point of the 1981 revival was hearing the blues sung by Handy's daughter, Katherine Handy Lewis, as she had sung forty-seven years earlier.

Another historical survey of African American music, conceived and staged at Carnegie Hall by music producer and critic John Hammond at two concerts in 1938 and 1939, began with a recording of African tribal music. The program ended with a rousing performance of swing by Count Basie and His Orchestra. In January 1967, Hammond repeated the second of these concerts at Carnegie Hall.

CABARET DIVAS

Cabaret music took its place in the black community as a special style of popular music and jazz in the early twentieth century. And though it received little public attention through the years, its performers developed their skills and carved out rewarding if not lucrative careers for themselves. Overwhelmingly female, the pianist-vocalists found employment in nightclubs, dance halls, hotel lounges and cafés, and even in the proverbial "holes in the wall." To their patrons the nightclubs offered intimate surroundings, food and / or drinks, and entertainment. The entertainers often were chic, elegant personalities who offered jazz storytelling of a quality that held listeners spellbound, but their numbers also included the nameless, downhome singers whose blues and folk ballads helped alleviate the loneliness of the black migrants who moved into the inner cities after World War II.

The memory of the early African-American cabaret scene in New York City has been perpetuated in watercolors by the American painter Charles Demuth. Dating from 1915–17, the paintings show patrons sitting at small tables in Harlem's basement clubrooms of Marshall's Hotel or Barron Wilkins's Cafe, entertained by a three-piece "jazz" ensemble composed of piano, banjo, and drums. One of the pictures, "Negro Girl Dancer" (1915), depicts a woman dancing to the music with a brooding expression on her face.[12] Another, "Negro Jazz Band" (1916), shows a woman singing the ballad "Bill Bailey" with great passion.

---

[12]A reproduction of a Demuth nightclub scene is published in Alvord Eiseman, "Negro Girl Dancer," dated 1915, *Charles Demuth* (New York, 1982), pl. 6.

The cabaret entertainers of the late twentieth century shared many experiences in common. As children, they had typically studied piano, started professional careers while still in their teens, and studied classical music at Fisk University, Howard University, the Juilliard School of Music, and the Oberlin Conservatory of Music, or a similar institution. Several left music for long periods of time to pursue other careers, such as teaching school or nursing, then returned to performing after a lapse of decades. In their early careers they toured with important bands, such as those of Benny Carter, Count Basie, Teddy Wilson, Mercer Ellington, and Fats Waller. The women were encouraged by jazzmen to pursue careers in jazz. Most toured in Europe on the nightclub circuit, as soloists or with bands, and several operated their own nightclubs, in Paris, Rome, and London. Finally, they all recorded regularly, though not prolifically.

Beginning in the 1920s, Lillian "Lil" Hardin Armstrong (1898–1971), Revella Hughes (1895–1987), Mabel Mercer (1900–1984), and Ada "Bricktop" Smith (1895–1984) were among the first women to win wide critical approval for their jazz skills—Hardin, especially, as the pianist in King Oliver's band and as leader of male groups and her own bands. The other women also led small jazz ensembles from time to time, and all four were highly rated as cabaret artists.

The somewhat younger women who began their careers during the 1930s and '40s came under the influence of the celebrated male big-band leaders, from whom they received the encouragement and mentoring that enabled them to move with ease from traditional jazz into swing and bebop. The icons were Billie Holiday, Ella Fitzgerald, and, later, Sarah Vaughan: these three women became celebrities early on and, despite their youth, were widely emulated, especially in the way they used their voices and projected the lyrics of the songs they sang. Best known of this generation were Una Mae Carlisle (1915–1956), Pearl Bailey (1918–1990), Lena Horne (b. 1917), Sylvia Symns (1917–1992), Adelaide Hall (1910–1993), Carmen McRae (1920–1994), Hazel Scott (1920–1981), Cleo Laine (1920–1994), and Helen Humes (1912–1981). All worked in nightclubs over several decades, attracting but little notice by the mainstream public except when their career paths took unusual turns, as when Bailey went on Broadway to star in *Hello, Dolly;* or Lena Horne took her show, *The Lady and Her Music,* to Broadway at the age of sixty-five; or Adelaide Hall achieved success with her cabaret in London; or when European café society in Paris and Rome made Bricktop's clubs the gathering places of royalty and pseudo-royalty.

The artists drew upon a standard repertory of cabaret ballads, theater songs, and other tunes—Cole Porter, the Gershwins, and Noel Coward were favorite songwriters—though each singer had her special flair in delivery. Popular among audiences were such sultry ballads as *Body and Soul, As Time Goes By, I Can't Give You Anything but Love, Miss Otis Regrets, Mean to Me, Walkin' by the River, Do It Again,* and *I Loves You, Porgy.*

The early club vocalists accompanied themselves, and several took as much pride in their piano artistry and virtuosity as in their vocal gifts. Scott and Hughes, particularly, were noted for the way they "jazzed the classics." In recent decades, the accompaniment was more likely provided by a double bass and drums, sometimes joined by a piano.

Obituaries for the cabaret divas appeared with increasing frequency during the 1980s and '90s, their careers having spanned the history of jazz. Notices of their deaths evoked considerable nostalgia in the music community, particularly in the café-society set, for the romantic ballads of the past. There were few young divas standing by, ready to replace the older women. Some of these women had begun their careers in nightclubs such as Harlem's Cotton Club; some, in Sissle and Blake Broadway musicals; and at least one toured with *La Revue Nègre* in 1924 when that production made Josephine Baker a star in Paris. A few cabaret artists whose performance reflects the influence of modern, if not contemporary jazz, carried on the tradition: Dorothy Donegan (b. 1926), Shirley Horn (1934–1994), Abbey Lincoln (b. 1930), Shirley Scott (b. 1934, who was inspired by jazz organist Jimmy Smith to specialize on the electronic organ), and Nina Simone (b. 1933).

One male, Robert "Bobby" Short (b. 1926), stands at the peak of the cabaret-music tradition with a lifetime of singing sophisticated, nostalgic, theater songs in a cabaret setting. Self-taught on the piano, he perfected the singing of the "story songs" written by Cole Porter, Noel Coward, Duke Ellington, the Gershwins, and Jerome Kern, among others.

RESOURCES OF THE PAST

Ragtime

Although the great revival of the 1980s swept along all styles of black music in its wake, both the recent and the not so recent, black musicians gave their primary attention to the "old fashioned" music of the 1960s and '70s. We have noted the ragtime revival, which occasioned the release of the album *The Eighty-Six Years of Eubie Blake* in 1969; the world premiere of Scott Joplin's *Treemonisha* in 1972; a movie, *The Sting,* which featured the Joplin rag *The Entertainer,* on its soundtrack; and ragtime lectures, concerts, and recordings.

Blues Revivals

Since the heyday of the "country blues" singers in the late 1920s and '30s, there have been two blues revivals, in the 1960s and in the 1980s. Two bluesmen, legendary guitarist Robert Johnson (ca. 1912–1938) and bassist Willie Dixon 1915–1992), sparked the later revivals. Johnson's popularity emerged when his recordings, including *Hell Hound on My Trail* and *I Believe I'll Dust My Broom,* were "discovered" by enthusiastic fans and then by the music industry, which withdrew them from archives and reissued them as CDs.

Dixon has been called the Architect of the Chicago Sound. As arranger and songwriter for the major Chicago blues people of his time, he infused the old downhome blues they were singing with elements of pop, jazz, spirituals, and gospel, producing a new sound that found new urban audiences. For established blues singers, such as Buddy Guy, John Lee Hooker, and B. B. King, the revival has meant more engagements in the clubs and at festivals, and more lucrative record contracts. For the newcomers, such as Kenny Neal, Walter "Wolfman" Washington, and Artie Moore, the popularity of the blues has meant survival in a demanding profession.

The revival also focused attention on another source of talented, though obscure, blues singers—the Mississippi Delta. Small, independent companies, such as Rooster Blues Records and Fat Possum Records (both founded in 1990), scoured the land, making recordings in the field and in the process uncovering new talent and rediscovering the forgotten seasoned artists.

Popular Music

Like jazz singers, many singers of popular music experienced slow periods during the 1970s, but most of the artists made successful comebacks in the eighties. Also, as in jazz, the older singers met with ever-increasing competition from younger ones—Paula Abdul, Anita Baker, Toni Braxton, Mariah Carey, Natalie Cole, Whitney Houston, and Janet Jackson, to name a few. Nevertheless, most of the older singers held their own. Aretha Franklin could announce confidently on her recording *Through the Storm* (1989), "I'm the Queen of Soul," and no one could contradict her. Tina Turner, another artist who made a comeback in the eighties—this time as a soloist—demonstrated her importance as a soul singer on such recordings as *What's Love Got to Do With It* and *Private Dancer.*

Prince Rogers Nelson moved into the nineties without a break in his continuing productivity. In September 1994 he surprised his fans with the announcement that he would no longer perform music dating from the period when he was called Prince (1958–93). The critics found his new name to be an unpronounceable glyph. His album *Come* (1994) was described as including "experimental and open-ended" music, but *The Gold Experience* (1995) was vintage Prince with the lyrics as explicit as ever. He continues to play personally all the instruments on his recordings except the horns.

Michael Jackson maintained his domination of the entertainment field as The Greatest Entertainer of All Time, not only because of the phenomenal sales of his records in the multi-millions and the immense sizes of his audiences, but also because he succeeded so well in a new form of television performance, the music video. Through the 1980s and into the 1990s, Jackson made important innovations, such as a new dance-music style in *Thril-*

ler (1982) that blends rock, disco, and bop. He returned with another new dance style in *Dangerous* (1992), which uses New Jack Swing, a style developed by composer-producer Teddy Riley that blends rap with rhythm 'n' blues.

The big pop-music winner in the 1980s was the old-fashioned love song, and Luther Vandross (b. 1951), called the Voice of His Generation, could also be dubbed the King of Love, based on the subject of several of his big hits, including *Never Too Much* (1981), *Hear and Now* (1990), and *Power of Love* (1991). A singer in the tradition of Nat King Cole and Johnny Mathis, he professed to have been inspired and influenced by women, particularly "soul divas" Dionne Warwick, Gladys Knight, and Patti LaBelle. Contemporaneous male "soul crooners" included James Ingram, Lionel Richie, Peabo Bryson, Freddie Jackson, and Marvin Gaye (1939–1984). Like several singers and songwriters of his generation, Vandross also worked as an arranger and producer.

Groups as well as individuals found ready audiences for their love songs; to name a few, the male quartet Boyz II Men, the Neville Brothers, and from the 1970s, the Pointer Sisters (Anita, June, and Ruth), still concertizing in the late 1990s. One journalist described the trio as having "a sound that is, by turns, exuberant, joyful, sultry, powerful, and unforgettable. . . . [They] jazz, they pop, they scat, they R & B, they rock, and they fly."[13] Another of the multi-talented performers who emerged during this period was Bobby (Robert) McFerrin, Jr. who attracted wide attention for his talent in reproducing instrumental-music sounds with his voice and other parts of his body; using only his voice, he performed cello sonatas with the concert cellist Yo-Yo Ma.

The New Pop Music: Rap

The new pop music of this period reflects the influence of several genres and styles that have effected significant changes in the sound of the music. This new music was the direct heir of R & B, soul, and funk, but its sound was altered and enriched by the use of advanced synthesizer technology and the absorption of unconventional musical and literary elements.

A Bronx (New York) disc jockey, Afrika Bambaataa, is credited with being one of the pivotal forces in the development of the music that early picked up the label of "rap." Bambaataa, an ex-gang member and self-taught student of black culture as well as the philosophy of Malcolm X and other black nationalist leaders, came to believe that the arts could be used to combat the rampant street violence of the youth gangs in his community (which included the Bronx River Project).

In 1973 he founded the Youth Organization at Adlai Stevenson High School (later renamed the Zulu Nation), which brought together large num-

[13] "The Pointer Sisters Still Going Strong," *Big Red News,* August 1, 1992.

bers of teenagers and young adults who shared his interest in the street arts. The artistic expression of youngsters in Bambaataa's groups prepared the way for the inner-city youth art movement of the 1970s, whose activities included break dancing, disc jockeying, rapping, and graffiti drawing. Practicing their arts wherever they could—at private basement parties, on street corners, in school playgrounds, in public parks, and at community centers— the street artists developed their skills to a high level under the tutelage of the "masters." Bambaataa pointed out, "I had them to battle against each other in a nonviolent way, like rapper against rapper rather than knife against knife." He may well have been the first person to apply the term "hip-hop" to the South Bronx street culture he helped bring about: he had heard a rapper at a Bronx party chanting:

"Hip-hop, you don't stop / that makes your body rock" and starting using the term himself. "Then," he said, "It caught on."[14]

By the mid-1970s, youths in black communities across the nation were "partying" to this new kind of dance music, having rejected disco as growing increasingly dull and impersonal. Challenged by the teenagers to produce something exciting to dance to and "hang out by," the local disc jockeys (DJs, or deejays) began using two turntables at the same time so that with the assistance of a sound mixer, they could lift fragments or passages of music from one record and insert them into another. To this mix they added a pre-recorded rhythm track, taken from the original record or another one; then, as the record was spinning, the disc jockey recited improvised verses over the sound of the music. This "sampling" and mixing became essential features of the disc jockey's performance, as did the technique known as "scratching" permitting the disc jockey to exploit a wide variety of sounds.

In 1975 the young Jamaican Clive Campbell began his disc-jockeying career in the South Bronx area of New York City under the name Kool D J Herc. He introduced some of the practices that contributed to the development of rap as a bona fide music genre.

> [Herc] would pick the most recognizable part of a hit or a soul classic and play it over and over again, integrating pieces of others songs while rhyming over them. . . . [He] became notorious for incorporating the most obscure records into his mixes. Anything was fair game for inclusion in a mix: a James Brown scream, a Wilson Pickett grunt, a funky bass line, a guitar riff, and even tidbits of jingles and theme songs from popular TV shows and movies. Soon partygoers were showing up at halls and clubs just to check out what the deejays were "dropping" on the mic and the turntable.[15]

[14]K. Maurice Jones, *The Story of Rap Music* (CT, 1995), p. 46. Let me express here my deep appreciation to the several rap enthusiasts who generously shared with me their personal rap experience, either via interview or unpublished paper, among them, Cheryl L. Keyes ("Rap Music and Its African Nexus," 1995) and April Reilly ("A History for Rap," 1996).

[15]Jones, *Story,* p. 46.

It soon became obvious that this dance music called for two kinds of skills: the deejay would have to concentrate on mixing the music and spinning the records, while the MC (Master of Ceremonies) or emcee, usually a young man, gave his attention to improvising rhymes over the music, or "rapping."

The popularity of rap swiftly spread through black inner-city neighborhoods, particularly in New York and Los Angeles, where teenagers could listen to the latest records and purchase inexpensive, homemade cassettes from local DJ's. As the genre was developing, so was its own distinctive hip-hop culture, which included a language that served to prevent outsiders from becoming insiders too easily and dress codes to further set members of the group apart from society at large. Great concern was taken for the images presented to the public. When the mainstream music industry became aware of the new music, it was moved into the recording studio, where professionals developed it into a commercial success.

Of the several professional musicians who influenced the evolution of rap through their inventiveness and performance practice, the strongest inspirations came from James Brown, Godfather of Soul; George Clinton, master of funk; Teddy Riley, who invented the music style called New Jack Swing, and others, including Larry Graham, Gil Scott Heron, Curtis Mayfield, and Sly Stone.

There have, of course, been milestones in the short history of this new genre. In 1979 Sugar Hill Records, a small, black, New York label, released the first rap single, "Rapper's Delight," which quickly sold over 500,000 copies. Rap clearly was destined for success—particularly as dance music.

By 1982 rap groups were touring widely, both at home and in Europe, to critical and public acclaim. The first crew abroad included deejays Afrika Bambaataa and Fab 5. In the United States, rap began for the first time to attract the wide attention of the pop music world, primarily because of its subject matter. No longer was it simply "party" music; it had taken on the character of a political movement that embraced themes of black nationalism. The first album to feature a "theme," *The Message* (1982), performed by the Bronx crew Grandmaster Flash and the Furious Five, gave a harsh and graphic picture of life in the nation's black slums.

The leading group of the 1980s was Run-D.M.C. (rappers Joseph Simmons and Darryl McDaniels and deejay Jason Mizell). Their first single, *It's Like That* (1983), pushed them into the ranks of celebrities—they were the first rappers to perform on American Bandstand and MTV—and they were still to be counted among the leading groups ten years later (although they had experienced some low periods in the interim). In 1987, an equally famous crew, Public Enemy, released its debut album, *Yo, Bum, Rush the Show* (the group's name was taken from a James Brown song). Public Enemy's ambition was to revive the black power movement, this time with its roots in hip-hop culture. In 1988, rap's first superstar, M. C. Hammer (Stanley Kirk Burrell), came on the scene, and his very first album, *Let's Get It Started,* sold more than a million copies.

Although rappers have generally had brief careers, a sizable number have made a big splash with a best-selling debut album and then disappeared, some to reappear years later with best sellers. In addition to the posses named above, other individuals and groups who have achieved prominence are Public Enemy's Chuck D. (Charles Riddenhour), Flavor-Flav (William Drayton), Terminator (Norman Rogers), De La Soul (rappers Maseo, Posdnuos, and Trugoy the Dove), Ice-T (Tracy Morrow), rapper and producer Dr. Dre, Ice Cube (O'Shea Jackson), Snoop Doggy Dogg (Calvin Broadus), and L L Cool J (James Todd Smith), whose name stands for "Ladies Love Cool James." Fresh Prince (Will Smith) became a celebrity through a television sitcom, "The Fresh Prince of Bel-Air," and a Broadway comedy.

Some women crews have developed loyal fans—although in smaller numbers than the men—among them Queen Latifah (Dana Owens), who stars in the television sitcom "Living Single," Salt 'N' Pepa (Cheryl James and Sandi Denton), and Sister Souljah (Lisa Williamson). Two popular white crews were Vanilla Ice and the Beastie Boys, whose debut album *Licensed to Ill* (1986) was a multi-million-dollar best seller.

Not surprisingly, the popularity of rap soon drew it from its original arena into the black community at large, and then into mainstream pop music. Originally a music for "break dancing," it was to be heard in the background of films such as *Flashdance, Breakdance,* and *Beat Street;* centering on the black community, such as Spike Lee's *Do the Right Thing* and John Singleton's *Boyz N the Hood,* in videos, and, of course, in the recording studio, on the concert stage, and even in the gospel church.

By the mid-1980s, rap had become fragmented into subsets that reflected the social class of the rappers. Los Angeles rappers, living in the inner city, were perceived as being uneducated but streetwise, and as being obsessed with violence, drugs, sex, gangs, and guns. Their rap acquired the label "gansta rap" (for gangster rap). Some New York rappers, high-school graduates and college students living in middle-class neighborhoods, were called "black Bohemians" because of their interest in the classics, the arts, poetry, and the sciences, and because genuine poets were among their number.

By 1990, rap had become far more musically complex than it had been in its early days, and it continued to evolve. One music critic observed:

> Layer after layer of sounds are placed on top of each other until the music becomes nearly tactile, with whisperings and murmurings placed carefully in the background while choruses sampled from other records act as riffs, and guitar noises repeated over and over again like an unattended machine gone beserk. It's the sound of urban alienation, where silence doesn't exist and sensory stimulation is oppressive and predatory. But Public Enemy has conquered it. . . .

> Through the mess comes the redemptive beat; the group makes some of the best dance records around. And in the mist of the sonic jungle, there's order. As if trying to complete a history of sound, the tracks have elements lifted from Public Enemy's own earlier songs, reminding listeners that the group itself is not only part of a tradition but has a history of its own.[16]

Like other African-American popular-music genres, rap was continually subjected to experimentation, most frequently by deejays who introduced foreign elements into the rap mix. The 1990 debut album of A Tribe Called Quest, entitled *People's Instinctive Travels and the Paths of Rhythm,* may have been the first to blend jazz elements with original rap. A year later, Tribe made rap history by becoming the first posse to collaborate on an album *(Low End Theory)* with a live musician, bassist Ron Carter. The practice of mixing rap with live jazz performance became common in the ensuing years.

Some crews displayed their interest in black-music history as a source of musical material by quoting from or alluding to such "elders" as Curtis Mayfield or Richard Pryor. One group, Digable Planets, attracted wide attention in 1994 with their album *Reachin' (A New Refutation of Time and Space)* and their interest in researching black-music history. Digable's two male rappers, Butterfly (Ishmael Butler) and Doodle Bug (Craig Irving), and one female rapper, Lady Bug (Mary Ann Vieira), performed with the backup of a live jazz quintet, consisting of trumpet, saxophone, guitar, drums, and bass fiddle.

The origins of rap can be traced to any number of sources, of which only a few need be cited here. First, there is a longstanding tradition in the black community of using language creatively in everyday life. "Pattin' juba," for example, which dates from the early nineteenth century, was often a two-person operation: the patter provided dance music and a second person accompanied him, or her, reciting verses that were made up on the spur of the moment. Then there is the modern ritual called "playing the dozens," which sets two males at each other's throats in exchanging clever insults via verses they improvise as the game proceeds. Influences from abroad on the development of rap include the "toasting" rites, a blend of rap and reggae, which were brought to the United States by Jamaican disc jockeys, and the practices of some rhythm 'n' blues singers of reciting lyrics while backed up only by a rhythm track.

> Rap's emphasis on rhythm rather than melody makes it easy to export. . . . It is catchy, visceral, danceable. Where pop songs offer solace from an increasingly perplexing world, rap engages it. Its beats are upfront and impolite, not content to be mere background music. Rap embraces chaos as art: complex drumbeats stagger and stutter, punctuated by dissonant samples using everything from

[16]Peter Watrous, "Public Enemy Makes Waves—and Compelling Music," *New York Times* (1993)

James Brown to obscure jazz to television commercials, the mix held together by a steady stream of intricate wordplay.[17]

As the black music world moved toward the twenty-first century, rap seemed likely to become its new pop music. Rap has become popular around the world, especially as protest music. As more than one critic has observed, rap possesses essential components that appeal across gender lines to all ages and ethnic groups.

To summarize the last quarter of the twentieth century, we may note that black musicians in all genres paid homage to the past even as they were forging new paths into a future of experimentation. In 1989, for example, Quincy Jones erected an appropriate milestone for the history of African-American music. Producer, songwriter, and arranger of such albums as Michael Jackson's *Thriller* (the best-selling album of all time) and his own *We Are the World,* Jones took his listeners back to the old inner-city neighborhood with his album *Back On The Block.* Described as a "lavish collage" of black-music styles, the album purports to tell the history of the music over a period of the last four decades.

Jones drew upon almost every known black-music style and genre, from a Zulu chant to the big band. Several of the album cuts begin with rap introductions that segue into jazz or other musics. There are speakers as well as musicians, including the Reverend Jesse Jackson.

To perform the music, Jones called upon many preeminent artists of the time, among them Ella Fitzgerald, Sarah Vaughan, Miles Davis, Dizzy Gillespie, Ray Charles, and Bobby McFerrin. The performance groups include the Andrae Crouch Singers (gospel), Take 6 (the harmonizing quartet), and rappers Big Daddy Kane, Melle Mel, Kool Moe Dee, and Ice-T.

WOMEN IN BLACK CHURCH MUSIC

Though rarely discussed in the literature, black women composers of church music have played an important role in the development of the genre ever since the first independent black churches in the United States were founded in the 1790s. The earliest reference to a black woman church organist dates from 1828, when the press noted that the St. Thomas Episcopal Church in Philadelphia had purchased an organ, and nineteen-year-old Ann Appo (1809–28) was appointed organist. Similar references are scattered throughout the historical record; for example, Susan Paul presented sacred music concerts with her juvenile choral groups during the 1830s at Boston's Belknap Church, and several of the black hymnals published for folk churches after Emancipation include hymns attributed to women.

[17]James Bernard, "A Newcomer Abroad, Rap Speaks Up," *New York Times* (August 23, 1992), p. 2.

While a few women attracted attention because of their great achievement in the field of church music—Eva Jessye, for example, as a choral conductor and composer of religious music, and Lucie Campbell as a composer of gospel songs—hundreds of black women, largely forgotten today, carried full responsibility for the music of their churches. Among those we know about are Loretta Manggrum (1896–1992), Evelyn Pittman (1910–1994?), Lena McLin (b. 1929), and Betty Jackson King (1928–1994).[18] These four women all graduated from college, and some pursued graduate studies; they all taught in the public schools, where they also had charge of music groups; and they all composed a large quantity of sacred music in both small and extended forms while also writing secular music. Two of the women published textbooks that related to their experiences as educators, and three of the women composed in the larger forms—oratorio and cantata. They were generally conservative in their approach to composition, relying heavily upon the use of Negro folksong elements, particularly in making spiritual arrangements for solo or choral forces. Beginning their careers at an early age, all four were encouraged by parents or other relatives who were professional musicians—McLin's uncle, Thomas A. Dorsey, was the Gospel King—and they won many honors and awards, as well as the undying appreciation of the black music community for their rich legacy of church music. The extent to which their lives were driven by their vocations is suggested by McLin's experience of writing, during one seven-year period of her life, an anthem, a call, and a hymn for *each* Sunday of the church year, fitting her text to the subject of the sermon for that Sunday.

GOSPEL SINCE THE 1980s

In 1980 Chicago celebrated the Golden Jubilee of Gospel Music with a series of events through the year, climaxing with "The Roots of Gospel," a pageant broadcast on television in November. Appropriately, gospel called forth its own performers, rather than mainstream scholars, to discuss its history—pioneers Dorsey and Sallie Martin; leading singers Jessy Dixon and Albertina Walker; and Clayton Laverne Hannah, official historian of the Gospel Academy of Recording Arts and Sciences. One of the highlights of the year's celebration was the outdoor concert in June, entitled "O For a Thousand Tongues to Sing," held at Grant Park, which included a 300-voice choir in addition to the featured singers and groups.

Hymnals and Performance Practice

With the year 1981 came the landmark publication *Songs of Zion,* sixty years after an earlier landmark, *Gospel Pearls,* had made the songs of the

[18]See further in Mildred Denby Green, *Black Women Composers: A Genesis* (Boston, 1983).

pioneer black gospel composer accessible for the first time. Like its predecessor, *Songs of Zion* made available, for the first time in a single source, all the various religious song-types belonging to the black tradition—spirituals and jubilees, both folk and arranged; early gospel hymns of Tindley, Campbell, and Dorsey; contemporary gospel songs of Bradford, Cleveland, Crouch, Hawkins, Martin, and Morris, to cite but a few names. Additionally, the hymnal includes the standard and gospel hymns by white writers that over the years have been "transposed and arranged and sung as new songs of Zion."[19] As the editors point out, the last named were as much a part of the black tradition as the songs composed by black Americans. Like Allen's hymnal of 1801 and *Gospel Pearls,* this collection cuts across denominational lines in its appeal to black Christians.

For scholars of black-church music, perhaps the biggest event of the 1980s was the publication, for the first time, of an official COGIC Church of God in Christ hymnal. According to a brief introductory note, the title of the hymnal, *Yes, Lord!,* reflects a practice of Charles H. Mason, founder of COGIC, Inc., in 1896: when Bishop Mason wanted "to pull the congregation together in commitment and spiritual communion," he would begin the singing of a dynamic, tuneful chant, the text of which repeated the phrase "Yes, Lord" a number of times.

Yes, Lord! makes a sharp break with the traditional past. In its collection of 506 songs, the handling of the accompaniment, in particular, reflects the importance given to instruments and polyphonic textures in the pentecostal tradition. Except for the old standard hymns (which retain their conventional, four-part harmonizations) the accompaniments are lively and imaginative, promising an extra dimension of richness and excitement to the performance of the songs.

The major gospel composers of four generations are represented in the hymnal, from Tindley to the generation of Roberta Martin, Kenneth Morris, Dorsey, and others, to the generation of Andrae Crouch. In addition there are numerous songs written by pentecostal composers whose names are not known outside the Church, such as Mattie Moss Clark and Iris Stevenson, among others.

The collection includes a wide variety of texts: standard hymns are interspersed with gospel hymns, spirituals, patriotic songs, gospel songs, and religious songs in the classical European tradition—for example, St. Francis of Assisi's "All Creatures of Our God and King" and songs of Beethoven, Mozart, and Handel. Turning the pages, one comes across delightful surprises, such as a charming three-part round written by Terrye Coelho, and occasionally a shocker—such as the full, four-part arrangement of the "Hallelujah Chorus" from Handel's *Messiah* (covering six pages).

The black folk-church adopted this work as if it were a jubilee or shout song: members of the congregation sang along with the choir when it was

---

[19]*Songs of Zion*, p. xv.

performed, taking whichever voice-part they preferred and missing not a note. The inclusion of the "Hallelujah Chorus" in a pentecostal hymnal legitimizes the establishing of yet another black-church-music tradition.

Contemporary Gospel

A number of young gospel figures contributed—as much by their actions as through their innovations—to the development of the "contemporary gospel" style (as distinguished from "traditional gospel") that began to emerge during the mid-century years. In the first place, many talented professionals, wooed by the pop-music industry, left the field of sacred song for the commercially greener fields of rhythm 'n' blues and pop. The first well-known artist to cross over into pop music, Sam Cooke (1931–1964), left the celebrated Soul Stirrers quartet in the mid-fifties to write and produce his own music, thus setting an example that enticed other gospel figures, many now famous, to emulate him. Among them were Aretha Franklin, Della Reese, Dinah Washington (née Ruth Jones), Gladys Knight, Lou Rawls, the Staple Singers ("Pop" Roebuck Staples and his three daughters), and two quartets, the Dominoes and the Isley Brothers.

When these gospel singers moved into the mainstream of concertizing— via church- and revival-circuit touring, concert-hall touring, jazz and blues festivals, dance halls, radio broadcasting, television telecasting, and nigh-club entertaining—they brought along their church-rooted performance practice and repertory items. To many listeners it seemed that the newly arrived pop singers were merely replacing religious texts with secular ones, for the sound was essentially the same. Particularly noticeable were the similarities between the gospel as preached and the gospel as sung. Commenting on a performance by Aretha Franklin, one listener noted:[20]

> You listen to her and it's like being in church. She does with her voice exactly what a preacher does when he moans to a congregation. That moan strikes a responsive chord in the congregation and somebody answers you back with their own moan, which means I know what you're moaning about because I feel the same way. So you have something sort of like a thread spinning out and touching and tieing [sic] everybody together in a shared experience just like the getting happy and shouting together in church.

Franklin brought the same fervency to her singing of a love song:

> She leans her head back, forehead gleaming with perspiration, features twisted by her intensity, and her voice—plangent and supple—pierces the hall: "You make me feel like a natural woman."

Earlier we discussed the importance of jazz as an element in traditional gospel music, particularly in regard to the infusions made by jazzmen

---

[20]Quoted in Bernice Johnson Reagon, *We'll Understand It Better By and By* (Washington, D.C., 1992), p. 29.

Thomas A. Dorsey in the 1920s and Kenneth Morris in 1934. Not surprisingly, gospel figures of the present era, in their continuing search for the novel and the expressive, have experimented with blending gospel elements with other genres. Jazzman Horace Silver, for example, might have anticipated things to come when he blended gospel and bop elements in his album, *The Preacher* (1955), but Edwin Hawkins (b. 1943), was the first gospel artist to produce a genuine "hybrid" with his rhythm 'n' blues arrangement of a Baptist hymn in *Oh, Happy Day* (1969), which sold more than two million copies. Aretha Franklin attracted even more attention with her "soul" version of the hymn *Amazing Grace* (1972), a multi-million record seller.

The popularity of gospel increased at an enormous rate during the last two decades of the century. Responding to the unprecedented commercial success of black-church music, the pop-music industry expanded the number of categories allotted to black-music genres on the charts—gospel, soul, pop, and spiritual (Contemporary Christian was generally reserved for white gospel). Black gospel artists consistently won places in all the categories on Top 10 lists of the sales charts and Top 40 on radio playlists. In addition to touring on the concert circuit, young gospel groups contribute songs to films, television sitcoms, and video soundtracks; provide back-up vocals for albums and live solo concerts; serve as introductory acts for concerts by the celebrated; write their own songs; and produce albums. Some of the groups that include evangelists as well as singers work only with Christian materials.

Throughout its history, the black church has been uncomfortably aware of the tensions within its walls between the traditionalists and the modernists, especially when it comes to musical practices. The church now holds both groups in an uneasy embrace, its music having survived the onslaught of both experimentation and prohibition. The conservatives cling to the old ways and, if they must experiment, seek to explore the potential of gospel within the church, avoiding secular venues while singing and preaching to the converted. Some of the established artists have tried singing in the new gospel style, only to discover that it did not work for them, and they found themselves returning to the church. Evangelist Shirley Caesar, for example, shuns "worldly" venues, describing herself and some of her contemporaries as "traditional gospel singers with a contemporary flavor."[21] Among a younger generation, Andrea Crouch (b. 1942) and Edwin Hawkins (b. 1943) have taken the lead in promoting innovation and experimentation in gospel, but within the parameters of the church or other sacred venues, and always for Christian audiences.

Crouch played piano in his father's holiness church as a child and sang with a group, the COGICs (Church of God in Christ) during his high-school years. Within the next decade he became one of the principal gospel singers

[21]Bob Darden, "Shirley Caesar, Singing Evangelist," *Rejoice* 2 (1990), p. 8.

of his time, appealing from the beginning to white as well as black audiences. He toured widely with his group, recorded extensively, and wrote numerous songs, some of which became gospel standards. He combined elements of popular music, rock, country music, and soul with traditional gospel; his accompanying forces consisted of both acoustical and electronic instruments, including synthesizers. Among his best-known songs were *The Blood Will Never Lose Its Power Through It All,* and *Take Me Back.*

The Edwin Hawkins Singers, the nucleus of which were members of his family, developed out of a youth choir in his father's Church of God in Christ. The singers toured widely from 1968 on, both in the United States and abroad, and much of its repertory was written by Hawkins or other members of the group. Its performance style was in the tradition of soul-gospel, including the use of electronic instruments and synthesizers.

The modernists, on the other hand, eagerly grasp the opportunity to use "contemporary gospel" as a way to reach wider audiences with its attractive, even seductive, music and messages of inspiration (which are sometimes ambiguous about the singer's relations to humanity and to God). The influential figures of this generation include BeBe & CeCe Winan—a brother-and-sister act—and other members of the Winan family; Walter Hawkins (b. 1949); Tramaine Davis Hawkins (b. 1957, Walter's wife); Danniebelle Hall; pianist Ben Tankard (b. 1964) and the Richard Smallwood Singers. Their songs primarily fuse gospel with jazz but also draw upon rhythm 'n' blues, pop, soul, disco, reggae, or rap. Their themes, which relate to everyday life concerns, are identified as "message music."

A GOSPEL GREEK MYTH

After viewing a performance of *The Gospel at Colonnus* in 1983, a music critic hailed it as "an exhilarating musical celebration that seamlessly blended the agony of Greek tragedy and the ecstasy of American gospel into a jubilant meditation on fate and redemption." Conceived and produced by whites and featuring an all-black cast, Sophocles' story of Oedipus the King is presented in the format of an old-time African-American church service. The story line is divided among several actors and soloists and four gospel groups. Of the ensembles that took part—The Brooklyn Institutional Choir, the J. D. Steele Singers, Clarence Fountain and the Five Blind Boys of Alabama, and J. J. Farley and the Original Soul Singers—the two mixed groups sang contemporary gospel and the two male groups sang in traditional quartet style. After touring for four years, *The Gospel* was adapted for television presentation, also to critical acclaim. The drama presents a glorious summary of the black gospel sound half a century after its emergence on the mainstream American music scene.

CODA

It has been 377 years—at the time of this writing—since black men and women first began to sing their "song in a strange land," the land that later became the United States of America. History has recorded many changes in that song as it moved from its African moorings toward a genuinely African-American music, which today encompasses a wide variety of genres, styles, forms, and performance practices. Indeed, the variety is at times bewildering. Contemporary composers and performers no longer fit neatly into stylistic categories as did their predecessors; they are traditionalists, modernists, expressionists, avant-gardists, and other kinds of "ists." Some experiment widely, improving the old, perhaps mixing the old and the new in producing a different music. At the same time, others are holding on to the past, continuing to compose and perform in the ways black musicians have done for decades.

Which way is the future? It is difficult to tell. It is unlikely, however, that black musical styles and genres will disappear, as some gloomy soothsayers have prophesied, once American society has rid itself of racial discrimination. The enduring feature of black music is neither protest nor self-expression; it is *communication,* and one cannot imagine a time when black musicians will have nothing to say, either to others or to God. Nor is it likely, as some have predicted, that the creative well of black people will run dry once blacks are integrated into American society and their music absorbed into American and world music. History does not support such an assumption.

Again and again black musical styles have passed over into American music, there to be diluted and altered in other ways to appeal to a wider public or to be used as the basis for developing new styles. There was the transformation of the slave songs, for example, into Ethiopian minstrel songs and, on another level, the assimilation of jazz elements into the music of a Gershwin or a Stravinsky. The black composer's response to such a transfer has been simply to invent a new music: thus spirituals were replaced by gospel; traditional jazz, by bebop; rhythm 'n' blues, by soul—to cite a few examples. The old is never totally discarded, however, but absorbed into the new. In summary, black music constantly renews itself at the same time as its innovations are being absorbed into the general language of Western music. And that is as it should be.

BIBLIOGRAPHY

DISCOGRAPHY

INDEX

ABBREVIATIONS

BPIM   *The Black Perspective in Music.* New York, 1973–

LB   *Living Blues.* Chicago, 1970–.

RBAM   *Readings in Black American Music.* Rev. ed. Ed. Eileen Southern. New York: W. W. Norton, 1983.

KATZ   *The Social Implications of Early Negro Music in the United States.* Ed. Bernard Katz. New York: Arno Press, 1969.

BIBLIOGRAPHY AND DISCOGRAPHY

GENERAL REFERENCE

Allen, Daniel. *Bibliography of Discographies.* Vol. 2: Jazz, 1935–1980. New York: R. R. Bowker, 1981. Discographies for individuals, composers, record labels, etc., as well as genres.

Annals of the Metropolitan Opera: The Complete Chronicle of Performances and Artists. Boston: G. K. Hall and The Metropolitan Opera Guild, Inc., 1989.

Archive of Folksong, Library of Congress Catalogue.

ASCAP Biographical Dictionary of Composers, Authors, and Publishers. Compiled and ed. by the Lynn Farnol Group. New York: American Society of Composers, Authors, and Publishers, 1948. 4th ed., 1980.

Baker's Biographical Dictionary of Musicians. 6th ed. Rev. by Nicholas Slonimsky. New York: Schirmer Books, 1978. For a list of the black musicians represented in Baker's see Dominique-René de Lerma, "A Concordance of Black Music Entries in Five Encyclopedias: Baker's, Ewen, Groves, MGG, and Rich," *Black Music Research Journal* (1981–82).

Bean, Calvert. "Retrospective: The Black Composers Series." *Black Music Research Newsletter* 4 (Spring 1981). Report on recordings of the classical works of black composers—Anderson, Baker, Coleridge-Taylor, Cordero, Hakim, Hailstork, Kay, Nuñes-Garcia, Saint-Georges, Hale Smith, Sowande, Still, Walker, José White, Wilson. Columbia Records, 1974–78.

Bloom, Ken. *American Song: The Complete Musical Theatre Companion, 1900–1994.* 2nd ed. New York: Schirmer Books, 1996.

Bordman, Gerald. *The American Musical Theatre.* New York: Oxford University Press, 1978.

Brooks, Tilford. *America's Black Musical Heritage.* Englewood Cliffs, NJ: Prentice-Hall, 1984.

Butcher, Margaret Just. *The Negro in American Culture.* 1956. Repr. New York: Alfred A. Knopf, 1966.

Chase, Gilbert. *America's Music from the Pilgrims to the Present.* 1955. 3rd rev. ed. New York: McGraw-Hill, 1987.

Creighton, James. *Discopaedia of the Violin, 1889–1971.* Toronto: University of Toronto Press, 1974. Includes references to recordings of the music of James Bland, Eubie Blake, Clarence Cameron White, Saint-Georges, and others.

Davis, Elizabeth A., comp. *Index to the New World Recorded Anthology of American Music: A User's Guide to the Initial One Hundred Records.* New York: W. W. Norton, 1981.

de Lerma, Dominique-René. *Bibliography of Black Music.* 4 vols. Westport, CT: Greenwood Press, 1981–84.

_____. *Black Concert and Recital Music: A Selective Discography.* Beverly Hills, CA: Theodore Front Musical Literature, 1976–82.

_____. "A Concordance of Black Music Entries in Five Encyclopedias: Baker's, Ewen, Groves, MGG, and Rich," *Black Music Research Journal.* (1981–82).

Dixon, Robert, and John Godrich. *Blues and Gospel Records, 1902–1942.* 1964. 3rd ed. London: Storyville Publications, 1982.

Encyclopedia of Black America. Ed. by W. A. Low and Virgil A. Clift. New York: McGraw-Hill, 1981.

Ewen, David. *New Encyclopedia of the Opera: Its Story.* Rev. ed. New York: Hill & Wang, 1971. Includes most of the important opera figures as of 1970.

_____, ed. *Musicians Since 1900: Performers in Concert and Opera.* New York: H. W. Wilson, 1978. For a list of the black musicians included see Dominique-René de Lerma, "A Concordance of Black Music Entries in Five Encyclopedias: Baker's, Ewen, Groves, MGG, and Rich," *Black Music Research Journal* (1981–82).

Feather, Leonard. *The Encyclopedia of Jazz in the Sixties.* New York: Horizon Press, 1966.

_____. *The New Edition of the Encyclopedia of Jazz.* New York: Horizon Press, 1960.

_____, and Ira Gitler. *The Encyclopedia of Jazz in the Seventies.* New York: Horizon Press, 1976.

Floyd, Samuel A., Jr., and Marsha J. Reisser. *Black Music Biography: An Annotated Bibliography.* White Plains, NY: Kraus International, 1987.

_____. *Black Music in the United States: An Annotated Bibliography of Selected Reference and Research Materials.* Millwood, NY: Kraus International, 1983.

Folkways Records Catalogue. Includes some jazz as well as folk-music listings.

Franklin, John Hope. *From Slavery to Freedom.* 1947. 7th ed. New York: Alfred A. Knopf, 1994.

Gelatt, Roland. *The Fabulous Phonograph: 1877–1977.* 2nd rev. ed. New York: Macmillan Publishing Co., 1977.

George, Zelma. "Negro Music in American Life," *The American Negro Reference Book.* Englewood Cliffs, NJ: Prentice-Hall, 1966.

Gray, John, comp. *Blacks in Classical Music: A Bibliographical Guide to Composers, Performers, and Ensembles.* Westport, CT: Greenwood Press, 1988.

Green, Stanley. *Encyclopedia of the Musical Theatre.* New York: Dodd, Mead & Co., 1976.

Hamm, Charles. *Music in the New World.* New York: W. W. Norton, 1983.

_____. *Yesterdays: Popular Song in America.* New York: W. W. Norton, 1979.

Hare, Maude Cuney. *Negro Musicians and Their Music.* 1936. Repr. New York: Da Capo Press, 1974.

Harris, Sheldon. *Blues Who's Who: A Biographical Dictionary of Blues Singers.* New Rochelle, NY: Arlington House, 1979.

Harrison, Max, *et al. Modern Jazz: The Essential Records.* A Critical Selection by Max

Harrison, Alun Morgan, Ronald Atkins, Michael James, Jack Cooke. London: Aquarius Books, 1975.

Hartel, Harold. "The H3 Chrono-Matrix File," *Record Research,* begins in Issue 175/6 (September 1980). Chronological listing, published serially, of the entries in Rust's *Jazz Records* and Dixon and Godrich's *Blues and Gospel Records,* beginning in the year 1897. Identifies artist, title, date, label, city, etc., with cross references to Rust and Dixon.

Hatch, James, and Omanii Abdullah. *Black Playwrights, 1823–1977: An Annotated Bibliography of Plays.* New York: R. R. Bowker Co., 1977. Includes black musicals.

Hayes, Cedric. *A Discography of Gospel Records, 1937–1971.* Copenhagen: Knudsen, 1973.

———, and Robert Laughton. *Gospel Records, 1943–1969: A Black Music Discography.* Milford, NH: Big Nickel Publications, 1993.

Herskovits, Melville J. *The Myth of the Negro Past.* 1941. Repr. Boston: Beacon Press, 1958.

Hitchcock, H. Wiley. *Music in the United States: A Historical Introduction.* 1969. 3rd ed. Englewood Cliffs, NJ: Prentice-Hall, 1988.

Horn, David. *The Literature of American Music in Books and Folk Music Collections: A Fully Annotated Bibliography.* Metuchen, NJ: Scarecrow Press, 1977. Supplement 1, by David Horn, with Richard Jackson, 1988. Extensive discussion of black music titles in all genres.

Howard, John Tasker, and George Kent Bellows. *A Short History of Music in America.* New York: Thomas Y. Crowell Co., 1957.

International Library of Negro Life and History. Washington, D.C.: Publishers Company, 1967. Multivolume set includes *The Negro in Music and Art, Anthology of the American Negro in the Theatre,* and *Historical Negro Biographies.*

Jackson, Irene V. *Afro-American Religious Music: A Bibliography and a Catalogue of Gospel Music.* Westport, CT: Greenwood Press, 1979.

Jackson, Richard. United States Music: Sources of Bibliography and Collective Biography. New York: Institute for Studies in American Music / Brooklyn College of the City University of New York, 1973.

Jepsen, Grunnet Jorgen. *Jazz Records: Discography, 1942–1968.* 11 vols. Copenhagen: Knudsen, 1963–70.

Kingman, Daniel. *American Music: A Panorama.* 2nd ed. New York: Schirmer Books, 1990.

Kinkle, Roger D. *The Complete Encyclopedia of Popular Music and Jazz, 1900–1950.* 4 vols. New Rochelle, NY: Arlington House Publishers, 1974.

Leadbitter, Mike, and Neil Slaven, eds. *Blues Records, January 1943–December 1966.* 1968. New York: Oak Publications, 1969.

Leder, Jan. *Women in Jazz: A Discography of Instrumentalists, 1913–1968.* Westport, CT: Greenwood Press, 1985.

Mapp, Edward. *Directory of Blacks in the Performing Arts.* Metuchen, NJ: Scarecrow Press, 1978. Includes biographical facts.

McCarthy, Albert, *et al. Jazz on Record: A Critical Guide to the First 50 Years, 1917–1967.* By Albert McCarthy, Alun Morgan, Paul Oliver, Max Harrison, with additional contributions by Ronald Atkins, *et al.* London: Hanover Books, 1968.

Meadows, Eddie S. *Jazz Reference and Research Materials: A Bibliography.* New York: Garland Publishing, 1981.

Mellers, Wilfred. *Music in a New Found Land: Themes and Developments in the History of American Music.* 1964. New York: Oxford University Press, 1987.

New Grove Dictionary of American Music, The. Ed. by Stanley Sadie and H. Wiley Hitchcock. 4 vols. New York: Macmillan Press, 1986.

New Grove Dictionary of Jazz, The. Ed. by Barry Kernfeld. 2 vols. New York: Macmillan Press, 1988.

New Grove Dictionary of Music and Musicians, The. Ed. by Stanley Sadie, 20 vols. London, 1980. For a list of the black musicians represented, see Dominique-René de Lerma, "A Concordance of Black Music Entries in Five Encyclopedias: Baker's, Ewen, Groves, MGG, and Rich," *Black Music Research Journal* (1981–82).

New York Times Directory of the Theatre, 1920–1970, The. New York: Arno Press, 1973.

Odell, George. *Annals of the New York Stage.* 15 vols. New York: Columbia University Press, 1927–49.

Peterson, Bernard L., Jr. *A Century of Musicals in Black and White: An Encyclopedia of Musical Stage Works By, About, or Involving African Americans.* Westport, CT: Greenwood Press, 1993.

Placksin, Sally. *American Women in Jazz 1900 to the Present: Their Words, Lives, and Music.* New York: Seaview Books, 1982.

Roach, Hildred. *Black American Music: Past and Present.* 2nd ed. Malabar, FL: Krieger Publishing Company, 1992.

Ruppli, Michel, comp. *Atlantic Records: A Discography.* 4 vols. Westport, CT: Greenwood Press, 1979. Good for jazz.

———, with assistance from Bob Porter. *The Savoy Label: A Discography.* ort, CT: Greenwood Press, 1980. Good for contemporary gospel.

———, with assistance from Bob Porter. *The Prestige Label: A Discography.* Westport, CT: Greenwood Press, 1980. Good for jazz.

Rust, Brian. *Jazz Records, 1897–1942.* 1962. 2 vols. 4th ed. New Rochelle, NY: Arlington House, 1978.

———. *Complete Entertainment Discography, from the Mid–1890s to 1942.* New Rochelle, NY: Arlington House, 1973. Similar to Rust's *Jazz Records,* except that it includes performers not classified as jazz figures, such as, for example, Lena Horne.

Sernett, Milton C., ed. *Afro-American Religious History: A Documentary Witness.* Durham, NC: Duke University Press, 1985.

———. *Black Religion and American Evangelicalism.* Metuchen, NJ: Scarecrow Press, 1975.

Simmons, William. *Men of Mark.* Cleveland: G. M. Rewell & Co., 1887. Biographical sketches of notable black men of the nineteenth century includes musicians.

Skowronski, JoAnn. *Black Music in America: A Bibliography.* Metuchen, NJ: Scarecrow Press, 1981. Includes articles as well as books.

Smithsonian Collection of Recordings Catalogue, The. Recordings of black jazzmen, gospel figures, folk singers.

Southern, Eileen. *Biographical Dictionary of Afro-American and African Musicians.* Westport, CT: Greenwood Press, 1983. Entries for more than 1,400 individuals and groups in all areas of musical activity.

———. *Music of Black Americans, The.* 1971, 1983. 3rd ed. New York: W. W. Norton, 1997.

———. *Readings in Black American Music.* 1971. 2nd ed. New York: W. W. Norton, 1983.

———, and Josephine Wright. *African-American Traditions in Song, Sermon, Tale, and Dance, 1600s–1920: An Annotated Bibliography of Literature, Collections, and Artworks.* Westport, CT: Greenwood Press, 1990. Almost 2,500 entries.

Spradling, Mary Mace, ed. *In Black and White: Afro-Americans in Print: A Guide to Magazine Articles, Newspaper Articles, and Books Concerning More than 15,000 Black Individuals and Groups.* 1971. 3rd ed. Detroit: Gale Research Co., 1980.

Stambler, Irwin. *Encyclopedia of Pop, Rock, and Soul.* New York: St. Martin's Press, 1974.

_____, and Grelum Landon. *Encyclopedia of Folk, Country, and Western Music.* New York: St. Martin's Press, 1969.

Szwed, John F., and Roger D. Abrahams. *Afro-American Folk Culture: An Annotated Bibliography of Materials from North, Central, and South America, and The West Indies.* Publications of the American Folklore Society. Philadelphia: Institute for the Study of Human Issues, 1978.

Tirro, Frank. *Jazz: A History.* 2nd ed. New York: W. W. Norton, 1993.

Tudor, Dean, and Nancy Tudor. *Black Music.* Littleton, CO: Libraries Unlimited, 1979. Annotated discography.

_____. *Jazz.* Littleton, CO: Libraries Unlimited, 1979. Annotated discography.

Turner, Patricia. *Dictionary of Afro-American Performers: 78 RPM and Cylinder Recordings of Opera, Choral Music, and Songs, c. 1919–49.* New York: Garland Publishing, 1990.

Voigt, John, and Randall Kane. *Jazz Music in Print.* 1975. 3rd ed. as *Jazz Music in Print and Jazz Books in Print.* Boston: Hornpipe Music Publishing Co., 1982.

Warner, Thomas E. *Periodical Literature on American Music, 1619–1920: A Classified Bibliography with Annotations.* Warren, MI: Harmonie Park Press, 1988.

Who's Who Among Black Americans, 1992–93, edited by Christa Brelin. 1975. 7th ed. Detroit: Gale Research, Inc., 1992.

Who's Who in Colored America. 1927. Ed. by Joseph J. Boris, *et al.* 7th ed. Ed. by G. James Fleming and Christian E. Burckel. Yonkers-on-Hudson, NY: Christian E. Burckel and Associates. 1950.

Who's Who in Opera. Ed. by Maria F. Rich. New York: Arno Press, 1976. For a list of the black musicians included see Dominique-René de Lerma, "A Concordance of Black Music Entries in Five Encyclopedias: Baker's, Ewen, Groves, MGG, and Rich," *Black Music Research Journal* (1981–82).

Who's Who in the Theatre. Ed. by Ian Herbert. 16th edition. Detroit: Gale Research Inc., 1977.

Woll, Allen. *Black Musical Theatre: From Coontown to Dreamgirls.* Baton Rouge: Louisiana State University Press, 1989.

_____. *Dictionary of the Black Theatre: Broadway, Off-Broadway, and Selected Harlem Theatres.* Westport, CT: Greenwood Press, 1983.

Woodson, Carter G. *The History of the Negro Church.* 1921. Repr. Washington, D.C.: The Associated Publishers, 1972.

Wright, Josephine, comp. "Selected Doctoral Dissertations: 1968–1988." *New Perspectives on Music: Essays in Honor of Eileen Southern.* Warren, MI: Harmonie Park Press, 1992.

_____. "New Music," BPIM 1973–90. List of new music of black composers published annually in the Fall issue of BPIM.

_____, ed. with Samuel A. Floyd, Jr. *New Perspectives on Music: Essays in Honor of Eileen Southern.* Warren, MI: Harmonie Park Press, 1992.

THE AFRICAN LEGACY

Atkins, John. *A Voyage to Guinea, Brasil, and the West Indies. . . .* London: Printed for Ward and Chandler, 1737. Contains information about John Conny, thus documenting the relationship between Conny, the West African, and the John Conny festivals in the New World.

Bebey, Francis. *African Music: A People's Art.* New York: Lawrence Hill & Co., 1975.

Bosman, William. *A New and Accurate Description of the Coast of Guinea, Divided into the Gold, the Slave, and the Ivory Coasts.* 1705. Written originally in Dutch . . . and now faithfully done into English. London, Printed for J. Knapton, 1721.

Bowdich, Edward. *Mission from Cape Coast Castle to Ashanti.* London, John Murray,

1819. Includes descriptions of instruments and performance practice, as well as melodies in notation and watercolor scenes.

Clapperton, Hugh. *Journal of a Second Expedition into the Interior of Africa from the Bight of Benin to Soccatoo*. 1826. Repr. London: Frank Cass & Co., 1966.

———, and Dixon Denham. *Narrative of Travels & Discoveries in Northern and Central Africa in the Years 1822, 1823, & 1824 by Major Denham, Captain Clapperton, and the Late Doctor Oudney*. . . . London: John Murray, 1826.

Conneau, Theophilus. *A Slaver's Log Book, Or 20 Years' Residence in Africa*. 1854. Ed., with an introduction, by Mable Smythe. Englewood Cliffs, NJ: Prentice-Hall, 1976. For this edition of the log book of Captain Conneau (or Captain Canot), the editor has gone back to the original manuscript of 1819. Earlier editions—by Brantz Mayer in 1854 and Malcolm Cowley in 1928—omitted details that are here included.

Donnan, Elizabeth. *Documents Illustrative of the History of the Slave Trade to America*. Washington, D.C.: Carnegie Institution of Washington, 1930–35.

Equiano, Olaudah. *The Interesting Narrative of the Life of Olaudah Equiano, or Gustavus Vassa, the African. Written by Himself*. 1789. New York: Printed by W. Durrell, 1791.

Hawkins, Joseph. *A History of a Voyage to the Coast of Africa, and Travels into the Interior of that Country*. . . . Troy, NY: Printed for the Author by Luther Pratt, 1797.

Jobson, Richard. *The Golden Trade, or a Discovery of the River Gambra and the Golden Trade of the Aethiopians*. London: Nicholas Okes, 1623.

Laing, Alexander Gordon. *Travels in the Timannee, Kooranko, and Soolima Countries in Western Africa*. London, John Murray, 1825.

Nketia, Joseph H. Kwabena. *African Music in Ghana*. Evanston, IL: Northwestern University Press, 1963.

———. *The Music of Africa*. New York: W. W. Norton, 1974.

Noris, Robert. *Memoirs of the Reign of Bossa Ahadee, King of Dahomey*. London: W. Lowndes, 1789. Repr. New York, 1968.

Park, Mungo. *The Journal of a Mission to the Interior of Africa in the Year 1805 by Mungo Park, together with Other documents, Official and Private, Relating to the Same Mission*. . . . London: Printed for John Murray, 1815.

Smith, William. *A Voyage to Guinea: Describing the Customs, Manners, Soil, Climate . . . and Whatever Else is Memorable among the Inhabitants*. London: Printed for John Nourse, 1744. Includes information about John Conny, thus pointing to the origin of the John Conny festivals.

Trotter, H. D., *et al. Narrative of the Expedition Sent by His Majesty's Government to the River Niger in 1841 Under the Command of Captain H. D. Trotter, Captain William Allen, and T. R. H. Thompson*. 2 vols. London: Richard Bentley, 1843. Contains many drawings of African instruments and also musical examples.

Waterman, Richard. "African Influence on the Music of the Americas," *Proceedings of the 29th Congress of Americanists, 1949. Selected Papers*. Ed. by Sol Tax. Vol. 2: *Acculturation in the Americas*, with an Introduction by Melville Herskovits. Chicago: University of Chicago Press.

Wilson, Olly. "The Significance of the Relationship Between Afro-American Music and West African Music," BPIM 2 (Spring 1974).

EIGHTEENTH AND EARLY NINETEENTH CENTURIES

Benson, Louis F. *The English Hymn: Its Development and Use in Worship*. 1915. Repr. Richmond, VA: John Knox Press, 1962.

Bridenbaugh, Carl. *Cities in Revolt: Urban Life in America, 1743–76.* New York: Alfred A. Knopf, 1955.

———. *Cities in the Wilderness: Urban Life in America, 1625–1742.* New York: Alfred A. Knopf, 1939.

Bruce, Philip Alexander, *Social Life of Virginia in the Seventeenth Century.* 1907. Repr. Richmond, VA: Printed for the Author, 1964.

Cappon, Lester, and Stella F. Duff. *Virginia Gazette Index, 1736–1780.* 2 vols. Williamsburg, VA: Institute of Early American History and Culture, 1950. Includes references to slave musicians.

Cohen, Hennig. *The South Carolina Gazette, 1732–1775.* Columbia: University of South Carolina Press, 1953. Good for slave-musician advertisements.

Cooper, James Fenimore. *Satanstoe: Or, the Littlepage Manuscripts. A Tale of the Colony.* 1845. New York: American Book Co., 1937. Includes a description of the Pinkster festival.

Cresswell, Nicholas. *The Journal of Nicholas Cresswell.* Introduction by Samuel Thornely, a descendent. New York: The Dial Press, 1924. Contains some of the earliest comments on black musicians and dancers in the United States.

Crèvecoeur, Hector St. John de. *Sketches of Eighteenth-Century America, Or More "Letters from an American Farmer."* Ed. by Henri Bourdin, *et al.* New Haven: Yale University Press, 1925.

Davies, Samuel. *Letters from the Rev. Samuel Davies and Others: Shewing the State of Religion in Virginia, S.C., &c., Particularly Among the Negroes.* London: Printed by J. & W. Oliver, 1761. Repr. of some letters in RBAM.

Earle, Alice Morse. *Colonial Days in Old New York.* New York: Charles Scribner's Sons, 1896.

———. *Customs and Fashions in Old New England.* New York: Charles Scribner's Sons, 1893.

———. *The Sabbath in Puritan New England.* New York: Charles Scribner's Sons, 1891.

"Eighteenth-Century Slaves as Advertised by Their Masters," *Journal of Negro History* 1 (April 1916): 162–216.

Epstein, Dena J. "African Music in British and French America," *Musical Quarterly* 59 (January 1973): 61–91.

Felt, Joseph. *Annals of Salem: From Its First Settlement.* Salem, MA: W & S. B. Ives, 1845. Includes discussion of the slave festival called 'Lection Day and of Negro governors.

Fithian, Philip Vickers. *Journal & Letters of Philip Vickers Fithian, 1773–1774: A Plantation Tutor of the Old Dominion.* 1900. Ed. with an Introduction, by Hunter Dickinson Farish. Williamsburg, VA: Colonial Williamsburg, 1957.

Greene, Lorenzo Johnston. *The Negro in Colonial New England, 1620–1776.* 1942. Reissue. Port Washington, NY: Kennikat Press, 1966.

Haraszti, Zoltan. *The Enigma of the Bay Psalm Book.* Chicago: University of Chicago Press, 1956.

Jernegan, Marcus Wilson. *Laboring and Dependent Classes in Colonial America, 1607–1783.* Chicago: University of Chicago Press, 1931.

Keefer, Lubov. *Baltimore's Music: The Haven of the American Composer.* Baltimore: J. H. Furst & Co., 1962.

Klingberg, Frank. *An Appraisal of the Negro in Colonial South Carolina.* Washington, D.C.: The Associated Publishers, 1941.

Levering, Joseph. *A History of Bethlehem, Pennsylvania, 1741–1892.* Bethlehem: Times Publishing Co., 1903. Includes discussion of the early black converts to the Moravian Church in Pennsylvania.

Mordecai, Samuel. *Richmond in By-Gone Days: Being Reminiscences of an Old Citizen.* Richmond: G. M. West, 1856.

Munsell, Joel. *The Annals of Albany.* 10 vols. Albany: J. Munsell, 1850–59. Vol. 5 includes discussion of the Pinkster festival.

Nell, William C. *The Colonial Patriots of the American Revolution, with Sketches of Several Distinguished Persons.* . . . With an Introduction by Harriet Beecher Stowe. Boston: Robert Wallcut, 1855.

Norwood, Frederick. *The Story of American Methodism.* Nashville, TN: Abingdon Press, 1974.

Pennington, Edgar. "Thomas Bray's Associates and Their Work Among the Negroes," *The American Antiquarian Society Proceedings,* New Series 48 (October 1938): 311–403.

Platt, Orville. "Negro Governors," *The New Haven Historical Society Quarterly* 6 (1900): 315–35. Discussion of the New England slave holiday called 'Lection Day.

Reynolds, Helen Wilkinson. "The Negro in Dutchess County in the Eighteenth Century," *Year Book of the Dutchess Historical Society* 26 (1941): 89–99.

Russell, John. *The Free Negro in Virginia, 1619–1865.* Baltimore: Johns Hopkins University Press, 1913.

Sewall, Samuel. *The Diary of Samuel Sewall, 1674–1729.* Collections of the Massachusetts Historical Society. Fifth Series, vols. 5–7. Boston, 1878–82.

Smyth, John F. *A Tour in the United States of America.* . . . 2 vols. London: Printed for G. Robinson, 1784. Reprint of Chapter 6, "Manner of Living of the Different Ranks of Inhabitants of Virginia," *American Museum* 1 (March 1787): 245–48.

Stuart, Isaac. *Hartford in the Olden Times: Its First Thirty Years.* Ed. by William B. Hartley. Hartford, CT: F. A. Brown, 1853.

Tate, Thad. *The Negro in Eighteenth-Century Williamsburg.* Williamsburg, VA: University Press of Virginia, Charlottesville, 1965.

Turner, Edward. *The Negro in Pennsylvania: Slavery, Servitude, Freedom, 1639–1861.* Washington, D.C.: American Historical Association, 1911.

Watson, John Fanning. *Annals and Occurrences of New York City and State in the Olden Time: Being a Collection of Memoirs, Anecdotes, and Incidents Concerning the City, County, and Inhabitants from the Days of the Founders.* Philadelphia: Henry F. Anners, 1846.

Watts, Isaac. *Hymns and Spiritual Songs in Three Books.* 1. Collected from the Scriptures. 2. Compos'd on Divine Subjects. 3. Prepared for the Lord's Supper. . . . London: Printed by J. Humfreys, 1707.

Watts, Isaac. *The Psalms of David, Imitated in the Language of the New Testament and Apply'd to the Christian State and Worship.* London, J. Clark, 1719.

Wilkes, Laura Eliza. *Missing Pages in American History Revealing the Services of Negroes in the Early Wars in the United States of America, 1641–1815.* Washington, D.C.: Printed for the Author, 1919.

THE NINETEENTH CENTURY

Aimwell, Absalom. "A Pinkster Ode, Albany, 1803." *New York Folklore Quarterly* 8 (Spring 1952): 31–45.

Armstrong, Orland Kay. *Old Massa's People: The Old Slaves Tell Their Story.* Indianapolis: Bobbs Merrill, 1931.

Austin, William. *Susanna, Jeanie, and The Old Folks at Home: The Songs of Stephen C. Foster from His Time to Ours.* New York: Macmillan Publishing Co., 1975. Includes information about Francis Johnson and other black musicians of the nineteenth century.

Avirett, James B. *The Old Plantation: How We Lived in Great House and Cabin Before the War.* New York: F. T. Neely, 1901.

Beasley, Delilah L. *The Negro Trail Blazers of California.* Los Angeles: Published by the Author, 1919. Chapter 17 is devoted to discussion of musicians.

Birdoff, Harry. *The World's Greatest Hit—Uncle Tom's Cabin.* New York: S. F. Vanni, 1947. Includes discussion of the first black actors to play leading roles in *Uncle Tom's Cabin* (Sam Lucas and Horace Weston) and the first black choral groups to appear in the productions, as well as history of the play.

Bishop, Julia Truitt. "Easter Morn in a Colored Convent," *Ladies Home Journal* (April 1899). Discussion of a visit to the Convent of the Holy Family in New Orleans.

Blassingame, John W. *The Slave Community: Plantation Life in the Antebellum South.* New York: Oxford University Press, 1972.

Botkin, B. A. *Lay My Burden Down: A Folk History of Slavery.* Chicago: University of Chicago Press, 1945.

Botume, Elizabeth Hyde. *First Days Amongst the Contrabands.* 1893. New York: Arno Press, 1968. Reports on a teacher's experiences with the ex-slaves in the 1860s.

Bremer, Fredrika. *The Homes of the New World: Impressions of America.* Transl. by Mary Howitt. New York: Harper & Brothers, 1853. Excellent for its discussion of slave life and music.

Brent, Linda [Harriet Jacobs]. *Incidents in the Life of a Slave Girl. Written by Herself.* Ed. by L. Maria Child. Boston: Published for the Author, 1861. Includes good description of the John Kuner festival.

Brown, William Wells. *The Anti-Slavery Harp: A Collection of Songs for Anti-Slavery Meetings.* Boston: B. Marsh, 1849. Texts only, but with suggestions for appropriate tunes.

——. *The Negro in the American Rebellion.* Boston: Lee & Shepard, 1867.

——. *My Southern Home: Or, The South and Its People.* Boston: A. G. Brown, 1880.

Cable, George. "Creole Slave Songs," *Century Magazine* 31, n.s. 9 (April 1886): 807–28. Repr. in KATZ.

——. "The Dance in Place Congo," *Century Magazine* 31 (February 1886): 517–32. Detailed description of the slave dancing in the Place Congo of New Orleans. Repr. in KATZ.

Damon, S. Foster. "The Negro in Early American Songsters," *Papers of the Bibliographical Society of America* 28 (1934): part 2, 132–63. Includes discussion of the earliest performers in blackface and the beginning of minstrelsy in the United States.

Dannett, Sylvia. *Profiles of Negro Womanhood.* Yonkers, NY: Educational Heritage, 1964. Includes most of the important female performers.

[Dazey, Charles T.]. *The Fine Book Circle Presents the First Book Appearance of Charles T. Dazey's Thrilling American Drama in Old Kentucky.* Forward by Barrett H. Clark. Introduction by the Author. A Historical Note and an All-Star Cast of Players Depicted in the Leading Roles by Paul McPharlin. Detroit: Fine Book Circle, 1937.

Delany, Martin Robison. *Blake: or, The Huts of America.* 1859. With an Introduction by Floyd Miller. Boston: Beacon Press, 1970. This novel, the first published by a black writer in the United States (two earlier novels of black authors were published in England), offers insight into slavery from the black perspective.

——. *The Condition, Elevation, Emigration, and Destiny of the Colored People of the United States.* Philadelphia: Published by the Author, 1852. Includes information about important black musicians of the early nineteenth century.

Desdunes, Rudolphe Lucien. *Nos Hommes et notre histoire.* 1911. Trans. by Dorothea Olga McCants: *Our People and Our History.* Baton Rouge: Louisiana State University Press, 1973. Chapter 7 is devoted to the musicians of New Orleans in the nineteenth century who were identified as "creoles of color."

Dichter, Harry, and Elliot Shapiro. *Early American Sheet Music: Its Lure and Its Lore.* New York: R. R. Bowker Co., 1941. Includes discussion of the so-called Negro songs sung by performers in blackface.

Douglass, Frederick. *Life and Times of Frederick Douglass, Written by Himself.* 1881. Repr. New York: Collier Books, 1962.

———. *My Bondage and My Freedom.* New York: Miller, Orton & Mulligan, 1855. Offers insight into the importance of music in slave life and culture.

———. *Narrative of the Life of Frederick Douglass, an American Slave. Written by Himself.* 1845. Repr. New York: Penguin Books, 1982.

Douglass, William. *Annals of the First African Church in the United States of America.* Philadelphia: King & Baird, 1862. History of the St. Thomas Episcopal Church in Philadelphia from its origin to mid-century.

Du Bois, William E. B. *The Souls of Black Folk.* 1903. New Introduction by Herbert Aptheker. Millwood, NY: Kraus-Thomson Organization, 1973. Discussion of Negro spirituals in a chapter entitled "Of the Sorrow Songs," which is reprinted in KATZ and RBAM.

Emery, Lynne Fauley. *Black Dance in the United States from 1619–1970.* Palo Alto, CA: National Press Books, 1972.

Epstein, Dena. *Sinful Tunes and Spirituals: Black Folk Music to the Civil War.* Urbana: University of Illinois Press, 1977.

Fisher, Miles. *Negro Slave Songs in the United States.* New York: American Historical Association, 1953. Discussion and analysis of the Negro spirituals, not a collection.

Fletcher, Tom. *The Tom Fletcher Story: 100 Years of the Negro in Show Business.* New York: Burdge, 1954. Discusses minstrelsy in the late nineteenth century.

Floyd, Samuel A. Jr. *The Power of Black Music: Interpreting Its History from Africa to the United States.* New York: Oxford University Press, 1995.

———, and Marsha J. Reisser. "The Sources and Resources of Classic Ragtime Music," *Black Music Research Journal* 4 (1984): 22–59.

Forten, Charlotte. *The Journal of Charlotte L. Forten.* Ed. by Ray Allen Billington. New York: Dryden Press, 1953. Detailed descriptions of the singing of ex-slaves during the 1860s in the Sea Islands, South Carolina.

Foster, George G. *New York by Gas-Light, with Here and There a Streak of Sunshine.* New York, 1850. Reprinted in his *New York by Gas-Light and Other Urban Sketches* (Berkeley: University of California Press, 1990.) Discussion of dance halls with black fiddlers in Chapters 7 and 9.

Fuld, James J. *The Book of World-Famous Music: Classical, Popular, and Folk.* 1966. 4th rev. and enlarged ed. New York: Dover, 1995.

Gaines, Francis Pendleton. *The Southern Plantation.* New York: Columbia University Press, 1924.

Handy, W. C. *Father of the Blues: An Autobiography.* Ed. by Arna Bontemps, with a Foreword by Abble Niles. 1941. London: Sedgwick & Jackson, 1957. Includes discussion of minstrelsy in the nineteenth century.

———. *Unsung Americans Sung.* New York: Handy Brothers Music Co., 1944. Includes information about the less well-known black musicians.

Harris, "Spike" M. A. *A Negro History Tour of Manhattan.* New York: Greenwood Publishing Co., 1968. Includes many references to black musicians.

Hearn, Lafcadio. *The Selected Writings of Lafcadio Hearn.* Ed. by Henry Goodman. New York: Citadel Press, 1949. Includes the article on "Levee Life" that was originally published in the *Cincinnati Commercial,* March 17, 1876.

Higginson, Thomas Wentworth. *Army Life in a Black Regiment.* Boston: Fields, Osgood & Co., 1870.

Hughes, Langston, and Milton Meltzer. *Black Magic: A Pictorial History of the Negro in American Entertainment.* Englewood Cliffs, NJ: Prentice-Hall, 1967.

Hughes, Rupert. "A Eulogy of Ragtime," *The Musical Record* (April 1, 1899): 157–59.

Hungerford, James. *The Old Plantation, and What I Gathered There in an Autumn*

Month. New York: Harper & Brothers, 1859. The author visits a plantation in Maryland.

Hutton, Lawrence. *Curiosities of the American Stage.* New York: Harper & Bros., 1891. Includes discussion of "the stage Negro" and Ethiopian minstrelsy. Also a program bill of the African Grove Theatre and a picture of actor Ira Aldridge.

Johnson, Guy B. *John Henry: Tracking Down a Negro Legend.* Chapel Hill: University of North Carolina Press, 1929. Discussion of the John Henry myths and songs.

Jones, Charles Colcock. *The Religious Instruction of the Negroes in the United States.* 1842. Repr. Freeport, NY: Books for Libraries Press, 1971.

Katz, Bernard, ed. *The Social Implications of Early Negro Music in the United States: With over 150 of the Songs, Many of Them with Their Music.* New York: Arno Press, 1969. Includes reprints of the first articles published about the slave songs in the post–Civil War period.

Keck, George R., and Sherrill V. Martin, eds. *Feel The Spirit: Studies in Nineteenth-Century Afro-American Music.* Westport, CT: Greenwood Press, 1988.

Kemble, Frances Anne. *Journal of a Residence on a Georgian Plantation in 1838–1839.* 1863. Repr. Ed. by John A. Scott. New York: Alfred A. Knopf, 1961.

King, Grace. *New Orleans: The Place and the People.* New York: Macmillan Publishing Co., 1895.

Kinnard, J. "Who Are Our National Poets," *Knickerbocker Magazine* 26 (October 1845): 331–41. Discussion of Ethiopian minstrelsy and its origin among the slaves. Repr. in BPIM 3 (Spring 1975): 83–94.

Kmen, Henry A. *Music in New Orleans: The Formative Years, 1791–1841.* Baton Rouge: Louisiana State University Press, 1966.

Krehbiel, Henry, *Afro-American Folksongs: A Study in Racial and National Music.* New York: G. Schirmer, 1914. Includes both analysis of the folk music and examples of songs.

Latrobe, Benjamin. *The Journal of Latrobe: Being the Notes and Sketches of an Architect, Naturalist and Traveler in the United States from 1796 to 1820.* With an Introduction by J. H. B. Latrobe. 1905. New York: Burt Franklin, 1971. Latrobe's journal is also published under the title *Impressions Respecting New Orleans: Diary & Sketches, 1818–1820* (1951).

Levine, Lawrence. *Black Culture and Black Consciousness: Afro-American Thought from Slavery to Freedom.* New York: Oxford University Press, 1977. Considerable attention given to black American folksong.

Long, John Dixon. *Pictures of Slavery in Church and State.* Philadelphia: Published by the Author, 1857.

Lovell, John. *Black Song: The Forge and the Flame. The Story of How the Afro-American Spiritual Was Hammered Out.* 1972. Repr. New York: Paragon House, 1986.

Majors, M. A. *Noted Negro Women.* Chicago: Donohue & Henneberry Printers, 1893. Includes discussion of the important female musicians of the period.

Mallard, Robert Q. *Plantation Life Before Emancipation.* Richmond: Whittet & Shepperson, 1892.

Marcuse, Maxwell. *Tin Pan Alley in Gaslight: Saga of the Songs that Made the Gray Nineties "Gay."* Watkins Glen, NY: Century House, 1959.

Marks, Edward B. *They All Sang: From Tony Pastor to Rudy Vallee.* New York: The Viking Press, 1935. Includes discussion of minstrelsy, ragtime, and such black songwriters as Gussie Davis.

Mathews, Charles. *The London Mathews: Containing an Account of This Celebrated Comedian's Trip to America.* Philadelphia: Morgan & Yaeger, 1824. Includes discussion of Mathew's visit to the African Grove Theatre in New York.

_____. *Sketches of Mr. Mathew's Celebrated Trip to America . . . with the most Laughable of the Stories and Adventures, and Eight Original Comic Songs.* Written for Charles Mathews by James Smith. London: Printed for J. Limbird, 1824.

Meltzer, Milton, ed. *In Their Own Words: A History of the American Negro, 1619–1865.* New York: Thomas Y. Crowell Co., 1964.

Mitchell, Loften. *Black Drama.* New York: Hawthorne Publishers, 1967. Discusses the African Grove Theatre in New York during the 1820s.

Munsell, Joel. *Annals of Albany.* 9 vols. Albany: J. Munsell, 1852. Scattered discussion of Pinkster festivals, black itinerant musicians, Elizabeth Taylor Greenville (vol. 4), Frank Johnson (vol. 9), and others.

_____. *Collections on the History of Albany from Its Discovery to the Present Time.* . . . 4 vols. Albany: J. Munsell, 1865–71. Vol. 2 includes detailed descriptions of the Pinkster festival.

Nathan, Hans. *Dan Emmett and the Rise of Early Negro Minstrelsy.* Norman: University of Oklahoma Press, 1962. Very little attention given to black minstrels except for Master Juba.

Northup, Solomon. *Twelve Years a Slave: The Narrative of Solomon Northup, A Citizen of New York, Kidnapped in Washington City in 1841 and Rescued in 1853, from a Cotton Plantation near the Red River in Louisiana.* Auburn, NY: Derby and Miller, 1853. A violinist, Northup offers insight into the lifestyle of slave and free black musicians. Repr. of relevant passages in RBAM.

Oberholtzer, Ellis Paxon. *Philadelphia: A History of the City and Its People.* 4 vols. Philadelphia: S. J. Clarke Publishing Co., 1912. Information about Frank Johnson and other black bandleaders, also about black street criers.

Olmsted, Frederick. *A Journey in the Seaboard Slave States in the Years 1853–1854, with Remarks on Their Economy.* . . . 1856. New York: G. P. Putnam's Sons, 1904.

Ottley, Roi, and William Weatherby. *The Negro in New York: An Informal Social History.* New York: New York Public Library, 1967. Includes extensive discussion of musical matters.

Paine, Lewis W. *Six Years in a Georgia Prison. Narrative of Lewis W. Paine, Who Suffered Imprisonment Six Years in Georgia, for the Crime of Aiding the Escape of a Fellowman from that State, after He had Fled from Slavery. Written by Himself.* New York: Printed for the Author, 1851. Repr. of relevant passages in RBAM.

Parks, H. B. *Follow de Drinkin' Gou'd.* Publications of the Texas Folk Lore Society, No. 7. Ed. by J. Frank Dobie. Austin: Published by the Texas Folk Lore Society, 1928. Discussion of the different versions of the folksong and a story about its origin.

Payne, Daniel. *History of the African Methodist Episcopal Church.* Two parts, in one volume. Nashville, TN: Publishing House of the A.M.E. Sunday School Union, 1891.

_____. *Recollections of Seventy Years.* With an Introduction by F. J. Grimké. Nashville, TN: Published by the A.M.E. Sunday School Union, 1888. Includes detailed discussion of church music, both formal and informal spirituals and shouts. Repr. of selected passages in RBAM.

Ping, Nancy R. "Black Musical Activities in Antebellum Wilmington, North Carolina," BPIM 8 (Fall 1980): 139–60. Includes discussion of the John Conny festival.

Platt, Orville. "Negro Governors," *The New Haven Historical Society Quarterly* 6 (1900): 315–35.

Puckett, Newbell Niles. *Folk Beliefs of the Southern Negro.* Chapel Hill: University of North Carolina, 1926.

Raboteau, Albert. *Slave Religion: The "Invisible Institution" in the Antebellum South.* New York: Oxford University Press, 1978.

Rawick, George P., ed. *The American Slave: A Composite Autobiography.* 48 vols. Westport, CT: Greenwood Press, 1977–79. A compilation of the slave narratives collected during the years 1936–38 by interviewers who were employed by the Federal Writer's Project. The narratives were assembled and processed at the Library of Congress under the Works Progress Administration.

Reid, Ira De A. "The John Canoe Festival," *Phylon* 3 (1942): 349–77.

Rice, Edward LeRoy. *Monarchs of Minstrelsy from "Daddy" Rice to Date.* New York:

Kenny Publishing Co., 1911. Includes discussion of Picayune Butler, Master Juba, Horace Weston, and Bert Williams.

Richardson, Harry V. *Dark Glory: A Picture of the Church Among Negroes in the Rural South*. New York: Friendship Press, 1947.

Sampson, Henry. *Blacks in Blackface: A Source Book on Early Black Musical Shows*. Metuchen, NJ: Scarecrow Press, 1980. Also includes discussion of black minstrelsy.

Scharf, John Thomas, and Thompson Westcott. *History of Philadelphia, 1609–1884*. Philadelphia: L. H. Everts & Co., 1884. Much information about black culture, especially good for Frank Johnson.

Scruggs, Lawson. *Women of Distinction*. Raleigh, NC: Published by the Author, 1893. Includes discussion of the important female musicians of the period.

Sears, Ann. "Keyboard Music by Nineteenth-Century Afro-American Composers." *Feel The Spirit: Studies in Nineteenth-Century Afro-American Music*. Ed. by George R. Keck and Sherrill V. Martin. Westport, CT: Greenwood Press, 1988.

Simond, Ike. *Old Slack's Reminiscence and Pocket History of the Colored Profession from 1865 to 1891*. 1891. Repr. with Preface by Francis Lee Utley and Introduction by Robert C. Toll. Bowling Green, OH: Bowling Green University Popular Press, 1974.

Snipe, Simon [pseud.]. *Sports of New York: Containing an Evening at the African Theatre*. New York, 1823.

Sojourner Truth. *Narrative of Sojourner Truth*. 1878. Repr. New York: Arno Press and the New York Times, 1968.

Southern, Eileen. "The Georgia Minstrels: The Early Years." *Inter-American Music Review* 10 (1989, Spring–Summer): 157–67.

Stuckey, Sterling. *Slave Culture: Nationalist Theory and the Foundations of Black America*. New York: Oxford University Press, 1987.

Svin'in, Pavel. *Picturesque United States of America, 1811, 1812, 1813, Being a Memoir on Paul Svin'in . . . by Avraham Yarmolinsky*. New York: W. E. Rudge, 1930. In addition to discussing his visit to a black church in Philadelphia, Svin'in painted two watercolor scenes that included blacks.

Tallant, Robert. *Voodoo in New Orleans*. New York: Macmillan Publishing Co., 1946.

Todd, Robert W. *Methodism of the Peninsula*. Philadelphia: Methodist Episcopal Book Rooms, 1886.

Toll, Robert C. *Blacking Up: The Minstrel Show in Nineteenth-Century America*. New York: Oxford University Press, 1974.

Towne, Laura M. *Letters and Diary of Laura M. Towne, Written from the Sea Islands of South Carolina, 1862–1884*. Ed. by Rupert S. Holland. Cambridge, MA: Riverside Press, 1912.

Trotter, James M. *Music and Some Highly Musical People; With Sketches of the Lives of Remarkable Musicians of the Colored Race: With Portraits, and an Appendix Containing Copies of Music Composed by Colored Men*. 1878. Repr. New York: Johnson Publishing Co., 1968.

Wade, Richard. *Slavery in the Cities: The South, 1820–1860*. New York: Oxford University Press, 1964.

White, Newman Ivey. *American Negro Folk-Songs*. Cambridge: Harvard University Press, 1928.

White, William Carter. *A History of Military Music in America*. New York: Exposition Press, 1944. References to the band of Francis Johnson and other black bands.

Wiley, Bell. *Southern Negroes, 1861–1865*. New York, 1938.

Williams, Isaac. *Sunshine and Shadow of Slave Life: Reminiscences as Told by Isaac Williams to "Tege."* East Saginaw, MI: Printed for the Author, 1885.

Willson, Joseph [Willson, Joseph]. *Sketches of the Higher Classes of Colored Society in Philadelphia. By a Southerner*. Philadelphia: Merrihew & Thompson, 1841.

Wilson, Olly. "The Heterogeneous Sound Ideal in African-American Music." *New Per-*

spectives on Music: Essays in Honor of Eileen Southern. Ed. by Josephine Wright, with Samuel A. Floyd, Jr. Warren, MI: Harmonie Park Press, 1992.

Yoder, Don. *Pennsylvania Spirituals.* Lancaster, PA: Pennsylvania Folklife Society, 1961. Includes detailed discussion of black religious music.

NINETEENTH-CENTURY COLLECTIONS: MUSIC SCORES

Allen, William, Charles Ware, and Lucy Garrison. *Slave Songs of the United States.* 1867. Repr. New York, 1967. Repr. of Preface in RBAM (and some songs).

Armstrong, Mary Frances, and Helen Ludlow. *Hampton and Its Students. By Two of Its Teachers. . . . With Fifty Cabin and Plantation Songs, arranged by Thomas P. Fenner. . . .* New York: G. P. Putnam's Sons, 1874.

Barton, William. *Old Plantation Hymns.* Boston: Lamson, Wolffe & Company, 1899. Repr. in KATZ.

Jackson, George Pullen. *White and Negro Spirituals: Their Life Span and Kinship.* Locust Valley, NY: J. J. Augustin Publisher, 1943.

James, Willis Laurence. *Stars in De Elements, A Study of Negro Folk Music.* Ed. by Jon Michael Spencer. Durham, NC: Duke University Press, 1995.

[Johnson, Frank]. *A Choice Collection of the Works of Francis Johnson.* 2 vols. Ed. by Charles Jones and Lorenzo K. Greenwich. New York: Point Two Publications, 1932–37.

Marsh, J. B. T. *The Story of the Jubilee Singers, With Their Songs.* 1876. Repr. New York, 1969. Numerous editions of the songs of the Jubilee Singers were published during the years 1872–1903.

Parrish, Lydia A. *Slave Songs of the Georgia Sea Islands.* Music transcribed by Creighton Churchill and Robert MacGimsey. New York: Creative Age Press, 1942.

Scarborough, Dorothy. *On the Trail of Negro Folk-Songs.* 1925. Repr. Hatboro, PA: Folklore Associates, 1963.

Southern, Eileen, ed. *African American Theater: Out of Bondage (1876)* and *Peculiar Sam; or, The Underground Railroad (1879).* New York: Garland Publishing, 1994. Spirituals and minstrel songs.

Trotter, James M. *Music and Some Highly Musical People. . . .* 1878. Repr. New York: Johnson Publishing Company, 1968. Contains thirteen musical pieces, including three sacred, one for guitar, two art songs, and the remainder for piano.

THE TWENTIETH CENTURY

Abdul, Raoul. *Blacks in Classical Music.* New York: Dodd, Mead & Co., 1977.

_____. *Famous Black Entertainers of Today.* New York: Dodd, Mead & Co., 1974.

Anderson, Jervis. *Harlem The Great Black Way, 1919–50.* London: Orbis Publishing, Limited, 1982.

Austin, William. *Music in the Twentieth Century: From Debussy to Stravinsky.* New York: W. W. Norton, 1966. Especially good for scholarly analysis and discussion of black jazz composers.

Baker, David, Lida Belt, and Herman C. Hudson. *The Black Composer Speaks.* Metuchen, NJ: Scarecrow Press, 1978. Interviews with fifteen contemporary composers.

Balliett, Whitney. *Improvising: Sixteen Jazz Musicians and Their Art.* New York: Oxford University Press, 1977.

_____. *Jelly Roll, Jabbo, and Fats: 19 Portraits in Jazz.* New York: Oxford University Press, 1983.

Baraka, Imamu Amiri (LeRoi Jones). *Black Music.* New York: William Morrow, 1967.

Primarily articles about contemporary jazz (for that period) previously published in magazines and record-liner notes.

Barbour, Glenn. *Afro-American Classical Music: A New Awareness.* Atlanta: C. Noland Publishing Co., 1985.

Bastin, Bruce. *Red River Blues: The Blues Tradition in the Southeast.* Urbana: University of Illinois Press, 1986.

Belz, Carl. *The Story of Rock.* 1969. 2nd ed. New York: Oxford University Press, 1972. Historical survey from the time of the origins of rock. Also includes some discussion of rhythm 'n' blues.

Berendt, Joachim E. *The Jazz Book: From Ragtime to Fusion and Beyond.* Transl. by Helmut and Barbara Bredigkeit with Dan Morgenstern. 1975 (English language ed.). Rev. and exp. Westport, CT: Lawrence Hill & Company, 1982.

Berlin, Edward. *Ragtime: A Musical and Cultural History.* Berkeley: University of California Press, 1980.

Berry, Jason, Jonathan Foose, and Tad Jones. *Up from the Cradle of Jazz: New Orleans Music Since World War II.* Athens: University of Georgia Press, 1986.

Bishop, Cardell. *Opera at the Hippodrome in New York City.* Santa Monica, CA: Published by Cardell Bishop, 1979. Includes information about opera singers Jules Bledsoe, Minto Cato, Caterina Jarboro, and Charlotte Murray.

Blesh, Rudi. *Combo: U. S. A.: Eight Lives in Jazz.* 1971. Repr. New York: Da Capo Press, 1979.

Blesh, Rudi. *Shining Trumpets: A History of Jazz.* 2nd ed. New York: Alfred A. Knopf, 1958. Repr. New York: Da Capo Press, 1975.

Blesh, Rudi, and Harriet Janis. *They All Played Ragtime: The True Story of an American Music.* 1950. 4th ed. New York: Oak Publications, 1971.

Bogle, Donald. *Eighty Years of America's Black Superstars.* New York: Harmony Books, 1980.

Bontemps, Arna. "Rock, Church, Rock." *Common Ground* 8 (1942).

Booker, Queen. "Congregational Music in a Pentecostal Church." BPIM 18 (Fall 1990): 31–44.

Boyer, Horace Clarence. *How Sweet the Sound: The Golden Age of Gospel.* Washington, D.C.: Elliott & Clark Publishing Company, 1995.

Brawley, Benjamin. *The Negro Genius: A New Appraisal of the Achievement of the American Negro in Literature and the Fine Arts.* 1937. Repr. New York: Biblio & Tannen, 1966. Detailed in discussion of musicians but general omission of jazz and folk artists.

Broughton, Viv. *Black Gospel: An Illustrated History of the Gospel Sound.* Poole, Dorset, [England]: Blandford Press, 1985.

Brown, Charles T. *The Art of Rock and Roll.* Englewood Cliffs, NJ: Prentice-Hall, 1983.

Budds, Michael J. *Jazz in the Sixties: The Expansion of Musical Resources and Techniques.* Iowa City: University of Iowa Press, 1978.

Burton, Jack. *The Blue Book of Broadway Musicals.* 1952. With additions by Larry Freeman. Watkins Glen, NY: Century House, 1969.

Burton, Jack. *The Blues Book of Tin Pan Alley: A Human Interest Anthology of American Popular Music.* 2 vols. 1950. With 1950–65 Supplement by Larry Freeman. Watkins Glen, NY: Century House, 1965.

Charters, Samuel, and Leonard Kundstdt. *Jazz: History of the New York Scene.* 1962. Repr. New York: Da Capo Press, 1982. Discussion of black dance music in New York from the turn of the century through the 1950s.

Charters, Samuel. *The Country Blues.* 1959. Repr. New York: Da Capo Press, 1975.

Cherry, Gwendolyn, Ruby Thomas, and Pauline Willis. *Portraits in Color: The Lives of Colorful Negro Women.* New York: Pageant Press, 1962.

Chilton, John. *Who's Who of Jazz: Storyville to Swing Street.* 1970. 4th ed. New York: Da Capo Press, 1985.

Cobbins, Otho B., ed. *History of the Church of Christ (Holiness) U. S. A., 1895–1965.* New York: Vantage Press, 1966.

Collier, James. *The Making of Jazz: A Comprehensive History.* Boston: Houghton Mifflin Co., 1978.

Cone, James. *The Spirituals and the Blues: An Interpretation.* New York: Seabury Press, 1972.

Courlander, Harold. *A Treasury of Afro-American Folklore.* New York: Crown Publishers, 1976.

Crawford, Richard. "Notes on Jazz Standards by Black Authors and Composers, 1899–1942." *New Perspectives on Music: Essays in Honor of Eileen Southern.* Ed. by Josephine Wright with Samuel A. Floyd, Jr. Warren, MI: Harmonie Park Press, 1992.

Dahl, Linda. *Stormy Weather: The Music and Lives of a Century of Jazzwomen.* New York: Pantheon Books, 1984.

Dance, Stanley. *The World of Count Basie.* New York: Charles Scribner's Sons, 1980.

———. *The World of Duke Ellington.* New York: Charles Scribner's Sons, 1970.

———. *The World of Earl Hines.* New York: Charles Scribner's Sons, 1977.

———. *The World of Swing.* New York: Charles Scribner's Sons, 1974.

Dannett, Sylvia. *Profiles of Negro Womanhood.* Yonkers, NY: Educational Heritage, 1964.

Davis, Francis. *In The Moment: Jazz in the 1980s.* New York: Oxford University Press, 1986.

Douglass, Frederick. *Life and Times of Frederick Douglass, Written by Himself.* 1881. Repr. New York: Collier Books, 1962.

———. *Narrative of the Life of Frederick Douglass, an American Slave. Written by Himself.* 1845. Repr. New York: Penguin Books, 1982.

Dunbar, Ernest. *The Black Expatriates.* New York: E. P. Dutton, 1968. Includes discussion of several important black musicians who settled abroad: among them, Gloria Davy, Dean Dixon, and Reri Grist.

Ellison, Ralph. *Shadow and Act.* New York: Random House, 1964.

Emery, Lynne Fauley. *Black Dance in the United States from 1619 to 1970.* Palo Alto, CA: National Press Books, 1972.

Evans, David. *Big Road Blues.* Berkeley: University of California Press, 1982. Historical survey and analytical study of the blues.

"Evolution of the Jazz Composer, The." *BMI: The Many Worlds of Music.* Issue no. 3 (1981). Entire issue given over to jazz, including articles by Burt Korall and Dan Morgenstern and biographical sketches of major jazzmen and women.

Feather, Leonard. *From Satchmo to Miles.* New York: Stein & Day, 1972. Historical survey of jazz from Louis Armstrong to Miles Davis.

———. *Inside Be-Bop.* Reissued as *Inside Jazz.* New York: J. J. Robbins, 1949.

Fernett, Gene. *Swing Out: Great Negro Dance Bands.* Midland, MI: Pendell, Co., 1970.

———. *A Thousand Golden Horns: The Exciting Age of America's Greatest Dance Bands.* Midland, MI: The Pendell Co., 1966. Includes discussion of the big bands of black jazzmen, primarily during the 1920s–40s.

Ferris, William. *Blues form the Delta: An Illustrated Documentary on the Music and Musicians of the Mississippi Delta.* Garden City, NY: Anchor Press / Doubleday, 1978.

Fletcher, Tom. *The Tom Fletcher Story: 100 Years of the Negro in Show Business.* New York: Burdge, 1954. Especially good for the early twentieth century.

Fox, Ted. *Showtime at the Apollo.* New York: Holt, Rinehart and Winston, 1983.

Garland, Phyl. *The Sound of Soul.* Chicago: Henry Regnery Co., 1969.

Gart, Galen, ed. *First Pressings: Rock History as Chronicled in Billboard Magazine.* Milford, NH: Big Nickel Publications, 1986.

_____. *The History of Rhythm & Blues: 1953.* Milford, NH: Big Nickel Publications, 1989.

Giddins, Gary. *Rhythm-a-ning: Jazz Tradition and Innovation in the '80s.* New York: Oxford University Press, 1985.

_____. *Riding on a Blue Note: Jazz and American Popular Music.* New York: Oxford University Press, 1981.

Gitler, Ira. *Jazz Masters of the Forties.* 1966. Repr. New York: Collier Books, 1974.

_____. *Swing to Bop: An Oral History of the Transition in Jazz in the 1940s.* New York: Oxford University Press, 1985.

Given, Dave. *The Dave Given Rock 'n' Roll Stars Handbook.* Smithtown, NY: Exposition Press, 1980. Includes also rhythm 'n' blues figures and groups.

Green, Mildred Denby. *Black Women Composers: A Genesis.* Boston, MA: Twayne Publishers, 1983.

Greene, Robert Ewell. *Black Defenders of America, 1775–1973.* Chicago: Johnson Publishing Co., 1974. Includes discussion of military musicians.

Gridley, Mark. *Jazz Style.* Englewood Cliffs, NJ: Prentice-Hall, 1978. Historical survey and musical analysis.

Guralnick, Peter. *Sweet Soul Music: Rhythm and Blues and the Southern Dream of Freedom.* New York: Harper & Row, 1986.

Hadlock, Richard. *Jazz Masters of the Twenties.* New York: Macmillan Publishing Co., 1965.

Handy, D. Antoinette. *Black Conductors.* Metuchen, NJ: Scarecrow Press, 1995.

_____. *Black Women in American Bands and Orchestras.* Metuchen, NJ: Scarecrow Press, 1981.

_____. *The International Sweethearts of Rhythm.* Metuchen, NJ: Scarecrow Press, 1983.

Handy, W. C., ed. *Blues: An Anthology.* New York: A. and C. Boni, 1926.

_____. *Negro Authors and Composers of the United States.* New York: Handy Bros. Music Co., ca. 1938. Short listing (24 pages) of black musicians.

_____. *Unsung Americans Sung.* New York: Handy Brothers Music Co., 1944. Includes information about the less well-known black musicians.

Harrison, Daphne Duval. *Black Pearls: Blues Queens of the 1920s.* New Brunswick, NJ: Rutgers, The State University, 1988.

Haskins, Jim. *The Cotton Club.* New York: Random House, 1977.

Hasse, John Edward, ed. *Ragtime: Its History, Composers, and Music.* New York: Schirmer Books, 1985.

Heilbut, Tony. *The Gospel Sound: Good News and Bad Times.* New York: Anchor Press / Doubleday, 1985. Discussion of gospel style and biographical sketches of major figures of the period.

Hipsher, Edward Ellsworth. *American Opera and Its Composers: A Complete History of Serious American Opera, with a Summary of the Lighter Forms Which Led up to Its Birth.* 1927. Expanded ed. Philadelphia: Theodore Presser, 1934. Includes biographical sketches for Harry Lawrence Freeman and others.

Holt, Nora. "The Chronological History of the NANM," BPIM 2 (Fall 1974): 234–35. History of the origin of the National Association of Negro Musicians.

Huggins, Nathan Irvin. *Voices from the Harlem Renaissance.* New York: Oxford University Press, 1976.

Jasen, David A., and Trebor Tichenor. *Rags and Ragtime: A Musical History.* New York: Seabury Press, 1978.

Johnson, Francis Hall. "Notes on the Negro Spiritual," RBAM. Discussion of the spiritual from the point of view of a choral conductor and composer.

Johnson, James Weldon. *Black Manhattan.* 1930. Repr. New York: Atheneum, 1968. Especially good for the early twentieth century, but also discusses musical activity in the late nineteenth century.

Jones, John Paul. *The Black Man in Military Music of the United States*. [Jackson, MS: Westside Printers], 1978.

Jones, K. Maurice. *The Story of Rap Music*. Brookfield, CT: Millbrook Press, 1994.

Jones, LeRoi. (Baraka, Imamu Amiri). *Blues People: The Negro Experience in White America and the Music That Developed from It*. New York: William Morrow, 1963.

Keil, Charles. *Urban Blues*. Chicago: University of Chicago Press, 1966. Includes both sociological and historical discussion, as well as analysis of contemporary blues styles.

Kofsky, Frank. *Black Nationalism and the Revolution in Music*. New York: Pathfinder Press, 1970.

Layne, Maude Wanzer. *The Negro's Contribution to Music*. Philadelphia: Theodore Presser, 1942. Includes biographical sketches.

Leadbitter, Mike, ed. *Nothing but the Blues*. London: Hanover Books, 1971. Primarily reprints of articles originally published in the British magazine *Blues Unlimited*.

Lichtenstein, Grace, and Laura Dankner. *Musical Gumbo: The Music of New Orleans*. New York: W. W. Norton, 1993.

Little, Arthur. *From Harlem to the Rhine*. [1936]. Repr. New York: Haskell Book Sellers, Inc. 1974. Good for its discussion of James Reese Europe and his band overseas.

Locke, Alain. *The Negro and His Music*. 1936. Repr. New York: Arno Press, 1969.

Lotz, Rainer, and Ian Pegg, eds. *Under the Imperial Carpet: Essays in Black History 1780–1950*. Crawley, England: Rabbit Press Limited, 1986.

Lotz, Rainer E. and Ulrich Neuert. *The AFRS [The Armed Forces Radio Service] "Jubilee" Transcription Program: An Exploratory Discography*. Frankfurt, Germany: Norbert Ruecker, 1985.

Lovell, John. *Black Song: The Forge and the Flame. The Story of How the Afro-American Spiritual Was Hammered Out*. 1972. Repr. New York: Paragon House, 1986.

Lydon, Michael. *Boogie Lightning*. New York: Dial Press, 1974.

Lyons, Len. *The Great Jazz Pianists: Speaking of Their Lives and Music*. New York: William Morrow, 1983.

Machlis, Joseph. *Introduction to Contemporary Music*. 1961. 2nd. ed. New York: W. W. Norton, 1979.

Marks, Edward B. *They All Sang: From Tony Pastor to Rudi Vallee*. New York: The Viking Press, 1935. Includes discussion of the early black songwriters, among them Bob Cole, J. Rosamond Johnson, Irving Jones, Chris Smith.

Marsalis, Wynton, and Frank Stewart. *Sweet Swing Blues on the Road*. New York: W. W. Norton, 1994.

Mattfeld, Julius. *A Handbook of American Operatic Premieres, 1731–1962*. Detroit Studies in Music Bibliography, No. 5. Detroit: Information Service, 1963.

Maultsby, Portia K. *Afro-American Religious Music: A Study of Musical Diversity*. Papers of the Hymn Society of America. Springfield, OH: Hymn Society of American, [1981?]

McCarthy, Albert J. *Big Band Jazz*. New York: Putnam's Sons, 1974.

Meeker, David. *Jazz in the Movies: A Guide to Jazz Musicians, 1917–1977*. New Rochelle, NY: Arlington House, 1977.

Murray, Albert. *Stomping the Blues*. New York: McGraw-Hill, 1976.

Neff, Robert, and Anthony Connor. *Blues*. New York: David R. Godine, 1975.

Nettl, Bruno. *Folk Music in the United States: An Introduction*. 1960. 3rd ed., rev. and exp. by Helen Meyers. Detroit: Wayne State University Press, 1976.

Odum, Howard. "Folk-Song and Folk Poetry as Found in the Secular Songs of the Southern Negroes," *Journal of American Folklore* 24 (1911): 255–94, 351–96.

Oliver, Paul. *Aspects of the Blues Tradition*. Westport, CT: Hyperion Press, 1973.

———. *Blues Fell This Morning: The Meaning of the Blues*. New York: Cambridge University Press, 1990.

_____. *Blues Off the Record* New York: Hippocrene Books, 1984.

_____. *Savannah Syncopators: African Retentions in the Blues.* New York: Stein & Day, 1970.

_____. *Songsters and Saints: Vocal Traditions on Race Records.* Cambridge, England: Cambridge University Press, 1984.

_____. *The Story of the Blues.* Philadelphia: Chilton Book Co., 1969.

Osgood, Henry Osborne. *So This Is Jazz.* 1926. Repr. New York: Da Capo Press, 1978.

Oster, Harry. *Living Country Blues.* Detroit: Folklore Associates, 1969. Primarily a collection of blue texts.

Palmer, Robert. *Deep Blues.* New York: The Viking Press, 1981.

Panassie, Hugues. *Hot Jazz: The Guide to Swing Music.* New York: M. Witmark, 1936.

Peabody, Charles. "Notes on Negro Music," *Journal of American Folklore* 16 (July 1903): 148–52. Reprint in BPIM 4 (July 1976).

Perrow, Eber C. "Songs and Rhymes from the South," *Journal of American Folklore* 28 (1915): 129–90.

Ramsey, Frederic. *Been Here and Gone.* New Brunswick, NJ: Rutgers University Press, 1960.

Reagon, Bernice Johnson, ed. *We'll Understand It Better By and By: Pioneering African-American Gospel Composers.* Washington, D.C.: Smithsonian Institution Press, 1992.

"Rhythm and Blues," *BMI: The Many Worlds of Music* (Summer 1969). The issue is devoted to historical survey of blues and rhythm 'n' blues, including biographical sketches of major blues figures.

Ricks, George Robinson. *Some Aspects of the Religious Music of the United States Negro: An Ethnomusicological Study with Emphasis on the Gospel Tradition.* New York: Arno Press, 1977.

Riis, Thomas L. *Just Before Jazz: Black Musical Theater in New York 1890–1915.* Washington, D.C.: Smithsonian Institution Press, 1989.

Rose, Al, and Edmond Souchon. *New Orleans Jazz: A Family Album.* 1967. Rev. ed. Baton Rouge: Louisiana State University Press, 1978.

Rowe, Mike. *Chicago Blues.* New York, 1975. Repr. New York: Da Capo Press, 1981.

Russell, Ross. *Jazz Style in Kansas City and the Southwest.* Berkeley: University of California Press, 1971.

Russell, Tony. *Blacks, Whites and Blues: Negro and White Folk Traditions.* New York: Stein & Day, 1970.

Rust, Brian. *The American Record Label Book.* New Rochelle, NY: Arlington House, 1978. Includes discussion of "race records" of the 1920s and '30s.

Sampson, Henry. *Blacks in Blackface: A Source Book on Early Black Musical Shows.* Metuchen, NJ: Scarecrow Press, 1980.

Sanjek, David. "World Up On Rap." *Newsletter* 21:2 (1992). Institute For Studies In American Music / Conservatory of Music, Brooklyn College of the City University of New York. Contains a full bibliography on "Rap."

Schafer, William, and Johannes Riedel. *The Art of Ragtime: Form and Meaning of an Original Black American Art.* Baton Rouge: Louisiana State University Press, 1973.

Schiffman, Jack. *Uptown: The Story of Harlem's Apollo Theatre.* New York: Cowles Books, 1971.

Schuller, Gunther. *Early Jazz: Its Roots and Musical Development.* New York: Oxford University Press, 1968.

_____. *The Swing Era: The Development of Jazz, 1930–1945.* New York: Oxford University Press, 1989.

Scott, Emmett J. *Scott's Official History of the American Negro in the World War.* Washington, D.C., 1919. Discussion of black regimental bands in World War I at home and abroad.

Sears, Ann. "Keyboard Music by Nineteenth-Century Afro-American Composers." *Feel The Spirit: Studies in Nineteenth-Century Afro-American Music.* Ed. by George R. Keck and Sherrill V. Martin. Westport, CT: Greenwood Press, 1988.

Sears, Richard S. *V-Discs: A History and Discography.* Westport, CT: Greenwood Press, 1980.

Shapiro, Nat, and Nat Hentoff, eds. *Hear Me Talkin' to Ya: The Story of Jazz by the Men Who Made It.* New York: Rhinehart, 1955.

Shaw, Arnold. *Black Popular Music in America: From the Spirituals, Minstrels, and Ragtime to Soul, Disco, and Hip-Hop.* New York: Schirmer Books, 1986.

_____. *Dictionary of American Pop / Rock.* New York: Schirmer Books, 1982.

_____. *Honkers and Shouters: The Golden Years of Rhythm and Blues.* New York: Macmillan Publishing Co., 1978.

_____. *The Jazz Age: Popular Music in the 1920s.* New York: Oxford University Press, 1987.

_____. *The Rockin' '50s. The Decade That Transformed the Pop Music Scene.* New York: Hawthorne Books, 1974.

_____. *The Street That Never Slept.* New York: Coward, McCann, and Geoghegan, 1971.

_____. *The World of Soul. Black America's Contribution to the Pop Music Scene.* New York: Cowles Books, 1970.

Simon, George. *The Big Bands.* 1967. Rev. ed. New York: Macmillan Publishing Co., 1971. Detailed discussion of the big bands of the swing era in jazz history from the 1930s through the 1960s.

Spellman, A. B. *Black Music: Four Lives in the Bebop Business.* New York: Schocken Books, 1970.

Spencer, Jon Michael. *Sacred Symphony: The Chanted Sermon of the Black Preacher.* Westport, CT: Greenwood Press, 1987.

Standifer, James, and Barbara Reeder. *Source Book of African and Afro-American Materials for Music Educators.* Washington, D.C.: Contemporary Music Project, 1972.

Stearns, Marshall. *The Story of Jazz.* New York: Oxford University Press, 1956.

_____, and Jean Stearns. *Jazz Dance: The Story of American Vernacular Dance.* New York: Macmillan Publishing Co., 1968.

Tate, Greg. *Flyboys in the Buttermilk.* New York: Simon & Schuster, 1992. Discussion of "rap."

Thomson, Virgil. *Virgil Thomson.* New York: Alfred A. Knopf, 1966. Includes discussion of the opera *Four Saints in Three Acts.*

Tischler, Alice. *Fifteen Black American Composers: A Bibliography of Their Works.* Detroit Studies in Music Bibliography, 45. Detroit: Information Coordinators, 1981.

Titon, Jeff Todd, ed. *Downhome Blues Lyrics: An Anthology from the Post–World War II Era.* 2nd ed. Urbana: University of Illinois Press, 1990.

Titon, Jeff. *Early Downhome Blues: A Musical and Cultural Analysis.* Urbana: University of Illinois Press, 1977.

Ullman, Michael. *Jazz Lives.* Metuchen, NJ: Scarecrow Press, 1980.

Vincent, Ted. "The Social Context of Black Swan Records" LB 86 (May–June 1989): 34–40.

Waldo, Terry. *This Is Ragtime.* New York: Hawthorne Books, 1976.

Walker, Wyatt Tee. *Somebody's Calling My Name: Black Sacred Music and Social Change.* Valley Forge, PA: Judson Press, 1979.

White, Evelyn Davidson, comp. *Choral Music by Afro-American Composers: A Selected, Annotated Bibliography.* Metuchen, NJ: Scarecrow Press, 1981.

Williams, Martin. *Jazz Heritage.* New York: Oxford University Press, 1985.

_____. *Jazz Masters in Transition, 1957–69.* 1970. New York: Da Capo Press, 1982.

Williams, Ora. *American Black Women in the Arts and Social Sciences.* 1973. Rev. ed.

Metuchen, NJ: Scarecrow Press, 1981. Lists compositions of the major composers—for example, Margaret Bonds, Julia Perry, Florence Price, among others—and includes biographical sketches for selected musicians.

Wilson, John S. *Jazz: The Transition Years, 1940–1960*. New York: Appleton, Century, Crofts, 1966.

Wilson, Olly. "The Heterogeneous Sound Ideal in African-American Music." *New Perspectives on Music: Essays in Honor of Eileen Southern*. Ed. by Josephine Wright, with Samuel A. Floyd, Jr. Warren, MI: Harmonie Park Press, 1992.

Work, John W. "Changing Patterns in Negro Folk Songs," *Journal of American Folklore* 62 (1949): 136–44. Description of the religious music that later would be called gospel.

_____. "Plantation Meistersinger," *The Musical Quarterly* 17 (1941): 97–106. Discussion of shape-note singing in the South among blacks, particularly in Alabama.

TWENTIETH-CENTURY COLLECTIONS: MUSIC SCORES

Albertson, Chris, ed. *Bessie Smith, Empress of the Blues*. New York: Walter Kane, 1975. Collection of thirty songs arranged for voice and piano.

Ballanta, Nicholas. *Saint Helena Island Spirituals: Recorded and Transcribed at Penn Normal Industrial and Agricultural School . . . South Carolina*. New York: G. Schimer, 1925.

Charters, Ann, ed. *The Ragtime Songbook: Songs of the Ragtime Era by Scott Joplin, Will Marion Cook, Alex Rogers, and Others. With Historical Notes Concerning the Songs and Times*. New York: Oak Publications, 1955.

Coleridge-Taylor, Samuel. *Twenty-Four Negro Melodies*. With a Preface by Booker T. Washington. Bryn Mawr, PA, 1905. Piano arrangements of Negro spirituals and African melodies.

Cook, Will Marion. *In Dahomey: A Negro Musical Comedy*. Produced at the Shaftesbury Theater (London). May 16, 1903. Jesse A. Shipp, book; Paul Lawrence Dunbar & others, lyrics.

Dett, R. Nathaniel. *The Collected Piano Works*. With Introductions by Dominique-René de Lerma and Vivian McBrier. Evanston, IL, 1973.

Handy, W. C., ed. *Blues: An Anthology; With an Historical and Critical Text by Abbe Niles. . . . 1926. Blues . . . Complete Words and Music of 53 Great Songs*. Rev. by Jerry Silverman. New York: Macmillan Publishing Co., 1972.

Jazz Master Series, The. New York: Consolidated Music Publishers, 1981. Includes transcriptions of solo piano pieces of Art Tatum and Thelonious Monk, among others.

Johnson, J. Rosamond, arr. *Rolling Along in Song*. New York: The Viking Press, 1937.

Johnson, James Weldon, and J. Rosamond Johnson. *The Book of American Negro Spirituals*. 2 vol. 1926–27. Repr. New York: Da Capo Press, 1977.

Joplin, Scott. *The Complete Works of Scott Joplin*. Ed. by Vera Brodsky Lawrence. New York: New York Public Library. 1971. With Introduction by Rudi Blesh and Preface by Carman Moore. New York, 1981.

Joplin, Scott. *Treemonisha*. Piano score for the opera is in Vera Lawrence, *The Complete Works of Scott Joplin*, vol. 2.

Morton, Ferdinand "Jelly Roll." *The Collected Piano Music*. Ed. by James Dapogny. New York: G. Schirmer, 1982.

Patterson, Willis. *Anthology of Art Songs By Black American Composers*. New York: Edward B. Marks, 1977. Collection of forty-one art songs.

Scott, James. *The Music of James Scott*. Ed. by Scott, Deveaux and William Howland Kenney. Washington, D.C.: Smithsonian Institution Press, 1992.

Niles, John Jacob. *Singing Soldiers*. New York: Charles Scribner's Sons, 1927. Text of songs sung by black soldiers in the European theater during World War I.

Silverman, Jerry, comp. and ed. *Folk Blues.* 1958. Repr. New York: Macmillan Publishing Co., 1971.

Songs of Zion. Comp. and ed. by J. Jefferson Cleveland and Verolga Nix. Preface by William B. McClain. Nashville, TN: Abingdon Press, 1981. Collection includes contemporary gospel songs and traditional as well as spirituals and other black religious songs.

White, Newman Ivey. *American Negro Folk-Songs.* 1928. Repr. Hatboro, PA: Folklore Associates, 1965. Primarily song texts of all types, religious and secular.

Work, John W. *American Negro Songs and Spirituals.* New York: Bonanza Books, 1940.

Yes, Lord! Church of God in Christ Hymnal. Comp. and ed. by Norman N. Quick, Memphis, TN: The Church of God in Christ Publishing Board, 1982. Traditional and contemporary gospel songs.

PERIODICALS

American Music (1983–)
Annual Review of Jazz Studies (1982–)
Black Music Research Journal (1978–)
Black Perspective in Music, The (1973–90)
Cadence (1976–)
[New York] Clipper (1853–1923)
Down Beat (1934–)
Ebony (1945–)
Ethnomusicology (1953–)
Journal of American Folklore (1887–)
Journal of the American Musicological Society (1948–)
Journal of Jazz Studies (1973–79). Continued as *Annual Review* . . .
Journal of Negro History (1916–)
Keyboard (1975–)
Living Blues (1970–)
Musical Quarterly, The (1915–)
Newsletter, Institute for Studies in American Music (1970–)
Record Research (1955–)
Rejoice: The Gospel Music Magazine (1987–1994)
Southern Workman, The (1872–)

BIOGRAPHIES

ALDRIDGE, IRA
Marshall, Herbert, and Mildred Stock. *Ira Aldridge, the Negro Tragedian.* London, 1958. Also discussion of James Hewlett.

ALLEN, RICHARD
Allen, Richard. *The Life and Experience and Gospel Labors of the Rt. Rev. Richard Allen,* Philadelphia, 1988.

Braithwaite, J. Roland, ed. *Richard Allen: A Collection of Hymns and Spiritual Songs.* Nashville, TN, 1987.

Wesley, Charles H. *Richard Allen, Apostle of Freedom.* Washington, D.C., 1935.

ANDERSON, MARIAN
Anderson, Marian. *My Lord, What a Morning.* New York, 1956.

Newman, Shirlee. *Marian Anderson, the Lady from Philadelphia.* Philadelphia, 1965.

Sims, Janet. *Marian Anderson: An Annotated Bibliography and Discography.* Westport, CT, 1981.

Vehanen, Kosti. *Marian Anderson: A Portrait.* New York, 1941.

ANDERSON, T.J.
Thompson, Bruce. "Musical Style and Compositional Techniques in Selected Works of T. J. Anderson" (Ph.D. diss., Indiana University, 1979).

ARMSTRONG, LOUIS "SATCHMO"
Armstrong, Louis. *Satchmo: My Life in New Orleans.* 1954. Repr. New York, 1961.
_____. *Swing That Music.* New York, 1936.
Collier, James Lincoln. *Louis Armstrong: An American Genius.* New York, 1983.
Giddins, Gary. *Satchmo.* New York, 1988.
Jones, Max, and John Chilton. *Louis: The Louis Armstrong Story, 1900–1971.* Boston, 1971.
Miller, Marc H. *Louis Armstrong: A Cultural Legacy.* Seattle, 1995.

ARROYO, MARTINA
Abdul, Raoul. *Famous Black Entertainers of Today.* New York, 1974.

BAILEY, DEFORD
Morton, David C. with Charles K. Wolfe. *DeFord Bailey: A Black Star in Early Country Music.* Knoxville, TN, 1991.

BAILEY, PEARL
Bailey, Pearl. *The Raw Pearl.* New York, 1968.
_____. *Talking to Myself.* New York, 1971.

BAKER, JOSEPHINE
Baker, Josephine, and Jo Bouillon. *Josephine.* 1977. Transl. by Mariana Fitzpatrick. New York, 1988.
Haney, Lynn. *Naked at the Feast: A Biography of Josephine Baker.* New York, 1981.

BALLARD, FLORENCE
Wilson, Randall. *Forever Faithful: A Study of Florence Ballard and The Supremes.* San Francisco, 1987.

BARKER, DANNY
Barker, Danny, with Jack Buerkle, *Bourbon Street Black: The New Orleans Black Jazzman.* New York, 1973.

BASIE, WILLIAM "COUNT"
Basie, William "Count," with Albert Murray. *Good Morning Blues: The Autobiography of Count Basie.* New York, 1985.
Dance, Stanley. *The World of Count Basie.* New York, 1980.
Horricks, Raymond. *Count Basie and His Orchestra: Its Music and Musicians.* 1957. Repr. Westport, CT, 1971.
Morgan, Alun. *Count Basie.* New York, 1984.
Sheridan, Chris, comp. *Count Basie: A Bio-Discography.* Westport, CT, 1986.

BECHET, SIDNEY
Bechet, Sidney. *Treat It Gentle.* London, 1960.
Blesh, Rudi. *Combo: U.S.A.: Eight Lives in Jazz.* Philadelphia, 1971.
Chilton, John. *Sidney Bechet: The Wizard of Jazz.* New York, 1987.

BERNHARDT, CLYDE E. B.
Bernhardt, Clyde E. B. *I Remember: Eighty Years of Black Entertainment, Big Bands, and the Blues: An Autobiography . . . as Told to Sheldon Harris.* Philadelphia, 1986.

BERRY, CHARLES EDWARD ANDERSON "CHUCK"
Berry, Chuck. *Chuck Berry: The Autobiography.* New York, 1987.
Dewitt, Howard A. *Chuck Berry: Rock 'n' Roll Music.* 1981. 2nd ed. Ann Arbor, MI, 1985.

BETHUNE, TOM "BLIND TOM"
Southall, Geneva. *Blind Tom: The Post-Civil War Enslavement of a Black Musical Genius.* Minneapolis, 1979. Book 1.
Southall, Geneva A. *The Continuing Enslavement of Blind Tom, the Black Pianist-Composer (1865–1887).* Book 2. Minneapolis, 1983.

BIGARD, BARNEY

Bigard, Barney. *With Louis and the Duke: The Autobiography of a Jazz Clarinetist.* Ed. by Barry Martyn. New York, 1986.

BLAKE, EUBIE

Carter, Lawrence. *Eubie Blake: Keys of Memory.* Detroit, 1980.

Kimball, Robert, and William Bolcom. *Reminiscing with Sissle and Blake.* New York, 1972.

Rose, Al. *Eubie Blake.* New York, 1979.

BLAND, JAMES

Daly, John J. *A Song in His Heart.* Philadelphia, 1951.

Haywood, Charles. *The James A. Bland Album of Outstanding Songs.* New York, 1947.

Geary, Lynnette G. "Jules Bledsoe: The Original Ol' Man River," BPIM 17 (1989): 27–54.

BOLDEN, CHARLES "BUDDY"

Marquis, Donald. *In Search of Buddy Bolden: First Man of Jazz.* 1978. New York, 1980.

BONDS, MARGARET

Bonds, Margaret. "A Reminiscence," in *The Negro in Music and Art.* Ed. by Lindsay Patterson. New York, 1968.

Green, Mildred. "A Study of the Lives and Works of Five Black Women Composers in America" (Ph.D. diss., University of Oklahoma, 1975.

BOONE, JOHN WILLIAM "BLIND"

Fuell, Melissa. *Blind Boone, His Early Life and His Achievements.* Kansas City, MO, 1915.

BRADFORD ALEX

Abdul, Raoul. *Famous Black Entertainers of Today.* New York, 1974.

BRADFORD, PERRY

Bradford, Perry. *Born with the Blues: The True Story of the Pioneering Blues Singers and Musicians in the Early Days of Jazz.* New York, 1965.

BRAXTON, ANTHONY

Lock, Graham. *Forces in Motion: Anthony Braxton and the Meta-Reality of Creative Music.* London, 1988.

Ullman, Michael. *Jazz Lives.* Washington, D.C., 1980.

BRICKTOP

Smith, Ada Beatrice Smith (pseud. "Bricktop"), with James Haskins. *Bricktop.* New York, 1983.

BROONZY, WILLIAM

Broonzy, William. *Big Bill Blues: William Broonzy's Story as Told to Yannick Bruynoghe.* 1955. Repr. New York, 1964.

BROWN, JAMES

Brown, James, with Bruce Tucker. *James Brown: The Godfather of Soul.* New York, 1986.

BROWN, MARION

Brown, Marion. *Recollections: Essays, Drawings, Miscellaneous.* Frankfurt, Germany, 1984.

CAESAR, SHIRLEY

Darden, Bob. "Shirley Caesar: Singing Evangelist," *Rejoice* 2 (Summer 1990): 8–11.

BURLEIGH, HARRY T.

Janifer, Ellsworth. "H. T. Burleigh Ten Years Later," *Phylon* 21 (1960).

CALLOWAY, CABELL "CAB"

Calloway, Cab, with Bryant Rollins. *Of Minnie the Moocher and Me.* New York, 1976.

CAMPBELL, LUCY

Reagon, Bernice Johnon, ed. *We'll Understand It Better By and By: Pioneering African-American Gospel Composers.* Washington, D.C., 1992.
Washington, William, ed. *Miss Lucy Speaks.* Nashville, TN, 1971.
CARTER, BENNY
Berger, Monroe, Edward Berger, and James Patrick. *Benny Carter: A Life in American Music.* Studies in Jazz, No. 1. 2 vols. Metuchen, NJ, 1982. Includes discography and filmography.
CARTER, BETTY
Ullman, Michael. *Jazz Lives.* Washington, D.C., 1980.
CHARLES, RAY
Charles, Ray, with David Ritz. *Brother Ray: Ray Charles' Own Story.* New York, 1978.
CHEATHAM, ADOLPHUS "DOC"
Ullman, Michael. *Jazz Lives.* Washington, D.C., 1980.
CHRISTIAN, CHARLIE
Blesh, Rudi. *Combo: U.S.A.: Eight Lives in Jazz.* Philadelphia, 1971.
COLE, NATHANIEL "NAT"
Cole, Maria, with Louie Robinson. *Nat King Cole: An Intimate Biography.* New York, 1971.
COLEMAN, ORNETTE
Spellman, A. B. *Four Lives in the Bebop Business.* 1967. New York, 1971 (with new title *Black Music*).
COLERIDGE-TAYLOR, SAMUEL
Coleridge-Taylor, Avril. *The Heritage of Samuel Coleridge-Taylor.* London, 1979.
Sayers, William C. Berwick. *Samuel Coleridge-Taylor: His Life and Letters.* 1915. 2nd ed. London, 1927.
Tortolano, William. *Samuel Coleridge-Taylor: Anglo-Black Composer, 1875–1912.* Metuchen, NJ, 1977.
COLLINS, LEE
Gillis, Frank, and John Miner, eds. *Oh, Didn't He Ramble: The Life Story of Lee Collins, as Told to Mary Collins.* Urbana, IL, 1974.
COLTRANE, JOHN
Cole, Bill. *John Coltrane.* New York, 1976.
Thomas, J. C. *Chasin' the Trane: The Music and Mystique of John Coltrane.* Garden City, NJ, 1975.
White, Andrew Nathaniel. *Trane 'n' Me: A Semi-Autography. A Treatise on the Music of John Coltrane.* Washington, D.C., 1981.
COOK, WILL MARION
Carter, Marva Griffin. "The Life and Music of Will Marion Cook." (Ph.D. diss., University of Illinois, Urbana-Champaign, 1985).
CLAYTON, BUCK
Clayton, Buck, with Nancy Miller Elliott. *Buck Clayton's Jazz World.* London, 1986.
CROUCH, ANDRAE
Crouch, Andrae, with Nina Ball. *Through It All.* Waco, TX, [1974].
DACOSTA, NOEL
Baker, David, Lida Belt, and Herman C. Hudson. *The Black Composer Speaks.* Metuchen, NJ, 1978.
DANDRIDGE, DOROTHY
Dandridge, Dorothy, and Earl Conrad. *Everything and Nothing: The Dorothy Dandridge Tragedy.* New York, 1970.
DAVIS, GUSSIE LORD
Wright, Josephine. "In Retrospect: Gussie Lord Davis (1863–1899)," BPIM 6 (Fall 1978).
DAVIS, MILES

Carr, Ian. *Miles Davis: A Biography*. New York, 1982.

Chambers, Jack. *Milestones: The Music and Times of Miles Davis*. Vol. 1, 1983. Vol 2, 1985. New York, 1989.

Cole, Bill. *Miles Davis: A Musical Biography*. 1974. Repr. New York, 1980.

Davis, Miles, with Quincy Troupe. *Miles: The Autobiography*. New York, 1989.

James, Michael. *Miles, Davis*. London, 1961.

Nisenson, Eric. *'Round About Midnight: A Portrait of Miles Davis*. New York, 1982.

DAVIS, SAMMY, JR.

Davis, Sammy, Jr. *Hollywood in a Suitcase*. New York, 1980.

Davis, Sammy, Jr. *Yes I Can*. New York, 1965.

DEPREIST, JAMES

Abdul, Raoul. *Famous Black Entertainers of Today*. New York, 1974.

DETT, R. NATHANIEL

McBrier, Vivian Flagg. *R. Nathaniel Dett: His Life and Works*. Washington, D.C., 1977.

DODDS, JOHN

Lambert, G. E. *Johnny Dodds*. London, 1971.

DODDS, WARREN "BABY"

Gary, Larry. *The Baby Dodds Story, as Told to Larry Gary*. Los Angeles, 1959.

DOLPHY, ERIC

Simosko, Vladimir, and Barry Tepperman. *Eric Dolphy: A Musical Biography and Discography*. Washington, D.C., 1974.

DORSEY, THOMAS A.

Boyer, Horace Clarence. *How Sweet the Sound: The Golden Age of Gospel*. Washington, D.C., 1995.

Harris, Michael Wesley. *The Rise of Gospel Blues: The Music of Thomas Andrew Dorsey in the Urban Church*. New York, 1992.

O'Neal, Jim and Amy. "Georgia Tom Dorsey," LB 20 (March–April 1975).

Reagon, Bernice Johnson, ed. *We'll Understand It Better By and By: Pioneering African-American Gospel Composers*. Washington, D.C., 1992.

ECKSTINE, WILLIAM "BILLY"

Southern, Eileen. "Conversation with William Clarence (Billy) Eckstine," BPIM 7 (Fall 1979): BPIM 8 (Spring 1980).

ELLINGTON, EDWARD KENNEDY "DUKE"

Collier, James Lincoln. *Duke Ellington*. New York, 1987.

Ellington, Duke. *Music Is My Mistress*. New York, 1973.

Ellington, Mercer, and Stanley Dance. *Duke Ellington in Person: An Intimate Memoir*. New York, 1978.

Gammond, Peter. *Duke Ellington: His Life and Music*. 1958. Repr. New York, 1977.

George, Don. *Sweet Man—The Real Duke Ellington*. New York, 1981.

Jewell, Derek. *Duke: A Portrait of Duke Ellington*. New York, 1977.

Rattenbury, Ken. *Duke Ellington, Jazz Composer*. New Haven, 1993.

Tucker, Mark. *Ellington: The Early Years*. Urbana, IL, 1991.

Ulanov, Berry. *Duke Ellington*. 1946. Repr. New York, 1975.

EUROPE, JAMES REESE

Sissle, Noble Lee. *Memoirs of Lieutenant "Jim" Europe*. (Unpublished manuscript, Library of Congress, 1942).

FITZGERALD, ELLA

Colin, Sid. *Ella: The Life and Times of Ella Fitzgerald*. London, 1986.

FLANAGAN, TOMMY

Ullmann, Michael. *Jazz Lives*. Washington, D.C., 1980.

FLETCHER, TOM

Fletcher, Tom. *100 Years of the Negro in Show Business*. New York, 1954.

FRANKLIN, ARETHA
Abdul, Raoul. *Famous Black Entertainers of Today.* New York, 1974.
Bego, Mark. *Aretha Franklin: Queen of Soul. New York, 1989.*
FOSTER, GEORGE MURPHY
Foster, George Murphy. *Pops Foster: The Autobiography of a New Orleans Jazzman, as Told to Tom Stoddard.* Berkeley, 1971.
Lydon, Michael. *Boogie Lightning.* New York, 1974.
GARDNER, NEWPORT
Ferguson, John. *Memoir of the Life and Character of Rev. Samuel Hopkins, D.D., formerly Pastor of the First Congregational Church in Newport, Rhode Island.* Boston, 1830. Reprint of passages about Gardner in BPIM 4 (July 1976).
Mason, George. *Reminiscences of Newport.* Newport, RI, 1884. Repr. of chapter about Newport Gardner in RBAM.
GILLESPIE, DIZZY
Gillespie, Dizzy, with Al Fraser. *To Be or Not to Bop. Memoirs.* 1979. Repr. New York, 1985.
GORDON, DEXTER
Ullman, Michael. *Jazz Lives.* Washington, D.C., 1980.
GRANT, MICKI
Abdul, Raoul. *Famous Black Entertainers of Today,* New York, 1974.
GREENFIELD, ELIZABETH TAYLOR
LaBrew, Arthur. *The Black Swan.* Detroit, 1969.
HACKLEY, E. AZALIA
Davenport, M. Marguerite. *The Life of Madame E. Azalia Hackley.* Boston, 1947.
HAKIM, TALIB
Baker, David, Lida Belt, and Herman Hudson. *The Black Composer Speaks.* Metuchen, NJ, 1978.
HANCOCK, HERBIE
Baker, David, Lida Belt, and Herman C. Hudson. *The Black Composer Speaks.* Metuchen, NJ, 1978.
HANDY, W. C.
Handy, W. C. *Father of the Blues.* 1941. Repr. New York, 1970.
HARRIS, WYNONIE
Collins, Tony. *Rock Mr. Blues: The Life & Music of Wynonie Harris.* New Milford, NH, 1995.
HAWES, HAMPTON
Hawes, Hampton and Don Asher. *Raise Up Off Me: Autobiography of a Black Jazz Pianist.* 1975. Repr. New York, 1979.
HAWKINS, COLEMAN
DeVeaux, Scott Knowles. "Jazz in Transition: Coleman Hawkins and Howard McGhee, 1935–1945." (Ph.D. diss. Berkeley: University of California, 1985.)
HAYES, ROLAND
Hayden, Robert C. *Singing for All People, Roland Hayes: A Biography.* Boston, 1989.
Hayes, Roland. *My Songs; Afro-American Religious Folk Songs.* Boston, 1948.
MacKinley, Helen. *Angel Mo and Her Son, Roland Hayes.* Boston, 1942.
HENDERSON, FLETCHER
Allen, Walter C. *Hendersonia: The Music of Fletcher Henderson and His Musicians: A Bio-Discography.* Highland Park, NJ, 1973.
Magee, Jeffrey. "The Music of Fletcher Henderson and His Orchestra in the 1920s." (Ph.D. diss., University of Michigan, 1992).
HENDRIX, JIMI
Knight, Curtis. *Jimi.* New York, 1975.
HINES, EARL
Dance, Stanley. *The World of Earl Hines.* New York, 1977.

HINTON, MILT
Hinton, Milt, and David G. Berger. *Bass Line: The Stories and Photographs of Milt Hinton*. Philadelphia, 1988.
HOLIDAY, BILLIE
Blesh, Rudi. *Combo: U.S.A.: Eight Lives in Jazz*. Philadelphia, 1971.
Chilton, John. *Billie's Blues: A Survey of Billie Holiday's Career, 1933–1959*. New York, 1975.
Holiday, Billie, with William Duffy. *Lady Sings the Blues*. 1956. Repr. London, 1973.
HOOKER, JOHN LEE
Lydon, Michael. *Boogie Lightning*. New York, 1975.
HOPKINS, CLAUDE
Vaché, Warren W., Sr. *Crazy Fingers: Claude Hopkins' Life in Jazz*. Washington, D.C., 1992.
HORNE, LENA
Buckley, Gail L. *The Hornes: An American Family*. New York, 1986.
HUNTER, ALBERTA
Taylor, Frank C., with Gerald Cook. *Alberta Hunter: A Celebration in Blues*. New York, 1987.
HYERS, ANNA MADAH AND EMMA LOUISE
Southern, Eileen, ed. *African American Theatre: Out of Bondage* (1876) and *Peculiar Sam; or The Underground Railroad* (1879). New York, 1994.
———. "An Early Black Concert Company: The Hyers Sisters Combination." *A Celebration of American Music: Words and Music in Honor of H. Wiley Hitchcock*. Ed. by Richard Crawford, R. Allen Lott, and Carol J. Oja. Ann Arbor, MI, 1990.
JACKSON, MAHALIA
Cornell, Jean Gay. *Mahalia Jackson: Queen of Gospel Song*. Champaign, IL, 1974.
Dunham, Montrew. *Mahalia Jackson: Young Gospel Singer*. Indianapolis, [1974].
Goreau, Laurraine. *Just Mahalia, Baby*. Waco, TX, 1975.
Jackson, Mahalia, with Evan McLeod Wylie. *Movin' On Up*. New York, 1969.
JENKINS, EDMUND THORNTON
Green, Jeffrey. *Edmund Thornton Jenkins: The Life and Times of an American Black Composer, 1894–1926*. Westport, CT, 1982.
JOHNSON, FRANCIS "FRANK"
Jones, Charles K. and Lorenzo K. Greenwich II, eds. *A Choice Collection of the Works of Francis Johnson*. 2 vols. New York, 1982–87.
Mackey, Philip English, ed. *A Gentleman of Much Promise. The Diary of Isaac Mickle, 1837–1845*. 2 vols. Philadelphia, 1977. Good source of information for Johnson and Isaac Hazzard.
Southern, Eileen. "Frank Johnson and His Promenade Concerts." BPIM 5 (Spring 1977): 3–29.
Waln, Robert (pseud.) *The Hermit in America on a Visit to Philadelphia*. Philadelphia, 1818. Passages about Johnson reprinted in RBAM.
JOHNSON, FRANCIS HALL
Carter, Marva Griffin. "Hall Johnson: Preserver of the Old Negro Spiritual." (Unpublished M.A. thesis, Boston University, 1975).
JOHNSON, JAMES P.
Brown, Scott E., and Robert Hilbert. *James P. Johnson: A Case of Mistaken Identity*. Metuchen, NJ, 1986.
Davin, Tom. "Conversations with James P. Johnson," *Jazz Review* (June, July 1959).
JOHNSON, TOMMY
Evans, David. *Tommy Johnson [Mississippi bluesman]*. London, 1971.
JOHNSON, WILLIAM "BUNK"
Sonnier, Austin. *Willie Geary "Bunk" Johnson*. New York, 1977.

JONES, BESSIE
For the Ancestors: Autobiographical Memories. Collected and ed. by John Stewart. Urbana, IL, 1983.

JONES, M. SISSIERETTA
Daughtry, Willia. "Sissieretta Jones: A Study of the Negro's Contributions to Nineteenth-Century American Concert and Theatrical Life" (Ph.D. diss., Syracuse University, 1968).

JONES, QUINCY
Horricks, Raymond. *Quincy Jones.* New York, 1985.

JOPLIN, SCOTT
Berlin, Edward A. *King of Ragtime: Scott Joplin and His Era.* New York, 1994.

Gammond, Peter. *Scott Joplin and the Ragtime Era.* New York, 1978.

Haskins, James, with Kathleen Benson. *Scott Joplin: The Man Who Made Ragtime.* Garden City, NY, 1978.

Lawrence, Vera Brodsky, ed. *The Collected Works of Scott Joplin.* 2 vols. New York, 1971.

KAY, ULYSSES
Baker, David, Lida Belt, and Herman C. Hudson. *The Black Composer Speaks.* Metuchen, NJ, 1978.

Hayes, Laurence. "The Music of Ulysses Kay, 1939–1963," (Ph.D. diss., University of Wisconsin, 1971).

Hadley, Richard. "The Published Choral Music of Ulysses Simpson Kay, 1943–1968" (Ph.D. diss., University of Iowa, 1972).

KING, RILEY "B. B."
Sawyer, Charles. *The Arrival of B. B. King.* New York, 1980.

KIRK, ANDY
Kirk, Andy. As Told to Amy Lee. *Twenty Years on Wheels.* Ann Arbor, MI, 1989.

KIRK, RAHSAAN ROLAND
Ullman, Michael. *Jazz Lives.* Washington, D.C., 1980.

LANE, WILLIAM "Master JUBA"
Dickens, Charles. *Notes on America.* New York, 1842. Relevant passages reprinted in BPIM 3 (Spring 1975): 81–82.

Winter, Marian Hannah. "Juba and American Minstrelsy," *Chronicles of the American Dance.* Ed. by Paul Magriel. New York, 1948.

LEDBETTER, HUDDIE WILLIAM "LEADBELLY"
Garvin, Richard, and Edmond G. Addeo. *The Midnight Special: The Legend of Lead-BELLY.* New York, 1971.

LEWIS, GEORGE
Bethell, Tom. *George Lewis: A Jazzman from New Orleans.* Berkeley, 1977.

LUCAS, SAM
Holly, Ellistine Perkins. "Sam Lucas, 1840–1916: A Bibliographic Study." *Feel The Spirit: Studies in Nineteenth-Century Afro-American Music.* Ed. by George R. Keck and Sherrill V. Martin. Westport, CT, 1988.

MARSALIS, WYNTON
Marsalis, Wynton, and Frank Stewart. *Sweet Swing Blues on the Road.* New York, 1994.

McDANIEL, ELLAS "BO DIDDLEY"
Lydon, Michael. *Boogie Lightning.* New York, 1974.

McGHEE, HOWARD
DeVeaux, Scott Knowles. "Jazz in Transition: Coleman Hawkins and Howard McGhee, 1935–1945." (Ph.D. diss. Berkeley: University of California, 1985).

McLEAN, JACKIE
Spellman, A. B. *Four Lives in the Bebop Business.* 1967. New York, 1971 (with new title *Black Music*).

MINGUS, CHARLES
Mingus, Charles. *Beneath the Underdog: His World as Composed by Mingus.* Ed. by Nel King. New York, 1971.
MITCHELL, GEORGE
Mitchell, George. *Blow My Blues Away.* Baton Rouge, LA, 1971.
MOORE, CARMAN
Abdul, Raoul. *Famous Black Entertainers of Today.* New York, 1974.
MOORE, UNDINE SMITH
Baker, David, Lida Belt, and Herman C. Hudson. *The Black Composer Speaks.* Metuchen, NJ, 1978.
MORTON, FERDINAND "JELLY ROLL"
Dapogny, James. *Ferdinand "Jelly Roll" Morton: The Collected Piano Music.* New York, 1982.
Lomax, Alan. *Mister Jelly Roll: The Fortunes of Jelly Morton, New Orleans Creole and "Inventor of Jazz."* 1950. Repr. Berkeley, 1973.
NELSON, OLIVER
Baker, David, Lida Belt, and Herman C. Hudson. *The Black Composer Speaks.* Metuchen, NJ, 1978.
OLIVER, JOSEPH "KING"
Allen, Walter, and Brian Rust. *King Joe Oliver.* Belleville, NJ, 1955. London, 1957.
PARKER, CHARLIE
Giddons, Gary. *Celebrating Bird: The Triumph of Charlie Parker.* New York, 1987.
Harrison, Max. *Charles Parker.* London, 1960.
Priestley, Brian. *Charlie Parker.* New York, 1984.
Reisner, R. G. *Bird: The Legend of Charlie Parker.* New York, 1962.
Russell, Ross. *Bird Lives: The High Life and Hard Times of Charlie (Yardbird) Parker.* New York, 1973.
PEEBLES, MELVIN Van
Abdul, Raoul. *Famous Black Entertainers of Today.* New York, 1974.
PERKINSON, COLERIDGE T.
Baker, David, Lida Belt, and Herman C. Hudson. *The Black Composer Speaks.* Metuchen, NJ, 1978.
PERRY, JULIA
Green, Mildred. "A Study of the Lives and Works of Five Black Women Composers in America," (Ph.D. diss., University of Oklahoma, 1975).
Palmer, Richard. *Oscar Peterson.* New York, 1984.
PITTMAN, Evelyn Larue
Green, Mildred. "A Study of the Lives and Works of Five Black Women Composers in America" (Ph.D. diss., University of Oklahoma, 1975).
PRICE, FLORENCE
Brown, Rae Linda. "The Orchestral Music of Florence B. Price (1888–1953): A Stylistic Analysis." (Ph.D. diss., Yale University, 1987).
Green, Mildred. "A Study of the Lives and Works of Five Black Women Composers in America" (Ph.D. diss., University of Oklahoma, 1975).
Jackson, Barbara Garvey. "Florence Price, Composer," BPIM 5 (1977): 30.
PRICE, LEONTYNE
Lyon, H. L. *Leontyne Price: Highlights of a Prima Donna.* New York, 1975.
PRICE, SAMMY
Price, Sammy. *What Do They Want: A Jazz Autobiography.* Ed. by Caroline Richmond. Urbana, IL, 1990.
RAINY, GERTRUDE "MA"
Lieb, Sandra. *Mother of the Blues: A Study of Ma Rainey.* Amherst, MA, 1981.
Stewart-Baxter, Derrick. *Ma Rainey and the Classic Blues Singers.* New York, 1970.

RAZAF, ANDY
Singer, Barry. *Black and Blue: The Life and Lyrics of Andy Razaf.* New York, 1992.

RIVERS, SAM
Ullman, Michael. *Jazz Lives.* Washington, D.C., 1980.

ROBESON, PAUL
Duberman, Martin Bauml. *Paul Robeson: A Biography.* New York, 1989.
Robeson, Eslanda Goode. *Paul Robeson, Negro.* New York, 1930.
Robeson, Paul. *Here I Stand.* New York, 1958.
Seton, Marie. *Paul Robeson.* London, 1958.

ROBINSON, SMOKEY
Robinson, Smokey, with David Ritz. *Smokey: Inside My Life.* New York, 1989.

ROLLINS, SONNY
Ullman, Michael. *Jazz Lives.* Washington, D.C., 1980.

ROSS, DIANA
Abdul, Raoul. *Famous Black Entertainers of Today.* New York, 1974.

RUSSELL, GEORGE
Baker, David, Lida Belt, and Herman C. Hudson. *The Black Composer Speaks.* Metuchen, NJ, 1978.
Russell, George. *The Lydian Chromatic Concept of Tonal Organization.* New York, 1953.

SCHUYLER, PHILIPPA
Schuyler, Josephine. *Philippa, the Beautiful American: The Travelled History of a Troubadour.* New York, 1969.
Talalay, Kathryn. *Composition in Black and White: The Life of Philippa Schuyler.* New York, 1995.

SHEPP, ARCHIE
Baker, David, Lida Belt, and Herman C. Hudson. *The Black Composer Speaks.* Metuchen, NJ, 1978.

SHORT, BOBBY
Short, Bobby. *Black and White Baby.* New York, 1971.

SILVER, HORACE
Ullman, Michael. *Jazz Lives.* Washington, D.C., 1980.

SISSLE, NOBLE
Kimball, Robert and William Bolcom. *Reminiscing with Sissle and Blake.* New York, 1972.
Sissle, Noble Lee. *Memoirs of Lieutenant "Jim" Europe.* (Unpublished manuscript, Library of Congress, 1942).

SMITH, BESSIE
Albertson, Chris, ed. *Bessie Smith, Empress of the Blues.* New York, 1975.
Feinstein, Elaine. *Bessie Smith.* New York, 1985.
Moore, Carman. *Somebody's Angel Child: The Story of Bessie Smith.* New York, 1969.

SMITH, HALE
Baker, David, Lida Belt, and Herman C. Hudson. *The Black Composer Speaks.* Metuchen, NJ, 1978.
Breda, Malcolm Joseph. "Hale Smith: A Biographical and Analytical Study of the Man and His Music" (Ph.D. diss., University of Southern Mississippi, 1975).

SMITH, "STUFF" HEZEKIAH
Barnett, Anthony. *Desert Sands: The Recordings and Performances of Stuff Smith: An Annotated Discography and Biography Source Book.* East Sussex, England, 1995.

SMITH, WILLIAM "WILLIE"
Smith, Willie "the Lion" with George Hoefer. *Music on My Mind: The Memoirs of an American Pianist.* 1964. Repr. New York, 1975.

STILL, WILLIAM GRANT

Arvey, Verna. *In One Lifetime*. Fayetteville, AK, 1984.

A Birthday Offering to William Grant Still, full issue of BPIM (May 1975).

Detels, Claire, ed. *William Grant Still Studies at the University of Arkansas: A 1984 Congress Report*. Fayetteville, AK, 1985.

Haas, Robert Bartlett, ed. *William Grant Still and the Fusion of Cultures in American Music*. Los Angeles, 1972.

SWANSON, HOWARD

Baker, David, Lida Belt, and Herman C. Hudson. *The Black Composer Speaks*. Metuchen, NJ, 1978.

Ennett, Dorothy. "An Analysis and Comparison of Selected Piano Sonatas by Three Contemporary Black Composers: George Walker, Howard Swanson, and Roque Cordero" (Ph.D. diss., New York University, 1973).

Jackson, Raymond. "The Piano Music of Twentieth-Century Black Americans as Illustrated Mainly in the Works of Three Composers [Dett, Swanson, and Walker]" (Ph.D. diss., Juilliard School of Music, 1973).

TATUM, ART

Howlett, Felicity. "The Piano Style of Art Tatum" (Ph.D. diss., Cornell University, 1981).

Laubich, Arnold, and Ray Spencer. *Art Tatum: A Guide to His Recorded Music*. Studies in Jazz, No. 2. Metuchen, NJ, 1982.

Lester, James. *Too Marvelous for Words: The Life and Genius of Art Tatum*. New York, 1994.

TAYLOR, BILLY

Taylor, Billy. *Jazz Piano: A Jazz History*. Dubuque, IA, 1983.

TAYLOR, CECIL

Spellman, A. B. *Four Lives in the Bebop Business*. 1967. New York, 1971 (with new title *Black Music*).

THOMPSON, LESLIE.

Leslie Thompson: An Autobiography, as Told to Jeffrey P. Green. Crawley, Sussex, [England], 1985.

TINDLEY, CHARLES

Reagon, Bernice Johnson, ed. *We'll Understand It Better By and By: Pioneering African-American Gospel Composers*. Washington, D.C., 1992.

Jones, Ralph. *Charles Albert Tindley: Prince of Preachers*. Nashville, TN, 1982.

TURNER, TINA

Turner, Tina, with Kurt Loder. *I, Tina*. New York, 1986.

Fissinger, Laura. *Tina Turner*. New York, 1985.

WALKER, AARON THIBEAUX "T-BONE"

Dance, Helen Oakley. *Stormy Monday: The T-Bone Walker Story*. Baton Rouge, LA, 1987.

WALKER, GEORGE

Baker, David, Lida Belt, and Herman C. Hudson. *The Black Composer Speaks*. Metuchen, NJ, 1978.

Ennett, Dorothy. "An Analysis and Comparison of Selected Piano Sonatas by Three Contemporary Black Composers: George Walker, Howard Swanson, and Roque Cordero" (Ph.D. diss., New York University, 1973).

Newson, Roosevelt. "A Style Analysis of the Three Piano Sonatas of George Theophilus Walker" (D.M.A., Peabody Conservatory, 1977).

WALLER, THOMAS "FATS"

Fox, Charles. *Fats Waller*. New York, 1961.

Kirkeby, W. T. *Ain't Misbehavin': The Story of Fats Waller*. London, 1966.

Machlin, Paul S. *Stride: The Music of Fats Waller*. Boston, 1985.

Waller, Maurice, and Anthony Calabrese. *Fat Waller*. New York, 1977.

WASHINGTON, DINAH
Haskins, James. *Queen of the Blues: A Biography of Dinah Washington*. New York, 1987.
WATERS, ETHEL
Waters, Ethel, with Charles Samuels. *His Eye Is on the Sparrow*. 1951. Repr. New York, 1978.
Waters, Ethel. *To Me It's Wonderful*. 1972. Repr. New York, 1975.
WATTS, ANDRÉ
Abdul, Raoul. *Famous Black Entertainers of Today*. New York, 1974.
WELLS, WILLIAM "DICKY"
Wells, Dicky, as told to Stanley Dance. *The Night People: Reminiscences of a Jazzman*. Boston, 1971.
WILLIAMS, CLARENCE
Lord, Tom. *Clarence Williams*. Chigwell, England, 1976.
WILLIAMS, EGBERT "BERT"
Charters, Ann. *Nobody: The Story of Bert Williams*. New York, 1970.
Rowland, Mable. *Bert Williams*. New York, 1923.
WILLIAMS, JOE
Gourse, Leslie. *Every Day: The Story of Joe Williams*. London, 1985.
WILLIAMS, MARY LOU
Handy, D. Antoinette. "Conversation with Mary Lou Williams: First Lady of the Jazz Keyboard," BPIM (Fall 1980): 194–214.
WILSON, OLLY
Baker, David, Lida Belt, and Herman Hudson. *The Black Composer Speaks*. Metuchen, NJ, 1978.
Southern, Eileen. "Conversation with Olly Wilson," BPIM 5 (Spring 1977): 90–103: 6 (Spring 1978): 7–70.
WONDER, STEVIE
Haskins, James. *The Story of Stevie Wonder*. New York, 1976.
WORK, JOHN WESLEY III
Garcia, William B. "The Life and Choral Music of John Wesley Work" (Ph.D. diss., University of Iowa, 1973).
YOUNG, LESTER
Blesh, Rudi. *Combo: U.S.A.: Eight Lives in Jazz*. Philadelphia, 1971.
Delannoy, Luc. Transl. by Elna B. Odio. *Press: The Story of Lester Young*. Fayetteville, AK, 1993.
Gelly, Dave. *Lester Young*. New York, 1984.
Porter, Lewis, ed. *A Lester Young Reader*. Washington, D.C., 1991.

SOUND RECORDINGS

Black Composers Series. Columbia Records. Detroit Symphony Orchestra, Paul Freeman, conductor. 1974–78.
Ellington, Duke. *Sacred Music Concert*. Recorded at the Presbyterian Church (Fifth Avenue, New York). December 26, 1965.
Folk Music in America. 15 records (LBC 1–15). Recorded from field and commercial sources: published in celebration of the American Revolution Bicentennial by the Library of Congress.
New American Music. Folkway Records, 4 vols.
New World Records. Recorded Anthology of American Music. Index prepared by Elizabeth A. Davis. New York: W. W. Norton, 1981. More than 100 albums. Recordings of works of black composers listed below:

NW 201 Cecil Taylor

NW 211 *Music for Wind Ensemble:* Hale Smith

NW 216 Avant-Garde: Duke Ellington, John Lewis

NW 217 Big Bands and Territory Bands of the '30s: Ellington, Earl Hines, Dizzy Gillespie, Cab Calloway.

NW 224 Black Hymnody: Rosetta Tharpe

NW 235 *Maple Leaf Rag* (1899): Scott Joplin

NW 242 Small Jazz Groups of the '50s and Early '60s

NW 247 The American Art Song: H. T. Burleigh, J. Rosamond Johnson

NW 249 Rock 'n' Roll in the 1950s

NW 250 Small Groups in the 1930s: Eddie South, Henry Allen

NW 252 Roots of the Blues

NW 256 Big Bands and Territory Bands of the '20s

NW 259 Piano Blues and Boogie-Woogie (1926–1941)

NW 260 Shuffle Along: Sissle & Blake

NW 261 Rhythm & Blues

NW 265 Types & Stereotypes in American Musical Theater: James A. Bland

NW 269 Rags to Jazz: James Reese Europe

NW 271 Bebop

NW 272 American Composers: W. C. Handy, Duke Ellington

NW 274 Stylemakers of Jazz: Count Basie

NW 275 Neglected Jazz Figures of the 1950s and Early 1960s: Jaki Byard, Cecil Taylor, Thelonious Monk

NW 278 Georgia Sea Island Songs

NW 279 Golden Years of Tin Pan Alley: Thomas "Fats" Waller

NW 284 Jazz in Revolution: The Big Bands in the 1940s

NW 290 Folk and Popular Blues Styles to the Early 1940s

NW 293 Instrumental Dance Music 1780s–1920s: Francis Johnson

NW 295 Jazz Vocalists 1938–1961

NW Videmus (a Boston-based chamber organization established in 1986 to promote
the music of minority and women composers). Includes recordings of works by
T. J. Anderson, David Baker, R. Nathaniel Dett, Donal Fox, William Grant Still,
and Olly Wilson.

Natalie Hinderas Plays Music by Black Composers.

Norton Anthology of Jazz, The.

Patterson, Willis, comp. *Art Songs by Black Composers* (SMOO15), 1982. Music scores
of many of the songs are in Patterson's *Anthology of Art Songs by Black American
Composers.*

Smithsonian Collection of Classic Jazz.

Time-Life Records: Giants of Jazz. Albums for major jazz figures of the past; also booklets containing biographical facts and style analysis.

Index